An Improbable Life

Memoirs by

Vanderbilt University Press • *Nashville*

An
Improbable
Life

Robert Craft

Published by Vanderbilt University Press
Copyright © 2002 by Robert Craft
All rights reserved
First Edition 2002

This book is printed on acid-free paper.
Manufactured in the United States of America

Design by Gary Gore

Library of Congress Cataloging-in-Publication Data

Craft, Robert.
    An improbable life : memoirs / by Robert Craft.
        p. cm.
Includes index.
ISBN 0-8265-1381-6 (cloth : alk. paper)
    1. Craft, Robert. 2. Conductors (Music)—
United States—Biography. I. Title.
ML422.C91 A3 2002
784.2'092—dc21

                                        2002011653

Also by Robert Craft

Stravinsky: Chronicle of a Friendship
Stravinsky: Glimpses of a Life
Present Perspectives
Prejudices in Disguise
Current Convictions
Small Craft Advisories
The Moment of Existence
Places

Parts I and II are dedicated with love to
My sister Phyllis Crawford

Part III is dedicated with love to
My wife Alva

Contents

List of Illustrations   ix

Acknowledgments   xi

PART I GROWING UP

Chapter 1   A Sense of Self   3

Chapter 2   Prep School   20

Chapter 3   Juilliard, the War, Tanglewood   33

PART II THE STRAVINSKY YEARS

Chapter 4   "Dear Bobsky"   59

Chapter 5   Wetherly Drive Regulars   112

Chapter 6   The 1950s   142

Chapter 7   Isaiah Berlin and Stravinsky's *Abraham and Isaac*   220

Chapter 8   The Final Years   242

PART III SURVIVING THE LEGACY

Chapter 9   Confrontations   301

Chapter 10   Three Deaths and a New Life   334

Chapter 11   My Return to Music   371

Chapter 12   Not Going Gently   415

Index   441

Illustrations

(Black and white insert following page 130)

1880s. John Craft, the author's great-grandfather.

1864. Thomas Gibbs, the author's great-grandfather (father's maternal side).

1927. Robert, age four, Phyllis age six, Shetland pony.

1931. Family photo.

1931. Phyllis, Robert, Patricia.

1932. The St. John's Episcopal Church Choir, Kingston.

December 1937. In a New York Military Academy winter cape.

April 1943. Waiting for a train in Poughkeepsie.

August 1946. Tanglewood.

July 16, 1951. Dinner at the Aldous Huxleys'.

September 1951. Venice, on the Accademia Bridge with Vera Stravinsky.

1952. Santa Monica Boulevard, Beverly Hills.

October 20, 1954. Drawing of "BOB" by Stravinsky,
with music notation, "Happy Birthday," in his hand.

May 1954. Postcard from Stravinsky in Lisbon.

August 1957. Villa Valsanzibio, Euganean Hills.

1958. Hollywood. Recording *Le Marteau sans maître*.

1958. 1260 North Wetherly Drive. "Trio con brio."

November 1958. Vienna. Rehearsing Schoenberg's Five Pieces for Orchestra.

December 1959. Town Hall, New York. Rehearsing *Les Noces*.

In 1963, Isaiah Berlin presented the author
with a personally inscribed copy of *Karl Marx*.

October 1962. Rome. With Stravinsky during intermission
in a rehearsal of his *Movements*.

Winter 1997. In Recording Studio 1, Abbey Road, London.

(Color insert following page 258)

1928. Kingston.

Château de Joux (Pontarlier), the home of the Doyeaux,
the author's French ancestors on his mother's side.

Civil War medals of Thomas Gibbs and Isaac Lawrence.

1962. The last page of Stravinsky's working libretto for *Abraham and Isaac*.

1973. In the Stravinsky apartment, 920 Fifth Avenue, New York.

April 1989. With Alexander at Villa Lante, Lazio, Italy.

December 1989. New York. Rehearsing Elliott Carter's Double Concerto.

January 1990. Alexander with Nepalese children on a road to Mount Everest.

November 1992. Xi'an, China.

November 1992. Beijing, China.

November 1992. On the Great Wall of China.

October 1995. Stilo, Calabria.

1993. Venice. The façade of SS Giovanni e Paolo.

September 28, 1994. Todì, Umbria.

December 1996. Borobudur, Java.

March 2001. Banteay Shrei, Cambodia.

April 2001. Viterbo. Thomas Aquinas's open-air pulpit.

January 2002. Gulf Stream.

Acknowledgments

I thank my beloved wife, Alva, who shared, and helped me through, all of the more recent experiences related in the book. I also thank my sister Phyllis Crawford for her lifelong support and for proofreading the manuscript. The Vanderbilt University Press, its director Michael Ames, and his colleague Dariel Mayer, deserve the highest praise for the handsome layout of the volume, the beautiful reproduction of the illustrations, and the superb quality of the printing. Olivia Pittet cannot be sufficiently complimented for her perceptive suggestions of improvements, for miraculously deciphering my handwriting, for typing and retyping the text, and for preparing the index. I am grateful to Mrs. Gladys Krenek for permission to publish Ernst Krenek's letters to me, and to Barbara Epstein for permission to reprint four excerpts that originally appeared in *The New York Review of Books*. I am also deeply indebted to Lady Aline Berlin, who kindly encouraged me to publish her late husband's letters to me. Selections are reproduced with permission of Curtis Brown Group Ltd., London, copyright Isaiah Berlin Literary Trust 2002. (Henry Hardy of the Isaiah Berlin Literary Trust verified my transcripts of them with the originals.)

An Improbable Life

Part I

Growing Up

Chapter 1

A Sense of Self

My mother's book, *Baby's Days and Baby's Ways*, reveals that I was born at 3:10 P.M. on October 20, 1923, in Kingston City Hospital, Kingston, New York. I remained anonymous for three days, possibly for the reason that my arrival was as much as a month premature, though several weeks earlier my mother's friends had held a "stork shower" to help furnish my layette. "Robert" was her choice of names, she told me, because I could be called "Bobby" in the lallation phase, "Bob" as an adolescent, and "Robert" during the decline that begins with maturity.

Whether or not "I" had been striving to emerge ahead of schedule, I believe that "essence" precedes "existence," and that "it," Groddeck's *"Es,"* directed me to get on with my life. Being in a hurry has been a lifelong character trait. (In contrast, my sister, Phyllis, who preceded me by two years and a month, had not wanted to depart and finally did so only reluctantly, buttocks-first.) On delivery, "when light / First strikes the new awakened sense," I measured twenty inches lengthwise and weighed six pounds and twelve ounces, which had shrunk by four ounces at the end of a week.

What is consciousness, and when does it begin? I do not know, of course, and like everyone else only hope for enlightenment from advances in neurobiology, or what Antonio Damasio, in *The Feeling of What Happens*, calls "cognitive neuroscience." Meanwhile, minds studying themselves, Aristotle's "thought thinking itself," have discovered something about the embryogenesis of the nervous system (the formation of the neural plate), and about brain structure (amygdalas, the hippocampi—the ridge in the limbic system involved in emotions of fear and aggression). But while science enlightens about the chemistry and some of the measurable functions of the brain, it tells us virtually nothing about mind. We can be certain only that our earliest impressions of our sensations have been revised for us by our parents and others, that all memories are revisionist, and most retrospections are rationalizings.

I was attended in the hospital by our family physician, Dr. Frederick Snyder, and nurse, Florence Baxter, and not released until October 29, a week longer than would be allowed today. Nothing is said in *Baby's Days* about breast-feeding, but in 1923 the subject may have been taboo. About sixty years later I learned that I had been fed that way, and hence received the hormones and amino acids, unknown at that time.

We lived at 70 Green Street, which had replaced the west wall of the seventeenth-century city; Kingston celebrated its 350th anniversary in 1952. In 1925 we moved to 30 Janet Street, and in the summer of 1928, a year after the birth of my sister, Patricia, whose creation, I suspect, was unpremeditated, to a much larger house at the corner of Johnston Avenue and Lounsberry Place. The new house, only two blocks away, was at a greater social, as well as topographical, elevation.

Baby's Days inventories my birthday gifts: rattles, rompers, booties, silk moccasins, silk stockings, jackets, kimonos, brushes, flowers. It notes that my first outdoor nap took place on November 12, 1923, and that on Thanksgiving, at my maternal grandmother's, I was a "very good boy," which could have been because I liked her. On November 26 a "torn nail" was "poulticed with bread and milk." The gifts at my first Christmas included a silver spoon and several five-dollar gold pieces. The medical record mentions whooping-cough, January 22, 1924, falling out of bed, July 13, 1924, chickenpox, August 24, 1926, and measles, May 3, 1929. Between March and December 1924 eight teeth were cut. My "eye teeth" did not emerge until February and March 1925.

In July 1924, I had crawled backwards—*before* forwards, my propensity ever since. I "very soon learned to remove pans from the kitchen cabinet," a premonition, perhaps, of my predilection for the percussion music of Stravinsky and Varèse. On May 19, 1924, I said "Momma," a week later "Daddy," and "See" (sister) soon after, but my earliest vocabulary is quite unimpressive. By July 1924 I was doing "pat-a-cake." On September 9, I climbed two steps and the next day made my way to the top of the stairs. I walked alone for the first time on November 3, 1924. *Baby's Days* enshrines two locks of hair, dark brown at two months, light blond at ten. The book says nothing about Baptism, but on June 14, 1925 my name was entered on the Sunday School Cradle Roll of St. James Methodist-Episcopal Church. My mother was an Episcopalian and a member of St. John's Episcopal Church. I have a Certificate of Confirmation from there dated May 9, 1937, signed by the Bishop of Liberia! (When the English in New York succeeded the Dutch, the colonial Governor of the Province, Lord Edward Hyde Cornbury, supplanted the Dutch Colonist Church with the Anglican Established Church.)

My earliest memories, in the ordinary sense, are of my mother lifting me from and returning me to my nursery crib. I was not fed at our dinner table until I was three or four, and then in a highchair, but table manners were inculcated as early as the bib-and-rattle stage. As I gurgled my alphabet soup, my mother would hold my hand and the curved-handle baby spoon, saying: "We sail the boat from the harbor toward the opposite shore, lift it to our lips, and unload it from the side." After dinner my nurse, Pearl, would bathe me, launch my balsa boats, and ignite the dollop of Sterno which powered the tiny "put-put" vessel that I navigated around the tub with my fingers and toes. Pearl washed me, lingering, I recall, on my genitalia, which, pediatric opinion notwithstanding, induced a tingling sensation. She dried and powdered me, safety-pinned my diapers to me, helped me into my one-piece flannels with the buttoned-up rear, and after listening to my prayers ("Now I lay me down to sleep . . . and if I die before I wake . . ."—why should an infant, so new to life, be obliged to wonder about the *finale?*) and tucking me and my toy terrier under the sheets, switched off my bed lamp. Then my mother would come and in her lulling, musical voice recite verses and tell stories about Robin Hood and King Arthur. When I was a little older she read to me, *Uncle Wiggly, Br'er Rabbit,* and the now politically incorrect *Little Black Sambo.* Then came *A Child's Garden of Verses, The Little Engine That Could, Sharp Eyes The Silver Fox,* and, after she had taught me some American history, *Washington's Young Aides.* She sang lullabies and songs as well, American, then Schubert and Brahms. My mother's sweet voice allured me to music forever.

If I think about the remote past, I long for those readings and for her goodnight kiss. On going-out nights it was perfumed. In the early 1920s young parents of their class often spent Saturday nights ballroom dancing—I see her in a red evening gown with bare shoulders—and on New Year's Eve went to parties in New York, where on at least one occasion Paul Whiteman's orchestra provided the music. I fell asleep with the distant hoots of Hudson River boats and the closer ones of U and D trains (Ulster and Delaware, the "Useless and Dilapidated," my father said), insinuating themselves into my dreams.

How I loved the clothes my mother made for me, above all the black satin knee-length suit with white silk cuffs and collar and six large mother-of-pearl buttons in three rows of two across the front! I still have a studio photograph of myself in this Fauntleroy outfit, taken when I was four, standing with right hand resting on the back of a white wicker chair, knitted socks rolled below the knees, laced patent-leather shoes. My head seems too large for the rest of me, and the photographer, Mr. Pennington, has retinted my blond bangs and retouched my dark eyebrows. My mother also made scarves and coats and woolen winter hats for me, a crepe-de-Chine admiral's hat, and a lavender chenille bedspread and window valances that matched the lilac bushes outside.

I have no recollection of locomotion in a perambulator but clearly remember my mother pulling me on my sled in winter and playing croquet with me on the side lawn in summer. There was a rabbit hutch here, as well, but not for very long, since my mother was afraid of myxomatosis. The ground behind our house had several flower gardens, and one for water-melons, which I tended under her supervision, and which we ate, together with pears, apples, plums, and grapes from our own trees and vines. She also picked berries with me in nearby woods and fields, and taught me how to trim the vines in our rose arbor. The house was surrounded by trees, the largest of them a dark red Norwegian maple and a horse chestnut, with a swing suspended from a low branch. My mother placed me in its boxed-in seat and gently pushed me a few feet aloft. In autumn, my birthday season, she would help me gather and shell the prickly husks from the glossy brown and white nuts.

The apple tree in the northwest corner of the yard became my hideout. I built a hut on its lower limbs and dug a rectangular hole about six feet deep in the ground underneath, a fortress for myself and friends. The clos-est of these, Robert Gross, my slightly younger next-door neighbor on the Lounsberry side, had partly modeled his renegade personality on mine. He would remain a good friend through my early New York years, at which time he introduced me to many books, including *Ulysses*, the Dos Passos trilogy, Michael Gold's *Jews Without Money*, Ludwig Lewisohn's *The Island Within*, and Thorstein Veblen's *Theory of the Leisure Class*. One of my most vivid memories of him is as my impresario when I was eight or nine years old. With a combination of chutzpah and entrepreneurial adroitness, this boy of seven or eight convinced the manager of Kingston's Orpheum movie theater to present me playing the trumpet as part of a vaudeville act. At this time feature films were generally preceded by newsreels, "selected short-sub-jects"—"Our Gang" comedies, "Laurel and Hardy," Chaplin—and animated cartoons. But live shows were also provided: tap-dancers, singers, acrobats, jugglers, dogs walking on their hind legs, and so forth—this was the era of Major Bowes's amateur nights. I actually appeared in one of these presenta-tions, walking on stage in a darkened theater and into a blinding spotlight, where I played a solo without piano accompaniment and was warmly ap-plauded. When a cartoon of me in my act appeared in the local newspaper the next day, my mother was displeased because I had not told her and had not worn my best clothes (short pants in the cartoon and moccasins instead of proper shoes). I split the four dollars received with Bobby Gross.

One day during the construction of my apple-tree house I filled a toolbox with a hammer, nails, pliers, a monkey wrench, a chisel, a saw, and a shovel, and tried to carry it from the basement of our house to the building site. Suddenly feeling a sharp pain just above my right knee, I dropped it, and seeing blood pulsing from a wound there, limped to my mother, who washed and dabbed it with stinging iodine. Finding a rusty, bloodied nail extruding from the underside of the box, she summoned Dr. Snyder, who came quickly and injected me with anti-tetanus. At this time, lockjaw (tetanus) was usu-ally a fatal disease, one of the terrors of the ante-antibiotic age. I proved to be allergic to the horse serum, and my body was soon covered with wheals so itchy that my arms had to be strapped to the bed to prevent me from scratching. My parents, as well as Dr. Snyder and his consultants, failed to conceal their concerns that I would die, but after about seventy-two hours, the hives began to subside. The apple tree was cut down after that, as if to punish it, but another reason was that my father wanted to use that part of the property for a tennis court.

In 1933 I underwent a tonsillectomy, that unnecessary trauma suffered by most children at the time. I recall the experience primarily because it was my first lesson in deception. Once the mask had been fastened over my mouth and nose, the surgeon kept telling me to "blow away the ether if you don't like it."

In Indian summer we raked the gorgeous red, gold, and orange leaves on our lawn into large piles on the side of the street where they were collected by men in ill-fitting, crumpled, dirty-white uniforms who shoveled them into wagons. In this and other seasonably warm weather these street cleaners pushed broad brooms and propelled wheeled refuse barrels in which they emptied scooped-up horse manure. When I was small, horse-drawn vehicles were more common than motor trucks. A sculpted tethering stone with water trough hollowed in the center marked the curb in front of our house. Horses drank and were fed there, heads buried to the eyes in oat-filled canvas bags. Our milkmen stopped there every weekday morning to deliver three or four quarts to our backdoor, and so did our ice men, toting two large blocks of it with iron tongs; electric refrigerators were still a year or two in the future. These delivery wagons, like those of the tinker and the scissors- and knife-sharpener, who came through our neighborhood every few weeks, were horse-drawn. A farrier was located on a side street near the center of the city, a half-hour walk from where we lived. I remember the whinnying of horses through the open doors here, the smithy hammering shoes for them, and watching him retrieve the red-hot metal from his flaming forge.

The propaedeutic stage of my education began at Miss Dora Costello's kindergarten, at 301 Washington Avenue. I remember her as a hefty woman who wore her hair-braids coiled around the sides of her head, like earphones. Her school may have fostered an anti-social tendency in me, since she was constantly comparing me unfavorably to my sister, who had preceded me by two years, had been more adept at her lessons than I was, and better behaved. This was to be a pattern throughout my academic life. Like my father, Phyllis was a model student, always first in her class, whereas I, having no interest in schoolwork, received the lowest passing grades, passing, no doubt, only because my teachers wished to pass the problem along. In our art class I was slow to accept and adapt to the artificial square or rectangular field of the drawing paper, and acquired a bad reputation for my choices of colors in crayons for my image-making. The objects in my pictures were radically wrong, Miss Costello said, my sun not being yellow or orange, my sky not blue, but reds and purples. Innocent herself of any experience of art, Miss Costello insisted that her pupils' landscapes have conventional green pastures and standard black, brown, or dappled cows.

Occasionally my mother would fetch me at Miss Costello's to join her on a shopping expedition. I have vague memories of at least one of the establishments visited, a "dry goods" store, which in this pre-polyester paradise meant not only silk, velvet, cotton, but also wool, organdy, rayon, voile (say "vo-il"), dimity, calico, and other dressmaking materials. The movements and the mannerisms of the clerk, Mr. Skepmoes, a pernickety Dutchman wearing a black suit and horn-rimmed glasses, fascinated me, as he placed money from sales in a metal box attached to wires that conveyed it to an upstairs office and brought back change and receipts.

On other occasions my mother took me from kindergarten to nearby Forsyth Park, which had a carousel with wooden ponies for seats, horrible music, and a zoo that encaged Catskill Mountain bears, deer, and wildcats. Years later, when the upkeep on our tennis court became too bothersome, we played the game on one of several cement courts in another part of this park. I remember it most clearly now for walks there in the woods with my father, where I would unintentionally make his blood curdle by trying out my two-note Tarzan yodel, an imitation of Johnny Weissmuller. The park adjoined a stadium in which, before Thanksgiving Day dinners, we watched the annual Kingston-Newburgh high school football game.

In the summer of 1929 my father took me with him for an airplane ride on a Ford trimotor excursion flight. The altitude probably did not exceed 2000 feet, since we could see every building of the city below and even people walking. My mother's permission had not been sought, my father knowing that it would be refused, and when we returned and described the adventure she fainted.

After a year of kindergarten, I was enrolled at Public School No. 7, of which I will say only that I hated every minute of the eight years wasted there. Girls entered the classrooms from a basement on the Green Street side, boys from a basement on the Crown Street side, both sexes marching single-file, as in a reformatory. The atmosphere was not unlike Squeers's Dotheboys Hall, the learning process largely a matter of memorizing hard dates and facts, for which, perhaps, something might once again be said. History and geography "stuck" this way, at least in my case, and so did grammar and multiplication tables. The classroom walls were part blackboards and part pullout maps on which a large part of the world was British-red. One important difference between "grammar schools" then and now is that we had music classes. Solfeggio was taught, even in the lowest grades, as it was in France; my Hollywood landlady in the 1950s, the French-born and educated Baroness d'Erlanger, was non-musical, but could do *solfège*.

Miss Quimby, the music teacher, appeared twice a week with a pitch pipe to teach us to sing songs in unison and to read notes, which reminds me that each school morning began with the class standing and droning "My country 'tis of thee, sweet land of liberty."

The experience of School No. 7 had a disturbing effect on Phyllis. At this time we slept in twin, bird's-eye-maple beds with blue coverlets, and I remember that she suffered crying spells at night and difficulty in breathing, with the asthmatic's fear of suffocation. Our parents transferred her to the only private school in the vicinity, the Academy of St. Ursula, where the teachers were Belgian nuns. It stood on a high hill near the Cordts mansion, overlooking the Rondout Creek at the point where it debouches into the Hudson River. The pupils wore uniforms of below-the-knees jumpers, light tan blouses, and brown jackets, and were taxied there and back home every day. The curriculum required French and Latin, and the teaching of English was at a much higher level than in the public schools, which were paced to the slowest students. Patricia would also attend St. Ursula's, and, like her sister, leave it with a good groundwork education, but, being nominally Protestant, confused about religion, and frustrated with the nuns' pretense that the onset of adolescence could be ignored.

A more important part of my life than school was the St. John's Choir. I became a member and a soprano soloist when I was six, and remained one until age twelve, when my voice changed and I was sent to a boarding school. We rehearsed on Wednesday afternoons, a half-hour after school hours, and on Friday evenings, and were paid on the last Friday of the month, according to tenure, attendance, and ability. After a year the salary rose from one dollar a month to a dollar and a half, and so on up to as much as three dollars. On payday, many of us would go to Cople Barnowitz's Pharmacy on Broadway to devour gooey maraschino-topped banana splits, or chocolate sundaes dusted with malt. My father being a friend of the Barnowitz brothers, I was given a charge account.

The choir director and organist, Robert D. Williams, lived and taught in Newburgh and hence had to drive from there and back three times a week, a long commute in pre-Thruway days. He was too fond of some of the better-looking boys, whom he would hug during rest periods or disappear with them into the basement to "check the furnace." But he also kept strict discipline. More important, he was a good musician, with a keen sense of pitch, and an inspiring teacher. His lifetime ambition, never realized, was to conduct César Franck's Symphony in D-minor, heard everywhere then and nowhere now. I learned the B-minor Mass and St. Matthew Passion under his tutelage, as well as sacred classics by Haydn, Mozart, Mendelssohn, Gounod, Tchaikovsky, Franck, and, of course, Stainer's *Crucifixion*. He convinced my parents that my musical talents merited training. The choir maintained a summer camp in the Catskill Mountains north of Saugerties. In 1931 I was packed off to this depressing retreat, but as soon

as my parents had deposited me there, I felt desperately homesick and resolved to flee. After dark on day two I exited from a tent shared with five
other boys and walked and hitchhiked back to 41 Johnston Avenue, some
twenty-eight miles away. Reaching home in midmorning, I learned that my
parents had received telephone calls from the camp and that the police
were searching for me.

During Advent a tall Christmas tree was fixed in a heavy iron standard in
the library of our home, where we decorated it with chains of colored lights,
tinsel, icicles, and the heavy, heirloom, eighteenth-century gold and silver
balls that had to be delicately unwrapped and handled like priceless porcelain. On Christmas Eve, I was sent to bed at six o'clock, to nap before the
long midnight service, which I loved for its music—the Bach chorales, Handel
choruses, Mozart Mass, Tchaikovsky anthem, and, during Communion, unison
medieval plainchant in squared meters.

One Christmas morning I came downstairs to find a Lionel electric
train, blue engine, passenger cars, cattle cars, coal cars, and a caboose rac-
ing over tracks that tunneled through mountains and crossed bridges to
stations where my father controlled the signals and switches. A year or two
later I received a chemistry set, and thereafter spent my time doing experi-
ments that on two occasions started fires in my room.

Easter was another musical celebration, requiring extra choir rehearsals. Starting on Ash Wednesday we sang twice a week at Evensong. The
music was dolorous, and the sermons made little sense to me. During Lent,
my sisters and I filled "mite boxes" for the poor from our allowance money.
At home, my mother plotted Easter-egg hunts, leaving a trail of cryptic
notes that led from one hiding place to another: "Near the side window in
the attic," "Inside the door of the food cellar," "On the upper shelf of the
dumb waiter in the butler's pantry."

I recall that one day after one choir rehearsal as I passed the impressive
residence of Henri Abramowitz next door to our church on Albany Avenue, his front door opened and he asked me to come inside. I was frightened because on the few occasions I had seen him he was angrily protesting
the noise of the choirboys playing football in the churchyard. Moreover,
he was known to be a fur trader, originally from Russia, and contemptuous
of the religion indoctrinated on the church side of the property line. I responded to his beckoning, nevertheless, entered his home, and stopped
with him in the entresol before a pedestaled marble bust of a bewigged
figure he identified as "Monsieur François-Marie Arouet de Voltaire."
Mr. Abramowitz then told me about this freethinker and instructed me
in the virtues of his reasonableness, as compared to the ignorance and
superstition propagated in our church. The incident made an impression
on me, not the substance of what he said, since it did not fit into any corner

of my tiny, circumscribed mental world, but the reverence of this alien, or at least un-Kingstonian, type for the sharp-featured philosopher. I told my parents about the experience but learned no more from them than that Voltaire, and therefore Mr. Abramowitz, were atheists, a new concept for me. My father was an atheist, too, but in this instance a hypocritical one.

Apropos of nothing, I remember that, through a magazine, Phyllis corresponded with a young West African girl until one day a furry swatch of monkey skin arrived in the mail, which my mother refused to have in the house. Fantasies about foreign places always excited me. I recall that my father returned from a Holland-America Line cruise with Dutch gifts for Phyllis and me, including wooden shoes that did not fit.

Suddenly, too, without connection I picture our mother marching my sisters and me in tandem from room to room singing "the cod liver oil brigade," one of her many medicine-taking games. We were rewarded at the end of this procession with a chocolate for having swallowed large spoonfuls of the revoltingly fishy fluid. Also out of nowhere comes a picture of telephone conversations of the time. On lifting the hearing apparatus the caller engaged in neighborly small talk with the operator on a first-name basis, then after making the connection the operator monitored all exchanges of gossip that interested her and of course spread the news around the city. Any long-distance call was certain to be reported in full.

My mother made paper hats for me and my guests at my birthday parties, as well as favorite foods and a pink-icing cake. We opened presents, played pin-the-tail-on-the-donkey and musical chairs, looked at pictures in a magic lantern, and, in the basement recreation room, engaged in Ping-Pong matches. For my seventeenth birthday, she gave the large Breitkopf und Härtel score of Tchaikovsky's Fifth Symphony to me, after having had it autographed by Serge Koussevitzky (how did she manage that?). But by then I was away at school.

In front of me is a family photograph taken in 1931—surprisingly, since the photographer had come from Fifth Avenue, New York, which I would suppose, after the Wall Street crash of 1929 in which my father lost his money and had to begin his work life anew, to have been beyond our means. Whether by the photographer's intuition or simple accident, the composition reflects our underlying family relationships. My mother leans over her family at the exact center. My father sits in front of and a little to her right, Patricia reclining in his lap, head resting on his right shoulder. Phyllis, standing, rests her head on her mother's left shoulder. I am seated in front of Phyllis in the foreground, at the lowest elevation, my father's left hand resting on my left shoulder. But I am somewhat detached from the group. My mother and sisters are smiling, but father and son are skeptical. The females wear bracelets on their left wrists, and the daughters pearl necklaces. An opal ring adorns my right middle finger. I lost it in a snowbank in the coming winter and spent hours in a vain search. Even now, looking at the photo, I feel a pang of regret for the ring, despite a replacement by a garnet, another October stone. Obviously the affinities captured in the photograph are coincidental, except that the cameraman may have observed that Phyllis looks like her mother, I like my father. I have the largish ears of a musician. The picture could have been an ad for a middle-class family insurance plan.

My parents had become friends at Kingston Academy, founded in 1774 and reputedly the best classical secondary school in New York State; out-of-town students boarded in the city in order to attend. My father and mother were members of the last graduating class (1915) before the building was demolished. Recently, sorting our mother's effects, Phyllis discovered two love letters to her from my father, both of them written when they were twenty. I quote the first of them because the combination of innocence and formality is scarcely believable today. He wrote from 308 Wall Street, Kingston, March 15, 1918, to Miss Arpha J. Lawson, Box 370, Cornwall, New York, where she was teaching: "Dearest Arpha: This is to reassure you that you are to be my fiancée after 12 o'clock a week from next Saturday night, my little darling, and that *next* September first will find us united as one . . . [They were actually married July 16th.] I'm endeavoring to collect my wits and prepare for that wonderful day. As you say, it's all been a dream . . . I think your next trip home will mean a lot to you for you'll go back with a ring of promise on your finger. Sweetheart, there's not a blessed bit of news except that the new chauffeur seems good.[1] Oh, I hope time will fly from now until next Friday and that life will have a thousand times more pleasant future in store for us. Night and day my thoughts are of you, Arpha dearest. The only thing left to write is—I love you, my sweetie, I love you."

My mother's personality changed after the premature heart-attack death of her father, kept from me at first because I was too young to know. She no longer played the piano, or sang, or laughed. Eventually she tried to enlighten me on his translation to Heaven, but only succeeded in disturbing me more, because she had said the year before that Tweetie, our canary, had gone there, and I did not think the same place could be appropriate for people. The other part was that I loved my grandfather, who had shown me his father-in-law's Civil War rifle and the 120th Regiment uniform worn when he was wounded at Antietam. The Civil War was real to me as a

---

1. He was still there during my early years and the Cadillac lasted until the stock-market crash. The only car I was ever fond of; it had broad running boards, jump seats for my sister and myself, and a speaking tube to the driver through the glass partition.

child, and when I was small, veterans of the conflict still marched on Broadway in Memorial Day parades. Two or three years later an ever-dwindling few were driven in open automobiles.

Phyllis told me that our mother's sudden, mysterious absences were caused by crying spells over her father's death. One day during our second summer at Willowbrook Heights, our summer home south of Poughkeepsie, she went for a walk by herself and did not return for more than three hours. Phyllis told me of fears that she might have drowned herself, the thought of which made me cry. If Willowbrook comes to mind now, that afternoon comes first. I was happier the next summer when we vacationed at Lake Katrine, but by then I was deeper into music.

Kingston had been a thriving Hudson River port since the seventeenth century, remaining so throughout my childhood. The pace of life was slow, the economy based on farming, river trade, cement and stone quarrying, and textile manufacturing. New York City, ninety miles away, was another world, to be visited only on special occasions for viewing skyscrapers, Chinatown, the Bronx Zoo, the Museum of Natural History, and riding on double-decker Fifth Avenue buses and elevated Sixth Avenue trains.

Uptown Kingston is bounded on the north by the Esopus Creek, named for the Indians who had lived nearby, and on the south by the Rondout Creek, a Dutch name. Both estuaries flooded their banks every spring; I remember seeing newsreel footage of the Esopus valley under water and being amused by the commentator's mispronunciation of the name, giving it a tonic accent, instead of on the second syllable. Rondout, the name of the downtown section of the city bordering the Hudson River, was the harbor for the ferry to Rhinebeck and the New York Central railway. It boasted attractive old buildings, notably a synagogue from the 1840s, where I sometimes attended Friday night services with Robert Gross. Its Rabbi, Herbert Bloom, was an extraordinarily intelligent, well-read man, though he refused to talk about the apostasy of Portuguese-Dutch Spinoza—Baruch into Benedict—who just at that time interested me very much. In 1942, one of the elders of Kingston's beautiful Reformed Dutch Church, whose spire is still the city's chief landmark, earned the admiration of Wallace Stevens for having written a pamphlet with the phrase, "When Spinoza's logic went searching for God." The cemetery that fills the churchyard contains the grave of George Clinton, first Governor of the State and second Vice-President of the United States.

The first Senate House of New York State—Kingston was the capital before Albany—was within the walled precincts of uptown Kingston, along with more than a score of seventeenth- and eighteenth-century stone houses still today in good condition. The nearby villages of Marbletown, Hurley, and Stone Ridge contain as many more, one in Stone Ridge now a National Historical Site because General Washington stayed there in 1777.

John Craft, my paternal great-grandfather, a bearded Biblical patriarch in appearance, was a prodigious reader and failed writer. His son established stores in San Francisco and other cities in the Far West for the Great Atlantic and Pacific Tea Company, which imported from China, and barely escaped with his life during the San Francisco earthquake of 1905. According to family lore—no documentation has been found—my grandmother Craft's maternal great-grandfather Gibbs was a member of the Royal Philharmonic in London. His widow and two children emigrated to the United States, where the young son, my great-grandfather, a volunteer in the Grand Army of the Republic, was captured, but survived the plagues and ill-treatment of Andersonville.

My mother's paternal ancestors came to America with a grant from Queen Anne for what is now Coney Island. (In 1866, M. D. Conway wrote that Walt Whitman had two studies where he read: "One was the top of an omnibus, and the other a small mass of sand, entirely uninhabited, far out in the ocean, called Coney Island.") My lineage on the maternal side is French, from Chateau de Joux, in the Jura. Two centuries later Honoré, Comte de Mirabeau, was incarcerated in the Fort-de-Joux. Toussaint L'Ouverture, following him, died in the dungeon there. It seems that shortly before the Revocation of the Edict of Nantes, one Hugo Frère, together with the father and son Chrétien and Pierre Deyo, fled with other Huguenots to Calais, and from there to New Amsterdam and up the Hudson River to what is now Kingston. Seeking to maintain their French culture as separate from the Dutch, they soon left and in 1678 founded the town of New Paltz, whose Huguenot Street is also a National Historic Site. The same Hugo was the progenitor of Charles Lang Freer of Freer Gallery–Smithsonian fame, whose grave is near that of my parents in Wiltwyck Cemetery, Kingston. My other maternal ancestors were early Dutch and English settlers, some of whom fought in the French and Indian, Revolutionary, and Civil Wars. My mother was a member of the Daughters of the American Revolution when I was growing up. I protested against her membership, and at the time of the Marion Anderson scandal published an inflammatory anti-DAR article titled "Unconstitutional Hall," yet despite the DAR she was a woman totally without prejudice. On my father's side, I am reputed to be a descendant of William Bradford, the first Governor of the Massachusetts Bay Colony.

For their time and class, my parents were somewhat better educated than most of their Kingston peers, my father having attended Syracuse University and my mother a teachers' college. As a stock investor, my father was sufficiently prosperous to afford private schooling for his children, a gardener, and a live-in maid—the trappings, in other words, of the bourgeoisie. I did not become aware of my actual lowly social status until I went to boarding school, where my classmates included James Farley, Jr., son of the Postmaster General, the wealthy Shattucks of Schrafft's, the Philadelphia Annenbergs, and the scions of Venezuelan and Colombian dictators. Therein was born a lifelong social unease that turned me inward and led me to join Earl Browder's Communist Party for a short period.

Both my parents were musically gifted and could play the piano, my mother with sufficient promise to win acceptance at the New England Conservatory of Music. Phyllis was also talented, giving piano recitals in her early teens before majoring in music in college. There, however, she transferred to English literature, wrote for and edited the literary magazine of the University of Rochester, and graduated Phi Beta Kappa. For many years she was a social worker in adoption and child welfare, eventually on the faculty at SUNY, New Paltz, in its mental health program. Post-retirement she became the docent for the Ulster County Historical Society Museum and the Huguenot Historical Society. Surviving two disastrous marriages that ended in divorce, she is the mother of Diane and Kristin; Diane is the mother of Wendy and Jonathan and grandmother of Matthew.

As youngsters we were taken to concerts in New York, as well as to local musical events. But the most important factor in our early education was our mother's dedication to her profession of teaching school. She read to us and made us study, taught us to speak grammatically, to attend church, and, above all, to be punctual—the root, I think, of my "deadline" neurosis. My father, too, always stressed the importance of knowledge and education, taking us to every historically interesting location and cultural event within the New England to Virginia radius. Some of these were nearby, in Ulster County and on the east bank of the Hudson. Benjamin Franklin stayed in Kingston in 1754 on his way to form the Albany Plan of Union. We drove to Saratoga, Ticonderoga, to the country of the "Green Mountain Boys" of Vermont, and to the Plains of Abraham above Québec. Our first visit to Washington, D.C. was in the late 1920s. (I returned to the same hotel, the Harrington, in 1948 when I went to the city to meet Igor Stravinsky.) We visited Valley Forge, Gettysburg, and other battlegrounds, as well as historical sites in Philadelphia, Boston, Concord, and Walden. My lifelong absorption in history was kindled early on.

The principal stimulus, nevertheless, came from the contents of our own home, a handsome late-Victorian residence with secret passageways, tiled fireplaces, bay window seats, and a hideout attic-above-the attic. My memories of our move to this new home remain clear because it occurred during a record heat wave that prevented the delivery of our beds and obliged us to sleep on mattresses. I remember that we had a Jamaican housekeeper whose appearance frightened my infant younger sister. I also recall that in several rooms gas lamps had to be replaced by electric lights, a late date for this change.

The previous owner had been an Orientalist, sometime resident of Egypt,

India, Burma, Siam, China, and Japan. She had collected art, most of which my father purchased along with the house. As I gradually became conscious of the exotic bric-a-brac surrounding us, I began to fantasize about the four-legged holders for incense burners carved out of single pieces of teakwood, the cobra-shaped candelabra, the tooled brass and copper wares, the carved Chinese dragon chair, the samurai swords, the hookahs from Arab countries, and the Persian rugs. Our few European antiques, in contrast, were some faded French tapestries—distinctly not the fashion in a 1920s provincial American town. None of these objects reflected the tastes of my parents—did they recognize themselves and their world in the novels of Sinclair Lewis, which they read on publication day?—but they were the foundation of my desire to travel in the Far East, and my late-in-life love of Kangra paintings, of which I have a modest collection.

The previous owner's legacy also included a large library, with editions of Shakespeare, sets of Byron, Dickens, Wilkie Collins, Thackeray, Scott, Jane Austen, George Eliot, the Brontës, Ruskin, Disraeli, Stevenson, Cooper, Hawthorne, Mark Twain; the 1893 Emily Dickinson *Letters;* and my mother's favorite, *Elizabeth and Her German Garden.* Travel histories, especially those by and about Hakluyt, Mungo Park, Stanley and Livingstone, Burton, and Prescott's Mexico and Peru, filled many of the shelves, as did the four-volume *World of Today,* a young people's compendium illustrated with color photographs. To these my parents added dictionaries, Compton's *Picture Encyclopedia,* and *My Book House,* an anthology of fairy tales, myths; and fables. No music corner existed until I began to read biographies of composers—Berlioz's *Memoirs,* first and best—and to collect Eulenburg pocket scores. In the enjoyment of all of this, I had the guidance of a sister two years older whose dominant interests were also literature and music. Together, over the years, we added Everyman, the Modern Library, and the Loeb Classical Library.

Most of the summers of 1936 and 1937 were spent at the Ernest Williams School of Music, Pine Grove, West Saugerties, New York, a few miles east of Woodstock in the direction of the Hudson River. Woodstock was a renowned art colony early in the century, though not a notorious one until 1968. Well-known painters lived, worked, and exhibited there. A summer-stock theater, directed by the actress Elissa Landi, presented works by Ibsen, Noel Coward, and the time-to-time resident Eugene O'Neil. His son, a Greek scholar and translator, also lived there. Hart Crane was a visitor, as was Garcia Lorca, who wrote part of *Poet in New York* in Woodstock. In the summer, chamber music concerts were given at the Maverick Theater, an open-at-the-sides shed with a stage. The main street was lined with art galleries, the side streets with houses and ateliers. A cold, rocky creek runs through the town.

Pine Grove was not a village, nor even a hamlet, but simply a postal stop with a dozen mailboxes clustered together at the side of the road. The Williams School consisted of a concert hall and stage, and a wooden dormitory with a kitchen and dining room. These buildings stood on the top of a hill on the south side of the highway. In the surrounding woods were screened-in summer cottages for teachers and barrack-type living quarters for students, most of whom were boys of my age or older. Girl students had their own quarters.

Overlook, Indian Head, and other Catskill Mountains extended into the distance on the north side of the road. A short walk back toward Woodstock was the school's concrete and brick swimming pool with a diving board. I splashed about here at every opportunity, since my prowess at performing double flips from, and standing at length on my hands at the end of, the diving board drew the attention of older and taller boys unable to manage these acrobatics. One day, during one of my fancy dives, the left side of my skull struck the side of the pool. When I regained consciousness, and was lifted from the water, I noticed that it had turned incarnadine. I remember being in great pain, the school nurse bandaging me, and a faculty member driving me to Kingston, where a surgeon in the principal hospital closed the gash with several stitches. When we reached Johnston Avenue my mother fainted at the sight of my turbaned head. I did not receive anti-tetanus this time, and was soon back at Pine Grove, my status elevated to that of private pupil of Dr. Williams.

He had been the first trumpet player in Leopold Stokowski's Philadelphia Orchestra, and his trumpeter's embouchure was the distinguishing feature of his face. I asked him about playing *Petrushka* in Philadelphia and told him that I wanted some day to study with Stravinsky. He was not expecting so grand an aspiration but did not ridicule it, while making me understand that for him Stravinsky's music was cacophony. Williams possessed a musical gift, certainly, but no school supervising ability. I now suspect that he was afflicted with satyriasis, since his intelligent and sensitive eyes, moving in a nervous tic between a squint and wide openness, carefully appraised the contours of the symmetries fore and aft of every attractive female student. I had quickly deduced that the young woman who lived with him was not his wife but an unusually mature private pupil. But I liked him and was fascinated by his talk about life in a symphony orchestra.

Some of New York's leading musicians were among the faculty in this pre-summer-festival era. They included members of the New York Philharmonic and the Metropolitan Opera Orchestra. Pierre Henrotte, concertmaster of the latter, and Horace Britt, its first cellist, had homes in Woodstock. A small, bald, pink-faced, pixyish character, Henrotte conducted Gounod's *Faust* on July 29 and 30, 1936, the first live opera performances I had ever seen, and on August 23 gave a recital that included César Franck's Sonata, which I loved. Our most famous teacher was Georges Barrère, a distinguished-looking man with beard and pince-nez, much resembling Eric Satie; together with Marcel Möyse, Stravinsky's Paris friend, they were the two preeminent flutists of the day. When I learned that, in New York in 1919, Serge Prokofiev had coached a performance of Stravinsky's *Pribaoutki* in which Barrère was the flutist, Barrère became one of my heroes.

All students attended classes in general music education, meaning harmony, counterpoint, "form," composition, and orchestration, and in these departments the faculty included some comparatively well-known figures. First among them was Percy Grainger, the Australian-bred composer, pianist, folk-music collector, and editor—an expert on Reratoryan heterophony—remembered today for his arrangement of "Country Gardens." He was the first eccentric I had had an opportunity to observe, and the first who had been a close associate of a major composer, Edvard Grieg; a great deal more is now known about this strange, foppish character, and his fanatic devotion to a mother whose suicide would destroy his mental and emotional equilibrium. We short-pants students delighted in his lecture demonstrations, though sometimes the temptation to laugh at, rather than with, him was hard to suppress.

Henry Cowell, a much less flamboyant friend of Grainger's, lived in Shady, New York, west of Woodstock. As a member of Dr. Williams's teaching staff, this prolific American composer was experimenting with tone clusters at the time—striking the keyboard with his flattened forearms—and with harp-like strumming of the strings of a lidless piano. I thought the sounds beautiful and became as absorbed in his art and the structure of his complex chords as he was himself. Cowell's secondary uses of the piano are now recognized as pioneering contributions to "new music," and he himself is acknowledged as a forerunner of his young friend John Cage.

Unfortunately Cowell's personal life would soon attract more publicity than his music. He was convicted of sexually molesting a young boy and incarcerated in San Quentin. Finally, after four years, his case was reopened by a group of artists and musicians who eventually proved that the charges against him were false, and obtained his release. We now know that he organized and conducted a chorus of inmates during his confinement and also taught classes in various subjects. One of those who helped vindicate him was Peter Yates, the founder of Los Angeles's Evenings on the Roof and a good friend of mine. The outcome of this brutal story is that Cowell began a new, productive life as composer and critic in Woodstock and New York, and married an understanding woman, as I can verify, his wife Sydney having been my niece Diane's occasional baby-sitter. Henry Cowell used to cut out paper dolls to amuse the child.

In concerts we played Tchaikovsky symphonies, excerpts from Wagner, the *Ocean* Symphony by Anton Rubinstein, Henry Litolff's *Robespierre* Overture, *Scheherazade* and other Rimsky-Korsakov pieces, as well as American music of the Chadwick, Charles Wakefield Cadman genre, plus, of course, pieces by Grainger, Cowell, and another of the teachers, Erik Leidzen, a humorless, disagreeable Swede who gave me lessons in orchestration and belittled my first attempt to write an orchestra piece—a tone poem, naturally, since the orchestra was performing *Till Eulenspiegel* and *Don Juan.*

My happiest musical discoveries in the summer of 1936 were in my piano lessons with Professor E. Cassius Gould, above all in Schumann's *Kinderszenen* and in movements from Mozart sonatas. I remember that when not playing, he used to splay his fingers as Egon Schiele does in his self-portraits, the middle two straight and close together, widely spaced between the index and the small finger—and rest them on his knees (as well as on mine). The only fellow-students of whom I have any recollection are "Stumpy" Brown, the truncated trombone-playing brother of the jazz-band leader, Les Brown, and Carter Harman, the editor of the school's *News*, who in the 1950s would become music critic of *Time* magazine and a composer from whom Lincoln Kirstein commissioned the ballet *Blackface*, performed by Ballet Society in 1947.

Chapter 2

Prep School

In September 1937 I became a cadet at the New York Military Academy (NYMA) in Cornwall-on-Hudson. My parents believed that the education available there was superior to the one Kingston High School offered, and both of my sisters were already in a private school for the same reason. I was also thought to be in need of a more structured, disciplined life and a broader range of activities, my immersion in music and my compulsive reading having introverted me to an unhealthy degree. Playing tennis and swimming, which I did with competitive zeal, were the only branches of "physical culture" in which I had had any experience.

My mother taught in a school in Cornwall on her graduation from college and had perhaps heard favorable comments about NYMA at that time. Its location, less than an hour's drive from Kingston, recommended it as well, and after interviews with school officials and inspections of facilities and accommodations, I was enrolled and unwittingly sentenced to four years of humiliating regimentation, incarceration, and stigmatization. Another factor in the decision was that I received a scholarship to play in the school band, without which my family could not have afforded the tuition at that time. Band members, I soon discovered, were regarded as an inferior, even a segregated, class. They could not participate in equestrian sports, nor could they, on free days, ride any of the thirty or so horses that belonged to the upper-class D Company Troop, which paid for their grooming and stable upkeep. In sum, I became class-conscious at NYMA, and after graduating and reaching voting age, I registered with the American Labor Party, thereby horrifying my parents and ostracizing myself from their social circle. Later, at Juilliard, I would take a teaching degree as a fallback, and in a straitened period, applying for an interim job as a music teacher in Kingston High, I was rejected because of my politics. But I am ahead of my story.

"Situated on a bluff and run on the same principle" was my adaptation of the school motto, but only a handful of the 250 or so "jocks" who made up the student body subscribed to this subversive attitude. To the south of the bluff, Storm King Mountain encroaches on the Hudson River from the west, its narrowest passage between Albany and New York. In the late 1770s, or thereabouts, the American Revolutionary Army laid an iron chain across the river here to prevent British warships from sailing to Albany. A few large links from this cordon are displayed at Washington's Headquarters in nearby Newburgh, but whether or not the barrier was ever tested I do not know. From the upper floors of the school's main academic building the view extends to the east shore of the river and the contours of the mountains beyond. In the warm days of late spring some of us would make our way through a steep ravine at the end of the football field and hike to the river to swim in its chilly, but not yet polluted, waters, though they were off-bounds, and it was a serious breach of rules and regulations to go near them.

My mother preserved nearly a hundred of my letters sent from this citadel of philistinism, which has been best described in its European counterpart in Robert Musil's classic *Young Törless*. It is unwise to read old letters. The disappearance of family and friends is saddening, the confrontation with one's stupidity discouraging. Moreover, the past never much enlightens us about the present. My first letter, September 23, 1937, describes my living quarters and the activities of freshman-orientation week—drills, camp-outs, and such absurdities. It adds that we have movies on Friday and Saturday nights, chapel on Sunday. Though promised a private room, I did not receive one until my second year, sharing instead a large communal one with seven other boys. Our beds were double-deckers, and we had metal footlockers and small, uncomfortable study desks. When my parents left me immured in this grim place and drove beyond the gates, my first impulse, as at choir camp, was to run away. Then I realized I would have to adjust. One advantage of being quartered in this high-story enormous room was that those who wished to smoke, which of course was forbidden, had egress to a secluded part of the roof through a secret panel, never discovered during inspections, at the top of a spiral staircase.

My letters are almost entirely concerned with my musical interests in the outside world and contain only scanty information about school life. Classes were small, limited to about a dozen, but I was an inattentive student even in these small groups. Though the faculty lived on the campus and, theoretically, could be consulted, student visits were not encouraged, and all but one of my teachers was formal and remote. There were no disciplinary problems. A student who failed consistently in his grades, or could not adapt to the exaggerated orderliness and regimentation, was "sent down," meaning kicked out. The military side was robotic. We marched to and from the dining room, where the meals, planned by a dietitian, were varied and not terrible. Water, milk, and cocoa—full of saltpeter, the masturbating older boys warned—were the only beverages. After dinner, announcements were made about school functions. On Friday nights we marched to the laundry, bags over our shoulders, and on Saturday mornings submitted to pompous inspections of our living quarters.

NYMA, like most other schools of the kind, was essentially about athletics. Physical education was "manly" but reading was not. In all my four years there I never saw anyone perusing a book beyond the minimal requirements of a course. Football came first, and the difference between winning and losing meant the reward of a free day or the punishment of an extra workday. Lacrosse was more important than tennis, and everyone had to try out for the track team. At some early stage we took boxing lessons and competed for a "golden gloves" tournament. I preferred fencing and actually attained a certain skill in the art. But swimming and tennis were my sports.

I learn from my letters, but could have guessed, that between the ages of twelve and sixteen I was a fanatic Wagnerian. Almost every letter refers to forthcoming performances of Wagner's music dramas at the Metropolitan Opera and asks my father to procure tickets for those that occurred during school vacations. Every letter, without exception, contains a count of days until the next school break, some subdivided into hours and some with drawn-in calendar months for my mother's convenience in crossing off the days. I was homesick from my first to my last day at NYMA.

Hazing was nasty for new students during the first semester, and they were vilely treated as factotums. The system required them to shine the shoes and hang up the clothes of the upper classmen. One of my letters says that during "hell week," the last before Christmas furlough,

> Plebs must strip their beds every morning, remake them at night, and stand at attention in company formation in front of their barracks during a cold hour before breakfast. They are not permitted to speak, must wear parade dress uniform with cross webbing at all times, and walk at attention, taking all corners at straight right or left angles, and, at the command of an upper classman, "freeze" in whatever position they happen to be. Finally, they must run the gauntlet, which means that their sophomore, junior, and senior classmen hit them from both sides with buckled belts and paddles, a local barbarity borrowed from American Indian culture.

What I most hated in my first semester were the Saturday football games. True, the bus rides to them provided a few hours away from the bluff, but we were required to stand in the bleachers and cheer during most of the game. Since I had absolutely no esprit de corps and no interest in the sport, I had to restrain myself from contributing Bronx cheers. I learn from my letters that the first game, against Iona, took place in mid-October in a stadium in Mount Vernon, New York, and that we were given home leave for the weekend following our victory, as we were again after the one with Admiral Farragut Academy, pretentiously called "the little Army-Navy game."

A letter dated November 3, 1937 announces that I am on the swimming team and, except for algebra, have passed my bi-weekly exams. The swimming coach, Floyd Hade, who was also the biology teacher, had decreed that in or out of the pool, and in the showers, bathing suits were not permitted. The reason for this did not become clear until one night on his rounds—a check of all dormitory rooms took place at about 10:30 by faculty members—he was caught in bed with a handsome, epicene boy. Biologist Hade was hustled away, but his picture is in the 1941 yearbook, of which I was one of the editors and which was appropriately named *The Shrapnel*. I was aware of homosexual attachments and related activities taking place after lights out, natural enough in this adolescent male society, but in 1937 even the word was taboo, and I knew nothing about the subject. Rumors were rife about other student-teacher, as well as student-student, relationships, but apart from talk about "wet-dreams," which I experienced frequently, I was deaf to sex gossip. My own most ardent feelings were sublimated in my passion for *Tristan und Isolde*, which I saw several times at the Metropolitan Opera during paroles from NYMA.

In December I continued my studies in harmony and counterpoint with our bandmaster, Arthur Fredin, and took lessons on the viola with him. During Christmas vacation my father took Phyllis and me to a performance of *Tannhäuser* at the old, elegant, Thirty-ninth Street Metropolitan Opera, for me a lifetime experience. I was transported, first of all by the red and gold curtain and the red plush carpets and upholstery. As the house lights dimmed and the audience fell silent when the conductor entered the pit, the anticipation mounted to an almost unbearable degree. The sound of the unseen horns and clarinets playing that noble melody was thrilling, glorious, euphoric. The Venusberg scene, the first ballet I had ever beheld, and, first and last, the most erotic, was choreographed by George Balanchine, a new name even in New York, before this scandalous production made him infamous overnight. Venus's sirens wore skin-colored body suits, and their movements were sexually explicit. If Tannhäuser and his hapless pilgrims found them irresistible, so did I, and Wagner's Bacchanale, with the offstage female chorus, was ecstasy. At intermission I could not speak, and my reserved father, clearly embarrassed, also said nothing. My libido had been awakened before this, to be sure, partly by older boys' descriptions of female conquests—fantasies, of course—and by reading the *Decameron*, Rabelais, and *Fanny Hill*, passages of which provoked unintermittent rigidity.

I returned to Kingston that first Christmas vacation determined to undertake a tactile exploration of the voluptuous chassis of my mother's eighteen-year-old maid, Florence, not necessarily to seduce her, being reasonably certain that that had already been accomplished. Several times in the past, I had approached her from behind, thrust my right hand inside her dress at the neck, and squeezed her bosoms without incurring any serious reprimand but only a slow-in-coming "stop that." I decided to go further, and accordingly, in the middle of a bitter cold night, took the risk of slowly climbing the dangerously creaky stairs from my second-floor to her third-floor room. Having correctly calculated that she would not scream, I asked to lie next to her for a moment because I was shivering. "Go back to bed," she said, but I persisted. She relented, as expected, "so long as you do not touch me." But she wanted me as much as I wanted to oblige, and after some amorous clipping and kissing, intromission was soon achieved. Feeling the immanence of crisis on my part, she ejected me in what was already mid-spasm. I managed to creep downstairs to the bathroom without waking anyone, feeling no post-coital *triste* but only a strong desire for repetition.

My letters from school after returning there in January 1938 are formal—"please accept this excuse for a letter," "faithfully yours"—and they sink with adolescent sententiousness about "philosophy," the meaning of life and death, and ravings about Beethoven's Ninth and *Götterdämmerung*. Nothing is said about school functions, but I claim that, even though my homework time is spent entirely on music, I am managing to keep up with my studies. In French class we read *L'Abbé Constantin*, Alphonse Daudet's *Moulin*, and in English class *Macbeth*, *Silas Marner*, and a novel by Thomas Hardy. I also spent considerable time in the school library, the librarian, Mme Boisseau, the dishy wife of our Spanish professor, being an inducement as strong as the verse of the Earl of Rochester, which was not on the shelves. My friends and I used to run to our dormitory windows to watch her sashaying haunches as she walked from her apartment house on the opposite side of the quadrangle to the main classroom building.

I spent part of the summer of 1938 at the music school in West Saugerties and attending Boston Symphony concerts in Tanglewood. Miniature scores were on sale at a store there, and I shoplifted one of Tchaikovsky's Fourth Symphony in order to follow the performance.

My autumn 1938 letters from school are mellower. I am surprised to find one to my mother dated October 9 that begins: "I must admit that seeing you today made me terribly homesick. I tried not to but couldn't help crying." Down from my "high horse," as my mother would say, I now sign simply, "With love." The same letter tells her that the limousine she saw on

Sunday afternoon at the school belonged to James A. Farley, the Post-master General, who was visiting his son. At my graduation, in 1941, I received my diploma from this powerful Tammany Hall politician. But per-haps I am unfair in blaming the school for indulging the rich. Morgan Shattuck, whose family owned the restaurant chain of Schrafft's (see Auden's *New Yorker* verse on lunching at one of their links), was a quiet, reserved, good student, and so were those aforementioned sons of Venezuelan and Co-lombian dictators, though when they entered the student body, a portrait of Simón Bolívar in stained glass replaced one of the plain windows in the school chapel. I do not know what the school's most famous alumnus, Donald Trump, has bequeathed to it, but surely nothing less than an oil portrait, or an equestrian statue of himself as prosperity American-style.

From another letter I learn that Phyllis has memorized Bach's Two- and Three-Part Inventions and that my mother is practicing "the fourth con-certo"—I do not know whose—to play four-hands with me: "Practice for rhythm especially," I wrote to her, "where your part is in eighths against my triplets." My letter of November 10 explains how, at Fredin's request, I am trying to arrange Berlioz's *Roman Carnival* Overture for band instruments. The composer's *Treatise of Instrumentation* was my guide, and I claimed to have learned from it the characteristic sonorities and color effects in every range of every instrumental part that I have rewritten, the violins transposed for clarinets, the violas, bassoons, and cellos for saxophones. In addition I had to "transpose the whole score a half-tone lower." The remainder of the long letter speaks of a new ambition to enter the Paris Conservatoire next year, NYMA being "drudgery and an utter waste of time." The concluding line is rebellious: "I am looking forward to doing what I want, when I want, and where I want."

Francophilia overshadows the next letters, and my reading of French history is obnoxiously evident. I mention the composer Samuel Barber win-ning the Prix de Rome and being "played by Toscanini," and my writing book reports for a friend in order to earn money to buy the score of Brahms's Fourth Symphony. During Christmas vacation I heard Artur Rodzinsky con-duct the NBC Symphony, but I had already heard him in Tchaikovsky's Fifth with the touring Cleveland Orchestra in Kingston.

In New York during a school break I accompanied three classmate cro-nies to Minsky's Burlesque to see the strip-tease artiste Gypsy Rose Lee, whose entire act, as well as the finale and totally nude exit, so madly ex-cited us that we had to remain seated after it for subsidence and a cooling-off interval. (Since she later became a tenant in the famous Brooklyn board-inghouse whose other occupants included W. H. Auden, Christopher Isherwood, Benjamin Britten, Paul Bowles, Carson McCullers, and Truman Capote, I regret that I did not ask the first two writers if they ever spoke to her. Auden rarely noticed women, however. Elizabeth Hardwick, who was strikingly good-looking and knew him well, once told me that he had passed her many times on the sidewalk without showing any sign of recognition.)

My parents were loving, generous, well-intentioned, middle-class, middle-brow people. They wanted their children to enter respectable professions, and music was below that level. But by 1939 I think they knew I would not be deterred from it and realized that I actually was in the wrong school and should be in classes with other music students, and teachers sensitive to my talents, as well as to my personal and emotional needs.

The 1939 letters continue to vent frustrations. I decided to audition for the Curtis School of Music in Philadelphia, but whether as a student of composition, conducting, or playing an instrument, I do not remember. A letter of January 10 remarks that "if I am admitted I won't have to come back here," and this negative reason for switching schools seemed to be as strong as the positive ones. At the end of the mid-winter vacation break, on the afternoon scheduled for my return to NYMA, I disappeared into the woods behind Kingston's Kaufman's Pond with my score of Brahms's Fourth Symphony. I did not go home until after dark and at that time defiantly said that I would not go back. In fact I returned three days late, giving, instead of "a cold" or "flu," the serious excuse that a right inguinal hernia had been discovered, and that I had had to be fitted for a truss. (In fact the hernia had appeared long before, as a result of attempting to carry something very heavy, and had not been treated. It did not bother me much and finally healed itself.)

The auditions at Curtis were not until April, my next letter states, hence "I have ample time to worry." It adds that I am very pleased with my viola lessons, and that I have received high marks for an essay on Thackeray's *Vanity Fair*, which I had read in our family copy of the original Tauchnitz edition. I also wrote and sent home a parody of Ruskin's *Ethics of the Dust*, which is about spick-and-span housekeeping. Ruskin's complete works were in our library at home; I read several volumes before finding the great books, *Unto This Last* and *Praeterita*. My next letter, one of the few to my sister Patricia, offers advice about the importance of breath control to a singer, as she wanted to be. I congratulated her on her good grades; for, as aforesaid, she was a victim of my father's overemphasis on the importance of academic distinction. He and his mother had been valedictorians. In a letter written to Phyllis a few days later I quote Bacon's priggish "There is no stond or impediment in the wit but which may be wrought out by fit studies," and cite the example of Rimsky-Korsakov's autodidactic cure for his ignorance of counterpoint: compose sixty-four fugues one summer. I mention an application form from Curtis, but most of the letter is about Berlioz, including his famous description, pedestrian-sounding now, of the flute solo in Gluck's *Orfeo*.

The next letter urges my mother to listen to the New York Philharmonic on Sunday afternoon for George Enescu's performance of Beethoven's

Seventh. But most of the communication is a paean for Wagner and pro-Roosevelt propaganda, the school being right-wing and anti the latter. I refer to the Met's broadcast of *Simone Boccanegra*, to Barbirolli's of Tchaikovsky's Fifth, and to swirling winter winds from the snow-hooded mountains above our bluff. I shall have to be tutored in algebra, I say, but so will the rest of the class; "the teacher is being replaced." I "received the highest mark in my class in English," I add, to offset the lows. Changing the subject, I note that after the coming weekend, Spring Hop, I will be able to rest. The next letter scolds my mother for sending the banal program of her music club, and instructs her to listen to Toscanini's Wagner program on Saturday night.

My Curtis audition took place on the last Tuesday in April 1939. My parents fetched me after drill the day before, and we stayed in a hotel in Philadelphia. I knew at once that I had flunked. By way of consolation, a member of the Philadelphia Orchestra told me that "everyone knows it is all a matter of pull." Still, the experience was enlightening, and while there I happened to hear Fritz Reiner rehearse the school orchestra in the *Freischütz* Overture. The horn quartet and the clarinet solo became, with *Tannhäuser*, other seraphic, unforgettable experiences. In the Philadelphia Art Museum, too, we happened to see the *Petrushka* puppet that Stokowski had introduced into his performance of the piece—on a wire across the stage, synchronized with the solo trumpet music at the end—and the costume worn by Martha Graham in his and her 1931 performance of *The Rite of Spring*. By Tuesday night I was back in school, studying trigonometry and logarithms.

On March 24 we attended the New York Philharmonic concert in Carnegie Hall *en famille*, hearing John Barbirolli conduct and José Iturbi play Liszt's E-flat Concerto. An April 6 letter home protests that "I do not belong in a school like this, where, for whatever reasons, most of the boys have never enjoyed any home life, and many of them are motherless or fatherless because of divorces. Some of the boys actually want to be West Point cadets, an appalling thought. After two years, I am more homesick than ever and feel as if I am serving a jail term."

I had foolishly invited a girlfriend, Joan Craig, from Kingston Public School No. 7, to the Mother's Day weekend hop. Single-sex schools tended to force these events, one of the penances for the greater concentration and achievement they falsely claimed to offer. Visits by females at NYMA were normally restricted to Sunday afternoon strolls on the campus. Girls were regarded as trophies rather than objects of desire, and this was my attitude to J.C., who may also have thought that she had to come because her father was my father's accountant. As for desire, "loose women" could be found off campus and therefore only long after "lights out" and at the risk, if caught, of being expelled. But I could not dance, both because I had not learned the steps and because I immediately became tumescent, which was undisguisable in the tight "tartan trews" of our braided dress uniforms. I had to find a substitute partner for her, which, fortunately, she did not think insulting, and to pay him, which I did by taking his guard duty that night. I asked my mother to make a reservation for her in Cornwall and to send money, since "She will have to eat and must have a corsage . . . I expect her at about 3 o'clock Saturday. How I wish this were over."

After undergoing a U.S. Government inspection, for which we had to scrub every inch of our dormitories and look immaculate ourselves, we were bused to the World's Fair on Long Island (May 18). One letter describes this as a combination of amusement park and commercial expo involving miles of walking from and to remote parking areas. "The commercial buildings, like 'Heinz 57', are boring, and the exhibits from the foreign countries are purely commercial." On May 22, Wagner's birthday, I wrote a dozen terrible couplets beginning

> Small of stature, large of head,
> Disease of the skin, hair colored red.

Also on the 22nd I confided to my sister that my English teacher, Wallace Norvell Simpson, whom I liked partly because he addressed us as "morons," wrote on one of my papers: "You are a walking encyclopedia." In the week after school closed for the summer on June 10, I attended an outdoor Philharmonic concert in Lewisohn Stadium.

We spent part of the summer in the Berkshires and at Tanglewood concerts, and on Labor Day weekend drove to Cape Ann—Eliot's *Dry Salvages*—listening to the automobile radio for political news. I remember hearing King George VI declare war on Germany, which had invaded Poland the day before, and then hearing the Ninth Symphony immediately after the King. Our vacation was cut short by the tail end of a hurricane.

The autumn 1939 letters mention Stravinsky for the first time, distinguishing him from the Wagner epigones. A year or two earlier I had heard the *Firebird* Suite in Kingston played by the touring Rochester Philharmonic under José Iturbi, with whom I chatted after the concert. Since he and Ernest Ansermet had played the premiere of Stravinsky's *Pièces faciles* in Lausanne in 1919, I asked him to describe Stravinsky, but he could not. The other letters are unremarkable.

The first 1940 letter to my sister is entirely about Stravinsky, but I cannot tell from it how much of his music I had actually heard. I ask her, as I do my mother, to listen to an NBC Symphony broadcast performance of *Petrushka*. All letters from this time forward speculate about the European War, the likelihood that the United States would soon enter it, and what would happen to students. One early consequence was that our curricula suddenly became more strenuous. I now had seven classes a day: advanced algebra, economics, modern history, English, French, biology with laboratory. We also learned some military maneuvers. I was looking forward to seeing *Die Walküre* at the Met with my father, and *Tristan* with my mother.

The event of the spring of 1940, and indeed of my early life, was hearing the Sunday afternoon, April 7, New York Philharmonic broadcast of *The Rite of Spring* conducted by Stravinsky.[1] I listened to it on the radio of my father's automobile, following the performance in the 1933 Kalmus miniature score that I still own. I lost my place three or four times, and lost it for good near the end of the *Danse sacrale*, but no matter: this was the most exciting music I had ever heard, and its violent emotions, rhythms, harmonies, orchestral sonorities were electrifyingly new and wonderful. My world changed during this half-hour, and I had a new lodestar. My next letter to my mother fatuously praises the composer, whose "free mind, spirit, and inspiration overthrew the démodé language of his predecessors." She hadn't yet heard *The Rite* but would hear it for the rest of her life—once, in 1962, conducted by me with the New York Philharmonic. She disliked it at first, saying that it unsettled her nerves. When she realized that it had killed the absolutism of the Wagner of my earlier years, an unacknowledged emotional rift opened up between us. Even in her eighties she would sit through *Parsifal* all alone at the Metropolitan Opera.

Meanwhile, I had been reading Schopenhauer, who, with Nietzsche, still seems to me the most readable in English of all the great German philosophers, and thirsted for more knowledge, but not of the kind found in our school textbooks. I set out to read the whole of the Harvard classics, the infamous (as Eliot calls it) "five-foot shelf," devouring the books associated with music, Goethe's *Egmont*, first. I had become friendly with a professor endowed with a musical background, and when I told him that *L'Après-midi d'un faune* was my favorite poem (in Aldous Huxley's translation), he expatiated on Mallarmé. I read at night by flashlight, under my blankets.

My letter to my mother of April 25 quotes Schopenhauer: "The musician reveals to us the hidden spirit of the world, he makes himself the interpreter of the profoundest wisdom, whilst speaking in a language which reason does not understand." It also contains an invitation from the school to all parents to dine at Schrafft's on Fifty-seventh Street before our upcoming Sunday Fifth Avenue parade, ending at a church that must have been St. Thomas's, since very few students were Roman Catholics. On May 8 I wrote

---

1. I have always regretted not having seen that concert, partly because Stravinsky's podium manners revealed so much about him, partly because his physical gestures are in his music. Sixteen years later, seeing him conduct for the first time—the Symphony in Three Movements—I was fascinated by the way he stood on his toes, which suggested the suspension of his syncopated, off-the-beat music. He licked his left thumb before turning the pages of his score and gave no preparatory beats, indeed no beats either, but a kind of clawing at the instruments. He did not smile at the end when bowing. In 1948, Goddard Lieberson, who produced the recording of the 1940 performance, told me that the orchestra hated the music, and the players behaved rudely to Stravinsky. When my own MusicMasters recording was released, the timing of the performance was only a few seconds different from Stravinsky's a half-century earlier.

to say that I was applying to enter a summer conducting class at Juilliard taught by Fritz Mahler, a relative of Gustav, whom he resembled in facial features and shape of head. I wrote to him, received a courteous invitation to visit him, and did so on June 10. His wife, the dancer and choreographer Pauline Kohner, was distractingly present at my audition. Mahler asked me to sing the beginning of the second movement of Beethoven's Fifth, expecting to catch me out on the one sixteenth note after all the thirty-second notes following double-dotted notes. He did not succeed in this, but he said that I needed more work reading orchestra scores at the piano. He was encouraging and kind, but I did not attend his class. Later I learned that he had assisted Schoenberg in his Society for Private Musical Performances, Vienna, 1921.

My final letter of the semester brags that "I never opened a book in any of my school subjects," and that I received "hundreds on two algebra tests, a perfect mark in biology, and 90 in English." I am reading Whitman, am enthusiastic about Roy Harris's Third Symphony, and I discuss the "mainly pecuniary"—I have become florid—problems that "beset" me.

The tone of the fall letters, the beginning of my senior year, is more mature, but also arrogant. I am now quite indifferent to the school: "I find geometry and chemistry hard but interesting, and I can pass the other subjects without effort." I am less interested in Wagner than in a forthcoming Boston Symphony performance of Stravinsky's Symphony in C, conducted by him. "Our classes are 48 minutes long," I write, "but during the three minutes between them I think about Bach, Beethoven, Stravinsky." I am now conducting the band. "I start them, set the tempo, signal when to repeat, and stop them, since Fredin is rarely here, or, if here, too inebriated to be entrusted with the job." I go into hokey raptures about the resplendence of nature in this season. To Phyllis I mention the non-sectarian communion services in the school chapel and talk about the breakdown of belief and value systems; about reading Darwin, Marx, Nietzsche; about my espousal of socialism and atheism; about Carlyle's *Essay on Hero Worship*, which seemed to have been written with me in mind; and my worship of strange gods, "the Bach of the B-minor, Beethoven of the Ninth, Wagner of *Tristan*, Stravinsky of the *Sacre*." I also register surprise at finding lubricious passages in my copy of the *Decameron* marked by her friend Gloria Avigo—"interesting," "sorta cute," etc. By November 1940 I was listening every day to *The Rite of Spring*, Stravinsky's recording made during the two days *before* the April 7 broadcast.

On November 6 I announce my intention of visiting Edward Hail, a member of the Company D cavalry, at his home in Providence. He was a friend of one of the professors who possessed a collection of classical recordings, including Beethoven quartets, which he shared with us. (In fact I went to Rhode Island, where we spent our time listening to Schumann's

Second Symphony.) My letter to Phyllis of November 7 is high on Strauss's *Salome*, which I must have heard in a broadcast; the Met had banned it not long before. Meanwhile, my father had taken us to see *Der Rosenkavalier* at the Met, but I did not much like it and found it hard to follow. On December 2, I acknowledge the receipt of Stravinsky's *Noces* recording. It would soon ensorcelate me even more deeply than the *Rite*.

On the following Sunday, at 6:05 P.M., I heard the broadcast premiere of Schoenberg's Second Chamber Symphony, presented by the New Friends of Music at Town Hall. The tune of the first movement stuck with me—it is repeated more than any other in Schoenberg, I think—and my next letter announces that Schoenberg has entered my pantheon. My last letter of the year warns that "I am probably going to flunk chemistry, but very few are passing it," and that "I have been made manager of Intramural Sports for the winter season, supposedly an honor, but one that will consume all of my free time." I mention the arrival at the school of a movie actress, Rita Johnson, after her marriage in Las Vegas to a movie mogul named Kahn, whose son, a friend of mine, did not know in advance that she had become his new mother.

In January 1941, back in school, I applied for admission to Juilliard in the coming autumn. A letter of the 14th indicates that I sent Bertrand Russell's *Why I Am Not a Christian* to my parents for their edification: "Certainly you do not have to agree with him, but don't be so narrow as not to read it." It shocked them so much that they arranged for the Reverend Maurice Venno of St. John's, an open-minded and very likable minister, to meet with me during my next furlough. The same letter says that I am reading, and overwhelmed by, *War and Peace*. The next day I wrote to Phyllis echoing some of Russell's arguments and propounding the Darwinian theory of the adaptation of living creatures to the environment *vs.* the Church's, and Pangloss's, doctrine of the creation of forms of life to fit the environment, but of course she had been aware of this years before me. As for music, I praised a passage in a Shostakovich piano prelude, said that I was doing counterpoint exercises from Cherubini's treatise, and was conducting the school jazz band as accompaniment to a play that probably wouldn't be performed because so many in the cast were in the infirmary, the consequence of an influenza epidemic.

On January 20 I received congratulations from Professor Simpson for an essay on "the allegorical in music." Stravinsky and Schoenberg figure in it. A New York Philharmonic broadcast of Bruckner's Symphony No. 8 had enthralled me, especially the slow movement, but my letter of February 3 could have been written by a convict: "45 more 24-hour periods before Spring break and 67 of them after." "Mom," I say, "you must listen to *Tristan* on Saturday, and I must get a scholarship to Juilliard, but if I don't I won't quit." On February 10 I wrote to Phyllis: "I have 6 out of 6 periods full plus two extra chemistry periods in the afternoon. I do not have five free minutes a week, and I got into trouble for skipping things on Saturday to hear *Tristan.*" Fickle, as always, I declare that my new "idol" is Schoenberg.

On the 25th I confessed that I had borrowed money "to buy the score of Shostakovich's Fifth Symphony," and that "I played piano in the jazz band at an informal hop. I am in pretty deep water with Joan Craig, and I must extricate myself or I'll be dancing with her." The letter home of February 26 announces that "I passed my chemistry retest and am as good as graduated." In a March 10 letter I use the word "adscititious" correctly, indicating that my vocabulary is growing. I mention that school policy has changed, based now on the certainty of war in the next six months, and that one of our army reserve captains had been called to active service.

In New York on March 22, a Saturday night, I escorted Joan to *Götterdämmerung,* from and back to Kingston by bus. She had a seat for the performance, but as usual I stood under an exit light in order to follow the score. This involved nine and a half hours standing for me, three and a half of them outside in a queue, but standing-room tickets cost only $1.50. By March 16 I was comparing my frugality to H. D. Thoreau's. On April 23 I sent four themes from my string quartet, very chromatic stuff for the time. One of them, for the viola, is not at all bad but far closer to early Schoenberg than to Stravinsky, who must have seemed inimitable to me. At the beginning of May a woman from Juilliard came to interview me. She left me feeling elated, telling me that I was exactly right for the school. In a letter home I described our band's participation in a Fifth Avenue parade, ending at St. Thomas's, where we discovered that an expensive musical instrument had been stolen.

In the summer of 1941 we were at Tanglewood again for Boston Symphony concerts. I saw Hindemith there for the first time.

Chapter 3

Juilliard, the War, Tanglewood

On Sunday afternoon, December 7, 1941, my father and I were watching a football game in Rockville Center, Long Island, when a loudspeaker announced the bombing of Pearl Harbor. The game went on as though the statement had not been understood, or taken for another Orson Welles radio hoax, but when twice repeated, the stunned, disbelieving crowd in the bleachers began to drift away. As we drove back to Manhattan, the automobile radio sputtered news bulletins, one of which said that the Museum of Fine Arts in Boston had been cordoned by police because of concern that its great collection of Japanese Art might be endangered by reprisals.

The next morning, when I arrived at the Juilliard School of Music, in which I had been a student for less than three months, I was told to go to the concert hall, where everyone had assembled to hear President Roosevelt address Congress from a radio placed on a center-stage table. The now-televised world is so remote from this that I find it difficult to be certain that I did not actually see him, as I and most people did later that day and the next in the newsreel theaters that were common in midtown Manhattan, and in news clips shown before feature movies.

The wailing of air-raid sirens on Tuesday, December 9, shut New York's public schools. Juilliard followed the next day with a more musical, or at least rhythmic, public alarm that began with two long and six short buzzes, followed by the extinguishing of lights, the closing and taping down of window shades, and another gathering in the concert hall. Reports had been broadcast of a U-boat sighting off the New Jersey coast, which seemed at least credible, but talk of air raids was patently preposterous, the Germans having no aircraft carriers and no bases within range. Though all able-bodied males between eighteen and thirty-eight were immediately required to register for the draft, students were deferred, I myself for fourteen months, until February 1943.

From my letters to Phyllis I learn that on December 5 I had seen *Don Giovanni* conducted by Bruno Walter at the Met Opera, and on the 11th would see *The Magic Flute* there, also conducted by him. On the 6th I heard a Met broadcast of *Die Walküre*, and afterward went from Pennsylvania Station to Rockville Center to stay with friends. On the morning of the 7th I walked alone in snow flurries on Jones Beach.

My letters home that month claim that I am at the top of most of my classes and am especially proficient in counterpoint and French. This must have pleased my parents, since my grades at NYMA, with the exceptions of English and business law (!), were deplorable. At that time I had done no homework, spending all of my study time reading and learning orchestral scores in the small yellow Eulenberg editions. Indeed, my qualifications for admission to Juilliard on the strictly academic level were so poor that my father had to appeal to an influential acquaintance for help. As a part-time Woodstock resident, the eminent historian and Columbia professor James T. Shotwell[1] knew both my father and Ernest Huchinson, the pianist and President of Juilliard.

My first letter, October 7, 1941, describes my musical aptitude entrance exams, as directed by Igor Buketoff, who played intervals and chords at the piano, examples of music in different rhythms and in a variety of meters, and asked me to identify their pitches and time signatures. At the end he said: "You have a perfect ear and your ear-training and sight-reading are far in advance of the others in your class. You could be graduated tomorrow, except that you must be equipped with the traditional academic music education." I liked this one-time pupil of Rakhmaninov, the first Russian I had ever known, and was charmed by his musical Russian accent and voice. After a chance meeting with him in London fifteen years later, in December 1956, we dined together at the South Audley Street Arts Centre, where I was rehearsing for a concert in St. Martin-in-the-Fields. I did not hear of him again until 1997, when his reorchestration of *Boris Godunov* was performed by the Metropolitan Opera. He was eighty-two.

My letter also says, "We have been learning Bach's *Magnificat* in our chorus rehearsals. I sing bass and I never want the music of '*Omnes, omnes generationes*' to stop. Buketoff conducts it." Even so (this is by the end of my first Juilliard semester), I announce that, after hearing all of Mozart's Piano Concertos on WQXR, he is my favorite composer. I give reports on New

1. Together with Max Beloff, also of Columbia, Shotwell published a study of the demographic problems of the region bordering the Curzon Line, which defined the boundaries between Russia and Poland, the nation created by the Treaty of Versailles. Coincidentally, the Curzon Line relocated some seventy miles of the western Ukraine inside Poland, which included Stravinsky's summer home in Ustilug (at the confluence of the Bug and the Lug), thus enabling him to sell the property as Polish territory in the mid-1930s. In September 1939 the U.S.S.R. annexed the land, then quickly lost it to Germany, and repossessed it shortly before the end of World War II.

York Philharmonic concerts by Artur Rodzinski and Boston Symphony concerts by Serge Koussevitzky, and I describe a new friend, a flutist from Oklahoma, Albert Weatherly, who, besides teaching me much about musical interpretation, initiated me into the trick of squeezing through subway turnstiles together, two for the price of one. His older brother was the first trumpet player in the Radio City Music Hall Symphony, as well as the star player of the instrument at Juilliard, an important connection for me, since I was studying it as well as piano and organ. In December 1941 the Weatherly brothers took me to the New York premiere of Shostakovich's Sixth Symphony. With the Soviet Union as our wartime ally, Shostakovich had momentarily become very popular in America. I saw every Soviet film screened at the Ninety-sixth Street Thalia Theater, and in the Russian neighborhood on East Fourteenth Street. Some of them, including *The Young Maxim*, about Gorky, had music by Shostakovich. I purchased the score of his Piano Concerto for strings and trumpet at Am-Rus on Fifty-seventh Street, and learned to play it, as well as his piano Preludes. But Fourteenth Street Russian culture became a more integral part of my life after the war.

One of my letters to Phyllis states that "Juilliard is all that it is supposed to be" and explains that I had become a member of the school orchestra, which was then rehearsing César Franck's Symphony, Haydn's 104th, and *Till Eulenspiegel*. In music theory and composition "I am in a better than beginning" class, though the other students are older. Ninety percent of them are commuters, I add, most from Brooklyn, but some from other Boroughs and New Jersey, and I explain that, as the only member of my German class who does not know Yiddish, the assignments are more difficult for me than for them.

A few days before enrolling at Juilliard I rented a room from Mrs. Ruth Brown, my mother's college sorority sister, and her husband, Dr. Emmet Brown, a professor at Teachers' College, Columbia University. This was in their Morningside apartment, two blocks from Juilliard. The Browns had two children—a son of my age, Hugh, who died tragically in an automobile accident a few years later, and a slightly younger daughter, Marcia, who resided with her parents and with whom I immediately fell in love. I became part of the family, abiding by the rules of the cramped, one bathroom residence, but I took meals with them only exceptionally, ordinarily patronizing one of the small restaurants catering to the thousands of students in the area, as well as at International House, a student dormitory on Riverside Drive near Grant's Tomb. With the Browns, I attended concerts, plays, and functions at the Museum of Modern Art, and saw movies (*Citizen Kane*). Dr. Brown, a music lover, often accompanied me to the Columbia library where we listened to Beethoven on records through earphones in stuffy little carrels adjoining the main reading room.

The Browns lived at 130 Morningside Drive, the name for the continuation of 122nd Street east of Amsterdam Avenue as it curves in steep acclivity to Morningside Heights. Farther south Morningside slopes down to 110th Street and the Cathedral of St. John the Divine, where I had once sung on a visit of our Kingston St. John's Church choir. The area below the Drive, Morningside Park, leads from the Columbia campus to Harlem, which fascinated me, and with which I soon became familiar. I frequented 125th Street, used its post office and subway stations, and even saw films in the Apollo Theater, despite the Browns' admonitions that this could be unsafe. Columbia University, Barnard College, and the Union Theological Seminary border Broadway from 114th Street to 122nd. At that time, Juilliard—now the Manhattan School of Music—occupied the block immediately to the north of 122nd, facing the Hebrew Theological Seminary on the other side of Broadway.

My early letters comment extensively on ballet, to which my only previous exposure had been Balanchine's staging of the Venusberg scene in *Tannhäuser*. In the autumn of 1941, Léonide Massine and the Ballets Russes de Monte Carlo presented a season at the Metropolitan Opera. In October I saw *Jeu de cartes* there and Dali's *Labyrinth*, which used Schubert's C-major symphony and featured Tamara Toumanova as Ariadne. I remember that, though we were not yet at war, "The Star-Spangled Banner" was played at the start of each performance, followed, embarrassingly, by the first four notes of Beethoven's Fifth, while a "V" for victory was flashed on the curtain. My greatest musical delights of this period were the New Opera Company's *Così fan tutte*, conducted by Fritz Busch, and the Sunday afternoon recorded concerts of late medieval (Pérotín) to early Renaissance (Josquin) music that I heard at the Cloisters in upper Manhattan throughout my Juilliard and later years. Not many years later I persuaded Stravinsky to acquire the *Anthologie Sonore*.

On October 15 I wrote describing a class in music theory which I had ruffled by insisting that a certain chord was superior to the teacher's preferred one, and by pointing out a hidden tritone that he had failed to notice. In the orchestra rehearsal that followed, the red-faced, cantankerous Dutch conductor, Willem Willeke, asked me to play a passage alone, then actually complimented me. That same day I rode the subway with Marcia to midtown, where we saw the stage spectacle at Radio City. The following week I heard a concert by Eugene Ormandy and the Philadelphia Orchestra at Carnegie Hall, finding standing room behind Oscar Levant, who was in the last row aisle seat parterre, stage right, in order to see the hands of the piano soloist, Serge Rakhmaninov, who performed his *Paganini Variations*. I was less impressed by the music than by his playing of it and his dignified but dour bearing. He walked directly to the piano, sat without acknowledging the deluge of applause that greeted him, and remained distant at the end, bowing to the waist, his right hand over his heart. When I finally saw Stravinsky in Carnegie Hall, in January 1946, he entered, bowed, and exited in exactly the same way, also with no camera smiles.

On November 4 I heard Leopold Stokowski conduct Schoenberg's *Pelleas und Melisande* with the NBC Symphony in the Fifty-fifth Street Cosmopolitan Theater (now the Mosque). His experimental seating arrangement, winds and percussion in front and strings in the rear, did not suit Brahms's Third Symphony with which the concert began and which was the only piece broadcast. After it, when "Stokie" announced to the audience that he would play the Schoenberg, many people departed, and I found a better seat in the fourth row, where I noticed that an English hornist missed a cue in a passage for woodwinds alone, whereupon "Stokie" stopped the performance, pronounced the last rehearsal number before the mistake, and started again from it. Nobody else, including the *Times* critic, seemed to have been aware of the hiatus. The remainder of my letter raves about the piece, the polyphonic web, the gorgeous sound: "Of course the music owes everything to *Tristan*, but every composer in his early stages resembles somebody else . . . Soon I'll be hearing Mozart's *Requiem* with Bruno Walter. William Vacchiano, my trumpet teacher from the New York Philharmonic, told me I would have had a scholarship, except that none was available." A note just before Christmas describes a bombing alert, which closed all schools, and the evacuation of all civilian personnel from Mitchell Field.

After the holiday I heard Otto Klemperer conduct Mozart's *Impresario* and Léon Barzin a performance of the *Seraglio* with the National Orchestral Association. I received an A in a counterpoint exam. My teacher, Vittorio Giannini, the younger brother of the singer Drusilla Giannini, was an academic composer, but I liked him, and he could make voice-leading and harmonic functions very clear. My letters written by the end of January mention that "enlistments to take advantage of the options—Army, Navy, Air Force, Marines—have decimated the male student population, and, what is regrettable, many will not come back to music after living away from it for a long time. Girls are almost the only students left. The boys who remain say they will finish the year but not return in the autumn." The train back to New York from Kingston, or rather Rhinecliff, on the east bank of the Hudson, was mobbed with soldiers, but I found a seat with one of them, who told me about a cushy job he had landed, living in the McAlpin Hotel to work for the First Air Command.

A letter of January 27 describes my piano exam (Mozart's A-major Sonata), theory exam, and sight-reading class, in which I received the highest mark. The weather being unusually warm, I walked through Central Park from 110th Street to see the Rembrandt exposition at the Metropolitan Museum of Art, but the exciting events of the month were hearing Bertrand Russell lecture on Spinoza's *Ethics* and on D. H. Lawrence at the New School for Social Research. He contended, perversely, that Frieda Lawrence really wrote her husband's books. The movements of Russell's mind were so swift,

his manner so direct, particularly during the audience's question period—
"Very silly question and you are unable to say what you mean," he told one
unlucky hand-raiser—his behavior so unorthodox—arriving late, dropping
his overcoat on the floor, beginning to talk before reaching the dais—that
my mental image of him has never blurred.

My reading at this time centered on Proust and Mann, above all on the
colloquies of Naphta and Settembrini in *The Magic Mountain*. I did not read
methodically but simply stumbled along discovering new authors unrelated
to each other. Never in later years would I give so much time to fiction.

The capsizing of the SS *Normandie* on February 9, in its berth in the
Hudson following a fire that broke out mid-ships, darkened the mood of
the city. Since subways, buses, and automobile transportation to the area
had been blocked, I walked from 122nd to Fifty-Seventh Street to see the
gutted luxury liner. A catastrophe of this magnitude in the center of New
York was shocking but also unreal. By the end of the month sixty Juilliard
students had been drafted.

My musical highs at the time were Bruno Walter's *Don Giovanni* at the
Met, and a *Götterdämmerung* there on February 13, the third time that I saw
the opera in the standing-room section in the corridor adjoining the front
rows, stage left. A few days later Mrs. Brown stood with me through *Siegfried*.
At about the same time I heard Mahler's *Resurrection* Symphony conducted
by Walter, and I played in the Juilliard Opera Orchestra in Gluck's *Iphigenia
in Tauris* conducted by Albert Stoessel. The most exciting concert was one
of a series conducted by Koussevitzky with the New York Philharmonic, in
which Copland's uninteresting *Quiet City* was performed. The trumpet soloist, Harry Glantz, an idol of mine, played in the Los Angeles pick-up orchestra with which, fifteen years later, I made the first commercial recording of Schoenberg's Variations, Opus 31.

In the spring I heard Toscanini's Beethoven cycle and *The Magic Flute* at
the Met. The standing-room line had become my spiritual bread line. I
remember a Haydn Symphony cycle on WQXR, a lecture on Montesquieu
by my sponsor Dr. Shotwell, and a Sunday morning Mahler cycle conducted by Erno Rapée with the Radio City orchestra.

In the autumn I rented a room in another apartment in the same building, Hugh Brown having returned to his parents' home. Mr. Cox, my new
landlord, was head of the physics department at NYU, his wife, a painter,
had seen *The Rite of Spring* in Paris in 1920. Phyllis gave the Koussevitzky–
Sanroma recording of Stravinsky's Capriccio to me for my birthday, and I
gave books by Plato, Pascal, Nietzsche, and Joyce to her.

At the beginning of February 1943 I went to Albany to enlist in the U.S.
Navy, but was rejected because of poor eyesight and drafted into the U.S.
Army instead. At 6 A.M. on a bitterly cold February 23rd, together with

more than a hundred other eighteen- and nineteen-year-old students, I left Kingston by train for the processing center at Camp Upton, Long Island. Traffic was halted on Kingston's Broadway as we walked across the railroad tracks to the west side from a government building two blocks away and entered a three-car train that had pulled into the station. We carried self-addressed bags in which our civilian clothes would be sent home. For the present they contained the regulation toiletries, underclothes, and a few other possessions, in my case some books and scores. The day was dismal. Our families had come to see us off, and some of the women were weeping, my mother among them, I think, but I could not bear to look in her direction.

I sat with friends, all of us scared and unsuccessfully trying to make jokes. Several were from my uptown neighborhood, including Julian Ronder, who lived near us on Johnston Avenue. I never saw him again, nor did his family. He was captured by Germans in the Italian campaign near the end of the war, and, being Jewish, was shot.

The normally two-hour ride to Weehawken and two more to the Long Island depot lasted the entire day. At that time railroad cars had to be ferried across the river, and traffic in Grand Central Station was paralyzed by mismanagement. Finally arriving at Camp Upton, we received packages of sandwiches and were made to strip, undergo "short-arm" inspections—move the prepuce back to detect possible venereal infections—and bend forward to facilitate a similar examination of the anus. We were assigned double-decker bunks and lights were extinguished early. The barracks were very crowded. Loud talk of the most obscene kind that I had ever heard continued throughout the night from older men in a far part of the room who singled out some of the handsomer students and vulgarly threatened to "brown them."

Awakened at 5 A.M., we spent the entire day filling out forms, taking I.Q. and aptitude tests, and receiving fever-provoking vaccinations, dog-tags, ill-fitting uniforms, socks, underwear, shoes, pajamas, knapsacks. Feeling ill and exhausted, we were finally fed and allowed to go to bed.

Sometime in the predawn we were dispatched to an unknown destination, the window shades of the train drawn tightly closed—as if Germany, having suffered the greatest defeat in its history at Stalingrad, the turning point in the war, would be employing spies in New York to report on the movements of first-day recruits among the 11 million superfluous ones already in American uniforms. We peeked around the window shades, nevertheless, and recognized the hideous railroad yards of Trenton, Philadelphia, Baltimore, Washington, and Richmond. At the last we were shunted to a siding and finally deposited at Blackstone, in southwestern Virginia. Here we piled into army trucks that dropped us at Camp Pickett, specifically at "C-9 MATC, Bldg. 824." At first, and compared to Camp Upton, this new shelter, in a pine forest, seemed almost pleasant, though it had been built in a hurry, obviously, and was not adequately heated. Patches of snow were on the ground. I felt lucky in that two Kingston friends, Douglas Mathers and William Burns, were with me. I staked claim to an upper berth against the wall nearest the latrine and the front door, repacked my duffel bag in a footlocker, endured an irascible and illiterate welcome from a moronic drill sergeant, a klutz of a captain, and a medical-idiot major. I went to sleep that night vowing to part company with the army as soon as possible, dead or alive.

In the middle of the third or fourth night, an exceptionally cold one, we were wakened and marched, shivering, to open ground in the middle of a forest to witness an insultingly inept example of U.S. propaganda. Huge, monstrously distorted effigies of Tojo, Hitler, and Mussolini were floodlighted at the opposite side of the field, Tojo with a toothy, cartoon-style grin and "comically" large spectacles, the Duce with grotesquely exaggerated chin. During this exhibition banal speeches exhorting us to hate this villainous trio and exult in our natural superiority as Americans were blasted in our direction through loudspeakers. The spectacle succeeded only in convincing me and my friends that in the presentation of propaganda we were surely less efficient than our enemies.

My next shock was the discovery that "colored servicemen," the Army's designation, were segregated as strictly as if there had never been an Emancipation Proclamation and a Civil War. The living quarters of black soldiers, as well as their food, were of a lower quality than ours, and their work was degradingly menial: they emptied the latrines of their outranking whites, collected garbage cans, shoveled coal, and were sent out on humiliating work "details" such as sweeping streets and picking up refuse. Chiefly they did K.P. (kitchen labor), peeling potatoes, dishwashing, and ladling and dolloping food on the trays of the whites as they filed past in the mess hall. From a young Columbia University student named George Washington, the most sophisticated soldier that I met during my army experience, I learned of worse and more abusive treatment. A New Yorker, this was his first taste of life on the wrong side of the Mason–Dixon line. One can hardly imagine the humiliation and anger he must have felt on seeing the sign reading "Coloreds to the rear of the bus." Unbelievable as it seems now, there was a rule against fraternization with "coloreds." In fact we were not allowed to speak to them. For ignoring this I was punished by being assigned to clean boiler rooms on free evenings. Private Washington told me that when chicken was the fare for third mess, "white soldiers are given breasts, wings, legs, while blacks receive necks, knees, elbows, and ass-holes." He and I talked literature and radical political philosophy. I resolved to write a piece for the *Daily Worker* protesting the treatment of black men fighting for the same cause as whites and paying the same price. But at that time nineteen-year-old draftees did not even have the right to vote. George was well read—

Michelet, Benjamin Constant, Sainte-Beuve, Comte, Locke, Gibbon, Fox, Paine, and Jefferson, whose bigotry at that remote time was not suspected.

I wrote home later in the week:

> Today we had a sixteen-mile hike, the last quarter of it a "forced march" that had to be covered in 35 minutes. Before the end, half of our unit lay prone in the dirt road, but I was not among them . . . I spoke on the Richmond Radio last evening. It seems that civilians have been complaining about the boorish-ness of G.I.'s "on the town" and someone at Pickett conceived a project to redeem the reputation of the unfortunate slobs and gobs doing penal servi-tude here by having slightly better behaved and educated types lecture on the Richmond radio. The records of university students were researched and from them I and three others were chosen for this Richmond assignment. My sub-ject was Spengler. A certain Sergeant Waldig, who plays recordings of classi-cal music in his office and invites me to hear them and the Toscanini broad-casts, is in charge of the Richmond project; he drove me there, together with a parasitologist from the University of Michigan, a Herrick scholar, and a young lawyer, a Heidelberg graduate who knows more music and more about it than anyone I have met since Juilliard. *Aller* and *retour*, we sang Mozart, Bach, and Beethoven, but I doubt that the image of the G.I. as loutish and delin-quent has been improved.

During the second or third week at Pickett I awoke one morning with acute nasal pharyngitis and a high fever. I did not go on sick call until three days later, because if suspected of goldbricking, one was put on extra work details. I was sent to a hospital ward, filled beyond capacity because of an epidemic of spinal meningitis. During my first night here the young man in the bed next to mine died of it. I remember nothing else about the hospital except that, while standing on a long line in the corridor outside the mess hall, I saw a pile of Richmond newspapers with a front-page story announc-ing the death of Rakhmaninov. On my discharge three days later I met someone who said it was possible to obtain a pass from Saturday afternoon to late Sunday night to go to Washington or New York. Cars would take six men from Pickett to the Washington railroad station for ninety dollars each— several hundred dollars today—and for the same outrageous price return them after their twenty-four-hour reprieves. A letter to my younger sister reminds me that:

> Saturday I went home. The cost of only 6¹/₄ hours there was 28 hours of travel, a much larger figure than that in dollars, and no sleep in all that time. Since I did not know until 5 P.M. Saturday that I would receive the pass, I could not notify mother, who swooned seeing me, perhaps thinking I was AWOL. The most galling waste of time was the long wait for the train from New York to

Poughkeepsie. Since the Washington–New York–Washington trains carried more than twice the number of G.I. passengers than there were seats, the floors were impassable.

Reveille at Pickett is in the dark, at five o'clock. A few minutes later, after washing, shaving, dressing, and making our beds, we march to first mess. Toilet and shower facilities can accommodate only about a third of us at a time. The toilets have no seats, and, instead of being at least semi-enclosed in stalls, are only inches apart, as in Roman baths. When I can hold out, I wait to use them until the middle of the night. The worst of the Army, otherwise, is the endless waiting to do nothing, the absence of conversation, the bullying and ignorance of "superior" professional soldiers. Night marches and maneuvers are preferable to evenings in the PXs and Service Clubs, though on one occasion in one of the latter I sat at a piano and played part of the Prelude to *Tristan*, softly, for myself, but not out of the earshot of another draftee who introduced himself as Jonathan Sternberg.[2]

We march with rifles, and I am required to do target practice, even though I have registered as a Conscientious Objector who would disobey any order to shoot at a human being. I almost enjoy the obstacle course, in which we swarm up and down a rope grid suspended from the top of a wall sixty feet tall, an exercise intended to prepare us to board and abandon ships.

In the first days at Pickett we were shown the sickening, never-to-be-forgotten documentary film on venereal diseases and their consequences. During the scenes of gonorrhea patients and strapped-down syphilitics in mental hospitals, one in ten tough men passed out or "threw up." Condoms were unavailable at that time, though prostitutes usually provided them. A prophylactic cream could be bought, but it had to be inserted like a catheter and the intussusception was said to sting both participants. Camp-following women were procurable in Blackstone—indeed they accosted most men in uniform—but the film was so frightening that during the ninety-day Basic Training period few men resorted to them. Furthermore, most of us were too tired in the evenings. I spent my leisure time reading *The Idiot, Crime and Punishment, The Possessed,* and *The Charterhouse of Parma.* I had a few scores as well and studied those of *The Rite of Spring* and *Pierrot Lunaire* until they were engraved in my memory.

My next letter home was posted from New Orleans on June 7:

2. He would become well known for his recordings of Haydn in Vienna immediately after the war. I saw him in Tanglewood in 1946 and after that occasionally in New York, his girlfriend being a friend of the Kassman sisters, of whom more will be said later. On June 11, 1998, he came to a lecture that I gave at the Morgan Library in New York. On this last occasion I asked him where he was conducting. "Wherever they will have me," he said, "which at present seems to be Uzbekistan and Ecuador."

I am in a Hospital Unit in a Camp called The New Orleans Staging Area, about ten miles up-river from the city . . . The bandmaster at Pickett had promised that I would be named as his co-conductor in two weeks, but I was already on the shipping list for here and here I am. The journey could hardly have been more roundabout. We rode in Pullman cars to Lynchburg and Roanoke, then switched to triple-decker bunkers in West Virginia, waking up in Cincinnati—though of course no one slept. I doubt that our railroad engineers had had any training at all. Each stop and start was so abrupt that many men tumbled to the floor. Several times we were shunted to sidings to allow more important trains to speed by. At Cincinnati we got out and did group exercises on the station platform, limbering up again at Louisville, Nashville, and Huntsville. We passed through Birmingham and Jackson in the night, arriving in New Orleans at 5 A.M. in fierce heat and humidity.

The city could be attractive if its soldier and sailor populations were reduced by half a million each. Like Trinidad, and because of its location in a swamp, it seems to be a training area for the South Pacific. The camp is ill-equipped and disorganized. We do not have clothes lockers, or even foot-lockers for our other possessions, but only duffel bags. Army barracks are the same size everywhere, but 105 men are crammed into this new one as compared to 50 at Pickett. There is no telephone on the grounds. Because of the overcrowding, married men are permitted to live in the city from 5:30 P.M. to 4:30 A.M. (Please find a wife for me.) Most of our time is spent on queues carrying laundry bags or waiting—an hour on average—for meals. Rotation seems not to have been heard of here.

Worst of all, my barracks "buddies" are totally uneducated, coarse, Midwest hayseeds and Deep South rednecks. The scarcely edible food is the best they have ever tasted. I thought the Pickett people pretty scruffy, but many of them had been students, at least, and all were New Yorkers or Pennsylvanians, better educated and from socially more advantaged backgrounds than these Arkansas and Missouri farmhands. They do not know what to make of me, but openly regard me with suspicion, particularly when I am reading. They peek at the titles of my books, as though suspecting something subversive, except that the *Social Contract* or Marx's *Capital* would mean nothing to them. I heard one of them whisper about me: "He's some kind of religious nut, probably." A large number of them are Seventh Day Adventists who, inexplicably, are allowed to follow the calendar of their religion of the Sabbath. I don't think Jewish holidays are observed, but there are no Jews.[3] Well, just one, Hyman Sidorsky, from Brooklyn, who has become my best friend. I love his bitching about the waste of time, the pettiness, the blank stupidity of the higher echelons of military feudalism. His accent makes me homesick. The Southern drawl grates on my nerves.

3. Kenneth Starr, the Clinton Special Prosecutor, had tried and failed to pass a law to allow Jewish soldiers to wear yarmulkes.

The camp has been erected over a paludal wasteland and we have been warned about snakes—there were two snakebite deaths this week—and malaria. Soldiers transferred from Panama and Trinidad insist that the mosquitoes in those places are smaller and less predatory. Fortunately, our bunks are encased in mosquito netting.

We are to become a hospital unit, the 182nd General, but this will take a long time. The one compensation for the life here is that evening bus service to and from New Orleans is provided at a token sum. Please send me ten-dollar money orders. The twenty-dollar denomination and checks cannot be cashed. Don't send food, which would either be stolen or devoured by ants.

I have begun to explore New Orleans on Mississippi excursion boats, and through long walks in the Vieux Carré and the streets around Jackson Square, the Cathedral of St. Louis, and Cabildo. I have found a good library but not the time to reread *Manon Lescaut,* let alone Kate Chopin—remember our Johnston Avenue collection of George Washington Cable's books, and Stark Young's *So Red the Rose?* I failed to find Edgar Dégas's Musson house—he lived here in 1872–1873—but learned that a liaison in his mother's family resulted in a mixed-race first cousin.

My next letter, to my sister Patricia, is dated June 15:

We take concentrated salt tablets every morning because men are collapsing from over-perspiration. On all of our marches we carry full packs and wear gas masks, some doltish general having predicted that in the last ditch the Germans and Japanese will resort to poison gas, though we seem closer to last-resorting than they do. The part of the mask that fits over the skin is made of rubber or some other exacerbating non-absorbent material, and every hour or so we are given a pause to rub or scratch our sore faces. I am writing during one of these breaks after marching across the Huey Long Bridge, near the Staging Area, and sitting on a levee about five feet above the Mississippi.

We had a ghastly experience a few days ago. After spending a night lying on the floors of cattle cars, we reached a live-ammunition obstacle course on the north shore of Lake Pontchartrain. Here we crawled around on our bellies under barbed wire, and slithered over watery patches and bramble, machine-gun bullets whistling two or three inches overhead. One must be careful not to look up or to raise one's helmet. Casualties occur, but it is thought that soldiers killed in this way are probably suicides. The reason for this exercise is that the first American soldiers in North Africa panicked under fire. The next day we were exposed to poison gases, such as picric acid and phosgene, and were obliged to remove our masks for a time in a room full of tear gas, which was unpleasant.

There are evening discussions about the conduct of the war in Europe, but, being optional, they are ill-attended. The average soldier has absolutely no knowledge of geography and little or no interest in the war. The presiding colonels and generals do not know much more: "Military Intelligence" is still the perfect oxymoron. These superiors have been told to propagandize the case for invading Italy, though of course there isn't one, and trying to conquer its steep, solidly fortified mountains will be a disastrous mistake. Mark Clark, a boob and a dunce, with no concern for human life, but a talent for garnering publicity, is expected to be in charge. I hate military science, but have at least read Clausewitz, and therefore stood up at one of these sessions and propounded the view that an Allied front from Naples to Bari is exactly what the Germans want, since they would know exactly where we are and not have to tie down twenty divisions around the lower peninsula. I said that we should land in Yugoslavia, our true ally, since the "Jug" partisans are holding down thirty or more German divisions. But the top American brass regards the "Jugs" as Communists. No doubt a memo was entered in my dossier suspecting me of Leftist sympathies.

Did you know that most of New Orleans is only 4 1/2 feet above sea-level and that if the levees gave way, it would turn into Venice, strictly in the sense of flooding, of course? Far out on such old streets as St. Charles and Carondelet are antebellum houses with the huge trees that Walt Whitman loved. Some of this architecture is attractive, as are the early nineteenth-century buildings around Jackson Square and the wrought iron balconies on Royal Street, but Benjamin Latrobe built the best of the city, as he did of Washington. The outlying neighborhoods, and Audubon Park, my favorite retreat, are dark, and the air is cloying with flower perfumes, which is at least a relief from the chicory (roots of endive used in coffee) and molasses. The quiet here, mentioned by Whitman, is welcome, too, after the noisy blare from bars on Bourbon Street. But the side-by-side wealth and poverty are distressing, and the "color" barrier is intolerable, though not to the rednecks in my unit.

Now that you are out of school for the summer, why don't you follow the example of your boyfriend and read *The Brothers Karamazov*? Did mother really like *Petrushka*, or was this reported reaction only for my sake?

Ordered to get rid of my books and music, I have found a place in New Orleans where I can store them. Au revoir Tacitus, Thucydides, Shakespeare, Pushkin, Lermontov, Dostoyevsky.

The rest of the letter expresses my discouragement at the extremely slow pace of the war: "We are still fighting in the Solomon Islands after ten months and have made no progress in New Guinea after a year."

A letter to my mother on Red Cross stationery from the Station Hospital, New Orleans, dated Thursday night, June 22, clarifies the events of five days before. While the conscripts in my unit, the future 182nd General, were at third mess on June 17, I swallowed the entire contents of a large bottle of aspirin, assuming that the dose would be strong enough to kill me. I soon felt the increasing speed of my heartbeat reaching exploding point, then became unconscious. Evidently someone found me and the empty bottle, and I was taken to La Garde Hospital's mental ward, where I was held for psychiatric observation, but not, so far as I know, stomach-pumped or treated medically in any way. Whether or not I really wanted to die, I found the vacuum of my present existence—isolated, friendless—unbearable. In truth, the suicidal act had an element of Russian roulette in that death by this means was not a certainty. (The only death by an aspirin overdose known to me was in P. D. James's 2001 novel, *Death in Holy Orders*.) The New Orleans pharmacist who sold me the bottle warned me that the dose would be fatal if I could keep it down, but I told him that I intended to take the pills during an extended period because of frequent headaches. I have never mentioned this episode to anyone and only recently found out that it was reported to my mother and sister when they visited me. I wrote to my father three weeks later revealing no more than my state of mind: "I had stopped thinking of consequences and began to obey impulses that could lead to my own destruction."

Meanwhile, on July 6, I was discharged from the hospital and returned to the 182nd General Hospital. That same day I applied for and obtained a pass to visit New Orleans in the evening. I did not return to the Staging Area until July 13, when I had run out of money.

New Orleans was a capital of vice on the scale of Bangkok, with venereal disease prevention stations on many downtown blocks. During my vagabond week in the city I slept in two hotel-bordellos and after that on a bench in Audubon Park. In the lobby of the first of these establishments I walked between two rows of seated young women, legs and bosoms all but fully exposed. A few seconds after I entered my room one of them knocked on my door, opened it herself, and asked if I "wanted" her, at the same time naming a price of fifteen dollars. I gulped "yes," though I would have preferred a more lissome type. In the room and out of her clothes in an instant, she told me to take mine off, including my dog-tags. After ordering me to sit down, she proceeded to inspect my by now rigid, throbbing member, on which she complimented me ("cute"). Thereupon she nimbly rolled a condom down over me, the first in my life. Then, sprawling on her back on the bed, she instructed me on how to shove myself in, obviously realizing that I had had next-to-no experience. A very few minutes later, she became vituperative, accusing me of having had a "free" second orgasm. This might have been true, for at that age detumescence does not invariably occur after a single climax. The only words exchanged afterwards were those of our ages. We were both nineteen. The next night I saw her in a bar with another client. She quickly looked away and they left the establishment.

Roving the streets one night, I encountered a fellow-draftee friend, Jack Sharot, who, mathematically improbable as it sounds, had been in the St. John's Church Choir with me. I confided my predicament to him, as he, I would discover later, did to all Kingston. The next day, tired, hungry, and covered with mosquito bites from sleeping in the open, I turned myself in at an M.P. Station. A guard trained his cocked rifle on me while confiscating my belt, shoelaces, and spectacles, and I spent the night on a mattress in a cell with two other occupants and innumerable cockroaches. In the morning I was returned to La Garde Hospital, this time to a ward for the criminally insane: the windows were barred, the cells locked, and the toilets, washbowls, tables, and chairs riveted to the floor. Some of the twenty-five or so men confined here had police records, and all, with one exception, were quite evidently mentally subnormal. Three were catatonics, two spoke only gibberish, some were in shock, one suffered frequent attacks of *petit mal*, another, a Baptist, believed himself to be "possessed" (energumen). New patients, myself among them, were straitjacketed for twenty-four hours. Five of the inmates were from my barracks. But Ward 48 was at least racially integrated.

The most important event in my army career, its termination, was set in motion during my second or third day in this mental ward with the visit of an intelligent and sympathetic chaplain, a young man from Tennessee named Louis D. Ferrell. He explained that discharge boards were working overtime all over the country, that small towns like Kingston drafted everybody, especially students, after superficial physical and no psychological evaluation; and that I should have been processed at Grand Central Annex in New York, where personality tests separated psychoneurotics from, well, normal neurotics. It seems that already 750,000 had had to be discharged. Ferrell would eventually prevail on the army brass to obtain my honorable discharge. As he later wrote to my mother, "I knew from the first that Bob didn't have any business in the army and I wanted to get him out." In fact he wrote immediately to my parents, saying it was necessary for them to come to New Orleans because I was in trouble. He asked me to write to him explaining my life, philosophy, interests, and he gave me a copy of Thomas à Kempis. He forwarded a letter I had written, at his request, to the head chaplain of the New Orleans Port of Embarkation, a Colonel Kirkpatrick, who became interested in the case, and with whom Ferrell put my parents in direct communication.

At the hospital we sat on a screened-in, steel-barricaded porch. I met a criminal type here, Louis Nonast, who had somehow fashioned a tool to dislodge part of the screen and carry out a mad plan of escape. Confident that he could swim the Mississippi River, about a hundred yards away and here comparatively narrow, he talked of making his way through eastern Texas to Mexico and invited me to come with him. I did not think his scheme feasible—his only clothes, after all, were his one-piece pajamas—

and I tried to avoid him. When his tampering with the screen was discovered, both of us were transferred to the Staging Area stockade and questioned about it. As the instigator and elder, he was locked up for several days in the "black box," a tiny, airless cell with no light and a bread-and-water diet.

I was awarded twenty-five days of incarceration and the forfeit of two-thirds of a month's pay, or about thirty-three dollars. We slaved here from 5 A.M. to 8 P.M., collecting latrines from around the base at gunpoint on the back of a truck and emptying them in a concrete cesspool. I never described this revolting activity to anyone, but told my younger sister in a letter that the work I was forced to do was "very menial in character." Exhausting as this was, we were still forced to drill for another hour after the evening meal. I remember almost nothing else about the place except that it was controlled by kangaroo courts and that, outside the barbed wire enclosing it, military police patrolled the area with submachine guns night and day. Inside, in front of the barracks, was a grassy compound, where on Sunday afternoons visitors could be received for two-hour visits. Here, on July 28 and August 4, deeply ashamed and humiliated, I embraced my mother and sister Phyllis, a wrenching experience. As an indication of how unbalanced I had become, the day after they left I wrote to them at the Roosevelt Hotel, where they were staying, asking them to go to the Schirmer music store in the city and "listen to the *Sacre* for me." On their second visit, they brought books for me, which were admitted only after examination by illiterate guards. My mother was devastated, having endured such a tiring trip and being obliged to wait an entire week between two brief visits conducted as though I were a murderer or dangerous criminal.

I had been moved to the stockade on July 23, a day before my mother and sister had arrived in the filthy city. Evidently they met with Ferrell and two other chaplains and, soon after that, with a psychiatrist, who explained to them that whereas food and shelter were all that the average soldier needed, I had lost the reason for my existence.

My two meetings with my mother and sister took place on successive Sunday afternoons on that empty patch of ground in the stockade, in other words in full view of the especially attentive (since they were females) convict population. I learned from them that they had been forced to stand for most of the train trip from New York and, on arriving in New Orleans, were unable to find accommodations except for a large room in a YWCA, most of its space occupied by female welders. Ferrell came to the rescue and found rooms for them in the Roosevelt. During their second visit they were able to tell me that I would be returned to La Garde Hospital on the 19th, to a kind of annex for patients scheduled to be severed from the service. I was officially discharged by a board of doctors on September 24 and told that I would receive papers to this effect in two weeks, but I spent seven weeks there, all of them in pajamas. On October 15, I was given my uniform, accumulated pay, a document of honorable discharge, a train ticket, and an automobile ride to the railroad station.

One day before, I had written to my mother asking her to call Miss Cervenik at Juilliard and enroll me as a student majoring in conducting, but also taking other subjects toward a degree. Since my birthday was approaching, I asked for the Fritz Busch albums of Brandenburg Concertos, for other music and many books, and asked to see on my arrival the *Well-Tempered Clavichord* on the keyboard and Mengelberg's recording of the *Egmont* Overture on the turntable.

As those last weeks in the hospital dragged on and on, so did the correspondence between my parents and Ferrell. One of his letters to them, dated October 5, promises that "If Robert is not home by the 10th, send me a telegram and I will go over again and stay until he gets out . . . If I know anything about human nature, you will be proud of your son some day." The routine was at least restful. Every morning a Red Cross volunteer social worker stopped to converse with me. One of them, a Radcliffe graduate, had actually studied with Nadia Boulanger and could play Stravinsky's *Sérenade en la*. A country-and-western-style group visited twice a week and sang "You Are My Sunshine" and other depressing hillbilly classics. Movies were shown every evening, but I preferred to read: Dos Passos, *Buddenbrooks*, all of Ibsen, John Addington Symonds's overly florid *Renaissance*, Chekhov, and Sholokov's glorification of the U.S.S.R., *And Quiet Flows the Don*.

I was home two days before my birthday, unburdened of the innocence with which I had left it, not at all grateful for the knowledge and experiences of the world I had acquired, but, as I left the train at the Poughkeepsie railroad station, redivivus. A month later my grandfather Craft died of cancer, a sad event for me, though I scarcely knew him.

The student body at Juilliard was much diminished in 1944 from the one I had left, and overwhelmingly female. Since the faculty was partly new, as well, I felt like a stranger. I found a room in a run-down apartment house on Amsterdam Avenue a block north of Morningside Drive which I shared amicably with Gilbert Mitchell, who would later become the conductor of the Northern Virginia Chamber Orchestra. Leading me to our new quarters, he said, "Are you ready for a shock?" In fact, I wasn't when he opened the door of a room on the way and exposed the body of a naked elderly man lying dead on his bed. Mitchell explained that it was a natural death and that the police and an ambulance were on the way. I remember only one experience with Mitchell, a matinée Philharmonic concert in Carnegie Hall in which Fritz Reiner conducted Stravinsky's *Song of the Nightingale*. Years later I learned from one of Reiner's letters to Stravinsky that Béla Bartók had been in the audience that day and was delighted with the music.

Mitchell soon left our apartment for a job in the Symphony Orchestra in New Orleans, of all places. Massimo Freccia, the conductor there, had become a friend of Stravinsky, through Fifi Tarafa in Cuba.[4] Through this connection, Mitchell obtained an autographed photo of the composer and became a lifetime Stravinskyan.

My sister Phyllis, doing war work and studying English at Columbia, had now moved to 506 West 122nd Street, just east of Broadway, living with three career women of very different temperaments and interests: Betty Lickert, whose family had been missionaries in India, and who went there herself to reverse the conversions of Christians back to Hinduism; Catherine Johnk, a harpist studying at Juilliard, who married Robert Gottlieb, a friend of mine there, and eventually moved with him to Los Angeles, where she occasionally played in recordings with me; and Julie Rider, who married someone in the State Department and spent most of her life in Central and South America. I mention these people because I found their company more stimulating than that of the musicians in my classes at Juilliard. A letter from this period tells me that I met and became a friend of a certain John Brossard, who had taught French at the University of California, and whose mother had attended the premiere of Le Sacre du printemps, keeping a souvenir of the occasion in the form of a hat that had been stomped upon.

Only one experience in my first and second terms at the school remains clear to me: my attraction to a young woman, a pianist, who was in three of my classes. A flirtation began and soon became an affair. She became pregnant, and, abortion being out of the question, we talked of marriage, openly and with our respective families as well. Her father, a prosperous Brooklyn physician, did not want a gentile son-in-law and told me I would have to convert. I must have agreed, since his daughter and her mother drove to Kingston one Sunday to meet my family. Dr. N. received me graciously in his Brooklyn home and summerhouse at Patchogue. At his behest I received instruction from a rabbi, and eventually, in a private ceremony in the N. home, I was circumcised by the doctor himself, the second time for me, since in the era of my birth New York State health laws required it. But Dr. N. wanted the ritual, and I obliged by submitting to a needle puncture on my prepuce. Two or three drops of blood fell on the cover of a Bible, and were then wiped away. I repeated a few phrases in Hebrew, but to this day do not know whether or not I can be considered a Jew. (I never had a Bar Mitzvah.) In any event, we did not marry, and Dr. N. terminated the pregnancy with an injection. The relationship continued until the end of August 1945, when we had a "tiff." I remember giving a piece of jewelry to her at Hanukkah, nevertheless.

Earlier in the year I joined Erno Rapée's Radio City Music Hall orches-

---

4. See the entry for 1951 in my book, Stravinsky: The Chronicle of a Friendship, 1948-1971 (New York: Alfred A. Knopf, 1972, revised and expanded, Nashville: Vanderbilt University Press, 1994).

tra and, with Albert Weatherly, played with it on an ill-fated, weather-wise, three-week tour. We were snowed in at Buffalo for three days, and delayed again from the same cause in Pittsburgh and Baltimore. In the latter two cities, I was able to watch rehearsals of the local Symphony orchestras conducted by, respectively, Fritz Reiner and Reginald Stewart. Theodore Bloomfield, who in later years was music director of the Hannover (Germany) Opera, was also a member of this touring orchestra, as a horn player.

In the summer of 1945 I drove my mother to Portsmouth, Virginia, where Phyllis was living, unhappily, with her naval officer husband. The trip involved an overnight ride on a ferry from the Delaware side to Norfolk. I also recall being alone with my father somewhere in a hotel on the New Jersey coast on VJ Day, but of the circumstances only that we became aware of the news when shouts rose from the street, windows opened, and people poured out of buildings, the noise developing into a roar.

In the winter session of 1945–6 I was enrolled as an extension philosophy student at Columbia. Irwin Edman, a Santayana disciple, was one of my teachers, and, like his master, homosexual. He made "a pass" at me, and though I brusquely rebuffed him, he gave me an A for the course. I do not remember the name of my professor in logic, but his class was much smaller, and I found the subject riveting, the texts used being from G. E. Moore and Bertrand Russell. In the previous summer I had been in Ruth Benedict's anthropology class at Columbia and in Robert Weaver's famous course in literature. I found Benedict bright and stimulating but egregious. Weaver, who has a place in literary history as the "discoverer" and editor of Melville, was the most inspiring teacher I have ever known. He made performances out of comparing Chaucer's and Shakespeare's *Troilus*, reciting the *Roman de la Rose* and Dante, and giving huge reading assignments that included *Swann's Way*. But he ridiculed Joyce and Eliot (an "inconsiderable poet"), just when I was becoming mesmerized by them.

The main event of 1946 was the birth of my niece, Diane, March 20. The following month, I applied for a teaching job at Antioch College, which I describe in a letter to Phyllis as "a good liberal progressive school," and met a very bright Barnard College student, Betty Rubinstein, through my Kingston friend Robert Gross. She had attended W. H. Auden's lectures at Bennington College, was bewitched by him, and invited me to hear him at Barnard. Ignoring the strict rule against admitting persons of my gender to the premises, she smuggled me in, encircled by six classmates on their way to the same small room. Auden arrived promptly at the appointed hour, removed his jacket, dropped it on the floor, then, without any greeting, began his homily in what seemed to be *in medias res*. From time to time he looked in the general direction of the students, but never directly at any one of them. The atmosphere was a little strained, as the girls did not understand his British pronunciations of some words, to say nothing of the words themselves. When hands were raised and he was asked to explain or repeat, he turned to the blackboard, and, muttering unflattering comments on the students that made them titter, chalked up "Arete," the only one I remember. Betty was also a friend of Robert's on-and-off girlfriend, Judy Horowitz. The most "liberated" female I had ever met, Judy proposed that I go to bed with her and Betty at the same time, which we did, the most stupid experiment in which I have ever been engaged, doomed from the first grope.

Otherwise, I was spending more and more time that spring in the Metropolitan and Frick Museums, and more evenings in the Fourteenth Street area, where I could eat Russian food and see foreign movies. I read Kafka for the first time, Flaubert's *Trois Contes*, and, with the help of the Campbell and Robinson guide, *Finnegans Wake.*

I duly graduated from Juilliard—after passing an exam in vocal training, of all things, singing Ravel's baritone songs, *Don Quichotte à la Dulcinée*— and received my degree from William Schuman, the school's new president.

Meanwhile I had been accepted as a conducting student at the new Tanglewood Music Center in Lenox, Massachusetts. I rented a room in a small private home in the center of town, next to the one occupied by Canadian tenor Joseph Laderoute, who sang the title role in the American premiere of Benjamin Britten's *Peter Grimes*, the summer's main attraction. Morris Levine, a violinist and later a leading conductor of Broadway musicals, also boarded there.

On the first day at the center I attended a conducting class by Stanley Chapple, a British teacher who talked purposefully about the art at both the technical and practical levels, but, lacking an orchestra or smaller ensemble, was unable to demonstrate his nostrums and offer his students opportunities for experience. During this first session I met Claudio Spies, a coeval and close friend from that day to the present. We immediately discovered a common passion for Stravinsky's music. Claudio had actually met the composer, having been introduced to him by Nadia Boulanger in New York in 1943. Claudio was born in Santiago, Chile, to which his father had emigrated from Germany in 1913. Since a cousin of his was a member of the Boston Symphony, Claudio had been able to attend Stravinsky's rehearsals with the orchestra. Next to this sophisticated, multilingual, well-bred student I felt an utter bumpkin, but we became fast friends. Together with his friend Mordekhai Sheinkman, pianist, we formed a Stravinsky fan club, the three of us hanging on every word of the slightly older Harold Shapero, a wunderkind who had won the Gershwin Prize in Composition at age twenty, and was regarded as the most promising composer of his generation by Stravinsky himself. Harold had written a symphony, a string serenade, and three appealing piano sonatas. In one area I was slightly ahead of Claudio, and had an influence on *him*: already in 1940 I had realized that

Arnold Schoenberg was the "other" in what would become the two hege-
monies of the century's music. In the general shift toward Schoenberg and
expressionism a few years later, Shapero stopped composing, while Claudio
graduated from Harvard and went on to teach at Vassar, Swarthmore, and,
as Milton Babbitt's colleague, Princeton, where he remained for three decades.

Among other longtime friends met at Tanglewood was the composer
Irving Fine, an attractive man, composer, and teacher (at Harvard), who
would die very prematurely of a heart attack in 1963. I also remember with
affection Phyllis Curtin, a clear-voiced soprano and impeccable musician,
and now the director of vocal music at Boston University. Two years after
Tanglewood she recorded the part of Parasha in Stravinsky's *Mavra* with
me, along with Eunice Alberts, a contralto and another good friend, who
also sang in my *Mavra*.

Closer than both of these was Vera Kassman, an attractive, pleasant,
good-natured, vocal student, who spoke Russian and whose father was the
Boston Symphony's assistant concertmaster. We became instant friends. While
walking with her one hot afternoon in the forest half a mile or so from the
open-air concert auditorium, we rested on a grassy knoll, dallied, and were
soon stumbled over by, of all people, Aaron Copland, who, so he said, was
on an inspirational ramble. He affected not to have noticed anything and
began a serious conversation with us about the Tanglewood Summer School
and what we thought of it. Each time I saw Copland in later years, at concerts, at the Stravinskys' in Hollywood and, with them, in New York, he
mentioned the incident in a kindly, joking way: "Do you remember when
we first met in the tangled woods?"

Conducting students were required to attend Serge Koussevitzky's Boston
Symphony rehearsals, during which a select few were given a little time to
work with the orchestra, Leonard Bernstein far more than anyone else, but
also Harold Shapero, Seymour Lipkin (Sibelius's Fifth Symphony), and the
gifted Brazilian, Eleazar de Carvalho, by far the most interesting student
discovery of the summer. His forte, of course, was the music of Heitor
Villa-Lobos, but later in life he gave exciting and rhythmically precise performances of *The Rite of Spring*. (He had been the tuba player in the Rio de
Janeiro Symphony in 1936 when Stravinsky conducted it.) Koussevitzky
himself was not highly esteemed. His clothes—white flannels, black, red-
silk-lined capes, sporty tweed caps—were garish beyond description, and
he was surrounded by flunkeys and sycophants, who cordoned him off from
students. The orchestra players, over whom he had life-and-death power,
did not respect him or even look at his ham histrionics while conducting,
following Richard Burgin, the concertmaster, instead. Further, his English
was rudimentary, virtually without syntax. It seems that when he dismissed
a player during a rehearsal one day, the victim, before leaving, angrily shouted

vulgar profanities at him, to which Koussevitzy responded: "It is too late to apologize." It was widely known that underlings did most of the initial work of rehearsing and an open secret that Koussevitzky learned new scores by having Lukas Foss, or another pianist, play them for him. The Boston Symphony, nevertheless, was rated the country's best, and it was commissioning more new music than any other in the United States.

Symposia took place in the evenings, but most of them were limited to "amusing" anecdotes. I enjoyed one of these soirées very much, a friendly disagreement between Shapero and the celebrated cellist Gregor Piatigorsky. The discussion centered on Piatigorsky's close friend Jascha Heifetz and his refusal to learn Stravinsky's Violin Concerto. He could not play the first chord, Piatigorsky said in his comically thick Russian accent, following the statement by a droll pantomime of the struggling violinist. Shapero, making a case for the neglect of the contemporary composer by the contemporary virtuoso-tycoon, argued that younger violinists had played the chord without trouble and in fact found that it was the root of the piece, as Samuel Dushkin had realized fifteen years earlier. Piatigorsky had come to Tanglewood to play Hindemith's new Cello Concerto, and Hindemith had come to teach composition. He also conducted his short opera, *Hin und Zurück*, which goes forward, then backwards from the denouement, like the rewinding of a movie reel.

The Koussevitzky Foundation had commissioned Benjamin Britten's *Peter Grimes*, and contracted to give its American premiere. The work had launched a new musical era in England and established Britten as the country's leading composer. Claudio and I attended his rehearsals, without much interest in the music. At the performance, conducted by Leonard Bernstein, Britten was accompanied by Auden, who had come up from New York. After it, they went to a reception in the composer's honor, during which "Lenny B.," burning with envy over the success of the opera, began to play pop tunes on a piano in another part of the room, thus drawing attention from Britten. Shy, gracious, deferential, and unknown personally hereabouts, the composer became a captive onlooker at Bernstein's exhibition.

In the autumn of 1946 I returned to Juilliard as a scholarship conducting student. My teacher, Edgar Shenkman, conveyed much useful technical knowledge about the "art" to me, and to three or four other students, but since we had no opportunity to work with an orchestra, the classes were confined to theoretical-hypothetical discussions. The outstanding musical experience of the school year was a visit by René Leibowitz, proselytizing for the music of Anton Webern and conducting his Concerto for nine instruments as an illustration to an analytical talk about the work. This event changed my life, and from that day I tried to learn all available music by the composer, which was very little. I heard many interesting concerts in midtown, the most memorable of these being Bernstein's performance of *Oedi-*

pus Rex with a cantor in the title role, and of Stravinsky's Violin Concerto, with Tossy Spivakovsky as soloist. I did not care for Darius Milhaud's four cantatas presented at Juilliard, though the occasion brought his wife, Madeleine, to New York, thereby enabling Stravinsky to perform *Perséphone* with her as *diseuse* on a late-night CBS broadcast.

I was paid by the school to visit colleges and other schools and give lectures on music and the humanities. At Juilliard, too, I became friendly with an English teacher, Elbert Lenrow, whose standards were higher than those of anyone else I had encountered since Robert Weaver. He had edited an edition of Wagner's correspondence with Anton Pusinelli, acquiring therefrom a name as a musicologist. He wrote to me after seeing me conduct on the opening night of the New York City Ballet's Stravinsky Festival in 1972, and this led to a literary association when I first began to publish review articles in the *New York Review of Books*. In the late 1970s I sent the manuscripts to him of almost every essay I wrote, and I owe much to his editing advice.

Also in the autumn of 1946, I moved to 313 West Ninety-first Street, between West End Avenue and Riverside Drive. Vera Kassman, who had an apartment there, found a top-floor cold-water flat—a loft—for me to rent. I moved in with my Juilliard friend, Elden Gatwood, an oboist from Nashville who had played in the Manila Symphony at the end of the war under the excellent conductor Herbert Zipper. Elden would spend several years as an oboist in the Cleveland Symphony and as first oboe in the Pittsburgh Orchestra. He later became a close friend of my parents, sisters, and elder niece. After retiring, he switched to the viola da gamba, which he still plays in an "old music" ensemble.

Our Ninety-first Street living arrangements were Bohemian. At bedtime Elden moved to Vera's room, and she to his part of mine. I never knew whether or not he shared the other back room, whose tenant was an attractive young woman called Rosalind. Unfortunately, the only bathroom facilities had to be shared among the residents of all three rooms.

On January 29, 1947, I conducted a piece by Poulenc and another by the Juilliard composition student William Bergsma in a Juilliard concert. The next day I returned to my old job as conductor of the Lyndon Wright Choral Society in Yonkers. I had resigned after a spat with the accompanist, but was persuaded to return by the president of the organization, a Mr. Mittler. Juilliard had found this ill-paid employment for me months before. It entailed one or two nights of rehearsing each week, and long subway rides to the end of the line at 300th Street, the southern end of the suburban city, the site of the Broadway musical *Hello, Dolly.* The chorus was hopelessly amateur, but I learned from the work. We gave two concerts in the year, and to add more musical interest to them I invited Morris Levine (from Tanglewood) and Frank Glazer, a friend of Elly Kassman, to perform César

Franck's violin sonata. These memories of the experiences have been revived by the discovery of a note from my Kingston tailor, Hyman Rafalowsky: "Pants measurements: 30½ crotch to end of cuff; 30 for the waist." He was fitting a tuxedo for me to wear in my Yonkers concerts.

In the summer of 1947 I briefly attended Pierre Monteux's summer classes for conductors at Hancock, Maine. There I quickly realized that I did not want to become an all-purpose standard-repertory conductor, but, instead, something of a specialist in modern music. On August 20, 1947, I wrote to Stravinsky asking for assistance in procuring the score of his *Symphonies of Wind Instruments*. Years later, Stravinsky, who was deeply superstitious, told me that my letter came on the very day he had begun work on a new version of the piece and that he foresaw some significance in the coincidence.

Part II

The Stravinsky Years

Chapter 4

"Dear Bobsky"

Correspondence 1947–1949[1]

Avant-Propos

Chrysippus believed that all events are determined by "a seamless web of interrelated causes, and no event occurs randomly." But he also acknowledged that "obscure causes are working under the surface." I do not know whether my connection with Igor Stravinsky was the result of "interrelated causes" or fortuitously and by coincidences of circumstance. Certainly a convergence of factors took place. Stravinsky understood from my April 1948 conducting of his Symphony in C, *Symphonies of Winds*, and Capriccio, however crude, that I understood the spirit and knew the letter of his music well enough to be able to rehearse for him, as I did before that first concert. He also realized from those days together in April 1948 that I was conversant with new tendencies (and new contrivances) in music from which he felt isolated, including the awakening interest in Arnold Schoenberg and his school.

Another element that contributed to the relationship that quickly developed between Stravinsky and myself was that, since the next work on his agenda was an opera in English, I might be of some help to him vis-à-vis the libretto of *The Rake's Progress*, which Wystan Auden delivered to him in the same instance that I delivered myself. Further, while most of Stravinsky's fellow refugee friends in the United States were planning to return to Europe after the war, he had made up his mind as early as February 1942 to settle in California[2] and even to "Americanize" himself, in the best sense of

1. The letters have been published before, but in a text rife with chronological and other errors, and in limited, now long out of print, editions. The present version has been corrected to the best of my abilities, and I have expanded my commentaries to the letters.

2. On the 20th of that month he wrote to Ernest Voigt, of Associated Music Publishers, "I have decided to remain. I have purchased a house here in Hollywood, and, already two years ago, I took out my first [citizenship] papers. My musical activities have been transferred here by events, and there seems to be absolutely no reason to hope for a return to a normal life in Europe when this gigantic conflict ends."

the word (if there is one). I was the only born-and-bred American among both his California and New York friends. Hence the very handicap of my ignorance of his languages worked to my advantage: he wanted to develop his command of English and would be forced to do so in order to communicate with me, while at the same time he would be able to speak privately with his wife and other Russians in my presence. The "fortuitous" begins to seem inseparable from the "interrelated causes."

Though Stravinsky could be said to have dominated modern music in America at the end of World War II, his music, the early ballets excepted, was little known, and performances of his other compositions were rare. This helps to explain his remarkably cordial response to the letters of a young conductor steeped in and intent on performing them.

I knew from Tanglewood friends and from Samuel Dushkin, whom I had met independently in New York, that Stravinsky made factotums of everyone close to him. Thus his younger son wrote to me, December 8, 1949: "Father says he does not trust anybody except you. As such a compliment cannot be received just gratis, he would ask you . . ." etc. I am not ashamed of the appellation "Adlatus," and from the composer's earliest letters I could see that I was on the way to becoming just that.

Like others surprised at the confidence Stravinsky placed in me, I continue to speculate about the question. The reader will quickly discover Stravinsky's psychological powers as a manipulator: most of his letters ask me to perform tasks that he could not do. At the same time, he learns from me and uses my expressions. I first perceived his verbal wit in a letter about the pianist Gary Graffman playing the *Sérenade en la* on a program with two preludes by Rakhmaninov. "What a neighborhood!," was Stravinsky's comment. The correspondence after our first meetings reveals that he had understood things about me that had escaped my progenitors.

My musical background and training were unexceptional, as I have already indicated, and I had no precocity of any kind. My quest for knowledge of and about great music, and my discoveries in it, were entirely my own, and certainly no one led me in the direction of Stravinsky. By the time I entered the Juilliard School of Music, the pillars of my musical world were *The Rite of Spring* and *Pierrot Lunaire.* The logical path of study for an aspiring composer, I believed, was to be found in the works of the masters of modern music. Hence my disappointment in those super-conservative classrooms where Stravinsky was mentioned only derogatorily, Schoenberg not at all, and Hindemith as a reckless radical. No doubt my choice of a Hindemith sonata for my Juilliard entrance audition earned me extra demerits.

I studied conducting in order to learn contemporary music, but had so few opportunities to practice the métier before the concert I shared with Stravinsky in New York, April 11, 1948, that my total experience with a full orchestra consisted of a fifteen-minute rehearsal of the *Oberon* Overture with the Juilliard student ensemble. Stravinsky was aware of my technical insufficiencies, of course, if not of their extent. But no matter. I managed to perform his Symphony in C by the grace, as he recognized, of a profound love of the music.

On February 22, 1944 I sent a letter to Stravinsky in Hollywood,[3] asking a few general and several technical questions, one of which concerned the articulation of the trumpet's groups-of-fives in the "Royal March" from *Histoire du Soldat*. On February 27 he dictated a reply to his secretary, Mrs. Adolph Bolm, and corrected it in pencil. He had not understood the question about the *Soldat* ("I am completely baffled by it"), and as for the scores that I had hoped to borrow, he himself did not have them and would "like to purchase any extra copies you might find." He added:

> My son Sviatoslav, according to latest news received through his brother Theodore who is in Switzerland, is, as before, in Paris teaching my music . . . My younger daughter, Milene, from the last letter by Theodore, has returned to the health clinic in Upper Savoie, France, for further treatment of her lungs . . . I did not attend the reception you mention for Proust . . . [4]
>
> Sincerely,
>
> Igor Stravinsky
>
> P.S. Enclosed your letter of which you have no copy for your guidance.[5]

He then decided not to post the two letters, mine to him and his answer, but, twenty years later, gave them to me as a memento, recalling that he had not mailed them at the time, assuming that I had no copy of my letter, and fearing that it could be lost. But what was most curious about my letter is that I had neglected to sign it. Stravinsky was intrigued by it, and asked Nicolas Nabokov to try to track me down.

I wrote again on March 29, reporting on performances of his music in New York as well as on the lack of them at Juilliard,[6] "except for the *Sérenade*

---

3. With the exception of the letter of March 9, 1949, all of Stravinsky's communications published here, entirely or in part, were sent from 1260 North Wetherly Drive, Hollywood 46, California. All were written in English.

4. This was the famous party after the premiere of *Renard*. Both Proust and Joyce were there—and so was Stravinsky, as Clive Bell's biography of Proust establishes. Stravinsky's denial suggests that, unlike Diaghilev, he was unaware of Proust even four months before his death.

5. My letter was handwritten.

6. A change of attitude toward Stravinsky came about in 1946 with the presidency of William Schuman, who, on June 28, 1947, invited him to accept a commission to compose a piece for the Juilliard String Quartet. Stravinsky answered on July 10, saying that he would "love to do the work for Juilliard," but that he was "overcrowded with work" at present. On September 26 Schuman wrote that a Stravinsky Festival would be held at the

en la, which Josef and Rosina Lhevinne teach to their better pupils." I also expressed the hope that he would include *Oedipus Rex* or *Perséphone* in the programs for his forthcoming appearances with the New York Philharmonic. My next letter, August 15, 1944, requested the loan of a score and gave my name and address. He replied on the 19th: "I am sorry not to be able to give you a satisfactory answer about the orchestra score of my Capriccio. I am exactly in your case."

I wrote to him again on December 21, 1946, this time at the Ambassador Hotel, New York, where he was staying briefly during a concert tour. Eleven months earlier I had heard him conduct the premiere of his Symphony in Three Movements in Carnegie Hall. In the autumn I heard *Oedipus Rex* for the first time, conducted by Leonard Bernstein at City Center (the Fifty-fifth Street Mosque) and narrated by Norman Corwin. My December letter repeated the request to borrow and photocopy scores. I could fetch them from his hotel "either before Cleveland, or between Cleveland and Philadelphia," I said, which indicates that I knew his schedule. The letter mentions an "air-check" recording[7] that I had made of his 1945 broadcast of the "Chorale" from the *Symphonies of Winds* and asks if he has rearranged any more of the piece. I also identify myself for the first time: "I have a conducting fellowship and am working for a degree in philosophy at Columbia." The latter is not true. I had taken only two courses in philosophy, one in logic, and one on aesthetics. I was fascinated by logic, particularly by such questions as the distinction of the validity of an argument and the truth of its conclusion, and by the more famous philosophical paradoxes.

Hollywood
February 10, 1947
Dear Mr. Craft: Returning home from my concert tour I hasten to answer your very kind letter of December 21 (!!).[8] Sorry for this delay.

---

school in 1948–49, and that "we should like to have you with us . . . to conduct one concert, or portion of a concert. . . Obviously, the pleasure of having you here could not be measured in money." (It could be for Stravinsky, of course.) His answer of October 6 places the emphasis on Juilliard's agreement to a postponement of the quartet. In the last week of January 1948 Schuman visited Stravinsky in Hollywood, at which time Stravinsky revealed that he was working on an opera, and that the quartet would have to be put aside indefinitely. On May 22, 1950, Stravinsky wrote withdrawing all hope for the quartet.

7. Recordings of broadcasts on acetate. Many small companies made them at the time.

8. Mark Schubart, the dean of Juilliard, told me that he had met Stravinsky at a Christmas Eve dinner with the Darius Milhauds, and that Stravinsky had mentioned my letter and said that he would be delighted to see me, and that I could borrow the score of *Perséphone* from CBS after his broadcast of it in January. I wrote to my sister on January 4, 1947, that I had planned to call on Stravinsky at the Ambassador Hotel "next Tuesday," but when the time came I lost my nerve, and, anyway, Stravinsky was already in Boston. On

I have recently signed a long-term contract with Boosey & Hawkes (668 5th Ave.), who are preparing to publish the works you mention in your letter. I advise you to contact Mr. H. W. Heinsheimer, who, I am sure, will be helpful in the matter.

Wishing you the very best of success,

                                        Sincerely,
                                        Igor Stravinsky

My letter of March 1, 1947, sent from 313 West Ninety-first Street, New York, requests permission to photostat a copyist's score of *Perséphone* procured from Boosey & Hawkes by Mark Schubart of the Juilliard administrative staff. I had been studying it at the school, I told Stravinsky, and "I have an excellent recording from your broadcast." Whether or not Stravinsky agreed, Schubart kindly entrusted the score to me. My letter goes on:

> You will be interested to know that I went to Boston, Wednesday, February 26, to hear Irving Fine's performance of your Kyrie and Gloria.[9] The music was well received by a packed hall and by many musicians, Copland among them . . . Some remarks about your tour this winter. Of the performances of the new Symphony, I preferred yours with the New York Philharmonic, in spite of the trouble with the clef in the cello part. [Richard] Burgin's performance with the Boston was good, first because the orchestra knew it, second because the piano was up front and very clear. This was the main fault with the Cleveland performance. I like the faster tempo of the first movement that you are implementing this year. But the Philadelphia concerts were the best. I followed you on foot to and from the Academy of Music, from and to the Warwick Hotel.

The poor man must have thought he was being stalked by a lunatic.

In my aforementioned letter to Stravinsky of August 20, 1947, I offered to send the Soulima Stravinsky–Oubradous recording of his Piano Concerto, made in Paris in 1943 but only just received, in exchange for comments on tempi and other matters in the performance of the piece. The pianist Elly Kassman[10] had invited me to conduct the work in her Town Hall recital, December 28, 1947. In the meantime Stravinsky had apparently heard favorable reports of my broadcast performances of his Octet at

---

February 2, at 1 P.M., WNYC broadcast my concert (Stravinsky's Octet) from the Brooklyn Museum. Meanwhile, my friend George Brackman and I played in a performance of Bach's Christmas Oratorio in Bethlehem, Pennsylvania.

9. The wind parts were arranged for two pianos by Claudio Spies. He still has the manuscript with markings in Stravinsky's hand.

10. Elly Kassman, Vera's older sister, was married to an eminent psychiatrist, Dr. Bernard Meyer; they are the parents of Nicholas Meyer, author of *The Seven Per-Cent-Solution*.

the Brooklyn Museum (February 2) and at Juilliard (May 2). He answered on August 29:

41 Johnston Avenue
Kingston, New York[11]
Dear Mr. Craft: Just read yours of August 20.
You will be disappointed to know that at present it is impossible to get the orchestra material of the *Symphony for Wind Instruments*. All I have of this work is a very dirty proof of the orch. score in the last revision made before the war, sent to me by my son Sviatoslav upon my request. I have my doubt that it ever was published.[12] As to its last movement, the Choral, I reorchestrated it omitting the clarinet group for the special purpose to be played in addition to *Psalms* broadcast[13] in order to use the same instruments as in this symphony.

I shall be more than glad receiving Sviatoslav's record of my Piano Concerto, which you so generously offer me. Concerning the orch. score of this Piano Concerto, I corrected the very poorly published old score of which I have a photostatic copy here.

Surprised that you do not know of the change of date in the *Orpheus* premiere. Instead of October or November, it will be given in the early spring (probably about the end of April at City Center Theater).[14]

What is *Speculations* by T. E. Hulme, have no idea. And Souvtchinsky's new essay on me, do you mean his article of the last year in *Contrepoint?* This latter, I read it. Do you know Gisèle Brêlet's *Esthétique et création musicale*—an important essay [that] recently appeared in the Presses Universitaires de France? I recommend you this work.

All best sincerely,
Igor Stravinsky

On September 5 I wrote that I had obtained the Piano Concerto records

11. Unless otherwise indicated, all of Stravinsky's letters were sent to me at this address.
12. It wasn't.
13. This indicates that he had not received, or not read, my letter of December 21, 1946. The broadcast was part of CBS's late-night "Invitation to Music" series. When Stravinsky conducted *Perséphone* in the same series, January 15, 1947, with Madeleine Milhaud as *diseuse*, he was photographed on the podium during the interval between the rehearsal and the broadcast, flanked by younger musicians, including Walter Hendl, Lukas Foss, Claudio Spies, and myself. In a muckraking book about Stravinsky that appeared in 1972, the photo is captioned "Historic Encounter," meaning between Stravinsky and myself, but I did not meet or in any way "encounter" Stravinsky on that occasion, and I had been in closer physical proximity to him during a rehearsal of *Renard* at Hunter College Playhouse two days earlier (January 13, 1947). At no time before March 31, 1948, did I present myself to Stravinsky.
14. The Fifty-fifth Street "Mosque" between Sixth and Seventh Avenues.

through friends in Paris and London, and that the discs had survived a long odyssey, eventually reaching New York in a diplomatic pouch. I also asked permission to send W. R. Inge's *Plotinus*, in addition to the Hulme, as well as one of Ralph Mannheim's books of sociology and some English commentaries on Bossuet (the great "Sermon on the Dignity of the Poor"), whose *Méditations sur l'Evangile*[15] was always at Stravinsky's bedside. He replied as follows:

October 7, 1947

Dear Robert Craft: I apologize for my long silence. Your good letter of Sept. 5 received and also Sviatoslav's records and also Hulme's *Speculations*. Thank you heartily. I was overcrowded with thousand matters. Happy to have these records and this so important book. *Tell me by return mail how much I owe you for all that.*

Although Sviatoslav's records (his playing) are good on the whole, there are many things to say about—correctness for tempis (too hurriedly), the balance of wind instruments (Oubradou) [sic],[16] and the technical side (engineering) of the records. I already wrote to Sviatoslav about it.

As to the *Symphony for Wind Instruments*, I already started to rewrite it, as I am far from satisfied with the one I have here in proofs. When this will be done, I hope not far away, I shall then be ready to have it performed.

I heard here the test [pressings] of L.B.[17] recordings to *Octuor* and *Histoire du Soldat*. I wonder why he did not follow the very good cutting of my own European Columbia records. The only explanation for his odd cutting is that he took in various parts of these two works absolutely arbitrary tempis against my indications and against already established tradition. You are right, he used the pedal drum (*H. du Soldat*) to ease the job of the percussion; that is, of course, not a solution of the problem. Wrong also—the whole drum coda, the pitch of the different drums—entirely entangled! I am praying these records would never be published. I spoke to Mr. Gilbert of RCA Victor who understands my worry, but he is the only one in this Company and I am afraid he would not be able to impede the publication of these records of which L.B. is so proud. What an intolerable situation for a living author!

I heard about Mrs. Tangeman's[18] excellent Jocasta performance, but what can she do alone to save *Oedipus* this fall while under K.'s[19] baton?

15. In a 1922 edition published by the Librairie Garnier Frères.
16. Ferdinand Oubradous conducted the recorded performance.
17. Leonard Bernstein.
18. Four years later Nell Tangeman sang the role of Mother Goose in the Venice premiere of *The Rake's Progress*. Her husband, Robert Tangeman, wrote to Stravinsky, March 9, 1958: "Robert Craft was in one of my most interesting classes as its most interesting student the first year I taught at Juilliard."
19. Serge Koussevitzky. Stravinsky's March 15, 1948 letter to him expresses a con-

Have you heard my *Dumbarton Oaks* records (Keynote Corporation)?[20]
Why is it so difficult to get it in retail shops? Can you investigate?[21]
     Would be glad to hear from you soon.

All best sincerely,
Igor Stravinsky

P.S. No, the last 8th in the 5th bar after 86 in my Piano Concerto is a G-sharp,
only in the next bar comes the G-natural.

My October 11 answer describes Leonard Bernstein's performance of
Oedipus Rex in a Stravinsky concert at City Center as "maudlin," a word he
evidently did not know, since he wrote *"affecté, sentimental"* in the margin.
(He also provided the Russian equivalent for my word "fixation.") On October 18 I sent a report on the Keynote mystery, telling Stravinsky that the
first records, issued six weeks before, "were made of pure vinylite, some of
which developed boils and cracks. They will be reprocessed with an alloy."
I also tried to explain that the RCA employee's job was to "understand
Stravinsky's worry and to sympathize with him," but the business-minded
composer never grasped the reasons for the contradictory positions taken
by the public relations and budgeting departments of the same company.
His next communication was a telegram:

October 21, 1947 (8 A.M.)

Many thanks, could you get *Dumbarton Oaks* album for my son handing it over
to Arthur Sachs Waldorf Astoria who leaves October 22 for Paris.

Greetings,
Igor Stravinsky

------

flicting attitude toward his ability to perform the piece: "Your telegram touched me deeply
and made me happy. I have just received words from friends in Boston of the brilliant
performance of *Oedipus Rex*, and I am sincerely sorry that I was unable to be there and to
thank you in person. But I thank you from here. After much fluctuating and fretting, I have
decided not to go to Europe this year. I cannot risk it. The situation is too uneasy, and who
can assure us that we can get out in the event of an emergency. . . This week I conduct the
Philharmonic here [Los Angeles] and then am in Washington and all of April in New York."

20. The Concerto was recorded in New York between April 27 and 30, 1947. John
Hammond, president of Keynote—and brother-in-law of Benny Goodman (but no relation to Richard Hammond, discussed in the next chapter)—promised test pressings by
May 14, but they did not come until late June. (Stravinsky had known John Hammond
since 1925, when Koussevitzky escorted him to Hammond's home in Gloucester, Massachusetts.) The album was released in early September. On October 3 Stravinsky wrote to
the composer David Diamond: "Am delighted you like my *Dumbarton Oaks* records. Are
they now on sale, because Alexei Haieff could not get them recently when leaving for
Rome?" Diamond answered (October 9) that he had found a copy "at Rabson's."

21. On December 8, 1947, Stravinsky wrote to Nicolas Nabokov: "Bring three albums
of *Dumbarton Oaks* Concerto, which, so far, has still not arrived here in stores. Tell this to
Sasha Schneider [Alexander Schneider, violinist], who so zealously defends Keynote."

I delivered the *Dumbarton Oaks* recording to Sachs at the Waldorf and described this adventure to Stravinsky on October 24. I did not leave the album at the front desk, fearing it might be lost, but went directly to Sachs's suite. After I rang the bell, he appeared in a tell-tale loose dressing gown and in bare feet, evidently expecting room or bar service, but seeing me and perhaps suspecting that I might be a private detective, did not remove the chain on the door of his room. Passing the recording through the narrow opening, I caught a glimpse of a sparsely clad young woman.[22]

My letter also mentions that I had heard an air-check recording of Leopold Stokowski's attempt to conduct Stravinsky's Symphony in C[23] with the NBC Symphony, in which the third movement was unrecognizable. Sachs, meanwhile, had telephoned to Stravinsky, who sent the following telegram to me:

October 26, 1947 (7:43 A.M.)

Thousand thanks for *Dumbarton Oaks* records. Will write you next week hoping to finish before that time reorchestration of my *Wind Instrument Symphony.*

All best,

Igor Stravinsky

On November 1, I wrote inviting Stravinsky to conduct the new version in a program of my "Chamber Arts Society"[24] in Town Hall, New York. Stravinsky telegraphed his reply to my proposal:

November 4, 1947

Washington Concert April fourth. Could conduct *Wind Symphony* your request after Washington. Advise contact Columbia Concerts for arrangement. Two-Piano Concerto recorded in Paris Columbia before war my son and my-

---

22. For an account of Sachs's extramarital liaison, see Vera Stravinsky's correspondence with Sachs's wife in *Dearest Bubushkin.*

23. When Samuel Dushkin sent an enthusiastic telegram to Stravinsky after hearing this broadcast, the composer answered, February 23, 1943: "*Mon cher* Samsky: . . . I ask only what anyone could understand in this performance. . . The first movement—well, he got through that. But with the second, he began to spoil everything (pitilessly dragging in spite of all my verbal instructions [Stokowski had recently spent a day working with Stravinsky in Hollywood] and against the evidence of the music itself): the music was deformed because of the insensitivity to tempo that is innate in this man. As for the third movement, this was simply beyond his technique, and instead of going to the source of the problem (rhythmic relationships), he plunged the music into a chaos of disordered sounds. I tell you that by this time my patience was a little tried, and it is not necessary to tell you that although the last movement was less badly presented, this by no means made me forget the torture of the two proceeding ones."

24. Founded in New York City in 1947 by myself and Eugene Kassman, brother of Vera. Through him Koussevitzky became one of the sponsors.

self try to get them. Glad friends my music not fooled by Broadway music merchants.

Greetings,
Igor Stravinsky

The reference to "Broadway music merchants" is explained by an enclosed clipping, headed "A Run of Half Notes," from the *Los Angeles Times*, November 9, 1947. The article, heavily underscored by the composer, says, in part: "Igor Stravinsky is *very much disturbed* over reports that he has sold out to the juke boxes. The fact of the matter is that the original version of *Firebird*, from which the "Ronde des princesses" was drawn to make a popular song, has always been in the public domain in the United States. The only existing American copyright is that of the revised version, to which all rights are held by the Leeds Music Corp., which exercised its privilege to use the material for a popular song. Stravinsky did not write the popular arrangement, known as "Summer Moon," nor did he see it until after it was printed."[25]

On November 19, 1947, Stravinsky wrote to Louise Frey, his agent and the assistant to Arthur Judson of Columbia Concerts: "Please tell the Chamber Arts Society that I accept the sponsorship and would be glad to conduct my *Wind Instrument Symphony* for nothing provided it does not interfere with my engagements in April, 'Invitation to Music' and Pittsburgh, if any.[26] Up to you to arrange the dates."

On November 24, at Hunter College Playhouse, my chamber music ensemble performed the second Brandenburg Concerto, Mozart's Serenade, K. 388, the *Dumbarton Oaks* Concerto, and *Histoire du Soldat*. Arthur Berger reviewed the concert very favorably in the *New York Herald Tribune*, and evidently some of Stravinsky's friends in the audience reported to him enthusiastically. On December 10 he informed his publisher Ralph Hawkes of a promise "to conduct this *Symphony* on the program of my works in April, when in N.Y. I am doing this gratis to help that young and gifted Robert Craft and by the way to hear myself how it sounds. You will understand that in such a case even Ansermet, who used to be a faithful interpreter of my works, conducting the same piece and preceding me, is out of the question."

Boosey & Hawkes, unaware of the ten-year-old rift between Stravinsky and Ernest Ansermet, had chosen the Swiss conductor to give the premiere of the new version of the *Symphonies*, although Ansermet greatly preferred

25. Stravinsky sued Leeds for $250,000 on grounds that "Summer Moon" was "devoid of musical merit," and that Lou Levy, president of Leeds, had remarked in an interview that Stravinsky was "making a bid for juke-box popularity." Murray Schumach's detailed account of the suit was published on the front page of *The New York Times*, July 30, 1948.
26. Neither engagement materialized.

and wanted to perform the old one, with which he was familiar.[27] The composer was angry that he had not been consulted.

Stravinsky's next letter to me turns down my request to include the Kyrie and Gloria from the Mass in the program with the *Symphonies*, despite the Boston performance of February 26, 1947:

December 10, 1947

Dear Mr. Craft: Just a short note concerning your April program of my works.

I would prefer that fragments of my Mass yet not finished (I have now completed the Credo) would not be played before the whole work is ready, and that is precisely what I don't know. Before April, after April?—*aucune idée.*

The entire orchestra material of the newly revised and reorchestrated version of my *Wind Instruments Symphony* will be available at Boosey & Hawkes in about 10 days. Will you enquire? Bear in mind—it lasts about 9 minutes *only.* The Mass numbers excluded, you have only 20 minutes of the Piano Concerto and 22 or 23 minutes of *Les Noces*—a total of 51 or 52 minutes. What will you do with the 40 min. missing? Because you told me the concert will last 1 1/2 hour, I suggest to play twice the *Wind Symphony* with the addition of the Octet and *Dumbarton Oaks* Concerto, which I shall do with pleasure. Do you really intend to come here? This will be nice.

Sincerely,

I. Stravinsky

The composer's next message was a Christmas greeting, forerunner of a gift: "Merry Christmas, dear Mr. Craft. I sent you some days ago for this occasion the summary sketches of *Orpheus* which you will receive probably with some delay.[28] Hope you will like it."

On December 26 New York City was paralyzed by the heaviest blizzard in its history. I was stranded on a bus in New Jersey about ten miles from the Lincoln Tunnel and missed the only rehearsal of the Piano Concerto. Fortunately, it was possible to arrange another one for the morning of the day of the concert. The performance had a considerable success.

27. When Stravinsky refused Ansermet's request to play the "original version" of the *Symphonies* on his January 31 NBC Symphony broadcast, the composer was inevitably "preceded" in performing the new version. Ansermet wrote to Stravinsky from the Essex House, New York, January 13, 1948: "Mr. Craft has given me to understand that this does not make any difference to him, since he will have the first public performance." The late Minna Lederman, Editor of *Modern Music*, had introduced me to Ansermet at a Balanchine ballet performance.

28. On January 2, 1948, Stravinsky wrote to Nicolas Nabokov: "If you see Harold Shapero, ask him whether or not he received my *Orpheus*, which I sent to him as a present . . . [Vittorio] Rieti and Craft got them and answered me, but not Shapero (original in Russian).

January 5, 1948

Dear Robert Craft: Many thanks for your telegram and New Year wishes (your letter of Jan. 1 I just received). Glad you have my *Orpheus* and you like it.

As to the April concert settled for the 14th, it seems to me all right. But concerning the program (*Mavra* or String Concerto in D), let me think it over, I shall write you later on. At any case I do not think it is a good idea to perform *Pribaoutki* in this concert, because these three[29] very short pieces will be completely lost in the vicinity of their neighbors. For the chorus of *Les Noces* I always had a number not exceeding the modest figure of 30, sometimes less (24). Are you singing it in English?

The discovery of my Piano Concerto after my own and multiple performances in this country (NY Phil.—twice, Boston—twice, Chicago—twice, Cleveland, Detroit, Philadelphia . . .) twenty-three years ago and at the NY Philharmonic with B. Webster[30] three years ago, as it appears, does not disturb the ignorant press at all. An old story, indeed. Glad you had a personal success with this "intricate" (as always) and "full of barbaric rhythms" (as always) score. How was Miss Kassman in your opinion, and who is she?[31]

I heard about the English *Horizon* of November, but I did not get this issue.[32] Kindly send for my information, although it already causes me a nausea.

Please give me news about the K.[33] performance of Nabokov's *Elegy*. Nabokov spent here the Christmas week and played me his charming work. Get in touch with him, you will not regret. His address is: 1350 Madison Avenue, New York 28, NY, ph: Sacram 2.5782.

I wrote from Florida on January 21, asking Stravinsky if he still approved of the very fast tempo in the first movement of his Duo Arte player-piano recording of the Piano Concerto, and proposing a change of program for Town Hall. The composer replied to the second question by telegram:

February 1, 1948 (9:07 A.M.)

22 North Lakeside
Lake Worth
Florida

Danses concertantes preferable but only if you prepare it in order not to lose time with musicians in reading the music during my rehearsals.

Greetings,
Igor Stravinsky

29. Actually four pieces.
30. The pianist Beveridge Webster was a close friend of the Stravinsky family from the late-1920s.
31. See n. 10 above.
32. It contained an article about him by Eric Walter White.
33. Koussevitzky.

Stravinsky conducted concerts in San Francisco on February 12, 13, and 14 and in Mexico City on February 27 and 29. He received my next letter, dated New York February 27, on his return to Los Angeles, March 2. It contained examples of English word-setting by Purcell, including ribald canons of the kind that amused the adolescent Mozart. I also sent Purcell's *Funeral Music for Queen Mary*, which so impressed Stravinsky that he hand-copied it. He telegraphed:

March 3, 1948

Halmans Agency
119 West 57 Street
New York, New York
    Accept new dates rehearsals and concerts April 9 to 11.

IS

The next envelope from Wetherly Drive contained a clipping from *Time* magazine about Ansermet in which the composer had underlined the following lines: "Between premieres and table-pounding talk with Picasso, Diaghilev, Prokofiev, and Stravinsky ('a man of great culture—and the best businessman I ever knew'[34]), Ansermet mastered the classics—without losing his appetite for the moderns."

Stravinsky wrote again on March 9:

Dear Robert Craft: Just to thank you for your kind letter of February 27 (also for the previous one from Palm Beach).

Arriving in Washington D.C. on Tuesday, March 30 at 8:25 A.M. Staying there at the Hotel Raleigh.

Will be nice to you see you on the same day, a free day, because the rest of the week—working every morning (four rehearsals all together), unless you planned to come later in the week.

Delighted you enjoy reading dictionaries, so do I. I found the other day in a French dictionary the following definition of *sex*: "*Conformation particulière de l'être vivant, qui lui assigne un rôle spécial dans l'acte de génération.*"

OK for the change of dates (rehearsals and concert April 9 to 11)—I wired March 3 to the Halmans Agency, as you asked.

All best,
Igor Stravinsky

I had sent a selection of Samuel Johnson's more eccentric definitions, and after receiving this letter sent the dictionary itself.

---

34. Stravinsky wrote to Ansermet on January 31, 1948: "Do you really think I am a good businessman composing such music?"

Stravinsky completed the Agnus Dei of his Mass on March 15 and on March 19 conducted the Los Angeles Philharmonic. He wrote a few days later before leaving for Washington via Chicago and Pittsburgh:

> Dear Robert Craft: Since my letter of March 9, some changes have occurred, first—I am arriving in Washington only on March 31 (Hotel Raleigh), then Wystan Auden coming expressly to work with me on his libretto for *Rake's Progress*, very urgent in view of his departure for Europe on April 7.
>
> In spite of all this rush I hope to have time for you too, but want to let you know of all this.
>
> Have you attended the so "reputed" Boston performance of *Oedipus*? Am curious to know your own reaction?
>
> Sincerely,
Igor Stravinsky

My *Chronicle of a Friendship* describes my first meeting with Stravinsky. Mrs. Stravinsky's diary records the, to me momentous, occasion without comment:

> *March 31.* On arrival in Washington to the Hotel Raleigh. We spend all day with Auden and Craft.
>
> *April 1.* Igor goes to his 10:00 A.M. rehearsal with Craft (Auden returned to NY last night). In the evening we go to a Mozart concert at Dumbarton Oaks and a reception by John Thatcher. "Power corrupts, absolute power corrupts absolutely."

I had used Lord Acton's dictum in conversation with her. Discovering it in her handwriting after her death, I was pleased to see that I had made at least some impression on her.

In Washington I accompanied Stravinsky to and from his National Symphony Orchestra rehearsals, to a concert of Mozart chamber music at Dumbarton Oaks on April 1, and to parties and receptions—one of them by the director of the Byzantine collection there, Dr. John Seymour Thatcher, whom I nicknamed "Chicher-Yacher" (after the song "*Chicher yacher soberalaya vecher*" in Stravinsky's *Souvenirs de mon enfance*), a soubriquet that Stravinsky never forgot. I seconded him at an interview, the first of hundreds, following one of his rehearsals: "Mr. Stravinsky poured himself a [whiskey] and soda . . . Someone suggested he hide the pint of [whiskey] so as not to afford any free advertising. He obliged, caressing his drink: 'My friend,' he said, meaningfully . . . He admonished the photographer not to photograph him with an open mouth. "I look terrible photographed with an open mouth—

like a tenor . . . I studied under Rimsky-Korsakov. He taught me everything—even how to erase."[35]

I returned to New York to attend to the organization of my concert,
but returned to Washington with Vera Kassman for Stravinsky's concert on
April 4 (*Scènes de Ballet*, Symphony in Three Movements, Divertimento from
Le Baiser de la fée, "Dance, Lullaby, and Finale" from *Firebird*). We accompanied
the Stravinskys to their hotel afterward. Nicolas Nabokov and his new wife,
Patricia Blake, were already there, and the Stravinskys were about to invite
us to join the four of them at dinner, but thought better of it when they
discovered that Miss Kassman spoke Russian. Meanwhile, Stravinsky had
drafted a program note for the *Symphonies of Wind Instruments*, postdating it
April 10, the day before our Town Hall concert:

> The *Wind Instrument Symphony* was composed in France [in] 1920 and played in
> 1921, and thereafter very little, mostly by Ansermet who performed it last
> January at NBC. I don't know if there was any concert performance in this
> country before this NBC broadcast.[36]
>
> This work was composed to the memory of Debussy who died in 1918.
> The title "SYMPHONY" given to this short composition must not be taken in the
> usual sense of the word. There are various short sections, a kind of litanies in
> close tempo relations succeeding one another; and various instrumental groups
> (woodwinds and brasses) succeeding one another; and some rhythmical dia-
> logues between separate woodwind instruments, such as flute and clarinet.
>
> The whole peculiar structure of this work required a special title. This
> title is very easily rendered in French—*Symphonies* (in plural) *d'instruments à vent*—
> but in English we can find only an approximate translation, which is *Sympho-
> nies of Wind Instruments*, the togetherness of wind instruments.

Miss Kassman and I were on the same night train to New York, April 4–5,
as the Stravinskys and Nabokovs, however, and on April 6, in New York,
Stravinsky handed me his program note. The next four dates are from Mrs.
Stravinsky's diary:

> *April 7.* New York. Igor goes with Haieff to Craft's rehearsal at the Nola Stu-
> dios, 1657 Broadway.
> *April 9.* From 10–1 Igor rehearses his *Symphonies of Wind Instruments*. Lunch with
> Craft and Lisa.
> *April 10.* Abram Chasins interviews Stravinsky, Balanchine, Kirstein, and Craft
> at 7:30 P.M. on WQXR.[37]

35. *George Washington University Hatchet*, May 6, 1948.
36. The *Symphonies* was performed in New York and Philadelphia in 1924 and 1925 by
Stokowski and the Philadelphia Orchestra.
37. Chasins was a well-known pianist. A recording of the talk, most of which was
contributed by Stravinsky, is preserved at the Paul Sacher Stiftung in Basel. The purpose of

April 11. Rehearsal in Town Hall from 10–1. Tickets to Balanchine, Nabokovs, Harold Shapero, Stark Young and Bill Bowman,[38] Kyriena[39] and friend, Pavlik Tchelichev.[40] Concert at Town Hall at 5.

Actually *I* rehearsed the *Symphonies* while Stravinsky listened. Lisa, wife of the actor Vladimir Sokolov—his face was one of the most familiar in Hollywood at the time—was Vera Stravinsky's closest California friend from the mid-1940s. The two women were partners in managing the art gallery on La Cienega Boulevard called La Boutique.

As I wrote to a friend, the next four weeks in New York were

the most exciting in my life. I was with Stravinsky every day, early morning to late night, at rehearsals for *Orpheus* as well as for our concert. I absorbed his talk with Balanchine,[41] Kirstein, and others, accompanied him to the theater and to parties, went with him and the Nabokovs to a debate at the Rand School (Mary McCarthy was brilliant), ate multiple-decker sandwiches with the composer at Reuben's, but, chiefly, basked in the man himself, whose energy, alertness, and vivacity left everyone else behind. He dominated not only gatherings of people, but even his physical surroundings . . . One hurdle was that before meals he obliged me to join him in eating *saumon fumé* and swallowing large, straight slugs of *eau de ginèvre* that he poured from a terracotta bottle, which made rehearsing the Symphony in C, with a scratch orchestra and with its composer sitting directly behind me, difficult indeed.

---

the interview was to publicize my concert the next day (April 11) and the forthcoming premiere of the Stravinsky–Balanchine *Orpheus*. I had met Balanchine in the Stravinsky apartment in the Ambassador Hotel, Park Avenue and Fifty-second Street, on April 5, and Kirstein in 1947, when I became a member of his Ballet Society.

38. Stark Young (1881–1963). This drama critic for the *New York Times* and the *New Republic* was also a novelist, essayist, and playwright. Among his books are *So Red the Rose*, *Immortal Shadows*, and *The Pavilion*. Part of this last was excerpted for inclusion in Anne Fremantle's and W. H. Auden's *The Protestant Mystics*. When I first met the Stravinskys, Stark Young and his lifelong friend, Bill Bowman, were among their closest New York friends. I recall more than one bibulous evening in their apartment.

39. Kyriena Siloti, daughter of Alexander Siloti, the conductor, pianist, pupil of Liszt, intimate of Tchaikovsky, knew Stravinsky in St. Petersburg and was present at the first performance of his *Fireworks*, which her father conducted. When her family moved to New York, she gave piano lessons there. In my period she came for tea at least once on Stravinsky's every visit to the city and, in her cheerful, high, lilting voice, told me fascinating stories about Stravinsky in Russia.

40. The painter Pavel Tchelichev was a close friend of the Stravinskys long before my time. I met him and his companion, Charles-Henri Ford, the actress Ruth Ford's younger brother, only once, with Stravinsky, December 3, 1956, in the Ritz Hotel, Paris.

41. Stravinsky and Balanchine conversed in Russian, but in front of me and Maria Tallchief, the choreographer's wife, they spoke slow-going English.

Mrs. Stravinsky's diary does not mention me in connection with what in fact was my concert, or say that it was only the second time in Stravinsky's American career that he shared a program with another conductor—the first had been with Klemperer in Los Angeles at the end of World War II. Moreover, I am emboldened to claim that his performance of the *Symphonies*, a premiere of a revised version (only), was musically less significant than my performance of the Symphony in C, which had been conducted in America heretofore only by the composer and once, chaotically, by Leopold Stokowski.

I count some eighteen other occasions during the Stravinskys' remaining twenty-four days in the city at which I was present but am not included in the diary. Indeed, my name appears only four more times, though it does progress from "Craft" to "R. Craft" to "Bob Craft." I quite see, of course, that the monosyllabic bark, "Craft," and its suggestions of the lowest associations—wiliness, Freemasonry, processed cheese—would be grossly out of place next to the glitter and social allure of "Prince Troubetzkoy," or the musical glamour, at that time, of "Koussevitzky," but I was there, nonetheless, and more conspicuously than a dipterous insect on the wall. Perhaps the late Lucia Davidova, who translated the diary for me, felt as I did, since she has transposed a party after the *Orpheus* premiere from Harold Clurman's address to her own.

On April 20th, I accompanied Stravinsky to watch and hear Balanchine conduct the orchestra in his Tchaikovsky ballet *Theme and Variations* (Ballet Theatre, Metropolitan Opera).[42] I accompanied the Stravinskys on the 21st to a staged performance of *Oedipus Rex* at Juilliard and on April 27 sat with him in his dressing room before he conducted *Apollo* for Ballet Theatre. The premiere of *Orpheus* took place on April 28, on a program that began with *Renard* and the *Elégie* for solo viola (played by two violas), and concluded with Mozart's *Symphonie concertante*.

Stravinsky's first written communication to me after we had been together for a month in New York was an inscription in a miniature score of his Symphony in C:

To Robert Craft
    In remembrance of his noble and discriminated performance in April 1948 (Town Hall, N.Y.)

> Cordially
> I. Stravinsky
> May/48

---

42. My close friend from Juilliard, Samuel Baron (1925–1997), the flutist, told me that the orchestra thought Balanchine "the most musical conductor they had ever had."

I understood the compliment as subtly evasive. As his inscriptions of this sort go, it is warm and generous, but "noble" actually means courageous, *i.e.*, foolhardy, to have undertaken the venture at all, while "discriminated" simply concedes that I knew the work. He does not say that the performance was good, and it was not.

Stravinsky returned to California on May 4, after inviting me to stay with him there. Five days later I conducted *Histoire du Soldat* in Times Hall (Forty-fourth Street), and on May 12 I wrote to accept the invitation and to send reading lists that both Stravinskys had requested. I wrote again on May 18, describing Stokowski's performance of the String Concerto, and on May 30 told of an afternoon with Goddard Lieberson[43] of Columbia Records listening to test pressings of Stravinsky's *Ode*.

The composer's next messages, a telegram and a covering letter, are both dated June 1:

> Can you be in New York to meet and help my son arriving with wife and baby by plane June 17 at 11 A.M. Am mailing details.
>
> > Greetings.
> > Igor Stravinsky.

> Bob: Too bad. I had no time at all these last weeks to answer your letter of May 12 and to thank you for the "Concert Hall" album.[44] So I do it now in this short note which will let you know that my son Sviatoslav with his wife and their baby arrive at La Guardia field on June 17 at 11 A.M., NY time, airplane No. AF-009.
>
> It would be wonderful if you could meet them there and help them at their arrival. Am afraid our friends V. Rieti and S. Dushkin will be not in New York to meet and help them as they planned to do, the former coming here the next week and the latter—probably in Paris, by now.
>
> Could you also ask Mr. W. E. Brown, the Manager of the Ambassador Hotel, to make a reservation for them, one room with a double bed and a small one for the baby (two years old).
>
> Enclosed a pocket score of my Symphony in C, which, as you see, finally arrived from Mainz after four months of traveling.
>
> Don't pay attention to the gossips about Sviatoslav; fortunately I know too well what they are worth and their source.[45]

---

43. I had met Lieberson two years before, through my Barnard College friend Betty Rubinstein, who had been his secretary. He asked me to edit the CBS recording of the *Ode* because of a technicality in Stravinsky's contract with RCA.

44. Of Stravinsky's Sonata for Two Pianos played by Robert Fizdale and Arthur Gold.

45. The reference is to Soulima Stravinsky's activities during the Occupation, and in particular to his ambition to give concerts in Germany in 1941; the "sources" were Pierre Souvtchinsky, Nicolas Nabokov, and French friends of Stravinsky. At the end of the war, a

Thanks again and let me know if it is OK. 100,000 cordialities from both of us.

ISTR

P.S. They will stay till Tuesday June 22 in NY.

I met Soulima and his family on June 17 and five days later helped them entrain for California. Meanwhile, a note had come from Mrs. Stravinsky:

June 2, 1948

Dear Bob: Thank you for your nice letter. I am waiting for the book list. Please write me the next time who is who in *Lions and Shadows*, and if Homer Lane really existed. You know everything—that is why I ask *you*. At this moment we are terribly busy and happy with the arrival of Sviatoslav (Soulima, Nini, Svetik—his other nicknames), his wife and the baby. My husband will ask you to help them on their arrival, just to find them a room in the Ambassador and show them the Italian restaurant Maria (on the 52 Str?). I hope they speak almost fluently English and you will enjoy to meet them.

It would be nice if you can come to Hollywood this summer. The Denver concert will be on July 23. Before and afterward we are in Hollywood.

With all my best wishes,
dear Bob,
Vera Stravinsky

Stravinsky wrote:

June 6, 1948

Thank you, dear Bob—very, very kind of you. Am so glad you can meet Sviatoslav at his arrival.

In saying "Brahms had more feeling than Beethoven" the ridiculous old man[46] seems to be for once right, but beware—*unfortunately* for Brahms and *fortunately* for Beethoven. However, doubtful he, the old man, had exactly that in mind.

U.S. government official gave the composer a letter from Willy Strecker, director of B. Schott in Mainz, Stravinsky's publisher, to the Nazi musician, Hans Gebhardt (b. 1895), dated April 17, 1941, saying that he had received a request from Soulima Stravinsky to arrange concerts for him in Germany and asking Gebhardt to reply and explain that this was not possible at present. Strecker says that he has heard only indirectly that Soulima's father is faring well in the United States and adds that: "It makes me happy that [Soulima] has found in Paris so much musical activity." A letter from Olga Sallard to Vera Stravinsky, December 30, 1946, reveals that Stravinsky's niece, Ira Beliankina (Belline), could not bring herself to "forgive Soulima the mistake of publishing two articles in the German newspapers during the Occupation of Paris."

46. Koussevitzky. The quotation is from an interview in the *Los Angeles Times* that Stravinsky had clipped and enclosed.

Miteleuropulos[47]—I already heard about his charming behavior in *Histoire du Soldat*. Disgusting, including his conducting without music.[48] Mass—am also a little bit distrustful as to Westminster Choir or the Washington Cathedral project. You are right in mistrusting the ppppp-fffff technic of this kind of organization.

No more time to write—so long.[49]

Best wishes,
ISTR

June 24, 1948

Dear Bob: Today, the evening of Sviatoslav's arrival, we were at the funeral of our best friend, Mrs. Lisa Sokolov, who died from a heart attack two days ago.[50]

It is terrible.

Affectionately,
ISTR

On July 3, 1948, Stravinsky telegraphed: "Arriving Denver 7:50 A.M. July 20 morning. Rehearsals the following three days. Leaving Denver July 25 evening. Longing to see you. Affectionately, Igor Stravinsky."

On July 7 the Stravinskys, Schoenbergs, and Thomas Manns, among other notables (see the *Los Angeles Times*, Thursday, July 8), attended a dinner honoring Alma Mahler-Werfel in the Crystal Ballroom of the Beverly Hills Hotel. On July 20 the Stravinskys were in Denver, at the Brown Palace Hotel. I was there, too, and in the following days spent many hours with the composer poring over the libretto of the *Rake*. He had already written the music for much of the first scene. On July 24 we attended a University

47. Dimitri Mitropoulos (1896–1960), conductor of the Minneapolis Symphony Orchestra at this time, later of the New York Philharmonic. He added crescendo-decrescendo "hairpins" to the violin part in the "Scene by the Brook" in the *Soldat* and distorted the piece in other places, but the reference here is to his capers on stage throughout the work.

48. Stravinsky, like Schoenberg, distrusted conductors who performed from memory.

49. Stravinsky's use of such American expressions, acquired from orchestra musicians, the cinema, and his reading, seemed droll in their incongruity and more so in his accent.

50. The Sokolovs had traveled by train to Mexico with the Stravinskys in July 1946, at which time Lisa contracted amoebic dysentery and the jaundice from which she never entirely recovered. From January 1950 to April 1952 I rented the Sokolov guest house, at 8624 Holloway Drive at the foot of a small hill behind the actor's own home and about seven blocks from the Stravinskys. (In 1952 I moved from there to another, much smaller guest house—actually a two-room apartment over a garage—on the property of the Baroness Catherine d'Erlanger, a short distance below the Stravinsky house on the same street, North Wetherly Drive.) After Lisa's death, the Stravinskys abruptly and, I thought, in spite of Sokolov's brooding, moody personality, rather cruelly "dropped" him. I was present at the last dinner with him in the Stravinsky home.

of Colorado performance of Virgil Thomson's *The Mother of Us All*, and on July 22, a performance of *Così fan tutte*, Stravinsky's favorite opera of the time. When I saw Thomson shortly after the performance of his opera, he asked, "How's Papa?" and "Did he like *The Mother?*" I ducked the question: "He saw many things in it." Thomson was not pleased that Stravinsky was writing an opera.

On July 23 Stravinsky led the Denver Symphony in a concert in Red Rocks, an open-air theater about twenty miles from the city. The program consisted of the Overture to *Ruslan and Lyudmila*, Tchaikovsky's Second Symphony,[51] the Capriccio (with Soulima as soloist), and the Divertimento. In spite of her nice letter of June 2, Mrs. Stravinsky's diary of the week in Denver, a crucial one in my life, does not mention me.

The Stravinskys left for California on July 25, and when I joined them there a week later, by way of Mexico City, the relationship with her improved. The composer's letter to Ralph Hawkes, August 2, is the first that may show traces of having been written with my assistance, as in the following passage: "In my whole career I have never been so concerned about launching a work [the Mass]. This is why I am so cautious about a possible wrong presentation for the huge NBC radio audience. This is, of course, nothing deprecatory in reference to our friend Ansermet, but even he cannot be aware of my incommunicable intentions."

Her diary records events in Hollywood as follows:

July 30. Hollywood. Bob Craft for dinner, directly from Mexico.

August 1. Party here: Father McLane (3), Hammond (2), Berman (1), Bob Craft, the children.

August 2. Bob here for lunch.

August 3. Lunch at the Farmers' Market with Bob. Dinner at Françoise's[52] with Edel and Craft.

August 4. For lunch here, Bob and Edel. To buy books at Pickwick with Bob Craft.

August 6. Lunch with Bob at the Farmers' Market. Drive Bob to Bel Air and UCLA. Here for dinner: the Dahls, Grau,[53] and Bob.

August 7. For lunch here Bob and Max Edel.[54] With Bob and Françoise to the

---

51. A letter from Païchadze to Stravinsky, April 25, 1939, reveals that the composer had paid the publisher to have the orchestral parts extracted for both the first and the second symphonies of Tchaikovsky. Stravinsky rented these parts to the orchestras with whom he conducted the symphonies.

52. Wife of Soulima Stravinsky.

53. Gilbert Grau was a film composer and orchestrator. In 1950 I conducted a piece by him for Evenings on the Roof in the Wilshire-Ebell Chamber Music Hall.

54. The Stravinskys' physician at the time. They had introduced me to him at the premiere of *Orpheus* in New York. See chapter 5.

bookshop to buy, as he calls them, "investments." Very gay lobster dinner with Bob at the ocean.[55]

August 8. For lunch here . . . Berman and Bob. Then to the ancient film, *The Birth of a Nation.* We dine at the Naples restaurant.

August 9. Drive Bob to Burbank airfield.

August 22. Write to Bob Craft: "Merthi for your letter, your literary and kind letter. Thank you also for all of the books coming from London. I became more and more a Waugh fan. E.W. is somebody from the family. I imagine how he would react on this: You are certainly not a cousin of mine. Nevertheless, he *is* one. Everybody here is all right but I, who have a sore finger, and Popka, who is very irritated."

Popka, Stravinsky's parrot, was the favorite among his feathered pets, which included forty lovebirds.

Some of the people mentioned here played large roles in the Stravinskys' lives as well as in my own.[56] The "children" refers to Stravinsky's younger son and younger daughter and their spouses. In the autumn of 1946 Vera Stravinsky invited Milene Marion, and her husband, Andre, to live in Hollywood in order to care for the composer in the event of her death or incapacitation.[57]

From New York, on August 16, 1948, I thanked my hosts for "every gilded moment" with them. I also enclosed a copy that I had made of Bach's fughetta *"Christum wir sollen loben schon,"* mentioning "the entrance on the subdominant in the fifth bar; the 6th-chord on the downbeat of bar 9; the relation to the same chord in bar 17 (first beat); and the cadence from the diminished chord to the final E major—in a very short piece that begins in D minor!"

Stravinsky's next communication consisted of only three lines:

August 30, 1948

Dear Bob: Can you answer this letter if you have time?[58]

55. In a small restaurant on the Santa Monica pier. Iris Tree, the poet and niece of Max Beerbohm, lived in an apartment across the street and above a noisy merry-go-round.

56. See chapter 5.

57. See chapter 9 in my book *Stravinsky: Glimpses from a Life* (New York: St. Martin's Press, 1992).

58. A number of questions from Michael Steinberg, a ci-devant Princeton student, later music critic of *The Boston Globe,* about Stravinsky's Mass and his reasons for writing it. In 1968 Steinberg and I were interested in the same woman, the Boston flutist Eleanor Preble, whom I had met in Lima, Peru, in 1960, where she was the star in the otherwise dark sky of the local symphony orchestra.

Thanks 100,000 times for the scrapbook which I will send back at my earliest. No answer yet from Hawkes!!

He wrote again on September 8:

Dear Bob: Nini will see you in NY next week and discuss with you all details of the Mass premiere on which I shall roughly write you now. What you say about Detroit, primarily the absence of a children's choir, and also the fact that they have not yet written me formally, make a Detroit premiere doubtful? As time is short, decisions must be made, and here is [mine]:

Between Kirstein's Ballet Society Productions and your Chamber Art Society Concerts I prefer the latter as a strictly musical event. So it would be your production. We will start our program with the Octet conducted by you, followed by Soulima's solos. After the intermission the choir master presenting the three Russian Church choruses and finally the Mass conducted by myself. It goes without saying that none of us, neither I nor Soulima, expect any financial remuneration. Should there be any profit (let us hope) it will go toward your musical production fund.

Here is another thought. I am informed that soon things will get going with Petrillo.[59] So I suggest that you see Richard Gilbert of RCA Victor.[60] They ought to be interested to take advantage of the occasion and make records of the already prepared Mass and also to help you with the actual concert of the premiere.

As to Detroit, it can be done later with the "handsome fee," if such it would be without a world premiere.

Try to prepare all dates, Town Hall (last week of February), Westminster or other Choir, Boosey & Hawkes material (hope gratis for premiere); to discuss and settle as much as possible details with Nini to save time.

Glad you are doing *Mavra* (and what else in this your opening concert?) and blessings for successful translation by the brother[61] of NN "the Bulwark of Baltimore" and the taming of the "brother" . . . Ralph Hawkes if he kicks about a $75 translation. Keep me abreast.

Love—kisses,
ISTR

59. James C. Petrillo, president of the Musicians Union, then on strike against the recording companies.

60. Richard Gilbert was director of artists and repertory at RCA.

61. Vladimir Nabokov, who was the cousin, not the brother, of Nicolas. Little-known at the time, and until *Pnin*, Vladimir had been suggested as a translator for *Mavra*, since the story is by Pushkin. It now seems incredible that this renowned writer could have been offered a fee of $75. The "Bulwark of Baltimore" was my term for Nicolas, who taught classics at St. John's College.

September 13, 1948

Nini arriving this Friday 1 P.M. New York time La Guardia his plane is Air France please fix with Baldwin for afternoon going there directly from airfield.

Stravinsky

Soulima was in New York to play Mozart's Concerto K. 503, with the CBS Symphony conducted by Alfredo Antonini. On September 23 Stravinsky wrote to Nicolas Nabokov that "[Soulima] couldn't bring the conductor, Antonini, evidently rather a primitive gentleman, to see any reason for avoiding a Strauss [doubling] of instruments to play Mozart; additional rehearsals would also have been useful" (original in Russian).

September 25, 1948

Dear Bob: This is just to inform you about my correspondence re: Mass with this people (am writing Betty [Bean][62] also). But are you or not in touch with the Westminster Chorus?

All best,
ISTR

[Enclosure: the carbon copy of a telegram from Stravinsky to Eugene Ormandy saying that the American premiere of the Mass had already been promised.]

September 27, 1948

Dear Bob: Is it too much to ask you to fill up these forms[63] (with Betty if you cannot do it yourself), and send them back for signature. Many thanks.

Love,
ISTR

October 8, 1948

Hello, Bob: Yes, am glad to hear from you for I too miss you greatly. Please, do come at Christmas, please, please! Please answer YES.

As for Minna Lederman,[64] on Oct. 3 there was a wire from her: "Working hard on book full cooperation of Rieti Berger Balanchine Craft. All feel material about new opera vitally important for book. Urgently need reply to my questions of Sept. 18 . . . And here is my answer, which I did not wire her: Air mailed you yesterday (Oct. 3) regret not able collaborate for absolute lack of time. Don't find expedient to speak about my opera before completely fin-

62. Director of Boosey & Hawkes, New York, and a friend of Ralph Hawkes.
63. A curriculum vitae.
64. Lederman was preparing her book *Stravinsky in the Theatre* (New York: Pellegrini and Cudahy, 1949).

ished." So you see, I am in complete agreement with you not to speak at all about *Rake*. You better show her this not wired telegram.

What are the "important things you learned by being in the B & H vicinity"?[65] What happened? Am somewhat troubled.

The Jewish parade picketing before Lifar (City Center)[66] can only be a profit for the latter . . .

Very interesting (and important) what you say about Olivier's *Hamlet*. Hope they are coming here.

Nini gave his greatly successful recital (Evenings on the Roof on Sept. 27) well packed small hall (Wilshire-Ebell Theater) and a very enthusiastic audience and critics. And one week later he took part in a whole Stravinsky program (same place but the big hall) playing with Ingolf Dahl the two-piano concerto and with Sol Babitz the Duo concertant.[67]

My *Rake* makes progress (starting the 2nd scene), but not as fast as Ralph Hawkes wants it.

Love–Kisses,
I Str

P.S. A letter from Charles-Albert Cingria[68] with this "P.S.: *Ansermet est l'être le plus faux du globe.*"
P.S. No. 2. No broadcasts this year for the Boston Symphony. So much the better for composing programs, but the worse for Basler Concerto and also for my and Nini's pockets. Airmailed R. Gilbert asking him to get in touch with Boston to record *Orpheus*. Wonder if Mass will prevent it. Try to see Gilbert and write to me about it. That is important.

October 9, 1948

Dear Bob: Just to tell you that Richard Gilbert is no longer at RCA Victor. Too bad! I wrote him the other day about the necessity of the *Orpheus* recordings during my performances with the Boston Symphony and received today an answer from a certain Richard A. Mohr[69] (Artists & Repertoire Department) that he thinks a "definite decision could be reached within the next two weeks"

---

65. I do not remember to what this refers. I spent several hours in the Boosey & Hawkes rental library at Lynbrook, Long Island, trying to sort out the several editions of parts and scores of *The Rite of Spring*, but not long after a fire destroyed the building and most of its contents.

66. I had sent a New York newspaper photograph and article on the subject to Stravinsky. Lifar had been a flagrant Nazi collaborator, even dancing for German troops.

67. See chapter 5 for Babitz and Dahl.

68. One of Stravinsky's closest friends in his Swiss and French years, and the author of a book on Petrarch (see FN 137) that deeply influenced Stravinsky. In 1986 I gave Stravinsky's copies of Cingria's Collected Works to the Sacher Foundation in Basel.

69. Gilbert's successor.

by his (Gilbert's) successor, who is not yet named. Am worried. Wonder if the Mass recording is still holding. Please check up and advise me quickly (see my last letter of Oct. 8—the P.S.).

In hurry—no time to speak with you about interesting things in your letter to Vera (Oct. 9th) just received.[70]

Houston concert—on January 31. Program not yet discussed (!?) February 1 leaving for NY. Boston rehearsals will start February 7, on Monday as usual.

Affectionately,
ISTR

Stravinsky's next letter shows that he had not yet changed his mind about *Falstaff*, which did not happen until the mid-1950s.

October 20, 1948

Dear Bob—Greetings!

Heard yesterday Verdi's *Falstaff*—very discomfortable sensation feeling myself a poor cretin in what I am able to give the crowd, a sensation which does not exist when listening to *Traviata* or *Trovatore*. Hope will be happier today with *Elixir of Love* (Donizetti).[71]

Now expecting news after your visit to RCA Victor Monday.

Love,
ISTR

P.S. The lady you often see with Rieti is la Marquise de Casafuerte. She is a violinist.[72]

October 28, 1948

Dear Bob: Enclosed a new nonsense from B. & H. which they probably call *catalogue*. Even as a proof it is not acceptable. In order to avoid writing them a letter with high words which they deserve, please explain them, as you can, their utmost stupidity and neglect. You will be an Angel! Please send me back this "catalogue" with my remarks.

Good news—at last the Petrillo ban is lifted. Many thanks for your phone the other day. Will it be possible to record as well my Basler Concerto (13 minutes)?

In a big hurry—going downtown to hear *Don Giovanni*.

Love,
ISTR

---

70. I had acquired the habit, at my hated prep-school, of advancing the dates of my letters.

71. Stravinsky is referring to performances by the visiting San Francisco Opera.

72. Yvonne de Casafuerte played in the pit orchestra of *South Pacific*. At a party celebrating the thousandth performance of the musical, she startled Mary Martin by revealing that she had attended all of them.

This San Francisco Opera performance of *Don Giovanni* in the Los Angeles Shrine Auditorium was the first of three that Stravinsky attended. The conductor, Paul Breisach,[73] made a good impression, and became the composer's first choice to conduct *The Rake's Progress*, but he died before the opera was completed.

After a meeting with Mohr I telegraphed to Stravinsky that *Orpheus* could not be recorded with the Boston Symphony, but it could be done with a pick-up RCA orchestra.

October 29, 1948

[Telegram]

Delighted record *Orpheus* with Victor orchestra. Finishing my Boston Symphony tour in New York Feb. 19. Can start rehearsals next day. Try arrange Basler Concerto too. Igor Stravinsky.

He wrote again on November 3, 1948:

Dearest Bob: Thanks a lot for your nice letter (Sunday–October 31).

Am a little bit worried about the fate of my thin sheet music with a few bars of the Jocasta aria's ending for Nell Tangeman. Did you receive it? How was her performance?[74]

Delighted you are hopeful not only for RCA recording of my Basler Concerto but also they are willing to record *Apollo* too. Provided they agree!

OK with your schedule for my recordings and my Mass rehearsals. Provided R. Shaw[75] will be ready before my starting rehearsals (Feb. 23, 24, 25)!

Just received the published vocal (and when the full?) score of my Mass. As was to be expected, B. & H. disfigured my original (black) negative and printed under its *Instrumentation*—"Duration: 17 minutes"! Where comes this figure from? My timing was, as you remember, 23 minutes and I recollect (unfortunately too late) I never was asked about it by them. Is it possible to print the right timing in the orchestra score?[76] Please, inquire.

---

73. Stravinsky had been introduced to Paul Breisach at the home of the composer Eric Zeisl. A letter from Willy Strecker to Stravinsky, August 7, 1930, refers to Breisach as a *"sehr gute, bisher Dirigent."*

74. Stravinsky composed a concert ending for Jocasta's aria and sent it to me to give to Mrs. Tangeman for a recital performance in Town Hall. I mistakenly let her borrow it and never saw it again.

75. Robert Shaw (1916–1999), choral director.

76. Publishers' timings are notoriously longer than the actual ones because their rental and recording fees are based on length in minutes. But Stravinsky's obsession to determine the exact timings of his music amounted to a neurosis. His sketchbooks contain split-second timings for even the shortest entries. In the case of the Mass, he calculated the duration from his reading at the piano, which was six minutes longer than any performance he ever conducted. Although admitting that performances inevitably vary in length, he continued to plan programs based on the timings given in his scores, all of which are mistaken.

Sorry a healthy lady died from a heart attack listening to a Mitteleuropulos performance of Arnold Schönberg's music. I did not know the 12-tone system were not good for healthy people neither.[77]

More than glad to meet Evelyn Waugh in February. Delighted he is coming. What a marvel his *Scott-King's Modern Europe!*

Please do write, don't be lazy—write or typewrite, as you want.

Grüss aus Hollywood,
ISTR

November 9, 1948

Dearest Bob: Your good letter concerning the Milan premiere of my Mass somehow confused me. The discrepancy between the enclosed cables I received a week ago and *Time's* report seems rather complete.[78] Hawkes and Ansermet suspiciously silent. Is there the key to this riddle? Who, good heavens, provided *Time* reporter with this ridiculous (and useless for the public) information about 17 min., and why?

Better I keep silent and answer by my own performance* with children (am sure Ansermet had female voices) on February 26, 1949, and by my own records, provided RCA Victor not impressed *Time's* jeer and not renounced to record it.

If possible, send me two or three clippings of the *Time* issue and its date.

Love,
ISTR

* of 23 minutes duration[79]

When his late-in-life recordings lopped minutes from earlier estimates, he would write in the score, parenthetically, "Today I do it in . . ." and give his latest timing, as if the discrepancy required an explanation. No less surprising was his inability to foresee the approximate amount of music still to be composed in a work-in-progress. The most famous instance of this is found in the sketches of *The Rite of Spring*, where he writes "Curtain" and "End" before the *Danse Sacrale.* On February 11, 1955, he wrote to Nicolas Nabokov: "I have composed barely half of *Agon.*" In fact only the first two numbers had been composed, and these not in final form. Writing to Nabokov, February 19, 1958, Stravinsky says: "The composition of *Threni* is slowly coming to an end, but the length of what is already composed is not so great as Bob tells you, as he always tends to exaggerate." At that time, and though Stravinsky estimated that the piece would not last more than twenty minutes, it was already considerably longer. On March 27, he wrote to Nabokov: "The *Threni* are finished. The music lasts longer than I had thought, 35, not 20 minutes." Its actual duration is about twenty-eight minutes.

77. An elderly woman had died of a heart attack at a New York Philharmonic Friday matinée subscription concert during Dimitri Mitropoulos's performance of Schoenberg's Five Pieces for Orchestra. Stravinsky's mistaken classification of the piece as "12-tone" reveals that he knew nothing about the 12-tone method.

78. *Time* had reported that Ansermet conducted the Mass on the stage of La Scala with a chorus of a hundred and twenty.

79. It actually lasts seventeen minutes.

One of the cables enclosed was from Antonio Ghiringhelli, *sovrintendente* of the reconstructed—it had been bombed in World War II—La Scala. He still held that position three years later when La Scala provided the chorus and orchestra for the premiere of *The Rake's Progress* in Venice.

November 10, 1948

Dearest Bob: Please check up immediately at Boosey & Hawkes [and see] *whether orchestra parts of my Piano Concerto* (with winds) which were made here by my copyist and after which I conducted the work with B. Webster at piano in Carnegie Hall, Febr. 1 and 2, 1945, *are still at B. & H.*

A year ago I sold B. & H. this my material. Now I need it in Boston for my performances of it with Soulima. So, please, see to it that B. & H. deliver to the Boston Symphony *precisely this corrected set* and not an old one (from Galaxy[80] or London-Paris), which will undoubtedly cause me much trouble.[81]

Thank you a million.

Love,
ISTR

On November 12, Stravinsky wrote to Ralph Hawkes: "I continue to receive from everywhere (England, Switzerland, France) very enthusiastic letters about my Mass heard in the broadcast from Milan. From everybody except Ansermet . . . I do not approve this La Scala performance . . . This large opera-house was no place to present an absolutely liturgical piece of chamber music proportions."

At Boosey & Hawkes in New York, I was shown a letter from Ansermet to Erwin Stein, the firm's principal editor, saying that some hissing was heard during the Mass performance and explaining that "I can teach the chorus pitches, but, after years of *Aida*, not the whole style of singing a motet." The letter also quoted a phrase from a review by Domenico de' Paoli, Stravinsky's Italian biographer at the time of *Perséphone* (1933–34): "A work of humility and submission and diabolical pride." I did not repeat these remarks to Stravinsky.

Dearest Bob: How to thank you for Lorenzo da Ponte's Memoires. Exceedingly happy to have it. Thanks also for your Kingston Nov. 24 letter. No time to answer these days: Nov. 29 & 30—Ralph Hawkes visit, Dec. 1 & 2—Poulenc, Bernac, Dec. 3—Ald. Huxley.

80. Galaxy Music Corporation was the New York branch of Editions Russes de Musique. On June 25, 1945, Stravinsky wrote to Koussevitzky informing him that "Galaxy paid an advance of $1,000 in January 1940, the last and only payment received from them," *i.e.*, from Koussevitzky's defunct Editions Russes.

81. A note in Stravinsky's archives reads: "Piano Concerto orch. score and parts; Ralph Hawkes took it for revision and publication May 1, 1948, NY City."

Today only to complain: a very bad mistake in my Mass—Kyrie, No. 9, 4th measure, Discanti, on the 3rd beat a sharp is missing at F (see trumpet) in the full score. In the vocal score also, which makes it worse because London editor put (in plus) a precaution at F. Really too bad!

Finally—a letter from Ansermet (from Geneva). A very empty letter, indeed, excuses for writing so late, not a word, of course, about his personal reaction to the work (neither about that of the public). The only thing he said was: "singers, instrumentalists, and the conductor did their best" (sic). How very kind of them![82] All best for you and *Mavra* (who will be the tenor, Hess?)[83]

Love,
ISTR

Ansermet had written to Stravinsky on November 20 with questions about the pitches in several places in the Mass, and Stravinsky answered in the margin of the letter. On November 30 I sent copies that I had made of Purcell's catches. But the next letter to me was from Mrs. Stravinsky:

December 1948

We are terribly busy all this last time. People was (or were?) coming in and out. Sometimes boring, sometimes amusing. We saw the whole Orchestre de Paris, a lunch with them in a French restaurant, garden party with them, organized by the French Consul, with Charlie Chaplin, the [Edward G.] Robinsons,[84] and movie people. Poulenc and Bernac had lunch in our garden. Sun and strawberries in December! Their concert had a continental style, like a concert in a *salon de la princesse de Polignac*. We also had a party for Charles Bayly.[85]

Finally, we were so tired that we went with Nini *et* Françoise for two days to Palm Springs and I send you a picture. Also to have a little rest before Ralph Hawkes's arrival. Huxleys are here now, but he has bronchitis and teeth troubles, so we did not see them.

---

82. See Stravinsky's reply, November 27, 1948, in *Stravinsky: Selected Correspondence*, Vol. I (New York: Alfred A. Knopf, 1982).

83. William Hess had sung Eumolpus in *Perséphone* in Stravinsky's January 1947 broadcast, but Robert Harmon, who had sung the role of Oedipus at Juilliard in the April 1948 performance that Stravinsky heard and liked, was the tenor in *Mavra*.

84. Robinson was the Stravinskys' witness when they took out first papers for U.S. citizenship in 1940. When asked to show his own papers, however, he was compelled to admit that he had jumped ship in New York during the Russian Revolution and did not have any.

85. Stravinsky had met Charles Bayly, a direct descendent of Henri Beyle (Stendhal), in 1935, when the composer and Samuel Dushkin gave a recital in Denver. I met him in Denver in July 1948.

The composer wrote shortly afterward:

December 4, 1948

Greetings, dearest Bob: Have a letter from Mr. Mohr and yours of Nov. 30 and your books—*The Steps of Humility*[86] and the *Sewanee Review*[87]—many, many thanks. When will I only have time to read all this. Just finished to read P. Valéry's remarkable *Faust*. Is it translated? You must read it.[88]

Orpheus—of course it would be suicide to rehearse and record it in one four-hours session. So tell Mr. Mohr that I agree for Feb. 22 but need another date (Feb. 23 or 24) to let the musicians and myself do the job in more human conditions. *Danses concertantes* (19 minutes) was recorded a year ago in 2 three hours sessions, the same for Divertimento (23 minutes), and everybody agreed that it was a *tour de force* on my part to do it in such a short time.[89]

Mass—that is quite different, because we will use the last rehearsal (Feb 25) of our February 26 concert. O.K. But what can I put on the sixth side? Mr. Mohr suggests one or two of my a cappella choruses. I suppose Pater Noster and Ave Maria will not exceed 4'25", so let us go ahead. By the way, in what language will it be sung? It is my feeling that the original Russian text must be used, this text being printed in Latin letters. Please airmail me an immediate reply on this. No more time except for

Love,
ISTR

Please explain all this to Mr. Mohr—have no time to typewrite for him a new letter.

Played what is composed of *Rake* to Ralph Hawkes—he is enthusiastic about it. I told him I heard in July a very good performance of *Così fan tutte* in [Central] City, Colorado, and we conceived the project to give the world premiere-preview *there*. Am sure of your reaction to this.

December 14, 1948

Dearest Bob: Received your letters (Dec. 10 & 11)—will answer in a few days (Auden—a good idea).[90] Maybe the Mass—twice?

86. Bernard of Clairvaux's Latin classic with facing English, published by Harvard University Press.

87. This issue contained Eliot's "Poe and Valéry."

88. In 1958 Stravinsky contributed a preface to a volume of Valéry's plays that included *Mon Faust*.

89. Stravinsky recorded *Danses concertantes* and Divertimento in Hollywood in 1947. A recording of a performance of *Danses concertantes*, conducted by Vladimir Golschmann in the Museum of Modern Art, had been issued by Mary Howard Recordings, 37 East 49th Street, but Stravinsky criticized its tempi as "often too nervous and unsteady." (Letter to Nabokov, October 5, 1943.)

90. Now that the collaboration in *The Rake's Progress* had been publicized, I suggested that we invite Auden to read three new poems in our February 26 concert.

Read the inclosure and tell him (Gary Graffman)[91] I have absolutely no time to correspond. Why not use my records? He surely can ask Arthur Berger to let him hear them . . . Just typewriting these last words I received his [Graffman's] records which I immediately played. Not bad the whole thing, but why not follow my records? The degree of closeness to my records—as follows: 4th part, 2nd part, 1st part, and 3rd part (too turbulent indeed*).[92]

OK for *Orpheus* recording on Feb. 22 in two 3¹/₂ hour sessions.

Will check Mass's timing again; afraid you are right—we made a wrong estimation of the duration of each number and in plus we made a wrong total (with wrong figures). What a shame! Ansermet will be delighted with R. H.[93] triumphant. What a shame!

Love,
ISTR

* and too *fast*

December 15, 1948

Dearest Bob: Enclosed is a letter from Merle Armitage,[94] which I ask you to send back after reading it. Try, if possible, to bring up the matter with this, although nice, but rather unreliable man.

Nini is writing to you. Please send us the photos of the *Harpers Bazaar* (Zizi[95] & family) impossible to find the right issue. What is the date of it?

Pre-Christmas love,
ISTR

[Here is] my answer to Mr. Eric Walter White about Beethoven (his article* in *Tempo*, Summer 1948—London)

1—It is wrong that I do not like Beethoven.

2—The reference to Ramuz is rather a weak argument, because Ramuz, who was not a musician, meant what he said about it quite differently.

3—After all, is it really obligatory for any composer to like Beethoven and what exactly does it mean? Also, I would like to know the reason Mr.

91. The second half of Graffman's program began with Stravinsky's Serenade and two Rakhmaninov preludes.

92. Stravinsky means that the fourth movement of Graffman's recording was the closest to his own recording, but Stravinsky's recording of the work had been unobtainable for many years.

93. Hawkes.

94. Merle Armitage, book designer, had published a volume of articles about Stravinsky in 1935, and was bringing out a revised edition described by Stravinsky in a letter to Nabokov, December 15, 1949: "The general appearance of the book, with its importunate, cheap, and provincial illustrations and vignettes, is as unacceptable as the price" (original in Russian). Armitage was a sponsor of my concerts. He lived in Santa Fe for a time and was a "friend" of Miranda Masocco (see chapter 5) who used to refer to him as "Merle Armpit."

95. John Stravinsky, the composer's grandson (b. 1945).

White is so interested in it. What will be his reaction if I tell him, for example, that I cheer the influence of Beethoven in Harold Shapero's work, and that I feel more than a little bit embarrassed by his influence in Romain Rolland's work. ISTR

* "Stravinsky as a Writer"

The next letter, December 22, 1948, was from Mrs. Stravinsky:

Dear Bob: I send you all the beginnings of my letters to you. The collage I made for you of the opening of the Philharmonic season to show you what kind of menagerie we have here and how Stravinsky is getting inspired by reading the dictionary.

I make miles and miles now before Christmas and my legs are now "strictly ornamental."

I wish you a nice Christmas time and the most successful 1949. It would be so nice to have you here for Christmas but I understand that you are very busy. We ordered for you some books but I am afraid that they will not get there on time. Forgive us the delay, but you will have it one day. It is Mozart, *Letters.*

Give our best wishes and greetings to your parents and your sisters. And our love to yourself,

Vera Stravinsky

Mrs. Stravinsky's collage consisted of clippings from the society pages of the *Los Angeles Times.* "Making miles" was her way of saying that she had been driving a great deal. "Strictly ornamental" was Aldous Huxley's expression, coined by him after he had been apprehended by the Beverly Hills Police on suspicion of vagrancy while walking in a residential neighborhood in that city of many automobiles and few pedestrians. The three-volume edition of Mozart's letters, one of Stravinsky's sacred books, arrived on December 25.

Stravinsky's next note was inscribed on the carbon copy of a telegram he had sent to Richard Mohr:

December 26, 1948

Mr. Mohr in his letter to [Aaron] Sapiro[96] asked for Manhattan Center, gave only 3 1/2 hours for each session, did not speak about a good rest between, and finally mentioned Mass recording on *4 sides* (sic). Is it a trick or a mistake, I wonder. Please clear it up dear Bob. We missed you yesterday.

Love,
ISTR

96. Stravinsky's attorney from the early 1940s until 1959.

Stravinsky's next three messages were telegraphed:

December 28, 1948

Town Hall, 113 West 43 St.
NYC
Dearest Bob: If you have time please call collect after the concert. Longing to have immediate news. Needless to say how intensely we are with you. The four Stravinskys.

January 2, 1949

Perplexed your silence after *Mavra* performance wired you Tuesday Town Hall.[97] Best wishes for success asking to phone me collect. Have you ever received it?   Stravinsky

January 3, 1949

Happy your *Mavra* success. Congratulations. Delighted Auden participation and your program suggestion. Just yesterday wired Richard Mohr my acceptance to record Mass on five sides with Russian choruses on the sixth one. Now if these choruses eliminated, wonder how to cut Mass without harm otherwise than if five sides.

Igor Stravinsky

Each movement of the Mass was composed to fit a record side (four to five minutes). The next two envelopes from Wetherly Drive contained one request and two clippings:

January 5, 1949

Dear Bob: Please send me the program of your Dec. 29 concert (*Mavra*).

Love,
ISTR

[Enclosures: (a) A photograph from the *Los Angeles Times*, Tuesday morning, January 5, 1949, of five-year-old Marjoe Gortner signing a marriage license after performing a wedding ceremony. Stravinsky wrote in the upper margin: "for the Evelyn Waugh collection, ISTR." (b) An article from the *Los Angeles Times*, Friday, January 7, 1949, entitled "Orchestra Welcomed After Month's Rest," in which Stravinsky had underlined the following sentence: "David Diamond's Symphony No. 4 had a bit of rough going in meeting the competition of Mozart's masterpiece—the Sinfonia Concertante in E-flat major—and Tchaikovsky's overwhelming *Pathétique* Symphony which ended the con-

97. Stravinsky had failed to notice that the December 29 concert took place at the YMHA auditorium on Lexington Avenue at Ninety-second Street and not in Town Hall. On the 30th Auden wrote to Chester Kallman in Ischia: "Went to the Yiddish Y yesterday to hear a concert performance of *Mavra*, which I thought a lovely work, all about a huzzah [hussar] in drag."

cert, though Mr. Wallenstein, with his usual discretion in programming, gave it first chance on the auditors' approval and spared no pains in giving the new work an illuminating performance."]

January 10, 1949

[Telegram]
Received yours, sixth and eighth. Airmailing you Betty's letter just received strictly confidential. Wired her there is no question to renounce Mass premiere February 26.

Igor Stravinsky.

January 10, 1949

Dearest Bob: Just sent you a Night Letter; herewith are copies of the letters from Betty Bean and Andrew Tietjen.

Why did Tietjen write to Betty Bean (who understands nothing about technical matters) and not to you? What a shrewd people all those Betties and Boosies. Unhealthy atmosphere indeed.

Have you obtained with Tietjen the number of soprano boys to get a good balance? I guess you did. Otherwise you would not write me (Jan. 8) "Notified both, Mohr and B. Bean." Please reassure me.

LOVE LOVE LOVE,
ISTR

[Enclosures: (a) copy of a letter from Betty Bean regarding the forthcoming recording of the Mass; (b) program of a Carnegie Hall piano recital by Gary Graffman and letter from him to Stravinsky inviting him to attend.]

My letter of January 11 discusses the distribution of singers in the Mass, cites J. S. Bach on the numbers of sopranos, altos, tenors, and basses in his Leipzig churches, and goes on to say that "polyphonic singing is unknown here. The soprano line, the only one that anyone expects to hear, is always overloaded . . . Furthermore, plainsong is shoe-horned into 4/4 hymn-tunes."

January 22, 1949

Dearest Bob: Yours Jan. 20 at hand. Thanks.
We will stay in Houston at Rice Hotel. Ave Maria and Pater Noster without Credo under Shaw's baton perfectly all right.

Have no opinion concerning your *Renard* project. We will speak about it Feb. 3. However, I think Octet more fitting.

Do your best in casting Ballet Society musicians for Victor recording of *Orpheus*. I trust you will.[98]

98. Hugo Fiorato, the concert master of the orchestra, called me about this several times.

Nini's concerts very successful. He called yesterday from San Francisco. We will see him today at 11 P.M.

Happy to see you soon.

> Love,
> ISTR

On the morning of January 23, 1949, the Stravinskys left Los Angeles for Houston on the *Sunset Limited*. Soulima Stravinsky wrote to me the same day:

> Dear Bob: Father and Vera left this morning for Houston. I'm glad they will have at least 36 hours of complete relax in the train—they deserve it so much.
>
> Thank you very much for the [Hotel] Berkshire reservation. We are very excited by this next visit to N.Y. but still we have much to do in these few days before leaving.
>
> Father will play *Rake*'s score to you and Auden, nobody else. So keep it in absolute secret, don't tell anybody (even Rieti or Nabokov, for instance) anything which can reveal it. And you will arrange this meeting of strictly you, Auden, Father and Vera, at the Baldwin house, to make it absolutely incognito, sometime in the afternoon on February 3.[99]
>
> So, dear, dear Bob, see you in only ten days![100]
>
>> Love,
>> Soulima

In the Rice Hotel, on the afternoon of January 25, Stravinsky gave an interview to Hubert Roussel: "'Neo-classicism?' he scoffed. 'A label that means nothing whatever. I will show you where you should put it'—and he gave his derrière a firm pat . . . 'The only dance company in the United States is Lincoln Kirstein's Ballet Society in New York and it doesn't travel. The Ballet Russe? Many excellent dancers, but the music . . . Who could make music with that orchestra? At the premiere [of *Danses concertantes*], they did it right. Never since. I heard it in Los Angeles recently and I took my head in my hands.' "[101] On January 31 Stravinsky conducted the Houston Sym-

---

99. The Baldwin Piano Company did not have a room available for the requested time, and eventually the audition took place in the apartment of the violinist Alexander Schneider. Auden, who had been on jury duty that afternoon, dined with the Stravinskys and myself in their rooms at the Ambassador Hotel; we taxied from there to Schneider's, where Stravinsky was furious to find Balanchine, Nicolas Nabokov, his wife Patricia, and Rieti waiting.

100. He came east to play his father's Piano Concerto and Capriccio in a series of concerts with the Boston Symphony Orchestra, at home and on tour, and to play Stravinsky's Concerto for Two Pianos with Beveridge Webster in my Town Hall Concert, February 26, 1949.

101. *Houston Post*, January 26, 1949.

phony in a concert consisting of the String Concerto, *Apollo*, the Divertimento, and the 1945 *Firebird* Suite.

Auden and I met the Stravinskys on their arrival at Pennsylvania Station at 6:55 A.M., February 3. On February 6 the Stravinskys and I traveled to Boston, the Sheraton Hotel, by train. He rehearsed the Boston Symphony on the 7th and 8th and conducted a concert in Symphony Hall on the 8th, going afterward to a late supper at Edward Forbes', the first time I had been in the house. On the 9th the Stravinskys and I contracted food poisoning from a dinner at the Amalfi restaurant. Dr. Max Reinkel came at 7 A.M. and three hours later Stravinsky was able to rehearse the Boston Symphony for his concert in Sanders Theater, Cambridge, on February 11 (*Ode*, Capriccio, String Concerto, Divertimento). On the 14th and 15th he rehearsed again for his concerts with the orchestra in Carnegie Hall, New York (the 16th and 19th), the Mosque Theater in Newark (the 17th) and the Brooklyn Academy of Music (the 18th), each with a partly different program (the Overture to *Ruslan and Lyudmila*, Tchaikovsky's Second Symphony, the Capriccio, and the Divertimento).

I attended all of the rehearsals and concerts, learning a good deal about Stravinsky's stylistic concerns in the performance of his music. I also took note of such personal idiosyncrasies as his habit of wearing a beret Basque as he slept, of rolling his own cigarettes, and, at every rehearsal break, changing his perspiration-drenched shirt and underwear top, removing for a moment the religious medals and gold cross that hung around his neck on fine gold chains, then dousing himself with 4711 Eau de Cologne.

In New York on February 20 we rehearsed the St. Thomas Church choir in Stravinsky's Mass, and on the 21st attended a birthday party for Auden at his apartment.

On February 21, Auden wrote to Chester Kallman in Ischia:

> I went off to the Ambassador Hotel to go through Act One [of *The Rake*]. All your suggestions were conveyed and enthusiastically received; I wish you had been there to get the credit. I'm afraid you'll have to swallow my couplet for the Cabaletta:
>
> *Time cannot alter*
> *My loving heart*
> *My ever-loving heart.*
>
> I was faced with fitting it into the music and it was the only thing I could think up that would fit. The performance was from the piano score with the maestro at the piano, Bob Craft, Balanchine, self, etc., screaming parts. Craft (a very intelligent young conductor), is writing out an analysis of Act One to send you.[102]

---

102. Dorothy Farnan, *Auden in Love*, (New York: Simon and Schuster, 1984), p. 186.

My collaboration with Stravinsky as a writer began during this Boston sojourn. After reading the usual negative reviews of his music following the
concerts of February 10, 11, and 12, he asked me to draft a telegram to
Koussevitzky, who was vacationing in Arizona, that would attack the Boston critics and eulogize him. Mrs. Stravinsky composed the salutation: "Your
orchestra is wonderful." The text of my own contribution is as follows:
"Your incomparable orchestra gave me great pleasure and we achieved a
huge success. Unfortunately the twenty-four years of your brilliant influence taught the press nothing. It remained provincial and hostile." Stravinsky's
contribution, no less characteristic, added precision: the date, "Feb 14 / 49,"
clearly, meticulously drawn.

On February 24, Auden wrote to Kallman:

> There is a new plan about the *Rake*. To have the premiere in Central City,
> Colorado, in the summer of 1950. A nuisance for us, but there might be the
> consolation that Stravinsky has agreed that you and I shall direct the staging,
> for which we shall get paid . . . [103]

On February 22 and 23 Stravinsky recorded *Orpheus* in Manhattan Center
(West Thirty-fourth Street) with an orchestra of freelance musicians. On
February 24 and 25 he recorded the Mass and his new Latin versions of
Pater Noster and *Ave Maria* in Town Hall. At the performance of the Mass
there on the 26th, Dame Edith and Sir Osbert Sitwell shared a loge with
Mrs. Stravinsky. On March 5 Dame Edith wrote to the composer: "My
brother and I will remember the evening of the 26th of February for the rest
of our lives . . . It was a great privilege to us to meet the man whom we
know to be the greatest living creator in any of the arts."

The Brown Palace
Denver, Colorado
March 9, 1949

O Bob! Two (2) wonderful concerts:
    Urbana[104]
    Denver[105]
See you June 1, 1949. Going home.

Love, kisses,
ISTR & family

103. *Ibid.*

104. The concert, March 3, consisted of the String Concerto, *Apollo*, the Suite from
Pulcinella, and the Piano Concerto. On the afternoon of March 2, Stravinsky gave a press
conference at the Urbana-Lincoln Hotel.

105. Stravinsky conducted the Denver Symphony on March 8 in the String Concerto, *Apollo*, the Piano Concerto, and the *Firebird* Suite.

June 1 had been set as the date on which I would begin to work regularly for Stravinsky, as well as live in his house. My first task was to catalog the manuscripts and archival materials that he had lately received from his apartment in Paris.

March 13, 1949

Dearest Bob: I'll write you soon. 1000 thanks for yours of March 8.

Love Kisses Love Love,
I Str

[Enclosure: Address of Victoria Ocampo.[106]]

March 16, 1949

Dearest Bob: I wanted you to know that I received the following wire from Olin Downes: "Will you join with other outstanding American musicians in sending the following cable of greetings to Dimitri Shostakovich:[107] 'We are delighted to learn of your forthcoming visit to the United States and welcome you as one of the outstanding composers of the world. Music is an international language and your visit will serve to symbolize the bond which music can create among all peoples. We welcome your visit also in the hope that this kind of cultural interchange can aid understanding among our peoples and thereby make possible an enduring peace.' Please wire me . . . Olin Downes."[108]

The old fool! (*Rake's Progress*)

I answered him as follows:

106. Argentine writer (1890–1979), publisher of *Sur,* biographer of T. E. Lawrence, and a close friend of Stravinsky. He had asked me to invite her to narrate the part of *Perséphone,* which she had performed with him in Buenos Aires and Rio de Janeiro in 1936, and in Florence in 1938. I had planned to perform the piece in Carnegie Hall in November.

107. On March 6, the U.S. State Department granted permission for Shostakovich and twenty-one other delegates from Russia and the Soviet bloc to attend a peace conference in New York. Stravinsky received Downes's telegram on March 13. His telegram of refusal was published in the world press on March 18, and the next day the Soviet paper *Red Star* denounced him as a "traitor and enemy of our fatherland." This, too, appeared in the world press and among other reactions divided Americans into supporters either of Shostakovich or of Stravinsky. On March 25 reporters converged on Stravinsky in his home and asked if he would debate with Shostakovich on political or artistic issues. Stravinsky replied: "How can you talk to them? They are not free. There is no discussion possible with people who are not free." On March 27, in Madison Square Garden, Shostakovich played a piano transcription of the second movement of his Fifth Symphony. Nicolas Nabokov, who was in the audience of nineteen thousand, asked Shostakovich from the floor if he was in agreement with "the denunciation by Soviet critics of the works of Stravinsky, Hindemith, and Schoenberg." Shostakovich replied: "I am in accord with the denunciation of Stravinsky and Hindemith, and Schoenberg, too."

108. Stravinsky detested Downes (1886–1955), music critic for *The New York Times* from 1924 to 1955, and quarrels between them in the press were frequent. On December

Regret not to be able to join welcomers of Soviet artists coming this country. But all my ethic and esthetic convictions oppose such gesture.

Love, kisses,
I Stravinsky

March 22, 1949

Bob dearest: Yours of March 18 at hand. Strangely enough—not a word in it about your good wire you sent me the very same day. [Only] from this wire I learned that Olin Downes [gave] my answer (to him) to the A[ssociated] P[ress]. Do you know where it appeared?

Best thanks to Auden for his touching interest in this unsuccessful, alas, trial.[109] Of course Sapiro will retake it on a more solid basis this time. He is now in Chicago for a week, where he met R. Hawkes. The latter, stubborn as ever, proved once more to be the less accommodating person Sapiro met in his life. Disgusting!

Wise arrangement for singers and instruments of *Les Noces*.

Ocampo! She planned to be again in NY only at Christmas and, as she cannot dispose of her Argentine money in the USA, I wonder if she will be able to come here at all. Who else, in this case, could be the lady narrator? Madeleine Milhaud? But she too cannot do it for nothing.

Second act of *Rake* not yet started—till now am really overloaded by so many things in hand. Just made a final Latin version of Pater Noster and Ave

---

14, 1949, Stravinsky wrote to Nabokov: "I heard Prokofiev's Sixth Symphony. Nothing justifies its dullness and it shows neither esthetic nor technical novelty. This is clear to everyone except Comrade Olin Downes" (original in Russian).

109. On March 9 Los Angeles Judge Joseph Vickers ruled that Stravinsky's attorney, Harold Fendler, should have brought the action against the Leeds Music Corporation "not on tort but on contract." According to the *Los Angeles Daily News*, February 18, 1949, F. F. Spielman had testified that the Leeds Music Corporation hired him to make the arrangement published as "Summer Moon." He added: "I didn't want to use hillbilly harmonics [*sic*] because I wanted to come as close as possible to the master's feelings in the music. Max Fink, attorney for Leeds, contended that the company was trying to "bridge the gap" between the classical and the popular. "Experts say it's a void, not a gap," Judge Vickers answered. The experts were Eric Zeisl, who said that "in the classical world, Igor Stravinsky is the greatest living composer," and Ingolf Dahl, who said that "Stravinsky is the greatest contribution to modern musical culture." The newspaper report continues: "The judge grabbed his dictionary, read the definitions of harmonics, started on 'harmonica,' but ruled this out as irrelevant and immaterial. 'I did my best, as I thought it would be shown to Stravinsky whom I hope to meet sometime,' Spielman said. . . [He] da-daed a few bars [from his and Stravinsky's versions]. . . 'By the way,' the Judge said, 'you've never sung professionally, have you?' . . . The arranger admitted he changed the . . . harmonies . . . but [claimed] that his adaptation still conveyed the same feelings." The *Summer Moon* version was recorded by the Wagnerian tenor Lauritz Melchior.

Maria, now in B. & H. hands. Sent them a corrected score of my Mass with a newly photographed cover and the Basler Concerto with all my corrections in the full score and in the newly engraved pages (additional measures) I received from London. Lots of things, as you see.

Vera busy with flowers in the garden after her cold (two weeks). Nini-Françoise for two days out (pleasure trip). Milene-Andre every day here. Andre very helpful (correspondence).

Thanks also for clippings (in your previous letter). Convey my sincerest sympathy to Harold Shapero.[110] His contact with the "pompiers" of the "radicalism" of the "20s" is as symptomatic as this old, very old story.

And what about Dr. Koussevitzky and his enthusiasm for Shostakovich?

I. Stravinsky

[Enclosure: A clipping from the *Los Angeles Times*, Tuesday, March 22, 1949, of Stravinsky's letter to the newspaper correcting its misprinted version of his telegram to Olin Downes: "I said it was against 'my ethic and esthetic convictions.' Ethic was omitted." The quoted phrase is underlined by Stravinsky.]

On March 28 I wrote to thank Stravinsky for two drawings, one of them, in the margin of his March 22 letter, of a desert landscape, the other a profile portrait of me showing two bars of *Les Noces* sounding in my right ear. I went on to say: "I am sorry you did not have more information about the fate of your O. Downes wire. I assumed you would be bombarded. Lowell Thomas read your wire on the evening news, and both the *Times* and *Tribune* carried the story on p. 2. I had also supposed that Nabokov had called you, since he is so prominent in the affair. Downes clearly gave your wire to the press thinking it would put you in an unpopular (illiberal) position, but he miscalculated, because in the last three days the great majority of self-proclaimed 'intellectuals' have formed an anti-Stalinist conference, in which Nabokov and the *Partisan Review* people are involved. The supporters include many Jews who now realize that both their temples and their civil liberties are at risk in Stalin's U.S.S.R."[111]

110. I had sent Stravinsky a clipping from the *New York Herald-Tribune*, March 13, 1949, which reported that while Henry Cowell—see chapter 1—was reminiscing about the radical music of the 1920s in one New York concert hall, in another one, Harold Shapero's "half-hour long sonata in F-minor was being hissed . . . for daring to attempt a reinstatement of late-Beethoven principles, instead of adding to musical evolution with new sonorities." Stravinsky underlined the statement in red and blue pencil.

111. This is my only complete letter to Stravinsky that escaped the auto-da-fé that I made of my correspondence when I left Hollywood for New York in 1969. I am pleased to discover that my view in the last sentence replicates that of George Orwell.

April 2, 1949

Dearest Bob! 100,000 thanks for your wonderful March 28 letter.

Please send me your full score *Perséphone* (Nini's letter). Almost finished the corrections on the proofs.

Please ask Nabokov to write me a letter.

Love, kisses,
ISTR

[Enclosure: A letter to Stravinsky from Vladimir Horowitz, president of an Artists Committee for Koussevitzky: "Dear Mr. Stravinsky: . . . You belong to the group of artists who have had the great privilege of working with Dr. Koussevitzky . . ." Stravinsky underlined this in red and blue and wrote in the margin: "!!!!!!?????? How polite!"]

Stravinsky's next note was attached to a new Boosey & Hawkes catalog of his works:

April 5, 1949

Dear Bob: Have you or Betty my old *corrected* copy?—Because the new copies I just received are absolutely identical to the old stuff full of mistakes. Please answer, I am disturbed.

Love,
ISTR

At Town Hall on April 19 I conducted *Les Noces, Histoire du Soldat,* and the Pastorale for violin and wind quartet on a program with Bartók's Sonata for Two Pianos and Percussion. I wrote two days later, mentioning a letter from Lincoln Kirstein saying that Baba the Turk was modeled on Christian Bérard.[112] Stravinsky responded:

April 27, 1949

Dearest Bob: So glad to have at last your letter, 2 days ago—a very nice one [came] from E. Berman, who was enchanted by your concert. But there never was a call from Nabokov.

Am enthusiastic about your November program (*Perséphone, Pulcinella* & Violin Concerto).

Heard Robert Shaw's Mass performance by transcription.—Chorus from beginning to end covered by instruments. A very bad balance, indeed, and annoying lack of reasonable stoppages between phrases. Disappointed.

When exactly will you do this Mass?[113] Don't know the date.

112. This seems unlikely, though Kirstein was close to Auden at this time, and Bérard much in fashion, albeit of a kind that did not interest Auden.

113. This refers to a performance that I conducted at Columbia University's McMillan

Everybody here eager to see you soon, very soon. Hope not later than
June 1. Yes.

Love, kisses by millions,
ISTR

What a wonderful book that of Bernard de Clairvaux.
[Enclosure: A clipping from the *Los Angeles Times*, the "Music Mail Box," Sunday, April 24, 1949, quotes a letter from Arnold Schoenberg. An editor has
divided Schoenberg's text into three parts, subtitling the second "Very Characteristic," and the third "Happened Rather Often." Stravinsky has circled these
editorial headings in red pencil, added question marks, and inscribed the whole:
"Most idiotic titles I read in my life."]

May 5, 1949

Dear Bob: Enclosed is a sample of Hawkes's stupid and mean behavior, as well
as my answer to him.

Thank you so much for yours of Tuesday A.M.:

1. The [orchestra] parts of *Babel* are probably with Nathan Shilkret.[114]
Where is he now? . . .

2. Your brilliant article I had already read in *Musical America*. Has it been
printed in full there? . . . I doubt it. Remember—June 1st.

Love,
ISTR

[Enclosure: A copy of a letter from Ralph Hawkes to Aaron Sapiro: "I am
disturbed to hear that Mr. Strawinsky has authorized the free performance of
his works recently at the Town Hall concert given by Robert Craft at which
Mr. Strawinsky also conducted. . . ." and a copy of Stravinsky's reply: " . . .
Your grievances against me seem to be rather directed against Robert Craft
who, though not a 'star' (God forbid), is regarded by myself and by many pure
bred and really *'éprouvés'* musicians as a most excellent, reliable and devoted
interpreter of my music. This of course is, unfortunately, and very often, the
contrary of 'big money.' "]

Theatre on May 19 on a program, apparently chosen by Virgil Thomson, with prepared
piano pieces by John Cage, Palestinian Songs by Stefan Wolpe, and string pieces by Louis
Menini. Robert Shaw had prepared the chorus. "Kiki" Ocampo, Victoria Ocampo's brother,
came backstage after the performance. He had just seen Stravinsky in Hollywood and
brought news of him.

114. The Hollywood film composer Nathaniel Shilkret had commissioned Stravinsky,
Schoenberg, and other composers to contribute five-minute pieces, to fit on a 78 RPM
record side—and comprise a *Genesis* Suite.

May 10, 1949

Dearest Bob: How very consolatory an attitude like yours (the only one possible) in front of this ludicrous celebration of an old, experienced megalomaniac[115] by his fellow-travellers of the younger generation.

Eagerly expecting news after this Saturday's Mass performance.

Much thanks for this letter.

League of Composers condition (in buying tickets for your concert) is no surprise to me. I know them well already twenty-five years; it is why I never accepted their membership.[116]

Does really exist a portrait of me by Shagal [sic]? I never heard about it.[117]

Praising *Mavra* reprise with Monteverdi's *Orfeo*.

Love, love,
ISTR

[Enclosure: An article about Sartre and Existentialism.]

May 29, 1949

[Telegram]

Happy to see you, dearest Bob. Please come directly Wetherly Drive for early breakfast with us.

Stravinsky

I arrived in Hollywood at the beginning of June 1949 and recall that a few days later Stravinsky played the first scene of Act 2 of the *Rake* for me. He had composed it at the beginning of April, on his return from his Denver concert. The mood of the music, utterly different from that of Act 1, perfectly conveys the hero's weariness and disillusionment, partly by expanding the dimensions of the *da capo* aria in the previous act. The dotted rhythm and downward octave plunge at the beginning forebode ominous developments.

I left his studio thinking about the odd juxtaposition, the opposite of a concatenation, of his choice of wall art: five or six icons, some twelve drawings and paintings by Picasso, and, among the many photographs, the Turin Shroud and the daguerreotype of Chopin, swollen from the medications he was taking for his tuberculosis; the insane Nietzsche recumbent on his deathbed; Oscar Wilde doting on the young Lord Alfred Douglas; Verlaine in the Café François Premier sitting alone on a banquette, Silenus-like, head

115. Koussevitzky.

116. The League of Composers had agreed to buy a block of tickets on condition that a work by another composer besides Stravinsky be included in the program.

117. Marc Chagall's portrait of Stravinsky, dated 1949, was drawn from memory and a photograph.

back, eyes closed in a stupor, a glass of absinthe on the marble-topped table in front of him. Stravinsky believed the Shroud (and, later, the one in Oviedo) to be a genuine artifact. He admired the Nietzsche photograph as art—the black hair and mustache against the white bedlinen—and the pederasty of the others intrigued him, as the subject always did. One of his beliefs about the nature of the art world was that "taste is for pederasts." He also talked about the homosexuality of Diaghilev and Cocteau. Ravel was not homosexual, he said, indeed had no sex life at all. Because his autobiography mentions sleeping in the same bed with Ravel in a hotel near Como, people used to ask him what it was like, to which his answer was: "You will have to ask Ravel." Satie was homosexual, Stravinsky would affirm, and explain that the *Gymnopédies* refer to a ceremony outside the temple of Apollo Karneis in which naked boys danced and sang paeans to the patron of Palaestra.

On June 3 the composer David Diamond came for luncheon at the Stravinskys'. Forty-six years later, he wrote to me: "I remember that Friday, June 3, 1949. Mme Stravinsky's delicious food . . . the master, as we listened to his music, conducted quietly . . . The outdoor, back-patio, meal began with caviar and *crème sour* in halves of avocado, and continued with *kulebiaka*."

In a letter to my sister, dated August 1, 1949, I reveal some of my own reactions to life in Southern California after two months: "I like many things here, but I must live in older places and older cities. I hate the sprawl, the vacant lots, the lack of a center to this godless horror. We drove to San Diego yesterday to visit the art museum and zoo. Del Mar and Laguna are pleasant places, no doubt, but the civilization is twenty years old, only, and completely empty."

The main events of June, July, and August 1949 are described in my *Chronicle of a Friendship*. I returned to New York on September 7, and Stravinsky's next letter reached me in Kingston:

September 10, 1949

Dearest Bob: Happy to have your wire—1000 thanks. Provided you keep your word and *we see you here in Dec.*

Enclosed an incredible letter from an unknown idiot after the *Orpheus* broadcast. Send it back for my collection, please.

Expecting now your letters.

Much love,
ISTR

[Enclosure: An article from the *Los Angeles Times*, Wednesday, September 7, 1949, in which Stravinsky maliciously underlined the following comment on a speech by Koussevitzky at the Beverly Hills Hotel: "As is always the case with great men, his message was concise and asked no quarter . . . for it had a warning, too . . . All those here must work together and without thought of personal gain or aggrandizement."]

Stravinsky's next message was written in the margins of his carbon copy of a letter to Boosey & Hawkes regarding their receipt of the score of Act 2, scene 1 of *The Rake's Progress:*

September 13, 1949[118]

Dearest Bob: Please see to it that they send me a *decent acknowledgment.* Also, inquire at AMP if Hugo Winter[119] is coming here (he wanted to be here Sept. 10). Just received yours of Sept. 11. How disgusting![120]

[Enclosure: An announcement from the *Los Angeles Times* of a forthcoming performance of *Pierrot Lunaire* at Evenings on the Roof, and an article from the same newspaper, Sunday, September 13, 1949, about Koussevitzky's twenty-five years with the Boston Symphony.]

September 18, 1949

Bob dearest: Hope we'll hear from you (your impressions) before Nini's arrival. How was it? Eager to know. L.K.[121]

ISTR

[Enclosure: The *Los Angeles Times* review of *Living Music of the Americas* by Lazare Saminsky and *Music to My Ears* by Deems Taylor. These books, targets of Stravinsky's ridicule, received the *Los Angeles Times's* highest accolades.]

The impressions that Stravinsky wanted before his son's return to California were of a ballet that Soulima Stravinsky had "pieced together . . . from his favorite Scarlatti sonatas for a revised version of choreographer Antonia Cobos'[122] . . . *The Mute Wife*." (*Time,* September 26, 1949.) Stravinsky feared that the arrangement of Scarlatti would be compared with *Pulcinella.* When at the last minute Stravinsky telephoned me asking for a report, I said that the "choreography has some good points, hampered by idiotic

118. This letter and those of September 18 and 20 were addressed to me c/o Boosey & Hawkes, 30 West 47th Street, New York.

119. Hugo Winter, publisher of Stravinsky in New York during the war and a close friend of Anton Webern in Vienna.

120. I have no recollection of this reference.

121. L[ove] K[isses].

122. I had met Ms. Cobos at the time of the Royce Hall performance of *Histoire du Soldat* in June 1949. She appeared to be quite close to the Stravinskys, but I never knew the background of their relationship. Her real name was Phyllis Nahl.

costumes. The choice of the sonatas is discriminating, and the orchestrations are simple. The question is whether these keyboard pieces can be transferred so literally, since the even and continuous keyboard line cannot be reproduced in the strings unless they are reapportioned." The reviews condemned the performances, which Soulima conducted, as "ragged." As *Time* noted, "About the most charitable word the critics could find . . . was 'drab.' " Nevertheless, it was after this engagement—according to Vera Stravinsky's diary (October 5)—that the Soulima Stravinskys decided to move to New York.

On September 20 Stravinsky sent a clipping of Leonard Lyons's column in the *Daily News*, New York, September 17. Stravinsky had marked and queried the statement: "Judy Garland promised to return to New York for a Carnegie Hall appearance, and recite Stravinsky's *Perséphone* with Leonard Bernstein conducting the New York Philharmonic."

October 7, 1949

Dearest Bobsky: Today, just this: By now you must have received the *Pribaoutki* material I sent you one week ago via B & H. Please acknowledge!

Paul Sacher (of Basel) was here the other day—on his way (from Mexico) to New York. He will be there on October 10 at the Ambassador Hotel. I promised him to write you—he wanted so much to get in touch with you and to come at your concert. He leaves New York on October 26.

Let us hear from you very soon.

ISTR

[Enclosure: The *Los Angeles Times* obituary for Richard Strauss, September 25, 1949.]

On October 7 Ralph Hawkes wrote to Stravinsky inquiring about the Preludium and Canon announced for my October 22 concert. Stravinsky replied on October 17. "The 'Preludium' is a 1-minute piece of music which I composed in 1937 at the request of a certain Reichman (jazz leader) . . . I made a piano solo reduction of this music which Bob wanted to be played at his concerts. As to the 'Hommage à Nadia Boulanger,' this is just a very short canon (just a few measures) which I sent her for her birthday and I did not intend to be publicly performed. I know Bob liked it very much. That is why he will probably try to squeeze it between other short vocal pieces in one of his programs." This misleadingly suggests that Stravinsky made the arrangement of the "Preludium" for my concert. In fact the manuscript of the original had not been published when I found it in the sketchbook of *Jeu de cartes*. Stravinsky's 1953 orchestration of it was made for my thirtieth birthday concert, October 19, 1953.

Stravinsky's next two communications were telegrams:

October 13, 1949

[Telegram]

Dearest Bob: What a joy for us you're coming here December hope for a long time. Soulimas definitely leaving Hollywood for New York mid-December.

Affectionately,
Stravinsky

October 21, 1949

[Telegram]

Care Mrs. Frederick Hyde
Morningside Dr., NY[123]

Happy birthday to you dearest Bob, wishing you heartily a very very successful concert, all the Booseys, Beans, Betties, and Hawkes notwithstanding. Love, kisses, Stravinskys.

My Town Hall program on October 22 at 5:30, between a matinée and an evening concert, included Stravinsky's *Renard* and Suite No. 1 for Small Orchestra, Mozart's Clarinet Concerto (with Reginald Kell), Falla's Harpsichord Concerto (with Sylvia Marlowe), a Duo for violin (Joseph Fuchs) and piano (Leo Smit) by Arthur Berger, and Alban Berg's Chamber Concerto (with Isidore Cohen, violin, and Robert Cornman, piano). The Preludium and Canon were not performed because the program was already too long. After the concert I dined with Auden and a young cellist friend of his, then flew to Los Angeles for four days. On October 24 Auden wrote to Stravinsky: "Bob Craft's concert last Saturday went quite nicely, with the usual impatience of the management to throw us out. The voices in *Renard* were a bit frightened." In fact the stage manager could be seen gesturing threateningly in the wings during the last movement of the Berg, but we finished the piece.

November 14, 1949

[Telegram]

Glad am able to give you good news. Money at your disposal. Where to send it and to whom exactly? Shall write my bank on hearing from you. Affectionately, Stravinsky.

·

123. I lived on Morningside Drive at 122nd Street during the first part of my Juilliard period (see chapter 3). In 1949 I briefly rented a room in the same building from the addressee of the letter. The mystery is how the communication reached me without the street number.

On November 1, 1949, in an effort to raise money for my *Perséphone* performance,[124] Stravinsky wrote to Arthur Sachs, then in his home at Faugeras, Corrèzes, asking him for "the sum of $900.00 to permit me to keep my word *vis-à-vis de Robert Craft, qui a organisé ce concert en tablant sur mon aide* . . . I will reimburse you from the receipts, or, if these are not sufficient, I will make up the balance by giving one of my manuscripts to you." Sachs had been a friend of the composer since 1923, and, during World War II, his frequent host at Santa Barbara's Hope Ranch.[125] He was a senior partner of the investment-banking firm of Goldman, Sachs, which had sold at the peak before the Wall Street Crash in 1929. He replied to Stravinsky on November 9, 1949, " I accept your proposition cheerfully, in the way that you have indicated," but he inquired if the gift would be tax-deductible. Stravinsky replied on November 15 that his lawyer, Aaron Sapiro, had given assurances that the money for the purchase of the manuscript could be deducted. The letter went on to say that *"Hollywood est devenue si mort* . . . because the economic prosperity created by the war has given place to a *marasme* . . . and because all of the most interesting people whom we knew and frequented had come to California only as a temporary residence and have now returned to Europe."

November 15, 1949

Here is a check dear Bob, just received yours of Sat. Nov. 12.

Will write you today or tomorrow—*tell me your address in NY*—have your dates but not the address.

Love,
ISTR

124. Stravinsky's generosity to me extended even to the pocketbook level and belies his reputation for parsimony. In 1958 he asked me to rehearse *Threni, Oedipus Rex, The Rite of Spring*, and other pieces for him in Hamburg for his concerts in Venice, but the Norddeutscher Rundfunk turned down my request for enough money to cover expenses. Stravinsky wrote to Nicolas Nabokov, June 16: "Hamburg refused Bob the 750 dollars and offered him only 500. With this money he'll pay for the trip, Venice to Hamburg, and rehearse [for two weeks]. These conditions seem to me very poor. . . Is it possible that [Rolf] Liebermann did not agree, or else that you forgot to ask him about it? I told Bob that I would write to you. If this does not bring results, I will pay the 250 dollars to him from my own pocket, since he is doing this Hamburg business only for me, and, what is more, he would be paying for it."

125. See chapter 11 for a fuller account of the Sachs–Stravinsky relationship.

November 15, 1949

Dear Bob:

1. I sent you this morning a check of $900.00 because Sachs answered me in the way we all expected—*i.e.*, he will transfer the money to my bank. One point has yet to be cleared in order to help Sachs get the most out of his gesture in relation with his taxes. That point is: are you or are you not a "Non-Profit Organization"? Just let me know by return mail.

2. I hope that you are not too worried regarding your Carnegie Hall-*Perséphone* finances. Have you to wait until your father returns to get that money from him? Or did you find some other way out?

3. If Auden leaves on March 13 [1950] I figure I shall arrive in New York on the 10th in order to be able to work with him on the 11th and 12th. This means that we will have to start from here on March 1, so that we do not get too tired driving too fast across the country.[126]

4. If you think that my bad terms with Toscanini would not become an obstacle to his consent to invite you, I am quite ready to write him.[127] I'd like you to suggest the best argumentation to convince him: your talent as a young American conductor or my wish of having a good and correct performance of my Symphony.

5. As to the concert planned for April, I think it is better not to start worrying about it until you are through with *Perséphone*.

6. Of course if you have the possibility to do *Pulcinella* I will be delighted. Please answer me immediately before going to New York.

Love to you dearest Bob,

ISTR

November 20, 1949

[Telegram]
Carnegie Hall NY

Our thoughts are with you ever and especially this evening. Convey best

---

126. The Stravinskys and I had planned to drive to New York, where he had conducting engagements, needed to discuss questions in the *Rake* libretto with Auden, and had agreed to pose for Marino Marini's two bronze portraits of his head. We left Hollywood on February 6, 1950, stayed in El Centro, Las Cruces, El Paso, Del Rio, Beaumont, New Orleans, Tallahassee, Sarasota, Miami, Daytona, Charleston, Williamsburg, Philadelphia, arriving in New York on February 18.

127. Toscanini's NBC Symphony had many guest conductors at this time but Stravinsky was played only by Ansermet. Stravinsky's wish to have his Symphony in C performed was such that he went to the length of writing to Toscanini, November 28, 1949: "Dear Maestro, . . . I would like to recommend to you a very talented, cultured, young musician and conductor, Mr. Robert Craft. . . He knows my music so well . . . he is able to handle any of my works."

wishes to Zorina[128] and Hess. Please call us collect after concert. With love,
The Stravinskys and Max[129]

Auden was ruffled because Stravinsky had forgotten to include his name. I
dined with him before the concert and was amazed that he could gulp three
martinis and still not slur a syllable in the poems he read.

On November 22, Auden wrote to Kallman in Ischia:

Last night I had to put on tails and recite at Carnegie Hall in the midst of a
Stravinsky programme. *Pulcinella* (better than I thought though too long) and
Perséphone, which is very remarkable. Some of the Princeton choir who
took part were very fetching. It conflicted with opening night at the Met.
Rosenkavalier . . .[130]

The complete *Pulcinella*, Four Etudes for Orchestra, and *Zvezdolikiy* had not
been performed before in America, and Harold Schonberg's favorable review of the concert, in the *New York Sun*, November 22, 1949, mentioned
the importance of these novelties in programming, while acclaiming *Perséphone*
as one of Stravinsky's greatest works.

November 28, 1949

Dearest Bob: I have your 3 letters (Nov. 22, 25, 26).

Poor Bob! . . . I prefer to talk all this over with you when you will be here
again.[131] Today only these lines.

1. Enclosed a copy of my letter to Toscanini to which I shall await the
reply anxiously.[132]

2. What happened with Berger?[133] He was the only friendly critic of your
activities; and what is your trouble with him? I'd like to know all about it as
soon as possible.

3. RCA Victor. Tell Mohr that it is imperative to make *Apollo* and Basler
Concerto in one single album as the cutting of the Concerto in four sides

128. After hearing Vera Zorina in Honegger's *Jeanne d'Arc au bûcher* at Hollywood Bowl
in the summer, I invited her to narrate the part of *Perséphone*. William Hess sang the part of
Eumolpus, as he had done with Stravinsky in the 1947 CBS broadcast performance.

129. Dr. Maximilian Edel.

130. Dorothy Farnan, *Auden in Love*, p. 187.

131. I had lost three thousand dollars on this concert.

132. Toscanini did not answer.

133. Arthur Berger had criticized the performances in the *Herald-Tribune* as under-rehearsed. This was true. The dress rehearsal had had to be canceled because Toscanini suddenly commandeered the hall for a recording session.

would be real mutilation to which I shall never agree. It is also imperative I do it before others would.

4. If you don't need the *Pribaoutki* material anymore, please bring it with you or send it back.

5. The Mass yesterday with Byrnes[134] was very good and attracted a good public. Goldberg very elogious,[135] the others not mean, but stupid. What a terrible hall that Wilshire-Ebell Theatre! . . . All the voices sounded like behind the curtain.

6. Did you go to the premiere of the City Center *Firebird* with new setting of Balanchine? He called me up yesterday night just while I was at the Mass and I received a very enthusiastic telegram from Berman. That's all for today.

Love

[Enclosure: An article from the *Los Angeles Times*, November 25, 1949: "Britten Conducts Own and Purcell's Works."[136]]

Stravinsky wrote on December 2 to thank Arthur Sachs: "All musical enterprises here are in an ultraprecarious situation at the moment. Only large and long-established organizations, with their committees, patrons and subscriptions, can survive. And, unfortunately, these societies offer only the most popular repertory. *Ceci nous oblige à compter sur le sacrifice héroïque de quelques apôtres du genre de Robert Craft."*

On December 8 I conducted the New York City Ballet in *Orpheus*, but without a rehearsal in which to correct a serious mistake. As I wrote to Stravinsky on December 6, "Barzin conducts the music between [77] and [79] not as equal bars but as three-eighths and two-eighths."

Then, on December 10, in Town Hall, I conducted *Mavra* and Monteverdi's *Orfeo*, playing the continuo part of the latter on the piano. A few days later I disbanded my New York concert organization and boarded a

134. Harold Bernstein, a German-born conductor who lived in Hollywood during the war. Stravinsky liked him, but Schoenberg, after hearing him conduct his first Chamber Symphony, forbade him to perform any of his music ever again.

135. This was one of Stravinsky's favorite words.

136. On the same day Stravinsky wrote to Nicolas Nabokov: "All week here I've listened to aunt Britten and uncle Pears. . . Britten himself makes quite a favorable impression as a performer, especially at the piano" (original in Russian). Stravinsky had heard him conduct the Los Angeles Philharmonic on November 24 (Interludes from *Peter Grimes*, Serenade, *Young Person's Guide to the Orchestra*), and had heard his opera *Albert Herring* at Bovard Auditorium, U.S.C., on December 9. The Los Angeles *Times* review of the opera is vigorously underscored by Stravinsky in red and blue pencil expressing strong disagreement with Albert Goldberg's laudatory remarks.

bus, the only transportation I could afford, for Los Angeles, where I arrived with double pleurisy and pneumonia. At Christmas, Stravinsky presented me with the most marvelous gift I have ever received, a hand-copy by him of the manuscript score of his unfinished *Dialogue Between Joy and Reason*,[137] inscribed to me. I gave it to the Paul Sacher Stiftung in Basel in 1990.

137. The text is of an early French translation (No. 244, Bibliothèque Nationale, Paris) of Petrarch's most popular Latin verse dialogue (from *De Remedii utriusque fortunae*, 1358). After Stravinsky and Dushkin had played the *Duo concertant* in the Salle Pleyel on December 8, 1932, C.-A. Cingria wrote to the composer: "What a triumph, the Cantilène, Eglogue I, Eglogue II! The music is wise . . . in a way achieved by no one before. . . It is Petrarch. You have captured the equivalence, set Petrarch in the same voice as that of the *Duo concertant*. Perhaps the title would even make people understand. . . How good the music was! It absorbs me entirely. . . My *Pétrarque* has been published. It will be sent to you from Lausanne." Stravinsky was profoundly influenced by this book, particularly the passage, which he underscored, beginning *"Le lyrisme n'existe pas sans règles . . . autrement ce n'est qu'une faculté de lyrisme et elle existe partout."* He was also influenced by its musical examples, a sestina by Arnauld Daniel (the manuscript, in the Ambrosiana, was transcribed, in lozenge notes, by Johann D. Beck), and pieces by Bardi, Caccini, and Gluck. Cingria inscribed Stravinsky's copy of the volume: *"A l'auteur du Duo concertant qui va si bien avec Pétrarque. . ."* Stravinsky conceived the *Dialogue* for two voices and a keyboard instrument, but put it aside to compose *Perséphone*.

Chapter 5

Wetherly Drive Regulars

T he portrait sketches and vignettes that follow are of Stravinsky's closest but, with exceptions, less well known friends in his California years. Because of disparities in language, age, and professional and cultural interests, these frequent *invités* do not form a "circle," nor, with the exception of the Huxley, Isherwood, and Heard firmament, can they be thought of as "intimates." Stravinsky was both sociable—he enjoyed parties, but tended to converse with only one person—and withdrawn. He would suddenly retreat into an inner core that he shared with no one, not fully even with his beloved second wife, for the reason that she did not go back far enough in his past.

The people discussed here were brought together only in the large gatherings traditionally held at Easter, on the composer's birthday, June 18, the Fourth of July, and on Mrs. Stravinsky's name day (September 30) and birthday (Christmas).

In 1948, the Stravinskys' Hollywood social acquaintance was more Russian than would be the case a few years later. In the early 1940s they frequently dined with the Prince and Princess Galitzin (he was Stravinsky's physician), Prince Mdivani, the Sergei Bertensens (he was the son of the doctor who attended Tchaikovsky on his deathbed), the Edward G. Robinsons (an old friend, he had been the witness to Stravinsky's application for U.S. citizenship), the Artur Rubinsteins (a good friend since 1914), Zosia Kochanska (widow of the violinist Paul Kochansky), the Akim Tamirovs, the Gregory Ratoffs, Misha Auer, the Vladimir Sokolovs, Zoya Karabanova (Mrs. Stravinsky's friend from the Chauve-Souris), sometimes at Romanov's in Beverly Hills, but more often at the less formal Bublichki, a Russian restaurant only three blocks away on Sunset Boulevard.

The Stravinsky household was entirely Russian when I first lived with them. Even their masseuse, Xenia Liamina, Mrs. Stravinsky's confidante, was Russian. Yevgenia Petrovna, the live-in cook-housekeeper from 1946 to 1964—she had been preceded by Masha and by Elizaveta Alexandrovna—lavished her attentions on Igor Fyodorovich, but tended to be chary of them with Vera Arturovna, who would have preferred an Italian-Parisian cuisine to a Russo-American one as well as less rigidity in the designated hours for breakfast, lunch, *Chai*, and dinner. Yevgenia Petrovna was not generous, and could be curmudgeonly with the two Russian gardeners. Vassily Varzhinsky, who was hardworking and wrote plays on the side, deserved better, and if, occasionally, Dmitri Stepanovich did not, he should always have been forgiven. True, he was overly fond of vodka and more inclined to boss than to help his partner, but he was in his late sixties when I met him. A Stravinsky retainer since 1941, this gentleman refugee had a Kaiser Wilhelm II beard and an aristocratic appearance. He resembled the German monarch so closely, in fact, that a Hollywood talent scout, who had been casing the property, asked him to play the part in a war movie. (He did not land the job because he spoke no English, but Mrs. Stravinsky, who had seen him act, said he was a terrible "ham," and that his performance would have been much too heavily scented.) His gallantry toward the taskmistress in the kitchen went unrewarded. She never offered either of these Ostrovskyan characters a glass of tea and a pirozhki, or one of the delicious feather-weight meringues freshly made every Friday by Vera Arturovna. Since I knew no Russian, and since neither of them spoke English, I did not understand Yevgenia Petrovna's cavils or their responses. Gospodin Stravinsky was kinder, and he personally chose the flowers for the fresh bouquet that would be placed in his studio at least twice a week.

Alexei Haieff

Claudio Spies introduced me to Alexei Haieff during Stravinsky's dress rehearsal for his CBS broadcast performance of *Perséphone* in New York in January 1947. He had been a pupil of Rakhmaninov but by 1945 was Stravinsky's closest musical associate. Russian-born, Haieff had come to the United States by way of Harbin, China, during the Russian Revolution. In 1939 he was living in Boston when Stravinsky delivered his Charles Eliot Norton Lectures. He became the composer's confidant at Harvard, briefing him in Russian about people encountered there, which ones were important, which "sticky"—a much-used Stravinsky expression—and who was a professor of what. Haieff accompanied the Stravinskys on concert tours, as I did later; and, during the war when train berths, or indeed seats, were nearly impossible to find, he slept on the floor of the Stravinsky compartment between Los Angeles and New York. In 1946 he conducted the *Ebony* Concerto on tour with the Woody Herman Band, and for a time after that he lived in the Hollywood house that Stravinsky purchased and furnished for his daughter and her husband, during the months before their arrival from France in 1947. The writers Katherine Anne Porter and Eleanor Clark lived there as well, before, after, and during Haieff's tenancy.

Alyosha, as the Stravinskys called him, assisted the composer at the rehearsals for my April 1948 New York concert with him, and, so I believe, helped to avert friction. In June 1952 he and I accompanied the Stravinskys on an automobile trip from Flint, Michigan to Lake Louise, Banff, in the Canadian Rockies, and on to Los Angeles. Since we shared motel rooms en route, I came to know him well at that time. Unlike me, this compulsive giggler did not complain of the inconveniences and *longeurs* of crossing the prairies, and he managed to entertain the Stravinskys with Russian stories. Later in the 1950s he married his English paramour, the Duchess of Brontë, heiress of the estate below Mt. Etna on the Taormina side—D. H. Lawrence's Fontana Vecchia, created by the Bourbons of Naples for a descendant of Lord Nelson. Haieff, whom we called the "Duke of Brontë" thereafter, lived with her in Rome, but Stravinsky, jealously possessive of his friends and not wanting his associates to marry, lost track of Alyosha thereafter. In March 1969 he was teaching at the University of Utah and paid two visits to Stravinsky in Hollywood. I last saw him during the intermission of a concert in Rome in April 1987.

The Bolms

The longest-time close friends of the Stravinskys when I arrived were Adolph and Beata Bolm. As a member of Diaghilev's original Ballets Russes, Bolm had danced in the first *Firebird*, though, to judge from a 1915 letter from the composer to Misia Sert, Stravinsky scarcely knew him at that time. Bolm had been Vaslav Nijinsky's best man at his wedding to Romola Pulski in Montevideo in 1913, and in March 1916, at Diaghilev's request, Beata had journeyed from Paris to Switzerland to chaperone Nijinsky, recently released from wartime internment in Budapest, to Paris and New York, where the Diaghilev troupe was performing none too successfully without its most famous dancer.

The Bolms, who were Swedish, did not return to Europe after the war but founded ballet schools in Chicago and, later, Los Angeles, where he choreographed a performance of *Firebird* in Hollywood Bowl that Stravinsky conducted in August 1940. In the early 1940s, Bolm became the Stravinskys' West Coast cicerone, touring every part of the state with them and initiating them into the movie-land mode of life, the endless vacant-lot boulevards, the forlorn beaches, the deluxe vulgarity of Bel-Air and Beverly Hills, and the Farmers' Market.[1]

1. In this book the "Farmers' Market" refers exclusively to the Italian restaurant called Yolanda, named for an attractive young friend of Aldous and Maria Huxley. The Stravinskys

Beata Bolm's English was correct and fluent. She had learned it, as well as Russian, French, and German, from governesses and tutors during her childhood in Persia, and it was for her linguistic abilities that Stravinsky engaged her to help with his polyglot correspondence. That was in 1943, after he had temporarily broken with Bolm for siding with the majority of a Hollywood Bowl audience that booed the conductor Dimitri Mitropoulos for kissing the hand of his soloist Marian Anderson.

During my first two years with the Stravinskys, the Bolms were dinner guests at least once a week. Their scandalous anecdotes about the early Diaghilev years fascinated me but bored Stravinsky, who would retire to his studio to work. Bolm died of a heart attack in the spring of 1951, but his petite, blue-eyed, blonde widow lunched with us periodically for the remainder of her long life (1967). Her impeccable manners did not prevent her from calling me "Bobby" and usually adding a chuckle.

"The Baron"

Baron Fred Osten-Sacken (1888–March 19, 1974) lived in California during World War II, and as early as October 1940 he and the Stravinskys began to see each other frequently. He had known both Vera and Igor since the first decade of the century, his brother, Maximilian, having been a classmate of the composer in the Gureyvich Gymnasium in St. Petersburg. His sister, Baroness Illa, was a later, post-Revolution acquaintance, dating from her residence as a refugee in Baden-Baden. Baron Fred had fallen in love at sight with Vera de Bosset in Moscow, December 3, 1908, and courted her when she was a student at Berlin University. With Stravinsky's ascendancy in 1921, the Baron redirected his ardor as best he could to another lady from among his wide acquaintance of the well-born kind. Then, in the mid-1930s, when Stravinsky's infidelities with Dagmar Godowsky during one South American and two North American concert tours became newspaper gossip, Vera Sudeykina resumed her liaison with Baron Fred. Photos survive of him with her in her hotel room in a health resort near Munich in the summer of 1936, while Stravinsky was in Paris composing *Jeu de cartes*. (Dagmar was the daughter of Leopold, the pianist, and sister of Leopold Jr., who married George Gershwin's sister Frances.)

The Baron seemed to have stepped out of the Almanach de Gotha, and in his blue-bloodedness was so different from anyone I had ever met that I felt sorry for him in what I assumed to be his loneliness. His imperious

---

dined there at least once a week in the early 1950s, at which time it was sufficiently secluded to serve as a haven for movie actors, who gaped with greater interest at the composer and the writer than the other way around. Cary Grant was one of the habitués. (When I became the ombudsman of the Stravinskys' social life, my first, self-appointed task was to cut down on movie people.)

bearing set him apart, as did his preposterous personal stories from a remote past. (He told me that as an adolescent he had hidden behind a curtain in his uncle's bedchamber and become a Peeping Tom during one of his amorous consummations, but, unable to stifle his laughter on hearing the seducer explain, *"und das, Amalie, sind die Eier,"* was caught out and punished.) I liked him and always spoke of him to the Stravinskys as the "Baron Noblesse Oblige."

I met him at the Stravinskys' in January 1950, on one of his trips from his new home in Mexico, and drove him to Wetherly Drive from Hollywood's Roosevelt Hotel, as I would do on other occasions. I did not know him well until much later in Lexington, Kentucky, where Marcel Boussac, a wealthy Parisian friend, employed the Baron to look after his thoroughbreds. After each season at Churchill Downs he would return to Paris and Longchamps. In April 1967 I conducted a concert with the Lexington Symphony Orchestra and during rehearsal week dined with him every evening and twice took him to the movies. In Kentucky as in Hollywood, I drove him home, but not all the way: he feigned a desire to walk the last blocks, not wanting me to see the poverty of his neighborhood. Lexingtonians regarded him affectionately as a "character," but also as a mystery: why was such a perfect gentleman so impecunious and conspicuously not a Kentucky Colonel? (Ironically, I was one, having been involuntarily inducted into the organization after a concert in Louisville the year before.) To an acquaintance of his who had asked this question, I explained that the baronial fortune had vanished with the Russian Revolution and that his only expertise, apart from his wide knowledge of Italian Old Masters, was in horse-breeding.

The Baron, a Lithuanian—*Kein Deutscher, echter Littauer,* the reverse of Eliot's line—spoke Russian with the Stravinskys, slipping into French and German only from time to time, during which lapses I learned that he had been a close friend of the Furtwänglers, archaeologist father as well as conductor son. The Stravinskys were unusually voluble with him, I think to stem the tide of his reminiscences. I saw him last in the Stravinsky apartment in New York. One of my nieces, then in her teens, joined us there for dinner and has not yet completely recovered from seeing the elderly aristocrat rise to his feet, bow, take her hand, and make the hand-kissing gesture. Baron Fred starved himself to death with a photograph of the young Vera de Bosset before his eyes, a still from the 1915 Russian film *War and Peace,* in which she played the role of *la belle Hélène.* Or so his doctor wrote to her when sending the picture, which the Baron had framed in a gold medallion on maroon velvet enclosed behind two small wooden doors, a traveler's altar.

"The Baroness"

The Baroness d'Erlanger lived in the fourth house below the Stravinskys on the same side of Wetherly Drive. Born Catherine de Rochegude, she became a lady-in-waiting to Queen Victoria. In 1895 she married the Baron Frederick d'Erlanger (1868–1943), a British composer and banker. As the heiress of a French banker herself, her fortune was so large that she tried to purchase Stonehenge. In fact she owned Byron's St. James's Street house and a larger residence in Portland Square (Enid Bagnold's autobiography includes a vivid description of the Baroness's life there), as well as Palladio's Villa Malcontenta on the Brenta Canal (where I met the Grand Duchess Olga with the Stravinskys in September 1951, driven there by the young composer Baron Raffaello de Banfield), and a magnificent palazzo on the Grand Canal. Stravinsky had known her husband slightly and even heard some of his music, which, he said, had "good manners."

The Baroness herself had known Diaghilev and been a patroness of the Ballets Russes from before World War I. Happening to be in Venice at the time of the impresario's death, she had paid for his funeral there, as well as his hotel and other bills, and kept the documents testamentary to this in a bedroom vault. I first heard about her during my initial stay with the Stravinskys in New York in April 1948. Her name was in newspaper headlines because of a robbery. The *Herald Tribune* for the 25th said: "The Baroness Catherine d'Erlanger, portrait painter and active London society figure, reported today the loss of $31,900 in jewelry and $5000 in cash in a burglary of her rambling Hollywood house." I should explain that her paintings were caricatures, genre Marie Laurençin, of Cocteau, Les Six, the Sitwells, et al. I did not meet her until 1949 and knew her well only when she became my landlady.

Between 1952 and 1969 I lived in a tiny apartment behind her house over the garage next to her pool, earning my rent by reading to her for four dollars an hour. In fact, this was my only source of income for about two years, but at least I chose the books. The house smelled strongly of sandalwood, she herself of vetiver, neither fragrance at all to my taste, but the place was so untidy that strong perfumes were probably necessary. By the mid-1950s the once wealthy woman had given her properties to ex-lovers and squandered her other assets. Most of her bibelots had price tags attached to them. To a new visitor it must have seemed odd to lift a saucer from a tea tray and discover that it was for sale at, say, three hundred dollars.

The Stravinskys and I dined with her quite frequently in my early years in California, sometimes in her home, more often, and as to cuisine, preferably, in one of two French restaurants that she owned on Sunset Boulevard, the Café Gala—she gave a party there for Stravinsky after he conducted *Petrushka* in Hollywood Bowl, August 31, 1944—and the Deauville, whose chef, Marie Le Put, later became Aldous Huxley's cook. Also in 1944, the Baroness occasionally became Stravinsky's "babysitter" and "telephone-girl"; he could not be left alone when his wife went shopping and would not trust anyone in the house he did not know. The Baroness's social acquaintance was largely *tapette*, the most distinguished and nattiest of whom was Cole Porter, who was always very shy with Stravinsky. The Baroness gave late-night pool parties, for which this famously eccentric dresser wore a tiara and a bathrobe.

I did not see her after 1958, when her son, Sir Gerald d'Erlanger, the director of BOAC, as I think the airline was called then, transported her to Paris to live with him and be near her French beau monde daughter, the Princesse Faucigny-Lucinge. The old lady died there the following year.

Richard Hammond

The independently wealthy Dick Hammond was a composition pupil of Nadia Boulanger in Paris in the 1920s, when he met Stravinsky. Nadia reintroduced them in New York on January 24, 1941, at a party Hammond gave after the second performance of Balanchine's ballet *Balustrade* (the Violin Concerto). By the end of that year Hammond and his lifelong companion, George Martin, were neighbors of the Stravinskys in the Hollywood hills, but at a slightly higher altitude, and the two couples frequently dined in each other's houses. Leopold Stokowski had lived next door to "the Hammonds" during the period of his infatuation with Garbo and his cinema-star turns—*Fantasia* ("Pleased to meet you, Mickey Mouse") and *A Hundred Men and a Girl* (Deanna Durbin). As a board member of New York's League of Composers, Hammond had sponsored Stokowski's 1931 Metropolitan Opera performance of *The Rite of Spring* with Martha Graham. In the 1950s and 1960s Dick and George spent part of their summers in Venice, where the Stravinskys saw them almost daily and often dined with them at Harry's Bar or the Ristorante Martini. In Septembers, Dick and George, "I Due Foscari," as I referred to them, reduced their cholesterol levels, or whatever this was called in the 1950s, by taking the "cure" in the Euganean Hills *terme* made famous by Shelley. In the early 1960s they moved to New York, where meetings with the Stravinskys were less frequent. They attended the private funeral service for the composer in the evening of the day he died, with Balanchine, Kirstein, the Elliott Carters, Lucia Davidova, Natasha Nabokov (Princess Natalie Shakhovskoy), and Paul Horgan.

Eugene Berman

Vera Stravinsky had known the Berman family in the second decade of the twentieth century when they were St. Petersburg bankers, and had sympathized with the sufferings from anti-Semitism of the brothers, Léonid and

Eugene, both of them painters, which had so emotionally scarred the latter as a young man that he spoke Russian only reluctantly, even with the Stravinskys. Stravinsky always addressed him in that language, but Berman would slip into Italian at the first opportunity, or, depending on the company, French or English.

Genia Berman was the best friend to me among the Stravinsky Old Guard. I made his acquaintance at one of the composer's Sunday afternoon lawn parties, which tended to spill into the arbors and gardens on the hill behind the small residence. I also met the painters Rico Lebrun and Corrado Cagli there, both of them fellow-refugee friends of the Stravinskys and Berman. In the summer of 1949, Berman invited me to tea and to see paintings and drawings he had done recently in Mexico. At this time Mexican Baroque architecture was the main subject of his art, but he also collected pre-Columbians and had amassed a trove of *objets d'or.* Mrs. Stravinsky drove me to his studio, in a residential hotel, the Villa Carlotta, in the center of Hollywood, a curiously incongruous neighborhood for a man of his urbanity, I thought, and as we watched him displaying his pictures, I wondered what he was doing in California at all, learning later that it was because the actress Ona Munson resided there. I left the studio commenting on his work to Mrs. Stravinsky, who had known him well in Paris in 1920. Her opinions were encouraging, but candid, whereas Stravinsky's were outspoken to the extent of advising the elimination of the "decorative blots" that amounted to the artist's logo. Berman nevertheless welcomed Stravinsky's criticisms, which in the case of the costumes and decor for *Danses concertantes* were severe. What struck me most in his work that afternoon, and I had not seen much of it together before, was his evident inability to paint faces. The alms-begging Mexican children, the mendicants inching their way to churches on their knees, the people in the marketplaces were always seen from the back. The only direct facial portraits he ever attempted, before the cartoons of Stravinsky in 1966–67, were of Ona, and in one of his watercolors of her that I still possess, the corners of her eyes are filled with pendant, pearl-like tears. As we left, he held up three drawings and asked me to choose one as a gift. Since I scarcely knew him, this seemed almost too generous, but I assumed he was testing my taste.

Berman had been infatuated with Ona since her appearance as Belle Watkins, the prostitute in *Gone with the Wind,* and had courted her ever since. Her boyish appearance appealed to his predominantly feminine side, nor was he deterred by her crushes on young girls. No doubt he had a lesbian-gay arrangement in mind from the beginning. What disturbed me was his poor judgment in not seeing that since she took no interest in the visual arts, even mistaking him for a major painter, their marriage would be a dubious proposition. By 1950, suffering from the rejection so common in the lives of middle-aged female actresses, and by this time easily wounded, she began to consider marriage to Berman as a refuge and accepted it. One night when we were with them at Reuben's restaurant on Fifty-ninth Street, which catered to actors and named its multideckered sandwiches after them, she noticed that the "Ona Munson" sandwich had been discontinued, reached for her hanky, and wept some of those jewel-like tears.

After the wedding, which took place in the Stravinsky house with myself as best man, the Bermans moved to an apartment on West Fifty-fifth Street that soon became suffocatingly full of art. When Genia received commissions for stage-designing at the Teatro Piccolo alla Scala in Milan, the Bermans began to live part-time in Italy, which Ona hated, as she told me the last time I saw her, in Siena in 1954. Less than a year later, in January 1955, she committed suicide in their New York apartment, leaving a brutal note instructing her husband not to follow her. Hearing the story in California, the Stravinskys tried to stop him from blaming himself, saying that she had been temporarily insane, and inviting him to stay with them. Instead, he returned to Rome, this time permanently, except to design sets for Metropolitan Opera productions of *Don Giovanni, Otello, Rigoletto,* and, in 1972, Balanchine's *Pulcinella.*

Berman loved the Stravinskys. He met them on their every arrival in Venice, or followed in a day or so, renting a room or studio near their hotel. He was our companion and guide on visits to the towns of the Po delta, Ferrara, and the great Benedictine Abbey and bell tower of Santa Maria Pomposa. On summer Sundays he accompanied us on visits to the Palladian villas in the Veneto and near Monselice, hours of architectural and landscaping enjoyment to which the Stravinskys always looked forward, exhausting as it was. In other seasons, in Rome, Naples, and Sicily, he conducted us through palaces and churches, excavation sites and museums. I remember trips with him to the *scavi* at Palestrina, and, on a tour of the Castelli Romaní, a view of the floor mosaic in the Cathedral of Anagni now thought to be the world's oldest fractal construction ("a Sierpensky gasket in the fourth order of iteration"). His apartment in the Palazzo Doria-Pamphili was a museum, one of the richest in Etruscan art in private hands. I also remember that one of his palatial walls sustained a gilded baroque altar that he had found in Calabria. While crossing the Ponte Vecchio one day he recognized an unidentified painting of a landscape in a souvenir shop as a Corot and acquired it for a few hundred dollars. He died alone, of diabetes, without designated heirs, and his entire collection was stolen, then disposed of by art thieves beyond the possibility of replevying.

In November 1960, after two weeks of rehearsals and concerts in Genoa, the Stravinskys and I arrived in Rome for more of the same. Berman gave a gala party for them, at which he introduced me to an attractive divorcée, Signora Crespi. A "romance," as Aldous sarcastically referred to such enterprises, developed that same evening. Before I was aware of what had happened, the comely lady was living in New York in the same hotel, the St.

Regis, as the Stravinskys and myself. She also traveled with us to Washington for concerts, where I realized, and she as well, that we were not meant for each other. On returning to New York, I provided a ticket for her back to Rome. But we continued to talk on the telephone. In October 1961, the story not yet at an end, I called Genia from Zurich, saying that I needed his guidance. He came from Rome, sat up with me all night, and convinced me that Stravinsky was my "destiny" and I could not leave him, which, however unlikely it may seem now, I must have contemplated doing. He understood my desire for a family and a life of my own, my fears of having to live alone later, and the responsibilities of my position vis-à-vis Stravinsky.

Eugene Berman was with Vera Stravinsky and myself during every moment of Stravinsky's funeral, and the pre- and post-funeral ordeal; he wrote a letter to his brother describing those days that remains one of the most important documents in Stravinsky biography.

Aldous Huxley

Stravinsky and Aldous Huxley were introduced in London, in July 1934, by Victoria Ocampo, the Argentine writer and publisher of *Sur*. She had known Aldous for several years and published Spanish translations of some of his books. Huxley's letters to her are among his most interesting: "I was very fond of [Valéry] personally and always derived much pleasure and profit from that almost incomprehensibly rapid and elliptic conversation . . . But some of [his poetry] had a certain quality of forced imagination and *voulu* phantasy . . . there was always a tendency in Valéry to pretend to a philosophical-mathematical profundity and precision of thought which in many cases he did not have. The result was a curious incongruity between form and substance—dense and inspissated sentences expressing light, vapid generalizations . . ."

The case with Stravinsky was very different. Victoria had been in love with him since the 1920s, as she revealed to Coco Chanel. In 1934 Victoria contracted to publish a Spanish translation of his *Chroniques de ma vie*, and in 1936 invited him to give concerts in Argentina, Uruguay, and Brazil, with herself as Narrator in *Perséphone*. Both Huxley and Stravinsky visited Mme Ocampo in her Rio Plata home, and throughout the 1940s and 1950s the three of them exchanged news about each other from remote parts of the world. Stravinsky wrote to her, April 10, 1941: "Aldous is here in Hollywood"; she had been with the Stravinskys at the beginning of January and contributed a dappled cowhide rug to the furnishings of their new home. Huxley's last letter to Victoria, in 1959, ends with *"J'ai vu les Stravinskys l'autre soir et les trouve en bonne forme."*

The close relationship between the Stravinskys and the Huxleys began in the autumn of 1946, thanks, in part, to Anita Loos, a long-time Huxley friend and Mrs. Stravinsky's English tutor. At that time the Huxleys actually lived on the same street, not Wetherly Drive but its southern extension into Doheny Drive. After that their long-time home at North Kings Road (now best known for a famous house by the Viennese architect Rudolph Schindler), where the Huxleys lived during most of my period, gave them greater propinquity to the Stravinskys than any of their other friends except the Baroness.

By the time of my arrival, Aldous had become the Stravinskys' intellectual index, guiding their ingestion of books from works of science, psychology (F.W.H. Myers' *Human Personality*), and philosophy, to the new British fiction, Angus Wilson's *Such Darling Dodos*, Kingsley Amis's *Lucky Jim*, and John Braine's *Room at the Top*, before these writers were known in America. Moreover, Aldous kept us abreast of the latest recordings of Baroque and Old Music (Dufay), as well as lauding the Mozart String Quintets to Stravinsky before even he knew them well. Aldous had been the music critic of *The Westminster Gazette* in 1922–23, publishing more than a hundred review articles there in that time.

A beacon in our lives, this almost blind prophet ("From those that have not shall be taken away even that which they have") and great humanist was the most considerate, the most dignified, gentle, and humble of all our friends. As an example of this last, he wrote to the author of a blurb for *The Perennial Philosophy:* "I am not a great philosopher and not a great novelist. In fact I am some sort of essayist sufficiently ingenious to get away with writing a very limited kind of fiction and sufficiently cautious to avoid long-drawn metaphysical disquisitions and logical arguments in which I should eventually break down."

But he could not have denied that he became a skilled hypnotist. More than once he succeeded in relieving Stravinsky's spells of insomnia with this technique, and it is partly because of the intimacy required during this experience ("success depends . . . on a satisfactory relation between the hypnotized person and the operator," Huxley wrote) that I consider him the most valued of the composer's Hollywood friends. What happens during hypnosis, in Huxley's words, is that "the ego is able to let go, to get out of the way, to stop interfering with the beneficent action of the entelechy . . . hypnosis is a cathartic and mildly abreactive bringing up into awareness of material which is disturbing on the lower levels of the mind. Remembering, in an impersonal, scientific-observerish way, is intrinsically relaxing . . . Moreover, the memory of pleasant events can be used as a method for inducing hypnosis."

The McLanes

Stravinsky had met the Reverend James McLane in Denver and Colorado Springs in 1935 during a concert tour with Samuel Dushkin. Before taking orders in the Episcopal Church, McLane had been a Harvard classmate of Lincoln Kirstein and Elliott Carter. As a cousin of C. K. Scott Moncrieff, he had a large literary acquaintance, and, until discouraged by Marianne Moore's rejection slips, wrote poetry. He married in the early 1930s, honeymooned in Sicily, settled in Denver for his wife's health, then moved to Los Angeles, where he renewed his acquaintanceship with Stravinsky through Alexander Schneider and Mischa Kroyt, both members of the Budapest String Quartet, for which McLane had helped to procure Los Angeles engagements. (Throughout the 1970s, Sonya Kroyt, widow of Mischa, was Vera Stravinsky's art dealer in New York.) Another musician friend of the Reverend was Ralph Kirkpatrick, the harpsichordist, Scarlatti scholar, and gentleman, whom McLane introduced to Stravinsky in 1944.

The Stravinskys dined with the McLanes on an average of two Sundays a month over a period of eight years, usually at the McLane home but sometimes at Perino's, Los Angeles's only four-star restaurant. The Reverend was well known for his art collection, acquired through Pierre Matisse and including ten of the most famous Chagalls, several excellent Klees and Giacomettis, Dubuffet cows, Picasso owl sculptures, and paintings by Balthus, whom Stravinsky, encouraged by McLane, proposed as set designer for *The Rake's Progress* premiere, thereby provoking a protest from Stravinsky's son, Theodore, who denounced the artist as a decadent and sexual pervert. Next to the huge private gallery (now in Philadelphia) of Walter Arensberg, to which, and to whom, McLane introduced us, and the Galka Scheyer collection in Pasadena, it was the most distinguished home museum of modern art in the Southern California of the day. McLane brought about the meeting between the Stravinskys and the artist Ben Shahn.

Here I should add that McLane introduced Paco Lagerstrom, a scientist at the California Institute of Technology, to Stravinsky. Lagerstrom does not qualify as a Wetherly Drive Regular, but as a music-lover attended most concerts that included pieces by Schoenberg and Stravinsky, and was a good friend of Alma Mahler, as well as of Milton Babbitt during a period when the latter was steeped in mathematics.

Mary McLane, the Reverend's wife, was shy and retiring, Augusta, his adolescent daughter, was flirtatious, and Louis, his teenage son, who coined the name "Big Vera" for Mrs. Stravinsky, was unstable. Another, decade-older member of the household, Brainerd Smith, to whom Stravinsky gave a page of the 1943 *Danse sacrale* manuscript—he gave another page to Alma Mahler—was the chief acolyte at St. Matthias church, next door to the McLane residence, but by the time the Stravinskys left California, he was a practicing psychiatrist. I recall a fierce argument between him and Isherwood's sometimes truculent friend Bill Caskey in the Stravinsky home concerning the desirability of clerical celibacy, Smith, of course, defending the family life of Father McLane.

A Mahler fanatic long before the composer's popularity, McLane was on good terms with his widow, whom Stravinsky referred to as "Alma Redemptoris Mater." McLane regularly visited her in her Beverly Hills home. (Improbably, his other long-time friends in the neighborhood were George Burns and Gracie Allen.) He would even play Mahler recordings for Stravinsky's edification, with only a modicum of success (*Kindertotenlieder*). The sprawling forms and *Weltschmerz* of the symphonies remained alien to him. But in truth, it was Vera, not Igor, Stravinsky who sustained the relationship with the Reverend. She thought him an original and amusing character with an informed eye for art, and, unlike Stravinsky, did not complain about the carryover into private life of the preacher's pulpit voice. Stravinsky winced at being called "Igor" by the younger members of the family and was ill at ease as well with the Reverend's campy clerical style, the ostentatious on-stage changes of vestments during Communion, the wide swinging of the thurifer, the prolonged ringing of the sanctus bell at the elevation of the host, the choreographed movements in the offices of the ritual, and the display of Balthus's portrait of the prepubescent nude "Georgette" adjoining a crucifix on the wall over his bed.

McLane had urged Stravinsky to base a work on the Book of Tobit. The dedication to his memory of the final movement of *A Sermon, a Narrative, and a Prayer*, from the collection *Four Birds of Noah's Ark* by Thomas Dekkar (sic, on the original edition of the book which Stravinsky used, now in the Sacher Stiftung, Basel), may be thought of as a substitute for this unrealized project, but it came about partly because McLane had read the prayer during one of his poetry-declaimings that were a staple of their Sunday evenings. After the Stravinskys had ceased to observe Orthodox services at Hollywood's Russian churches—they were married a second time in the one on Micheltorena[2]—they attended Good Friday, Easter, and Christmas Eve Mass at St. Matthias, which was in a derelict downtown Los Angeles neighborhood and supported mainly, perhaps entirely, by McLane himself. His parishioners were beatniks, gays, motorcyclists of the James Dean–Jack Kerouac era. At Huxley's request, McLane officiated at Maria Huxley's funeral. She had asked in her last hours for a service in the Church of her Belgian childhood, and to have McLane perform it, and to be buried in St. Matthias churchyard. (Alma Mahler expressed the same wish, and so did the Stravinskys, if they should happen to die in Los Angeles, but all three expired in New York and outlived the Reverend.) The real-life "survivor from Warsaw," an old, lonely man whom we saw at Yolanda's, where he came to

2. This was across the street from "the Roof" of Peter Yates's Evenings on the Roof concerts. (See below.)

know McLane, the man who told his horrific and heroic story to Arnold Schoenberg, also asked the Reverend to conduct his funeral service.

The Louriés

Genia and Laure Lourié were frequent dinner guests at the Stravinsky house from before my time—Stravinsky had attended Lourié's naturalization party in 1947, and another for the christening of his daughter, Anita—and, with hiatuses, through 1969. Decades earlier, in Paris, Stravinsky had recommended Lourié as a stage designer, with a letter February 18, 1932 to his concert agent, Dr. Enrique Telemaco Susini, describing him as a "young and very talented Russian painter who recently achieved great success with his work in René Clair's film *A Nous la liberté.*" At that date, Laure was married to John Ferren, an American painter in Paris. After they divorced, she married Lourié, moving with him at the beginning of the war to Hollywood. Here he became Jean Renoir's art director for films, one of which, Rumer Godden's *The River,* took him to India for more than a year.

Lourié spoke Russian exclusively with Stravinsky during the couple's weekly visits, for which reason, in part, I became a closer friend of his younger, vivacious, occasionally scrappy but intelligent wife, who was Stravinsky's first choice to prepare the English translation of his *Poétique Musicale.* I admired her gumption. One day when the Baroness d'Erlanger asked her about her "lineage," Laure scratched back with *"Je suis métèque, madame."* Laure was a music lover and a regular member of the Monday Evening Concert audience. She gave a party for me after a concert that I conducted on the eve of my thirtieth birthday.

The Lourié's daughter, Anita, was an intellectually precocious child and a gifted artist. In fact, Stravinsky purchased one of her drawings, made when she was eight, and kept it on a wall of his studio until the end of his life, not far from his Picassos, Klees, and Giacomettis.

In later years Laure proved to be one of Vera Stravinsky's truest friends. As a dinner guest of Stravinsky's daughter and her husband, Andre Marion, as well as of the Stravinskys, Laure warned her that her stepchildren were duplicitous and, in matters of inheritance and the distribution of Stravinsky's royalties, which increased exponentially in the mid-1960s, dangerous. But Mrs. Stravinsky refused to see the obvious; when Marion removed Stravinsky's manuscripts from his house during one of his concert tours and placed them in a bank vault under the Marion name, she refused to recognize the nefarious intent behind the action.

In the years after Mrs. Stravinsky's death, Laure telephoned to me in New York from her Los Angeles home about once a month for several years (she died in 2001), and was therefore my last source of information about friends and life in the city where I had spent so many years.

Lucia Davidova

Lucia Davidova knew Vera de Bosset (Sudeykina) as a stage actress and film star when she was herself a member of Nikita Baliyev's pre-Revolution Moscow Art Theatre. Lucia, as she asked me to call her early on, had met the Stravinskys in Paris in the 1920s, but they became friends only in the 1940s, though from then to the ends of their lives close ones. She was a good friend to me from 1948 and until her death in the 1990s. On renewing acquaintance with Vera de Bosset in Paris, she was dismayed to learn of her marriage—de facto or pretended is not known—to Sergey Sudeykin, whom Lucia detested because of his influence over Diaghilev during a 1908 Paris excursion together, and because of Sudeykin's treatment of Anna Akhmatova during his term as her lover. Sudeykin, Lucia told me, practiced sodomy with both sexes.

Lucia had come to the United States from Paris at the same time as Balanchine, the unrequited love of her life. (She had been married to the husband of the ballerina Tamara Geva while Geva was living with Balanchine.) But the choreographer did not care for older, and especially officious women. Moreover, Lucia's accurate, almost too precisely enunciated English, with a barely detectable Russian-Armenian accent, inhibited him. Nevertheless, Lucia sided with Balanchine against Stravinsky in 1937 when the choreographer came to dinner with two long-saved-up-for bottles of Bordeaux and the composer bluntly stated his preference for another *ticket*.

During the 1930s Depression, and thanks to tips from inside investors, Lucia made a fortune on Wall Street. She purchased a five-story townhouse with brick-walled garden and gazebo at 11 East Seventy-seventh Street, a few paces from Fifth Avenue. Lucia had been the mistress of Igor Sikorsky in his Connecticut years, and through him bought an airplane, learned to fly, and crossed the Atlantic in it.

Small, slender, with large dark eyes and jet-black hair coiled at the back, she stood very erect and with a proprietary air. Even in her nineties she held her head high, dyed her hair shoe-polish black, and managed to avoid wrinkles, not by cosmetic surgery, I think, since her skin did not have the telltale tight look resulting from lifts. She would have been the perfect hostess if she could have restrained herself from speaking harshly to her kitchen help and servers in front of her guests. Her evening purse always contained the three-pronged silver swizzle-stick which, twirled between the palms, extirpates the bubbles in champagne.

Her dinner guests included movie and stage actors, writers and painters. She courted intellectual company, but rarely, and then only on Stravinsky's account, managed to snare a top quarry (Auden). Cecil Beaton made excellent photographs of her and was a frequent dinner guest, along with Richard Burgi, a shy, very likeable man of sterling qualities from Troy, New York, who was a Princeton professor of Russian and Greek.

In Hollywood, Lucia stayed with the transfixingly beautiful—red hair, green eyes, pale white skin—Nadia Petrova, whose British husband, Reginald Gardner, was an actor often on tour or doing one-man Broadway stints of impersonations, "the orchestra conductor" most famously. We saw Lucia more often in Venice, where she resided with British friends in a palazzo on the Grand Canal side of Campo S. Maurizio. After suffering a heart attack on an airplane, she was invariably accompanied by Robert Sandbach, a tall, rugged, studsy type from Rochester, New York, whom she retained as a traveling companion, but who trod on her and her friends' nerves by gate-crashing conversations on artistic subjects over his head.

In 1939 Lucia was staying with Goddard Lieberson in the Beekman Arms, "the oldest hotel in America," in Rhinebeck, New York. The pair was checking out one morning at the same time as the movie star Vera Zorina (*I Married An Angel, The Goldwyn Follies*, etc.), whom Lieberson then saw for the first time but would marry as soon thereafter as she could obtain a divorce from Balanchine. All parties managed to remain close friends of the Stravinskys.

In November 1961 we spent two weeks in Egypt with Lucia, who was en route to stay with the diplomat Moore Crosthwaite at the British Embassy in Lebanon. After Stravinsky's death, Lucia was his widow's most faithful friend, visiting her two or three times a week. A close friend as well of Alice De La Mar, the daughter of a railroad tycoon, Lucia wintered in the thirty-six-room De La Mar Palm Beach mansion, where, in the late 1970s, Vera Stravinsky and I were her sometime luncheon guests. After Vera Stravinsky's death, Lucia translated her Russian diaries and correspondence for me. I had confidence in her discretion, but now suspect that she may have omitted seamier passages about Sergey Sudeykin.

Dr. Max Edel

I met Maximilian Edel at the premiere of *Orpheus* in New York in April 1948 and liked him immediately. By the summer of 1949 he had become my California confidant. I remember a lively weekend with him at the Soulima Stravinsky home in Montecito, where the composer's son was teaching at the Music Academy of the West. With Dr. Sigfrid Knauer, Max Edel was Stravinsky's principal West Coast physician for nineteen years (with interregnums) beginning in 1946, when he was recommended by the Baroness d'Erlanger. A refugee from Vienna, Edel was a Trotskyite, Freudian, Mahlerian, Frankfurt School sociologist, and a tireless polemicist in the causes of all four. But Stravinsky was fond of him and enjoyed chatting with him. During the long period between his first and second marriages, Mrs. Stravinsky advised him on his choices of girlfriends. He was *au courant* about many things, but more passionate about politics than about medicine. He would pay house calls at the Stravinskys' during all hours of the night, and receive the composer through a back door to his office ahead of his other patients, movie actors included. Marlene Dietrich and Charles Boyer, both friends of the Stravinskys as well, could often be seen in his waiting room, for the reason, I suspect, that he charged them less than other Beverly Hills physicians. Stravinsky was in his office as often as three times a week to receive B12 and Vitamin C *piqûres*, "boosters" as they were called, the fashion of the time. Edel dispensed these to everyone, and knowing that I fancied Ursula Andress, the star of the Bond film, *Dr. No*, he slipped me into a doctor's white smock so that I could remain in the room while he injected her shapely, maddeningly attractive posterior. He gave the long basal metabolism tests to me and the Stravinskys, and cured me of infectious mononucleosis, known at the time as "the kissing disease." In August 1954 we drove with him to Las Vegas for a holiday, and he visited us in Venice in August 1957, and again in 1958 for the premiere of *Threni*. In 1967, when he diagnosed a serious circulatory ailment in Stravinsky's left arm and hand as gout, Mrs. Stravinsky discharged him. Vindictively, he sold his files of Stravinsky's medical records to a college.

Sol Babitz

Sol Babitz was closer to the Stravinskys when I appeared on the scene than any of their other American musician friends. He had been a member of Otto Klemperer's Los Angeles Philharmonic in the 1930s and was in the orchestra when Schoenberg guest-conducted Brahms's Third Symphony, the first movement in a slow six- instead of the usual two-beat; according to Babitz, Schoenberg told the unbelieving orchestra that he had seen Brahms conduct it exactly that way. Eventually Babitz left the Philharmonic to freelance in the more lucrative Hollywood film-studio orchestras. In September 1940 he somehow gained access to Stravinsky and convinced the composer to help him with an analysis, published in *The Musical Quarterly*, of the just-completed Symphony in C. Babitz (*not* Dushkin, as some books have it) assisted Stravinsky with his violin and piano arrangement of the 1940 Tango. He also provided Woody Herman recordings as models for the *Ebony* Concerto, initiating Stravinsky, as well, into the prevalent "jazz" styles, swing, jitterbug, boogie-woogie, and acquainting him, in jazz hangouts, with such techniques as the trumpet lip glissando and the trombone "schmeer," which, in *Ebony*, sounds like yawning. On October 13, 1940, Stravinsky conducted his Violin Concerto with Babitz and a rehearsal orchestra recruited by him. Thereafter, Babitz became Stravinsky's guru on all questions of string-instrument performance. He participated in some of Stravinsky's *Histoire du Soldat* presentations and was a member of most of his Hollywood pick-up recording orchestras.

Sol married a gentle, soft-spoken lady from Louisiana, and Stravinsky became godfather to their daughters, Eve and Miriam. In my first years in California, the Stravinskys and I spent Thanksgivings and Christmases at the Babitzes'. In a 1970s book about Hollywood, Eve describes Stravinsky on these occasions passing glasses of Scotch under the table to her, aged thirteen or so. In fact the dinners were cozy family affairs shared with Sol's parents. Sol's strongest suit was his po-faced wit. I recall someone at a party trying to characterize the music of Eric Zeisl, a neighbor of mine 1949–1952, whose daughter later married the elder son of Arnold Schoenberg. Babitz described it as "Jewish Ernest Bloch."

The Babitzes loved Mexico and took many trips there. In Los Angeles they lived near the Mexican quarter, which they never tired of exploring. A typical, mildly ribald, Babitz story features a boastful resident there who tells his friends that he has been recognized locally as an accomplished "Latin lover." "On what grounds?" "When I went to a gringo drugstore the other day I heard the proprietor say, 'Here comes that fucking Mexican.'"

Sol was a friend of the Beatnik poets Gregory Corso, Kenneth Rexroth, Ginsberg, and the others, and had been a close friend of Laura Riding in her California period, pre- or post-Robert Graves, I no longer remember. More important was Sol's pioneering in the movement to recover Baroque performance style. He founded an early music laboratory to experiment with old instruments and apply the teachings of Leopold Mozart, Quantz, and Arnold Dolmetsch, whom G. B. Shaw had praised. Babitz was one of the first violinists to revive the curved bow, thereby discovering that articulation in Bach would have been more staccato than his music was currently played, the rise and fall of the "original instruments" movement notwithstanding. Babitz was one of the first to realize that greater rhythmic freedom within the beat is the basis of the Baroque style. He should also be credited for bringing Stravinsky's attention to the consort music of Matthew Locke, Henry Purcell's Restoration-period predecessor. The composer of *Agon* first encountered the dance forms *Bransle Simple* and *Bransle Gay*, under the corrupt English rubric "Brawl," in a collection of Locke's music given to him by Babitz.

Stravinsky became honorary president of Babitz's old music laboratory and attended some of his recital demonstrations in the salon of the Peter Yates home, and occasionally in the smaller home of Babitz's collaborator, the clavicembalist Wesley Kuhnle. Sol's discussions of ornamentation and unequal rhythm, the "long-short" and "short-long" execution of dotted rhythms, making them more like triplets, were enlightening, and his comparisons with the prevalent mechanical performance of what he called "sewing-machine Bach" were instructive and amusing. But if Sol's talks were a delight, his performances—on catgut strings and in mean-tone intonation—were not. He acknowledged this laughingly: "The music sounds horrible, just the way it should sound." He lecture-toured in both the United States and Europe and was finally recognized by academics as an original, scrimmage-line scholar. He edited the music by Monteverdi, Schütz, and Bach in my own recordings, and I still follow his ideas about double-dotting. We saw the Babitzes less frequently in later years, but Sol and his wife came to visit Stravinsky in Evian in the summer of 1970.

Ingolf Dahl

Walter Ingolf Marcus—Dahl was his Swedish mother's name—came to the United States in 1939 from Zurich, where two years earlier he had been the chief *repetiteur* for the first performance of Alban Berg's *Lulu*. Dahl was a versatile musician: composer, pianist, teacher (the conductor Michael Tilson Thomas was his pupil at the University of Southern California), and program annotator (Stravinsky's Symphony in Three Movements for the New York Philharmonic). Stravinsky commissioned him to make the piano reduction of *Scènes de Ballet*. Like me, he was also devoted to Schoenberg, who unfortunately approved his and Carl Beier's English translation of *Pierrot Lunaire*, conducted by Dahl at a Roof concert. On our first meeting at Stravinsky's in July 1948, he enthusiastically agreed with me that Schoenberg's Five Pieces for Orchestra was long overdue in the standard repertory. Dahl and his wife, Etta, were frequent dinner guests in the early years. Then, after a sabbatical in Austria, his composing style and musical philosophy changed. Hearing a concert of the new work in Los Angeles, I wrote to Stravinsky in New York, January 12, 1954: "The best piece, the suite for brass, which you know, was the earliest. Even Morton was disappointed."

In 1957–58, the trendy direction taken by the Monday Evening Concerts disaffected him. Dorothy Crawford's *Evenings On and Off the Roof* quotes an angry remark from his diary: "An article in *The New York Times* has quoted Boulez as saying: 'I am not interested in how it sounds, I am only interested in how it was made,' to which Dahl wrote in silent rebuttal: 'That should be *exactly* reversed! Who the hell cares how it was made?"[3] (*Ars est celare artem.*)

Dahl's wife Etta died of cancer in Fretingen, Switzerland at the beginning of August 1970. Shortly thereafter Ingolf himself succumbed, aged fifty-seven, to grief and his lifelong struggle against asthma.

3. Dorothy Lamb Crawford, *Evenings On and Off the Roof: Pioneering Concerts in Los Angeles, 1939-1971* (Berkeley: University of California Press, 1995), p. 266.

John Craft (1830–1922). Writer, teacher. New York, 1880s. The author's great-grandfather. He is buried in Laramie, Wyoming.

1864. Thomas Gibbs, the author's great-grandfather (father's maternal side), in the uniform of the Grand Army of the Republic. Born in Brooklyn, New York, in 1839.

1927. Robert, age four, Phyllis age six, Shetland pony. Janet Street, Kingston, New York.

1931. Family photo,
41 Johnston Avenue,
Kingston, New York.

Phyllis, Robert,
Patricia, *ibid.*

1932. The St. John's Episcopal Church Choir, Kingston. The author is the smallest boy in the front row, center.

December 1937. In a New York Military Academy winter cape.

April 1943. Poughkeepsie, New York. Waiting for a train to Camp Pickett, Virginia, with fellow U.S. Army Private Douglas Mathers.

R. CRAFT 1947-48

August 1946. Tanglewood, Massachusetts. Photo by Ruth Orkin. The caption, in Stravinsky's hand, misdates the picture.

July 16, 1951. Hollywood. The astronomer Edwin Hubble is engaged in a scientific discussion with Julian Huxley (not shown). Maria Huxley is seated at Hubble's left. The standing figures are Mrs. Igor Stravinsky and the author. The occasion is a dinner at the home of Aldous and Maria Huxley in the open lean-to behind their house on King's Road.

September 1951. Venice, on the Accademia Bridge with Vera Stravinsky. Photo by Claudio Spies.

1952. Santa Monica Boulevard, Beverly Hills. Photo by Vera Stravinsky.

October 20, 1954. Drawing of "Bob" by Stravinsky, with music notation, "Happy Birthday," in his hand.

May 1954. Postcard from Stravinsky in Lisbon to the author in Hollywood.

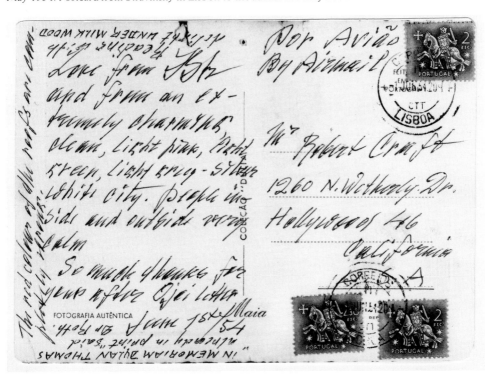

August 1957. Villa Valsanzibio, Euganean Hills, Italy.

1958. Hollywood. Recording *Le Marteau sans maître*. Ernst Krenek, in the background, is partly obscured by the guitar.

1958. 1260 North Wetherly Drive. The book is the newly published *Conversations with Stravinsky*. Stravinsky captioned the photo *"Trio con Brio."*

November 1958. Vienna. Rehearsing Schoenberg's Five Pieces for Orchestra.

December 1959. Town Hall, New York, rehearsing *Les Noces*. The pianists, left to right, are Lukas Foss, Samuel Barber, Aaron Copland, Roger Sessions.

KARL MARX

HIS LIFE AND ENVIRONMENT

ISAIAH BERLIN
M.A, F.B.A.

*Chichele Professor of Social and
Political Theory in the University
of Oxford*

Third Edition

For Bob   With total devotion
           for Isaiah
                        1963

LONDON
OXFORD UNIVERSITY PRESS
NEW YORK TORONTO
1963

In 1963, Isaiah Berlin presented the author with a personally inscribed copy of the reprint of his *Karl Marx*: "For Bob, with total devotion from Isaiah."

October 1962. Rome. With Stravinsky during intermission in a rehearsal of his *Movements* at the Accademia Philharmonica Romana.

Winter 1997. Control Room of Recording Studio 1, Abbey Road, London.

Christopher Isherwood

Between 1949 and 1969 Christopher Isherwood became the only truly intimate non-musical witness to the composer's life in California. The Stravinskys saw him more frequently than any other California friend, partly because he provided relief from musical talk.

By the 1960s Christopher and Don Bachardy, successor to Bill Caskey, had moved to a house on a hillside overlooking the Santa Monica canyon not far from the beach, in what was then known as the "slide area." The Stravinskys thought the dwelling and its location great improvements over the smaller, cramped, sea-level residences, but the barbecue, a few steps down from the front door, seemed precariously close to the steep drop down the canyon. Dinners there, after martinis, scotches, and hors d'oeuvres, were informal, to say the least, and the table often rocked with raucous laughter. Christopher himself drank less at his home than in the Stravinskys', where he had passed out on the floor during his first visit, after imbibing a snifter of the eau de vie Marc de Bourgogne. Stravinsky kept a shelf of marcs, grappas, and other *digestifs*, from which he drank almost daily. Isherwood seemed not to know that Marc was distilled from the lees, as well as the pips and skins—the pomace—left after pressing grapes to make wine, and that the pips are used as crusts on such cheeses as *tome de Savoie*. Evenings with Chris and Don were invariably pleasurable, relaxing, affectionate, more so than when Aldous or Gerald came as well and seemed to bring a whiff of disapproval. When Stravinsky would announce that he was tired, we would depart within five minutes for the half-hour drive home, dropping Aldous on the way.

Isherwood's talk focused on the movie world, gossip about actors, directors, scriptwriters. He seldom strayed into "literature" but could quote poetry copiously. He disliked Eliot for the reason that "all of the most interesting young men were interested in him." Yeats and D. H. Lawrence were icons, the latter for having been the first major writer to employ the first person. Lawrence was also the first to locate some of his novellas in the American Southwest, and Christopher rated *The Woman Who Rode Away* and *St. Mawr* the best "American" literature of the 1920s. Conrad was a hero, the main reason for the trip with Don to Singapore and the Orient. Isherwood was a relative of Robert Louis Stevenson and Graham Greene, but never said anything about either one. It is not generally known that both Aldous and Auden sent their work to Christopher to read before publication. His reservations about the later Huxley fictions were shared with us only inferentially, but, then, they were "brothers" in religion. Together they discussed the doings of the Swamis, the budgetary problems of the Ivar Avenue temple, the improvidence of the Vedanta Society and of the retreat at Trabuco.

I remember a dinner at Isherwood's with Aldous and Laura Huxley when Aldous, forgetfully, made an embarrassing remark about "queers," to the effect that "the world's artistic and cultural organizations are infiltrated by homosexuals to the extent that nobody who is vulgar enough to like women stands a chance." Christopher and Don pretended not to notice, and the Stravinskys were silent, whereupon Laura Huxley began to speak to her husband in Italian.

Miranda

Miranda Masocco was born in Venice, the youngest of four daughters. Their widowed mother had moved with them to the United States, but she died during the cross-country trip to San Francisco in the early 1920s. At Lamy, New Mexico, the girls were taken from the train to St. Vincent's Orphanage in Santa Fe. In time, the poet Witter Bynner, who lived nearby, recognized Miranda's intelligence and talents and became a foster-father to her. As a young woman she began to design jewelry and clothes, and was soon working in the Thunderbird Shop. In 1958 she married Ralph Levy, a Hollywood movie and television director, who produced numerous films with Jack Benny. Levy was the scion of a wealthy family of Philadelphia lawyers, one of whom Stravinsky once consulted about an income-tax questions.

The Stravinskys met Miranda and her boyfriend Robert Davidson, a writer, in Taos, New Mexico, in July 1950.[4] Later in the same summer, they came to Hollywood where we saw them frequently. By this time Davidson was working for the as yet unmarried Ralph, but not having been paid for some months, he went to the latter's hillside Hollywood home and, with my help, sank the patio furniture in the swimming pool.

We next saw the pair in Santa Fe at the beginning of March 1951, returning by automobile from a concert trip to Havana. The Stravinskys and I arrived at La Fonda Hotel in a snowstorm, after a seven-hundred-mile drive from Oklahoma City. Miranda, who was staying with Frieda Lawrence in Taos, insisted that we come to a party in Santa Fe that same evening hosted by herself and Davidson. There we met William Theophilus Brown, a painter and for the next twenty years one of the Stravinskys' and my closest friends. [Mr. Brown was, in truth, closer to the Stravinskys and myself than any other friend for many years, but after Vera Stravinsky's death, in 1982, he severed all connections with me. I have no idea why.]

We saw Miranda and Davidson again in New York in April 1952, before our flight to Paris and Nicolas Nabokov's Festival, "The Arts of the Twentieth Century." The Stravinskys and I continued to see Miranda, and in 1957 she convinced Stravinsky to come to the newly formed Santa Fe

4. See chapter 6.

Opera to oversee its production of *The Rake's Progress*. Thereafter the Stravinskys returned to Santa Fe for part of every summer from 1959 to 1963, largely as a result of Miranda's friendship with Vera Stravinsky, who enjoyed her company. (Stravinsky did, too, but not her hoydenish side.) In 1957 Miranda generously moved out of her charming hillside residence outside Santa Fe and put it at the Stravinskys' disposal.

After her marriage to Ralph Levy, the couple moved to Hollywood and purchased a house one ledge above Sunset Boulevard and two ledges below the Stravinskys' home at 1218 North Wetherly Drive. Living only a thousand yards or so away from the Stravinskys throughout their last years in Hollywood, Miranda came for lunch or tea two or three times a week, bringing such oddly assorted friends as Dorothy Parker, Roddy McDowell, and Rex Evans. When the Stravinskys sold the house, they entrusted Miranda to dispose of its contents.

Miranda understood that on Stravinsky's death I would be thrown to the wolves. In the summer of 1970, she traveled from her London home to Evian to impress on Vera Stravinsky how little she could expect in the way of family appreciation and support. A year later, after the death, she spent three weeks with Vera Stravinsky in Biarritz, trying to divert her from her personal loss and family troubles. More than once we drove across the border to St. Sebastian and Pamplona together.

Gerald Heard

In August 1952 the Stravinskys joined the Sunday morning congregation in Hollywood's Ivar Avenue Buddhist Temple to hear the sermons of [Honey Fitz-] Gerald Heard. Slim, red-bearded—resembling D. H. Lawrence in this if in no other way—he would emerge from a kind of vestry room at a watch-setting eleven o'clock, mount a pulpit, and stand for a minute of silence, transparent blue eyes peering into a high remoteness. His entrance was catlike, and as rapid as the squirrels and foxes that were among the props in his fiction, for under the name H. F. Heard he was a best-selling author of mystery and detective novels. In fact, he earned his livelihood writing them, though during the period of our friendship with him his book on UFOs, *Is Another World Watching?*, published under the Gerald name, outsold all of his other books together.

The room was invariably full, and some of the audience, which included former movie actors (Janet Gaynor), Pasadena scientists, Ramakrishnan mystics, and the aptly named Gayelord Hauser (*Look Younger, Live Longer*), had arrived as long as an hour earlier to be certain of finding seats. Gerald was the most accomplished extempore speaker I have ever observed. In the late 1920s and early 1930s he had been a science commentator for the

BBC, with Shaw, Wells, and Julian Huxley among his regular guests. He was Harold Nicolson's source for the futurisms, atomic energy and such, in his 1932 novel *Public Faces*. The young Evelyn Waugh's diary for July 8, 1930 records that "John Betjeman brought Gerald Heard to dinner, who is said to be the cleverest man in the world. He was well informed about theology and spiritualism. Clearly an active and retentive mind." He was also a mentor and crucial influence on the young W. H. Auden, and had toured the United States in the mid-1930s, giving public lecture-discussions with Aldous Huxley. Both men settled in Southern California in 1937.

Gerald's opening statements were often paradoxical. Often, too, they announced a subject of general scientific interest, but only rarely a political one. Among favorite topics were the danger of our becoming "sessile organisms"; the high incidence of "senile optimism," which he defined as "the triumph of hope over experience"; and "the refusal to hope when we have settled comfortably down to despair." He spoke in well-formed sentences, and his vocabulary, like his provision of quotations from poetry, was richly resourceful. The balanced paragraphs succeeded each other at a faster pace than most of his audience could have read them in print. This helped to compensate for a thin, high-pitched, nasal voice, lacking in dynamic range. He did not gesticulate, or resort to facial expression, but he talked over heads literally, as well as intellectually, and at intense moments in his arguments gripped the pulpit until the whites of his knuckles showed. His expositions and developments were logically ordered, his modulations smooth, his recapitulations well timed. He digressed, of course, and occasionally wandered into labyrinthine paths, but in his perorations always managed to find his way out and bring loose ends together. In private conversation, shortcutting, he tended to leap too quickly from hypothesis to fact, but in these Sunday morning seances intermediate steps were set forth in full. The subject matter of a typical sermon would shuttle from Plato to the identity of Samsara and Nirvana, to the Sanskrit psychologist-saints.

The talk ended, Gerald would disappear behind his pulpit while his manciple, Michael Barrie, a bald-pated monk in mufti, looking like Disney's seventh dwarf, would pass a collection plate. Gerald would then reappear and improvise a prayer based on something from Christian soteriology, after which we would proceed with him to the Bel Air Hotel for a far-from-ascetic lunch.

In the 1960s Gerald was the guru of Frank Lloyd Wright and spent weeks at a time with him and the Henry and Clare Boothe Luces in Scottsdale, Arizona, going from there to Honolulu with the Luces for the winter months. We saw him rarely thereafter. He died a few months after Stravinsky, following a series of strokes.

Edward James

The Stravinskys had first known Edward James (1907–1984) as the principal patron of Balanchine's "Les Ballets 1933." Edward VII's illegitimate child by his favorite mistress, Lady James, Edward was brought up in the great manorial house of West Dene, an estate of 12,000 acres, now a museum housing Edward's collection of Surrealist art. After Eton and Oxford, he inherited an immense fortune, bought a town house on Wimpole Street, and became a compulsive spender. He transformed Edwin Lutyens's Monkton House into a surrealist fantasy, and purchased a *finca*, "Las Posas," near the town of Xilitla in the Mexican jungle, which he tried to turn into an orchid farm. John Huston filmed *Treasure of the Sierra Madre* on this property and later filmed *Beat the Devil* at Edward's neo-classical villa at Rapallo. Edward also owned a house in Hollywood that became a repository of his Dali collection. For several years Dali was under contract to sell his entire output to him.

I met Edward when the Stravinskys invited him to dinner in July 1952. He had a small, wispy beard and was wearing a foppish raw-silk gray suit, but the feet in his shoes were without socks. Thus caparisoned, I did not recognize him from René Magritte's mirror portrait, or from the photographs by Cecil Beaton and Man Ray, in which, moreover, clean-shaven, he looks more female than male. He spoke French exclusively that evening, telling and impersonating amusing stories about his eccentric aunt Fenicia. He must have repeated this repertory countless times but nevertheless burst into high-register laughter himself after each anecdote. He said that he and Tilly Losch, the Austrian ballerina to whom he was married for a few months in 1931, had spent their wedding night on the Orient Express, and that when he came into her compartment, she seemed surprised and said, "Oh, I wasn't expecting there would be any fun." Tilly was one of Gerald Heard's faithful, but she and Edward passed each other arriving at his "Sundays" withholding any sign of recognition.

Stravinsky liked James to the extent that in 1953 he accepted his offer to accompany him from New York to Baltimore for a week of rehearsals and concerts, in which Stravinsky conducted the Schumann Piano Concerto. I suppose that James "defrayed" his own expenses, to use Stravinsky's word, but his capriciousness, masochism, indulgence of his every whim, and self-destructiveness were hard to take in large doses. He would leave manuscripts of his poems under the cushions of the Stravinskys' chairs, where they might go undiscovered for months (no reflection on Yevgenia Petrovna intended), and on returning proceed directly to the hiding place and retrieve the autograph—of perfectly correct innocuous verse in an antiquated style but without content. Edward probably thought of himself as a significant poet who would be discovered posthumously.

Edward divided his time between his Mexican retreat and the Bel Air Hotel in Los Angeles. (He never lived in his Hollywood house, which we saw only when he stopped by to collect a picture.) He gave lavish dinner parties in a villa attached to and rented from the Bel Air Hotel, then went to the monastery at Trabuco, the Heard–Isherwood–Swami Prabhavananda Ashram south of the city. Aldous was convinced that Edward's forays into this celibate community had exactly the opposite motivation. Edward was rarely without younger male friends who, whatever their occupational aptitudes, were introduced as "secretaries." Some of them were procured through Clifton Webb.

The reason for the July 1952 visit was that he wished to commission Stravinsky to set one of his poems to music. I regret to say that the composer was not indifferent to the project, but he had fortunately instructed his son-in-law, Andre Marion, to negotiate the terms, and when Marion informed James that the *"tariffe"* was too low, the greatly offended royal bastard disappeared for several months.

One of Edward's best imitations was of Maria Huxley. I recall being in a car with him, Aldous, and the Stravinskys on the way to visit Edwin Hubble, the space-age genius, whom we saw frequently in the early 1950s. En route, James asked Aldous some questions of the kind that Maria might have put to him, and in such a perfect imitation of her voice that we all giggled. But Hubble was an agelast, serious, sober, tight-lipped, and not receptive to James's jokes.

I learned that James was an "Indian giver" when he gave Dali's 1938 drawing of Freud's head to me, then came to reclaim it a few months later. The Stravinskys were very annoyed with him when, after two years, he took back the title to a ranch near Taos that he had made a great ceremony of presenting to them. He was also a far-from-perfect host, seeming deliberately to mismatch his guests. (He used to complain that Beverly Hills hostesses, on being introduced to him, would say, "Edward James? Now that would be a changed name, wouldn't it?") Once he invited us and about thirty movie stars to the La Rue restaurant on Sunset Boulevard. We were seated at small tables, Stravinsky awkwardly with Gertrud Schoenberg, Zachary Scott silently with Ruth Ford (they had recently been separated), Harry Brown, who wrote the script of *A Walk in the Sun*, with Marguerite Lamkin (ditto).

Plutarco, Edward's majordomo in Xilitla, named for the dictator President Plutarco Colles, was a married man, the father of several children, but also Edward's longest-lasting lover anywhere. Plutarco was the subject of many of Edward's stories, and so was Mexico, where he appeared to be happier than in New York or Hollywood. In one of them, a young Mexican housewife on a TV quiz show, a single answer away from the sixty-four-thousand-dollar prize, is asked the meaning of NaCl. She looks crestfallen, and the interlocutor tries to provide hints. Eventually he says, "What does your husband put on his eggs in the morning?" whereupon, brightening up, she blurts out *"talco."*

The Stravinskys and I saw Edward for the last time at morning twilight after a midnight Good Friday pageant in the Church of Santa Prisca in Taxco, Mexico. He was fleeing a group of boys dressed as Roman legionnaires and chasing and beating him with sticks. Edward was in ecstasy.

Lawrence Morton

I met Lawrence Morton at Ingolf Dahl's in the late spring of 1951. I remember making remarks about *Pierrot Lunaire* that he challenged. "It is impossible to hear all of the pitches," he argued, and I retorted that this was true as well of much Mahler and of a great deal of other music. But, Stravinsky excepted, Lawrence found all modern music arid. That his career as impresario should have cast him in the role of one of its most prominent advocates and patrons is a considerable irony. I did not see him again until after my return from Europe in 1952, and I do not recall the occasion. He had written favorable reviews of my performances of works by Schoenberg and Webern for the International Society of Contemporary Music at the University of Southern California, and his partner-director of the Evenings on the Roof concerts, Peter Yates, had approached me to conduct four concerts in Schoenberg's memory after his death in July 1951. As I recall, the programs were worked out by Lawrence and myself in the summer of 1952 at his house, which at that time was near Santa Monica Boulevard at the Doheny Drive intersection in the valley below the Stravinsky house. (North of Sunset Boulevard, Doheny bifurcates, the eastern branch becoming North Wetherly Drive, on which the Stravinsky house was the sixth or seventh on the right side of the steeply curving street.)

In November 1952, after the Schoenberg series, Stravinsky conducted a Los Angeles Chamber Symphony concert that included the premiere of his new "Cantata on Anonymous Elizabethan Lyrics." The piece was savaged by Mildred Norton, a Los Angeles reviewer, because of the line in the Christmas Carol "Tomorrow shall be my dancing day," an allegory of the crucifixion: "The Jews on me / they made great suit . . . they prefer darkness to light." Stravinsky contended that the offending line amounted to dogma at the time it was written, and that the poem was an untouchable classic. Nevertheless, he subtitled the tenor Ricercar in which it occurs as a "sacred history" and announced this change to the press, pacifying no one. Lawrence wished to program the Cantata in one of his 1953 concerts and asked me to discuss with him the possibility of changing the line and of convincing Stravinsky to accept it. After much thought and a slight adjustment of the musical rhythm, we agreed to substitute the phrase "My enemies on me made great suit." I took him to see Stravinsky, whom he did not know, and who said that he had not intended to hurt or affront anyone and that the reaction had surprised him. By this time he had received a letter from Alexander Tansman, his biographer in the early California years, then living in

Paris, criticizing him for having set such a text only seven years after the opening of the death camps. Stravinsky did not answer and never spoke to Tansman again, but he consented to my Evenings on the Roof performance with the emended text. It is not printed in the score, and the only recorded performance that uses it is mine. When Stravinsky recorded the piece in 1965, the English tenor Alexander Young refused to "desecrate one of the most beautiful poems in the language."

In any case, Lawrence had now met Stravinsky and become good friends with me. We saw more of him in 1953 and with increasing frequency after that. In 1954 he engaged me to conduct the weekend of concerts known as the Ojai Festival, of which he had become artistic director, his closest friend, William Vanderhoef, being an influential member of the board. In 1955 and 1956 he re-engaged me, but with Stravinsky as guest conductor. No one of Stravinsky's eminence had ever appeared before in this hazy, hidden inland town, more devoted to Krishnamurti by the wealthy, retired population, than to music, but Stravinsky's appearance made the place internationally famous. In November 1956 the Los Angeles Music Festival, which took place at about the same time as the Ojai Festival, invited Stravinsky to present the world premiere of *Agon* on his seventy-fifth birthday, June 1957, and he accepted (though I conducted it). Relations with Lawrence cooled after this with, as contributing factors, Stravinsky's increasing absences from California and correspondingly longer periods abroad. When Stravinsky was hospitalized in Hollywood for many weeks in 1967, Lawrence did not visit him, but he was helpful to Mrs. Stravinsky in the difficult years 1968 and 1969.

Lawrence was old-maidish, and could be acidulous and cranky, but he was also very intelligent, well-read, a good writer, a good cook, and hardworking to the detriment of his health. Being neither composer nor conductor, he was frustrated musically, and he preferred the music of Monteverdi, Bach, Haydn, Mozart, Beethoven to that of the twentieth-century—with that one exception. He had the highest integrity and the lowest income of any of Stravinsky's friends, did not own an automobile, and depended on participating musicians for his transportation to rehearsals and concerts. He did more to raise the level of musical culture in Los Angeles than anyone after Otto Klemperer and Ernst Krenek.

I remember him affectionately, the way we used to signal each other when he arrived at the foot of the stairs from the street to the Stravinsky house, he by whistling the first eight notes of the motto of Berg's Chamber Concerto, I, from inside through an open window or by opening the front door, whistling the remaining ten notes, meaning that I was on my way down.

The Kreneks

Stravinsky's most notable musician friends in Hollywood when I arrived had been Otto Klemperer, Artur Rubinstein, Joseph Szigeti, and Gregor Piatigorsky. Of significant composers, he admired only Krenek and Hanns Eisler. Stravinsky wrote to the latter, congratulating him on his incidental music for Brecht's *Galileo*, which had been performed in a theater on La Cienega Boulevard. I do not know whether the two composers ever met, but when Evenings on the Roof presented a program of Eisler's music on December 14, 1947, Stravinsky did not attend, fearing that his presence at a concert honoring the politically prominent Communist composer would be publicized.

Stravinsky was on good terms only with Rakhmaninov, during the last two years of his life in California (d. 1943), but this fellow Russian's high opinion of *Firebird* was not reciprocated by any Stravinsky interest in the older composer's concertos, symphonies, and C-sharp minor preludes. Stravinsky's connection with Italo Montemezzi, whose *L'Amore dei Tre Re* was still in the repertory of the Metropolitan Opera, and with Mario Castelnuovo-Tedesco, a kindly man who wrote a guitar concerto for Andrés Segovia, was purely social. Among resident Californian composers, Darius Milhaud was Stravinsky's closest personal friend. The Stravinskys stayed in his Mills College, Oakland home more than once, and in 1941 Stravinsky began to send money to his children in France through Milhaud's mother in Aix-en-Provence. A cable from Milhaud in Oakland with the code words "Stravinsky's health good" meant that his mother was to forward thirty thousand francs from her bank in Aix to Stravinsky's daughter in Sancellmoz; for which Stravinsky would reimburse his California colleague.

Stravinsky scarcely knew Ernst Krenek when I arrived on the scene, though a concerto by Krenek had shared the program with the German premiere of Stravinsky's *Geschichte vom Soldaten* at the Bauhaus in Weimar in August 1923. In the summer of 1925 Krenek visited Stravinsky in Nice, but no further meetings are recorded before the American years, and in 1938, in a book called *Music Here and Now*, Krenek criticized Stravinsky's *Autobiography* for explaining everything except his decline from *The Rite of Spring* to *Jeu de cartes*, a remark I carefully kept from Stravinsky. On April 1, 1945, Krenek and his champion, the conductor Dimitri Mitropoulos, performed Stravinsky's new Two-Piano Sonata in a concert in Minneapolis.

At the beginning of September 1949 I escorted Stravinsky to a concert by the Los Angeles Chapter of the International Society for Contemporary Music, whose most famous member was Krenek. The dingy, sparsely populated Hollywood hall increased Stravinsky's already glaring conspicuousness in this enemy territory. (ISCM members were almost entirely Central European refugee "twelve-tone composers.") Here it should be recalled that the sociologist–musicologist Theodor Wiesengrund-Adorno had recently published *The Philosophy of Modern Music,* a determinist polemic in the cause of Schoenberg, who, naturally, misunderstood it as an attack on him.[5]

Krenek was the ISCM's "intellectual," and Stravinsky had come that night primarily to see and hear him. Some chamber music pieces were played, after which Krenek read a paper. The atmosphere at these events—I had conducted under ISCM auspices more than once—was die-hard and grim, and Krenek could not lighten it. But Stravinsky admired him for his knowledge, modesty, and high intelligence. I arranged for the two composers to meet.

Starting in the fall of 1952 Krenek became a patron of, and eventually a participant in, the Evenings on the Roof and Monday Evening concerts, where he often met Stravinsky. At one of these he invited us to hear a tape of his opera *Karl V,* and a week or so later, in his Los Angeles apartment, we followed the score while listening to a German broadcast performance of it. The work held Stravinsky's interest, and he noted in his diary soon after: "Krenek came this afternoon and played me his electronic composition, *St. Augustine.*" Eventually the Kreneks moved to Tujunga, in the San Fernando Valley, I think because Gladys Krenek, a pupil of her husband and a composer herself, taught school there, which was probably their main means of support. Krenek's income from his compositions, books, and lectures was modest. He played and conducted at the Monday Evening Concerts for the same fees as everyone else, which is to say ten dollars per performing unit, and did not grumble. Since Tujunga was nearly an hour's drive from the Stravinsky home, we alternated visits for dinners in each other's houses and spent many enjoyable musical evenings together.

The advent of Ernst Krenek in Stravinsky's life coincided with the older composer's absorption in hexachord techniques, but equally in their common immersion in Renaissance polyphony. Krenek was far more knowledgeable in both areas, but Stravinsky, on occasion, did read scholarly publications, often provided by Babitz, and he corresponded with such musicologists as Hans T. David, Willi Apel, Arthur Mendel, Glenn Watkins, and Edward Lowinsky, whose *Secret Chromatic Art of the Netherlands Motet,* given to him by its author and now considered anachronistic, was one of his most treasured books. So was Krenek's *Hamline Studies,* and his *Lamentations of Jeremiah* served to a degree as a model for Stravinsky's *Threni.*

Apart from their mutual interests in new developments in music, the two men had common religious beliefs. Both read theology and the Christian mystics, and both set religious texts to music. They also liked the same Swiss white wine, Aigle les Murailles, and their capacity to consume it in

5. "So modern music has a philosophy—it would be enough if it had a philosopher . . . it is disgusting, by the way, how he treats Stravinsky. . . The book is very difficult to read, for it uses this quasi-philosophical jargon in which modern professors of philosophy hide the absence of an idea. . ."

quantity was commensurate. Both spoke German as well as English, and both were trained in classical languages, though Krenek's Latin was fluent, which cannot be said of Stravinsky's. As for the Stravinsky influence, he successfully encouraged Krenek, as he did Aaron Copland, to conduct his own music, both to ensure its authentic performance and to augment his income. This eventually led to Krenek spending more time in Europe, where he was more highly esteemed than in the United States, and his works were more frequently performed.

A typical evening at Krenek's would include listening to new pieces by younger musicians. Tapes of Stockhausen's *Gruppen* and *Caree* were played and discussed. Stravinsky had copies of both scores, the former given to him by Stockhausen with additions, changes, and revisions in his hand. Krenek would analyze and explain his compositional procedures in a new piece, from concepts to parameters and musical choices. Stravinsky was proud to see a photograph of himself and one of Arnold Schoenberg—and of no others—side by side on the wall of Krenek's studio. The Kreneks remained dear and close friends of the Stravinskys until the latter moved to New York in 1969. I shared a concert with Krenek in Milwaukee in May 1977 and was pleased to find him and his wife in good form and just as kind to me as they had been a decade before when I had last seen them in California.

Chapter 6

The 1950s

Christopher Isherwood's diary[1] for July 9, 1950, says that "yesterday" he, Bill Caskey, the Stravinskys, and I drove to Sequoia for a picnic and that, during the ride, while "Igor was in deep meditation on his opera, I had some valuable ideas for my novel." I remember this excursion very clearly. Vera Stravinsky, in her pre-air-conditioning greenish-gray secondhand Dodge, drove most of the way across the one-hundred-degree San Fernando Valley to Bakersfield. As usually the case when she was at the wheel, Stravinsky sat next to her. We were dressed casually, Stravinsky in blue jeans, short-sleeved shirt, and sandals. After about an hour-and-a-half he said he wanted to think about his work and asked us not to talk, at which time Isherwood concentrated on his novel. After forty-five silent minutes Stravinsky said he had been thinking of the problem of Baba the Turk, and Christopher announced that he had been considering a completely different approach to his book and would probably start all over again. Isherwood's diary notes that "Bob felt wonderful, because the air was so dry." (A chronic sufferer from sinusitis in humid climates, I feel euphoric in dry ones.) "[Bob] drove all the way home," Isherwood says, and so I did, but much too fast for him. His diary entry also observes that "Igor has a huge appetite." In truth, he had a small but ravenous one, and when hungry demanded food immediately.

Our picnic lunch, prepared by Yevgenia Petrovna and packed by her in two panniers, included Kievski cutlets, chicken breasts, bread and cheese. Bottles of Livermore Valley white wine were in ice buckets, and Stravinsky had flasks of Armagnac and Scotch. All of this was spread out on a tablecloth in a clearing below Moro Rock. Not inclined to undertake more mountain climbing, we then rested at the foot of the General Sherman tree be-

1. All citations from Isherwood's diaries are from *Christopher Isherwood Diaries, Volume I* (*1939–1960*), edited by Katherine Bucknell (London: Methuen Publishing Company, 1996).

fore beginning the long return drive. Famished again before dark, Stravinsky asked me to stop at a roadside restaurant. We reached the Stravinsky garage, where Isherwood had left his car, at about 1 A.M.

Between July 25 and 29, the Stravinskys and I drove to Aspen, staying in Salinas the first night; somewhere in the forests of Oregon—not finding a motel until 5 A.M.—the second night; Olympia the third; Coeur d'Alene the fourth; and on the fifth we dined in Aspen with Stranvinsky's old friends, the duo-pianists Vitya Vronsky and Victor Babin.

Stravinsky's concert clothes, sent to Aspen by train a day or two before a wildcat railroad strike, had not arrived, and he conducted in sandals and blue jeans. Since the concert hall was a circus tent, this did not seem inappropriate, and I thought the audience enjoyed the spectacle and the music more than they might have if he had appeared in formal clothes. At the first rehearsal he had given a downbeat intended to launch the dolorous beginning of Tchaikovsky's Second Symphony, but the orchestra played the upbeat—and the remainder—of "Happy Birthday" to celebrate the fact that one of the musicians had become a father during the night. But the jarring change of moods had destroyed Stravinsky's musical equilibrium, and he complained that someone should have warned him of the planned *plaisanterie*. What surprised me was that he seemed not to have recognized the tune without the words.

The concert was to be repeated on August 8, and, at the invitation of the duo-pianists, we visited Santa Fe with them in the interim. Driving in two cars, we found part of the road blocked by snow at the nine-thousand-foot level in Independence Pass. At Taos, Miranda Masocco and her friend Bob Davidson were waiting for us at the Sage Brush Inn, where we spent the night.

The next day, August 4, we called on Mabel Dodge, Frieda Lawrence— the "Q-B," as D.H.L. referred to her—and Tony Ravagli, her husband and the model for Lady Chatterley's lover. The storm that started in 1922–1923 between these two possessive women was still swirling. Stravinsky was uncharacteristically uncomfortable with Frieda, partly because her voice was abrasive,[2] but also because of the anti-Christian philosophy in Lawrence's *Apocalypse,* which I had read aloud to him during the automobile trip while Mrs. Stravinsky was driving. In Santa Fe the Babins took us to a shop selling Indian "Santos," primitive wood-panel paintings of saints, angels, Christs, and Marys. Stravinsky bought one for me, and, at The Thunderbird, whose proprietress was Miranda, a silver cross inlaid with turquoise. These gifts, intended to bring me into the fold—I subscribed to Huxley's "Religion can survive only as a consciously accepted system of make-believe"—sharpened my realization of how deep and doctrinaire Stravinsky's Russian Or-

2. Aldous Huxley wrote that "being with her makes me believe that Buddha was right when he numbered stupidity among the deadly sins" (letter, May 4, 1930).

thodoxy remained. The Stravinskys slept at the Babins' Rancho Piano in Tesuque, and I at the Bishop's Lodge, though I lost my way there on a dirt road and drove for a mile or so in an arroyo seco.

On August 5, the poet Witter Bynner displayed his famous Chinese jade collection and presented specimens from it to us, a belt buckle to me. He and his boyfriend Bob Hunt were with D. H. L. in Mexico while he was writing his novel about Aztec ophiolatry, *The Plumed Serpent*. Bynner published a malicious memoir about the adventure under the title *Portrait of a Genius, But . . .*

On the 6th we left for Aspen in late afternoon via Mesa Verde and arrived at night exhausted at the desert town of Cortez. Unable thus far to find any accommodations, we rented a single room, the only one available, in a squalid and decrepit posada. All three of us slept in our clothes and in the same bed, myself on its right side, the only side on which I *can* sleep. Stravinsky fortified himself with Armagnac, but both Stravinskys were better at roughing it than I was. The posada lacked a bathroom, but Mrs. Stravinsky had learned how to deal with that problem during the Russian Revolution: go outside with a blanket, find the low limb of a tree on which to suspend it, and hide behind.

On our first Sunday afternoon back in Beverly Hills, we attended an afternoon benefit concert on the spacious lawn of Artur Rubinstein's mansion just off Benedict Canyon. He played a Mozart Concerto with Harold Byrns and his Los Angeles Chamber Symphony. Most of the audience of about two hundred were movie stars. I had never seen so many familiar faces in one place.

Seldom separated from Stravinsky in 1950, and crossing the continent *aller-retour* with him and his wife, I began to know his habits much more intimately than in the summer of 1949, about which I have written in *Stravinsky: Chronicle of a Friendship*. He was a cinema buff—he never used the word "movies"—and one or two evenings a week would be sacrificed to this distraction, more than that if he could find someone to take him, as, from 1952, Edward James sometimes did. Even on our automobile trips he would insist on stopping in towns large enough to have cinemas. (We saw *Stromboli* in Philadelphia and a year later Ingrid Bergman herself, by that time a social outcast, in Jean Renoir's apartment in Rome.) After composing all day, Stravinsky needed the wit-dulling diversion. It could be torture for Mrs. Stravinsky and/or myself, because he preferred cowboy and gangster films, good and bad guys clearly delineated. He liked animated cartoons as well, but not the Looney Tunes ending "That's all, folks!" (I once heard him reply to an interviewer's question "What do you dislike most about America?" with "I don't like to be called 'folks.' ") In Hollywood, after the cinema we would eat in a popular restaurant, Melody Lane, which did not serve his brands of beverages and compelled him to bring flasks of Scotch and a thermos of a St. Emilion or St. Estephe, which he referred to as "grap juice." No fellow diner ever recognized him, and no waiter ever complained about the redolence of alcohol.

When we dined at home and alone, I often spent the evenings reading to the Stravinskys. Shaw's music criticism was among the favorites of these sessions, and Mme Calderón de la Barca's *Life in Mexico*. In the early years Stravinsky liked to hear Russian classics in English—Lermontov, Pushkin, Gogol, Leskov, Chekhov, Schedrin, Rozanov, and so on—thinking that since he knew the story lines and the substance, he would enrich his vocabulary.

Stravinsky had compiled an English–Russian dictionary in Paris in 1932 in preparation for his 1935 American concert tour. Many of the definitions are in French and German as well as English, and these languages as well as Italian and Spanish are resorted to in his examples of pronunciation. Thus the word "earn (*öpbb*)" is followed by an explanation in Russian and a sentence illustrating English usage. So far as I can tell, not all of the definitions are reliable. "At length," for instance, means more than "*enfin*," and of the three French words provided for "available," "*utile, profitable, procurable,*" only the last fits. He edited three extra, mimeographed pages on the conditional and subjunctive, presumably by a Berlitz tutor, and not surprisingly, his changes are in the interests of directness and economy: "I cannot oblige you to write exercises" becomes "I cannot make you write . . ." He complained about the lack of the Latin ablative absolute in English. The musical notations for accents, >, sfz, the dynamic markings *forte* and *piano*, and the hairpins for *crescendo* and *diminuendo*, found in his drafts for talks to women's music clubs in America in the 1930s, are not found in the dictionary. The book is a small thesaurus of synonyms and antonyms, as well as a calligraphic treasure that should be published in facsimile. How infinitely painstaking Stravinsky was!

My readings of Russian literature began with *Memoirs of a Sportsman*, a book Stravinsky's father had given to him on his tenth birthday, but, as I might have predicted, Turgenev was no longer to his liking. *The Death of Ivan Ilyitch* was also a failure, I think because it reminded him of the similar death of his father. I did not know *Oblomov* and thought the title character a marvelous creation, but Goncharov's other translated books disappointed me. We read *The Fables of Krilov*, two volumes by the early "existentialist" Shestov, a book by Valery Brussov, and *The Clock* by Remizov, a personal friend of Stravinsky, who contributed to the writer's support in his later, Paris years.

I also read aloud books by their friends, Auden's poetry, Isherwood's *Berlin Stories*, Huxley's *The Doors of Perception* and his book on the Bates Method of eye exercises. Thrillers and spies were Stravinsky's own favorite reading, Eric Ambler's *A Coffin for Dimitrios* and *Judgment on Delchev*, Erle Stanley Gardner, Raymond Chandler's *The Big Sleep*, and, later, everything by Friedrich

Dürrenmatt. The Stravinskys had a complete set of *Der Querschnitt* and enjoyed leafing through it.

We dined out at least once but more often twice a week, and the Stravinskys entertained guests at home two or even three times a week. All of this changed in later years, when many evenings were occupied by rehearsals for the Monday Evening Concerts, which took place at late hours when players under contract to film studios were more likely to be free. Stravinsky's attendance at these *Jour Fixe* affairs would depend on the music, meaning: his own, Orlando di Lasso's, Monteverdi's, Couperin's, Bach's, Mozart's, Webern's, Schoenberg's. When the ensembles were small, as in the Webern and Dallapiccolo instrumental songs, rehearsals often took place in the Stravinsky home. His own *Shakespeare Songs, Septet,* and *In Memoriam: Dylan Thomas* were heard there for the first time. We spent many evenings listening to recordings or playing the piano. Stravinsky had two pianos in his tiny studio in the house at 1260 North Wetherly Drive, the small upright at which he composed and a baby grand with a bench for two players. I heard him play and "sing" the Tchaikovsky ballets and operas, relaxation music and pure pleasure for him, on this larger instrument. A third, grander piano, for more public music-making—the one seen in the 1957 NBC Wisdom Series documentary—was in the adjoining den. The upright, on which he composed *Requiem Canticles,* was the only piano in his much roomier studio at 1218 North Wetherly, when he moved there in 1965.

When I first lived in the Stravinsky home, moments of friction were not infrequent during his bad moods, but I recall only one clash. I happened to be in the kitchen one morning while he was at work in his studio at the other end of the house. This arena, Stravinsky's and his Muse's, was sound-proofed, thickly carpeted, and protected by four doors: one to the studio itself, another to his bathroom adjoining it, a third at the end of a small corridor leading to the backyard, and, opposite this, the fourth, to a library-den. All of these were locked when he was working. On the day in question the telephone in the den rang persistently. After eight or nine times Stravinsky came charging out from his fortress, almost colliding with me as I ran toward the phone, which suddenly stopped. He looked furious and began to yell at me, "The telephone has to be answered *immediately.*"

Trembling with anger, I fled through the front door, slamming it after me, and intending to leave, which I would have done except that in this moment Mrs. Stravinsky drove into the garage. I told her that I would not be talked to in such a manner, and that it would not happen again because I would not be there. (In New York, before I left for California, Samuel Dushkin, who, in their months-at-a-time concert tours, had spent more time alone with Stravinsky than anyone else, warned me that such temper tantrums were not uncommon, but never having witnessed one, let alone been its object, I was deeply upset.) Mrs. Stravinsky, begging me to stay, went to her husband in his studio. Eventually, the two of them emerged together. The storm had blown over. He embraced me and went back to his piano.

Stravinsky's religion puzzled me. He believed in the salvific birth and death, and believed his genius was God-given: he prayed before an icon on the left wall of his studio each morning before beginning to compose; I was present once, but at the other end of the room, and he had not noticed me. He prayed to an icon over his bed each night and, before departing on our automobile trips, ceremoniously crossed himself, his wife, and me. (When I shared my first concert with him in 1948, he made the sign of the Cross in front of me before I went on stage to conduct, which unnerved me.)

During my first three years with him in Hollywood, he was a practicing Orthodoxist but attended church services only at Easter and confessed only on his birthday. The ritual of the latter was long and painful. There were no seats, pews, or cushions, and a great deal of bobbing up and down was involved, as well as, for the penitent, a half-hour spread-eagled and in kow-tow, all of this in thick, choking incense. In 1953 he broke off his connection with Hollywood's two Russian churches, for the reason that the priest-confessor had asked him for an autograph. His daughter had converted to Roman Catholicism, as had his elder son, Theodore, in both cases because of their marriages to Catholics. I think that his personal connection with John XXIII, first as patriarch of Venice, then as pope, then as conferrer of the St. Sylvester knighthood, impelled him toward the Church of Rome. In any case, this does not account for his decision before that, in 1944, to compose, uncommissioned, a Roman Catholic Mass. His explanation was simply that he needed musical instruments, prohibited by the Russian church. He was deeply disappointed that his Mass was rarely used liturgically, and when he conducted it himself in Santa Maria Sopra Minerva in Rome on the day of John F. Kennedy's funeral, it was as a concert piece, not a sacred service. The R.C. clergy in attendance hated it.

Like Diaghilev, Stravinsky had a morbid fear of death. The subject itself was taboo. He refused to attend the funeral of even such a longtime friend as Adolph Bolm. If he felt poorly, Mrs. Stravinsky withheld the news of the death of any coeval, or close friend of whatever age. When he received a letter, valedictory in tone, from his former intimate Ernest Ansermet, expressing a desire to forget their differences, he could not bring himself to reply. He had been on bad terms with Diaghilev when he died, and this upset him for many years, but he held a grudge against Ansermet.

In the summer of 1949 Stravinsky had received a visit from his London music publisher, Ralph Hawkes, who had suffered a heart attack on his airborne way home from Australia and been hospitalized in Honolulu for two weeks. I had met him in New York a few months earlier, during Stravinsky's tour there with the Boston Symphony, and shared a loge with him in Carnegie Hall at a Stravinsky performance of *Orpheus*. During intermission Hawkes asked me, quite seriously, to try to convince Stravinsky to make a suite out of the piece, on grounds that the full ballet was too episodic for concert programs. The Interludes could be cut, he suggested, especially since it is in them that "he hits you with a few nasty ones," meaning dissonant chords. He told Stravinsky that he wanted the premiere of *The Rake's Progress* to go to the 1951 Edinburgh Festival, or if not there, to the Royal Opera House in Covent Garden. Stravinsky did not welcome this opinion, having already decided that he wanted a small theater of the capacity of La Fenice in Venice. But he said nothing and never again saw Hawkes, whose next heart attack, in July 1950, killed him. After Hawkes's departure that afternoon in 1949, Stravinsky began to address himself to the prospects of a Venetian premiere. He also invited me to attend it with him and his wife, and for the next year I lived happy and excited with this anticipation.

But no response from the Italian cultural authorities was forthcoming. Lack of funds was a major obstacle, but apart from that, the Fenice orchestra and chorus were second-rate. The cast would have to be imported. Stravinsky began to think about an American debut, even a local one. The opera department at the University of Southern California had an excellent reputation and had presented professional-standard stagings by Carl Ebert (who would eventually direct the Fenice premiere). Further, Otto Klemperer was in Los Angeles and could be invited to conduct it. (Stravinsky actually played some of the opera for him, but Klemperer told other people that he found the music somewhat "thin.") The dean of the music department, Raymond Kendall, insisted on seeing the score and asked his assistant, Ingolf Dahl, to borrow it from the composer. Reluctant to let it out of his hands, Stravinsky arranged for an audition to take place one evening in my Holloway Drive house. Having been the home of the Soulima Stravinskys until their move to New York in January 1950, this domicile had sufficient living-room space for chamber music concerts, which had in fact taken place there, and a good piano. The arrangement of the piano score, begun by Erwin Stein, completed by Leopold Spinner, but extensively rewritten by Stravinsky, was never far behind the composition of the orchestral score. Stravinsky taught the piece to Dahl, and asked him to play what he could of the vocal lines. Since no singers were asked to participate, the opera as opera could not be fairly judged, or judged at all.

After a week or so of this coaching, a time was set and a few guests were invited, the Babitzes, Kendalls, and Max Edel among them. Afterward Stravinsky told me that he had realized from the beginning that Kendall did not understand the music. This was true, but the evening was worthwhile for me, Dahl's playing having conveyed a concrete idea of the score, which Stravinsky's renditions of fragments on his tiny muted piano, and his "singing" of the vocal lines with mispronounced words could not do.

The most important event of 1950, a cosmic one for me that would redirect the course of my life as a musician, was my meeting on July 5 with Arnold Schoenberg. I had written to him—in pencil and on poor-quality stationery, making me wonder why he kept the note (the original is now at the Schoenberg Institute in Vienna)—explaining that I intended to conduct his Septet-Suite and *Pierrot Lunaire* in a Town Hall, New York, concert in October, and that I would be grateful if he could find time to answer a few performance questions for me. (I did not say that Satie's *Le Piège de Méduse* was also on the program, but no matter: Eduard Steuermann, his pupil and my pianist, quickly persuaded me to abandon this inappropriate featherweight opus.) By the time of my first visit to Schoenberg, I felt confident of knowing his two pieces, but after listening with him to his privately recorded 1927 performance of the Septet, and taking mental notes on his comments as we heard it together, I realized that I would need many more hours of study.

What I still cannot understand is the irony of my coming under the thralldom of Schoenberg's music at exactly the same time as my virtual adoption, personally speaking, by Stravinsky. Like most other young musicians at that remote date, I knew recordings of *Verklärte Nacht*, Stokowski's of *Gurre-Lieder*, and Schoenberg's own of *Pierrot Lunaire*. I had been under the spell of this last since 1940. But the effects on me in 1949 of Dimitri Mitropoulos's New York rehearsals and recording of Schoenberg's *Serenade* and of Rafael Kubelik's Chicago Symphony recording of the *Five Pieces for Orchestra* were different and overwhelming. The *Five Pieces* seemed to me the greatest creation for orchestra since *The Rite of Spring* and, being entirely new, even greater than that by then very familiar opus. My love of Stravinsky's music continued, of course—*Oedipus, Noces, Psalms, Perséphone, Apollo,* the Two-Piano Concerto—and I knew all of it, whereas my knowledge of the Schoenberg repertory was small and would increase only through the experience of recording it myself in the 1950s and early 1960s.[3]

My personal position in 1950 was awkward in that I had to keep my feelings to myself, only gradually exposing a toned-down version of them to Stravinsky, and not in words but through performing Schoenberg's music. In fact, I did not tell Stravinsky about my October New York concert until shortly before it took place. I said I had been asked to conduct the two

3. In February 1931, in the course of a debate with Heinrich Strobel, Schoenberg showed his great prescience by remarking that "The circle which surrounds me . . . will grow through the curiosity of an idealistic youth. . ."

Schoenberg pieces by New York musician friends (Isadore Cohen, the violinist, Seymour Barab, the cellist, and the late Samuel Baron,[4] flutist and my
closest friend at Juilliard), and also that I was trying to expand my limited
conducting technique. Stravinsky did not conceal some surprise but said
nothing, and I promised to return in a week. Back in California, I told him
that I greatly admired the Schoenberg music I had conducted. (Let me jump
ahead of my story to say that only three years later, when I first recorded
the Septet-Suite, in December 1953, Stravinsky, who had attended every
one of the twenty-five rehearsals, supervised the session from the control
room.)

The year 1951 would become pivotal in Stravinsky's later musical life. His
return to Europe, and especially to Germany, after twelve years in the desert,
took him to radio stations where, as I have written elsewhere, he heard
tapes of Schoenberg's and Webern's music, as well as countless discussions
of it by respected musicians. Indeed, the first person with whom we dined
in Germany, the leading music critic Hans Stuckenschmidt, who came from
Berlin to Cologne to interview Stravinsky, was an early Schoenbergian and
would become his biographer. He knew about me from the Schoenberg
side, which surprised me as much as it did Stravinsky. He wanted to know
all that I could tell him about the composer's death (on July 13, a week after
my last visit to him), and of the well being of the family. He did not know
that a small concert dedicated to the great composer's memory had been
performed in Los Angeles shortly after his death, at which the soprano
Marni Nixon sang *Herzgewaechse*, its exotic ensemble conducted by her husband, the film composer Ernest Gold. I had persuaded a colleague of his,
Julius Toldi, to make a recording of it for me. The music, hauntingly, deca-
dently beautiful, could hardly be further from the bright, new, young *Rake's
Progress*, performed a few weeks later in Venice, but it persisted just as stub-
bornly in my mind.

After this first reunion with Europe, the Stravinskys returned annually,
except 1953, 1967, and 1969, three years plagued by illnesses. In aggre-
gate, we spent at least a quarter of our time outside the United States, and
during the 1960s half or more of it outside California, moving permanently
to New York in September 1969.

1951

We were in Italy from mid-August for the premiere of the *Rake*,[5] some of
the most exciting days of my life, above all the Venetian ones, as I look

4. He had stayed with me in California for several days in August 1950.
5. See my *Stravinsky: Chronicle of a Friendship*.

back on them now. Against strong odds, the opera was a genuine success. We did not know at the time that one of the greatest living poets was in the audience reviewing the occasion for the *Corriere della Sera* (September 19, 1951). Here are Eugenio Montale's notes about the premiere, originally published under the title "On the Trail of Stravinsky":[6]

> *Venice, September 8.* I have a lovely room overlooking the Riva degli Schiavoni, and an endless Canaletto, teeming and alive, unfolds before my eyes. . . . But God only knows whether I'll be able to get near Stravinsky . . . The Maestro, it seems, is rather *"arancino,"*[7] as they say in Florence, with journalists. At Naples after questioning him at length, they described him as "the great violinist"; *inde irae*[8] which discourages any direct approach . . .
>
> *September 8, evening.* I have managed to obtain a copy of the libretto of *The Rake's Progress,* which is a jewel of its genre and may contain Auden's most beautiful verse . . . I fear there will always be an imbalance between Auden's highly ramified and allusive intelligence and the naked, almost abstract intelligence of the late Stravinsky . . .
>
> *September 10.* From a loge at La Fenice I watched the dress rehearsal of the *Rake.* [Ferdinand] Leitner conducts, like a man of experience: tomorrow, when the composer will take the podium, it's said that everything will be more diluted.[9] I don't presume to make a judgment on Stravinsky's new work, but I cannot fail to note with satisfaction the reappearance, after so many years, of an opera with *parts* for the singers . . . Another welcome innovation is the abolition of the large orchestra, of symphonic padding. Here the devil is accompanied by a piano, and it's enough . . .
>
> *September 11.* Grand triumph of *The Rake's Progress* at La Fenice. Stravinsky was called to the stage, where he bounced up and down like a rubber puppet. When he conducts, with large imprecise gestures, preoccupied and absent, he looks like Benedetto Croce bent over an old codex. Like Croce, moreover, he belongs to the past, a great past. Through Stravinsky's filter Auden's libretto has lost much of its modern coloring but has gained in density of style . . . With *The Rake's Progress* a great European by choice warns Europeans not to become barbarians. I foresee, however, that many born and not made Europeans will respond that, without barbarians, Europe will lack a new face, and they will continue to write tedious musical dramas, not operas constructed like a chamber sonata.

6. The text printed here is Jonathan Galassi's translation published in Montale's *The Second Life of Art*, New York, 1982.

7. A small, bitter orange; hence sharp, haughty. Footnote by Montale.

8. "Whence the wrath" (Juvenal, *Satires*, I, 68).

9. Leitner's *tempi* were more brisk, the ensembles more secure.

September 12. A vermouth in the composer's honor, given by the city. Stravinsky arrived at the *imbarcadero* at the Rialto . . . In a room of the City Hall we crowd around the Mayor,[10] who makes a well-received speech that makes mention of Aeschylus, Hugo, and Arrigo Boito. Stravinsky, who is seated, takes the beating and expresses his thanks. He . . . bows in the Russian manner, as if diving. I manage to exchange a few words with him and am not surprised to find him so simple and humanly solitary. Fame, Hollywood, and dollars have not marred in the slightest his personality which is that of a small *barine* who is afraid of the devil and would like his whole life to be a beautiful opera, closer to Tchaikovsky than to Wagner.

September 13. I return to Milan. At the airport I see Auden again, leaving for Rome to return to Ischia. He nearly speaks Italian, takes my snapshot, repeats his admiration for Dante, a poet whom the English cook in their own style (and with reason); then he jumps aboard the plane like a roebuck. His carrot-colored[11] head enters the cabin, disappears. A little later, the plane for Milan takes off, too. Seen from above, Venice is bathed in mist. It was worth it to end the *Rake's* epiphany with this vision.

Returning to New York on Thanksgiving Day, the Stravinskys were dissatisfied with their rooms in the Lombardy Hotel and found the price exorbitant. After one night they moved to the Gladstone Hotel on Fifty-second Street east of Park Avenue and adjacent to the Ambassador Hotel, which had also raised its prices. Owing to a longshoremen's strike, the baggage, consisting of summer clothes and European acquisitions, which had been shipped from Venice in September, had finally been unloaded in Halifax. Vera Stravinsky arranged for it to be forwarded from there to New York by train. Already on his second day in the city Stravinsky rehearsed the City Center Ballet orchestra in *Le Baiser de la fée* and conducted a performance of it the following night.

Three days later we attended the New York premiere of *I Am a Camera.* Isherwood was in his element, introducing Truman Capote to other odd characters. The next morning, a basket of red roses arrived at the Gladstone "For Igor, with love from Marlene." Dietrich had been a good friend of Stravinsky since the 1920s, and the flamboyant embrace she bestowed on him at the theater had upstaged the show.

At the beginning of December Stravinsky wrote to the Marions that he

---

10. A cousin of Michelangelo Spagno, the second husband of the painter Stephanie Guerzoni, mother of Theodore Stravinsky's wife, Denise.

11. Henna-ed.

would not be back until after the holidays: "I am on a strict diet, and Véra has embarked on a treatment of injections." Mrs. Stravinsky wrote to them that "Bob is sometimes in New York, sometimes in Kingston. He is sad because his parents will sell the house in which he has lived all his life . . . We saw Christopher Isherwood's play. The first act was very good, the last two much less so . . . From time to time we see Auden."

She does not say that we spent many evenings in General Manager Rudolph Bing's box at the Metropolitan Opera. Casting for the Metropolitan *Rake* premiere had not yet begun, though the contract had been signed while Stravinsky was still in Europe. His only prerogative was that Elizabeth Schwarzkopf be engaged for the soprano role. Bing said that this would not be possible because of her wartime connection with Governor-General Hans Frank of Poland. Stravinsky pointed out to no avail that she was singing in Britain and throughout Europe. Bing said that the protest would be too great to control, but the question remained open for weeks to come.

On December 17 Stravinsky played the *Rake* for Balanchine and discussed the staging with him. Neither Balanchine nor Auden wanted Berman as set designer, and Stravinsky failed to see that Horace Armistead was really Kirstein's choice, not theirs, Auden being blind to the visual arts, and Balanchine, at this date, almost always deferring to Kirstein where they are concerned.

On December 18 Stravinsky wrote again to the Marions apropos his January concert with the Los Angeles Chamber Orchestra: "Saul [sic] Babitz *est* OK for the *Soldat* but not for the Pastorale," which, in any case, Stravinsky proposed to drop because "the English horn plays for only three minutes and must be paid for the entire evening," and because "the preparation of the piece will take a half-hour of my insufficient rehearsal time." He had already distributed the checks for the inheritance from Walter Nouvel[12] to his sons but would hold the one for Marion until he returns because he has "forgotten whether I owe the $514 to you or whether you owe it to me."

1952

At the beginning of the year Stravinsky commissioned me and his son-in-law Andre Marion to translate Theodore Stravinsky's *Le Message d'Igor Strawinsky*. Neither of us wanted to become involved with this small exercise in hagiography, but in our positions we could hardly refuse and were unable to think of any excuse that would satisfy Stravinsky. Two-hour stretches

---

12. Diaghilev's closest friend, Walter Nouvel, who died in Paris in 1950, had bequeathed generous sums of money to Stravinsky and his family.

were set aside in late afternoons for the work, at which time Marion's wife joined us, coming early to cut her father's hair, as she did during all the years I knew him. (She often cut mine, too.) If guests were not expected, the couple would stay for dinner, to Yevgenia Petrovna's ill-concealed displeasure. The translation was finished in February and sent to Boosey & Hawkes, whose response was that Anthony Gishford, representing the Board of Directors, would discuss it with me in Amsterdam in June, when he and Lord and Lady Harewood were coming from London for the gala seventieth-birthday performances of *Nightingale* and *Oedipus Rex* as a double-bill at the Amsterdam Opera. Gishford candidly told me that he thought the book not only worthless but detrimental, yet he eventually published it.

We spent most of May in Paris, the Stravinskys' first stay there since 1939. The composer himself was the main attraction of Nicolas Nabokov's American-sponsored festival, *Les Arts du Vingtième Siècle*, but the most memorable event was the Vienna Opera's performance of Alban Berg's *Wozzeck.* William Faulkner was the principal literary magnet, and Malraux, Camus, Auden, Spender, Ignazio Silone, Salvador de Madariaga, and others who participated in a public symposium did so only because Faulkner had consented. French writers who had mistaken this deeply conservative Southern regionalist for a desegregationalist gave his very short talk a long ovation. According to Joseph Blottner's biography, Faulkner arrived in Paris on May 19 and was installed in the same hotel as the all-black cast of Virgil Thomson's *Four Saints in Three Acts.* Discovering this, Faulkner complained to Nicolas Nabokov about the accommodation, and Nabokov, whom we saw two or three times daily, said that the writer spent his time in his room, marinated in whiskey.

In Hollywood on September 15 I inaugurated the Evenings on the Roof concert season with Schoenberg's Serenade. Peter Yates[13] wrote to a friend: "Igor has become a devotee of his rival's music. He sat the whole evening score in hand following every note."[14] I also conducted the second concert, a piece by Haydn and Boulez's *Polyphonie* for eighteen instruments. Yates described Stravinsky's reaction to the latter to a friend of the concerts: "Igor practically took me on his lap. He wished to describe to me what is wrong aesthetically . . . it has no continuity. I explained that this is indeed the very purpose of the Boulez-Cage aesthetic as of present information, to break up continuity, to provide a set of discontinuous experiences. He listened pa-

13. Founder, in 1939, of Evenings on the Roof, a concert organization in Los Angeles that by the mid-1950s attained international prominence.

14. Crawford, *Evenings*, p.100. Stravinsky first attended a Roof concert on March 6, 1944.

tiently and resumed by pointing out that . . . 'it does not lead the ear and mind on.' "[15]

At the beginning of October, Stravinsky was greatly distressed by a letter from Theodore, then aged forty-five and earning no money. He answered on October 10:

> You say that you do not have sufficient money to build the garage and the fence, and you ask me for another $8,000 or $9,000. Although I have already told you how difficult it would be for me to exceed the sum of $15,000, I shall once again explain the state of my finances . . . If I send the money you request, I would be reducing to a dangerous level the small amount that I have put aside for Vera and myself in the event of my incapacitation. Do not forget, I am seventy years old. I live modestly, and, if comparatively comfortably, this is only because I am still conducting. How long I shall be able to go on conducting without running myself into the ground, I cannot say; but I do know that without the conducting, it would be difficult to make ends meet. My earnings as a composer are not enough to live on, and I will not conceal from you that *I live in constant fear of having no security* . . . The greater part of the savings that I made have been for all of you. I gave each of you $15,000 to buy or build a house. My own house cost $13,000.

It was also about this time that Stravinsky displayed to me the packets of photographs he kept in boxes in cupboards in his living room, each packet containing a dozen glassine envelopes with thin gray cardboard backs. Two or three photos, slightly smaller than playing cards, and their negatives, were in each of the dozen compartments, on which he had meticulously captioned the place, date, and occasion. The quality of the photographs, all taken by Vera or him, was excellent. What astonished me was that he had identified himself in each one—"MOI"—as if any doubt could be entertained about this. Whole chapters of autobiography about his life in the 1920s and 1930s might be compiled from these pictures and captions. They are the only source for many friendships, such as the one with Roger Martin du Gard.

1953

On March 30, soon after our return from the recording sessions of *The Rake's Progress* in New York, I conducted *Renard* and *Pribaoutki* at a Roof concert. Lawrence Morton wrote to Ingolf Dahl,[16] who was on sabbatical from USC: "Last night's *Renard* was wonderful and made a big hit . . . One of the

15. Crawford, *op. cit.*, p.101.
16. *Ibid.*, p.102.

best concerts we ever had . . . on the subject of Roof survival, everyone was hopeful. Bob [Craft] will have a hundred plums . . . We shall want you to play Stravinsky's Piano-Rag and *Tango* on a wonderful program . . . If you want to play piano in the Ragtime, [Stravinsky] will rewrite the cimbalom part."[17]

On July 29 I drove to Brentwood and the Schoenberg home, wondering whether Mrs. Schoenberg had invited me to a dinner with, and by, Balanchine, because she wanted help in bridging the cultural gap, or whether Balanchine had asked her to invite me because he would be so far out of his element. When I arrived he was busily barbecuing lamb shish-kebabs on the lawn at the far side of the house. The social relations were stiff and formal, and I did not help much, because Balanchine feared that I might regard him as a traitor, more so in that Stravinsky was in the hospital undergoing a prostatectomy. Mrs. Schoenberg and I sat at facing ends of the dinner table, with Balanchine on her right, Tanaquil LeClercq on my right, Richard Hoffmann and Nuria on my left. Balanchine was here to seek the widow's permission to base a ballet on one of her husband's twelve-tone works. Since he did not know any of them, I proposed the *Accompaniment to a Cinematographic Scene*, partly because it is short, employs a small orchestra, has a clearly defined tripartite structure, and is not excruciatingly difficult to play. This last point did not go down well with Dick Hoffmann, who said that it is much more difficult than any of the Stravinsky scores in the ballet repertory. Seeing that Balanchine was becoming livid, I answered this simply to keep him from doing so, and in the process sank the whole idea. The ballet orchestra is very good, I said, and plays more new music than the New York Philharmonic (which was not true of the Mitropoulos years), and Mr. Balanchine will see that it receives lots of rehearsal. I promised to work with him immediately, and we made a date for the next day to hear the piece and decide. The evening ended soon after.

On July 30, after his morning rehearsal in the Greek Theater, Balanchine came to the Stravinsky home in a good mood, showing no sign of the guilt I felt in him last night. I explained the pitch organization of the piece to him and the proportional tempo scheme, and we listened to the tape of a German performance three or four times. He immediately grasped the dramatic structure, and then and there, I think, decided that it should be staged twice, once as a purely abstract piece, and once as a scene of some anxious action. He wanted to know why an "atonal" piece began and ended in triadic harmony, a good question.

The 1953–54 Evenings on the Roof series featured Stravinsky's *Shakespeare Songs*, dedicated to the concert organization. He heard all of the rehearsals,

17. *Ibid.* He did rewrite it, but the whereabouts of the manuscript, sold at auction, is unknown.

many of them at his own home, of this and of the many "old music" pieces performed. He preferred to have his own works programmed in combination with old, rather than new, music.

Dorothy Crawford recalls that "one of Craft's projects was a series of sixteen Bach cantatas; another was the exploration of *Symphoniae sacrae* and the *Christmas Story* of Heinrich Schütz; he conducted and eventually recorded some sixty-five Gesualdo madrigals and motets. Other projects were groups of late Renaissance and early Baroque music for brass, the large Monteverdi works, Guillaume de Machaut's . . . *Messe de Nôtre Dame* [1364]."[18] With solo-voice ensembles we performed Thomas Tallis's *Lamentations* and François Couperin's *Leçons de Tenebrae*, as well as newly discovered works for winds by Haydn and Mozart.[19]

Dorothy Crawford goes on to say:

> Craft and Morton worked closely together to find and edit music not yet available in performing editions. From the [Library of Congress's] copy of the Pavoni edition (1613) of Gesualdo's madrigals (actually published in score, rather than in the customary part books) [. . .] Morton and Craft [. . .] transcribed for the singers from the original clefs.[20] Aldous and Laura Huxley translated the texts for three of the four recordings that Craft and the madrigal singers made of the Gesualdo works.[21] The strangeness of the music, and the stir caused by Gesualdo's life history, were noted in an article in *Time* magazine (September 10, 1956) that followed Huxley's brilliant article on Gesualdo in *Esquire*.[22] In it Huxley [. . .] discussed Gesualdo's indifference to the poeti-

18. Crawford, *op. cit.*, p.274.

19. The transcriptions from *Die Entführung aus dem Serail*.

20. To see and hear all of the parts in the densely chromatic harmony, full scores were required by the singers then as now, though full scores were virtually unheard of in 1590.

21. A letter from Huxley to me, June 10, 1958, containing several of his translations, includes a note by him on the texts:

> Gesualdo was a great musician; but for most of his extraordinary madrigals he chose (or perhaps himself composed) texts so grotesquely affected as to be almost incomprehensible, and at the same time so silly that, when at last they are interpreted, the twisted phrases turn out to be entirely pointless. But for Gesualdo this was of no importance. All that he asked of a text was that it should be full of startling antitheses and that it should contain, if possible, such words as "death," "pain," "woe," "martyrdom," "languish," "alas." The antitheses permitted him to display his amazing skill in modulating abruptly from one musical mood to another, and the vocabulary of disaster was his excuse for indulging in those excruciating harmonic progressions, of which he is the supreme master. A literal translation of Gesualdo's texts will not help us to enjoy his madrigals. On the contrary, it might prove a hindrance. Bad verse distracts from good music. For us, all that is necessary is to be on the watch for such key words as *morte* and *dolore*, as *languisco, oimè* and *martire*, and to listen, with pleasure and astonishment, to the mad prince's ever-novel variations on these monotonously dismal themes.

22. For which I was the main source.

cal quality of his texts, in spite of his personal friendship with the poet Torquato Tasso [. . .][23] In November 1957 the Gesualdo Singers and Craft performed some Gesualdo motets found in Naples and transcribed by Ruth Adams, a Los Angeles early-music scholar.[24]

Crawford adds that "the fusion of German and Italian, Renaissance and Baroque styles and attitudes in the music of the great seventeenth-century German composer Heinrich Schütz clearly fascinated Craft and Morton. The performance on November 9, 1953 of *Fili mi, Absalom*, with four trombones, was the beginning not only of Morton's 'four-trombone period' but of an extended period of exploration of the works of Schütz. This investigation was given added impetus by Robert Craft's desire to record for Columbia Records an overview of Schütz's sacred works for voice and instruments: two of the *Cantiones sacrae* (1625), *Symphoniae sacrae* from the three volumes of these pieces (1629, 1647, 1650), and the last motet in the collection of Schütz's old age, *Geistliche Chormusik* (1648)." When Columbia Records agreed, one of the performers who eagerly joined the group was Marilyn Horne.

"Robert Craft supplied many of the ideas for and performances of early music in the fifties," Morton commented:

> [Craft had] repertoire ideas that were far more interesting than anyone else's and there was no point in holding any of these in reserve . . . Bob Craft and I were having a sort of holiday with the music of Schütz, Bach, Monteverdi, some Gabrieli, and other early Baroque, late Renaissance composers.[25]

Some of the rehearsals of *Il Combattimento di Tancredi e Clorinda*, and many future ones of Couperin, Bach, and others, took place in the Benedict Canyon home of the harpsichordist Carol Rosenstiel.

I had been rehearsing Schoenberg's Septet-Suite to record it, and some of the readings took place in the Schoenberg house. After one of them, on October 22, I spent the night there. The session took place in Columbia Records Studio 5, at Sycamore and La Brea, on the evening of December 4, Stravinsky helping in the control room.

23. Tasso—Goethe's play of that name dramatizes his life—had been in the service of Gesualdo's father in his Naples palace, and wrote thirty-six texts for Gesualdo's express use, though the composer set only a single one of these, in addition to seven other Tasso texts, not so stipulated.

24. Crawford, *op. cit.*, pp. 274-75.

25. *Ibid.*

I remember seeing *Un Ballo in Maschera* with Stravinsky at the Shrine Auditorium on October 28, and going backstage with him afterward to congratulate Tullio Serafin, the conductor. I was back at the Shrine two days later to hear *Turandot*, a sadly uneven score, Ping, Peng, and Pong going on much too long. Yet Liu's *"Tanto amore, segreto"* aria and the Prince's *"Nessun dorma"* are too short to offset the weaknesses. During a dinner with Edward James at the Statler Hotel following the opera, the dance band played a tune from *The Rite of Spring*, after which one of the musicians asked Stravinsky if he minded. What he minded, of course, was being asked, but why did he allow such incidents to rile him? He had absolutely no Olympian, Goethean calm, and was patient only in the throes of composing.

At the beginning of November, I read *Ladies Whose Bright Eyes* to the Baroness, our umpteenth book by Ford Maddox Ford, of whom she was much fonder than I was. On the 4th the Stravinskys and I dined at Mrs. Schoenberg's, whose only subject of conversation was "Mr. Schoenberg." Afterward she showed us the sketch of a marching chorus for *The Biblical Way* and the manuscript book for *Opera 23–29*, which greatly interested Stravinsky. She also played recordings of Schoenberg being interviewed. Stravinsky was surprised by the softness of the voice and the Viennese accent, as if he had expected a counterpart to the savage indignation of the face in photographs.

On the 28th we drove to Twenty-Nine Palms, La Jolla, and Escondido, staying in La Jolla Shores. A radio announcement of the death of Eugene O'Neill brought to mind his son, Eugene O'Neill Junior, in Woodstock, and a reading by this classical scholar in a New York theater of Calderón's *Alcalde de Zalamea*. Not long after, he committed suicide as Tacitus describes the method in ancient Rome, by opening his veins in a hot bath.

On the last day of the month Aldous Huxley called and read a passage to and about me by Martin Mayer in the December issue of *Esquire*, "Igor Makes A Record" [*The Rake's Progress*]:

> The most formal man in the house was Robert Craft, a young conductor who is one of the few musicians Stravinsky has ever accepted . . . He sat against the wall in the control booth, his score on his lap, wearing glasses and a grey flannel suit, twitching his pale face and flanneled arms in time to the music. Stravinsky had asked him to come. "When I conduct I do not hear the music," he says. "Robert is my ears." Craft has remarkable ears; throughout the sessions [David] Oppenheim [the producer] and Stravinsky deferred to his judgment in matters of pitch.

We already knew about the article, Stravinsky having received an irate letter from Fritz Reiner in response to criticisms of his conducting of the opera attributed to the composer by *Esquire*.

On December 6 we attended an official lunch at the home of the Italian consul, Signor Ungaro, who presented Stravinsky with a badge and scroll in the name of the Italian Government. The other invités were Lion Feuchtwanger, Passinetti, the Venetian novelist (*The Red Priest*), who was teaching at UCLA—we later invited him to dinner with the Baroness—and the Principessa San Faustino, who seemed to have preserved her accent in mothballs.

On December 9 and 12 I accompanied the Stravinskys to the Royal Ballet's *Swan Lake* and *Sleeping Beauty* in downtown Los Angeles. Stravinsky was deeply moved by *Sleeping Beauty*, and Vera Stravinsky was in tears, partly because she had played the part of the Queen in the 1921 London revival, and because her love affair with Stravinsky was in full flame at that time. Handkerchiefs were not needed after *Swan Lake*. The next day, December 13, Stravinsky finished copying the Bach-Webern *Ricercar.* I helped him spray the transparencies of the manuscript, to keep the soft lead pencil from smudging. Stravinsky was in New York at New Year's, rehearsing for the premiere of the Septet at Dumbarton Oaks in Washington. On December 31, I received a New Year's greeting in music from him.

Dorothy Crawford wrote that the 1953 fall season of the Roof concerts "was of the greatest importance to Stravinsky . . . Craft's enthusiasm for and involvement with the music of Schoenberg roused Stravinsky's creative energies and boundless curiosity. He received crucial nourishment for his composing from the breadth of repertoire in these chamber concerts; and the prospect of rearranging older works[26] for immediate performances by the fine performers at hand kept him at work and productive in the seasons to come."

1954

In January Stravinsky conducted the premiere of his Septet at Dumbarton Oaks in Georgetown, Washington. It seems that the concert's intermission was extended when he did not receive his fee and threatened not to conduct the second part of the evening; the check was a long time in coming. Also in January, I addressed a letter to Stravinsky in New York suggesting that he set Dylan Thomas's "Do Not Go Gentle" to music. He completed it on March 19.

Meanwhile, in Hollywood, the choreographer Jack Cole took Mrs. Stravinsky and me to dinner at Perino's (a Lafite 1945) and an Agnes DeMille dance evening at the Shrine Auditorium. A little Americana goes a long way, but with Aggie's uncle, Cecil B. DeMille, in the seat next to mine, I

26. This refers to his instrumentation for flute, harp, and guitar of the piano accompaniments of his *Four Russian Songs;* to his scoring for string quartet, piano, pairs of flutes and clarinets of the *Balmont Songs;* and to his composition of the four-horn accompaniment for his *Russian Peasant Choruses.*

kept this opinion to myself. We also dined that week at the Schoenbergs', after which Nuria and I went to an Ingolf Dahl concert in Bovard Auditorium.

On January 12, I finished reading Isaiah Berlin's *The Hedgehog and the Fox* to the Baroness, who was a descendant of Joseph de Maistre, one of the book's subjects. She showed her family tree to me, and a large photograph of Queen Victoria with herself and four other ladies-in-waiting on the lawn at Windsor Castle. In the evening I took the Stravinskys—he had just returned from New York—to *The Little Fugitive*, the film by Ruth Orkin, my friend from Tanglewood. On January 18 I conducted part of the Roof concert, Bach's Cantata 54, on a program with classical Japanese music.

On February 12 I recorded Webern's *opera* 15, 16, 17, 22 in a nerve-wracking three-and-a-half-hour session. Stravinsky, in the control room, followed scores that Leonard Stein had borrowed from Schoenberg's library. Dorothy Crawford wrote: "Craft recorded his epoch-making set of the complete Webern with the Roof performers, and as Peter Yates described it . . . Stravinsky 'sat through the rehearsals, his nose in the score . . . then he came to the concerts and did the same thing over again. At more than 70 he retains a young man's capacity to hear music the first time, to take it all in as a new experience with all the excitement of discovery.' "[27]

On the 18th we received a visit from Witter Bynner. At one point Stravinsky said to him: "They liked my early work, and now they like *only* my early work. They liked me too soon. But I know that I like what I do now—and they will be liking it sometime, but I like it now. I am ahead of them. And I will always be ahead of them . . . I know and I don't have to know through anyone else."

The next evening we dined at Oscar Moss's, the principal sponsor of the Monday Evening concerts. Stravinsky gave the piano-score manuscript of his *Shakespeare Songs* to him, and a sketch page of the same to Peter Yates.

At the dress rehearsal of George Antheil's *Ballet Mécanique* at Royce Hall two days later I had an attack of nerves, whereupon Stravinsky fed his two-pill combination[28] to me, one to calm and one to stimulate, and I conducted the concert without jitters. The Stravinskys fetched me at the stage door after the concert. They had been to tea at Trude Schoenberg's to meet the German Consul. On the way home we ate ice cream sodas at Wil Wright's on Sunset Boulevard.

On February 23 I recorded Webern's Six Songs, Opus 14. The following week we visited the Schoenbergs', to bid them best wishes for the premiere of *Moses und Aron* in Hamburg. Less than a week later Nuria wrote to

27. Crawford, *op. cit.*

28. This formula was especially prepared for Stravinsky in November 1951 by Maurice Gilbert, the Stravinsky family physician in Geneva.

me from there, reporting a switch in conductors, Hans Rosbaud taking over from Hans Schmidt-Isserstedt.

On March 7 I conducted Stravinsky's Septet and Cantata in the Lobero Theater in Santa Barbara. Aldous Huxley was with us; I drove him home from the Stravinskys' at 1:30 A.M. The program was repeated in Hollywood the next evening, with the addition of *Three Songs from William Shakespeare.*

On March 15, when I showed my program for "Do Not Go Gentle" to Stravinsky, he promised to compose dirge canons for the four trombones who were playing in Schütz's *Absalom* earlier in the program.

The next day I flew to New York to see my family, a few days ahead of the Stravinskys. They arrived at midnight on March 25, fog having forced their plane to land in Washington, where, together with Jack Benny, they boarded a train so crowded that all three of them had to stand most of the way. Before flying on to Rome for Nabokov's Arts of the Twentieth Century festival, we saw the play *Tea and Sympathy*, which had one suspenseful moment, Deborah Kerr's partial unbuttoning of her blouse, this being intended to resolve the self-doubt of her young co-star, whose sexuality was the subject of the play. But in so cold-blooded an experiment would the sight of her bared breasts, or even the manipulation of them, prove anything?

Our first days in Rome, from April 4, were spent exploring the Etruscan necropolises in Cerveteri and Tarquinia. I picked up some conversational Italian from Signor Belfiore, the driver assigned to us by Rome Radio, and together with musical terminology and a smattering of phrases from opera libretti, began to make my way around in the language. We also drove to the Villa Farnese at Caprarola and the Villa Lante at Bagnaia. As for music, Stravinsky and I heard Bartók's *Cantata Profana* in the Teatro Argentina. He did not care for it, but we met his future biographer Roman Vlad at this concert. We also went to a party at the American Academy with Stephen Spender, Elliott and Helen Carter, Samuel Barber, Denis de Rougemont, Poulenc, Virgil Thomson, and Hans Werner Henze, who describes the affair in his autobiography, *Bohemian Fifths.*[29]

> The Accademia Americana held a reception for Stravinsky . . . The whole of Rome was there . . . The festival director Nicolas Nabokov came over to me and said: "Stravinsky would like to meet you." For the first (and last) time in my life, I knew beyond a shadow of a doubt that I was in the presence of a living legend, a figure of mythic status . . . The simplicity and directness with which Stravinsky expressed himself . . . I liked him enormously. He wanted to speak German, but I answered in English and so we stuck to English. His German sounded a little Baltic but was otherwise excellent—as I was later to

29. Hans Werner Henze, *Bohemian Fifths: An Autobiography*, trans. Stewart Spencer (Princeton: Princeton University Press, 1999), pp. 128–39.

have other occasions to remark. The first thing he wanted to know was what I thought of twelve-note composition. He himself was not entirely sure what to make of it at the time, although, if anything, he tended towards scepticism. I did not dare ask him what he himself was working on, but, since he insisted on knowing, I told him about the opera on which I myself was currently engaged and about the twelve-note and serial techniques that I had chosen to use in it. We arranged to meet the next evening, at the first night of [my] *Boulevard Solitude*.

Stravinsky and Vera duly appeared in the main entrance of the Rome Opera on the stroke of nine, but the liveried doormen refused to admit them—Stravinsky was not wearing a dinner jacket. (He said it had smelt of mothballs.) Such rotten luck. The incident made headline news,[30] and the Minister for Tourism and the Arts sent a letter of apology to the Hassler Hotel, where they were staying, with flowers for Madame. Stravinsky turned up for the second performance, this time the only person to wear a dinner jacket, since there was no requirement to wear formal dress for the later performances. Once again, therefore, he was inappositely attired. He came with our mutual publisher, Willy Strecker, who [that same evening] enticed him into saying a few words of praise for my piece . . .[31]

A few nights later, at the Foro Italico, Stravinsky and I heard Darius Milhaud conduct Satie's *Socrate*, a piece for which Stravinsky had always professed a high regard, but he found it boring. Gertrud and Nuria Schoenberg had arrived in our hotel from Hamburg that day, bursting with pride over the reception of *Moses und Aron*.

On the day that Stravinsky was due to leave for Turin to conduct his Violin Concerto with Jeanne Gauthier, and *Perséphone* with Madeleine Milhaud, Vera Stravinsky was in bed with flu. Andre Marion accompanied him instead (19th), and Milene Marion and I took the RAI car to Subiaco, Carsoli, Rieti, unsuccessfully looking for the church with the fresco in which the not yet canonized St. Francis is portrayed without halo. The next day Vera Stravinsky was able to visit Norma, the medieval town at the top of an escarpment, reached on a hairpin road blocked by overloaded women and

30. It was reported on the front page of the next day's *New York Times*.

31. In a review article in the *Times Literary Supplement*, March 10, 2000, Andrew Porter refers to Henze as a golden boy, and quotes Stravinsky: "If I were gay, I'd want you as my lover." No source for this is given, though Henze is implicated. Stravinsky did not know the word "gay," of course, and I doubt that the remark attributed to him was ever uttered. He liked Henze personally and attended a gay party at his Naples residence in October 1959, after our concert in the Teatro San Carlo. He drank quite a lot and talked almost exclusively with Henze, but he was able afterward to board an all-night sleeper with me to Bologna. Since his tête-à-tête with Henze was in German, I understood nothing of it. They saw each other only thrice more, a year later in Rome, in June 1962 in Hamburg, and in October 1964 in Berlin, and not alone.

donkeys; the castle at Sermoneta; and Ninfa, in the Pontian marshes, where, in the time of Pliny the Younger, artificial islands revolved to music in the lake, an Ancient Roman Disney World. After Barbarossa sacked Ninfa in the twelfth century, it was confiscated by the Frangipane, then by Boniface VIII, the Caetani Pope and Dante's enemy. At the beginning of the sixteenth century it became the property of Cesare and Lucrezia Borgia. Pope Julius II, Michelangelo's patron, restored it to the Caetani, who have owned it ever since.[32]

In May, I returned to California to conduct the Ojai Festival, a grand-sounding affair, but consisting of a mere five concerts taking place during a single weekend, the only time musicians from Los Angeles under contract to film studios were free to make the hundred-mile trip. I also conducted children's concerts in the nearby Ventura high school: a string piece by David Raksin, Tchaikovsky's Serenade, and Ravel's *Mother Goose.* The opening Ojai program presented the Lichine Ballet, for which I conducted Vivaldi's Concerto Opus 3, No. 11; two pieces for strings by Copland; Stravinsky's String Concerto; Mozart's Serenata Notturna; Bach's flute suite with Arthur Gleghorn as soloist. My first evening concert consisted of Berg's Chamber Concerto, played by Eudice Shapiro and Ingolf Dahl, and Bach's *Trauer-Ode.* My final program included Stravinsky's Piano Concerto, with Lukas Foss as soloist, preceded by the *Symphonies of Winds* and Gabrieli's *In Ecclesiis.*

On returning to Hollywood, I wrote to Stravinsky in Geneva: "We read about the incident at the London airport in several newspapers. By now you should be settled in Lisbon, but it will be ten more days before we hear about the London concert and the medal.[33] We gave a clean and spirited performance of the *Basler* Concerto at Ojai."

I wrote to Stravinsky in Lisbon[34] on June 2, telling him, "We will be doing the Shakespeare Songs, Septet, and Cantata at the Los Angeles County Museum on June 27 . . . [Heinrich] Strobel wrote asking for the address of Mercury Music Publishers for the new Tango arrangement. I sent it but

---

32. The historian Ferdinand Gregorovius, who effected the restoration of Castel del Monte (Apulia), was also partly responsible for the preservation of Ninfa. See the author's *Chronicle of a Friendship* for an account of a luncheon, April 17, 1954, with Don Roffredo Caetani and his wife, Princess Margherita Caetani, in their Botteghe Oscure palace (now the Spanish Embassy) in Rome. Margherita, *née* Chapin, was a cousin of T. S. Eliot and an aunt of Schuyler Chapin.

33. For reasons still mysterious, Stravinsky had been detained at Customs and Immigration in Heathrow. He threatened to return to Geneva, but was rescued and admitted with the help of an attorney for Boosey & Hawkes. The Royal Philharmonic presented its medal to him through Sir Arthur Bliss, and a silver-tipped rosewood baton, said to have been used by Joseph Haydn. Milton Babbitt was in the audience.

34. Stravinsky, in Portugal for concerts, was accompanied by the Marions. The three of them visited the Shrine of Fatima.

meanwhile a second set of proofs has come from Mercury for you to correct."

George Balanchine, arriving from New York at the beginning of July
for his ballet season at the Greek Theater, worked with Stravinsky on *Agon*
July 6, 9, 11, 12, 17. We were in Las Vegas from August 19 to 22 with Max
Edel. I was aware that the Stravinskys had been promoting this excursion in
order to divert me, or cool me off (in the desert heat) from my intensifying
romance with Jean Stein.[35]

Stravinsky was not a gambler. He regarded it as a sin contradictory to
his religion, rather like his attitude to insurance, which for him was the
ultimate cynicism. Neither he, nor anyone in his family, nor any property
of his had ever been insured, though his house, with all of his manuscripts,
was in a fire zone. He was miserable in Las Vegas.

On September 20 I opened the season of the Monday Evening Concerts, the organization that continued Evenings on the Roof, with Lawrence
Morton succeeding Peter Yates as artistic director. Of the many concerts I
conducted for this group, my favorite program was this one with the premiere of *In Memoriam: Dylan Thomas*, coupled with pieces for four trombones
by Andrea Gabrieli, Purcell, Willaert, and Schütz, a group of Gesualdo
madrigals, Bach's *Gottes Zeit* cantata.

After a matinée *Fidelio* by the touring San Francisco Opera, Stravinsky
wrote a note to Pierre Monteux, complimenting him on his conducting of
the opera. I left it in Monteux's box at the Ambassador Hotel.

On October 31 we listened to a recording of Carissimi's *Jephtha* at the
Huxleys'. On November 3 Jean Stein came to the Stravinskys' for dinner.

I conducted three Sacred Symphonies by Schütz and Bach's *Aus der Tiefe*
at the next Monday concert, and we spent Thanksgiving at the Huxleys',
with Aldous's closest friend, the Canadian Dr. Humphrey Osborne, who
talked endlessly about psychotropic drugs, mescaline, and altered states of
consciousness. Auden and Isherwood joined us after dinner, the former's
consciousness more than noticeably altered by martinis. Aldous and Gerald
allowed their disapproval to show, which, surely, was inconsistent, alcohol
being a drug, however vulgar, of the kind they had been discussing. The
next day Auden and Isherwood came for dinner at our house. Auden, on a
lecture/poetry-reading tour, was again sozzled, but held forth brightly on
the genius of Tolkien, whose whimsy Isherwood thought unreadable, but
held his peace.

I conducted Schütz's *Christmas Story* on December 6, and the Stravinskys,

35. This had run into trouble in late July because we were staying out too late at night.
Her parents summoned me to a meeting, in which they claimed no opposition to my friendship with their daughter. To prove this, they invited me to dinner the following week,
"black tie, of course." Not having the required clothing, I did not immediately respond, but
later sent what I considered a polite note, declining. See also my *Chronicle* for July 1954.

Morton, and I flew to San Francisco after it. We had good views of the moonlit Pacific coast and its sparkling towns. Morton told a friend that immediately after the performance: "Craft, the Stravinskys, and I . . . flew to San Francisco. As we got on the plane and sat down, Stravinsky began to sing the final chorus; and the three of us, Craft and Stravinsky and I, had a marvelous time all the way up to San Francisco singing that final chorus, faking it, of course, but having a marvelous time."

Stravinsky conducted *Petrushka* twice with the London Festival Ballet in San Francisco, Anton Dolin dancing the title role. I spent the intermissions chatting with Kyra Nijinsky, who said she remembered me from Rome three years ago, when she was a clerk in a haberdashery on the Via Condotti.

The Huxleys fetched us at the airport on our return to Los Angeles, Aldous exhilarated by a new biography of Madame Blavatsky. Two days later, we dined at their home with Gerald and Nancy Ross, the Buddhist scholar. Aldous tried out a sleep-inducing record on Stravinsky, but it affected me, too, and I drove home feeling groggy. Again at the Huxleys, a few days later, I rehearsed the *Ode to Napoleon* with Aldous, but he decided not to narrate it at my performance because "Byron's poem is too long and keeps saying the same thing over and over."

I drove the Stravinskys to Christmas midnight mass at St. Matthias, and on Christmas Day and New Year's Day to the Shrine Auditorium, where he conducted two more performances of *Petrushka*. A telegram from Auden wished the three of us a "Happy and Productive 1955."

In 1954 my long-dreamed-of project of recording the complete works of Anton Webern moved forward. The work it entailed, some of the most arduous in my life, was not part of the dream. Much of the music had never been published, and I had to copy scores from photostats of Webern's manuscripts, which Universal Edition, in Vienna, was willing to provide only because Stravinsky personally requested it. I also had to extract the instrumental parts, transposing some of them in the process. But the most difficult task was to convince musicians and singers to rehearse with me for concerts and recordings of the music. Since union rules did not permit the larger pieces—the three cantatas and the orchestral works—to be performed in our concerts, I had to rehearse each player and singer individually in his or her home. After solving the logistic problems of borrowing the Stravinsky automobile to adjust to the musicians' schedules, I had to drive countless miles.

Another obstacle was the musicians' generally negative attitude toward Webern, particularly when rehearsed alone and feeling like ciphers. Lawrence Morton's lure to a recalcitrant violinist, clarinetist, or other player was to offer a chance to perform a Beethoven, Brahms, or other classical solo work in a future concert. Gradually most of the musicians became engrossed in the music and were proud of their performances and recordings. Columbia

Records was persuaded to release the four-record, long-playing Webern album only on my guarantee to pay for it from future, but predictably never-forthcoming, royalties. Stravinsky helped by refusing to record his own music unless Columbia supported the Webern undertaking. His generous gift to me of time from his own recording sessions was responsible for the introduction to the public of this most influential twentieth-century composer's work, whose music was only rarely performed in concerts, if at all.[36]

In October we received a visit from Gasparo del Corso, proprietor of the Obelisco Gallery in Rome, and his wife, Irène Brin, the Italian correspondent for *Vogue.* Both of them were very elegant and chic (the word was a compliment then). I suppose she was my elder by ten years or more, but I fancied her. I saw her again a few times in Rome, but within the year she was dead of cancer.

1955

On January 9 I conducted a matinée Mozart and Beethoven concert in the State University at Tempe, Arizona, despite wooziness from a bumpy flight. The next morning I boarded an early train, the *Cascade,* from Los Angeles to Portland. Stravinsky was conducting the local orchestra in Tchaikovsky's Second Symphony, not there but in Salem, Oregon. The next day, we ate at "Jake's"—brass rails, paintings of opulent nudes and of tomahawking Indians—and boarded the Chicago-bound *City of Portland.* When we reached Laramie, I walked with Stravinsky in the icy, invigorating air, and told him that my father's younger brother died in infancy here and was buried in Greenwood Cemetery in 1899. In Chicago we separated, the Stravinskys going to Alabama, where he conducted his Symphony in E-flat, I heading home via Poughkeepsie on the *Wolverine.* On January 20 Stravinsky called me from the Hotel Tutweiler, Birmingham, to say that, to his surprise, he had enjoyed conducting his early opus. Two days later, in New York, Paul Rosenberg, Picasso's dealer, gave one of the Tauromachia engravings to Stravinsky. (It is now on the wall of my study.) That evening, we saw a terrifying play, *The Bad Seed.*

The next two days were spent with Balanchine in our hotel, the Gladstone, to discuss *Agon.* On the second day, while Vera Stravinsky was dining with the Eugene Bermans, Stravinsky, Mr. B., Kirstein, and I worked out an agreement to postpone the ballet until 1957; Stravinsky wanted to finish the *Canticum Sacrum* first. In the evening, unwisely ignoring Kirstein's warnings about the pretentiousness and preciousness of Truman Capote's *House of Flowers,*

36. "Mr. Craft attained worldwide fame in the mid-1950s with his set of the complete works of Schoenberg's disciple, Anton Webern, an album that soon became as essential to an intellectual's library as a copy of Joyce's *Ulysses*" (David Schiff, *The New York Times*, August 8, 1999).

we saw the first act of the play. Mr. B. had told us that he was getting six hundred dollars a week for the use of his name, "even though they don't use my choreography." After the theater we watched the ice-skaters at Rockefeller Center.

A few days later we were in Atlanta for a concert, in which Stravinsky conducted Mozart's Notturno. We were unable to escape a dinner with people whose Southern accents were wholly unintelligible to the Stravinskys and nearly so to me. One of them, a Mrs. Davison, made a gift to me of her uncle's book about the Duke of Rutland writing Shakespeare. We flew to New Orleans for the insane purpose of returning to Los Angeles on the *Southern Pacific*, wanting to see the Rio Grande, which flows close to the rails in a landscape that before the Pecos is almost totally deserted. The Stravinskys had not known that the town of Marfa was named for Marfa Ignatyevna, the old retainer in *The Brothers Karamazov*.

On arriving in Hollywood, we were told that Maria Huxley was near death, her "jaundice" having been diagnosed two weeks ago as cancer of the liver. Why did Aldous refuse for so long to acknowledge that her illness was cancer, as his friends knew years ago, quite soon after the first operation for the tumor in 1952? Today we call it "denial," but I now see his secrecy as supreme intelligence: he foresaw a dreadful period in which the speculations of everyone in his acquaintance would add to his anxieties. The end was foregone, and he could only hope for medical miracles. On February 6, we were at Gerald Heard's for tea when Aldous telephoned to tell him that it was hopeless, a matter of hours. Gerald cradled the receiver and burst out with: "At last the mask will be off. How much happier she will be out of the body." Stravinsky was horrified. That same day Aldous wrote to their son: "the malignancy is spreading almost explosively. I try not to cry when I see her, but it is difficult after thirty-six years." The next day he wrote to a friend: "Today she hardly recognizes anyone . . . It is hard to tell if she hears me; but I hope and think that something goes through the intervening barrier of physical disintegration and mental confusion. The *Bardo Thodal* maintains that something penetrates even after death . . . Think of her with love; it is the only thing we can do . . ."

On February 21 Stravinsky came to my concert of his flute, harp, guitar songs and Mozart's Adagio for Two Clarinets and Three Basset Horns. I turned pages for Ernst Krenek, who played his new piano piece.

On March 9 in Pittsburgh, where Stravinsky conducted concerts,[37] we celebrated their fifteenth wedding anniversary by seeing *Cinerama Holiday*. This includes one striking episode, a New Orleans jazz funeral. The procession *starts* in the aboveground cemetery, the same in which I once slept

---

37. In Pittsburgh in 1986 for the opening of an exhibition of Vera Stravinsky's paintings, a woman showed me several good ink portraits of Stravinsky that she had drawn during the March 1955 rehearsals and concert.

in 1943, and the players, with grace and great dignity of bearing, move, or strut, in a slow rhythm, not quite a dance. The simplicity of the music is indescribably touching.

At the beginning of April we flew to Rome. The Pincio was covered with Flowering Judas, wisteria was blooming everywhere, and in the Ethnographic Museum we saw a stunning gold crown on loan from Ethiopia. Agreeable hours were spent with the Carters, Licia and Roman Vlad, and with Nadia Boulanger and her aide-de-camp Annette Dieudonné. Vlad was promoting the notion that Schoenberg must have been familiar with the writings of Swedenborg when first experimenting with the 12-tone system. On April 6 Stravinsky conducted *Oedipus Rex* at the Foro Italico. The rehearsals had not gone well. At the one the night before, he shouted at the musicians, clapping his hands to emphasize the beat, conducting very badly, and, in a temper tantrum, storming out of the hall and wasting forty-five minutes of much-needed rehearsal time. At the rehearsal next morning the ensembles were ragged, and Stravinsky's promise the day before to beat a passage in 2 was today's certainty that he would do it in 4. After lunch with Nadia, we drove to the Campidoglio to see the equestrian of Marcus Aurelius, Michelangelo's *Moses* and his pavement design, going from there to Santa Prassede for the mosaics in the apse. The *Oedipus* performance somehow held together, and Magda Laszlo's Jocasta was inspiring, though too low for her voice. Henze came at intermission, and we ate at the Ristorante Fagiano with him, the Nabokovs, the Vlads, and Petrassi.

The next night, at Ranieri, the proprietor brought a 1937 guest book with Stravinsky's signature on the same page as Ribbentrop's. Stravinsky and Mme Sudeykina were en route to Positano at the time, not knowing that Stokowski and Garbo were there, drawing crowds.

April 9 being a warm spring day, we drove to Ostia Antiqua and hunted four-leaf-clovers in the acoustically live amphitheater. After Vera Stravinsky found one, we lunched at a seaside restaurant with the Panni family, Vlad, and Mario Peragallo, whose Violin Concerto had won a composition prize that was presented to him by Stravinsky at an official ceremony. During the meal, Fiora Peragallo, the composer's young wife, secretly arranged a late-evening rendezvous with me, explaining that she and her husband no longer regarded themselves as married. She would fetch me at the Hassler to see the film *The Barefoot Contessa*. In the event, she drove around the Pincio to a secluded spot and parked, whereupon her supposedly separated spouse suddenly appeared, slapped her, and took her home.

On April 16 Stravinsky came to my matinée concert in the Teatro Eliseo: Vlad's Divertimento; Webern's Five Orchestra Pieces; Dallapiccola's *Tre Laudi*; Stravinsky's Little Suites, *In Memoriam: Dylan Thomas*, songs for voice (Magda

Laszlo), flute, harp, and guitar, and the Concertino for 12. The dinner afterward, in the Excelsior, was for three hundred people.

In Venice on April 19 we heard the news of Albert Einstein's death. Later the same day we went to Verona to see San Zeno and Pisanello's *Annunciation* in San Fermo Maggiore, staying in a small, uncomfortable hotel. At midnight I taxied to the railroad station where Magda Laszlo had promised to emerge briefly during the stop of her Munich-bound sleeper. She failed to do so and I felt hurt. The next day I was in Milan for Vera Stravinsky's exhibition at the Del Sol Gallery. Denise Stravinsky was there with her stepfather, Michelangelo Spagno, who drove us to the Villa d'Este at Cernobbio, complaining all the way of his hellish marriage. I had liked him from the first, when he guided me around Rome in November 1951, and, earlier in the same year, in Venice, borrowed the *motoscafo* of his cousin, Mayor Spagno, for excursions to Chioggia and the lagoon islands. Since he was good-looking and vivacious, his marriage to the considerably older and plain Stephanie Guerzoni puzzled me. True, there was something of the gigolo, the Cagliostro, about him, but his suicide, a few years later, came as a shock.

From Milan, Mrs. Stravinsky and I went to Berne to see Mina Svitalski, the retired governess of Stravinsky's children, and to visit the Klee Museum. We then made a short trip through the Voralberg—onion-domed churches, roadside crucifixes, villages with sloping snow roofs—to Innsbruck and Webern's grave at Mittersill, returning on the *Alpine Express* to Milan, and from there by car to Lugano, where Stravinsky had a concert. This took place in the Teatro Kursaal with the excellent small orchestra of the Radio Della Svizzera-Italiana, whose principal cellist, Professor Engelbert Roentgen, a retired member of the Metropolitan Opera orchestra, was a good friend of my mother in his Woodstock years. He had a letter from her telling him to expect me. We dined with the orchestra's conductor, Otmar Nussio, who had prepared the program. While in Lugano we were taken to a private showing of the Thyssen Collection by its owner.

The day after the concert we went to Stuttgart, where Stravinsky conducted the Rundfunk orchestra and I recorded the Concertino, slow, uphill work. A limousine took us from there to Mannheim. There, in the Musiksaal im Rosengarten, Stravinsky conducted his Concerto for Piano and Winds with Shura Cherkassky. The composer knew his soloist well—he had praised his performance, in December 1943, of the *Three Movements from Petrushka*—and liked him personally, but had been rough on him in rehearsal, ridiculing him off-stage as a *"fificus"* (*tante*). The next day we flew from Frankfurt to Copenhagen in order to take one of the first trans-Arctic flights home. We spent an enjoyable hour with Frederick Ashton, who was staying in the same hotel, but after that Stravinsky was trapped by reporters and photographers. The long flight to the west coast of Greenland, to Winnipeg, and to Los Angeles began in the evening, but the sun never set and we had a clear view of "Greenland's icy mountains," as the hymn goes. We received little blocks of Greenland marble inscribed with our names and the date, souvenirs of this pioneering polar flight.

On our second day in California I began to rehearse the orchestra for the upcoming Ojai Festival, my second year as music director. The opening concert featured the San Francisco Ballet in *Le Gourmand* (Mozart's Divertimento, K. 247), William Walton's *Façade*, and *Renard*, this last with the original Esteban Frances costumes and Balanchine's choreography as reconstructed by Lew Christiansen. I conducted Bartók's Sonata for Percussion and Two Pianos on the matinée program of day two, and Monteverdi's *Vespers* that night. *Nigra sum*, sung by Marilyn Horne, received an ovation, an occasion that catapulted her to West Coast prominence. Ernst Krenek attended my rehearsals for *Vespers*, as well as the concert, and the following letter from him marks the beginning of our close friendship:

Dear Bob: I wanted very much to talk to you after yesterday's rehearsal at Ojai, but I knew you were rushed with the afternoon concert coming up on the heels of your exhausting rehearsal, and we had to return to Los Angeles without delay.

You may guess that I, of course, find the work by Monteverdi a masterpiece of extraordinary proportions. I was somewhat acquainted with it, but had not studied it closely, nor did I ever hear it. And I am full of admiration [for] this perfectly magnificent choir, which, in my opinion, was as well prepared as anybody could wish.[38] The soloists, too, were, on the whole, up to your and Monteverdi's demands, which is saying a great deal. The instrumental ensemble lived up to the customary Los Angeles pattern of the flesh being willing but the spirit sometimes weak (—or is it the other way around . . . ?). Just the same, the effect was overwhelming and the experience something I shall not forget soon.

There are many questions I should very much like to discuss with you if you find time for it: for instance, the relation of the Redlich adaptation to the Malipiero edition, which *prima facie* one would assume to be a sort of "original," and your decision to rearrange the whole thing the way you did. Also: where did the two pieces come from which were MSS? I was unable to check quickly whether they are in the Redlich score at all, and in what shape, if so. Finally, what is uppermost in my mind is the question of the rhythmic and metric style of the interpretation with reference to the significance of the bar lines. I could go on right here blossoming out in a whole essay on this point, especially if I had a score—but I think it would be better to talk about these

38. The Pomona College Chorus conducted by William Russell.

problems if you have time for it. Will you call me one of these days? The number is still Hollywood 5–6087.

Once more, compliments and congratulations, and all the best, yours,

Ernst

At the Sunday matinée concert I conducted Stravinsky's *Greeting Prelude*, Beethoven's *Egmont* Overture, Schoenberg's *Accompaniment to a Cinematographic Scene*, and Brahms's Symphony No. 2. Stravinsky conducted Eudice Shapiro in his Violin Concerto in the second half, thus establishing the Ojai Festival as a nationally newsworthy event. I still regard my performance of the Brahms as a peak of my life as a conductor.

In Hollywood, Stravinsky began work on the *Canticum Sacrum*, his cantata for San Marco in Venice. He explained his concept of the three theological virtues as the centerpiece of the opus, and asked me to help him find texts from the Bible about Hope, saying "there are not many." At the start he thought that this "San Marco Concerto" would require a male chorus, four male solo singers, three bassoons, five trumpets, five trombones, and solo strings. Perhaps he had one or two countertenors in mind, the duet, "Sound the Trumpet," in Purcell's *Come Ye Sons of Art* having made a lasting impression on him. He had been reading Edmund Wilson's *Dead Sea Scrolls* and was devastated by the idea of an Essene prototype Christ.

At the end of May and in early June I conducted five Mozart concerts in the Los Angeles County Museum, and played the glass harmonica piece on a celesta. (I later heard an air-check recording of this broadcast.) I was also busy recording Webern; and I supervised a long session of the songs with piano, sung, every note perfectly on pitch and each piece two or three times through, by Marni Nixon, accompanied by Leonard Stein. On June 24 Stravinsky wrote his *Hommage à Webern* for Universal Edition's memorial book for the tenth anniversary of the composer's death.

July began with a visit from Georg Solti, who sought coaching on *Oedipus Rex*, which he would conduct with the Los Angeles Philharmonic. I spent the next three weeks rehearsing each chorus singer in Webern's Second Cantata individually, and recorded the choral movement in Stravinsky's session on the 28th, during which he taped his four-horn version of *Podblyudnye* and the Three Childhood Songs.

Isherwood's diary for July 21[39] recounts a dinner with Tony Duquette and Ivan Moffat: "Igor and Vera were so sweet, as always. Igor got quite drunk, which was nice, because he likes to, but it was a pity in another way because I missed one more opportunity—and how many more will there be—of talking to him quietly." Isherwood and his companions were forever going on "wagons" and did not seem to understand that inebriation was not

39. Isherwood, *Diaries*.

a moral question for Russians, who drank vodka because (1) they liked it, and (2) cholera had been a constant threat throughout their early lives. Stravinsky himself took it only with caviar and preferred pure Dutch gin, *eau de ginèvre*, from terracotta bottles that were kept in refrigerators at maximum cold temperatures. Neither ice nor vermouth was ever mixed with this bracing one-gulp drink. When I met the Stravinskys, they were unaware of the blue laws still in force in New York, where alcoholic beverages were not available on Sundays until after church hours, and I recall a Sunday lunch in the Gladstone Hotel that began with harsh language from the composer to a waiter and a lunch that we carried upstairs to our rooms, room-service being unavailable on Sundays.

Isherwood's entry for August 1 describes "a charming evening with the Stravinskys last night. Igor is really one of the most uninhibitedly sweet people I know. He threw his arms around me and told me how fond he was of me. A conversation with slimy Lukas Voss [*sic*] under the impression that he was Michael Mann. Luckily I only asked: 'How's your father?' "[40] At one point Isherwood confessed to having written the *Souvenir des Vacances* in *Oxford Poetry 1927*, explaining that, not having been at Oxford, he had to appear anonymously. His parody of Eliot is the book's best contribution, just as, despite stiff competition, the preface by Auden and Cecil Day Lewis, writing alternate paragraphs, is the worst.

On the 4th of August we drove to the Mission of San Juan Bautista—where Alfred Hitchcock filmed *Vertigo*—spent the night in Carmel, and continued to Yosemite for a rest. Deaths overshadowed other events in August, as well as earlier and later in the year. Thomas Mann's in Zurich on August 12 saddened both Stravinskys, who sent an affectionate cable to his widow. At about the same time Oscar Moss, the Monday Evening Concerts' principal patron, died suddenly. Lawrence Morton formed an emergency committee, named Stravinsky honorary chairman, and wrote a letter over his signature: "In my opinion, Monday Evening Concerts are presenting the most valuable selection of music of any concert organization that I know of today. They give Los Angeles international prestige of a kind you would know about only if you traveled abroad as much as I do."

I conducted a memorial performance of Monteverdi's *Vespers* (October 3), after which Norton Simon assumed the responsibilities of sponsor. On August 26 we went to a surprise birthday party for Isherwood in Tony Duquette's theater.[41] The next day the Stravinsky kitchen was invaded by an opossum through the cat's back-door flap. The ratlike prehensile beast

40. As a Quaker conscientious objector during World War II, Isherwood had known Lukas Foss's father, a professor at Haverford College. The misspelling of the name is Isherwood's. Michael Mann, son of Thomas, was a violist and friend of Stravinsky, as well as of Isherwood.

41. Duquette and his wife "Beegle" (Elizabeth) were acquaintances of the Stravinskys

ran through the house and hid in Stravinsky's studio, from which I chased it with a broom to the side door, strategically left open as the only egress. Cornered, the animal snarled, but did not exit until hours later.

The next day we dined with the Joseph Szigetis in their Palos Verdes home, where he showed us his collection of Bartókiana and a letter to him from Rilke dated 1916. On September 5 Aldous came for dinner and gave the typescript of his "Heaven and Hell" essay to me. He stayed for my rehearsal of Gesualdo and Monteverdi in the Stravinsky living room. By the time of our next dinner with him, he had read both volumes of Alfred Einstein's *The Italian Madrigal*, apparently remembering everything in them. He wanted to know more about Bartolomeo Tromboncino, the great frottola composer and a friend of Michelangelo, but I knew only a few pieces of his music.

Stravinsky had hoped to finish the *Canticum*'s Three Virtues movement by September 30, his wife's name day (*Fides*), but was five days late. Betweentimes Aldous invited us to dinner at "The Captain's Table." He undertipped, as always, and Vera Stravinsky surreptitiously supplemented the perk.

On October 11 I recorded eight Gesualdo madrigals, and after the session went with Aldous to Hamburger Hamlet, where we talked until 1 A.M.; he liked not being recognized. He went on, as he had done before, about stirpiculture (adolescent boys introduced to sexual intercourse by post-menopausal women), as in the Oneida[42] and various other early-nineteenth-century utopian communities. The following afternoon he corrected in black ink the spelling mistakes that I found in his essay on "Music in the Court of Ferrara." He had typed it himself, wearing his celluloid Chinese goggles, which block out peripheral light and substitute pinpoint perforations for lenses, thus forcing the eyes to move, both exercising them and preventing staring.

Aldous came to most of our madrigal rehearsals at Stravinsky's house and became absorbed in the historical background of the music and the court of Ferrara. As Dorothy Crawford recounts, he seemed to relish "the gory details of Gesualdo's murder of his first wife, her lover, and the

---

for a time, through Isherwood, and we dined at their home at least twice. He was a renowned interior decorator and costume designer of "fake, vulgar, gilded baubles, bangles, and beads" (*New York Times* obituary), in other words, exactly what Hollywood wanted. Nevertheless, he had an exhibition in the Louvre in 1961, and in the same year shared a Tony Award for designing the musical *Camelot*. As an artist he was a magpie, but he perfectly represents the aesthetic of Hollywood in the 1960s. Beegle was beautiful, blond hair tight around her head, boyish in behavior and build, shy, silent. Duquette staged-designed operas for the San Francisco Opera that could be described as phantasmagorical.

42. See *Desire and Duty at Oneida*, edited by R. S. Fogarty (Indiana University Press, 2001).

son Gesualdo suspected of being illegitimate," and recounted them in a pre-concert lecture on October 17 to introduce the performance of ten more madrigals that Morton and I had transcribed. The music critic Albert Goldberg reported that there were not enough seats for the crowd, and that Huxley "spiced the dry bones of history with wit and even a shade of malice . . . [Gesualdo was described as] a masochist to a degree that one does not dare even quote Mr. Huxley on the subject in this family newspaper."

Our bass, Charles Scharbach, a piano-tuner by profession, had absolute pitch, which helped us through the difficulties of intonation in the madrigals. I pointed a finger up or down in anticipation of pitch difficulties, telling the singers to think higher or lower, as the context demanded. When the recording was released, *Time* magazine, to my surprise and embarrassment, featured me in an article titled "The Mad Madrigalist."

On October 20 Jerome Robbins arrived from New York to discuss the staging of *Noces* at La Scala with its composer. On the 22nd, Stravinsky received Auden's "Metalogue for the *Magic Flute*" in a letter from the poet, and was deeply moved by the lines about himself. On the 26th the three of us grieved at the news from the Marquesa de Slauzol in Madrid of Ortega y Gasset's death, and cabled condolences. In November we heard several San Francisco Opera performances at the Shrine, including one of *Don Giovanni* preceded by a bombastic speech about the reopening of the Vienna Opera, and a sloppy performance of the Third *Leonora* Overture, as if Mozart's overture were not enough. Elizabeth Schwarzkopf was a superb Donna Elvira, Cesare Siepi a great Don, but Leinsdorf's tempi were hell-bent, his reading perfunctory, and he actually cut the epilogue.

On the 28th I conducted Machaut's Mass, two of Schoenberg's male choruses, and Bach's Cantata 84, with Marilyn Horne. On the 30th David Raksin and his girlfriend, the singer Peggy Lee, accompanied Aldous and ourselves to Capitol Records on Sunset Boulevard to hear Gesualdo playbacks. The next day we left for New Orleans on the *Sunset Limited*, changing trains there for Chicago and New York.

Shortly after checking in at the Gladstone, the Stravinskys, who had admired Clouzot's film *The Wages of Fear*, insisted on seeing his *Les Diaboliques*, which failed to faze them but terrified me. On the 29th Stravinsky completed the first variation of his arrangement of *Vom Himmel hoch*, after which we went to a cocktail party at Robert Fizdale's and Arthur Gold's with Auden, Copland, Virgil Thomson, Jerome Robbins, and Sylvia Marlowe.

We spent the afternoon of the 30th in the Museum of Natural History with my nine-year-old niece, Diane, then took her to *Oklahoma!* On the last day of the year we listened to test pressings of my Webern album with Milton Babbitt and Arthur Berger. Just before midnight Balanchine called, inviting us to a party for Doris Duke, but we decided to go to bed early. He was looking for a City Ballet benefactress, but we did not believe she would be it, and Stravinsky did not like being used as society bait, even by Mr. B.

1956

I spent New Year's Day reading Chekhov's *Letters* and Harold Nicolson's *Diplomacy*. (An apothegm in the latter, "self-satisfaction leads first to a loss of adaptability and second to a decline in imagination.") Mr. B. dined with us. The next day I went to Kingston, with the usual tug at the heart and the ton of guilt because of my delinquency with regard to my family.

On January 11 Ernest Ansermet and his wife came for tea. Relations were apparently cordial, but the undertow was almost palpable. Ansermet pointedly gave his new recording of the string orchestra *Grosse Fuge* to me, not to Stravinsky. After they left, Sam Dushkin and David Protetch taxied us and our luggage to Pennsylvania Station for our journey to California. My niece Kristin was born that night.

The day after detraining in Pasadena, Stravinsky and I watched Balanchine's staging of the *Magic Flute* on the Marions' TV. (The Stravinskys did not have television until years later.) The tempi were plodding and the diction unclear, which made the Auden–Kallman text sound like a foreign language. After dining at Luau, we listened to a tape of Dylan Thomas's April 1953 talk at Harvard ("students doing their doctorates on Rilke and the gold standard"). The next evening at the Kantor Gallery I talked about Luigi Nono's *Incontri*, but too fast and nervously because the Stravinskys and Trude Schoenberg were sitting in the first row. When I conducted the piece at the next Monday concert, it was hissed, a rare occurrence with our audiences. Afterwards Frau Schoenberg collected the autographs of the performers and audience notables to send to Nono, now her son-in-law. She also came to a party at the Stravinskys'.

The composer completed his arrangement of the third *Himmel hoch* variation on January 26. Heard and Isherwood came for dinner. Afterward we heard Marilyn Horne sing Mozart's *Bella mia fiamma*, K. 528, and his *Requiem* in a Royce Hall concert conducted by Roger Wagner. The next evening, Aldous and I listened to the first part of an inept dramatization of *Brave New World* on the Stravinsky automobile radio, after which the four of us dined at Lawrence Morton's. On February 6 we lunched with Aldous at Yolanda's, and in the evening took him to the Monday concert.

Stravinsky completed Variation IV of *Vom Himmel hoch* on February 9. The same evening he presided in the control room as I recorded Webern's *Das Augenlicht* and the choral movements of his cantatas *opera* 29 and 31.

The remainder of February and beginning of March were occupied with an exhibition in the Santa Barbara Museum of Vera Stravinsky's paintings, and with the editing and recording of a fifteen-minute suite from *Petrushka* for synchronization to an animated-cartoon film. Stravinsky calibrated the timings of the excerpts to be used, chosen not by him but by the producers, and on March 2 I rehearsed and taped them during two hours and forty-five minutes of a recording session in the Warner Brothers Sound Studio on Santa Monica Boulevard. In the remaining quarter of an hour Stravinsky ran through this new "suite." Three days later we edited the tapes and went directly from the editing studio to the Monday concert, where I conducted Bach's *Weinen, Klagen, Sorgen, Fragen.*

Aldous was with us for the Santa Barbara vernissage on February 28. Meanwhile, I had conducted a Monday concert of Dallapiccolo's *Goethe Lieder* and Stockhausen's *Kontrapunkte* in another Monday concert. My final Webern recording session took place on March 8, from nine to midnight. The Ricercar consumed thirty-five minutes of recording time, the Concerto twenty-five, the Variations two hours. Stravinsky was in the control booth.

Transcribing Gesualdo from the photostat negatives of the Library of Congress score edition took most of my remaining time in March. I remember completing two madrigals during one night. I conducted only one concert during the month, which Stravinsky attended to hear Bach's Brandenburg Concerto No. 3. I remember only one visitor at the time, the composer Boris Blacher, from Berlin, who conversed with Stravinsky in Russian and with me in English about our forthcoming visit to his city. I read *Gods, Graves, and Scholars* to the Baroness. On Good Friday I drove the Stravinskys to St. Matthias, and from there, at three o'clock, to the Farmers' Market, where from a distance we saw Aldous and his new wife. On this only day of the year that Stravinsky abstained from alcohol, he made us feel the full pain of his deprivation. At night we listened to Schütz's *St. John Passion.*

On April 6 Stravinsky gave his manuscript copy of Gesualdo's *Io pur respiro* to me. That day Aldous and Laura came for dinner. The Stravinskys were impeccable hosts, but Isherwood and Gerald were subdued and aloof. Isherwood's diary reveals more:

> Supper at the Stravinskys'—Michael Barrie, Bill Stroud, Chris Wood, Gerald Heard, Aldous and Laura Huxley were also there. On first meeting (actually I met her first the day before yesterday, when I went around to the house to talk to Aldous) . . . I find I don't altogether like Laura. She is good-looking, smart and stylish in a "sensible way" and adequately intelligent; but she has a curious tactlessness . . . She tries, I think, to be friendly and man-to-man, and only succeeds in being rather rude. However, Aldous seems very happy with her. He was wearing a twenty-year-old tie (from Paris?), which he described as looking like an early Rouault.
>
> Talk about dreams. Igor had once dreamed a passage of music which he was able to use . . .
>
> Both Igor and Vera were adorable as usual; and Bob was in a friendly

mood.[43] They served magnums of champagne, which Gerald managed to drink and disapprove of simultaneously.[44] They're planning to go to Greece in June. Igor looked very well, but complained of all kinds of ailments. Michael kept Bill Stroud off in a corner, as if he weren't big enough to listen to grown-up conversation.

May, the month of the Ojai Festival, began with a late dinner at Ciro's on Sunset Boulevard, where Maurice Chevalier was performing. I did not know that he and Stravinsky had been friends, but he invited us, with Louis Jourdan and Jean-Pierre Aumont, to his table, where they reminisced about Paris until 3 A.M. The next night we saw Pirandello's *The Man with a Flower in His Mouth*[45] in a small theater on Melrose Boulevard.

On May 12 Lawrence Morton and I met Magda Laszlo's train from New York and installed her in the Tropicana Motel on Santa Monica Boulevard. Since she spoke just enough Franglais to make conversation impossible, the Stravinskys invited the Huxleys for dinner to converse with her in Italian.

Though none too pleased with the importing of this strikingly, if coldly, beautiful woman as the star vocalist of the festival, Marilyn Horne accommodatingly drove me to Pomona for rehearsals of Schütz's *Es ging ein Sämann aus*. Understanding the situation, the Stravinskys invited her with Laszlo to dinner at the Bel Air Hotel. The Ojai fog and cold dampened our spirits, but the programs were good: Mozart's Symphony No. 39; the Schubert-Webern Dances; Act 2, scene 7 of *Così fan tutte* (Laszlo); *The Rake*, Act 1, scene 3 (Laszlo); Beethoven's Second Symphony; Brahms's Serenade in A; Bartók's *Three Village Scenes* (Horne); Manuel de Falla's *Maese Pedro* (a nervous, freckled boy-soprano soloist); Mozart's Divertimento, K. 251; Dallapiccolo's *Sex Carmina Alcaei* and *Due Liriche di Anacreonte*; Bach's *Wedding* Cantata (Laszlo); the world premiere of *Vom Himmel hoch*; Schütz's *Es ging ein Sämann aus*; Bach's Cantata No. 18; the Sonata from Monteverdi's *Vespers*; and *Noces*, conducted by Stravinsky. The Huxleys gently criticized me for allowing the sentimental Schubert to come between the Mozart masterpieces.

In mid-June we left for New York on *The City of Los Angeles*. A few hours out, Las Vegas glittered from thirty miles away in the clear Nevada night. In New York the Stravinskys spent a day with Balanchine, Berman, and Davidova at Alice De Lamar's country home, but I remained in the city to hear a CBS broadcast of our Ojai performances on tape, and to dine with Jean Stein at her Sutton Place apartment. The street there was nearly blocked

43. Unusual?

44. Gerald was a teetotaler until he became a Wetherly Drive Regular. Thereafter he drank champagne (only) and always expected it.

45. Huxley had urged us to see this play about a man with cancer of the throat, the cause, a few years later, of his own death.

by reporters and photographers waiting for Marilyn Monroe and Arthur Miller, then residing in the same building, to emerge.

A scandal occurred when Stravinsky refused to release an interview he had given to Emily Coleman of *Newsweek*. Elliott Carter and Milton Babbitt came to the Gladstone to listen to a recording of Elliott's Orchestra Variations, and we went twice to the theater, to see *My Fair Lady* and *A Most Happy Fella*, from which (the latter) we fled after a few most unhappy minutes. Stravinsky finished reading David Magarshack's *Turgeniev*.

On June 27, joined by Lawrence Morton, we sailed for Patras on the SS *Vulcania*. On July 7, about six hours east of Barcelona, the ship acquired an escort of dolphins. We began to sing *"Zefiro torna,"* Monteverdi's marvelous setting of Petrarch's sonnet, which we had recently performed at a Monday concert, using Stravinsky's copy of Nadia Boulanger's transcription. What intrigued Stravinsky about the piece was the syncopated rhythm of the passacaglia basso ostinato. I slapped out the beats on the Vulcania's taffrail.[46]

In Venice, Stravinsky spent September 17 playing *Agon* for Balanchine, with whom we ate most of our meals during the next three days. The City Ballet was performing at La Fenice, but Stravinsky would not attend on the evening that had a work by Glazunov on the program. During the stay we also saw Arthur Sachs, Paco Lagerstrom, our scientist friend from the California Institute of Technology in Pasadena, and, frequently, Eugene Berman. One afternoon in Harry's Bar we saw Tony Gandarillas, nephew of Madame Errazuriz and homosexual husband of Juanita, with whom Stravinsky had had a passionate affair. Stravinsky told me that he first met Tony in the Chilean Embassy in St. Petersburg.

In the last week of September we were in Berlin for concerts. I remember a lunch with Boris Blacher, Hans Stuckenschmidt, Josef Rufer, Henze, and two senators. On Vera Stravinsky's name day we dined in a private room in the Aben Restaurant with Hans Von Benda and Senator Bach: caviar with schnapps, Mosel with *Lachs*, Chateau Latour with saddle of deer. Back in the hotel the composer Giselher Klebe, young, thin, bespectacled, and overwhelmed to meet Stravinsky, came for tea.

By October 5 we were installed in the Vier Jahreszeiten Hotel in Munich. Otto Klemperer was there as well, having come to be with his wife, who had had a severe heart attack and was not expected to live. Letters from Trude Schoenberg, Nadia Boulanger, and Marilyn Horne awaited us, and packages of books: Dodds's *The Greeks and the Irrational*; Ostrogorsky's *Byzantine History*; Svevo's *Hoax*; Char's *Hypnos Waking* (*"Notre héritage n'est précédé d'aucun testament"*; *"L'acte est vièrge, même repété"*); Kitto's *The Greeks*.

Early in November, I went to Paris to conduct a concert in Pierre Boulez's "Domaine Musicale," feeling very unhappy about leaving Stravinsky in the

---

46. Our experiences in Greece, Turkey, and Venice, in July and August, are described in my *Chronicle of a Friendship*.

hospital in Munich.[47] I was graciously looked after by Boulez and by his partner at the time, my New York schoolmate, the pianist Paul Jacobs, with earring and makeup, looking unrecognizably different than he did in the States.

In Paris at the beginning of December, during a stopover between Rome and London, I recorded the *Canticum Sacrum* and *Vom Himmel hoch* Variations. The solo singers, chorus, and orchestra were the same who had performed both pieces with me in my Domaine Musicale concert in November. Boulez was at the controls and ran the session expertly, except that in the *Surge aquilo* text he allowed a few wrong Latin words to get by him. Since the recording took place in a resonant church with a less than fine-tuned organ, we had to contend with acoustical problems. Entering the church, Stravinsky was greeted by Alexander Tansman, his close friend in Hollywood during the war years, and the author of the only biography of Stravinsky covering that time. Stravinsky cut him dead, ignored his outstretched hand, and did not utter a word in response to his welcome. After the first performance in Paris of the 1952 Cantata, Stravinsky had received a letter from him criticizing his choice of text for the tenor ricercar, and it was clear that Stravinsky was still unforgiving. Tansman was crushed.

1957

We remained in New York until the end of January, primarily because Stravinsky had to conduct a group of concerts with the New York Philharmonic. In the early days of the year Jean Stein introduced me to Philip Rahv, editor of *Partisan Review*, who asked me to interview Stravinsky for the magazine. I mention this because the idea of "Conversations with Stravinsky" was born in that moment, the series of five books that gave so much diversion to Stravinsky and provided so much lucrative employment to musicological hacks after his death. Following the Rahv meeting, I joined Lincoln Kirstein and Carleton Sprague Smith (flutist and musicologist) on the stage of Carnegie Hall in a panel discussion about Stravinsky's upcoming concerts. The Stravinskys went twice to the theater, first to *Happy Hunting*, starring the brassy-voiced and brazen Ethel Merman, whom the Stravinskys liked to the extent of asking their lawyer, Arnold Weissberger, to invite her to a dinner with them. The second occasion was *The Good Woman of Szechuan*, which we saw simply to appraise the Phoenix Theater as a possible home for a short run of *The Rake's Progress*, Kirstein's latest brainstorm.

On January 7 and 8 I rehearsed the New York Philharmonic for Stravinsky in *Petrushka* and *Perséphone*. Ansermet, in New York to conduct the NBC Symphony, came to both rehearsals, primarily to see the effects on Stravinsky of his stroke three months ago, or so I suspected, but also to revile the 1947

47. See *Stravinsky: Chronicle of a Friendship*.

version of *Petrushka* to me. January 7 was Vera Stravinsky's Russian-calendar birthday. Her husband, who had felt the shadow of mortality pass over him in recent months, gave her a very moving gift, a gold chain-bracelet, each link of which was a letter of "I LOVE YOU." He had designed it himself and gone with Lucia Davidova to Tiffany's shortly after our arrival in New York to have it made. The concerts had a revivifying effect on him and restored his confidence. I stayed backstage during them, talking to Dimitri Mitropoulos, the orchestra's music director, the phenomenal musician who conducted an entire season, rehearsals and concerts, without looking at a score. Luigi Dallapiccolo and Ansermet were in the audience, and on January 12, Stravinsky and I went with the former to hear a tape of his *An Mathilde* at the home of the Columbia Records engineer and photographer Fred Plaut. I remember a lunch at the Brussels restaurant on Fifty-sixth Street with two *Time* interviewers a few days later. We saw three more plays: Jean Anouilh's *Waltz of the Toreadors;* Graham Greene's *Potting Shed,* performed for an audience of priests; and *Waiting for Godot,* with Bert Lahr, a great realization of a great play.

Awaiting me on our return to Hollywood—by train: Stravinsky's cardiologist did not permit him to fly—was a letter from Souvtchinsky at 15, rue Saint-Saëns, discussing my projected book *Avec Stravinsky.* He wanted to invite Stockhausen, Boulez, André Schaeffner,[48] and Hermann Scherchen to contribute, and he concluded, graciously: *"Je n'ai pas besoin de vous dire comme j'étais heureux de vous avoir connu et d'avoir pu constater et comprendre votre immense valeur en tout que musicien et en tout qui homme."* My answer began, as always, with apologies for my tardiness:

> *Cher ami,* I have just returned from N.Y. where, among other work, I rehearsed the Philharmonic for Stravinsky. He has had a remarkable recovery and looks infinitely better, even transformed, since you saw him last.
>
> Let us keep the title *Avec Stravinsky.* Of course I do not want to be alone in such a book, so please ask Stockhausen to write something, preferably an analysis. (He can do that, but since he can also make metaphysical statements about musical missions I would not press him for a general article.) Boulez should contribute a piece on "Stravinsky and Debussy," perhaps limiting himself to *Rossignol-Sacre. You* should do an essay on the setting of Russian in *Renard* and *Noces.* Scherchen should be asked for his memoirs of Stravinsky at the 1923 Weimar *Histoire du Soldat.* Schaeffner is learned in areas that the rest of us know nothing about. If he could be persuaded to write about primitive sources, God knows what kind, it would be much more useful than yet another "appreciation."

48. An ethnomusicologist who had done fieldwork in Africa, and an early Stravinsky biographer.

Stravinsky is delighted to have Giacometti in the book. No, let us not ask Mme Stravinsky to do a drawing; no family this time. I will send a photograph of my ithyphallic Picasso, a single-line drawing from the "Ragtime" period of a man in a state of tumescence. Stravinsky gave it to me four years ago after a concert in which I conducted his "jazz" pieces. He will ask Schoenberg's widow for permission to use two letters to him from her husband.[49]

Let me propose a new idea. A Trotskyite New York magazine called *Partisan Review* asked me for an interview with Stravinsky. The format appeals to me because the subject can change with each question without connecting-material modulations. I can ask *Partisan* to let you print this in French, and it wouldn't be a reprint because our book would appear first. Let me know your reaction to this.

With all best wishes and with a *nostalgie terrible pour ces merveilleux jours avec vous*[50] *à Paris. Vous ne pouvez pas imaginer comme j'ai envie de quitter ce désert de luxe et de revenir.*

In February, I conducted two Monday concerts: on the 4th, Couperin's Third Tenebra Lesson, Bach's cantata, *Tritt auf die Glaubensbahn*, with soprano Grace-Lynn Martin and bass Robert Oliver; and on the 18th, Schoenberg's Serenade and Monteverdi's *Il Ballo dell'ingrate*, with Oliver singing the part of Pluto and Catherine Gayer that of An Ungrateful Soul. The Stravinskys gave parties after both evenings. We also received visits from Elliott Carter and Peter Brook. Gerald Heard, affectionate and gentle as a moth with Stravinsky, came daily to teach him breathing exercises.

At my insistence Pierre Boulez had been invited to conduct his *Le Marteau sans maître* at a Monday Concert, in which, in the first half, I would perform Thomas Tallis's *Lamentations*. Boulez had just arrived at the Plymouth Hotel, New York. To help defray the expense of the trip, UCLA offered him six hundred dollars to participate in a panel discussion with me and two members of their music staff. He wrote saying that he would travel via San Francisco, where he would stay with his friend Hans Popper.[51] Boulez's letter mentioned "long conversations" in New York with Jean Stein and described a new piece of his for flute and instruments, and his concept of "controlled improvisation." In another letter he asked me to arrange for him to stay in a hotel in order to work freely.

49. Stravinsky did ask and was refused.

50. After this letter Souvtchinsky and I adopted the *tu-toyer* form.

51. A Viennese refugee, Popper made a fortune in scrap metal at the end of World War II, removing smashed tanks and artillery from Okinawa and other Japanese islands. He lived in Japan part-time, the rest in San Francisco. We did not know him at this date but, at Boulez's instigation, met him in Vienna in 1958. He was a patron of the Domaine Musicale. We saw him several times in New York in 1959 and later that year in Tokyo, where he exchanged Stravinsky's concert-cachet yen for dollars.

The first two weeks of March belonged to Boulez. I met his flight from San Francisco at the Burbank Airport on March 2, drove him to the Tropicana Motel, where Magda Laszlo had stayed in 1956 and Glenn Watkins would stay in 1960, and then to lunch at the Stravinskys', which became a daily routine. He described a visit to Virgil Thomson in New York and his amusement on seeing that the eminent composer-critic was orchestrating Brahms's Chorale Variations for organ. I attended Boulez's rehearsals with him and learned his technique of double-beating the fermatas, the second to release the first and simultaneously give the new beat. On March 4 I rehearsed the Tallis *Lamentations* in the Stravinsky living room. Never having heard of the composer, Boulez, who had no musico-historical sense ("praise be amnesia"), was much relieved to discover that he was not a contemporary.[52] Afterward we drove with the Stravinskys to the Santa Monica beach to watch the annual migration of the grunions into the sea.

Meanwhile, a letter had come from Krenek:[53]

Dear Bob: I understand that Pierre Boulez will be in this area for some part of next week, and I assume you will be in close contact with him. Since we should very much like to see him and possibly to contribute to making his visit pleasant, I would appreciate if you would call me as soon as possible so that we may see what arrangements can be made. I am writing to you since I don't know how to reach you by telephone.

All the best, until soon, as ever yours,

Ernst Krenek

On March 5 I recorded the first, fifth, sixth, and seventh movements of Schoenberg's Serenade with, in the control room, Stravinsky, Boulez, Krenek, and Lawrence Morton. Afterward David Raksin took us to hear Oscar Peterson at the Peacock Club. Three days later the UCLA (Royce Hall) panel discussion took place, with Boulez, Lukas Foss, Paul Des Marais, and myself. Perhaps it was recorded—I do not know—but Stravinsky, in the third row, made a drawing of the four of us. On March 12 I drove Boulez to the airport for New York.

On March 27 the first copy of my Webern album arrived, and Stravinsky and I spent the evening playing the four records. He now thought the Concerto and String Quartet too arid, and was most intrigued by the last movement of the Second Cantata. In April letters came from Hermann Scherchen, inviting me to his electronic-music studio at Gravesano, and from Dallapiccola, sending the score of his *Concerto per la notte di Natale 1956*. Isherwood stopped

---

52. In 1995 Boulez invited the Tallis Scholars to perform Gesualdo's Responses for Holy Saturday on a program with his own *Répons*.

53. All letters from Ernst Krenek are from *Stravinsky: Selected Correspondence* edited by Robert Craft, Robert Gottlieb, and Eva Resnikova (New York: Alfred A. Knopf, 1985).

by one afternoon, bringing the typescript of E. M. Forster's *Maurice*; he was Forster's, as well as Somerset Maugham's, literary executor. I found it difficult to believe that Forster actually wrote it. Isherwood's diary for April 6 records:

> It was our Dorothy's cooking night. We invited Gerald, the Stravinskys and Bob Craft. Gerald arrived on time and at once began talking mescaline, which is becoming more and more irritating as he refuses to give us any. The Stravinskys were nearly three-quarters of an hour late—they hadn't been able to find the way—and Bob Craft was sick with a terrible headache in the car[54] . . . Igor and Vera were both greatly upset over this—he more than she—one sees how deeply they love him. Vera wanted to know didn't we have some Miltown or anything similar? So Don went down to the Masselinks and got some Equanil. Quite soon, Bob had apparently recovered and was with us at the table, laughing and eating stuffed chicken.
>
> Igor, in his seventy-fifth year, looks good but complains of insomnia. He asked Gerald how to meditate, saying that he might as well do this while he was lying awake. Igor said, "I am not sure I am creative, only inventive." He said, "All the time I am saying to myself—yes, I am thinking, but am I thinking well?" He was so sweet and touching.
>
> Dorothy had never heard of Stravinsky. She thought she recognized Igor as a Jewish comic on the Molly Goldberg show.

Letters came from Boulez thanking me for my *"accueil et l'amitié"*; from my *"reconnaissant et devoué ami,* Luigi Dallapiccolo"; and from my mother, reminding me of our Sunday family dinners and our drives in the Catskill mountains; how far, but also how little, have I grown away from my roots. On April 12 I read a thousand-word message for a "Voice of America" recording to be broadcast from Berlin, and we dined with Edward James at Bel-Air. A few days later Mrs. Schoenberg and Joseph Rufer[55] came to tea. She said that at Schoenberg's 1924 performance of *Pierrot Lunaire* in Venice the three piccolo G-flats, sounding like a train conductor's whistle, were followed by a voice from the audience shouting *"Partenza."*

On April 26 Stravinsky completed the full score of *Agon.* He also completed Gesualdo's seven-part *Illumina nos* on May 5. I had transcribed the five surviving parts of it the previous week, and would record it in late May (22). I remember driving Stravinsky to have the *Agon* reproduced by the ammoniac ozalid process. When his soft-pencil on onionskin manuscript

---

54. I have been subject all of my adult life to ophthalmic migraines, particularly at sunset after eye-straining afternoons.

55. A former pupil of Schoenberg in Berlin. He was in Los Angeles to compile a descriptive catalog of Schoenberg's manuscripts and paintings.

score began to slip from his hand rapidly page by page, he said "Slippery when dry," as if from the tip of his tongue, a reference to the "Slippery When Wet" signs on oily, rarely-rained-upon California highways. On the same day a note came from Krenek at Princeton:

> Dear Bob: I should like to congratulate you upon the Webern album. I was lucky enough to get a copy—it seems they are selling rapidly. So far I have played only the Symphony, which I found not only very clear, but also intense and sinewy, in welcome contrast to the pseudo-ethereal style that has already become a kind of convention for Webern's music. I am eagerly looking forward to playing the whole set.
>
> Your study on Webern is excellent in its fresh approach to a subject which in my opinion those who were too close to it have so far found too touchy to deal with intelligently.
>
> A tiny footnote to the translation of the poetry (who made it?[56]) in the first poem on p. 23, *"der Nagerlstock"* is not "the wanderer's cane," and no Tannhäuser-miracle is hinted at. *"Nagerl"* is Austrian for *"Nelke,"* which is "carnation." I was always intrigued by this association of the carnation flower with *"Nagel"* (nail), because it also exists in English, though not with reference to the flower, but to the spice, which is called "cloves," this obviously being derived from the Latin *"clovis"* (nail). The spice actually looks like little nails.
>
> My seminars are going well. I am holding forth on serial music—what else? In New York I heard a recital by David Tudor and a four-piano display of "randomized" music (as Milton [Babbitt] calls it). This I could do without, I am afraid.
>
> I hope very much we will see you at our house when I return (end of May). Please give my respects to the master.
>
> All the best, as always,
>
> Ernst

Isherwood's diary for May 12 describes a supper the day before with the Stravinskys: "A journalist once asked him: 'When you wrote *Orpheus* did you think about classical Greece?' And he replied, 'I thought about musical instruments, chiefly strings.' . . . I feel very warmly toward Bob Craft, and Vera, and Igor—they are all lovable. Igor complained of headaches. He works even after supper. Edward James was there." A letter from Ansermet (May 23) proposed a simplified barring for the *Danse sacrale* (from [198], bar 3), but Stravinsky ignored it.

A letter from Krenek came early in June with the translation of Gesualdo's *Sacra Cantione* I had asked for:

---

56. Dr. Maximilian Edel.

Dear Bob: Here is my attempt at translating those lines: Enlighten us, God of mercies, by the sevenfold grace of the Paraclete so that, through it, liberated from the darkness of sin, we may partake of the glory of life.

The only word I am not sure of without the aid of a dictionary is *"delictorum."* I have just guessed at its meaning. Within a few days I might be able to check on it, if you can wait that long.

In the tradition of the Church, the Holy Ghost has always been associated with the figure "seven" (this is, by the way, why in my electronic piece I have based the music of the "Spirit" on a seven-tone pattern). The source of it seems to be Isaiah XI, 2, where the "seven gifts" are attributed to the Spirit of the Lord.

All the best from both of us,

                                                      Ernst

June, the month of Stravinsky's seventy-fifth birthday, began with a photograph of him in the *New York Times* cutting a sumptuous cake "in the Beverly Hills home of Jack Warner's daughter." The cake was topped by a huge egg representing Kastchei in the *Firebird,* but I doubt that the connection was understood. Birthday presents began to arrive at Wetherly Drive, from Berman a statuette of a *"petit bonhomme pré-Columbien"* wearing what looked like a Venetian carnival mask, and, from Nadia Boulanger, a parchment page of medieval music manuscript from the Cathedral of Apt (Vaucluse).

In midmonth, NBC made a documentary film of Stravinsky at home for its "Wisdom" series, a complex undertaking at this time. Wetherly Drive had to be blocked off by the police and traffic redirected away from the intersection with Sunset Boulevard below. Huge trucks with electric generators and sound equipment appeared on Wetherly Drive, and for three days the entire Stravinsky house was covered with canvas. Camera positions had to be changed with each change of position, an inordinately slow and lengthy operation. In the evenings I rehearsed *Agon* at Royce Hall for the anniversary concert on the 17th, the eve of Stravinsky's birthday.

The program began with the *Greeting Prelude,* conducted by Franz Waxman. I conducted the *Symphonies of Winds, Canticum Sacrum,* the world premiere of *Agon,* and Stravinsky conducted *Vom Himmel hoch* and the *Symphony of Psalms.* Scrolls were presented to him by the Los Angeles City Council and the National Association for American Composers and Conductors. Isherwood's diary contains an account of the proceedings:

To the Stravinsky concert in the evening—for Igor's seventy-fifth birthday. Bob Craft, pale as a lily and quite beautiful in his exhaustion. He looked, as it were, purged through hard work and so curiously innocent and good. He said he hadn't had enough rehearsals with the orchestra of the *Canticum Sacrum* and *Agon.* Then Igor came on, limp with sweat but wonderfully svelte, although he had hurt his back against the corner of a couch. He conducts with the most graceful, campy gestures, like a ballerina. Bob is stiff, sudden, birdlike . . .

Of course I didn't enjoy the music. I didn't expect to. It seems chiefly to consist of nervous stabbing sounds, the creakings and squeaks of a door swaying in the wind. Little fizzes of energy from the violins. Short desert twisters of revolving noise, which soon pass.

Yet I believed it when Aldous—looking more beautifully slim and distinguished than I have ever seen him—called Igor "a great genius," a "saint of music," and the maker of "the Stravinsky revolution." . . . Eisenhower sent an asinine telegram . . .

Vera's sweetly lovable, dazed, innocent fatness. The bohemian mixture of languages they all speak—which somehow creates Paris in the twenties. Igor always scolds her in Russian.[57]

Lawrence Morton reviewed the concert in *The Musical Quarterly*: "*Agon* is a complex score. It is "learned" music in the sense that it is full of highly organized and carefully worked-out details of polyphony and harmony and sonority . . . It will doubtless be a more popular work than the *Canticum*, but that is only because most people (not excluding conductors) would rather dance than pray."

On the day following the birthday, Stravinsky recorded *Agon*, but he gave the first half-hour of the session to me, thereby allowing me to finish the last three minutes of Schoenberg's Variations, which, though nearly killing myself and the players, I had failed to complete in a session on June 4. This impingement on Stravinsky's time put David Oppenheim, the Columbia Records director, in a tizzy, but he did not stop me. (Thanks David.)

The next day I boarded the *Super Chief* for Boston, where I conducted three concerts (Symphony in Three Movements; the Capriccio with Soulima Stravinsky, piano; *Petrushka;* and *Renard,* for which Sarah Caldwell had prepared the singers). I stayed with Claudio Spies and his wife, who gave a luncheon for Harold Shapero and Soulima, and also drove me to Brandeis to see Harold and Esther, his wife. My father and mother attended the final concert, and we drove to Kingston together afterward. A few days later I boarded a train from Albany to Santa Fe, where I was to conduct *The Rake's Progress.* I stayed in the home of Miranda Masocco, where the Stravinskys, coming from Los Angeles, joined me for two weeks. At a candlelight dinner at Brinkerhoff Jackson's[58] ranch we met Paul Horgan.

57. Stravinsky never "scolded" his wife in any language, but in the nervous atmosphere backstage he might have spoken more sharply than at other times. Vera Stravinsky, a tall, large-boned woman, was not fat. Isherwood's diaries show an obsession with weight, especially his own.

58. Editor, d. 1996, of a quality magazine on architecture and landscaping in the American Southwest.

The first *Rake* performance was rained out. Prior to the next day's make-up of it, we dined with Vitya Vronsky and Victor Babin at their Rancho Piano. Isherwood, Don Bachardy, and Miranda were also there. Isherwood's diary does not mention the occasion but gives his impressions of the opera:

> We saw *The Rake's Progress* twice . . . The *Rake* grew on me. There is something heartlessly brisk in the music which suggests the eighteenth-century equiva-lent of *Bandwagon*. All aboard for London, sex, success. Oops—you fell off? Too bad! Goodbye—we won't be seeing you! . . .
>
> Don and I agree that Vera Stravinsky is one of the un-nastiest people we know. There seems absolutely nothing bad about her. She is sweet-tempered, funny, silly, kind, intelligent, and very industrious. She had a show in Santa Fe for her paintings. We bought one called *Reflections*.

On the first of August we sailed for Plymouth on the SS *Liberté*. In New York, just before leaving, I had received a letter from Luigi Dallapiccolo, in Florence, describing the performances on my Schoenberg album as *"d'un niveau extraordinaire."* Seeing the name of Ferruccio Busoni's son on the pas-senger list, we invited him for tea, but, because of class restrictions, had to obtain permission for him to cross from tourist to first. At Plymouth we landed in a tender and had a long wait on shore to find lost luggage. Finally in Dartington, we were installed in a private home, and introduced to our housekeeper and cook, a pretty girl, Judith Sutherland, one of the students at the summer music school, who provided breakfast in bed. On our first full day in Devon, I drove the Stravinskys to Exeter Cathedral and back in time to hear a concert by Julian Bream playing Dowland on lute and Falla's *Homenaje* on guitar. We loved the rich green landscape, but the Stravinskys wanted to spend the weekend in London, where we devoted our first after-noon to the Elgin marbles and the funerary steles in the British Museum.

Our return train was met at Newton Abbot, and the next day I con-ducted Dartington students in Bach's *Aus der Tiefe* in Totnes Parish Church, where the Stravinskys sat with Julian Huxley and Arthur Waley. We dined at Lord Chaplin's with the Elliott Carters and Priaulx Rainier, and the day after, before a performance of *Histoire du Soldat*, at the home of Leonard Knight Elmhirst, founder of Dartington Hall. The *Histoire* was staged in the Barn Theater by Christopher Hassall and Judith Jackson, pretty, perfectly proportioned, and a flirt, but I could not juggle two Judiths. Other outings took us to Tintagel—fern, gorse, and, on the heath, black ponies and sheep with blood-red dye on their necks—where the only village was aptly named Hexworthy, and to Bath, where our host was H. D. F. Kitto, author of *The Greeks*.

We left Dartington for London on the 21st in a Rolls-Royce sent, with the photographer Gjon Mili, by *Life* magazine. He posed Stravinsky in Wilton,

Salisbury Cathedral, Stonehenge, and accompanied us to Venice on the night train for more pictures. From our arrival at the Hotel Bauer-Grünwald, Stravinsky worked on *Threni* continuously. On one of our first nights in the city we heard Goldoni's and Cimarosa's *Il Mercato di marmontile* in the Teatro alla Fenice, kilometers of the same kind of pretty, four-square music that might have provoked Madame de Maintenon's *bon mot*, "We shall all die of symmetry." We saw the painter Bill Congdon often, chez nous and in his studio, near San Tomà, where he showed us how he painted with knives and spatulas, rarely using a brush, and, like Turner, mixed silver, gold, and bronze dust with most of his colors. We lunched almost daily at the Taverna Fenice, as did Maria Callas at the next table. At first Stravinsky did not remember meeting her with Bernstein after one of his New York concerts in January, but later they became friends. One evening we went to a party at Stella Adler's in her suite at the Hotel Cipriani. She greeted Stravinsky at the door with "Maestro, you can have anything here you want, including me."

We also dined at the Martini with Nabokov and Rolf Liebermann. In his book *Actes et entractes*,[59] the author recalled:

> Stravinsky's personality was complex and behind his gothic-gargoyle's face was an extraordinary intelligence and a charm *fou*. He could at the same time display the philanthropy of a Russian prince and the sordid avarice of a usurer. . . . Sometimes our business dealings turned into high comedy. In 1957 I went to see him in Venice on behalf of the Hamburg Radio to commission a work for chorus and orchestra. This became *Threni*, a too-rarely-performed masterpiece. I offered him $10,000, which he accepted without reservation. The next day at 7:00 A.M. I was awakened by a call from our mutual friend Nicolas Nabokov. "Listen: Igor did not close an eye the entire night. He wants $1,000 more and he is embarrassed to ask you for it." It would have been stupid to renounce a work by Stravinsky for a sum that our Hamburg Maecenases could find in a few minutes, and did find during the morning. Igor was so delighted that he invited us to the best restaurant in the city and ordered mountains of caviar and many bottles of champagne. The $1,000 were quickly spent, but he was gratified.
>
> The Teatro alla Fenice presented a new German opera by Werner Egk based on Gogol's play *The Inspector General*. At the end we walked very slowly towards Stravinsky's hotel without saying a word. We were bursting to vent our opinions about the opera but did not want to speak before the master. This silent promenade lasted half-an-hour, and, reaching the hotel, we embraced and wished each other good night. But when I turned to leave, Stravinsky, who had started to climb the staircase, turned around and said

---

59. Rolf Liebermann, *Actes et entractes* (Paris: PubEditions Stock, 1976).

"C'est très gênant." Not another word but only this so perfectly exact yet totally unexpected epithet to describe an opera. Moreover, since we always conversed together in English, he said *gênant* in French because it was absolutely untranslatable.

Shortly after his arrival in Venice, Stravinsky received a letter from his daughter defending her husband to him as *"simplement un grand nerveux,"* Stravinsky wrote in red pencil next to this phrase, *"un homme assez grossier."*

In Munich, at the beginning of October, Stravinsky conducted a make-up concert for the canceled one a year ago. The occasion was celebratory. Stravinsky had recovered from his stroke and was fulfilling his promise to return, which not many would have believed possible when he left the city the previous autumn. I shared in the jubilation, but found the return to the Vier Jahreszeiten hotel a dispiriting reminder of a perturbing period. The concert was followed by a formal dinner with thirty guests, a nine-course meal—ten, counting cigars—long speeches, toasts. At Stravinsky's request, Dagmar Schnecter, his nurse the previous year in the Rote Kreuz Hospital, was seated next to him.

The following day we were in Baden-Baden to rehearse the Rundfunk orchestra for the concert in Paris on November 11th. The first half, Schoenberg's Five Pieces, Berg's Three, and Webern's Six, was conducted by Hans Rosbaud; the second, *Agon,* was conducted by Stravinsky. The programming had been designed by Boulez to overwhelm *Agon,* but the elegance and freshness of invention in Stravinsky's thin-textured *ballet blanc* turned the tables on the Teutonic heavyweights,[60] and Stravinsky received a standing ovation. Cocteau and Giacometti came to the post-concert party, and I met Lucie Lambert there. It was decided that Giacometti would come to our hotel the next day and draw the first of his now famous series of Stravinsky heads.

Three days later the American Embassy gave a reception for Stravinsky. Artur and Nella Rubinstein were there, the Milhauds, and Florent Schmitt, whom Stravinsky was seeing for the first time since 1936, when Schmitt

60. Doda Conrad's book, *44 ans d'amitié avec Nadia Boulanger,* quotes Elliott Carter on the morning dress rehearsal: "When I entered the Salle Pleyel, the only other person in the immense hall was Nadia Boulanger . . . with the scores of the three [sic] works on the program." She "knew these three works," Carter says, "but disliked the Berg, which she called seasick music.' " But Carter must also have said that the reason for her presence was the principal event of the concert, Stravinsky conducting the European premiere of *Agon.* Further, when Carter entered the hall for the rehearsal, several people, including the present writer with David Oppenheim, were already there.

defeated him in an election for membership in the French Academy. The U.S. Ambassador, Arthur Houghton of Corning Glass, and his wife, were delighted to be speaking American with the Stravinskys, since, incredibly, neither of them knew any French. I left for Rome the next day, and the Stravinskys for Donaueschingen and Zurich. They flew from the Swiss city to Rome for my birthday. Both Stravinsky and I had concerts there. I conducted *Agon* and Haydn's Symphony No. 101 with the Filarmonica in the Teatro Eliseo, and Stravinsky a program of his music at the Foro Italico. We spent the evening afterward with Carlo Levi, Giorgio de Chirico, Alberto Moravia, and the latter's wife, Elsa Morante. During a two-day stopover in Paris, on our way to New York, we dined at the Berkeley with Giacometti, Boulez, Souvtchinsky, and Judith Sutherland, who had materialized suddenly, as she had in Venice at the end of August, and in Rome only a week earlier. Afterward, Boulez teased me about *"La Commendatora."* The next day we dined again with Boulez and Souvtchinsky at La Bourgogne, and the day after that sailed from Le Havre on the SS *Liberté.*

When we docked in New York, *Agon* was in rehearsal at the City Ballet, but Stravinsky was present only once, on November 10. He immediately formed a "eulogious" opinion of the choreography,[61] but, engrossed in *Threni*, refused to stay in New York for the premiere. Balanchine called us in Hollywood to say that *Agon* had been a success beyond all expectations and would be given many more performances than originally scheduled.

As always after active periods in Europe, Hollywood seemed dull. A few days after our return, we watched "Stravinsky at 75," the NBC film documentary. I looked like an ass in it, twitching nervously, unsuccessfully trying to keep my hands and legs still, and contributing nothing, except banal questions for Stravinsky fed to me by Robert Graff, the NBC producer. At one point, sitting with Stravinsky at his card table, he tried to calm me by patting the back of my left hand. At his piano I again sat next to him like a zombie as he demonstrated how Beethoven held a piece of wood to the sounding board to hear the vibrations of the stick in his mouth.

Two letters from Ernst Krenek awaited me:

Dear Bob: I hear that you are back in town from your adventures and I hope to see you sometime soon and to get a first-hand report on your observations. It is good to have you around again . . .

[My new] work is called *Sestina*. I wrote the poem myself (in German) according to the pattern used by Petrarca, Dante, and their predecessors in the Provençal School of the twelfth century. In it I have musically tried my own brand of "total determination," and the piece surely presents a number of

---

61. Paul Horgan's *Encounters with Stravinsky: A Personal Record* (New York: Farrar, Straus and Giroux, 1972) refers to Stravinsky's, Mrs. Stravinsky's, and my own attendance at many *Agon* rehearsals, but only Stravinsky went and only once.

unusual problems. The [vocal] range goes from [low G] to [high D]. In other words it takes a singer who can do *Herzgewächse* and is not bothered by problems of intonation no matter what happens around her. The piece will take 15 minutes . . .

Thank you ever so much—and I hope to see you soon. All the best, as always,

Ernst

P.S. Please give our love to the Stravinskys.

Dear Bob: . . . I am looking forward with much anticipation to your visit, when I can show you the score and we may talk things over. Next week all evenings are free, except Saturday (December 7). Thursday night is not too good, but available if necessary. All this could be talked over by telephone, but I know that you are very rarely at your place,[62] and I hesitate to disturb the peace of the Stravinsky household. So please call me as soon as you can. (Fl. 3–1378).

All the best as always yours,

Ernst

Only two dates in December are of any consequence. On the seventh Sol Babitz took us to a jazz club on Crenshaw Boulevard where Stravinsky heard Shorty Rogers play the flugelhorn. The next day he rewrote the trumpet part for this instrument in *Threni*. Two days later, at a Monday concert, I conducted Stravinsky's three strangely dissonant Gesualdo Sacred motets, Josquin's *Déploration de Jehan Ockeghem*, Lasso's twelve-voice *Laudate Dominum* (sung twice), and Bach's *Trauer-Ode*.

We celebrated New Year's with the Huxleys and Heard. Gerald was very sprightly, while Aldous talked about the myth that tall left-handed men suffer from sexual impotence, viz. Tiberius. The year 1957 had been a good one. Stravinsky, restored to health, had been musically rejuvenated as well: *Agon* was his greatest success since *The Rake's Progress*, and new projects were in the offing.

1958

In contrast, 1958 brought medical anxieties, family fractiousness, and artistic disappointments. Stravinsky's polycythemia loomed as more and more life-threatening. The phlebotomy treatments were more frequent, and the strain increasingly debilitating. In late spring radioactive phosphorous had to be risked, even though its long-term effects were unknown. Musically, too, the year brought no great satisfactions. *Threni* was well received at its Venetian premiere and, unexpectedly, in New York, but the difficulties in the vocal parts soon forced it into retirement.

62. I spent much more time in the Stravinsky house than in my own.

The publication of *Answers to 35 Questions,* an interview between Stravinsky and myself, published everywhere in English, and in a French translation by Boulez, placed Stravinsky in an awkward position. The tendentious questions aligned Stravinsky with an avant-garde that was deeply opposed to all that he stood for, and in which my own interest was rapidly evaporating. Some observers were accusing me of trying to create a Stravinsky-as-modernist persona, which did not concern him in the least, though he was annoyed at finding himself coupled with Hindemith.

In the first week of the year I began my recording of *Le Marteau sans maître* for Columbia Records, which had actually asked me to do it, whereas my Schoenberg, Berg, and Webern recordings were paid for by me from driblets of royalties, loans, and by writing innumerable album notes. Halfway through the session David Oppenheim appeared, noticed that the recording was not stereophonic, and obliged us to start over from the beginning and make the product at least technically au courant. Two days later I attended Bruno Walter's recording session of Mahler's Fourth Symphony at the American Legion Hall. When David introduced me to Walter after it, he graciously congratulated me on my Webern records, saying "I would not know even how to *begin* to do it."

In 1958 the Stravinskys and I became close friends of the Kreneks, as the following excerpts from his letters, which also give an accurate picture of the life of new music at the time, make clear:

Dear Bob: A few days ago I had a lengthy telephone conversation with Paul Fromm[63] through which I learned that you had not gone to New York after all because you had been sick with that damned flu, about which I am sorry. But he told me that in the meantime you had gone to Houston,[64] which pleased me, for apparently you were well again. Now I hear that you are back here and busy with rehearsals . . .

Paul talked to me also about the Princeton project as if it were settled for good. I hope he is right. More power to him. I certainly should be happy to join forces with you at the Ivy League . . .

Please give our love to the Stravinskys.

All the best as ever yours,

Ernst

Another letter came from him on January 20:

63. Chicago's Maecenas of modern music. He sponsored a seminar in contemporary music at Princeton in the summer of 1959 and underwrote my January 1959 New York concert, which included the local premiere of *Threni.*
64. Stravinsky had concerts in Houston and Mrs. Stravinsky an exhibition of her paintings, but I was not with them. Paul Horgan, who was, has described the visit in his book *Encounters with Stravinsky.*

Dear Bob: I am happy to hear that Lawrence wants to put on the *Sestina* next year under your direction. Of course it would be much better if Paul Fromm would not have to help financially in this project, and I agree that this should not be necessary. Certainly some sort of "moral" association with the Fromm Foundation would be mutually helpful. I will call Lawrence and discuss the matter with him . . .

I too wrote to Cologne and Hamburg about the *Sestina* . . . These outfits are taking on a Pentagon-like texture. (For instance, I have never met Mr. Winkler,[65] who has written to you.) With these octopuses (or octopi, octopodes) one never knows which πoùs may have developed in a minor subhead of dubious competence while you were looking the other way. Anyway, I am watching developments closely—whatever that means.

I knew [Hans] Schmidt-Isserstedt since we studied together in Berlin in 1921 or so, but I'm afraid he is a lazy blockhead.[66]

I shall be happy to get the Gesualdo record. I am playing over the music which you left with me, and it is truly amazing. I'll have to talk to you about a few details, and I should like to know more about the sources of these transcriptions.

I am not sure that I will be able to decipher Bo Nilsson's[67] esoteric runes, but I will try my best to be of assistance to you.

Certainly I want to listen to your Boulez recording sessions, no matter how tedious they might be. Did I read correctly that they will take place on February 4 and 7? Please call me about this and everything else (Florida 3–1378).

All the best from both of us, as ever,

Ernst

P.S. I am glad you found my guitar piece interesting, and that [Theodore] Norman is going to put it in circulation—but where?

On January 30, writing to T. S. Eliot, Stravinsky began the process of publishing the "Conversations" books:

Dear Mr. Eliot: I would like to send a manuscript to you of a short (about 40,000 words) book of Dialogues of mine. It will be published in Germany,

---

65. Eric Winkler, of the Westdeutscher Rundfunk in Cologne, was a pianist and Stravinsky's concert agent for Germany, 1951–1955. He had been in Dresden during the February 1945 bombing and told us horrifying stories about it. See also my own visit to Dresden, described in chapter 12.

66. Schmidt-Isserstedt, of the Hamburg Rundfunk, conducted Beethoven's Ninth Symphony in Zurich and two other Swiss cities on a program with *Threni* conducted by the composer.

67. An avant-garde Swedish composer in vogue at the time.

France, and Italy in the fall but I have not yet arranged for English publication . . . I think the dialogues are in the order in which they were written, not categorized, as perhaps they should be. I will greatly value your opinion, especially about what to cut . . .

Very sincerely yours,

Igor Stravinsky

In late January I had an alarming call from home: my mother was flung from her car on an icy road and taken unconscious to the hospital. She was bruised but otherwise all right.

On February 3 I completed the *Marteau* recording. Stravinsky, in the control room with Krenek, remarked that the main weakness of the piece was its lack of a strong bass-register part, not filled by the guitar, in other words its lack of masculinity. Krenek wrote to me in more analytical detail about the recording and the opus:

Dear Bob: I am sorry that we had to sneak away the other night so suddenly. Gladys has to get up at 7 A.M. these days, and you know how long a drive we have to get out here.

We were not just impressed, but even slightly appalled at the amount of work which you expended during that session. In fact, Gladys worried that you were working yourself to a frazzle, and [was] concerned about your well-being. Well, I am sure you know what you are doing, and I know that being really engaged in a project one can do more than seems humanly possible.

As to the business under consideration, it is difficult for me to distinguish clearly between the problems of the composition and those of its rendition. Off hand, I feel that some of the composer's dynamic specifications remain somewhat theoretical. I wonder whether it is actually possible for the performers to carry out so many dynamic nuances, especially in a fast tempo. Frankly, I am not sure that I was able to make out whether all dynamic prescriptions were carried out completely, in spite of the numerous repetitions . . . I was also disappointed with the percussion. Most of these "traps" to me seemed to sound very much alike. I believe this is the fault of the composition—there is simply too much of it, to my taste, at least.

Anyway, it was a most instructive and exhilarating session. Curiously enough the work sounds much less like "*Punktmusik*" than I thought, and frequently rather "romantic" and "impressionistic"—whatever that may mean, if anything.

I'm sorry I can't be there for the Friday session. But please do let me know as soon as possible when you do the Stockhausen *Zeitmasse*. I want to hear that by all means. Also I should very much like to see you at least briefly before you and I go to New York.

All the best, as ever, your friend,

Ernst

Another letter came a few days later:

> Dear Bob: . . . I forgot to tell you that I conferred briefly with Bill Kraft[68] about the Nilsson score, trying to answer some of his questions. As I remember it, some of the problems were: metronome markings. They are indicated on top of the score, and they frequently change from one bar to the next. How to make such changes as from 80 to 82.5 to 67.5 and similar for just one bar, I don't know . . . The abbreviation "Hz" means "Hertz," which is the German term for fragments (cycles, *i.e.*, pitches, after the physicist Hertz). In other words, this is how [Nilsson] wants his bongos, or whatever they are, to be tuned. 440 Hz indicates the normal A, and so forth. *"Pedalbecken"* is the sort of cymbals which the jazz-bandits operate by footwork. I imagine that just means hitting the two cymbals which are mounted one on top of the other together. It then should probably mean hitting another pair of higher pitch. I imagine this will mean as much headache to Craft as footache to Kraft . . . These are the problems I seem to remember. If you think I may be able to interpret any more of the tricky Eskimo's directions,[69] please ask me about it at the Stockhausen meeting.
>
> All the best, as ever,
>
> Ernst

Christopher Isherwood's diary for February 14 records: "Don and I had supper with the Stravinskys and Bob Craft last night. Chris Wood[70] was also there. A wonderful evening of joy and love, in which I felt we were all included. I never can remember what is said on these occasions—Oh, yes, we were looking through a book of very inadequate illustrations by Nicolas de Staël[71] to poems by René Char[72] but it was all joyful. We had fish soup.[73] Igor seemed much better and looked younger."

The Stravinskys gave a party following the premiere of Krenek's *Sestina*. I had received a letter from him two days before:

---

68. The composer William Kraft, the timpanist of the Los Angeles Philharmonic at the time. I called him "Bob" and he called me "Bill."

69. Born within the Arctic Circle, the Swedish composer would now be considered an Inuit.

70. A pianist friend of Gerald Heard, whom he had accompanied to the United States from England in 1937. The Stravinskys were fond of him, and he was a frequent dinner guest.

71. The Russian painter who committed suicide in 1955, while we were in Madrid. The Stravinskys had met him in New York through Nicolas Nabokov and admired his work.

72. Char, the poet—author of *Le Marteau sans maitre*—and, during World War II, Maquis hero, sent his books to Stravinsky and to me through Pierre Souvtchinsky.

73. Mrs. Stravinsky's *bouillabaisse* was famous.

Dear Bob: Many thanks for your note. If I don't hear from you, we'll be Friday the 21st at 7 P.M. at the same place as the last time to get our time properly measured.[74] I do hope you won't call it off, since I don't want to miss this application of the "roadhouse" treatment by any means. Looking perfunctorily at the score I could see that the problems are staggering. In comparison my *Sestina* is a rather primitive exercise. I am now in the process of putting together a few short pieces for chamber ensemble which I might produce in Darmstadt next fall. They will be perhaps a little more tricky than *Sestina*, but even then the conductor will have a comprehensive job. I've never believed that outrageous difficulty is a token of superior quality, as some people seem to do.

I am sorry that the "Boo"[75] piece is disappointing. Two years ago his *Frekoenser* was one of the more attractive pieces in Darmstadt. From what you say about Boulez, I gather that all these people seem to have got caught in the "roadhouse" and don't see how to get out of it. [Stockhausen's] *Gruppen* idea is not even particularly novel—Charles Ives dreamed of several orchestras working away on various hilltops . . .

All the best, until soon, as ever,

Ernst

The mail on February 17 brought a copy of Dagmar Godowsky's autobiography, in which the references to Stravinsky nearly brought on an attack of apoplexy: "He is the most devout man I have ever known," she wrote. "A Greek-Catholic, he crosses himself before conducting, before dinner, before everything—and I mean everything, everything, everything." The last "everything" too obviously means sexual intercourse. As the Prince asks in Lampedusa's *The Leopard*: "How can I find satisfaction with a woman who makes the sign of the Cross before every embrace and then at the critical moment just cries *Gesùmmaria?*"

Dagmar Godowsky was Stravinsky's mistress in New York in 1935, where he heard Shostakovich's *Lady Macbeth of Mtsensk* with her, in Rio de Janeiro in 1936, and again in New York in 1937 and the autumn of 1939. She had been the screen partner of, and sexual screen for, Rudolph Valentino.[76] Newspaper clippings in Stravinsky's files for 1938 tell the story of how she became a stowaway on the SS *Normandie* and followed him to France. In Paris she "pestered" him for money until he obliged Vera Sudeykina to take some to her, as well as some food (buttermilk); this was carried out on May

74. This refers to the recording session of Stockhausen's *Zeitmasse*. The problems are simply that the cadenzas for woodwind quintet are marked "as fast as possible" and "as slow as possible," both of which are impossible to know until it is too late.

75. Bo Nilsson's first name is pronounced "Boo." I conducted the piece by him in a Monday Evening Concert.

76. Alva and I visited his birthplace at Castellaneta, Apulia, in the spring of 1992.

22 and May 23, 1938, which means that the two women saw each other twice. Stravinsky himself refused to see her and sent a brutal letter accusing her of complicating his life, which, he did not say, was already bigamous. By the spring of 1939 the rift had been patched up, and Dagmar continued to represent him as his New York concert agent. In October 1939, when she visited him in Boston, he asked a stupefied hotel clerk if he could have a woman in his room—or so Alexei Haieff, who was present, told me. Sexual mores were different in New York, and no embarrassments seem to have been suffered when Stravinsky stayed with her at the Navarro Hotel on Central Park South, a name I still see on the wall to the east of my apartment. She fell in love with him and on the death of his first wife expected him to marry her.

After conducting the Monday Concert on February 24 (Tallis's *Lamentations*, Bach's *Ewigkeit zu Donnerwort*, the Vivaldi Concertos for two mandolins), I flew to New York for a concert in St. Thomas Church, Fifth Avenue, and on my arrival heard the news of the death in Venice of our dear friend Alessandro Piovesan. Balanchine came to my rehearsals, and I dined with Milton Babbitt, Lincoln Kirstein, Auden, and Kallman. Stravinsky was at the railroad station to meet me in Los Angeles, and to tell me of the death in Mainz of his friend Willy Strecker, which had deeply upset him.

Another letter from Krenek awaited me, this one from New York:

> Dear Bob: I am sorry I missed you and your concert here. I am sure Milton told you that I had just arrived and had to get a little organized so that I was not quite prepared to sit through this lengthy [St. Thomas sacred music] service . . . You might be interested in hearing that the *Sestina* so far has gone admirably well (keep your fingers crossed) . . . I might say that I am myself amazed at the piece. In a sense, it transcends my own power of perception in that it produces musical situations which I would hardly have thought up had I not somehow blindly relied on the constructive mechanism which I set in motion. Of course, arriving at this and no other mechanism was a soul-searching affair, and it was not easy for me at this point to determine exactly what prompted my choice, for the results at any given point were practically unforeseeable. Saying that an act of faith was involved would probably be an oversimplification which would stand in need of further analysis. For this I am not yet ready by a long shot . . .
>
> All the best now, as ever yours,
>
> Ernst
>
> P.S. Please give my love to the Stravinskys.

Stravinsky attended my Monday Concert of March 11: Varèse's *Ionisation*, Bo Nilsson's *Doubleplay*, Schütz's *Fili mi Absalom* and *Vox Populi*. The next day we dined with the Huxleys at Luau. Aldous used the word "inenarrable," which occurs more than once in his essays and seems to me a useful expression for "inexpressible." According to the Oxford English Dictionary, it was last in circulation in the time of Gower. Aldous's reference was to Chaucer, and he recited a beautiful passage in what I assumed was the correct pronunciation. He said that Chaucer misread *"naves ballatrices"* for *"naves bellatrices,"* "ballet ships" instead of "battle ships."

I did another Monday Concert on the 24th, with Bach's *Christ lag im Todesbanden* and Dallapiccola's *Cinque Canti* on the program. The next morning Stravinsky received a letter from Eliot about publishing the "Conversations" book:

> London. March 19, 1958.
> Dear Mr. Stravinsky, . . . While our critics feel that some of the material could bear a little reorganization so as to give a greater effect of continuity and less abrupt transitions we have not the slightest doubt that this is a book of the greatest value and interest and we are convinced that it is a book which we shall be proud to publish . . . At this stage . . . I am merely writing to say, first that we want to publish this text, and second that we should be very happy if more material could be included. I do not know whether you could be persuaded to continue the Conversations in the same vein . . .
>
> With best wishes,
>
> Yours very sincerely,
> T. S. Eliot

On April 7 and 8, I recorded Stockhausen's *Zeitmasse* and some remakes for *Le Marteau*, after which, for two hours, Stravinsky and I taped exchanges from the "Conversations" book, which was the real reason that Columbia had agreed to the session in the first place.[77] On the morning of April 9, Stravinsky underwent phlebotomy for his polycythemia, but was able to lunch with Milton Babbitt. While we were at table, a telegram came from Deborah Ishlon (Columbia Records) in New York: *Holiday* magazine will publish portions of the diary [mine] if we agree to the byline: "Written by Stravinsky, translated from the French by Robert Craft." Stravinsky angrily telegraphed his refusal.

The following week, Stravinsky conducted three concerts with the San Francisco Symphony: *Apollo, Scherzo fantastique*—which I was hearing for the first time—and *Firebird*. On the afternoon of the 17th, we drove to Muir Woods and walked between its ferns and fallen, overgrown, and partly fossilized tree trunks. On the next afternoon, the painter Afro escorted us through an exhibition of his work at Mills College, where Leon Kirchner joined us. After the matinée concert on the 18th, we drove to the Torre Inn,

77. We never heard this, but it must exist somewhere in cold storage.

Carmel, learning from our automobile radio that Ezra Pound had been released from St. Elizabeth's Hospital in Washington.

A letter from Boulez awaited me in Hollywood. He proposed two concerts for Paris, one on November 7, in which Stravinsky would conduct his songs with instruments and the 1947 *Symphonies of Winds*, leaving me to fill out the program with the 1920 *Symphonies* and the recent chamber music. In the second, on November 14, Stravinsky would conduct *Threni* and I music by Gesualdo and Heinrich Isaak, the latter as transcribed by Webern. Stravinsky did not respond, but the difficulties concerning the performance of *Threni* in Venice had begun to annoy him, as he wrote to Giovanni Ponti, Piovesan's successor: "I of course understand the problem of the small seating in the Scuola di San Rocco, but I understood it last September when I started to compose *Threni*. In spite of the large ensemble, it is chamber music . . . The concert could be changed to consist only of *Threni*, played twice with a different audience each time."

Meanwhile, we spent an evening at Isherwood's, which his diary describes: "Rosamond Lehmann[78] left today . . . I think her stay was a success, though. On Saturday we had the Stravinskys, Bob Craft, and the Huxleys to supper. Igor became wonderfully oracular, said, "Music is the art of time." Aldous talked mescaline, recommended *The Relic* by Eça de Queroz, and said that he had met Father Bruckburger recently . . . Rosamond did her best to keep up with the highbrow talk . . . she wore a most elaborate grey dress and was covered with makeup. Laura seemed less rude and more feminine than usual. Bob, as always, was lovable. Vera told me that the day before, when I phoned her, she had been napping in her studio and had actually been dreaming of me and Auden."

At the beginning of May, hoping to galvanize the organizers of the Venice concerts, Stravinsky wrote to Rolf Liebermann in Hamburg, who had contracted to prepare *Threni*, *The Rite of Spring*, and *Oedipus Rex* (or, rather, have me prepare them), complaining that Vittorio di Sica, who had promised to take the Speaker's part in *Oedipus*, had not been heard from: "Unless he can agree to commit himself now, I think I had better eliminate the Speaker entirely (which maybe I prefer because the text is rather pompous . . .). We would play only the last of the fanfares for four trumpets, just before the end, and then continue!"

When Aaron Copland came to Hollywood to conduct the Ojai Festival, we had a pleasant evening with him at the home of Lawrence Morton's brother-in-law. But two days later Stravinsky suffered a ruptured blood vessel—a hemorrhage—in the small intestine and was taken to Cedars of Lebanon Hospital, where his hematocrit count was found to be dangerously low. I

78. English novelist (*The Ballad and the Source*), sister of John Lehmann, the publisher, and mistress of Cecil Day Lewis, the poet and father of the actor.

went to a supper at La Rue given by Isherwood for Don's birthday, with Marguerite Lamkin, Paul Mallard, Don and Hope Murray. Don Murray was front-page news at the time because of his performance opposite Marilyn Monroe in *Bus Stop*. I had a crush on his wife, the actress Hope Lange, but made a terrific gaffe in saying that I thought the Germans came off better than the Americans in *The Young Lions*, thanks to the use of *Tristan* as background music, and to Brando in the lead. I had forgotten that Hope Lange was paired with Montgomery Clift in the film.

The *Beverly Hills Canyon Crier* published a photo of Stravinsky on May 29, captioned "Hillside Genius," as publicity for his appearance in the Los Angeles Music Festival. At Cedars of Lebanon Hospital the main ailment of the genius of the slopes, worryingly pale and weak and complaining of hot and cold flashes, had been diagnosed as a bleeding duodenal ulcer. He received two transfusions and was not released from the hospital until June 7, when his blood count was back to normal: the red corpuscles at 4 million, the hemoglobin at 82, the hematocrit at 40. These levels were expected to change soon, and it was decided to begin radioactive phosphate injections in three weeks, the full effects of which would manifest themselves only months later. (The first intravenous dose was given on June 25.) Meanwhile he had to take hourly medications for the ulcer, a consequence of the polycythemia, and the third recurrence for him since 1950. His blood was too rich, partly as a result of the vitamin B 12 injections received twice or thrice weekly between 1948 and 1956. But he was pleased to be home, allowed to eat and drink as he wished, and to resume composing.

The day before the concert a postcard came from Krenek supplying translations from the Vulgate Psalms that I had requested:

Dear Bob: The text [of the "Psalms of the Compline"] is the beginning of the famous Psalm 70 (71 in the Protestant counting):

> *In thee, O Lord, do I put my trust; let me never be put to confusion.*
> *Deliver me in thy righteousness . . .*
> *Be thou my strong habitation . . . to save me.*

(The translation, especially of the first verse, does not even approach the majesty and beauty of the Latin rhythm, but it's King James.)

The next verse must be taken from a different psalm which I cannot identify. It goes approximately like this:

> *Thou shalt free me from the snare which they have hidden from me,*
> *for thou art my protector.*
> *Glory to the Father and the Son and the Holy Ghost.*

My humble suggestion for the first verse would be:

In thee, O lord, have I set my hope:
I shall not be confounded in all eternity.

The concert, June 16, in Royce Hall, included *The Faun and the Shepherdess*, with Marina Koshetz as soprano soloist, and a staged *Mavra*. (Eugene Lourié was to have designed it, but at the last minute someone else was given the commission.) Stravinsky conducted his little opera, and I conducted the first half: Schubert–Webern *Dances*, Webern's Five Pieces for Strings, and Haydn's Symphony No. 101.

A Vera Stravinsky vernissage took place five days later. Isherwood's diary describes "a gruelling session with Gerald Heard and Michael Barrie" at the opening. "The strangest people were there: Father McLane's son firing off champagne corks in the background like rockets . . . A Russian lady of eighty who could stand on her head, another of about three feet high who couldn't, and, of course, lots of musicians . . . A Russian Jewish surgeon named Max Cutler . . . came with us."[79]

On the evening of June 24, and into the early hours of the 25th, we recorded pieces by Heinrich Schütz, with Grace-Lynn Martin, Marilyn Horne, Richard Robinson and Paul Salomunovich, tenors, and Robert Oliver, bass. Stravinsky monitored the session, and Lawrence Morton played the harpsichord, but the musicological input was the work of our violinist, Sol Babitz. I was due to leave for Santa Fe immediately after to conduct *Falstaff*, but, to my great chagrin, had to cancel, being overwhelmed with work in preparation for our European concerts. I went to Santa Fe later and conducted the opera orchestra on the stage of the theater in the *Eroica* Symphony, *Danses concertantes*, and Schoenberg's *Accompaniment to a Cinematographic Scene*, Opus 39.

The next letter from Krenek (July 4) reveals how little a world-renowned composer of "serious music" might know about the business aspect of the art:

Dear Bob: I was sorry to hear that you had to give up your New Mexico engagement because of your being so fatigued by the recording work. It is just the recording business about which I wanted to ask you for some advice. I am to do a recording of *Jonny spielt auf* in Germany next November for the Vox Company. My question is whether it is customary for the conductor of such a recording to receive royalties from the sales of the records apart from his fee for the conducting job? I should think that this must be so, for how else would

79. The short Russian lady was Beata Bolm. The headstanding one was the wife of Dr. Sigfrid Knauer. She had lived in India and did Yoga exercises, but was younger than eighty. The aptly named Dr. Cutler was Aldous Huxley's physician during the last months of his life.

Elvis Presley make his millions from record sales? So far I have not been offered any contract—just promised a certain not very impressive fee for the
conducting—and I should like to know what I am up [against], being unfortunately somewhat ignorant of these things, as the opportunity has not occurred
before. Would you be good enough to let me know what your own or Mr.
Stravinsky's experience is in such cases? I should be much obliged to you for
your information . . .

All good wishes for you, and all our love to the Stravinskys, as ever yours,

Ernst

We celebrated *le quatorze juillet*, which the Stravinskys counted as their
wedding night (1921), with Isherwood and Don. Isherwood's diary records
the occasion, though he was unaware of its significance:

All day I've been useless for work because I got drunk last night . . . we were
drunk because we had the Stravinskys for dinner; in a week they will be leaving on one of their long European tours, and of course the thought always
occurs, shall we ever see Igor again? Actually, he seemed in fine form last
night. He and Vera both drink far too much though . . .

A great sense of love and support between us and them. Vera and Igor
talked about Diaghilev. He used to tell Vera all about his boyfriends. Vera
thinks he killed himself by excessive drinking.[80] Igor said that Diaghilev surrounded himself with people who were inventive . . . Inventions, Igor added,
are the only things worth stealing.

On July 29, we sailed from New York for Genoa on the SS *Cristoforo Co-
lombo*. We were met in Genoa by a film crew and reporters, whom Stravinsky
ignored, while he counted his eighteen pieces of luggage.[81]

Only a week after our arrival in Venice, I left for Hamburg to rehearse
the North German Rundfunk orchestra, chorus, and solo singers for the
Threni premiere in Venice, and to rehearse *The Rite of Spring* and *Oedipus Rex*
for Stravinsky's concert in La Fenice. A letter from Boulez awaited me in the
Vier Jahreszeiten: he had just seen the review in *Time* about my recording of
Le Marteau and *Zeitmasse*. Another letter soon followed, saying that he had
just discovered from Brussels and Hamburg newspapers that *Threni* required
six solo singers. This augured ill for the Paris performance, revealing that at
this late date no one had been engaged. I worked arduously in Hamburg
trying to achieve in-tune singing. The chorus was excellent, as were the

80. She could not have said that, knowing the history of his diabetes and his refusal to
take insulin.

81. A clip of this scene appears in François Mitterand's 1994 television film *Les Grands
Amants*; it shows Stravinsky answering a question about "the young Turks" (the avant-garde),
with "I prefer to be old hat."

three male soloists from Los Angeles, but *The Rite of Spring* was quite unfamiliar to the orchestra. Stravinsky sent a letter from Venice:

> Dear Bob: Please insist this absurd bass-trumpet be replaced by my Flügelhorn called Bügel contralto in B (flat); this is even more important (because of its solo in the beginning with the tenor) than the sarrusophone problem. I make this request through you, because I am not quite sure to be understood by the Rundfunk people what I am speaking about.
>
> If possible, please correct in *Canon a 3* at the end of bar 182 the three soli this way:
>
> Bar 114, of course, $M = 58$–60
> "   322, V -6, C–6   mf > pp
>
>   All best,
>   Love,
>   IStr.

I also received a letter from Altgraf Salm, whom I had met in Baden-Baden in 1951, asking if the Stravinskys "intend to stay in the Schloss in Donaueschingen, and whether Prince Fürstenberg should send a car for them in Baden-Baden."

On September 12, I dined in a Brussels restaurant with the composer Henri Pousseur and the musicologist-gourmets André Souris and Robert Wangermée. The next day I rehearsed the Machaut and Stravinsky Masses. Between them, in the afternoon, I drove to the forest at Soigne with Jeanne Déroubaix, my contralto soloist in the next day's performance of these pieces for a musicological congress. After tea with her on the terrace of the Empress Carlotta's former villa, we climbed the earthenwork pyramid at Waterloo, with the huge black British lion, and on our return to Brussels stopped at the house of Justus Lipsius in a neighborhood of many *"pignon espagnol"* roofs.

My concert on the 15th, sponsored by the Festival de Liège, took place in the beautiful Collégiale Notre Dame de Huy, the Gothic masterpiece of the Meuse Valley. (Huy is renowned for the nearby convent of Clair-Lieu, founded in 1285 when the relics of St. Odile, one of Ursula's eleven thousand Virgins, were translated there. A richly endowed institution, its scriptorium flourished in the *quattrocento*.) I used Gilbert Reaney's edition of the Machaut, who is thought to have lived in the area with his royal patron. Reaney, who had heard my performance of the Mass in California, told me that he attributed the absence of melodic embellishments, melismas, and ornamentation to Machaut's acquaintance with older music in the pope's chapel in Avignon. The score calls for a small organ, a clavecin, two English horns, two oboes, two bassoons, one viol, eight singers (two on each part). What noble music, and how marvelous it sounded here! The brass in

Stravinsky's Sanctus rang out like the saucing bell. The first half of the program consisted of liturgical monodic chants from the French tradition, going back to the Roman orientation of Charlemagne, and embracing both the Ambrosian chant of Milan and the Visigothic chant of Toledo.

The curiosity of the nine pieces comprising the first part of the program was a *Conduit De L'Office Dit De La Circoncision*, dating from the late twelfth or early thirteenth century. It was in the latter part of this period that Thomas Aquinas, refuting Bernard of Clairvaux, who wished to abolish the ritual, argued in favor of it on grounds that the seed of Abraham is the connection between the two Testaments. The repetitions, rhymes, assonances, and alliterations in the verse are very beautiful,

> *Natus est, natus est, natus est hodie . . .*
> *Nec! nec! minuit quod erat . . .*
> *Sed carnis sumpto pullio /*
> *In virginis palatio / Ut sponsus e thalamo /*
> *Processit ex utero . . .*

Since *thalamo* means marriage, *utero* the womb, and *palatum* the vault of heaven, circumcision could well be the subject.

After the concert Mme Déroubaix's husband drove us to Liège in time to catch the midnight train to Cologne, where we switched to the one for Milan and Venice. After a half hour on the second train, she knocked on the door of my sleeper, came in to talk about marital problems, disrobed, and so forth.

Venice never seemed more beautiful, or the Fenice, where I rehearsed *Oedipus* and *The Rite of Spring* (with the 1943 *Danse sacrale*, the first time Stravinsky ever heard it). I conducted an "acoustical" dress rehearsal of *Threni* in the Scuola di San Rocco, and Stravinsky's performance was warmly received by the audience and sensitively reviewed by the poet Eugenio Montale:

> Venice. One cannot help but be moved year after year by the sight of the elderly Stravinsky mounting the conductor's podium to present to the citizens of Venice (a city that now considers him an adopted son) and the habitués of the Festival the latest product of his study. The seventy-six-year-old maestro embodies fifty years of musical experience and this imbues each of his reappearances with a warmth of feeling that overrides any purely critical considerations. No one, in fact, would have wanted to see him replaced yesterday evening by a conductor more expert than he is in the interpretation of Stravinskyan music even though in the dress rehearsal given yesterday afternoon for journalists, the frequent interruptions showed that the good preparatory work done by the young Craft in pulling it all together was thrown to the winds by the still younger Stravinsky, always unsure, always in search of

himself . . . Of the five elegies that go to make up the Lamentations of Jeremiah, Stravinsky has set to music fragments of the first, third, and fifth in the Latin. There are six soloists: soprano, alto, two tenors, a bass, and a basso profondo. The make-up of the orchestra is complex and rich in little-used instruments. The first fragment is broken up into five groups designated by Hebrew letters which are syllabized by the chorus; the chorus recites the whole text *sotto voce,* and it is then taken up by the tenor with counterpoint by the women's voices. And so it continues by groups, or sub-groups, for each of which the Hebrew letter is repeated.

The structure of the work was explained here yesterday by Maestro Roman Vlad . . . following the "fundamental twelve-tone constellation" of the work through all of its changes and bringing out the various songs to be found in it, the monody of the bass and all the architectonic symmetry till the final perfect consonance in which every motion of the soul is resolved. Needless to say, here, as in the *Cantos* of Pound, or the *Ulysses* of Joyce, the intelligence of the schema is of little assistance to one who listens, as the work should be listened to, with a kind of mental virginity. And the ingenuous impression left by *Threni* is this: that Stravinsky has not been suffocated by the technique and the format he has imposed on himself, for the score bears the stamp of his own personality, and he comes particularly alive whenever the undercurrent of normal tonality breaks as if by a miracle through the forest of discordant voices—which happens in many places with the chorus and in a few phrases with the soprano and alto. . . . We would not attempt to deny that from the complex of the sober and yet highly intricate score there emanates an afflatus of religious inspiration. Why should we deny to an intellect that has known all experience the right to a conversation with the Divine?

We did not see Montale's notice then, but only a morning headline, *"I Treni,"* which drew the comment from Stravinsky: "Successor to *Pacific 231,*[82] no doubt," and a report in *Time* magazine: "[The] big name-studded audience (poet W. H. Auden, composer Francis Poulenc, et al.) braved a motorboat strike and journeyed by gondola to Venice's 450-year-old Scuola di San Rocco, one of Italy's famed Renaissance religious schools, for the fall's most eagerly awaited musical event. In hushed expectation, beneath a Tintoretto ceiling, they watched 76-year-old Igor Stravinsky, with a claw-like motion of his right hand, launch the orchestra into the premiere of his latest work. What followed was some of the finest—and most complex—music of Stravinsky's career. To prepare the Hamburg Radio Chorus for the taxing job of staying on pitch, while unaccompanied, conductor Robert Craft rehearsed the group more than twenty times."

The next day Stravinsky left by automobile with his son Theodore and

82. This Swiss composer Arthur Honegger's most popular piece.

Dr. Ernst Roth of Boosey & Hawkes to conduct *Threni* in three Swiss cities, on a double-bill with Beethoven's Ninth Symphony (!) conducted by Hans Schmidt-Isserstedt. Mrs. Stravinsky, Eugene Berman, and I went to a party for Alec Guinness at Peggy Guggenheim's. André Peyre de Madariague was there and talked to me about his new book on Bomarzo. By the time Stravinsky had returned to Venice for a rest, before entraining for concerts in Vienna, I was in Brussels, staying at the home of the Baroness Hansi Lambert, and conducting a concert of Webern and Stravinsky under the auspices of the Brussels World's Fair. The next day I flew to Frankfurt with the elderly Princess Fürstenberg, another Lambert houseguest, and joined the Stravinskys at the Frankfurter Hof. They had come from Venice by car. We continued to Hamburg the next day, stopping briefly in Salz-der-Helden, an old Nieder-Sachsen town. Stravinsky repeated his Scuola di San Rocco concert in the Hamburger Musikhalle, and we heard the *Magic Flute* at the Staatsoper. Rolf Liebermann played the tape of the premiere of Schoenberg's *Moses und Aron* for us. At a reception in the Vier Jahreszeiten, I struggled to remember my German, sitting between a senator and Phillip Jarnach, Busoni's pupil.

We drove to Brenner's Park Hotel, Baden-Baden, stopping briefly at J. S. Bach's town of Celle, dining there with Stockhausen and Boulez, now acidly referred to by Stravinsky as "Goethe and Schiller." All that I remember of the conversation is that Stockhausen spoke contemptuously of the notion of composing at the piano. From Baden-Baden we were taken to Donaueschingen. At a morning concert by the Juilliard Quartet, Stockhausen, sitting with me, groaned aloud throughout Bartók's No. 4, but contained himself during Stravinsky's *Trois pièces*, which he cannot have liked any more. We attended Hans Rosbaud's matinée concert of Debussy's *Jeux*, which Stravinsky put down as *"trop laliqué,"* Schoenberg's Five Pieces, and Stockhausen's *Gruppen*, then drove to the Baur Au Lac, Zurich, with Hansi and Lucie Lambert and Souvtchinsky. The next day, François-Michel[83] and his friend André joined us from Paris for my birthday.

On the 21st the Stravinskys and I took the night train to Florence for three perfect autumn days, with the aroma of roasting chestnuts filling the streets. Since Florence did not have an airport, I was obliged to go to Rome to fly to Hamburg for my next concert. I felt feverish on arriving in Hamburg, and after rehearsing the NDR Symphony in the morning, canceled the afternoon session and the concert. Fortunately Ernst Krenek happened to be in the city and agreed to conduct his piece in my concert. Still weak from what must have been an influenza virus, I nevertheless flew to Vienna to fetch the Stravinskys, coming from Florence, at the railroad station. We

83. A fine pianist, sometime housemate of Boulez, and the most discriminating gourmet I have ever met. He was a devotee of Claudel, and, at the request of André Malraux, edited the *Dictionnaire Fasquelle.* André, his chauffeur and lover, was a handsome young man of whom the Stravinskys and I were deeply fond.

dined at Lucie Lambert's in Hietzing, near Schönnbrunn Palace. An invitation had arrived there from T. S. Eliot in London to attend a reception at Faber and Faber. We telegraphed our acceptance from the Sacher Hotel the same night. Lucie's doctor urged me to submit to an appendectomy immediately, but I took antibiotics and decided to postpone surgery until New York.[84] Stravinsky conducted his *Oedipus Rex* at the Wiener Staatsoper, and he and I shared a concert with the Wiener Symphoniker, Haydn No. 101 and Schoenberg's Five for my part, *Apollo* and *Pulcinella* for his.

Arriving in Paris November 9 on the night train, we were met by Boulez and François-Michel. Rehearsals for our Salle Pleyel concert on the 14th began immediately, but without progress. On the morning of the dress rehearsal, it was glaringly apparent that the chorus and soloists could not sing *Threni*. Boulez had not fulfilled his promise to rehearse the piece. But Stravinsky was at fault, too, in not immediately canceling the concert, as his friends pleaded with him to do, and as he was morally and artistically bound to do since his latest creation would not be heard in an acceptable manner. Shockingly, Stravinsky turned a deaf ear to his wife's, Nadia Boulanger's, and my entreaties, and for a paltry cachet went ahead with the fiasco. I wanted to cancel my two opening pieces as well, Webern's Passacaglia, and the Three Movements from Berg's *Lyric Suite*, which were also underrehearsed, though the strings of the Orchestre Lamoureux could not have played the latter with a hundred more hours of preparation. These two pieces, of course, should not have been chosen (by Boulez) to introduce *Threni*, since music more remote from and antipathetic to the Stravinsky opus is unimaginable.

The concert was a nightmare. *Threni* broke down several times and at the end was vociferously hissed and booed. Boulez came backstage to urge Stravinsky to bow nevertheless, but he angrily refused, and shouted at him a resolve never again to appear on any stage in Paris. Antoine Goléa's *Conversations With Boulez*, an attack on Stravinsky, was on sale in the foyer, together with my book, *Avec Stravinsky*. A copy of the Goléa had actually been placed on the piano in Stravinsky's dressing room. Seeing it, Boulez blenched and quickly snatched it out of sight, but Vera Stravinsky had purchased a copy, and, back in the hotel, read it, to her horror, but not to Stravinsky.

Before leaving for Rome, Stravinsky received a letter from Sonia Botkin, daughter of the doctor who perished with the Tsar at Ekaterinburg: "Dear Igor Fyodorovitch, I came to your concert with Dr. Chekhov, but we could not reach you. We have not seen each other for so many years and I so much wanted to know about you and your family, whom we knew and loved for such a long time . . . L. S. Chekhov died six years ago, and your godson, Alexis Chekhov, was killed in the War (1944) . . . My telephone is

84. The operation never took place.

Balzac 76–76 . . ." Greatly disliking intrusions from his past, Stravinsky did not call.

He bowed to pressure in another instance, however, when Heinrich Strobel, director of the Südwestfunk in Baden-Baden, asked him to explain his criticisms of the "German style" of playing his music, published in Strobel's magazine, *Melos*, in his absence, and provoking an uproar. Indeed, Stravinsky's interview had caused such offense that on his last visit the orchestra did not stand when he entered the rehearsal room. The affair was resolved by Strobel writing a letter in Stravinsky's name, with the composer's imprimatur. While in Paris I received a gracious letter from Igor Markevitch apropos my recording of Schoenberg's Orchestra Variations.

We were in Rome on November 21, but my room in the Hassler Hotel adjoined the suite of Fulgencio Batista, the ex-dictator of Cuba, and the bodyguards stationed at the end of the corridor added to my anxieties concerning my concert with Stravinsky in the Teatro Eliseo on the 27th. A handwritten letter awaited me in the Hassler from Glenn Gould, sent from the Hotel Am Zoo, Berlin:

> Dear Bob: After our conversation in Hamburg, I wrote a short note to the CBC in Toronto and had a reply last weekend. They are most interested and enthusiastic for the idea of your conducting the CBC Symphony. I told them that if my schedule permitted we would like to include the Schoenberg Concerto, and so they suggested the following dates . . . May is impossible for me but certain times in October would I think be quite all right . . . Would you drop me a line to the Hassler, Rome, for arrival November 18, or to the Metropole, Brussels, for arrival November 20. I am sorry that I shall miss you in Rome. I trust that Vienna was a great success and that you are quite recovered from the 'flu. P.S. . . . I think you will enjoy the [CBC] orchestra and having ploughed through the Schoenberg with considerable élan 5 years ago I [sic] imagine they will do a more than competent job this time. You might consider making me your manager. I'll bet even Judson can't get any conductor an engagement this quickly.

The day after our concert we took the night train to Paris, where we dined chez Suzanne Tézenas,[85] then continued by train to London. There, on December 4, we partook of a bibulous lunch with, among others, Sir Harold Nicolson. His diary reports the occasion accurately, except that he does not mention the presence of such other guests as Isaiah Berlin, Henry Green, Spender, Edward Crankshaw:

> I lunch in a private room at the Connaught at a luncheon given by David Astor for Igor Stravinsky. He greeted me warmly. He tells me how much he

---

85. A sponsor of the Domaine Musicale.

enjoyed *Some People,* and what a delight *Journey to Java* had been to him and his wife. I groan inwardly. "But, of course," he adds, putting his hand on my shoulder, "your best book is your life of your father."[86] I was overjoyed by that. He said that as a composer he admired technique, and that he felt my technique was superb. I swelled with pride. He said how much he envied us writers, who had finished our work when the book was published. It was so different for a composer. His compositions, when played at Buenos Aires or Melbourne, were often entirely different from anything he had composed or intended.

On December 9, Vera Stravinsky received a copy of Eliot's *Old Possum's Book of Practical Cats* from, and inscribed by, the author: "To Madame Igor Stravinsky in memory of a very happy evening."[87] The next day, Stravinsky conducted *Agon,* Symphony in Three Movements, and *Apollo* with the BBC Symphony in Festival Hall. Three days later, he and I lunched with Spender and Cyril Connolly at the Garrick Club, and the following day we boarded the SS *United States* at Southampton for New York.

1959

On January 4, 1959, I conducted a Paul Fromm concert in Town Hall consisting of *Threni,* Schoenberg's Five Pieces for Orchestra, and the American premiere of Berg's *Altenberg Lieder,* this last, incredibly, still unpublished and unknown. Dimitri Mitropoulos and Leopold Stokowski were in the audience, and at a reception afterward, in a restaurant whose proprietor was the father of the pianist Eugene Istomin, Stravinsky introduced me to Stokowski with the remark, "This is Stokowski, if you want to meet him." Stravinsky was contemptuous of conductors—"they are not original people"—but his rudeness in this case was unwarranted and extremely embarrassing.

The next two days were spent recording the concert in CBS's East Thirtieth Street studio. Richard Avedon photographed Stravinsky afterward in his *shuba* (fur coat) in the windy street. Between the sessions, Milton Babbitt and I went to the publisher, Peters, to check Milton's theory that the E in the canon in Schoenberg's "Premonitions" should be E-sharp, which is not in Schoenberg's manuscript but is found in the version for chamber ensemble by his son-in-law Felix Greissle. A day or so later Greissle visited Stravinsky to tell him that Schoenberg had admired *Histoire du Soldat* (in spite of his critical remarks in a copy of the score). On the 7th, we went to a double birthday dinner at Auden's for Vera Stravinsky and Chester

---

86. Lord Carnock had been British Ambassador to the Sublime Porte, to Spain, and to Tsarist Russia.

87. We had dined with the Eliots at Claridge's the night before. See *Stravinsky: Chronicle of a Friendship.*

Kallman. Lotte Lenya was there, telling salacious stories at the expense of Alma Mahler.

Back in Hollywood, on February 17, Andre Marion brought William Montapert, his close friend and choice of attorney for the Stravinskys, to meet his new clients. On the 20th, a special delivery arrived from the poet Theodore Roethke, in Seattle, containing a copy of his *Words for the Wind*, inscribed: "For Igor Stravinsky, master of finance, from Theodore Roethke (*Baron von und zu Gar Nichts*)." Has he gone around the bend?

On February 22, the Stravinskys gave a party for the Spenders, Huxleys, Gerald, and Isherwood, and a few days later another one for Isherwood alone. Why have I never said anything pertinent about him? Perhaps the answer is that having taken the role of observer for himself, he strove to remain invisible, and I, no Houdini, could not make him visible, or even bring him to life. The Stravinskys loved him, trusted him, counted him as a most loyal friend, and he loved them, Vera more than any woman he knew. He understood that the Stravinskys, as close friends of Serge Diaghilev, were latitudinarian in sexual matters, and he felt wholly at ease with them, as he did not with Aldous. (How can Aldous have lived and traveled so closely with Gerald?) Stravinsky once asked Isherwood point blank about Auden's sexual orientation and was given a point blank, well, blow-by-blow, answer. Isherwood loved Aldous but was envious of the way people congregated around him at parties and social events.

On March 23 I conducted the Monday concert with Vera Zorina as *récitante* in Debussy's *Chansons de Bilitis* and the Mallarmé–Hindemith *Hérodiade*. The next day Stravinsky received a letter from T. S. Eliot:

London. March 19, 1959.

Dear Stravinsky: My wife and I were recently in New York for four days on our way back from the Bahamas to England. While there I had a telephone conversation with Mr. Paul Horgan . . . and also talked on the same subject with a friend of Mr. Horgan's and mine, Mr. Robert Giroux . . . I understand that an organization, the name of which I failed to grasp,[88] is eager that I would write the libretto of an opera, of which you would compose the score, for a fee of $20,000 [each]. I also understood that you had been approached on the subject and that your answer was awaited.

I am more than doubtful of my own qualifications for such a task. I have no formal musical education, or I should say my education in performance on the piano was begun at the age of ten and ended at the age of twelve . . . At the age of twelve, I could, to some extent, read music . . . This knowledge has completely vanished. I am now unable to read a note, and it seems to me that some proficiency in music is the necessary part of the equipment of a libret-

88. The Santa Fe Opera.

tist. Nor have I at the moment any ideas for the theme of an opera. Nevertheless I am writing, before giving a definite refusal, to ask you for your views on the matter.

I am even doubtful whether distinction as a poet is any qualification for the task. To be quite frank I was not happy with Wystan Auden's libretto for *The Rake's Progress*. Apart from incidental criticisms, my chief objection was that I thought he had combined unsuccessfully two quite different themes, the first that of Hogarth and the second that of the traditional contract with the devil. I say this all the more freely because I much admire your score, but my opinion about Wystan's work makes me all the more doubtful of my own competence, since Wystan has much more knowledge of music than I can claim.

. . . Yours very sincerely,

T. S. Eliot

Eliot was well aware of the true disaster of the libretto, of course, but was too prudent to put it in writing. Stravinsky answered from the Imperial Hotel, Tokyo, on April 8:

The proposition from Mr. Paul Horgan came at a very bad moment for me and until your letter I had not thought seriously about it . . . I myself am not very attracted by the operatic form at present and I would certainly not undertake to write an opera like *The Rake's Progress* for any fee . . . Perhaps I can counter-propose another kind of work, a cantata, or static stage piece (genre my *Oedipus Rex*), a shorter work than an opera and one more suitable to my present non-operatic musical thought. Perhaps a Greek-subject piece in a contemporary reinterpretation . . . I will think about this. But of course it would be a pleasure and an honor to work with you and I think that we might invent something very interesting together. Would you give me your thoughts about this suggestion (it is not really a proposition) and let me manage what I can manage? . . .

. . . my wife joins me in sending our most affectionate regards.

I. Str.

P.S. I hope we can talk some day about the *Rake* libretto . . .

P.P.S. Do you have a copy of your article about Julien Benda? If not, do you know where I could get a photostat of it . . . It must be 20–25 years old [and] I do not remember the magazine, but I wish to say a few words about Benda, whom I met once on a transatlantic crossing.

Three days after returning to Hollywood, in the first part of May, Stravinsky composed his *Grabmal* for Prince Max Egon von Fürstenberg, our host at Donaueschingen the previous October. I had already begun to rehearse for the Ojai Festival, which was to take place on the next-to-last weekend of the month. This time the Stravinskys would not be with me, but in Copenhagen, where he received the Sonning Prize, conducted a concert, and lunched with Niels Bohr and Isaak Dinesen. My Ojai repertory this year was conspicuous for novelties: Haydn's Symphony No. 73; Mozart's No. 40 in the version without clarinets; a harp concerto by Dittersdorf; Schubert's Fifth Symphony; Purcell's *Come Ye Sons of Art* and a sonata for trumpet and strings; a Vivaldi concerto for two flutes and strings; Bach's *Nun ist das Heil* and Magnificat; and the *Tristan* Prelude (with the rarely played, but rightly, since it is a let-down, concert ending). I also conducted Debussy's *Faun*, Schoenberg's Five Pieces, and the complete *Petrushka*. At my invitation Natasha Spender gave a solo piano recital, but suffered a memory lapse and some harshly negative reviews. As she fled back to Los Angeles, Stephen arrived, and in a late-night talk with me in a roadside cafe in Ventura spelled out the already very evident problems in their marriage.

Another letter from Eliot came before the Stravinskys' return:

London.

May 21, 1959.

My dear Stravinsky, . . . I am interested to know that you do not wish to undertake another opera at the present time but that you are considering a cantata or something more in the nature of your *Oedipus Rex*, which I had the good fortune of hearing beautifully presented in Hamburg several years ago. Of course I do not know whether I am any more competent to provide the text for a cantata than I should be for an opera . . . However, if and when the subject comes to you and in any case when you have further thoughts about the subject, I should be delighted to hear from you again on this matter. I will also try to apply my mind to this suggestion.

I am sending you herewith a copy which my secretary has made of my article of December 1928 on Benda. I must, however, tell you emphatically that on rereading this piece I am extremely dissatisfied with it. I was, in fact, quite horrified to learn that in 1928 I held the opinion there presented about the prose writing of Charles Péguy. Why I held that opinion at that time must remain a mystery, but I want to make clear now that I am a fervent admirer of Péguy's prose writings and was under the impression that I always had been, ever since Alain-Fournier introduced me to the *Cahiers de la Quinzaine*. It may be that my opinion of Julien Benda would be modified by time, but although I haven't read anything of his for many years I remember *Belphégor* with satisfaction.

Christopher Isherwood's diary for June 9 reveals that "the Stravinskys came on Sunday. We had a very happy time together. Talked about Wystan—the sadistic anti-theater side of him which occasionally appears in the plays. The covering of Baba's head with a tea cozy in *The Rake's Progress*, for instance. Igor is fascinated by fire. He comes out with me when I barbecue the steaks and keeps up a running commentary: *'Etwas umdrehen. Wasser.'* Here also. 'Oh, bravo!' "

A letter from Rudolf Serkin invited me to conduct in his festival in Marlboro, Vermont. I proposed a program of Haydn, Mozart, Schubert, and *Pierrot Lunaire*. He replied agreeing to the classics but not to the Schoenberg because "it would be the players' first contact with new music." But this new music has been around since 1912!

I went to Santa Fe in mid-June to rehearse Donizetti's *Anna Bolena*. Paul Horgan tells the story from there:

All went well until Friday, June 26, when [John] Crosby[89] was obliged to telephone the Stravinskys at Hollywood that on the preceding day Craft "fell and dislocated his elbow," and was in the hospital. It seemed that [after the dress] rehearsal with the orchestra in the theatre, Craft, in high spirits at how well affairs were moving, vaulted the barrier between pit and first aisle.[90] His foot caught, he put out his right hand to break his fall, and put his right elbow out of commission. He was taken to St. Vincent's Hospital, X-rayed, equipped with a plaster cast on his conducting arm,[91] and ardently attended by a sumptuous mezzo-soprano of the company.[92] She readily assumed the spiritual costume of an inflexible Florence Nightingale, which he perhaps did not find so becoming as her incarnation as a romantic . . . companion . . .

On the following Monday I met the Maestro and Madame as they arrived at Lamy from California on the Super Chief. They were in a great state of concern over Craft, and were eager to go to him at the hospital . . .

I drove them there and we found Craft's room. He was propped up in bed with his cast on a lap pillow. Cordilleras of books flanked him. There was emotion close to tears at their reunion and I left, saying I would return in an hour to take them back to their guesthouse.

When I returned to the hospital and knocked at Craft's door, I entered to find a tableau of such woe that my heart felt like lead. There were signs of tears on Madame's face. Stravinsky was diffidently ingratiating over what I would soon hear. Craft was nervous and circuitous in stating the case which they hated to bring up but must.

89. Founder and Director of the Santa Fe Opera.

90. The wall was actually a rope at the darkened *entrance* to the theater. The barrier between the pit and the aisle was too high to be vaulted.

91. This neglects to mention four hours of surgery.

92. Regina Sarfaty, of the City Center Opera in New York, sang the title role. She was the company's best-known artiste at the time.

In brief, they had talked everything over all the time I was gone, and with every apology for seeming ungrateful, they begged to be delivered somehow from staying at [Witter Bynner's] guesthouse . . . The manager of [La Fonda Hotel] found a two-bedroom suite for the Maestro and Madame, who could occupy it immediately. I hurried back to the hospital with my good news, and was rewarded by joy like light as it broke over all their faces. I was embraced, I was their deliverer, and before dinner they were safely transferred, bags and all . . . Craft remained in the hospital . . . When released he would return to the room given him for the summer by two [elderly and retired] school-mistresses in their beautiful hillside house, where, to their witty indignation, his angel of mercy would continue to administer to him—with the *door closed,"* the ladies announced over Santa Fe, their sibilant delight over imagined dalliance as energetic as their definition of decorous hospitality . . .

It was characteristic of Stravinsky's strict professional discipline that he was ready to take the first cathedral rehearsal on the evening of the day—June 29, 1959—on which he arrived. All was serene. Craft was not seriously hurt,[93] the hotel suite was a great relief, and the cathedral event interested him.[94]

On returning to Hollywood after the concert, I received a letter from Boulez complimenting me on my recording of *Le Marteau,* together with Stockhausen's *Zeitmasse,* adding that "nationalism is *à la mode* in France, and one does not know whether it is Napoleon III, Charles X, Joan of Arc, Saint-Louis, or de Gaulle." To illustrate the remark as it pertains to the last, he had drawn a cartoon of the general, hands in the air, and captioned it "the sign of the cuckold."

At the beginning of August, Balanchine visited Stravinsky with the request to choreograph *Movements* for Suzanne Farrell. The composer was skeptical about the ballet orchestra's ability to play it, but consented. On the next day I began acupuncture treatments for my dead elbow with Dr. Knauer and immediately felt signs of life in it. Knowing that I regarded Knauer as a holistic quack, Stravinsky, who shared Aldous's high regard for him, and believed the practice of medicine to be a talent and an art, accompanied me and sat with me throughout this and subsequent treatments.

On August 6 Stravinsky sent a note to "Dear T. S. Eliot: I did not write . . . because I was anxious to complete my new composition,[95] and could

93. Perhaps not, but my arm, in a cast for several weeks, was revivified only by a month of acupuncture treatment at Aldous Huxley's urging.

94. From *Encounters with Stravinsky, op. cit.*

95. *Movements for Piano and Orchestra.*

not consider any other work . . . I have received a proposal from NBC television, meanwhile, that has helped me to see my direction."

In mid-August, while I was at Princeton, two letters came from Boulez, the first about my *Marteau* recording—"excellent, especially the second and fourth movements" (the two that Stravinsky preferred)—the second asking me to have Stravinsky sign a request for a copy of (Boulez's) *Pli selon Pli* tape, since "his signature will impress the Rundfunk and have a great importance and prestige." On August 28, the Stravinskys and I lunched at the Princeton Inn with Roger Sessions. After that the Stravinskys visited Robert Oppenheimer. "Even his feet," unshod because of the heat, "are intelligent," Stravinsky said. Oppenheimer had told him that he was the first guest to have recognized the Dürer drawing on the wall from a distance.

At the beginning of September we were in London, dining at Claridge's with the Eliots, and dining and lunching there with Stephen Spender, who introduced the Stravinskys to Ralph Richardson, whom they regarded as the greatest actor they had ever seen; he was at another table, but came to the Stravinskys' and graciously chatted with them. After two days at the Hotel Berkeley in Paris, followed by a lunch with François-Michel at Chez Francois (a great Richebourg), we went to the Soutine exhibition at the Galérie Charpentier, and from there to the Orient Express for Venice. This was a thrill every time for us, with the early morning arrival in Milan, the aroma of espresso on opening the windows, the vendors of *prosciutto crudo* sandwiches, the views of Lago di Garda, the trestle to the Venice station, and the ride through the canals to the hotel, where Stravinsky immediately set to work completing two Gesualdo sacred motets by filling in the lines of the missing part-books.

On September 26 Leonard Bernstein, on tour with the New York Philharmonic, called on Stravinsky to offer a commission for a piece to open the new Philharmonic Hall in Lincoln Center. Stravinsky curtly refused, saying that such things were "more in Elgar's line." Leaving the hotel, Bernstein, a thousand times richer than Stravinsky, asked me if it really was a question of money. I answered that Stravinsky was already at work on a new piece, but if the sum had been more generous, he might have accepted.

On October 10 Stravinsky composed a canon for flute and clarinet *A la Mémoire de Raoul Dufy*. The next day we were joined by Eugene Berman for a Sunday afternoon excursion to the Villa Manin,[96] Aquileia, Udine, and (Rilke's) Duino.

---

96. Vera Stravinsky took a number of photographs of the villa, dilapidated then and now over-restored, of its famous sculptures of (Sabine?) rapes, and of the extensive grounds. Developing the negatives months later, she was surprised to find a good, pensive portrait of Stravinsky in one of them, and had the picture enlarged from a negative the size of a postage stamp to a cover for a large tripartite screen. This adorned the Stravinsky home in Hollywood thereafter and is now in the living room of my New York apartment.

In Bologna, for a concert during the last week of October, we visited Giorgio Morandi in his atelier. He made a gift to Stravinsky of a characteristically pale, almost white, still life. Stravinsky had known this shy, humble, gracious man since the 1920s.

In Paris, en route to London, the Stravinskys and I saw Claudel's *Tête d'Or*, staged by and starring Jean-Louis Barrault. Understanding nothing in the long dialogue between Simon and Cébès, which comprises virtually the whole first act, I left after it. In the evening I flew with Lawrence Morton to Hamburg, where I conducted a radio concert. Lawrence and I saw performances at the Hamburg Opera of Handel's *Alexander's Feast*, admirably staged and sung, and of *Lohengrin*, whose conductor, Heinz Tietjen, director of Bayreuth for a time in the Nazi period, started the Prelude to Act 3, then stopped beating, letting the orchestra finish the piece by itself. My own conducting was of Dieter Schönbach's Concerto for Soprano and Instruments, Webern's Orchestra Variations, *Agon*, and Henze's *Three Dithyrambs*. I spent the intermission with the expressionist artist Hans Henny Jahn, builder of baroque organs, founder of Ugrino Verlag, which brought out the Watkins–Weismann *Gesamtausgabe* of Gesualdo, and author of *Das Holzschiff*.

On October 31 Lawrence returned to Paris and I flew to London, rejoining the Stravinskys at the Savoy Hotel. A letter from Berman awaited me: "I saw Mary McCarthy on her way to Tripoli and received her book on Florence . . . Florence better becomes Mary's turn of mind than Venice, which is too rich, too complex, too dazzling for her to grasp intellectually . . . Naples, Gesualdo, Paestum, the quiet dinners at the Excelsior seem already in the distant past."[97]

In London we dined at the Berkeley Hotel with Eugene Goossens, Paul Horgan, and Paul's friend Edward Bissett. Horgan wrote that "Stravinsky and Goossens had not met for [almost two] decades, and now spent almost the entire meal in a duet of reminiscence and remembrance . . . in Stravinsky's funny gaieties, Goossens's elegant and original rhetoric, and Craft's neat discernments, there was much camaraderie."[98]

Stravinsky's Festival Hall concert took place at the inconvenient hour of 11 P.M., following a Beethoven concert by Klemperer. Stravinsky conducted *Oedipus Rex* with Jean Cocteau as Speaker. William Glock, Director of BBC Music, told us that someone on his staff had mistakenly offered

97. We had been to these places together in the week of October 12 with Stravinsky and Berman's friend, the photographer Robert Emmet Bright. Berman and Bright met our flight from Treviso at the Rome airport, and Bright drove us from there to Sperlonga— where the pool in Tiberius' cave shimmered with shivering eels—and Naples, where Stravinsky and I shared a concert in the Teatro San Carlo. In Gesualdo, Bright photographed, in color, Giovanni Balducci's altarpiece *Il Perdono*, of Gesualdo kneeling by his uncle, Carlo Borromeo. The painting has subsequently been restored.

98. *Encounters with Stravinsky*.

Cocteau £75 for the performance, and that Cocteau had already wired his acceptance before this was corrected to £750. Two days later I conducted a BBC broadcast concert of Varèse and Stravinsky. The next day we sailed from Southampton on the *Liberté*. On the first day out we saw the film *The Bridge on the River Kwai*.

In New York, Stravinsky recomposed his Dufy Canon for string quartet (November 24). On the same day he wrote to Eliot:

> Dear T. S. Eliot: We were obliged to change our plans and sail back rather than fly. We therefore reached New York later than expected, in fact a day after you sailed . . . You have probably not had much time to consider our project, nor, frankly, have I, with all my concerts in the past two months . . . I am going to read the York Mystery Plays . . . I haven't had time to read the *Deluge* yet.
>
> I expect to see Mr. E. Martin Browne's *Cranmer* next week . . . I was interested by some remarks of yours in an interview (*The Paris Review*), that a poet puts his own voice in everything he writes. So, too, I think, does a composer write vocal music for his own voice.
>
> Kindest regards,
Igor Stravinsky

The same day we went to, but beat a rapid retreat from, the musical, *Gypsy*.

On December 7 I was taken to the Carnegie Hall premiere of Marvin David Levy's *For the Time Being*, a dull, empty setting of Auden's Nativity poem. Claude Raines's orotund narration provoked titters, but the audience had come to see him, not knowing whether he had ever returned from Morocco (*i.e., Casablanca*). We spent the following evening with John Gielgud at the Liebersons'. We had heard his weepy reading of Shakespeare the week before.

Eliot replied promptly about the "opera," the subject of which had now become Noah's Ark. He had told the Stravinskys about the *York Mystery Plays* and *The Deluge* at a dinner in his London (Kensington) apartment on September 7, 1959:

> London. December 8, 1959.
> Dear Stravinsky, . . . our liners appear to have crossed in the Atlantic . . . I . . . am still considering whether I can be of any use to you . . . I hope, however, that when you have read *The Deluge* (of which, as I said, a text appeared in the Everyman volume in the Everyman Library) you will let me know if you think you can make any use of it. I might be able to make further suggestions for its arrangement, and should be very happy to be of any use though, as I say, I think you will need another more expert librettist to help also.
>
> I hope you will not be overworking while you are in New York, and wish

that you could be in a more favorable climate at this time of year. Your programme of travel and work while in Europe astounded me. You are an older man than myself, but I should hesitate to undertake such commitments as you have done.

Stravinsky and I jointly conducted a Town Hall matinée concert on the 20th featuring *Les Noces*. After it we attended a reception with Auden, Kallman, the Edmund Wilsons,[99] and others. Wilson's account of the occasion in *The Sixties* is not without errors, but his quotes of Stravinsky's talk and descriptions of him are accurate, and his note to the effect that Stravinsky hoped the Dead Sea Scrolls would turn out to be spurious is true and revealing. The statement "Robert Craft has become to some extent Stravinsky's impresario and mentor" is also true of the time, I am ashamed to say, and it regrettably echoes what was thought of me, though others, Byzantinists, would have added "Paracoemomene." Wilson mistakes Margrit Weber, not named, as her husband's daughter, wrongly says that Stravinsky dealt directly with her husband for the commission of *Movements*—Nicolas Nabokov brokered it—gets the host's name wrong, hides a cruelly demeaning reference to Leo Lerman's homosexuality under his initials, and wrongly begins his guest list for the second party with me. (I was downtown recording Bach.) He spells Stravinsky's pronunciation of the "au" in the word "applaud" as "approud," but might have observed that all of his "au"s sound German. When I first knew Stravinsky, Auden was "Owden."

The next day Stravinsky received a gracious note from Gerald Murphy about the *Noces* concert, reminiscing about the party on his *peniche* in the Seine after the premiere of the piece. Stravinsky recalled that Michel Larionov introduced him to the Murphys, which is undoubtedly true, since Sara Murphy had studied painting with Larionov's wife, Natalie Goncharova. Stravinsky remembered the American couple fondly, and that he and his wife had dined at their home in New York (February 9, 1946). They were aware that the Murphys were models for Dick and Nicole Driver in *Tender Is the Night*, one of the first American novels that I read to the Stravinskys. They did not know that Picasso did nude portraits of Sara on the beach at La Garoupe, and that both Fitzgerald and Hemingway were in love with her. The Stravinskys could never afford to own such Murphy luxury products as Mark Cross luggage.

On December 31 Stravinsky signed a contract to conduct *Firebird* on Leonard Bernstein's January 31, 1960 telecast, for four thousand dollars. Money had been lost on the Town Hall concerts, and Stravinsky asked David Oppenheim to negotiate this sum to help make up the deficit.

99. Mrs. Wilson, née Helena Mumm, of the champagne family, had been a close friend of the Stravinskys in Germany in the 1920s. They conversed in Russian and German.

Chapter 7

Isaiah Berlin and
Stravinsky's *Abraham and Isaac*

S travinsky was introduced to Sir Isaiah Berlin by Nicolas Nabokov in the Savoy Hotel, London, December 10, 1956. Meeting again two or three times in Venice in mid-September 1958, they enjoyed each other's company. Not wishing to impose on the composer's time, Sir Isaiah conducted his decade-long correspondence with Stravinsky through me. Eventually he would transliterate the text of *Abraham and Isaac* for Stravinsky, as well as play the key role in commissioning the work. His letter containing his account of its first performance, Jerusalem, September 23, 1964, is certain to become a document of lasting importance in our cultural history.

Sir Isaiah's first note to me was posted at "5:50 P.M." from the Venice railway station, September 21, 1958:

> Ferrovia, Venezia. Heat. Hurry. Lost Tempers. Glad to leave this Sodom. Forgive me for plaguing you with messages: but (a) if we could go to *Threni*[1] in Paris, I really shd be grateful to you. I can come on the 13th evening if we cd attend a *rehearsal.* (b) I wrote a fan letter to S.: it is an absurdly pompous document which I regretted immediately . . . but I wished to say that I had had a most moving and bouleversant experience, *and* I am too anglicized to be able to do it simply & convincingly. So defend me if he mentions it: tell him I meant well and did what I could.[2] I should *never* have left before *Threni* if it weren't for illness & my stepchildren. More demanding than real children. And I much enjoyed our few brief conversations.
>
> Yrs,
Isaiah

1. The world premiere of Stravinsky's *Threni: The Lamentations of Jeremiah* would take place on September 23 in the Sala della Scuola Grande di San Rocco.
2. Nicolas Nabokov purloined the letter from Stravinsky's room in the Hotel Bauer Grunwald and returned it to the sender.

I had met Sir Isaiah after a concert by the Hamburg Radio Orchestra in the Teatro alla Fenice on September 17. We went from there to the Piazza, a ten-minute walk that he infused with drollery and wit. I had spent the afternoon of September 20 with the Berlins, the Stephen Spenders, the Baroness Hansi Lambert and her daughter Lucie, visiting the lagoon island of San Francesco del Deserto, a bird sanctuary, whose caretaker monks Isaiah thought depraved. Back on the *motoscafo*, he was silent and contemplative, Stephen talked eloquently about Browning and Venice, and I contributed a two-cents worth on Rembrandt Peale's 1830 Venetian diary.

The Stravinskys and I spent December 5 of that year at Headington House, the Berlins' home in Oxford, a day or so before Stravinsky began rehearsals for a BBC concert. The other luncheon guests were Mr. and Mrs. Edgar Wind, Stuart Hampshire, and John Sparrow, Warden of All Souls, who was in the newspapers because of his testimony in the trial to lift the ban on *Lady Chatterley's Lover*. I was seated next to him, but felt so intimidated by the elegant prose of his essay, "Latin Verse of the High Renaissance," which I had just read, that I lacked the courage to converse with him. At teatime, Lord David Cecil (I had read his life of Cowper, *The Stricken Deer*, to the Stravinskys) and Maurice Bowra joined the gathering, the latter conversing in Russian with Stravinsky. I took refuge in the Ashmolean to see Uccello's *Hunt*. Stuart Hampshire rode back to London with us, talking about George Painter's *Proust* the whole way.

I next heard from Isaiah in a letter dated January 30, 1959, just before our concert tour in Japan.

> Dear Mr. Craft (if you call me Sir Isaiah, that is all I can do; but I would much rather not)
>
> Thank you very much for your letter, and I apologise for sending you a typed letter, but believe me it is better so—remember what happened to my fan letter to Stravinsky—I was only too glad to retrieve it from Nabokov and quietly destroy it, before worse humiliation occurred. Please send me the book—when it appears—there is something absolutely unique about his style and content, the independence, consistency, coherence and general tightness and nutritive content of it all seems to me enormously high.
>
> [. . .]
>
> I envy you Japan . . ."Genji" is a splendid dull masterpiece—I read it with a kind of conscious pleasure with which one reads becalmed beautiful things. It is not the kind of thing I really like at all—I suspect that Arthur Waley, for all his great gifts, turns everything into a kind of flat Bloomsbury object of the 20s, and that his hatred of embellishment and rhetoric is not there in the original—that what we get is a kind of two-dimensional devulgarised version, but which also leaves out a certain amount of life and colour. However I may be wrong.

Life is very quiet here at present. I have neither seen nor heard from any members of the Lambert family.[3] I have seen no poets, no priests, no composers. I am trying to write a lecture on Russian ideas in the nineteenth century—it is an escape world such as has never been; they themselves escaped through reality to quite a considerable depth and to escape into their imaginative world from ours is a double act—something which only Stravinsky could express by means of sound.

Do write me again if ever you feel moved. I was very glad to receive your letter.

Yours sincerely,
Isaiah B.

P.S. I enclose Montesquieu, also my latest oeuvre, of which I do not think much. I did not like *Lolita*, although I signed a letter to the *Times* proclaiming the need for publishing it here, despite all calls for decency. I prefer *Zhivago*. It is something that at any rate no Soviet composer will write an opera on its libretto, but the thought of the inevitable film appalls me.

By this time I was aware of the radically different opinions of Stravinsky and Isaiah on the merits of the two books, published at about the same time, the main topic of talk wherever we went. Stravinsky did not like *Doctor Zhivago*, esteemed highly by Isaiah, and the situation was the reverse with *Lolita*. The subject never having been raised, I assumed that Nicolas Nabokov, cousin of the author of the latter, had briefed Isaiah.

On September 28, 1959, Isaiah wrote again, inviting the Stravinskys to Oxford and offering to find rooms for them in London:

Dear Robert: I was delighted to receive your letter. All that I could do about the Ritz I have done . . . The rooms . . . solid, bathrooms enormous, the service moderately good, old-fashioned but dependable, the porters excellent . . . the manager an idiot . . . the restaurant large, quiet and restful to the nerves, but the food dull and uninspiring to a degree—the owner . . . does not want it to be smart, efficient, or attract too much custom . . . Hence the restaurant is discouraged from tempting its clients and the food is kept deliberately British and tedious . . .

The 2nd November . . . will suit us very well, if that is when you all want to come. We shall be delighted, not have a formal reception as last time, but ask one or two people who are likely to give pleasure, for example, Prof. Ayer,[4] whom you ask for, who by that time will be living here . . . When you say Forster, you mean E. M.? He is a gentle old creature who speaks in a low, low voice, giggles like a schoolgirl, and likes flattening subjects to the lowest level

3. The Belgian bankers, affiliated with the Rothschilds. Baroness Hansi Lambert was a frequent hostess of the Spenders, Nabokov, and Cyril Connolly in her Brussels home.

4. Professor Freddie Ayer did come.

to which they can naturally attain if unsupported, in this respect rather like T. S. Eliot . . . he is very clever, charming, and deliberately provincial: his outlook is that of, let us say, the city of Guildford, where he comes from. He is very fond of Wagner, and is the most English of all English phenomena, somewhat self-consciously and deliberately so. Stephen could ask him easily, but if the evening or afternoon is not to end in a series of gentle whimpers, someone with a little vitality would have to be imported to keep him going, unless you or the Stravinskys are prepared to prod him into constant life. His principal interests in the world are what Mr. [Irving] Kolodin, in his notorious review of Spoleto,[5] so disagreeably refers to as the third sex. Whenever a book by one of its inhabitants is unfavourably reviewed by anyone known to Forster, he despatches a small postcard saying "How could you have brought yourself, in these days, to have written . . . etc." Isherwood's devotion to him rests entirely on this. Still, he is the best living English novelist without a doubt. If you have tea with him it is exactly like having one with an excellent character actor who pretends to be a distraught old aunt: "Oh dear, oh dear, where have I put my spectacles—what a lot of jam we have eaten! Electric torches are much more practical than candles, I never know how to ask for the right kind of batteries" etc. I should love to see him and Nicolas Nabokov in a room together, it would be a clash of cultures such as has never been.

I am not sure about the date of the Stravinskys' arrival vis-à-vis your own. Do please let me know these again . . .

A note from Isaiah dated November 4 awaited me in London:

I have secured the Royal Box for Friday night at Covent Garden, which makes ingress and egress much easier. It will also be possible to obtain a dull but adequate meal at the back of the box, which can be consumed during the intervals . . . Scotch will be provided. I enjoyed the visit enormously, I hope so did you and the Stravinskys. I shall see you on Thursday night—indeed I will come and fetch you if I may . . .

Lord Boothby shared the Royal Box with us, and the dinner was served at a table in the foyer. I remember that an usher stopped Stravinsky from returning to the loge with a glass of Scotch in his hand. The opera, I should add, was one of his favorites, *Ballo in Maschera*. It was superbly conducted by Rudolf Kempe.

We next saw the Berlins in New York. On Sunday, January 3, 1960, in Carnegie Hall, Stravinsky conducted *The Rite of Spring* (with the 1943 *Danse sacrale*), as the second half of a concert that began with me conducting Schoenberg's "film" music, Berg's *Three Pieces*, and Webern's *Six Pieces*. We dined afterward with the Berlins and the Goddard Liebersons. The next

5. In *The Saturday Review of Literature*.

morning *The Rite* was recorded in a double session in the ballroom of the St. George Hotel, Brooklyn. But the exhausted Stravinsky could manage only a single, much too slow, "take" of the *Danse sacrale*, in which the tam-tam did not play at all (the part is missing from the score), and the timpani played in the wrong places, as it did in all of the recorded rehearsal "takes" that I conducted. (I recorded Berg's *Three Pieces* in a late afternoon third session.)

On January 29, 1960, Isaiah described another performance:

> Dear Bob: This is only to say that the performance of *Oedipus* at Sadler's Wells was absolutely marvellous. Colin Davis conducted it well, & the Japanese masks produced by some Algerian designer worked very well . . . It is the best thing I have seen in London for a very long time, most moving and splendid, and except for the wildly exaggerated diction of Mr. Hordern, who was melodramatic in the extreme, it was a most epoch-making experience. I think on the whole that *Oedipus* is probably one of the greatest works of the twentieth century in any art and this came through (but don't tell S. that) more strongly in London than in Venice.[6] But do tell him that it was a genuine triumph, and that I have promised the Sadler's Wells authorities to let him know this.
>
> I am sorry that our meeting in New York was so brief. Could you not all come and take a house near Oxford one day and rest in peace and we could all conduct long agreeable conversations? Our love to I[gor] F[yodorovich] and Mme S[travinsky].

We saw the Sadler's Wells *Oedipus Rex* on October 18, 1961. After it, Stravinsky spent an hour with Colin Davis coaching him on the tempi.

The next communication, from Portofino on September 7, seems to have gone astray. It recounted a socially awkward experience in Rapallo, of being at a gathering that included Ezra Pound, who had returned there on his release from St. Elizabeth's in Washington. At that time the poet had taken a vow of total silence. This was followed on the same day by another communication from Portofino:

> Dear Robert: . . . You shall certainly get *Roots of Revolution*,[7] wrongly so called. It is a quarry of minute information, but dull to a degree, save for those who really want to know where a given obscure revolutionary was born: why; what he did: why; when imprisoned, hanged, eaten by Siberian wolves; how; etc. No general ideas. Our love to I.S. and V[era] A[rturovna] . . .

The next letter is dated October 10 [1960], Oxford:

6. Berlin had heard Stravinsky conduct it in the Teatro alla Fenice in September 1958.

7. Franco Venturi's *Roots of Revolution* (London: Weidenfeld and Nicolson, 1960; New York: Grosset and Dunlap, 1966). Isaiah Berlin wrote an introduction to this (pp. vii–xxx), which was reprinted as "Russian Populism" in *Encounter* 15 No. 1 (July 1960), pp. 13-28, and in *Russian Thinkers*.

Dear Robert: I know exactly the kind of quotation you want and cannot think of any offhand . . . There is a famous piece called "Conversation Between the Boy in Trousers and the Boy Without Trousers" by Saltykov-Shchedrin—*i.e.*, a dialogue between a Russian and a German boy, in which the Russian boy, dirty, in mud, starving, etc. explains why he nevertheless is not prepared to barter his soul for sixpence, like the tidy, clean, well-fed, conformist Germany boy—and because he has not sold his soul he can get it back again whenever he wants it which the German cannot. But this is not what you need either. The only thing which comes to my head is the most hackneyed of all patriotic Russian quotations which comes from Pushkin's *Russlan & Lyudmila,* very early in it, when, after describing various mythological creatures, he says "here is the Russian spirit . . . here it smells of Russia." I wish I could think of something more apt. The point is that the whole of Russian literature is absolutely self-preoccupied, from the comedies of the late eighteenth century to *Zhivago* and beyond. The Germans are pretty self-centred but they are as nothing compared to the Russians whose sole subject is Russia—and this even in the most Western and aesthetically pure novels of Turgenev. This seems so universal and taken for granted—almost unconscious at times—that one very seldom gets any conscious emphasis on the point that Russian artists are the most self-conscious in the world, and that when, for example, national Russian music was created in the sixties and earlier, this succeeded because it was not artificial Chauvinism, but merely the expression of a feeling which was in any case pervasive—the subject of constant debate—at the centre of awareness—and not a provincial admiration—conscious archaism, a deliberate attempt on the part of an isolated group to awaken dormant memories, etc. as it was in a good many other countries. As soon as the Russians feel that "the Russian spirit is present" they fall into natural and not artificial ecstasies, and the result, though often rhetorical and sometimes tortured, is not exotic or artificial. More than that I cannot do for you, alas, but there is no doubt that quotations of the kind you seek are in existence and the person to supply them would be any competent professor of Russian literature (the person who must abound in this is the critic Stasov)[8]—we haven't one in Oxford which is why I cannot ask him—still by the time this letter is typed and I sign it I may have discovered.* I hope you are well. My love and respects as always to the Master and Madame S.—I am very sorry you are not all coming to England. When will you? I am not well yet and avoid people but would have welcomed you most warmly.

Yours,
Isaiah

P.S. How much longer can you give me on this? & where will you be?
* no, alas, nothing

8. Vladimir Stasov was the doyen of the nationalist Slavophiles among literary and music critics (1824–1906).

A letter from Isaiah dated June 5, 1961 at All Souls' College reached me in California:

> Dear Robert: Forgive me for not replying to you before. I am delighted to think that you and the Master will be coming here again. I have not seen Nicolas [Nabokov] yet, but I propose to go to Israel with him in the beginning of September—I wonder what impact that will make on that versatile personality. There is, as you know, a music festival there, with Casals, Stern, etc. Rubinstein e tutti quanti. I shall be back in September with Aline and we shall look forward to your visit during the last eleven days of October with great eagerness . . . Do say when you want to come. All weekends are free. I shall lecture three times a week in October in order to be able to go to India for . . . the celebration of the worthless mauvaise epoque poet, Tagore, who would have been a hundred this year, only, unfortunately, not alive. With all the false surges of our century he probably made the biggest impact with the smallest means. Please remind me to tell you about Klemperer and the Soviet Delegation at *Fidelio*. There was a scene and quite an enjoyable one . . . Love from Aline and please convey our affectionate regards to Mr. and Mrs. S.
>
>   Yours,
>   Isaiah

On July 10, 1961, I received a note from Isaiah at Oxford:

> Dear Robert: . . . On Thursday we go to Glyndebourne to see the new Wystan work—he claims that Henze's music is marvelous.[9] I wonder, I wonder, I wonder. I am now off to Geneva for a week to preside over a very dubious Conference (contemporary reality in the Soviet mirror), then Portofino as usual, then to Israel . . .
>
> Do not forget us and we shall expect you all on the 20th October.

My diary for October 20 gives an account of this:

> Lunch at Isaiah's with Robert Graves, tall and military in bearing, large-eared, and, today anyway, for his inaugural lecture as Professor of Poetry, neatly shorn. Because of the nose, which, like Michelangelo's, has been broken, one thinks of a pugilist, and—doubtless as with the sculptor, too—the fingernails are rinded with dirt. When Stravinsky asks him about his present work, Graves says: "I am disguised as a professor, implausibly." When Graves asks the same question, Stravinsky tries to explain that he is engaged in "serial versification," to which Graves responds, "Poetry is less purely genial than that and more demonstrably linked to moral questions." He begins a story: "I started down the street this morning thinking about a woman when suddenly my breast

9. *Elegy for Young Lovers* by Hans Werner Henze, libretto by W. H. Auden and Chester Kallman.

pocket burst into flames . . ." But whether the fire was merely allegorical or actually incendiary we never find out, for he switches to "hallucinatory psilocybin mushrooms," claiming that they "can induce a state of grace." He also reports on a conversation with David Ben-Gurion, who told him that "Israelis are less good taxpayers than the citizens of Protestant countries, but rather better than those of Catholic countries." On Paul of Tarsus: "He was not a Jew, of course, but a Syrian; you remember the Ebionite Epistle?" And Plato, who "did more harm than any one man before Freud." Aristotle, as no one needs to be told, was "a thoroughly unpleasant character," and Alexander the Great— "Shall I tell you my new idea about him? It will take just three minutes." (He actually glances at his watch.)—"That legend of the Priest's serpent at Siwa is nonsense. Alexander decided to conquer the world entirely out of the jealous desire to surpass Dionysus. Like Dionysus, he had himself declared 'Son of Zeus.' " Graves puffs on his cheroot while this is allowed to sink in.

Composing a "tonal row" and accompanying words of dedication for the Berlins' guestbook, Stravinsky asks for an English equivalent to the Russian "kanitel." Literally, the word means a silver or gold skein, Isaiah says, but, commonly, a long, entangled argument—whereupon someone quotes "or ever the silver cord be loosed." Graves lobs this back—he is faster with words than anyone I have ever encountered—with "The Yiddish is 'magillah,' and the Greek and Latin are . . ." Nicolas Nabokov whispers to Stravinsky in Russian: "Do you suppose he knows the Etruscan, too?" Watching Graves listen enviously to the Russians, I ask which of his languages he would most readily exchange for it. "German," says, without hesitation. After he has left for his lecture, Isaiah remarks that "He would do anything to depose Jesus and crown the White Goddess, but he is a true poet."

> . . . What envious youth cares to compete
> With a lean sage hauled painfully upstage—
> Bowing, gasping, shuffling his frozen feet—
> A ribboned hearse parked plainly down the street?

Isaiah reads passages from the Bible for us in Hebrew, translating word for word and explaining, *El, Elim,* and *Elohim:* "*Elohim* is used to denote the lords of the others, the Hammurabis, the 'After Strange Gods' "—obviously he is aware that Eliot's title is not Biblical and not a quotation.[10] He promises to prepare a properly accented copy in Russian transliteration of the story of Abraham and Isaac, if this is the episode Stravinsky chooses for his cantata. But Isaiah urges him to consider the first and seventh days of the Creation, a suggestion that fails to attract the composer because of the length: "The music would be longer than a British weekend."

10. The title comes from Kipling's story "On the City Wall" (". . . go whoring after strange gods").

Graves's bluntness, rather than his wit and erudition, seemed to have a subduing effect on Isaiah, but he was preoccupied with an appointment later in the afternoon to discuss a commission from Israel for the Biblical work by Stravinsky. Nabokov had come in time to help negotiate this, and Stravinsky had already chosen Abraham and Isaac as his subject. Isaiah promised to transliterate the text from the Hebrew to Latin letters, as well as provide a Russian translation. When he sent the text to me in California, November 7, we were in the antipodes and did not receive it for another month:

Dear Robert: Herewith the text. I have adopted a fairly home-made method of transcription and there are no mysterious Orientalisms of pronunciation— nothing that cannot be comfortably pronounced by anyone we know. My system is:

To put in apostrophes between vowels where two vowels come together and are not a diphthong, say as in the name Jeal or Joel where each vowel is given its full value. So far as other vowel sounds are concerned, they are pronounced as they would be in German or Russian: 'a' as in 'father', 'e' as in 'bed' or the German 'mehl', 'ei' like the 'a' in 'bake', 'ai' like the 'i' in 'like', 'i' like 'ee' in 'keen', 'o' as 'aw' in 'bawl', 'u' as 'oo' in 'soon', and 'y' is simply used like a German 'j'—'ya' instead of 'a', 'ye' instead of 'e', etc.

As for consonants, that is slightly more tricky because the apostrophes between them indicate some kind of gap which could, for singing purposes, best be replaced by a very short 'e'. 'V'lekh should be pronounced ideally as a 'v' held for a second and then 'lekh' ('kh' is of course the Russian 'x' or the 'ch' in the Scottish 'loch') but quite often it is transliterated as 'velekh,' where the first 'e' is extremely short, and this is what I recommend. I didn't put in e's simply in order to avoid the trouble of putting squiggles for shortness above them, which would give the whole thing a Czech look. But whenever you see an apostrophe between consonants, a short 'e' may and perhaps should be substituted. I have also accented the thing as best I could, and I think both pieces—both the first Seven Days of Creation and the (non-) Sacrifice of Isaac—are now in order. So, for example, the complicated Hebrew pronunciation of the equivalent of Isaac—Yitzkhak—is most comfortably pronounced Yitzekhak, if the 'e' is not lingered on.

What more have I to tell you? I am sorry that I wasn't able to come to the concert in London. I enjoyed your visit very, very much indeed. I send my warmest love and affection to the Stravinskys and in five minutes I must go to India. And that will be that. Do let me know what is happening.

The fee for the composition will present no difficulties, I gather. I long to be secretly immortalised by the purely simple little piece of work that I have done with great hope and devotion. If you really want a tape recording, I could send you even that, it would not make me self-conscious, but I should send it even if it did.

> Yours,
> Isaiah

I responded on our return to California in December, and on January 3, 1962 received the following reply, dated December 28, 1961:

Dear Robert: I am delighted to hear about *Abraham–Isaac* and hope that it will go splendidly. Do let me know if there is anything further I can do towards it—to be associated in any way with creation is a rare privilege, the greatest I should say in my life. Given that one cannot write libretti, it is the nearest that one can come to it perhaps . . .

If you do go to Israel, remember the food is abominable—nothing in Jerusalem is edible, though Tel Aviv has one or two restaurants which are not as terrible as the others. This is due partly to social and partly to theological reasons, and the combination is repulsive. The inhabitants are of sterling character but lack everything in the nature of douceur de la vie. You must acquire a sympathetic cicerone not in the country but from outside. Otherwise really no go—personally, I mean, not musically.

As for *Perséphone*, it was bold and on the whole successful. Nabokov . . . said about Ghika's decor that it was by Philip Emanuel Bakst. It was garish and gaudy but at least un-British: and Frederick Ashton's choreography was exceedingly elaborate; and Miss Beriosova's microphones with which she was bespangled went wrong once or twice, sometimes crackled, sometimes went out of action . . . and the whole thing was, from the point of view of the public, a wild and triumphant success. I like the music very much and the text not at all. The shades of Ida Rubinstein hovered slightly over the whole thing. But . . . it was imaginative, coherent, and not a feeble British or Anglo-Saxon effort either to imitate some kind of appalling German or Italian modernism, nor mild pastiche of Russian choreography, nor English puritanism, nor its obverse, coarse English verismo, which at present disfigures our ballet stage through the medium of Messrs. Macmillan and Cranko. So all in all, it was a lively, worthy, rich, adequate affair: not marvellous or right. It rose to no heights, was not at all what anybody could have wanted at the time of composition, will not live for ever in anybody's memories . . . and marked no nadir and no apogee. But it was nothing to be ashamed of or to laugh at or to weep over. Surely that is, in these days, something? . . . I would really prefer the music without any dancing, décor, boys, girls—or anything. I like the score very much indeed—more, perhaps, than even the composer himself these days . . . India was quite wonderful: particularly the accent. It has entered my substance . . . They are a handsome, amiable, silly, exhausted race. Nepal is something out of Firbank crossed with Shaw. The Cabinet and Prime Minister are in jail, the King governs by direct democracy and the Ambassadors, of whom there are only five, plot and counterplot all the time. The appearance of everything is magnificent, the Himalayas wonderful and the whole unreal to the highest degree. Well worth a visit. India, on the other hand, is all too real and everything lasts a very long time indeed.

Yours ever,
Isaiah

P.S. Please give our fondest love to the S.s and say we are sorry we are not to see them this year—or rather the first part of this year, for in the Autumn I shall be at Harvard and then we shall all carouse (I hope) long and deep (I in my teetotal cups).

Isaiah himself was our cicerone in Israel, meeting us at Lod Airport on August 20, 1964 and remaining close to us for the next four days. It was at this time that we heard him say, as he would tell Ramin Jahanbegloo three decades later, "In Israel I don't particularly feel like a Jew, but in England I do." He told us, additionally, that "I am not a believer, but I will take my hat and prayer shawl and go to the synagogue all the same."

I should add that the Stravinskys and I had been in Israel from August 29 to September 7, 1962, giving concerts in Tel Aviv, Haifa, and Jerusalem. The next letter is dated January 12, 1962:

Dear Bob: Having just returned from London . . . I hasten to report the news.

It took the form of a visit by Mr. [Aron] Propes,[11] plus Mr. [Theodore] Kollek from Israel, and several telephone calls from Isaac Stern. The chief item of news which I hasten to communicate to you is that the commission for *Abraham and Isaac* is definitely settled—I mean that the Israeli authorities guarantee the sum stipulated (fifteen thousand) and that I am formally to communicate this fact . . . I doubt now if Casals will be there at any time—one of the conditions of acceptance is apparently that his Oratorio on the Infant Jesus in the Manger—which lasts three and a half hours and is not thought a work of unforgettable splendour—[though] these three and a half hours are apparently unforgettable—every minute seeming an eternity—be performed. This may be too much for the Israelis, both intrinsically and because of the subject—Casals wants it done in a church in Nazareth, but as all the Nazarenes— or a good portion of them—seem to be disgruntled Communists . . . the situation is, as you might say, fraught with problems . . . Certainly every effort will be made to make you happy and comfortable in Israel—I only hope not too much effort. The sense of measure in that country is somewhat lacking. It

11. He and his wife became affectionate friends of the Stravinskys and visited them on all of their visits to Los Angeles and New York until the last year of the composer's life.

is one of its great charms, but one has to have a considerable sense of irony to respond to it appropriately . . .

. . . But I must not run on.

Yours ever,
Isaiah

Nabokov had apprised Isaiah of Stravinsky's opinion of Casals. The next message is dated June 25, 1962:

Dear Bob: I sent you a letter care of Rolf Liebermann rather vaguely addressed, as indeed was my telegram on Mr. S.'s birthday. I do hope all this has been received—not that it would matter gravely if it was not, from anyone's point of view but my own. I really was deeply touched by the dedication in the Penguin which I discovered when I bought it last week.[12] This is undeserved immortality if ever there was a case of it. I feel like one of those figures who occur in Beethoven's correspondence—say Pastor Amenda—who never would have been heard of but for this lucky circumstance. Future scholars will doubt- less wonder what I am doing by the side of Madame Boulanger. Let them do so. Madame Boulanger probably wonders about it already.

Dear Nicolas seems to be not well. He writes often and sadly. Yesterday I talked to him on the telephone and discovered your address. He told me you would not all be likely to be going to Latin America.[13] If that is so, perhaps there is a ray of hope for the Israelis. It would be wonderful for them if the work could be completed—I gather Nicolas now refers to it as "the sacrifice of Sir Isaiah"—by say next April. Do you think this is at all feasible? . . . If there is anything I can do . . .

I think *The Flood* is magnificent and sent you an idiotic account of it from The Times which I hope arrived. Here there is much raving about Britten's *Requiem*—critics cannot write because they are too moved to set pen to paper and must allow themselves a week or two to recover from a transforming ex- perience which has determined their entire outlook etc., I wonder, I wonder. He is a gifted composer no doubt, but there is something wrong in the tone in which these reactions are communicated. Eddy Sackville-West, now Lord Sackville, sat in floods of tears from the beginning to the end; Mr. David Drew cannot trust himself to write; the *Times* man thinks that all works should be dated by this central event; will this read as one of the great curiosities of criticism, even less than in a hundred years' time? Your guess is as good as mine, but I have a feeling that we shall guess the same. The article in *The*

12. This refers to a paperback Pelican Book, *Stravinsky in Conversation with Robert Craft,* consisting of *Conversations with Igor Stravinsky* and *Igor Stravinsky: Memories and Commentaries.*

13. For a pair of concerts in Caracas after our return from the U.S.S.R.

Observer is splendid. What is the Maestro's attitude to his biographer, Eric Walter White?

Yours,
Isaiah

P.S. I shall look forward to our meetings in New York very much indeed.

Rolf Liebermann, director of the Hamburg Opera, had invited the New York City Ballet to perform three Stravinsky ballets on the composer's eightieth birthday: *Orpheus*, conducted by Leopold Ludwig, the chief Kappelmeister of the Oper; *Agon*, conducted by me; and *Apollo*, conducted by Stravinsky. The following note from Isaiah is dated July 23:

Dear Bob: I enclose a worthless story which the author—unknown to me—wishes Mr. Stravinsky to see. I see no reason why he should: it seems to be perfectly worthless although I did not have the courage to say so to the author. He begged me to forward it, and so I do, you can cast your eye over it and if you think as I do, you could throw it away or return it with a formal note. Alternatively do nothing at all . . .

May I draw your attention to the piece in the excellent *Mimesis* by Erich Auerbach (I am sure you know it)—in particular the chapter where there is a comparison of Homer's account of the recognition of Odysseus by the nurse Euryclea and Abraham's non-sacrifice of Isaac. It is quite well done and is worth reading. I think Igor Fyodorovich would think quite well of it, too.[14] The fact that if Auden were on a desert island the records that he would choose to take with him would be all by Wagner and Strauss depresses me no end. So did [Schoenberg's] *Erwartung*,[15] which seems to me a marvellously gifted piece of super-Kitsch. Am I quite wrong about both these things? You must tell me when we meet in New York in, I hope, September. I shall go straight to Boston, omitting New York when I arrive, and await a summons.

The subsequent letter is dated October 28:

Dear Bob: . . . I am sure you are right about Nicolas and the Germans, but I do not think one is allowed to tell him that. As for Yehudi [Menuhin], he is a great deal shrewder in his saintly, withdrawn, detached way, more realistic than a good many more committed persons; in spite of all the fantasies about Yoga and the common mystical roots of our and Indian music . . . Upon everyday matters he has a kind of childish perceptiveness, which also Einstein

14. Stravinsky had read the book, as well as Auerbach's *Dante*.
15. Solti had conducted a triple bill of *L'Heure Espagnol*, *Erwartung*, and *Gianni Schicchi* at Covent Garden.

had, and which is much more effective than more elaborate ironies. Nicolas reappears here at the beginning of December in order to discuss the 1966 Israel Festival—I do not know what will happen there. I do not know where the money is to come from for *Moses and Aaron.* Meanwhile, a furious dispute is going on here about whether the twelve letters of *Moses und Aron* are essential to the title of the opera, because of twelve tones, . . . and mystical mathematics—or whether one is allowed to call Aron (one "A"), Aaron (two "A"s). I do not propose to take much part in that dispute, but in order to confuse matters further have asked Dr. [Theodor] Adorno to contribute something to one of the publications about *Moses and Aaron* that Covent Garden is about to put out. Not a word will be understood, and it will be comical to see how our critics react to his profundities. Do you know him? You must know him well.[16] I knew him well in Oxford and cannot help thinking him a marvellously comical figure. I propose to invite him to Oxford to deliver a lecture, and that too I shall enjoy, though perhaps not in quite so direct a fashion as I should.

Thank you for the clippings.[17] I find Hebrew fiendishly difficult to read, but one of these nights . . . I shall torture myself by spelling it out word by word—it is far more difficult than the Bible—and as a soporific it may be stronger than anything I have tried yet.

All my love and affection to the Stravinskys and yourself. I shall appear in the United States in mid-March—in Washington, where I have to deliver those fatal lectures. Where will you be? Do let me know.

The next letter is dated March 26, 1963:

Dear Bob: Thank you for your postcard. I have not spoken to Nicolas or Propes or anyone else, and these are purely my individual reactions to what you say. I think they will go mad with frustration if *Abraham and Isaac* is done as part of

16. The sociologist-musicologist Theodor Adorno was very well known in Los Angeles when I arrived there in 1948 as the chief source for Thomas Mann's novel *Dr. Faustus.*

17. I had sent an article by Nicole Hirsch from the *Paris Express* (translation mine): "It all began three years ago. Stravinsky was at Oxford at the home of his friend, the philosopher Isaiah Berlin, who read some passages from the Bible for him in Hebrew and with ancient scansion. Deeply impressed by the musical qualities of the language, Stravinsky dreamed of using Hebrew in a vocal work. In 1962, invited by the Festival of Israel, Stravinsky made a memorable tour, and at that time the commission was proffered. . . Stravinsky later refused the money and gave it to the fund for the restoration of Massada. 'I wanted the Hebrew to be sung in a different manner than in the religious tradition, which is fixed,' Stravinsky said. . . 'I did the same thing in Russian. My *Noces* is not sung like Tchaikovsky or Rakhmaninov, after all. . . The baritone has a double role, that of a narrator, who tells the story, and that of a singer, who comments. . . The language led me to employ appoggiaturas, as in Arab chant. . . As for the serialism, that is perfectly natural; it is the other way that is exhausted. I cannot do otherwise. . . Schoenberg understood this.' "

the regular concert season. Already they are in a lunatic state because Margot Fonteyn will not come to their Festival this year but in some regular concert series and they think that everyone will spend money on going to see her and correspondingly not on the Festival—which is no doubt perfectly true. They would almost rather she didn't come at all this year; it is only after I told them that if she didn't come this year they would never get her again, that artists are "special" and cannot be played fast and loose with because of mysterious local Israeli considerations, that they have desisted from barring her. They still may: as you know, they are not very easily controlled.

Now as to *Abraham and Isaac:* I am sure it is not a Festival piece in the *Firebird* sense, but then nothing that I.S. would write or could have written in the last ten years would have been that from the point of view of the unsophisticated Israel audience. The mere thought that he had written something for them and to be presented there would excite them all so immeasurably that the actual content of the music would play relatively little part, especially if it lasts for twelve minutes, even if it is repeated again. Perhaps some more popular piece of Stravinsky could be inserted between the two performances of the new piece—anyway, their pride will know no bounds if it is done for and in the Festival—I do not think you need worry at all about the actual content of the piece, *i.e.*, from the point of view of its popular reception. When you say it is late, do you mean it cannot be rehearsed in sufficient time? If I were you, I really would acquaint Propes with the facts about the solo part, the requirements for the baritone . . . Could it all not be rehearsed in America and brought over, as it were, packaged? If it is a question of money—*i.e.*, paying for an extra number of rehearsals with peculiar intensity or acquiring the right baritone for a relevant price—I am sure that the Israelis would have friends in New York who would help them with that; but it is necessary to make the position clear not only to Propes but also to Kollek, who would understand it perfectly. I think if it is simply performed at a concert, say in October or November, it will fall relatively flat; it must be done as the climax—then it will acquire due publicity, which is what (I believe) they must long for, and show them the required sense of exaltation . . .

In London in late May, Isaiah invited us to Headington House once more:

Dear Bob: . . . I have asked Gilbert Ryle, partly in order to see what you and the Stravinskys think at the end of it all. He was not in the least surprised to be asked (he should have been), as he is rather a vain man; but he is very distinguished, though you will find, I think, a fairly militant lowbrow, albeit disguised.

I have indeed three tickets for Covent Garden and will disguise the fact of your presences if you really want me to. Otherwise I fear that all the inhabitants of the Directors' Box on that night—it is bound to contain Royal persons—will demand his presence. The person who chiefly wishes to be introduced to you at the moment is a very brilliant Russian philologist, critic, scholar, student of linguistics, . . . called Roman Jakobson, who is Professor simultaneously at Harvard and M.I.T., and whom you certainly will greatly enjoy meeting—he was one of the most exciting Formalist critics in the early twenties, and then "defected" and had an extraordinary career in Prague, Paris, Oslo, Columbia, Harvard, who bought him for an enormous sum—he was followed there by his pupils, like Abelard in the Middle Ages. He is at Stanford this year, in the Center of Behavioral Sciences, and I told him that it was unlikely that you would communicate with him and that it would be better for him to communicate with you—I think Mr. Stravinsky would enjoy a visit from him—he is a most imaginative and creative Russian scholar, who has just abandoned his Czech wife (by no means his first) and acquired a brand-new Polish one. In short, I recommend him.[18]

It will be very nice to see you. Please say if you want a motor-car sent—if so, nothing easier—to the Savoy. Do ring up, in fact, when you arrive. The only other persons in Covent Garden with us will be the Spenders, which I imagine will not be objected to.

My diary for May 29, 1963 contains an account of the Headington House luncheon:

Oxford. Lunch at the Berlins' with Professor Gilbert Ryle, a big-boned, major-in-mufti type, with bald, brindled cranium, thrusting jaw, and "intellectual" brow; one feels that without further make-up—he arrives in a parka, tweeds, specs, pipe ("Damn the dottle, let's get our teeth into the problem")—he could take to the stage playing a private eye (Bulldog Drummond). About two minutes of conversation make clear that the Professor is a purely British phenomenon, deeply suspicious of "continental intellectuals," and, indeed, of anyone from "abroad." If he were to make an exception, moreover, it would undoubtedly favor a lean, outdoor-type Australian pragmatist, say, over some pasty-faced Middle European logical positivist, even if the ideas of the latter on how to "do" philosophy were closer to those of the Professor.

"Why are your chaps always bringing up Dewey and James?" he asks me. "The world would have been so much better off without those "Great American Bores." No answer is expected, of course, and the impossibility of expostulation has already been conceded. Besides, more seriously offending countries have yet to be dealt with. (When they have been, one sees to what extent philosophy is a national and school bias. "Steeped in port and prejudice among the monks of Oxford," Gibbon wrote, escaping the fate.) Noncompetitive

18. Since this was written Jakobson's reputation declined, for having pilfered from, misinterpreted, and made a *bricolage* of Saussure, and for having supported postmodernism.

philosophers such as those of the U.S.S.R. rate only indulgent amusement, and, for open laughs, a Soviet philosophical journal is quoted on the Professor himself, cited as a 'bashful materialist" and "creeping empiricist." Stronger medicine is reserved for closer trans-Channel targets. "One of my greatest satisfactions as an editor was in publishing a review of the works of one Teilhard de Chardin, then rumored to be a biologist. What a lot of lemon juice we poured on *that* old teleological pancake." Merleau-Ponty fares no better: "French *clarté*, indeed. And, by the way, have you noticed how many French intellectuals have become retroactive heroes of the *maquis?*" Mention of Karl Popper provokes the remark: "The first person pronoun, found twice in Aristotle, occurs seventeen times in one of Herr P.'s shorter footnotes; he can hardly bear to use any other word." Two Israeli philosophers are dismissed with the comment, "Neither is actually very good at listening," and an over-enterprising British colleague is swept aside as a "literary civil servant. One wonders about these people who try to take the pulse of every new movement. Where do they get all the fingers?"

But the acid tickles more than it burns. On the subject of "philosophers' jamborees," he says, "The *real* philosophers are the translators. Picture two thousand of us in an auditorium in Brussels with Professor Gorgonzola on the rostrum being translated line for line: 'The ontological postulate of the, and . . . oh, pardon me, Professor, but I didn't get the last phrase.' Well, *I* got it. Rubbish, of course." Telling us of an invitation to a similar picnic "somewhere in the Great American West," he remarks that "they wanted me to 'express my views on philosophy,' as they put it, in a five-minute television interview, to which I replied that I doubted if I could make anything clear to anyone out there in less than five years."

Talking about the difficulty of trying to keep up with new publications, Stravinsky cites the case of a friend who has learned to read while he walks, even though he looks like the absent-minded professor, or the last eccentric. The notion of crossing the quad with a book to one's nose delights Professor Ryle—"Oh, jolly good, very impressive indeed, splendid, splendid"—but he does not agree that eccentrics are disappearing, "at least not when I look around at my colleagues in the common room." An aroma, unmistakably of that location, is twice uncorked, first when he replies to one of our queries with "That's a further question which I will answer when you have answered mine," and again when he illustrates a limitation of the word "correct," in the sense of behavior, with the example of Lord X, "who, when told that his wife had been killed, responded with 'What a pity.' This, you see, is perfectly 'correct,' but most people would probably agree that something is missing." Once or twice I wonder whether the best of his *aperçus* ("Every generation or so philosophical progress is set back by the appearance of a 'genius' ") roll off somewhat too readily, undermining confidence in their hundred-percent spontaneity, and arousing suspicion that a repertory is being worked off, in the manner of Tchichikov or Mr. Jingle.

After lunch, a bowl of cherries is handed round. (The Professor's appetite is commensurate with his frame, and when the main course is finally being cleared, he resists three attempts by the butler to remove his bread plate.) "I have a cherry tree of my own," he says—to my surprise, having pictured him in landless bachelor's digs—"but have not yet tasted its fruit because the birds get there first." Vera Stravinsky recommends a new kind of protective net, but the Professor's answer is that "The tree is thirty feet tall and I'm not," which is empirically verifiable, to be sure, as well as, one fears, an example of more than a little philosophical activity.

The only real mishap occurs when the word "music" slips out. The Professor glums thereat and is soon beating a retreat back to, as he says on the way out, "academe." (But when did he leave it? Can he have regarded the visit as an excursion into "real life," as he defines that concept in his new lecture, *A Rational Animal?*) When he has gone, Stravinsky compares him to "a very brilliant schoolboy who, without meaning to, has made us feel like very dull schoolboys." The truth is that whereas the Professor has enlightened and exhilarated us, we have failed to provide him with good cutting matter for his wit.

Isaiah's next letter, dated July 17, 1963, is about the Oxford Bach Festival and its Director, Lina Lalandi:[19]

Dear Bob: . . . Miss Lalandi asked me to accompany this with a "personal message." I do so. We can talk about all this when, as I hope, we meet at Christmas in New York. Any messages for Jerusalem? I shall be there for about ten days from July 25th. The Mass was performed very decently here at the Festival. I hear that Nicolas has found a baritone for you: I hope this is true . . . English antiquarianism on the subject of Bach is grotesque and I shall make a due protest. The St. John Passion was abominably performed by Dr. Thomas of the Thomas Kirche in Leipzig with some German singers from Frankfurt— the worst I have ever heard in my life, I think. Close to them comes the Oxford Bach Choir, conducted by the Kapellmeister [Jascha] Horenstein; the combination of the Oxford Choir, the conductor and Miss Lalandi, suffering from a crick in the neck but I do not think this made any real difference, gave the Festival whatever is the opposite of a flying start—a diving start, perhaps, so that we started below sea level. But Milstein played the Bach sonatas very well; [Ralph] Kirkpatrick was up to the mark (though he found the audience

19. The harpsichordist and founder of the Oxford Bach Festival. We met her at the Savoy Hotel, London, and saw her thereafter, over a period of several years, in Athens, Zurich, and London.

'cold'), and Fournier was marvellous—better, it seemed to me, than either Casals (now) or Rostropovich (an incredible statement, only worth making because true). Dr. Karl Haas, who between each movement of C.P.E., J.[S.], J.C. Bach etc. explained what was happening, was exactly like an Ustinov parody of an Austrian musicologist, exhibiting every speck of musical dust with adoring commentary.

Till Christmas!
I.B.

On September 17, 1963 I received a droll letter from Isaiah on the Israel Festival performance of *Fidelio* in Hebrew. He said that Jan Peerce lapsed into "the oily sound of the synagogue & produced a very oily flow" and that the gentiles sang the to-them-unintelligible syllables "most purely."

In New York, in December, we lunched with the Berlins in their suite at the Carlyle Hotel with their friend Alan Pryce-Jones, editor of *The Times Literary Supplement*.

The following communication, dated January 30, 1964, on Auden's lack of sympathy for the subject matter of Stravinsky's *Elegy for J.F.K.*, reached me in California:

Dear Bob: Wystan feels so much more strongly about Dag [Hammerskjöld] than about J.F.K. that I cannot believe his words will convey very much. On the other hand Tennyson probably did not feel very much about the Duke of Wellington, and yet the poem is very fine. And Wystan is a consummate crafts-man as well as poet.

I am glad to hear about the Cantor. Miss Lalandi I leave to you—I cannot cope with her. Her energy and emotion are admirable, but I feel that if I really did what she tells me I should perish like Sidney Herbert and Clough at the hands of Florence Nightingale (if Lytton Strachey and Miss Woodham-Smith are to be trusted).

Our love to the Stravinskys.

Yours,
Isaiah

The letter of September 7, historically the most important in this collec-tion, describes the Jerusalem premiere of *Abraham and Isaac*. Isaiah, of course, was perfectly aware that no more than three or four musicians in Israel would be able to keep pace with the latest proof of Stravinsky's powers of instauration:

Dear Bob: This is only to say that I thought the whole thing successful and not at all awful—which seldom happens on such occasions. The bad thing was, of course, that for an event of this kind the Israelis are too provincial to invite eminent critics, and have no idea what to do—this is one of the virtues of their vices, or vices of their virtues—I assume that all critics expect to come to Berlin[20]—still, never mind. I thought everyone behaved very reasonably and decently, and the whole thing was without the suffering normally to be expected on such occasions. I thought that I[gor]. F[yodorovich].'s condition was very sweet and good, particularly those whiskey-filled evenings when he melted so amiably and appeared to move without any strain or stress and saw himself as Igor Manteuffel. I was very sorry about his neuralgia—I hope it is better.

I hope to see you all somehow in April.

I shall never forget the extraordinary spectacle of the concert itself in Jerusalem: in all that crude, sincere, simple, touching but not exactly sophisticated audience, with all those odd faces and coarse white hair and open shirts and Populist appearances, the entrance of this exquisitely fashioned, porcelain figure, with the egg-like head, of the most fine and delicate artificially-wrought material, from an age totally removed from everything that had happened in the last quarter of a century, say—the last surviving voice of the *douceur de la vie* of the eighteenth century—appearing before an audience of, as it were, American peasants in some frontier town somewhere in the 1840s. I also enjoyed immensely our few conversations about Stephen, Wystan etc.— I wish they had been longer. I did not think that you hated it all too much— perhaps I was mistaken, but it seemed to me that you did not think the moral atmosphere detestable or the press conference anything other than harmlessly comical.[21] Anyway, do write to me again—I enjoyed our conversations this time in Jerusalem as much as anything in my life.

Yours ever and ever,
Isaiah

My love, respect, veneration, affection and gratitude to the S's.

On July 15, 1965, Isaiah wrote to Vera Stravinsky about the Oxford visit of Anna Akhmatova. He said that the poet had entrusted him with a profile portrait she had done of her in Petrograd before the Revolution. Isaiah promised, and did, deliver the portrait in person. Akhmatova had written on the obverse of it *"cattiva"* (naughty girl), for the reason that Sergey Sudeykin had left her for Vera.

On September 17, Isaiah wrote to me from the Carlyle Hotel, New York. His subject was a concert in Festival Hall, London, a few days before. The first half, the Variations and *Rite of Spring*, which I conducted, was used by a BBC television crew to rehearse the lighting, camera angles, and microphone placement for the second half of the *Firebird*, conducted by

20. See chapter 8. Dietrich Fischer-Dieskau sang it there on September 22 in a concert of the Berlin Festival.

21. He was annoyed with me for having involved myself during a press conference in a discussion with Peter Stadlen, the pianist, about performing Wagner in Israel.

Stravinsky. The conversation among the technicians was audible through most of the *Rite*, and at moments the stage was plunged in darkness.[22]

> Dear Bob: The Memorandum is this: you did the Sacre *beautifully* on the 14th and the nasty remarks of the *Times* critic (which I hope you took no notice of: Giulini *genuinely*—I admire him for it—does not read notices, & lives in his music and ignores them all: his fame is smaller than say Solti's . . . but his life and work are of far greater worth: & justice in the end will be done him)—I don't know who he is: [William] Mann? [Jeremy] Noble? If Mann, it is no different from the other rubbish—& vulgar rubbish—that he writes: I don't know what these people failed at: [Walter] Legge is a failed conductor; Martin Cooper is a failed minor composer: *don't* regard all this: your labours for, with, about the immortal figure whom you now know better than anyone, assure you a place not merely in heaven (on which I am a poor authority) but on earth too. As *I* say this to you—who have suffered one minor irritation at your hands—but who will always remain your friend and disinterested admirer: I say this to you not just to staunch what *must*—for you are a great *minder* I am sure, as I am, & cannot flick these things off as one should & the great heartless geniuses (and non-geniuses—Milhaud for example) do: I am afraid you will always wince: but if you didn't you would not be capable of entering into, integrating, understanding it all: & the pachydermatous aren't all that happy. The Huxley Variations were (for the moment at least) beyond me: they will come; the performance of Abraham & I. in London (Del Mar) was very good. To hell with them all: your prowess and deep musical understanding are not matters of doubt . . .
>
> Yours,
Isaiah

The subsequent letter is dated January 30, 1966:

> Dear Bob: Alas, that we should have missed each other. I should have been proud to be photographed with S. As it is undeserved, I have no right to regret this; but there is no one else except the late Herzen, and L. Tolstoy, about whom I truly feel this. I had no idea the Stravinskys were in New York when I was there,[23] and learned of it too late. But never mind, the future still exists. I shall be in New York at the end of March and for about three weeks in April . . .
>
> I hated appearing in Brandon's collection—I have neurotic feelings about that, and go too far, and cannot help it. All forms of public self-exposure of

22. See chapter 8.

23. Isaiah had missed the world premiere of *Requiem Canticles* at Princeton, but the performance had not been advertised or publicized in New York.

this kind appear to me a kind of branding (no pun intended) but [Sir Lewis] Namier I stand by, although I have had a very cross note about it from his graphologist, to whom, according to him, I do not pay nearly enough attention. I have read your lecture [on *The Rite of Spring*] with the greatest fascination—and long to talk to you about it. The transposition to 1912–13 is probably easier for me than for you, even though it cannot be said that at the age of four I was fully aware of what the Second Front then meant to the French composers, nauseated, I suppose, by Central Europeans, whose great champion, curiously enough, was Romain Rolland. Have you ever looked at the *Revue Wagnerienne?* It is a very queer publication, not much related to music . . . the hatred for Glazunov is just like Berlioz's hatred for Cherubini etc. but don't tell S. that. He hates Berlioz, and a comparison will not seem flattering, but the effect of Berlioz was not dissimilar; the measure of his influence has always been minimized, and Liszt's exaggerated, it seems to me . . . When you come back from Paris, will you not spend a few hours in New York? . . .

On April 7, 1971, the day after Stravinsky's death, Isaiah wrote to me:

Dear Bob: There is absolutely nothing one can say when really fateful events occur & one's life is altered for good. I am sure you must—in spite of all the long expectation of Stravinsky's death—in spite of the fact that both you and Madame S. must have gone over this in your minds over and over again—be undone all the same; when it actually *happens*, it is always much worse, as well I know. Nothing will, alas, ever be the same: but one cannot *say* anything: all words are like sticks, & not even sounds convey anything remotely adequate. You *are* the guardian of this great & marvellous heritage: but it is a retrospective sort of experience: & I only hope it does not hamper your own green shoots. Being here I cd not come on Friday nor to Venice: for I have to tend to my College—it is in some upheaval & the living take precedence over the dead, no matter how eminent: & then I return to New York on April 15 to teach at C.U.N.Y. as contracted. When will you return? when will Madame S.? I did not wish to bother her or you when I heard how I.S. was: I thought too many *now* do that: but then I could not bear it any longer & did telephone; I also asked for you, but you were out. I am in N.Y. at the Ritz Tower from April 15 to May 7 or so—I don't know now where to reach you—I shall send this via Bob Silvers, who gives me reports of you—I'd love to see you & to see Vera S.—but don't want to be a bore & a nuisance. Would you communicate—just say when you can be telephoned? The tiny part I played in *Abraham & Isaac* is literally the proudest recollection of my life . . . But do communicate. I shall not write to Madame S. I wd much rather entertain her somewhere when she is ready to see me—

yrs,
Isaiah.

Chapter 8

The Final Years

1960–1971

I n Carnegie Hall, Sunday, January 3, 1960, as aforesaid, Stravinsky conducted *The Rite of Spring* (with the 1943 *Danse sacrale*), as the
second half of a concert that began with Schoenberg's "film" music,
Berg's *Three Pieces*, and Webern's *Six Pieces*. We dined afterward with the Isaiah
Berlins and Goddard Liebersons. The next morning *The Rite* was recorded
in a double session in the ballroom of the St. George Hotel, Brooklyn. But
the exhausted composer could manage only a single, much too slow, "take"
of the *Danse sacrale*, in which the timpani played in wrong places, as it did in
all of the recorded rehearsal "takes" that I conducted. (I recorded Berg's
Three Pieces in a late afternoon third session.)

In Town Hall on the following Sunday, January 10, Stravinsky conducted the premiere of his *Movements*. The *Tres Sacrae Cantiones*, Stravinsky's
Gesualdo arrangements, also received their first performances in this concert, after which I met Glenn Watkins, the Gesualdo scholar, author of the
standard monograph of the composer.

On our return to Hollywood at the beginning of February, Stravinsky
found a telegram from Gian Carlo Menotti requesting him to contribute a
drawing to be auctioned at a benefit for the Spoleto Festival of Two Worlds.
Stravinsky obliged, entering a memento in a notebook: "Sent them a re-
drawing of Picasso's face by me. ISTR." I could only wonder when he found
the time to do it. On the 12th, 15th, and 18th of the month, I rehearsed
and he recorded *Petrushka*. At the beginning of March a letter came from
Krenek:

> Dear Bob: . . . Has Stravinsky's piece for piano and orchestra,[1] which was pre-
> sented in New York, been published, or, if not, is there some way for me to see
> the score? I have been asked tentatively whether I would consider conducting

1. *Movements.*

this piece in one of my concerts in Europe next year. Of course, I would consider it a very special honor if the master would entrust me with this task. But I should like to see the score so that I may decide whether I may be able to do it.

Please let me hear from you. As always,

Ernst

In March we drove to East Los Angeles State College to hear Isherwood lecture on Kipling. He was a fluent, no-notes speaker. His diary records, "The Stravinskys came to my lecture yesterday . . . We ate an expensive lunch at Lucy's . . . Bob Craft's idea is that I should narrate something for a Stravinsky composition—in 1962.[2]

The next day Isherwood brought his diaries, 1937 to 1950, typed pages in loose-leaf notebooks, and in the evening I read them to the Stravinskys. The completed book would be published posthumously to help support Don. The diaries revealed a prickly, vindictive side, and on Garbo, Bertrand Russell, Gerald Heard, drew blood. But from time to time he stumbled on a good aperçu. The same diary for March 25, 1960 records:

Last night, at the Stravinskys, Don did excellent drawings of Igor and Bob. Bob has hepatitis. He feels awful. He assures us that he dreads the South American trip . . . and that Vera dreads it, and that only Igor wants it.

Igor had taken something to stop the pain in his arm. He was quite lively and showed Don the Russian-character typewriter given him by Diaghilev. But later he complained of his headache. I rubbed the back of his neck. He exclaimed affectionately "Oh, you are so gentle! You know just where to touch the nerves." Bob showed me the rest of the proofs of their new book of conversations. He's afraid Chester [Kallman] will resent the way they make it clear that Wystan was alone responsible (with Igor) for the outline of The Rake's Progress libretto. Altogether one of our pleasantest and most "family" evenings together.

On March 30 we arrived in Mexico City for concerts and were met at the airport by Laura Villaseñor.[3] With Edward James as our host, we dined

2. The Flood, which at this time, 1960, was still in the donnée stage in Stravinsky's mind.

3. A ravishingly beautiful lady whom the Stravinskys had first known as Laura Wells, wife of the art collector Oppenheimer in San Antonio. She later (1940) married Eduardo Villaseñor, the Mexican banker, a writer who sent his manuscripts to Stravinsky. Villaseñor had known D. H. Lawrence in Mexico in the 1920s—unpublished letters to him from Lawrence survive. After Eduardo's and Stravinsky's deaths, Laura and her son Lorenzo regularly visited Mrs. Stravinsky and myself in New York. Laura, still a very attractive woman, was also a gifted violinist—pupil of Isaac Stern, who flew from New York to give her

with Dorothea Tanning and Leonor Fini, but Edward forgot to bring money and all of us had to empty our pockets to foot the bill. After our second, late-morning concert in the Auditorio Nacional, the two sons of the banker Prieto took Stravinsky and me to a corrida.

Back in Hollywood, a cable from France informed Vera Stravinsky that her closest friend, Olga Sallard, had been killed in an automobile accident. Isherwood's diary a week later mentions "a lovely snug Easter lunch at the Stravinskys' with wonderful Russian dishes. Igor, Don, and I drank up a whole bottle of some special old Scotch—General Grant—without ice or mix. Igor was adorable, as usual."

I was committed to a Varèse concert in Town Hall, New York, at the end of April, but received a letter from him: "The copyist is behind schedule and the score sent to me lacks two pages. Looking forward to next week, warm greetings." The next day, April 25, I drove Stravinsky to Glenn Gould's concert in the Wilshire-Ebell, but he disliked the Berg Sonata, and thought the Brahms Intermezzo, played as an encore, the best piece and best performance of the evening. Two days later I was in Toronto, conducting Tchaikovsky's Second Symphony. From there I went to New York and my Varèse rehearsals, in which I discovered that the composer could not say exactly what he wanted, in anything like concrete terms. His assistant, the composer Earle Brown, a kind and helpful man, played Varèse's pre-electronic instrument, a version of the Ondes Martenot. Alberto Ginastera, the Argentine composer, attended the dress rehearsal and brought greetings from Victoria Ocampo.

On May 18 Stravinsky arranged the Lullaby from the *Rake* for two recorders and gave his manuscript to a young architect, who would accept no other payment for building an addition to the Stravinsky living room. The architect-builder and his wife played duets on the instruments. On May 31, in the new CBS studio at Sunset and Vine, I recorded Schoenberg's *Die glückliche Hand* and the Songs, Opus 22 (the orchestra track only; Regina Sarfaty overdubbed the vocal part later in New York). A few days later Stravinsky taped his *Symphony of Psalms* in a double session, in which I played the bass drum to earn the union-scale wage. John McClure, Columbia's Artists and Repertory supervisor, predicted correctly that the recording would not be released because the sound in the new CBS studio was too dry. Three days later we appeared in a Los Angeles Music Festival concert in Royce Hall. Stravinsky conducted his Mass and *Noces*, and I conducted Gabrieli's *In Ecclesiis* and Berg's Chamber Concerto, with Pearl Kaufman and Israel Baker as the soloists. In the days following, Stravinsky recorded his *Monumentum* and Mass, and I recorded the Berg and Mozart's Gran Partita.

---

lessons—and a translator of Octavio Paz. Lorenzo, who aspired to a career as a singer (baritone), was on the board of the Metropolitan Opera. In Mexico he was a close friend of Edward James.

Isherwood's diary for June 12 and 18 states:

Yesterday, we went to a party held by Paul Sorel in his newly acquired room at
the Sunset Towers West . . . What a relief to go on to the (in every sense)
spacious Stravinskys', for supper! They have built a huge new living room
onto the house. Igor was quite reproachful because we're still not drinking . . .

Last night we had the Stravinskys and Bob Craft to dinner, because of
Igor's birthday . . . While we were barbecuing, a plane came in from the ocean—
from Hawaii, maybe. It was a dark blue night, very calm, not long after sunset.
The plane was a big one, but it made very little noise. As it flew overhead, it
switched on its ground lights and turned, beginning its approach pattern to
the airport. Igor watched it and said softly, "Welcome." After supper he seemed
drowsy and spoke very little. Vera assured Don more than once that it isn't
she or Bob who are set on this South American trip. It is Igor himself. He is so
accustomed to being a great celebrity that he feels he has to keep making
public appearances, she said.[4]

Isherwood's diary for June 28 recalls that "Yesterday evening we went with
the Stravinskys to the Kabuki . . . a terrible disappointment—so inferior to
the time we saw [it] in Tokyo . . . Poor Igor was suffering from diarrhea (he
had to go to the men's room during the first play and asked me to come
with him, but then he whispered, 'Don't hold my arm.' Bob and Vera are
increasingly worried about Igor's health and it seems as if the trip to South
America might still be cancelled. I have a sad presentiment that I might not
see him again if he goes."

We returned to Santa Fe in July. Stravinsky, Paul Horgan, and I spent
the first morning there rewriting e.e. cummings's grammatically confusing

4. Actually Stravinsky hated his "celebrity," which had plagued him since *Firebird* in
1910, and he did not "make public appearances." He conducted concerts to support himself and his family. The Stravinskys' reasons for undertaking the trip were to visit Vera
Stravinsky's stepmother and such friends as, in Buenos Aires, Victoria Ocampo, her sister,
brother, and the conductor Juan José Castro, and in Santiago, Delia del Carril. They had
known her in Paris during her two decampments, after she discovered the infidelities of her
husbands, the second of whom was the Nobel laureate Pablo Neruda. Del Carril was the
outstanding personality among the Popular Front Parisian intellectuals of the 1930s. (Mov-
iegoers will remember her in the portrayal of Neruda in *Il Postino*.) I do not know how the
Stravinskys reconciled her Parisian social status with her prominence in the Communist
Party—she was on personal terms with Stalin—but she was a woman of considerable talents, literary, graphic, and musical (a pupil of Gabriel Fauré). I spent an afternoon with her
and the Stravinskys in Santiago in August 1960. She outlived both Stravinskys and was
over a hundred at the time of her death. Vera Stravinsky's father lived in Santiago after the
Russian Revolution; he died and was buried there in 1937. Her uncle Theodore de Bosset,
an admiral during the Russo-Japanese War, who accompanied the Tsar during the first
months of his abdication, lived and died in Lima, where we visited his grave in August
1960.

translation of the Speaker's part in *Oedipus Rex*. Two days later, Stravinsky conducted the piece on a double bill with *Gianni Schicchi*, the title role of which was sung (?) by José Ferrer. On the 17th, in St. Francis Cathedral, Stravinsky conducted the *Symphony of Psalms* and I conducted Haydn's *Sinfonia Concertante* and Mozart's *Prague* Symphony. Afterward Paul Horgan gave a dinner at La Fonda Hotel. We shared a table with Ferrer and his wife Rosemary Clooney. Ferrer made an amusing speech about Stravinsky writing a futuristic opera and having it translated into medieval Latin.

By the end of the month we were home in Hollywood, en route to Mexico. Isherwood's diary for July 31 reads:

> Yesterday evening we had supper with the Stravinskys—they took us to The Oyster House. Igor . . . is so wonderful still—bright and sharp and full of warmth—so considerate, for instance, of Don. And setting forth tomorrow morning on his new musical safari—Mexico City, Bogotá, Lima, Santiago, Buenos Aires, Rio, Brasilia, Trinidad, New York, Venice. He spoke of his happiness at *The Rake's Progress*—they heard it again in Santa Fe with a very good cast. "A great opera!" Igor exclaimed delightedly, but added that he was speaking just as much of the libretto.
>
> Dear Vera drives worse than one can think possible, especially as she does so much of it. She terrified us utterly coming to and from the restaurant . . . I do love them both so much.

We flew to Mexico City on August 1 and spent our second evening there with the Prietos at the Villaseñors'—Eduardo, Laura, Lorenzo, Andrea. The Villaseñors had an immense library—a separate building—and a large record collection. Returning to the hotel, I was surprised to see Ruth Streifer, a close family friend from Kingston, here to obtain a divorce and marry the successful young attorney Martin Garbus. At night I received a visit from Marian Ostrovsky, the photographer at our *Threni* rehearsals in the Metropolitan Museum the preceding year. She was also there to obtain a quick divorce, and later I wondered if she had tricked up a hidden camera to provide evidence for adultery with me. The next morning, at our concert in the Coliseum, I conducted Beethoven's First and the *Lulu* Suite.

After our South American tour, we flew to Rome and drove to Venice, arriving on October 2. A note awaited Stravinsky from Barbara Hutton, staying not on her yacht but at Albergo Cipriani: "Dear Maestro: I learn with joy that you are still in Venice and if it would not tire you too much I should be happy to call one day to give you news and love from your niece, Ira Belline."[5] We called but she had already departed.

Stravinsky's last communication before leaving Venice was a letter to Virgil Thomson, 17 *bis* Quai Voltaire, asking him to purchase *"parégoric lafran"*

5. Barbara Hutton had known Ira Beliankina in Tangier for many years. Ira's house in Marrakesh was a gift from her.

for him and take it to New York, where it was unobtainable. On November 5 we left for our concerts in Genoa. The Colombia Excelsior Hotel had no attractions, but the intendant of the theater, Signora Lanfranchi, had two comely daughters. They had lost their father in the partisan fighting in the last months of World War II, and Signora Lanfranchi had been awarded her Genoa post as a pension in acknowledgment of her husband's heroism. Stravinsky's first order of business there was to cancel our Palermo concert on grounds that he must return to New York for medical treatment, but the real reason was that he had been deeply shocked by Dimitri Mitropoulos's heart-attack death in Milan three days earlier, while rehearsing Mahler's Third Symphony. We enjoyed our Genoa concerts, which were well received, but we were eager to be in Rome for our Accademia Filarmonica concert on the 24th. At a party there given by Eugene Berman on the 20th, I met Signora Mathilda Crespi. On the 26th, we were in Paris, at the Elysée Park Hotel, 2 Rue Jean-Mermoz. Rolf Liebermann[6] describes the most memorable incident there:

> I was trying to bring about a collaboration between Igor Stravinsky and Marc Chagall to give the first performance of Stravinsky's latest work, *The Flood*, at the Hamburg Opera. The piece [would be presented on American television] but we would give the first stage performances, with Günther Rennert as stage director and Robert Craft as conductor. We naturally thought of Chagall to do the décor for this simple biblical story and I went to Paris to see him in his Ile Saint-Louis apartment. He immediately agreed to participate and to meet with Stravinsky, for which occasion we chose Nicolas Nabokov's Paris apartment. Stravinsky came from Rome, I from Hamburg, and Chagall from Rouen, where he was working on the stained glass windows for the Synagogue of Jerusalem. The rendezvous was to be at 5:30 in the afternoon. Chagall, his wife, and I were there on time, but by 6:00 we were still alone. Shortly after 6:30 the telephone rang. It was Mme Stravinsky, distraught to have to tell us that her husband was dead drunk in bed after a lunch in which innumerable glasses of vodka and bottles of champagne were consumed. It was impossible to wake him, she told me. I asked her to let him sleep and to come with Robert Craft. I will try, she said, but that won't be easy because he also is completely *soûl*. A quarter of an hour later Vera Stravinsky made her entrance at Nabokov's. Chagall, being Russian and hence not unfamiliar with inebriation, took the situation quite well, but his wife reacted badly . . . I went to bed disappointed but at 2:00 A.M. the telephone rang. Stravinsky was awake, terribly thirsty, and wanted to *trinquer* with me. At his hotel I found him in his pajamas with two bottles of Dom Perignon on ice. Trying one last time to revive the affair, I said: "Listen, Igor, telephone Chagall or write a few words to him." He answered, "Impossible, I don't want any decor by this *con*."

6. *Actes et entractes, op. cit.*

On December 4, in Weehawken, we disembarked from the SS *Rotterdam*[7] to find Paul Horgan and Deborah Ishlon[8] waiting on the dock, each with a limousine. The Stravinskys went with Horgan to the St. Regis Hotel in one of them, Ishlon and myself with the baggage in the other. A few days later, in Manhattan Center, I recorded the *Lulu* Suite and, with Bethany Beardsley, Berg's *Sieben frühe Lieder*. On December 21, we drove to Washington, D.C., the Hotel Jefferson, the "we" now including Signora Crespi.

On Christmas Day we discovered that Washington was in many ways the most provincial city in America. It had closed down completely. The Jefferson had no room service and even no restaurant. We scoured the city for take-out sandwiches and Stravinsky's life-dependent beverages. No American official or organization so much as acknowledged Stravinsky's presence in the city, but the Austrian Embassy mounted a gala reception to follow our performances of the *Nightingale* and *Erwartung*.[9] On the last day of the year I recorded *Erwartung* in the morning, and we returned to New York by train. Helga Pilarczyk, who had sung the work more than a hundred times at the Hamburg Opera, gave a stunning performance, though she had not looked at a score for years. Our New Year's Eve party at the St. Regis Hotel was not a complete success. Milton Babbitt's name for Signora Crespi, "open city," had stuck.

1961

When we lunched with Auden on the 6th of January, he told us that he had just broken away from an interviewer, telling her: "Enough of journalism and knowingness. I want to write poetry." That evening Debbie Ishlon invited the Stravinskys and me to the Lawrence Olivier / Anthony Quinn *Becket*. The next day Babbitt demonstrated the electronic synthesizer for Stravinsky at Columbia University, but he suffered a dizzy spell. Debbie taxied him to Dr. David Protetch, who gave him an injection, drove him back to the hotel, and stayed for dinner, at which we celebrated Vera Stravinsky's Russian-calendar birthday.

7. *The Flood* scenario was written during the rough crossing on this steamship.

8. Vice President of Columbia Records.

9. On March 16, 2000, I received a letter from Glenn Watkins: "I remember Signora Crespi well from the *Erwartung* performance in Washington, where she could be seen backstage giving you a massage. I actually talked to her later when I was in Rome. I got her phone number from Eugene Berman, thinking that she could tell me where you were staying, as I was at the Hassler and saw Stravinsky's picture in the papers. He was just changing planes, however, and not staying over." This is not quite accurate. We spent two nights in Rome in early November 1963 en route to Sicily for concerts. We dined with Mrs. Goddard Lieberson, who was converting to Roman Catholicism. I remember the visit to Rome very clearly because of a world convocation of Cardinals. Toward the latter part of the afternoon we went to St. Peter's and the College of Cardinals to watch the flow of scarlet from the building at recess, an unforgettable sight.

On our return to Hollywood a few days later, Stravinsky wrote to Count Lerche-Lerchenborg, the Danish ethnomusicologist, thanking him for the "Royal Copenhagen porcelain plaques with the charming silhouette made by Hans Christian Andersen." Then on February 7 Stravinsky made his first notations for *The Flood*. On the 12th a cantankerous Stravinsky recorded his *Movements* with Charles Rosen, but failed to establish rapport with him. At one point Ingolf Dahl played the piano solo while I replaced him at the celeste.

At the same time, a letter came from Glenn Gould:

Dear Bob: Just a note to thank you for your card and to say how much I, too, enjoyed the recording[10] and working with you. I think that we have turned up a fairly distinguished result and I think it has much more spirit and magnetism than most of the recordings of this period of Schoenberg . . .

I will be in New York on March 6–7 and as I recall you were going to be there by the end of February, I thought it worth mentioning in case there should be some slight change in your schedule. I doubt that I would have time on either of these days to sit down with you or Joe and edit but it would be nice, at any rate, to talk with you if the occasion presents.

All the best for now,
Glenn

Unpredictably, Stravinsky liked Leonard Bernstein's CBS television presentation of *Oedipus Rex* on February 26 and was enthusiastic about Inge Borkh's Jocasta.

I was in New York at the beginning of March to conduct Carl Ruggles's *Portals, Angels,* and *Lilacs* in the Museum of Modern Art for Charles Schwartz's "Composers' Showcase." On the 6th, after editing the tapes of the Schoenberg Piano Concerto, I heard *Elektra* at the Met with David Protetch.

A letter from Glenn G. awaited me in Hollywood:

Dear Bob: First of all, thank you for your card and particularly for the lines from Mr. Stravinsky which I very much appreciate. I am dropping him a line in your care.

My shoulder was in wretched shape that week; in fact I canceled the San Francisco Symphony a few days before and only did Los Angeles because I couldn't bear disappointing Mrs. Huttenback[11] once again. It was one of my more disturbing setbacks but it seems to be coming around nicely again. Nonetheless, it was about the least happy performance I have played all year.

10. The Schoenberg Piano Concerto.
11. Dorothy Huttenback, a Los Angeles concert agent, had known the Stravinskys since the 1920s when she lived in Frankfurt.

Last month, Joe, Howard and I listened to the Schoenberg and I must say I was extremely pleased with it. I think you did a wonderful job in putting it together. One thing that surprised me a little, at least listening to it as I did in a small cubicle upstairs, was that the sound of Massey Hall, normally so resonant, was extraordinarily immediate, even a bit dry. Joe says that he miked the brass very closely and this may have a lot to do with it. We listened to it twice and, after the shock wore off, it really had a wonderfully analytical clarity—almost a textbook diagram of Schoenberg. Anyway, I am very proud of it and my congratulations to you.

On May 10 we received the English translation of Thomas Mann's *The Story of a Novel: The Genesis of Doctor Faustus*. Max Edel had given a copy of the German original to Stravinsky years ago, but he had not commented on it then and did not do so now. He actually seemed jealous of the compliment to his wife: "We had, as I hoped, come to see much more of Stravinsky and his wife—a thoroughgoing *belle Russe*, that is to say, an example of that specifically Russian beauty that radiates the most likable of human qualities. Talking with him at a gathering in our house, I was struck by things he said—with Gide as a starting point, and speaking alternately in German, English, and French—concerning *confession* as the product of various cultural spheres: the Greek Orthodox, the Roman Catholic, and the Protestant. In his opinion Tolstoy was essentially German and Protestant." Perhaps Stravinsky's silence is attributable to his realization that Mann was also seeing Schoenberg quite regularly during the same period, and that Mann's *Faustus* was inspired, if that is the word, by a Schoenberg figure, not a Stravinsky figure. But Stravinsky never read the novel.

I finished reading the *Dr. Faustus* diary in the evening, in spite of Mann's insufferable egotism: "A letter from Werfel arrived . . . He spoke of *Buddenbrooks* [as] an 'immortal masterpiece' . . . That [my novel] should have capitivated a first-rate artist's mind . . . was bound to touch me deeply." Then, "I went to see Werfel . . . With eyes fixed upon me he explained that it seemed almost incredible to him to see the author of *Buddenbrooks* standing so materially before him . . ." Further, "I think I may call myself a good colleague who does not look grudgingly at the good and great things that are being done alongside him . . ."; "I expounded the plan of [*Faustus*] to [Werfel], who was stunned to amazement." Etc., etc.

At the beginning of June a delegation of Soviet musicians came to invite Stravinsky to visit his native land on his eightieth birthday. Three of them, Tikhon Khrennikov, Kara Karayev, and Igor Bezrodny, came backstage after our Royce Hall concert on June 5 and introduced themselves to Stravinsky. I had conducted Schoenberg's *Die glückliche Hand* on the same program, which the Russians could not have liked. Surprisingly, Trude Schoenberg did, and gave me her highest marks for the performance.

Three days later, at a party for the Soviet musicians given by Bart Lytton at his 333 South Mapleton mansion, the host made an appalling speech, pointedly directed to the captive Russians, asking them, in effect, to look at his rich home and property—vulgar opulence, rather—and see what a poor American boy can do in the land of opportunity, real estate in his case. The next day the Russian threesome came to the Stravinskys', who gave them caviar, foie gras, Dom Perignon, as well as time for photographing and patriotic toasting ("We're all Russians, after all"). The guests asked to see Stravinsky's studio, to which he agreed only reluctantly, knowing what would be said in the U.S.S.R. about his icons and crucifixes. As of that hour Stravinsky was formally, officially, invited to Moscow for his eightieth birthday. We were greatly relieved when the "Reds" departed and Aldous and Gerald arrived for dinner.

On the morrow a letter arrived from Varèse saying that he was unable to come for my recording session of his *Arcana* because Columbia Records had postponed the date, but he wrote "I wish you all the satisfaction good work deserves. Please convey my best wishes, and regrets, to Stravinsky . . . *la main amie de Varèse*." The session, on the 28th, with only three-and-a half hours in which to tape the whole *Arcana* from sight-reading to finished product, and with the orchestra parts in poor shape, cuts not clearly indicated, etc., etc., was brutal, but the Koussevitzky Foundation, which sponsored it, did not provide for overtime. Stravinsky, in the control booth, was delighted to discover the piece's overt borrowings from *Firebird* and *Petrushka*.

We went to Santa Fe in early July for performances of *Perséphone* and *Oedipus Rex*, which the U.S. State Department would present in September in Berlin and Belgrade, on condition that Stravinsky conduct one or the other work on each program.

In Hollywood at the beginning of August, a letter from Varèse enclosed an excerpt from the revised *Deserts*, the tapes of which were "ready, waiting for your return." He also said that John McClure was satisfied with the *Arcana* recording. Again, the composer strangely signed himself "*La main amie de Varèse*." (Stravinsky abhorred this expression, and criticized Souvtchinsky for using the pomposity in introducing an article about him as being from "*la main d'André Schaeffner*.") The next letter from Varèse puzzled me: "No importance about the '*vide*' between 29 and 32." Apparently all *Arcana* scores are not marked this way, but was it really of no importance to him whether or not this section was played? He looked forward to having the Stravinskys for dinner at his 88 Sullivan Street apartment in New York on the 27th: "If there are any forbidden fruits please phone and they will be excluded for any culinary preference you may suggest—except lobsters which I cannot stomach."

In New York, a letter from Berman reminded me that he had played the "aging Cupid" between me and Signora Crespi, and adding that he had teased her about being in the Donna Anna, Donna Elvira, Zerlina line of succession. He expressed a desire to do *Pulcinella* with Stravinsky and Balanchine, but "when Stravinsky is involved, so much of the gravy goes to him that his collaborators receive nothing."

On the last day of August, before sailing on the SS *Kungsholm* for Göteborg, David Protetch drove me to Queens to visit the parents of Judith Chazin, my ballerina friend from the Sante Fe and the Metropolitan Operas.

Our flight from Stockholm[12] to Berlin stopped for an hour at Hamburg, where Rolf Liebermann visited with us. In Berlin, I went directly to an *Oedipus* rehearsal in the Theater des Westens. The next morning, Nicolas Nabokov, leaving the Stravinsky room in the Kempinski Hotel after breakfasting with them, collided in the corridor with Judith Chazin exiting from my room. Tongues would soon wag. For the opening performance of our double bill, I switched pieces with Stravinsky so that Vera Zorina could appear with him in *Perséphone.*

1962

Stravinsky and I shared a concert in Los Angeles's Wilshire-Ebell Theater on January 6, he conducting the *Soldat,* I the Verlaine songs, *Renard, Pribaoutki,* and *Dumbarton Oaks.* At the morning dress rehearsal a tiff occupied between Stravinsky and me over the bassoon part in the fourth *Pribaoutki* song. He suddenly claimed that the thirty-second notes are an error and too fast to be played clearly. Instead of keeping my peace, I said that he himself had always performed the work as printed, whereupon he took my score and rewrote the figure in triplets, which are arrantly wrong. Back at home the dust-up was ignored.

The next day we flew to Toronto, but to avoid a snowstorm in Chicago were rerouted to change planes in New York. When the Toronto airport announced the cancellation of the Chicago flight, our welcoming committee departed, and we arrived at the Hotel Park Plaza alone, in a taxi and very late. The next morning, Stravinsky and I recorded a "conversation" for the CBC, and Stravinsky signed a new royalty agreement for *The Rite of Spring* with the Société des Auteurs et Compositeurs Dramatiques: four-sixths for Stravinsky, one-sixth for Sviatoslav Roerich (son of Nicolas), and one-sixth for Léonide Massine, who choreographed the 1920 revival.

12. This was after we had conducted joint concerts in Helsinki—where I fell in love with Helena Lehtela, a beautiful red-headed violinist in the orchestra, as well as a major actress in Russian films—and in Stockholm, where we saw Ingmar Bergman's unforgettable staging of *The Rake's Progress.*

In Washington, D.C., on January 22, Stravinsky recorded *Oedipus Rex* in the morning and conducted the evening performance. I conducted Ravel's *L'Heure Espagnole* on the first half of this and the following two programs. We had seen Alexis St. Léger (St-John Perse) several times during the visit, and in New York, on January 25, Stravinsky received a letter from him, ending with *"faites mes bonnes amitiés à Craft."* On the 26th we recorded *Ragtime, Renard,* and Varèse's *Ecuatorial* at Manhattan Center (West Thirty-Fourth Street). On the 28th Kyriena Siloti came for lunch and the Carters for dinner. Kyriena said that after the premiere of *Fireworks,* conducted by her father in St. Petersburg, a maternal aunt of its young composer approached to congratulate him, or so he expected, instead of which she asked *"Kak Mama?"* ("How is mama?")

On February 10, in Hollywood, Stravinsky began the choreographic movement, "The Flood," continuing from the preliminary sketch of March 5, 1961 and adding more "rain" (violins and flute). Two days later, Stravinsky gave full power-of-attorney to Mr. and Mrs. William Montapert. These two lawyers were close friends of Stravinsky's son-in-law, Andre Marion. In 1959 Marion had convinced Stravinsky to replace his longtime attorney, Aaron Sapiro, with this Italian- and French-born couple. The Montaperts, thereafter, were constantly proposing schemes to make Stravinsky rich and themselves richer. One of these was the purchase of citrus groves in Arizona. Another was the establishment of "Verigor" (true gold). Seven years later a New York attorney, David G. Licht, would state in an affadavit:

> In October 1969, I was retained by Igor Stravinsky to prevent the theft or destruction of certain of his manuscripts which were then under the control of Andre Marion . . . Among other matters which Stravinsky asked me to investigate was the establishment and assets of a company called Verigor Incorporated, which appeared to have substantial oil, gas, ore, and mineral leases. Igor Stravinsky knew nothing about the company or its assets, but believed that Montapert and Marion had used the company as a method of diverting Igor Stravinsky's funds for their own use.

Not until the end of the year 1969, when some of Marion's check stubs were sent to the Stravinskys in New York, did they discover the extent of his skullduggery.

I conducted the Monday Concert on the 19th of February: *"O holder Tag"* (Bach's *Wedding Cantata*), with Grace-Lynn Martin, soprano; *The Dove Descending* (premiere),[13] which had been perfectly prepared by Gregg Smith;

13. Completed January 2, 1962. In an interview in New Zealand, published in the *Wellington Evening Post,* November 16, 1961, Stravinsky was asked "why he had never set to music a poem of his friend T. S. Eliot. [He] replied: 'I have thought about it. But his words do not need music. I can find notes for Shakespeare because he wrote words for singing. Eliot's words are for speaking.' "

Elliott Carter's Double Concerto, with Leonard Stein playing the harpsichord part, Karl Kohn the piano; and Schoenberg's first Chamber Symphony. Elliott wrote a description of a party at the Stravinskys' afterward:

> Robert Craft was conducting my Double Concerto in Los Angeles, and Mr.
> and Mrs. Stravinsky invited me to their house on North Wetherly Drive. A
> little discouraged and shy in the midst of such august figures as Spender,
> Isherwood, and Huxley, who were also there, I went off into a corner, soon to
> be joined by Stravinsky himself, and we began musicians' talk until I got up
> the courage to ask him how he composed. At which he took me to his work
> room, and showed me a large book of blank pages onto which short frag-
> ments of musical sketches, roughly torn out of larger sketch-pages, had been
> pasted. Since the original sketch-pages had been papers of different qualities
> and colors and the musical fragments (sometimes only two or three notes)
> had been written on staves that were hand-drawn, often in quite fanciful curves,
> the scrapbook itself gave a very arresting visual impression. This was the work-
> book for *The Flood*.[14]

Also on February 19 I received a letter from Lincoln Kirstein in Kyoto,
where he was trying to arrange for a demonstration of Samurai martial arts
at the Seattle World's Fair. He had seen the Washington *Oedipus Rex*.

On March 9, we listened to a tape of Paul Sacher's premiere performance of *A Sermon, a Narrative, and a Prayer*. On first impression, the most
interesting music is in the concluding chords of the "Narrative."

A week or so later Miklos Keleman came from Zagreb to invite us to
conduct there in May. The next day Stravinsky drew a self-portrait for an
article in *Encounter*. On March 26 I conducted the Monday Concert in Plummer
Park: five instrumental movements from Bach cantatas; Mozart's Adagio
and Rondo K. 617; Schoenberg's unfinished Three Little Pieces (1910); the
premiere of the first four of the Eight Miniatures; and, with Vera Zorina,
Hindemith's *Hérodiade* and Debussy's *Chansons de Bilitis*. On the 27th we spent
the day rehearsing the cast for *The Flood* with Kirk Browning (Director),
Elsa Lanchester (Noah's wife), Lawrence Harvey (Narrator), Sebastian Cabot
(Noah). In the evening we recorded the Debussy and Hindemith in Columbia's
new Vine Street studio.

On April 1, clearly not aware of what he was doing, and forgetting that
he and his wife had given full power of attorney to William Montapert,
Stravinsky signed an agreement, concocted by Montapert, bequeathing the
money in his Swiss bank to Theodore, Soulima, Milene, and their spouses
in equal amounts, but nothing to his wife. The testament was written in
such a way that Stravinsky was made to refer to "Vera and myself" at the

14. Elliott Carter, *Collected Essays and Lectures, 1937–1995* ed. Jonathan W. Bernard (Rochester: University of Rochester Press, 1998).

beginning but then did not define her position in the event that he predeceased her.

Four days later Stravinsky received a letter from Eliot:

London. March 28, 1962.

My Dear Stravinsky, It was with the greatest of delight to my wife and myself when we were in Barbados . . . that we received a letter from Faber & Faber telling me that you had completed the anthem[15] using the words from my poem, that it was to be performed in London, and that you had dedicated the anthem to myself, and, to make our pleasure complete, given me your original manuscript. As for the last, we have been making enquiries as to how it could be preserved, in a frame, as a trophy to hang on our walls, and my wife is to consult an official of the British Museum, who, I understand, can advise us as to how to treat this precious script. I must say again how overjoyed my wife and I are at this great compliment, and how keenly we look forward to hearing the anthem performed. You know already how happy it made me when I first heard that you might be interested in setting words of mine in your music . . .

Yours very gratefully,
T. S. Eliot

On April 6 I edited the *Flood* tapes during twelve unrelieved hours, though feeling ill from the yellow fever inoculation for our forthcoming tour in Africa. A letter came from Stephen Spender at the University of Virginia:

Dear Bob: Thank you tremendously for all you have done. I phoned London today and they told me you were content with the proofs. I wrote this afternoon to Mel Lasky suggesting Cocteau might do a special cover. If you think this is a *BAD* idea please write a card to London at once saying I asked your advice and it is contra. They say the self-portrait [of Stravinsky] is excellent, but very faint and the printers are in despair about it. I have suggested they have a full-size photograph made and that they then get a professional artist to go over Stravinsky's lines—on the photograph, I mean—with a pen or brush and then have a line block made of this adaptation and send a copy to Stravinsky and you for approval. I told them on no account to print this without your OK. I hope there will be something you can agree to.

Best love to you and many many embraces to all for all,

Stephen

I've reviewed Christopher in *The New Republic*. I hope you will like it.

On April 10 Balanchine arrived from New York for five days with us. After he left, we flew to Seattle, the Olympic Hotel, to rehearse for the

15. *The Dove Descending*.

opening concert of the Seattle World's Fair. At the morning run-through, Stravinsky's bag, containing changes of clothes and bottles of 4711 and Scotch, was alternately carried for him by Danny Kaye and Van Cliburn. The concert, on the 21st, opened with Beethoven's *Leonora No. 3* Overture, followed by Cliburn playing Rakhmaninov's Third Concerto. After intermission I conducted the Symphony in Three for a noticeably diminished audience, and Stravinsky the *Firebird.* The next afternoon we entrained for Vancouver, where we transferred to the night train for Toronto. The bird life along the shore of Puget Sound was abundant, and during the ride through the Canadian Rockies we saw many elk.

Our concert in Massey Hall, Toronto, began with Schoenberg's *Genesis* Prelude, *A Survivor from Warsaw,* and Violin Concerto, with Israel Baker, and ended with Stravinsky conducting his completed *Miniatures* and *A Sermon, a Narrative, and a Prayer.* After recording these pieces, we left for New York in a limousine with John McClure, the Columbia Records producer, fog having closed the airport. We reached the Pierre Hotel at 5:30 A.M. Mrs. Stravinsky's vernissage was at the Galérie Internationale that same day, and she had only a few hours in which to hang her pictures. I walked there with Stravinsky at 6 P.M. and found that Leonard Bernstein, the Elliott Carters, and Dushkins had purchased paintings.

Another exhibition, "Stravinsky and the Dance," opened at the Wildenstein Gallery on May 2. Before it we went to a dinner for Stravinsky at 2 Sutton Place with Balanchine, Bernstein, Mr. and Mrs. John D. Rockefeller III, Bill Lieberman (director of the Museum of Modern Art), and Jeanne Vanderbilt. At the gallery Max Edel was waiting for us, very proud of his too large Wotruba-style bronze head of Stravinsky in the exhibit.

In Paris on May 16, we lunched with Samuel Beckett at the Plaza-Athenée. He described it in a letter: "Had lunch with Stravinsky and his wife. Very pleasant. His lunch: smoked salmon and a double scotch." (Goddard Lieberson and I were also there.) During the afternoon Stravinsky and I visited Cocteau. The next day Stravinsky sent a case of Sancerre to Beckett, who had said it was his favorite white wine. He reciprocated with whiskey shortly after, attaching a card saying *"Affectueux hommages et voeux/S.B."* The following morning the Stravinskys and I were in Brazzaville on the Congo.

From June 6, we spent ten marvelous days in Rome, then flew to Hamburg for a celebration of Stravinsky's eightieth birthday. At the Staatsoper we saw the first act of Henze's *Der Prinz von Homburg.* Since the work was dedicated to Stravinsky, his by-no-means-unnoticed departure at the first intermission was embarrassing. Three subsequent evenings at the Oper gave us Balanchine's beautiful staging of *Eugene Onegin* and Walter Felsenstein's intelligent productions of *Gianni Schicchi* and *Rigoletto.* Then came the five successive early-morning performances of Stravinsky's Greek trilogy by the New York City Ballet, Stravinsky conducting *Apollo* at the end, Leopold

Ludwig conducting *Orpheus* at the beginning, and myself *Agon* in the middle. A *sehr grosse Erfolg.*

When we returned to New York and the Pierre Hotel on June 29, a letter awaited me from Martie Retief, the winsome reporter-interviewer in Johannesburg: "If you meet Witold Rowicki in Poland, please remember me to him. He was the only other visiting conductor who made our orchestra sound inspired." We ate in the Russian Tea Room almost every day and saw the film *Last Year in Marienbad,* which Mrs. Stravinsky loved and Mr. Stravinsky and I loathed. She purchased two handsome Coptic textiles as an eightieth birthday present for her husband. On July 12 we conducted a concert in Lewisohn Stadium. During rehearsals Marian Ostrovsky[16] photographed Stravinsky without letup. Because of a threat of rain, the order of the program was switched, with Stravinsky conducting the first half and I the second (*The Rite of Spring*). But of rain, or moisture, there was none. A dinner had supposedly been arranged at the Russian Tea Room afterward, and a *scandale* was ignited when Mrs. Stravinsky discovered that the manager of the establishment knew nothing about it.

On July 17 the Stravinskys embarked for Chicago and our concert in Ravinia. I joined the train in Poughkeepsie, coming from Kingston, where I had spent four days with my family. The concert went smoothly, though the two rehearsals were insufficient, as they were the following week for the one in Hollywood Bowl. Two days after the latter we were in Santa Fe, at the La Fonda Hotel, where I found a letter from Stephen Spender in London: "Dear Bob: Thank you for your kind postcards, which keep us laconically well informed. Wystan was here staying with us, and very sweet. When the Cocteau drawings are sent, I'll hang on to them and bring them to America in January, if that suits you. Natasha and I had a wonderful time with you all in Hamburg and shall always gratefully remember it."

On August 1 a Stravinsky Festival was officially opened in the patio of the Museum of New Mexico with a lecture by Thomas Messer, "Stravinsky and Twentieth-Century Painting and Design." That evening, Stravinsky conducted *Mavra* and *Renard,* and I conducted *Nightingale,* with Patricia Brooks as the avian of the title. I fancied her, but so did others ahead of me in line, and she was married. On August 2, Stravinsky made his first notations for *Abraham and Isaac,* in a room adjoining the cathedral that Paul Horgan had procured for him. Milton Babbitt's lecture, "Recent Developments in the Music of Igor Stravinsky," was attended, but not comprehended, by my three ballerinas, Judith Chazin, Nancy King, and Signora Cesare Siepi, who were very vexed with me for compelling them to go. Later, in revenge, while I was out rehearsing, they spilled flour on my kitchen table and finger-wrote in it the words "Professor Milton Babble." I redeemed myself the next day by enlightening them on the word pulchritudinous, which the

16. See under Mexico, August 1960.

local newspaper had used to describe them in their *Perséphone* performances.
I had conducted this on a double-bill with Stravinsky conducting *Oedipus
Rex*. Other lectures were by Carlos Chavez ("The Influence of Igor Stravinsky
on the Music of the Americas"), Roger Shattuck ("Stravinsky and Accents
of Style in the 20th Century"), and Virgil Thomson ("The Operatic Works
of Igor Stravinsky"), which I skipped in order to rest for my *Rake* performance, but from which the Stravinskys returned angry with him.

On August 19 Stravinsky conducted his Cantata in the cathedral, and I
conducted *The Flood*, which I did two more times in the Santa Fe Museum.
We flew to New York from Albuquerque, dined on the 26th with Balanchine
at Lucia Davidova's, and the next day were in Israel for a concert tour.

At the beginning of September, I had a letter from Glenn Gould:

Dear Bob: I gather that we will be seeing you in November in Toronto and I
certainly hope that I am here during that week. But, in the meantime, I wonder if you can give me some idea of your schedule for next summer. I know
that you are usually very heavily committed with Mr. Stravinsky and I have
braced myself for the expectation that you are not available at all. Nevertheless, we would dearly love to have you come to Stratford and participate in as
wide a sampling of our enterprises as you feel your time would afford.

Specifically, I would be delighted if you could spend about a week with
us and conduct at least one Chamber Orchestra Concert and, possibly (pend-
ing the formation of a new Choral Workshop which we are discussing at the
moment), one concert of Renaissance choral music. Our concerts are largely
thematic in planning and I would think that, although we are entirely open to
suggestions for the Chamber Orchestra Concert, a program which would be
built around Schoenberg would be ideal. What about the E-Major Chamber
Symphony, for instance, and perhaps you could introduce to our audience at
least one relatively "far out" selection of your own persuasion.

The music part of the Festival runs usually for six weeks and as we are
only now beginning to think in terms of dates and visitors, you could pretty
well choose your own week. Normally, we begin the second week of July and
proceed through the third of August. Please do let me know as soon as possible whether or not you can manage to come and, meantime, all the very
best.[17]

Sincerely,
Glenn Gould

On September 19, after Israel and Venice, we were at the Berkeley Hotel in
Paris, preparing for a three-week visit to Moscow and Leningrad. Stravinsky
lunched again with Sam Beckett.[18]

17. I accepted the invitation but a conflict arose with my performances of *Lulu* in
Santa Fe, for which I had contracted at an earlier date.
18. The account in James Knowlson's Beckett biography quotes from an interview by

1928. Kingston.

Château de Joux (Pontarlier), the home of the Doyeaux, the author's ancestors on his mother's side, who in the seventeenth century fled to America to escape persecution as Huguenots, and were founders of New Paltz, New York. Le Château de Joux is best known today as the prison and burial place of Touissant L'Ouverture.

The Grand Army of the Republic medal, on the left, was awarded to Isaac Lawrence, the author's maternal great-grandfather. The other medal was awarded to Thomas Gibbs, the author's paternal great-grandfather.

ET-HADAVAR HAZEH V'LO
the deed this one and didst not

KHASHAKHTA ET-BINKHA ET-YEKHIDEKHA
withhold. thy son Him only one.

17 KI VAREKH AVAREKH'KHA
That bless I will bless thee,

V'HARBA ARBEH ET-ZAR'AKHA
and multiply I will multiply, thy seed

K'KOKH(A)VEI HASHAMA'YIM V'KHAKHOL
as the stars of the heavens, and as the sand

ASHER AL-SFAT HAYAM V'YIRASH
which (is) on the shore of the sea; and (it) will inherit,

ZAR'AKHA ET-SHA'AR ÖIVAV:
thy seed the gate of his enemies.

18 V'HITBARKHU VZAR'AKHA KOL GOYEI
And (they) will be blessed in the seed all the nations

HA'ARETZ EKEV ASHER SHAMA'(A)TA
on the earth, because that thou hast hearkened

B'KOLI || VAYASHAV AVRAHAM EL-NA'ARAV
to my voice. And (he) returned Abraham to his boys,

VAYAKUMU VAYELKHU YAKHDAV
and they rose and went together

EL-B'ER SHEVA VA'YESHEV AVRAHAM
to Beer-Sheba and dwelt Abraham

BIV'-ER SHEVA.
in Beer-Sheba.

1962. The last page of Stravinsky's working libretto for *Abraham and Isaac*.

1973. In the Stravinsky apartment, 920 Fifth Avenue, New York.

April 1989. With Alexander at Villa Lante, Lazio, Italy.

December 1989. New York. Rehearsing Elliott Carter's Double Concerto. The composer is following the score in the background.

January 1990. Alexander with Nepalese children on a road to Mount Everest.

November 1992. Xi'an, China.

November 1992. Beijing, China.

November 1992. On the Great Wall of China.

October 1995. Stilo, Calabria.

1993. Venice.
The façade of
SS Giovanni e Paolo.

September 28, 1994. Todì, Umbria.

December 1996. Borobudur, Java.

April 2001. Viterbo. Thomas Aquinas's open-air pulpit.

March 2001. Banteay Shrei, Cambodia

January 2002. Gulf Stream.

After returning to Paris from Moscow on October 11, we went to Rome for a concert at the Eliseo on the 18th. Stravinsky did not know until his return to California that on the 17th Pope John XXIII had made him a Knight of St. Sylvester with star: *"INGUARUM Stravinsky Equitem Commendatorem Ordinis Sancti Sylvestri Papae."*

Our Rome concert was repeated in Perugia on my birthday. Stravinsky conducted the complete *Pulcinella* and his early orchestration of Beethoven's *The Flea*, the first time he had heard it. A reception was given in the Brufani Hotel, where we spent the night. The next day, during lunch with Bill Congdon in Assisi, we heard the news of Natalie Goncharova's death, which greatly upset Stravinsky. Back in Rome, we dined with both the American and Russian Ambassadors, but Stravinsky, tipsy and confused, said the wrong things politically to each in turn.[19]

In New York on October 27, the night before flying to Caracas, the Stravinskys and I dined with their lawyer, L. Arnold Weissberger, his friend Milton Goldman, and Rita Hayworth, who had been invited on my account by L.A.W., her attorney; Weissberger took some interest in the vicissitudes of my amorous life, previously having invited Rita Gam to one of his parties with me in mind.[20] As New York's leading theater lawyer, he found no difficulty in obtaining seats for the opening of *Beyond the Fringe*, separate ones for Ms. Hayworth and myself at some distance from his and the Stravinskys'. The ex-spouse of Orson Welles and the Aga Khan arrived slightly inebriated, as L.A.W. had told us to expect, since she was terrified of meeting Stravinsky, who was never in the least anxious about meeting anybody—kings, queens, American presidents, Soviet dictators, popes, and even T. S. Eliot, let alone movie stars. But he was always attracted to beautiful women, and Ms. Hayworth's brown eyes and soft features were mesmerizing. At dinner L.A.W. tactfully launched a conversation that could include everybody but failed to engage her. She ate little or nothing, took another drink or two, and we walked up the street to the theater. She wore a shawl around her head to conceal her face, but instead it compelled people to look at her more closely. As we entered the theater, Charles Addams, the cartoonist, and his wife Deborah Kerr recognized her, and as we took our seats people whispered her name and ogled her. The first *"Fringe"* skit began soon after and, with it, my serious troubles. Laughter was general and up-

---

Beckett's nephew Edward saying that "Stravinsky embraced him like a long-lost friend, reminding him that he would be honored to compose music for any opera that Beckett might wish to write. Before leaving for Russia, the composer sent a whole case of Sancerre over to Beckett's flat. Beckett was delighted, flattered, and moved, and, as a gesture of thanks, sent several bottles of Jameson whiskey to Stravinsky's hotel." The biography mislocates the first meeting in Amsterdam.

19. The Elliott Carters were present at both of these occasions and used to give a hilarious account of them.

20. Later I persuaded Brigitta Lieberson to invite Ms. Gam to dinner with me.

roarious with each outrageously over-accented Brit joke, but Ms. Hayworth's laughs lasted longer than all the others, and the audience began to look in our direction. I wanted to vanish or crawl under my seat, but could do nothing. She was wholly unaware of the spectacle she was creating, but mercifully L.A.W. came to my rescue at intermission and we left the theater.

On our return from Venezuela, we saw the Met's *Don Giovanni* with Eugene Berman, who designed the production. Three days later, we dined with Balanchine, who had returned from the U.S.S.R. to see his wife and talk with Stravinsky about their Russian experiences. Mr. B. hated everything about the country, above all its "arts" supervisors, and dreaded having to return. He was extremely nervous, blinking, clucking, twitching, snorting. On November 16 Isaiah Berlin came for lunch, and a few days later I was in Toronto. The Stravinskys joined me there, and he recorded his Symphony in C, essentially following my concert broadcast of it, but slower.

In Hollywood on December 10, I wrote the following letter at Vera Stravinsky's request. It is included here partly as a picture of the effect on Stravinsky of his Russian trip, but more importantly as a different perspective on his California home life.

Dear Volodya,[21]

. . . As to your request for an account of Igor's home life, I will begin with a description of the house itself, except that, as it has only one bedroom and is very small—the low ceilings might have been designed especially for Igor's height—it is really no more than a bungalow. When we moved here, twenty-one years ago, the valleys of Hollywood and Beverly Hills were in panoramic view from the front terrace, but now we can see no farther than our neighbors, thanks to smog and high-risers. Twenty years ago, we occasionally felt a touch of the wildness of the West, even here in Hollywood. Rattlesnakes were still found in the vicinity, especially when the jungle of the nearby Doheny estate was divided into hundreds of small properties and then terraced into what are known locally as "the Jewish rice paddies." During a drought, one hot August night in 1949, a wildcat sprang to our roof from the hill behind the house and clawed an awning. We kept chickens on that hill during the war, but the neighbors complained because our rooster crowed at 3 A.M. We locked it in our bedroom closet. When it flew out in the morning, like an airplane, Igor chased it out of the house with a broom. Its comb and crest reminded us of a French *révolutionnaire*'s cap. Adventures such as these are not only unlikely any more but hardly credible. The invasions we expect nowadays are from autograph-hunters and cadastral surveyors.

21. Vladimir Ivanovitch Petrov, Vera Stravinsky's cousin, son of her mother's sister Olga (*née* Malmgren), professor of radiology at the University of Moscow at the time.

Visitors say that it is a happy house. Certainly it is bright and cozy, with light-colored walls and ceilings, upholstery, pillows, rugs, and always a plentiful array of flowers. Even the floppy rubber plants in the dining- and living-rooms, though hunched by the ceiling, are pleasing. The furniture is recent, American, ordinary; we have no French dynastic chairs offering you their *"sentiments les plus distingués."* The house is brightened, too, by many windows and mirrors—like Igor's mind. But it is so crammed now that we have had to part with one of our three pianos, leaving one in the library so that visitors, potential souvenir-collectors, will not have an excuse to invade Igor's studio and "try the piano" there.

Since we have more than ten thousand books, every room in the house is a library. They are classified by language, author, and subject, of which the largest category is art books, followed by *romans policiers* and poetry. The Shakespeare section is extensive, and so is the collection of old Baedekers, but a catalog of all the shelves would reflect Igor's widespread and changing curiosities as much as his abiding philosophies. Varying and unpredictable as he can be, he is a steady reader, inclined to pursue an author or subject to a rut. You may be interested to hear that since his Russian trip he has been reading Pushkin again, and dipping into Blok, Anna Akhmatova, and Mandelstam. He also tends to converse in Russian now, more readily than at any time in the past twenty years, and he talks of orchestrating Musorgsky's *Sunless.*

The house bulges with art. What the visitor sees first are posters on the backs of the dining-room doors advertising *Oedipus* and *Perséphone* at the Warsaw Opera. The innumerable objects on tables and shelves include an antique atlas; glass obelisks from a bygone Murano, and glass *presse-papiers,* which I collect (marbrie weights, piedouche weights, torsades and swirls); clumps of coral (one because it resembles Bourdelle's Beethoven), and bits of lapis lazuli and other semi-precious stones; a Joseph Cornell box of New York's Museum of Natural History; several New Mexican "Santos"; Russian cups, spoons, samovars, pyrogravure boxes; Igor's family silverware, which includes huge tureens and ladles, all bearing the crown-shaped Kholodovsky coat-of-arms; Inca and Copt textiles; many squab and ugly pre-Columbian statuettes, the finest pieces having been smashed during a *terramoto* years ago: you probably know that California is susceptible to terrestrial heart attacks. We own some Early American antiques, including a pair of eighteenth-century decoy wood ducks from Long Island, the gift of our friends the McLanes; and a collection of entomological specimens taken from tropical boats that call at Monterey—horrid things, even when stuffed, mounted, and stored in glass cases, but they fascinate Igor.

The walls display paintings, Russian and Balkan icons, old maps, old cartoons (one of Rossini lighting a giant firecracker), new cartoons (an intentionally unreadable diploma drawn for Igor by Saul Steinberg and still the only academic credential in the house), photographs of friends and of people

Igor admires (Lincoln and Pope John). One of the inner walls of a closet in Igor's den contains marks for the heights of friends who have slept there, the shortest of them, Beata Bolm, widow of the dancer, and the tallest Aldous Huxley and the poet Charles Olson. Except for our hexagonal "Monsù Desiderio," all of our paintings are contemporary. Nearly everything we have, moreover, was the gift of the artist, a description that includes a dozen Picassos, among them the well-known full-face line portrait of Igor, and a Bakst of me, several Giacomettis, a considerable number of Larionovs and Goncharovas, Jacques Villon's palette, some good Tanguys, and two Klees, one of them a drawing given to Igor by Alma Mahler (who received it as a gift from Rilke): Henry Moore, Miró, Masson, Dufy, Tchelichev, Chagall, Vieira da Silva, Bérard, Léger. In fact, the only pictures we have ever purchased are by young painters we wished to encourage, but for a more complete catalog I would have to mention my own paintings, of which more than a score can be counted about the house.

Igor's day is carefully routined. It begins with a headache, usually dispelled or forgotten in the shower. After that he stands on his head for about fifteen minutes, like a Hatha yogi. His bathroom, incidentally, looks like the prescription department in a pharmacy, with all the blue-and-white porcelain apothecary jars. There are trays of syringes, too, and a mammalian display of hot-water bottles, while the vials of medicines, counteragents for every ailment, all neatly labeled in Russian by Igor himself, can be counted to the hundreds (and that, as Americans say, is an underexaggeration). A branch office drug store is in business on his night table, too, and the powders, the supponerals, the unguents and ointments, the drops, the herbs, and other *materia medica* are so mixed up with the sacred medals that his doctor fears he may swallow a Saint Christopher some night instead of a sleeping pill. Igor acquired his taste for medicines at an early age, since his parents kept a cupboard of such remedies as aconite, belladonna, calomel, centaury seeds, feverfew, henbane, senna leaves, valerian, veronal, and he soon learned to climb up to it and to "tranquillize" and otherwise unhinge himself.

The apparent totality of Igor's belief in medical materialism is the most curious dodge in his character. Pretending to believe that every ill, serious or slight, must have a chemical solvent, he will clock the action of an aspirin to test the claims of the advertisements. It follows that he is also concerned with the health of people near him. Puff your cheeks, and he will give you a carminative; or cough, from momentary dryness of the throat, and out comes one of his silver pillboxes, favorite *objets de virtù*, and from it a grain of anti-plague or other placebo (as I suppose them to be), which he will urge you to swallow. As for Igor's own coughs, *they* are forelaid long in advance with one of his colored treacles. No matter how well he feels, Igor will check his temperature at least once daily. A half-degree rise of the thermometer may forecast the flu to him, and thus warned he can batten down with his medicines and conquer it weeks ahead. It should come as no surprise that he rarely allows Nature to take its course, at least not until he has given it a nudge. Heavy dinners are dispatched with two tablets of "concentrated saliva," a Japanese peptic confection rumored to stimulate digestion.

Speaking for myself, I find it odd that a man of such wide medical experience has never developed a suspicion of doctors, yet he is always ready to rub out the whole of his own considerable medical knowledge and transfer his faith to the most transient new practitioner. One penalty of these peremptory transfers is that he sometimes finds himself on chastening diets—turnip juice, say—prescribed by younger medics appalled at his intake of alcohol. He will observe these regimens with Mohammedan strictness for a day or two, then, when he may be in danger of becoming really ill, a whiskey-approving physician of long acquaintance will be called to the rescue. In 1951, Dr. Maurice Gilbert, a friend of Igor in Geneva, concocted a special formula for him of one pill to stimulate and one to calm, and for years Igor swallowed this Swiss neutrality thirty minutes before each concert, with ideal effect. Need I tell you that I am not *frileuse* myself, that I abhor medicines, am not solicitous with invalids, and would be the world's worst nurse?

Igor's breakfast, which is later than mine, coincides with the arrival of the post, and by that time I try to be out of the house. Years ago in Paris we used to play a game of choosing apt substitute vocations for our friends. "Postman" was always mentioned for Igor, next after "pharmacist." (Other choices were carpenter, frame-maker, bookbinder, package-wrapper: Igor likes to work with his hands.) In fact, he is so keen about receiving and sending mail that the Sabbath, unless relieved by a Special Delivery, is a dull day for him. In his desire to hasten a letter on its way, any visitor is impressed into the postal service. If the President of the United States were to come to lunch, he would leave with two or three letters in his hand and Igor's request to "drop them in the corner mailbox."

The humors of the day are determined by the contents of the post, which, with books, music, letters, is generally large enough to fill a laundry basket. Most of the letters are from autograph hunters of the sort, "Dear Sir, I already have signed photos from Michelangelo, Schweitzer, and Stockhausen. Would you mind sending . . ." These are destined for a special outsized dining-room wastebin, as Igor will allow himself to be victimized by the autograph racket only when it seems the easiest way to get rid of a nuisance. I may add, too, that he has managed to keep the public-institution attitude at bay more successfully than any other eminent octogenarian. But he is *not* fond of the patriarch role, and much as he loves children he will not allow the neighbors' to call him "Gramps"—which one of them did when he appeared at the doorstep at Hallowe'en with candy.

If Igor feels compelled to answer letters immediately, he demands the same alacrity in his correspondents, sometimes calculating the minimum time in which an answer *could* be expected, and if not received by then, resending a copy of his original. His rooms must contain as many filing cabinets as the State Department of Liechtenstein. And no wonder. In addition to a mountain of correspondence going back sixty years, he has amassed a whole library of programs and articles concerning his music since 1906. Most of the articles are heavily underscored, and their margins filled with rubrics vehemently unflattering to the perceptiveness of critics.

The trauma of the mail leaves him only one or two hours for composition before lunch, but another three hours are set aside in the late afternoon, and as many as three more at night. At the moment he is composing a cantata in Hebrew, and he says that the musico-syllabic qualities of the language, as he understands them, have charged his musical enzymes; judging by the ardor with which he has worked of late, they must be highly charged. He starts each day by playing over the work of the day before, and while he complains of the meagerness of the daily yield, each new opus continues to appear with the regularity that has marked his production all his life, the genie never failing him. From what I have said of his impatience to post letters, you will not be surprised to hear that as soon as a dozen bars have been completed he will write them in score and send them to the publisher. He rarely rewrites in any depth, but will recopy an entire page of orchestra score rather than leave the smear of an erasure.

Igor cannot bear any odor while he is composing, for which reason his studio is the most distant room from the kitchen. Pungent smells interfere with his hearing, he claims. He composes at a tacky-sounding, often out-of-tune upright piano dampened with felt. Nevertheless, and though the studio is soundproofed and its double doors always tightly closed, little noises as if from mice on the keyboard float into the next room. A plywood drawing board is attached to the music rack of the piano, and quarto-size strips of thick white paper are clipped to it. These are used for the pencil-sketch manuscript. Smaller sheets of paper are pinned to the board around this central manuscript, like sputniks. They are the navigation charts of serial orders, the transposition tables, the calculations of permutations: "here the twelfth note becomes the second note." To the side of the piano stands a kind of surgeon's operating table, except that the cutlery consists of electric pencil-sharpeners, styluses—with which Igor draws his staves and of which he is the patented inventor—an electric metronome, colored pencils, gums, stopwatches.

Among the regular, established interruptions in Igor's day are the weekly visits to doctors, and the almost weekly late-afternoon visits by attorneys with whom he is sometimes closeted for hours at a time plotting ways of reducing the "fisc" (Igor's word for income tax); the current way is a "mineralogical development project," which is a euphemism for some desultory fossicking in a goldmine called "Verigor" (true gold). Among the late afternoon visitors is Robert Craft, whom Igor calls "Bobsky," and, dropping a "ch" from Gogol,

"Bobinsky," a version first put into circulation by our friend the culture generalissimo, Nicolas Nabokov. Bobinsky comes to help Igor with musical affairs, as well as to contribute copious if not exactly coruscating conversation on other matters; but in the last few years he has become as indispensable to Igor as his memory (which, in fact, he is). Sometimes he stops to dine with us, incidentally (though not entirely, for he is something of a chowhound). I like to cook and sometimes prepare the meals myself. Ordinarily they are prepared by Evgenia Petrovna, whose last name, Mrs. Gate, is used according to whether we are being Russians or Americans. The cooking is regularly French but periodically Russian: caviare blini, pirozhki, kulebiaka, borscht, stroganov, kasha, kissel.

To American observers, Igor's table talk and manners could seem unbecoming, but not, I think, to Russians. Thus he appears to relish dinner-time discussions of liver, bladder, and bowel troubles; but so did Tolstoy (see the Countess Sophia Tolstoy's *Journal*), and the same unseemly inclination is manifest in other Russians of my acquaintance. But, then, one also encounters it in the French, as in the Goncourts' famous description of a dinner with Flaubert, Zola, Turgenev, Daudet: "We began with a long discussion on the special aptitudes of writers suffering from constipation and diarrhoea." Dr. Glover (*The Significance of the Mouth in Psychoanalysis*) would classify Igor as a "sucker" rather than a "biter," which would explain his preference, among eating utensils, for deep spoons, as well as his apparent dislike of the occidental system of impaling and lifting. In Japan he quickly became adroit with chopsticks. He abhors oleaginous substances and will peel a frankfurter and pare a piece of *prosciutto* so finely that the result could be called a carving, but this is not characteristically Russian. The impressive capacity to imbibe liquids is shared with other cultures, of course, but the tendency to slosh alcoholic beverages about the mouth to flush the remoter taste buds is not rare among other Russians. Peculiar to Igor is the sound of rich fricatives accompanying the intake of *potages*, rich enough in his case to increase an *avant-garde* writer's store of siphonic onomatopoeia—but the ultimate stage, in which the bowl is hoisted in the manner of a wassailing Viking draining his mead, seems more Scandinavian than Slavic. Russian, too, may be the habit of beret-wearing during meals, as if from doctrinal duress like that of a pious Jew.

Igor escapes from his work by playing solitaire; by listening to recordings; by catching and caressing Celeste, our *pusspartout* cat; by watching television. He strolls several times a day on our patio, but rarely walks in Beverly Hills any more, partly because of the danger of being run over by the limousines of movie composers, partly because walking at all has become difficult for him since his three "cerebrovascular accidents" (as thromboses are described in California, where a janitor is a "maintenance engineer," and juvenile gangs are "unsponsored youth groups").

Afternoon tea, served between siesta time and composing time, is another relaxation. Igor likes *infusions* or *tisanes, tilleulmenthe* or *camomile*, but he will also lace these very mild brews with a tumbler of Scotch. His managerial cortex is very powerful and alcohol seems not to interfere with his work. In the Swiss years he drank white Neuchâtel while composing, and in the French years red Bordeaux. In America it has been Scotch, or a bumper of beer. Every morning, several empty bottles stand by the kitchen door, yet Igor shows no ill effects. Doctors have sometimes gasped in disbelief after pressing his liver and showing him its size, like the fish that got away.

We have almost no social life here now, but this was not always the case. In the *"Tagebuch"* for *Dr. Faustus,* Thomas Mann suggests that wartime Hollywood was a more stimulating and cosmopolitan city than prewar Paris or Munich, and improbable as that sounds to a European visiting the subtopia today, it may almost have been true. The ferment of composers, writers, scientists, artists, actors, philosophers *did* exist then, and we sometimes attended their lectures, exhibitions, concerts, and assorted other performances. To compare *that* Hollywood with the Hollywood of today, consider that the premiere of a version of Brecht's *Galileo,* with the collaboration of Hanns Eisler, Charles Laughton, and Brecht himself, took place on La Cienaga Boulevard, where I once had my own art gallery, "La Boutique," and think of how inconceivably remote are the prospects of such an event now. Igor was greatly impressed by *Galileo,* incidentally, and shortly after it he protested the deportation of Eisler because he was a Communist, saying he could see no possibility of harm from the man, whereas the exile of the artist, or of any artist, was a loss. But during the political fears of the late Forties, culture decamped like Cambyses' army—culture as we knew it, that is, for Hollywood continues to boom, unmindful of the phase I have attempted to distinguish.

But I must stop. I beg you to forgive the total absence of gravitas in this letter, and not to show it to anyone in the Union of Soviet Composers. We send our love to you and to Caterina.

Vera

Also in Hollywood, we attended a screening of Joseph Strick's film of Jean Genet's *The Balcony,* with Peter Falk, to determine whether *Histoire du Soldat* could be used as background music.[22] On the 18th, we dined at Isherwood's, with the Huxleys and Gavin Lambert, author of *The Slide Area,* a roman à clef about the Baroness d'Erlanger. At almost the same time, a letter came from Stephen Spender:

I see Francis Bacon quite often and he told me that he would be very glad to paint Stravinsky and also to give the portrait to him. The difficulty is that he

---

22. Eventually I recorded the sound track.

is completely tied to agents—the Marlborough Gallery. The one thing he won't do is be televised while painting, Ken Tynan's suggestion, that completely ruined the last lot of negotiations. My feeling is that a compromise might be reached, say on the basis of doing two portraits—one for sale and one to give to Stravinsky . . .

Love to all,
Stephen

1963

On January 5 we lunched with Jean Renoir, whose face is still that of his father's pictures of him as a baby, except for the flushed, Bordeaux-drinker's complexion. He did all of the talking, in franglais, and was suspenseful and interesting on the subject of his escape from Paris in 1940. But he could be prickly, too, even confrontational, and he paid no attention to his dark, mysterious, attractive Brazilian wife, Dido.

On the 10th we dined at the Huxleys' with George Cukor and Gerald Heard, who went on and on about the hypothalamus.

As requested in a letter from the Paris music critic, and former Stravinsky nemesis, Boris de Schloezer, Alexander Scriabin's son-in-law, Stravinsky wrote (January 23) to Dr. Henry Kissinger, Director of the Harvard International Seminar, recommending Scriabin's daughter Marina as eminently qualified, intellectually and linguistically, to attend his seminar.[23]

On February 8, a letter came from Glenn Gould: "Dear Bob: I have been very much under the weather for the last little while and am just now beginning to feel myself again . . . it appears that the simplest thing, both in terms of time and economy, would be to engage separate players for the [Schoenberg] Serenade performance (*i.e.*, those who could rehearse during such times as our Festival Orchestra was engaged in their daily baths of Gilbert and Sullivan)."

In early February, Ralph Parker, Hurok's representative in Moscow, wrote to me enthusiastically of David Oistrakh's performance of Stravinsky's Violin Concerto, and with news of his translation of Solzhenitsyn's *Ivan Denisovich*: "I think Max Hayward is ashamed of his part in the race [to publish the book in English] . . . But, knowing Solzhenitsyn and what he has been through, I simply couldn't stomach the thought of his royalties going to the International Rescue Committee and Frederick Praeger. As it is, I got my four guineas a thousand words on the English edition only, just enough to cover my fare to London and back.

At the beginning of March another note came from Glenn Gould: "Dear Bob: This is by way of being a fan letter for *Erwartung*—absolutely one of

23. Kissinger did not answer, possibly because he knew that Vyacheslav Molotov was Scriabin's nephew.

the most marvelous things you have ever done! In fact, the whole record is tremendous . . . All the best for now. I look forward to seeing you at the end of the month."

On March 3 Stravinsky completed *Abraham and Isaac*, after which we dined with Aldous and Laura Huxley at "Trader Vic's."[24] On the 17th, Stravinsky declined an invitation from Henry (*Time/Life*) Luce to dine with President Kennedy, and selected others, at the Waldorf. Meanwhile, a letter came from Stephen Spender in Evanston: "Wystan is supposed to be zooming around the mid-West next week reading poems to pay for a new room in his Austrian schloss."

On the 21st, at a snow-engulfed Oberlin College, Stravinsky conducted his *Psalms* on a program in which I conducted his Symphony in C and the two orchestral movements from *The Flood*. The student orchestra was superb. In New York two days later we saw *Otello* at the Met, with Berman's decor, after which Stravinsky bought two of the costume sketches. On the 25th we dined with Hurok at the Pavillon, then went to Peter Ustinov's play *Photo Finish*. On the 27th Stravinsky and I flew to Toronto for recording sessions, he taping his Suite No. 2 and *Vom Himmel hoch*, and I Schoenberg's *Kol Nidre* and *Pelleas und Melisande*.

At Balanchine's morning rehearsal of *Movements* (April 5), Stravinsky was delighted with its "human architecture" and asked me to write a blurb about it for him, which I did in the afternoon:

> Balanchine's realization of the *Movements* exposes relationships of which I had not been aware. Seeing it was like touring a building for which I had drawn the plans but not completely explored the result. Balanchine began by identifying familiar hallmarks of my style, of which I myself became conscious only through his eyes and ears. And as I watched him fastening on the tiniest repeated rhythmic figure (bars 155–156), I knew that he had joined the score to my other music with greater speed than it could ever get there by way of the concert hall. Beyond that, he discovered the music's lyricism. As in most ballets, his dramatic point is a love parable, and his coda has a suggestion of the ending of *Apollo*.
>
> The choreography is a musical composition, a double concerto for a solo male and a solo female dancer, both identified with the piano. The choric group is spare: a hexachord of those bee-like little girls—big thighs, nipped-in waists, pin-heads—who seem to be bred to the choreographer's specifications. Only in the Interludes does the full sextet dance as a unit, thereby projecting the shape of the entire opus with exceptional clarity.
>
> One head movement seemed obtrusive, a holdover from *Bugaku*, but of no consequence. What struck me most was that when Balanchine asked his

---

24. This was the last time we saw Aldous Huxley.

dancers to repeat a section without the music, they were able to count it by themselves, which is better than most orchestras can do, even with the music in front of them. Are the *Movements* ballet music? Barbarous question to a Balanchine, who says that he needs a motor impulse, not a *pas de deux*.

At 10 P.M. on April 8 we boarded the SS *Bremen* with Wolf König, Roman Kroiter, and the camera and sound technicians of the Canadian National Film Board. At midnight Mr. B. and Lucia Davidova came to see us off. Before docking at Bremen, on April 16, a gangplank was lowered to allow reporters, interviewers, photographers, and Rolf Liebermann aboard. A limousine took us through heavy rain to the Vier Jahreszeiten in Hamburg, where we discussed ideas for *Oedipus Rex* and *The Flood* with the stage director Günther Rennert. The next day I rehearsed the opera orchestra twice. The musicians could not play, and balked at trying to play, the *Flood* movements that the Oberlin students performed perfectly with little rehearsal. Nevertheless, the first staged performances of *The Flood* and *Oedipus Rex* took place on April 30. Afterwards, Nabokov and Dagmar Hader, a stunning, twenty-three-year-old blond, came to dinner at the hotel.

Two weeks later I conducted *The Flood* in Zagreb with the touring Hamburg Opera, and Stravinsky shared an orchestra concert with me. "Stravinsky had to the highest degree the sense of knowing how to delight his audiences. All of the spectators at his concert for the Biennale of Zagreb were in shirtsleeves, and, though accustomed to *tenues plus mondaines*, Igor betrayed no surprise. On the contrary, at the end of the thunderous applause that greeted his entrance, he turned to the audience and said: 'Excuse me, but I too am very hot.' And, with perfect composure, he removed his tails, vest, white tie, and began to unbutton his shirt. The enthusiasm in the hall augmented with each step in this striptease."[25]

From Zagreb, we flew via Munich to Paris. Stravinsky was to have opened a festival in Bergen, Norway, with the King in attendance, but, enjoying Paris in the spring, cancelled the Scandinavian expedition on grounds of illness and sent me in his stead. Before going, I remember a pleasant lunch with Ambassador Charles Bohlen at the American Embassy, a stimulating dinner with the writer Michel Butor, and an audition in Nicolas Nabokov's apartment of his opera *Rasputin*, taped in Cologne. My flight to Bergen (May 19) included changes of plane in Copenhagen and in Oslo, but I was jealous at not being with Stravinsky in Paris while he examined *The Rite of Spring* sketches in the André Meyer collection. During rehearsals, and before and after them, Norwegian journalists waylaid me demanding an explanation for the photos in their newspapers of the supposedly ailing Stravinsky enjoying life on the Boulevards.

25. Liebermann, *op. cit.*

I spent a week in London at the beginning of June, then a week in Dublin, where Stravinsky and I shared a concert. Our next engagements were in Hamburg, where Stravinsky conducted *Oedipus* at the Staatsoper, and Stockholm, where he received the Sibelius Prize (twenty-five thousand dollars), and I conducted *The Flood* and, with the beautiful, sloe-eyed Estonian pianist Käbi Laretei (Mrs. Ingmar Bergman), the Capriccio. We flirted at the postconcert reception, the rumor being that she had already broken with Bergman and wanted a career as a pianist.

At the end of the month we returned to New York from Milan, where we had presented the *Flood* and *Oedipus Rex* on a double-bill at La Scala. A letter from Spender awaited me at the Hotel Pierre: "Henry Moore replaced the drawing with a small bronze of a figure like a goddess with a pleated tunic . . . We are very happy with the swap.[26] I have just finished dramatizing *The Golden Bowl* . . . I am going on writing my long poem about I-thou-we-they." Accompanying the letter was a copy of the catalog for the 1959 exhibition at the Tate Gallery, *The Romantic Movement*, inscribed on the flyleaf "To Robert Craft with affection and gratitude from Stephen Spender. June 63," and beneath this, in Moore's hand, "Souvenir de Henry Moore!"

In Hollywood at the beginning of July, John Walsh, who had inherited the Baroness d'Erlanger's house, proposed to sell it to the Stravinskys, who needed more room and a ground-level entrance (porte cochère) without step-climbing. The idea took root. On the 11th Stravinsky and I flew to Chicago for a Ravinia concert two days later. I conducted the *Tristan* Prelude (with the concert ending), Debussy's *Gigues*, and Schoenberg's *Five Pieces* (1909 version). On the 14th we flew to Albuquerque, where Paul Horgan met and drove us to Santa Fe. Vera Stravinsky and Bill (William Theophilus) Brown arrived later the same day in the Stravinsky car, after two days on the road from Hollywood. Paul Horgan describes the Albuquerque airport scene in his *Encounters with Stravinsky*:

> The airport was thronged . . . Stravinsky, looking fit, went with me to take a waiting-room bench. He was still full of the recent concert . . ."And Bop!" he said enthusiastically, referring to Craft. "You should have heard him conduct the *Tristan* Vorspiel . . . A wonderful piece! . . . Ja," he said, "Bop was vonderful . . . he was amazing in *Tristan*. My God! He drew out the first phrase, and held it. It was impossible to play, yet he made them play it," and in the bustling passenger crowd, Stravinsky suddenly gave a vocal demonstration of how Craft had paced the celebrated opening theme . . . The sound he made, with its

26. Moore asked Spender to give one of his pictures of sleeping figures in the London tube during the 1940s night-bombings to Stravinsky, promising a bargain exchange for the Spender collection. Stravinsky, in gratitude, sent a page of the *Abraham and Isaac* manuscript to the artist, and, after her husband's death, Mrs. Stravinsky gave the picture to the Henry Moore Foundation.

astounding hold and crescendo, was so loud that I had the impression of all movement in the airport coming to a halt, while a hundred and fifty people turned, startled, and stared to know what was happening. Stravinsky, oblivious, conducted his own sound as if giving instructions at rehearsal . . . Then again the second statement of the main theme, again in a voice growing so loud it echoed off the ceiling. The Chicago orchestra sat invisibly about him and he gave full expression to their imaginary playing. The energy he sent forth from his bench was astounding. It held almost everyone there motionless until, quite unaware of anyone about, he was finished with his demonstration. "There was not enough bow for them to play it, but Bop made them, and it was *épatant!*"

At our concert in St. Francis Cathedral in Santa Fe, Stravinsky conducted his Mass and I conducted eight excerpts from Monteverdi's *Vespers.* He was installed as a Knight Commander, with star, of the Papal Order of St. Sylvester, a ceremony that required him to kneel on one of the altar steps and receive taps on both shoulders with the flat blade of a sword. Horgan wore a uniform with gold buttons down the center of the tunic and stripes down the side of the trouser legs.

En route next day to Williams, Arizona, in intense heat, Mrs. Stravinsky fell asleep at the wheel, which I managed to grab just as the car started to veer off the road. If Stravinsky had been sitting with her, instead of me, the three of us would have been dead, since the speedometer was at 90 M.P.H.

At the end of August we were in New York preparing for concerts in Rio de Janeiro. Stravinsky cabled Oscar Alcazar:[27] "Please meet Friday morning flight 351 without journalists and photographers." In the evening of August 29 Eugene Smith,[28] of *Vogue,* photographed us leaving the New York airport. Our Rio concert took place in the beautiful church of the Igreja on September 8. We were back in New York the next day, and soon after in Hollywood, where I conducted a Monday Concert in Fiesta Hall, Plummer Park: Stravinsky's Miniatures and the premiere of his arrangement for eight instruments of Sibelius's string *Canzonetta,* Schoenberg's Septet-Suite, the original version of Wagner's *Siegfried Idyll,* a Haydn Cassation and his *Notturno II.*

On October 11 a cable came from Nadia Boulanger: "*Jean [Cocteau] est mort c'est seulement à vous que je puisse confier ma douleur.*" Stravinsky wept.

On October 25 we attended the opening of an exhibition of Schoenberg's paintings and drawings at a UCLA art gallery. Thirty of the fifty-eight pictures are self-portraits. Stravinsky, not knowing that Schoenberg was a painter,

---

27. Our Lima-based concert agent for Latin America.

28. Smith had married Phyllis Curtin, my friend from Tanglewood. In June 1966 he did many portraits of Stravinsky in the Hotel Lotti, Paris.

was much impressed by the self-portrait of the artist standing, from the rear.

A week later, in New York, Stravinsky saw and liked John Osborne's *Luther*, to his own surprise. On November 11 we flew to Rome on our way to Sicily for concerts. Landing at Ciampino on the 12th, Stravinsky left the airplane in a wheelchair to avoid the long walk to the terminal. Infuriated at the sight of paparazzi aiming cameras at him, he leapt up and swung his cane threateningly in their direction, thereby providing a more dramatic picture for the evening edition.

The mood in New York when we returned in December was unsettling. Our friends still seemed bewildered by the assassination of President Kennedy, partly because no one believed the official explanation of Jack Ruby's shooting of Oswald seen on television. We remained in the city during the holidays for a series of concerts with the Philadelphia Orchestra in January. On the last day of the year a letter from Spender thanked me "for your journals, your excellent memory, your incomparable intellect." *Oimè. We* celebrated New Year's Eve by ourselves in the Stravinsky suite at the Pierre.

1964

Stravinsky and I went alone to Philadelphia and Washington, giving Vera Stravinsky a vacation from concert touring and an opportunity to see friends in New York. When these concerts were over (January 25), I had conducted Schoenberg's *Five Pieces* and Stravinsky's Symphony in C five times, music no one else was performing with major orchestras. The Philadelphia management did not want this repertory, of course, any more than they wanted me, but if this was the only arrangement by which they could get Stravinsky, they were prepared to accept it. The orchestra was sympathetic to me, Eugene Ormandy kind and considerate. On January 28 Stravinsky saw Gian Carlo Menotti's *The Last Savage* at the Metropolitan Opera. Misinterpreting the satire on avant-garde music as an attack on him, he returned to the hotel saying, "We [*i.e.*, you] must do a paragraph about it for our next book."

In Hollywood on March 3 the Stravinskys deposited fifty-one thousand dollars in escrow for the purchase of the d'Erlanger house. Immediately afterward we were off again, this time to Cleveland, where I recorded Schoenberg's *Five Pieces* and Stravinsky his *Jeu de cartes* and *Ode*, the former unfortunately without his many revisions and corrections because he was using a rented score instead of his own, the *Ode* drooping badly at the end. We went by car to Cincinnati for an exhibition of Vera Stravinsky's paintings, and were met there by Fred Osten-Sacken, coming from Lexington. A radio commentator here introduced himself to me at the reception as my old Kingston friend and classmate William Burns. He reminded me that we were in Camp Pickett, Virginia, together in 1943.

The premiere of Stravinsky's *Elegy for J.F.K.* took place soon after our return to Hollywood. The *Los Angeles Times* critic described the piece generously as "expressive in its reticence." The singer, Richard Robinson, and the three clarinetists had seen the music for the first time only hours before the performance, and Robinson had a concert elsewhere slightly before this one. I rehearsed him in a dressing room just before we went on stage.[29]

The next day a letter from Boulez said that he hoped to see me in Europe and conveyed his *"bien cordiale sympathie."* On the 22nd Stravinsky wrote to Boosey & Hawkes, asking the publisher not to let the new recording of the *Rake* fall through: "The rental fee is too high, actually eight times what it was in 1953. Will you please cooperate in my interests, because a sale of only 5,000 copies of the old recording in eleven years does not justify making a new one . . . My stay in London in June depends on this."

In May Stravinsky recorded his Piano Concerto with Philippe Entremont in Manhattan Center. The pianist riled the composer throughout and managed to provoke three tantrums, all of them recorded, since Columbia Records kept the tape rolling throughout every Stravinsky session from about 1962 to the end of his recording career. I worked with a Cantor, Ephraim Biran, who would sing the premiere of *Abraham and Isaac* in Israel in September.

On our return to Hollywood, Max Edel took us to dinner with the film agent Paul Kohner, to discuss the possible use of Stravinsky's public-domain music in Dino de Laurentiis's *The Bible*, already referred to as "Good Book, bad movie."[30]

On our way to London we stopped in Denver, staying in the Brown Palace Hotel, full of ghosts of sixteen years before. Our concert, rained out from Red Rocks, was rescheduled in the Denver Coliseum. In London, Stravinsky recorded the *Rake*, and I recorded Schoenberg's *Von Heute auf Morgen* with the Royal Philharmonic and four very good German singers, who had performed the opera many times in Hannover. On June 27, we lunched in the Savoy Grill with Marie-José, the ex-Queen of Italy, House of Savoy, daughter of the "Red" Queen Elisabeth of Belgium. Two days later we were in Oxford for a concert in Lina Lalandi's Oxford Bach Festival. Miss Martie Retief, last seen in Johannesburg, drove me there three hours ahead of Stravinsky, so that I could rehearse for him. The Stravinskys had taken a room at the Randolph Hotel, where I was able to rest, but my totally unrehearsed *Trauer-Ode*, in spite of Janet Baker's gorgeous voice and matching art, was a disaster. After intermission, Miss Retief drove me back to the Savoy.

29. The first clarinetist Mitchell Lurie recalled that he walked with Stravinsky on the way from the parking lot to the hall: "I couldn't help remarking, as he walked with such difficulty to the hall just a few yards away, that he still traveled all over the world conducting orchestras. . . How did he do it? His answer: 'It is my new revenge.' I remember so well the wicked flash in his eyes." (UCLA Morton Collection)

30. Eugene Berman wrote from Rome: "I heard about the *Bible* project and was very skeptical, but John Huston assured me Igor would do the music!!"

In July 1964 a request to Stravinsky for money arrived from his daughter-in-law Françoise, wife of Soulima. She wrote that: "At Ann Arbor [in May] I asked Vera if it would be possible for you to help us financially with the work at my home, La Clidelle [France]. Her response was so kind and so full of warmth that I now permit myself to broach the subject with you." Stravinsky, much less kindly, not at all warmly, and, in truth, with embarrassing selfishness, wrote to his publisher in London: "Ashamed to ask me directly, [Françoise] spoke about it to Vera, breaking down into tears. But give the money to the poor girl, since taxes will not allow me to take it to my grave" (July 9, 1964).

On our arrival in New York, Stravinsky was deeply upset by news of the death of Pierre Monteux, the more so because the conductor had seemed so spry and happy when they met publicly in Albert Hall the year before, after Monteux's fiftieth anniversary concert of *The Rite of Spring*. On July 14 Vera Stravinsky flew to Los Angeles, Stravinsky and I to Chicago for a concert at Ravinia. The young Seiji Ozawa attended our Ravinia rehearsals and followed the scores with Stravinsky. While rehearsing *Orpheus*, Ozawa told Stravinsky that the harp "should sound more romantic, like a guitar." Claudio Spies and Glenn Watkins were there and heard this as well.

Two days after the concert I recorded Schoenberg's arrangement of Brahms's G-minor Quartet with the Chicago Symphony, without stops or inserts, then flew to Albuquerque and drove to Santa Fe. Stravinsky recorded *Orpheus* after me and flew to Los Angeles with John McClure. In Santa Fe, I received a most unexpected letter from Dagmar Hader, the young stage designer on the staff of the West Berlin Opera and secretary to Nicolas Nabokov, who had introduced her to us in Hamburg in the spring of 1963, and been her escort there, basking in the attention and gossip as he strode down the aisle of the Oper with the striking young blond on his arm.

The letter said that she was impatiently awaiting me in Berlin, where Stravinsky and I had a concert in late September. Since I was almost twice her age and could not imagine that she nourished any romantic interest in me, I considered every possible motive for the letter, without finding a plausible one. The mystery would have to wait until we were in Berlin. A few days before we left for Germany, the Stravinskys moved (on September 8) from 1260 to 1218 N. Wetherly Drive, the Baroness's former house. Stravinsky was more than a little sad and remained silent during the transfer.

Nabokov and Dagmar met us at the Berlin airport on September 17 in separate cars, and the tension between the two of them was all but palpable. He delegated me to ride to the hotel alone with her, telling me that I was to be her charge, that she would be responsible for seeing that I got to rehearsals and other functions on time. Though friendlier than she had been in Hamburg, our conversation en route was impersonal. And so it continued: the Stravinskys and I spent what little free time we had with such old friends as Auden, Spender, Nadia Boulanger, Nikita Magaloff (who played the Capriccio with Stravinsky in our concert), Eleazar and Joçy de Oliveira de Carvalho.

The sojourn in Berlin was largely uneventful until the last night. Hans Werner Henze took us to a performance of Jean Genet's *The Blacks*, but we left long before the end. We rehearsed *Abraham and Isaac* with Dietrich Fischer-Dieskau in his apartment. He had worked hard at the rhythms and mastered the pronunciation of Hebrew, but his pitches were imperfect, sevenths tending to become octaves, etc. To our great relief, he was never a prima-donna but always a hardworking musician. His recent autobiography compliments me but claims that at one of the orchestra rehearsals, I told Stravinsky, seated in the hall behind me and making fribbling interruptions every two minutes, to "sit down and shut up." Regrettably, this is true, but I uttered the words under my breath, and Fischer-Dieskau, standing a foot away from me, was the only one who heard them. Lorin Maazel, Music Director of the New York Philharmonic, watched the rehearsal from the side of the orchestra. The actual performance went smoothly. The Associated Press report on the concert, dated September 23, says that "Composer Igor Stravinsky won a standing ovation last night after he conducted the Berlin Philharmonic Orchestra. West German President Heinrich Luebke and West Berlin Mayor Willy Brandt personally congratulated the eighty-two-year-old maestro . . . Stravinsky's Biblical ballad *Abraham and Isaac* was performed for the first time in Europe, sung by Germany's best-known baritone, Dietrich Fischer-Dieskau. It was directed by the American conductor Robert Craft."

One evening Peter Heyworth, Otto Klemperer's biographer, invited me to go with him and Dagmar to the theater in East Berlin. On our return a dementedly enraged Nabokov was waiting in the Kempinksi Hotel parking lot, and Daggie, as he called her, had to slip out and run as if for her life. The next day she told me that he had been making her existence miserable with his jealousy, and that she wanted to go to New York, with which I realized where I came in. Returning to the hotel to change clothes after our *Abraham and Isaac* concert, I found Dagmar nestled in my bed. Since I had to put in an appearance at an official reception and was already late, I bade her good night before very long. On my arrival at the dinner, Auden said, "You look terribly pale." I must have looked even paler two hours later when, returning to my room, I found her still in the same place. At about 2 A.M., when my telephone rang, she hurried to answer it. The caller was, as she knew, Nicolas Nabokov. The next morning, in the Kempinski lobby, he threw her to the floor and began to whack her bottom with a "stick" of rolled-up newspapers, until stopped by porters and a policeman. He retreated to the Stravinskys' rooms, saying he was suffering a heart attack. As we had arrived in Berlin, so, that afternoon, we left—Dagmar and I to the airport in one car, the Stravinskys and Nabokov in another.

In Paris on September 26, we drove to Beauvais for lunch, and returned via Amiens and Chantilly. Our stay in New York was very brief, Stravinsky being eager to complete his Variations. He slept in his new Hollywood home for the first time on October 5. I conducted only one Monday concert that autumn, the nine-instrument version of Webern's Symphony, on a program with Haydn and Biber. Again in New York in late November, we heard *Falstaff* at the Met, well conducted, in Stravinsky's opinion, by Leonard Bernstein. I then introduced *Abraham and Isaac* in Toronto, on a program with Strauss's *Bourgeois Gentilhomme*, a program repeated the next day in Philharmonic Hall, New York, where Stravinsky conducted his *Pulcinella* Suite, *Berceuses du Chat*, and *Elegy for J.F.K.* This program was repeated in Constitution Hall, Washington, on December 7 and in Boston on the 9th. On the 11th Stravinsky recorded his vocal pieces with Cathy Berberian in New York. (A tape survives, B5 Masterworks GM 31/LXX 36940, of this unpleasant session, in which Stravinsky is heard crankily correcting the singer's English as well as her Russian. Her pitch and rhythm were indistinct, more so each time he shouted at her.) When we first heard her, Cathy Berberian, married to the composer Luciano Berio, had been one of the avant-garde's favorite interpreters. A personal friend of the Stravinskys and myself, she died prematurely.

1965

News of T. S. Eliot's death came in New York at the beginning of the year. In Hollywood on January 14, Stravinsky began to compose an *Introitus* to the memory, as he wrote, of "the unforgettable Eliot." We also rued the absence of Aldous Huxley during an evening at his widow's with Dr. Christian Volf, the renowned Danish expert on hearing. By playing recordings of synthetic sounds in low octaves through earphones, he sent vibrators through the bones and skull in a kind of internal massage that relieved sinus pains and congestion. In our case, Dr. Volf experimented with his "Reflex Theory of Acoustic Therapy." He believed that this could detect both cancer and schizophrenia. The waves generated by a vibrating C-128 tuning fork held to various nodules of the body travel directly to a cancerous area, he maintained, whereas they do not travel at all in schizophrenics, but exit through fingers and toes. Stravinsky consented to be strapped into a chair and even to having the *1812 Overture* blasted through his bones, all to no effect, which Dr. Volf accepted as proof that the composer was unafflicted by both the mental and the physical diseases.

On February 13 Rolf Liebermann arrived from Hamburg to discuss a Stravinsky Eurovision documentary. The only other event of the month was a dinner at Chasen's with Teddy Kollek, the mayor of Jerusalem, Gregor Piatigorsky, and Isaac Stern. Kollek gave an ancient shofar[31] to Stravinsky as a token of Israel's appreciation for his gift of the manuscript of *Abraham and Isaac.*

Near the end of the month Mrs. Stravinsky asked me once again to write in her name to her cousin in Moscow informing him of the move:

Dear Volodya:

As you see, we have changed houses! The climb up the hillside from the street had become too steep for Igor, and the cramped space was an increasing inconvenience for both of us. Fortunately, the new house is on the same street and only a two-minute walk away. Still, Igor was saddened at having to leave his old studio, and once the move was over he refused to re-enter the old residence. I now realize how deeply attached to objects he is, and how much security he derives from them; and as strongly as he had possessed them, they now turn on and possess him. Before he adjusted to the relocation of them in the new house, a fuzziness was noticeable in the edges of his ego. During that transitional period, the nightlight in his room had to be increased from his little blue *veilleuse* to a surgery-strength lamp.

The new property, more than twice as large as the old, extends through the block to the next street, on which we have a guesthouse. We also have many more trees: palms, pines, magnolias in front, avocados and oranges in the back, as well as some over-the-wall branches of the neighbors' eucalyptuses. One new feature is that we have a swimming pool. Igor was never much at aquatics, and in fact has a superstitious fear of water, staying below deck when at sea, like Goncharov on the *Frigat Palat.* But I like to swim—if the word fits my splashless turtle stroke—especially when the Santa Ana wind, our solano or mistral, dries our sinuses and the air for a hundred electric miles around.

The house has two storeys—three, counting the basement, which we have made into a music room, furnishing it with a piano, record-playing equipment, many shelves of music and music books. At the well of the basement staircase is a wine cellar. At the landing, conveniently suited for emergencies from either floor, is a w.c., one of five in the house. Salons, dining rooms, libraries are on the ground floor, and so, of course, is the kitchen, which, with pushbutton dishwashing, garbage disposal, gravity heat, is a triumph of automation. (Have you ever read Julien Offray de la Mettrie's 1746 *Man the Machine?*) The chief ornament of the living-room is a black marble fireplace, on whose mantelpiece Igor keeps silver bowls of white asters and wax gloxinias, but the only furnishing there from the old house is a triple-fold *paravant* papered with an enlarged 1956 photograph of Igor looking over the railing of a bridge at the Villa Manin.

31. It is now in Temple Emanuel in Kingston, New York.

The most effective improvements over our old house are upstairs, where Igor now has four connecting rooms, as well as a labyrinth of closets and alcoves, the Fort Knox of his filing systems. He can go from a central-bath-room-base-of-all-operations to his bedroom, office, or studio without interception, which is to say without leaving his lair. In the arrangement of furniture and bibelots, incidentally, his new studio is a near replica of the old, except that it and all of his rooms are more spacious.

I fancy that by this point you must be thinking of my description as the typical dream of the *petite bourgeoisie*. But we do not feel classified as such by our amenities. Nor do we mind being regarded by our Minutemen neighbors as "communists"—as we were regarded after our Russian visit—and by our politically progressive European friends as "imperialists," by the mere fact of our residence in the farthest-"right" neighborhood of the left-end of America.

We were familiar with the house during the tenancy of the former owner, a remarkable lady and friend of Igor's in ballet days, who paid for Diaghilev's funeral and interment when no one closer to him came forward. A very colorful woman herself—aspects of her fame have been established through the keyholes of more than one roman à clef (*Le Bal du Comte d'Orgel* among them)— her genealogy extended from the time of the First Crusade; on the dispensation of an Avignon Pope, she enjoyed an ancestral license to eat meat on Fridays. She had been prodigally rich, too, but her fortune had dwindled in the course of a lifetime shared with costly impermanent paramours. She was obliged to dispose of her homes in London, Paris, Venice, Stra (Palladio's Villa Malcontenta, no less, bequeathed to a former *cicisbeo*). The Hollywood house, her last property, had dwindled, too, by parceling and desuetude. Toward the end, in fact, it had become a kind of flea market. Practically all of the contents were for sale. Needless to say, the house had to be entirely refurbished before we could move in.

You ask about Igor's health. He is stooped and frail now, walks slowly, and only rarely without a cane. He uses a wheelchair in air terminals, which he would not have done a year ago. As you know, he was always an impatiently fast walker who only a few years ago used to trail me behind him like a Chinese wife. The greatest impediment to locomotion is not age, however, but a hernia, the result of an accident eight years ago, that, owing to partial paralysis on his right side, rendered him insensible to strain while lifting a suitcase. He says that at times he feels as if the right half of his body had been separated from the left, and that his right hand feels as if it were encased in a glove. Other parts of the dwelling are out of kilter, too, and there are other malfunctions, but the impaired walking bothers him more than anything else, and the threat of immobility, of the wheelchair as the only method of movement, is the most terrible of all his forebodings.

Even so, Igor does not look his years. His reddish hair is still unmixed with gray—on the top of the head, though it must be admitted that not many hairs of *any* complexion are to be found there—and his eyes and ears are as attentive and retentive as ever. The face has gained in flesh and lost in angularity, but is less striated than those of most other people of his age. That head, incidentally, is still the most striking I have ever seen. It is so small, for one thing, and so unlike the behemoth highbrow genius dear to nineteenth-century phrenology. In fact the frontal lobes are almost delinquently low and concave, the glabella and jaw are unheroically recessive, and the nether lip is too thick—a cranial picture that, so far as this description goes, seems to resemble the simian prototypes Igor refers to, and pronounces as, "aps." Yet it is a face of almost unbelievable power and sensitiveness.

The change in temperament in the last year or so is very marked. The carapace over the feelings appears to be harder than ever, but for the very reason, one suspects, that the contents have mellowed. Corresponding to this change is a loosening of the characteristic economy, in time, talk, money—in fact almost everything except music, where, on the contrary, the specificity is greater. He is forgetful, too, quick to reverse himself, and unduly suspicious—all ordinary signs of age. What is extraordinary is a new gentleness. In fact, the word *gentil* appears so regularly in his vocabulary now, and was so rare in the past, that I accustom myself to it with difficulty.

Rages and temper tantrums are rarer, too, and even the small eruptions quickly turn to embers. Contrast this with the bad old days when an explosion a week was the rule, some of them protracted detonations involving furniture overturning and crockery smashing *à la* Baba the Turk, though they could be noiseless, too, as occasion suited, for Igor was able to fill a room with his black mood simply by passing through it, like a cuttlefish spreading its ink. *That* Stravinsky wrote *The Rite of Spring*, one thought, retreating in awe until the mood had subsided (the debris settling or the dusky fluids dissipating). In truth, too, as you can see, I am a bit nostalgic and would welcome a small, symptomatic cyclone from time to time, the gods being too easily mollified now and the breezes too bland—nothing, in fact, but the Trades.

Reading Jules Renard's *Journal* the other day, I came across this passage which might have been written with Igor in mind:

> What remains is to pick up the pen, to rule the paper, patiently to fill it up. The strong do not hesitate. They settle down, they sweat, they go on to the end. They exhaust the ink, they use up the paper. There are only oxen. The biggest ones are geniuses—the ones who toil eighteen hours a day without tiring·

Sometimes the sound of Igor's piano can be heard from his sanctum sanctorum late at night, even while a party may be in progress, or decline, downstairs, a party at which he had imbibed as much as anyone else, though he alone is clearheaded and able to work an hour after. Last night, while I watched television, he typed a dozen letters; but he is *never* totally inactive, and even when ill in bed he will study a score or read or write. I have no way of estimating the amount of work he wrests from his time, but I doubt that many composers of his years (are there "many?") have surpassed him.

The unkindest way to behave with Igor is as if he were a being apart. Still, few people are themselves with him, which may be desirable in some cases, but not when the visitor, entering the presence, performs three bows and three stumbles, and departs gold-framing each word for a future conversation piece. The only possible compliment to offer such a man is the knowledge of his music. Yet many people humiliate him with flattery. No wonder he enjoys himself so much in the company of animals, and of people who have never heard of him. Still, he has not suffered from mental isolation or an insuscepti-bility to what philosophers call "other minds." Quite the contrary, Igor is amaz-ingly aware of and almost psychically able to read the contents of "other minds," and in fact some people even complain of his remarkable acquisitive powers, and of his habit of repeating *their* ideas back to them. My response to this is that he has a maieutic, improving mind himself.

I have also wondered about how oppressive to Igor must be the weight of posterity. In fact it has hung around his neck for so long now that for three-quarters of his life he must have felt as burdened with it as a belled cat. Imag-ine what it must be like to know that your letters are destined to be collected and sold, and that your most offhand remarks are certain to reappear, dis-torted and adapted to the purposes of other people's woolly memoirs. Igor tries to avenge himself on this fate in advance by, so to speak, entering into correspondence with it, framing in red ink the idiocies about himself in books and articles, as if by so doing he could rub posterity's nose in the dirt. But, to tell the truth, I think that bad reviews are important to Igor's security.

I have wondered recently if he is ever troubled by defections from his leadership, but concluded that he is too full of his own creations to give much thought to such matters. And what if he were to tell himself a few necessary lies? Who does not do that, and not only in old age but most of the time?

Now, at eighty-three, Igor receives about $10,000 for half a concert and part of a rehearsal. I have noticed that few people listen with much attention to the *music* in these concerts and that, in fact, few seem even to have come for that purpose. What they want is the numinous presence, and while $10,000 may be a lot of money, Igor is a lot of numen.

With love,
Vera

Filming for Rolf Liebermann began on March 16 by Richard Leacock, of the New York Leacock–Pennebaker firm. Stravinsky's interest not hav-ing been sparked, the first day's yield was meager. On the morrow Leacock appeared with a new sound engineer, a stunning young woman, Sarah Hudson, who galvanized Stravinsky. From then on the documenting proceeded with *brio*. Moving smoothly from English to German to French, Liebermann was the ideal interviewer for him. He understood music, and Stravinsky trusted him. Isherwood and Heard appeared at teatime, but added nothing. Stravinsky made some marvelous remarks: viz., "Everyone who makes something new does harm to something old." "I am always happy when I am awakened, and it is the same with composing . . . In the morning we think differently than in the evening . . . When I come to a difficulty, I wait until tomorrow; I can wait as an insect can wait." In answer to a question whether he cares if his music is performed, he replied: "Of course I am interested to hear if I was right or not."

The next day Pierre Boulez, in town for a concert, and Lawrence Morton came for lunch. Ms. Hudson, in a bikini, standing on the back terrace by the swimming pool, was the most delicious-looking hors d'oeuvre imaginable, but neither of these guests could bear even to look in her direction (whereas Stravinsky, at eighty-two, was unable to look anywhere else). After the meal, flipping through the score of *Noces*, Boulez talked an inebriated Stravinsky into canceling a bar of silence on the last page, mistakenly arguing that the original manuscript or a copy of the proofs would verify the bar as an error.

On the 21st Stravinsky wrote to Peter Bartok contradicting a statement by the widow of the cimbalomist Aladár Rácz that the instrument was abandoned in *Noces* "at the persuasion of Ernest Ansermet." On the 24th I went to a birthday party for Boulez at Morton's, and on the 25th, with Stravinsky, to Boulez's rehearsal of his *Eclat* in the Los Angeles County Museum.

At the beginning of April we were in Austin, Texas, for more filming, this time for a CBS documentary directed by David Oppenheim. It got off to a gimmicky start, with a reception for Stravinsky at the airport by a posse of cowboys, all of them twice as tall as he was. One of them placed his ten-gallon Stetson on the composer's head, decapitating him visually, as had happened in the Reinhart Museum in Wintherthur when he tried on Wagner's beret, which covered him to his shoulders. Another filmed scene of a drawing class with nude model at the University of Texas Arts Department had to be cut. On the last day I conducted a concert with the University Orchestra and was agreeably surprised to find one of my 1936–37 heroes in West Saugerties, New York, Frank Elsass, a faculty member here, playing in the brass section. After the program, which included *Orpheus* and excerpts from *The Flood*, we were driven to San Antonio for our flight to Los Angeles.

Chicago was the next venue for the CBS filming. We co-conducted a concert with the Chicago Symphony, but at the last minute the Musicians' Union did not allow a sound track to be made, and only the audience was photographed, especially Saul Bellow. I conducted the world premiere of

Stravinsky's Variations, the local premieres of Schoenberg's male choruses, his Opus 8 Songs, and the *Begleitmusik.* The next day, on the airplane to New York, Stravinsky gave his original manuscript of the Variations series to me as a memento, inscribing it affectionately. The Stephen Spenders came to the concert, and we encountered them at the Chicago Art Institute after one of the rehearsals. We also attended the premiere of Jerome Robbins's *Noces,* which moved the Stravinskys but also shocked them in that this peasant wedding was set in a vast, rich, and jewel-bedecked Russian church.

More filming took place in New York, most memorably for me a recording session of Benny Goodman, since I conducted him in all the rehearsal takes, playing the *Ebony* Concerto. Stravinsky was preserved on camera in a hansom crossing the 72nd Street bridge in Central Park midway between Fifth Avenue and Broadway; with Balanchine watching Suzanne Farrell dance on the stage of the New York State Theater; in the Guggenheim Museum serenaded from a balcony by the St. Thomas Boys' Choir; and with David and Ellen Oppenheim dining at the Café Chauveron.

On May 1 we sailed on the SS *Gripsholm* for Göteborg, with David Oppenheim, his cameraman Haskell Wexler, and their CBS crew. On arrival in Sweden, we flew to Copenhagen and, after a delay, to Paris. The next day we were in Fontainebleau and Barbizon, dining afterward at the Closerie des Lilas with Souvtchinsky. As always, Souvtchinsky changed his food order at the last minute and switched to the same as mine.[32]

Another, much shorter, tour began at the Los Angeles airport on June 28. Just before our flight to Indianapolis, the pianist Leo Smit[33] introduced us to the astronomer Fred Hoyle.[34] On arrival, a school car took us to Muncie, the locus of the landmark sociological study, *Middletown,* by Robert and Helen Lynd. I conducted *Histoire du Soldat* and *Oedipus Rex* at Ball State Teachers College, and after the performances we were driven to a Holiday Inn near Indianapolis. One of the baggage porters there, a fan of Stravinsky and in particular of the *Symphony of Psalms,* had opened the Gideon Bible in the composer's room to Psalm 150, the text of the last part of the piece. We flew to Chicago the next morning for a concert in Ravinia, in which I conducted Webern's *Six Pieces* and *The Rite of Spring.* Jack Bomer and his wife, Hilde, who later in the year underwrote my Russian-language recording of *Noces,* came from Minneapolis. Our last summer concert took place in Vancouver, and it was there, during rehearsals of *The Rite of Spring,* that Stravinsky made his final corrections to the score.

The day after our return to Hollywood, Goddard Lieberson visited us with Simone Signoret, with whom we had dined in Paris the night before

32. The events of the next six weeks in Switzerland, Poland, and Rome are described in my *Chronicle of a Friendship.*

33. He had been Stravinsky's *Jeu de cartes* rehearsal pianist in 1937.

34. d. 2001.

our African expedition three years earlier. On the 26th I recorded Stravinsky's Variations. Zubin Mehta attended part of the session to discuss our 1966 programs with the Los Angeles Philharmonic. After conducting in Hollywood Bowl on September 2, we flew to New York, where, feeling depleted, we decided to cancel the upcoming Hamburg recording sessions and filming, and cabled Rolf Liebermann to that effect. He promptly telephoned and, arguing that better now than in midwinter, changed Stravinsky's mind. The Hamburg sessions included my recording of *Introitus* and Variations, with twelve microphones for the twelve-part variations, and of "Terpsichore" from *Apollo*, conducted by Stravinsky, with whom Balanchine disagreed about the tempo. The 1928 tempo was right, Mr. B. contended, but Stravinsky said that his 1965 tempo was the only one for 1965, and that the wonderful dancer, Suzanne Farrell, would have to adjust, not him.

In London on the 10th, Balanchine and Stravinsky were filmed listening to the Hamburg recording of Variations and discussing it as a solo ballet for Farrell. A team from BBC television interviewed Stravinsky, then inexcusably destroyed the footage covering the following exchange: Interviewer: "Mr. Stravinsky, is it more difficult to compose in old age?" Stravinsky, smiling: "Ah, for you I am old, but not for me."

Franz Kramer, Alban Berg's pupil and our good friend from Toronto, came with us to the morning rehearsal for our woefully under-rehearsed Festival Hall concert. At the first intermission the virtuoso solo bassist, Knussen, asked me to introduce his son Oliver, aged fourteen, to Stravinsky. Since the boy was obviously precocious, bright, someone to watch, genuinely in love with and knowledgeable about Stravinsky's music, I did so. Unfortunately for me, the BBC used my *Rite of Spring* performance as a rehearsal for the filming of Stravinsky's second-half *Firebird*. Lights were switched on and off, the chatter of the cameramen was audible, and these distractions further ruined what amounted to a read-through. Stravinsky obliged me to conduct his Variations twice. At intermission Julian Huxley and Edward Heath came backstage, followed by Lydia Lopokova, the Diaghilev dancer and John Maynard Keynes's widow, who wept on Stravinsky's shoulder.

The morning after the concert, just as we were leaving for Heathrow and New York, Cyril Connolly called, inviting us to dinner, A letter from Stephen Spender awaited me at the Pierre Hotel: "We are coming to New York on Wednesday . . . Henry Moore is at the Stanhope Hotel . . . dinner together on Thursday . . . Wednesday night a party at Robert Lowell's." The Elliott Carters came for supper the night of our arrival. A few days later the Stravinskys and I went to Prokofiev's *The Flaming Angel* at City Center, but they insisted on leaving at intermission. At the beginning of October we were in Cincinnati, where Max Rudolf, the orchestra's regular conductor, stood close to me to watch my beat patterns in *The Rite of Spring*. After Stravinsky's evening talk to students at the University (four reels of tape), we hurried to the restaurant Pigalle, where the Stravinskys celebrated the twenty-fifth anniversary (the next day) of their Hollywood church wedding.

In Hollywood, I conducted Schoenberg's Serenade on a Monday program, with pieces by Haydn, Mozart, Brahms. On November 2 Trude Schoenberg came for dinner, bringing a facsimile of Schoenberg's *Jakobsleiter* manuscript for Stravinsky. On November 22 I accompanied Vera Stravinsky to the wedding of Ronald Schoenberg and Barbara Zeisl.

A few days later I heard Renata Tebaldi in *La Bohème* with the San Francisco Opera, and in the same week conducted Schoenberg's Septet-Suite in the Los Angeles County Museum. On the 30th I recorded the first two of Stravinsky's *Quatre Chants Russes*. In mid-December, I was in Toronto for a matinée concert, in which I gave the first performance of the brief Canon on the theme of the *Firebird* finale. A blizzard having closed the airports, I had to hire a car to reach the Ithaca College School of Music in time for a late-evening rehearsal of *Noces*. The next day, in New York, I recorded Schoenberg's *Friede auf Erde* and *Noces*. Stravinsky was in the control room for the latter, along with Nabokov, Charles Dutoit, and Jack Bomer, who had sponsored the recording and was justifiably annoyed that the singer engaged for the mezzo-soprano part had no voice. Kenneth Schermerhorn, now conductor of the Nashville Symphony, had rehearsed the instrumental ensemble for me. Predictably, Stravinsky flew into a rage when he discovered his mistaken deletion of the bar of rest, 3 before [135].

1966

Stravinsky had agreed to record the Capriccio with Philippe Entremont at Manhattan Center on New Year's Day, but recalling his experience with the pianist in his Concerto, decided not to appear, whereupon I had to conduct it. We were with Auden on the 7th, Vera Stravinsky's and Chester Kallman's birthday. Auden inscribed and gave to her a copy of George MacDonald's *The Princess and the Goblin*. We spent the evenings of the 8th and 11th with Balanchine. The next day brought news of Giacometti's death, which saddened us, though we had known of its imminence for many months. Stravinsky pasted the photo from the *Times* obit in his *Requiem Canticles* sketchbook and drew a cross at the head of the page. On the 13th we watched the NET television film of our December concert in Symphony Hall, Boston. The next day we were in Minneapolis for a concert on the 21st, except that Stravinsky remained in bed in the snowbound city reading Truman Capote's *In Cold Blood* until the last rehearsal. At the concert he did not beat the silent first-half of the first bar in the Pas de deux, in which the clarinet is supposed to, but did not, enter on the third beat, whereupon he stopped the orchestra, shouted a rehearsal number, and started again. After the concert we dined with Elliott Carter, here to give the John Lucas lecture at Carleton College.

On our return to Hollywood, Stravinsky recorded *Introitus*,[35] and I, Schoenberg's Opus 27 choruses. We flew to San Francisco for concerts, and again I did all of the rehearsing, but by concert time I had influenza. The orchestra physician gave me a morphine injection to ease my breathing and get me through the strenuous program of *The Rite of Spring* and Variations. I repeated the latter, following sustained applause.

A week later we were in Rochester for a concert with the Eastman School Orchestra, in which I conducted the Variations and "The Building of the Ark" from *The Flood*. Coming on stage to conduct *Firebird*, Stravinsky was received by two academics wearing mortarboards and gowns. They proceeded to confer a Doctorate of Humane Letters on him, not knowing that he had refused honorary degrees all his life on principle, and would have done so here if he had known beforehand. He had always mocked people who wore the Légion d'Honneur ("a concierge's distinction," he called it), a disdain that went back to his overwhelming defeat by Florent Schmitt in an election to the Académie des Beaux-Arts in Paris. At a postconcert reception given by Walter Hendl, conductor of the Eastman Orchestra, I was pleasantly surprised to see my niece Diane from Cornell.

In Hollywood on the last day of March, I drove Stravinsky and Lawrence Morton to the Los Angeles Music Center to hear Schoenberg's Variations for Orchestra. For reasons unknown, Zubin Mehta, who conducted it, introduced long pauses between each of the nine variations. Two weeks later I conducted two Bach cantatas at the Monday concert, and two weeks after that shared a program with Stravinsky in the Los Angeles Music Festival at Royce Hall. He conducted *Perséphone* with Vera Zorina, and I conducted Berg's *Altenberg Lieder* with Karen Armstrong, who had recently won the Metropolitan Opera auditions, had a sterling voice, perfect pitch, and a two-and-half octave range.

In mid-May we went to Paris, and from there to Athens for a concert with the London Symphony Orchestra in the amphitheater of Herodes Atticus, where I conducted the Symphony in Three Movements and Stravinsky conducted *Oedipus Rex*. The latter piece was repeated in Lisbon, with my friend from Santa Fe summers, Regina Sarfaty, as Jocasta. The local orchestra was surprisingly good, and Stravinsky graciously accepted the Order of Santiago from an admiral representing the dictator Salazar.

In Paris (Hotel Lotti), I became ill with, as a laboratory test confirmed, *fièvre de malte* (brucellosis), contracted in Greece or Portugal from, I think, non-pasteurized goat cheese. Our concerts in Luxembourg and Strasbourg

---

35. The French documentary film *Les Grands Amants du Siècle* contains footage of this session showing me conducting the piece, though the soundtrack is playing *Oedipus Rex*.

had to be cancelled, but the mayor of Strasbourg came in person to confirm Stravinsky's indisposition, and actually stalked into his bedroom without permission and even without knocking. In truth, the composer was suffering from no more than a mild cold, whereas I had a high fever.

In New York on June 30 we attended the opening concert of a month-long Stravinsky festival. Leonard Bernstein performed *The Rite of Spring*. After it, when he gestured to Stravinsky in his loge, we feared that the shouted "bravos" and standing-ovation applause would literally bring down the house.[36] The next day we returned to California for a concert in Hollywood Bowl. Then in mid-July the Stravinskys were back in New York for the last two weeks of the festival, which included a staged performance of the *Soldat* with John Cage as the Devil, Elliott Carter as the Soldier, Aaron Copland as the Narrator. The dance for the Princess was choreographed by Balanchine. I joined Stravinsky during a stolen weekend from Santa Fe. One evening the Stravinskys and Carters were dining at La Côte Basque when the by no means unfamiliar face of Frank Sinatra approached Stravinsky and humbly asked for an autograph. They had met before on transcontinental train trips in the early 1940s, but Stravinsky did not recognize him and simply inscribed his name on a piece of paper without dedicating it to "the voice," who then returned to his secluded private table and to Mia Farrow, with whom he eloped to Honolulu the next morning. The Carters were stunned, awed, disbelieving.

Our New York concert on July 24 was an emotional occasion, the audience clearly realizing that it was seeing Stravinsky for the last time. He conducted the *Symphony of Psalms*, and I the Symphony in Three Movements and the *Flood*, with the poet John Hollander as Narrator. I remember John Cage coming to visit Stravinsky in the Pierre Hotel on the afternoon of the concert to fetch a scrap of manuscript to auction for a charity. The next afternoon I flew to Dallas, slept for three hours in an airport motel, and proceeded from there at 5 A.M. in a very small, very slow, single-propeller airplane, which brought me to Santa Fe only a half-hour before my evening dress rehearsal of *The Rake's Progress*. Linda Anderson, meeting me in my rented car to drive me to La Posada, bumped into the car ahead at a stoplight, but fortunately without damage apart from the nuisance of reporting the accident and filling out insurance papers.

In Santa Fe in August, I conducted *Wozzeck* twice. On the evening of my return to Hollywood, I went with the Stravinskys to *Khartoum*, their third viewing of the film starring our Wetherly Drive neighbor Charleton Heston. By mid-September we were in Louisville for a concert (the first performance in the city of *The Rite of Spring*), then in New York to rehearse *Requiem Canticles* for the premiere in Princeton.[37] After that, on October 11,

36. See my *Chronicle of a Friendship*.
37. See Arnold Newman's book of photographs, *Bravo Stravinsky*, New York, 1967.

Stravinsky's doctors, Lewithin and Temple, pronounced him fit and able to fly to California on the morrow. At 1:30, as we were about to leave for a recording session in Manhattan Center, Isaiah and Aline Berlin arrived, and Stravinsky spent the afternoon with them instead. Coming to the session hours later, he refused to conduct his Mass, *Canticles*, and *Symphonies of Winds*, which I recorded instead. Vera Stravinsky made a scene, protesting Columbia's humiliating treatment of me in "allowing" me to record *Canticles* as a trade-off for "providing" Stravinsky to record the Mass, and for dismissing the professionals in the chorus after it was decided that I, not Stravinsky, would conduct, thereby reducing the choir to Ithaca College students.

For my birthday, in Hollywood, Stravinsky gave me a wonderful present, a sheet of motives from the Introduction to *The Rite of Spring*, drawn in different sizes with his styluses, beautifully arranged on the page. A few days later, a Mr. Jack Bernal came from New York to choose the underlay Stravinsky music for a United Airlines travelogue. The next week our concert at the Los Angeles County Museum presented the premiere of Stravinsky's *The Owl and the Pussy-Cat*, sung by Peggy Bonini with Ingolf Dahl at the piano. Dahl has described Stravinsky backstage:

> The old strength, flash, conviction, straightness of uncompromising, unpopular purpose arises as he stops me to talk about the song performance. I. S: "Everything is always too loud, too loud for me. More delicate—it should be like threads and it is like macaroni. On my piano upstairs, it *is* muted, you know, I can hear it right. It is like spiderwebs. One must speak softly in order to be understood *clearly.* The softer you sing, the clearer the syllables, syllables, syllables." I.D.: "And the softer you sing, the clearer the pitches." I.S.: "Yes, the pitches!"[38]

On the same program Michael Tilson Thomas played Beethoven's last Piano Sonata and William Kraft conducted his Double Trio.

In November, we were in Honolulu for a pair of concerts in which Itzhak Perlman performed Stravinsky's Violin Concerto with me. He played it again with me in Chicago on December 28. Soulima and Françoise Stravinsky came from Urbana for this concert.

1967

On February 19, in Miami to conduct a concert in Dade County Auditorium, we had a call from Nicolas Nabokov in New York telling us that Robert Oppenheimer had died and left a note requesting that the *Requiem Canticles* be played at a memorial service for him.

Among Vera Stravinsky's posthumous papers are three small pages from

---

38. From Crawford, *op. cit.*

a notepad with printed heading in red letters: "Don't Forget." Though not dated, they were written in late spring 1967, shortly after Stravinsky's eighty-fifth birthday:

> As old age approaches, life is becoming more and more difficult. Moving around is difficult. A plan to go to a cinema becomes a discussion. Everyone feels tired, and we think it may be better to stay home and watch TV. The climate is not energizing. I work all day, and go to the doctor to find out why I feel so tired. I am so rarely enthusiastic now. Perhaps I miss the kind of love that used to give me wings. I wake up at 6 A.M. worrying whether I will have enough energy to accomplish what should be done.
>
> Igor begins to feel hurt that his age prevents him from doing everything and taking part in conversations, especially if they are in English and about abstract subjects. He is continually asking me what we are talking about and I tell him as best I can, loudly and in Russian, which is embarrassing. Strangely, he reads English almost exclusively, but it is much easier for him to express his thoughts in Russian or French. But with whom, and who wants to hear about illness and taxes? He speaks Russian only with me and French only with Milene, who looks in for a few minutes only when she feels she has to. I am tired from trying to be diplomatic, trying to create a pleasant atmosphere at home, to protect Igor from business complications. The house is big and has a beautiful view. But I lack good help. After doing all of the cooking and cleaning for three weeks, I hired an expensive but incompetent cook. I have an enlargement of the aorta and high blood pressure. Both Igor and I are worried about it. Who will take care of him? In spite of all his illnesses he is very strong.

1968

On the next-to-last day of September, the Stravinskys and I arrived at the Dolder Hotel in Zurich. Rufina Ampenova, a representative of Boosey & Hawkes, came with Theodore Stravinsky and his wife on October 11 and presented a contract to Stravinsky for his signature authorizing Boosey & Hawkes to allot an annuity of three thousand pounds from his royalties to Pierre Souvtchinsky, "in consideration of [his] work with my archives." Stravinsky thought the sum far too high, saw no reason why he should finance the project, and, in any case, had changed his mind about publishing his papers. He balked, until his wife convinced him that the agreement was simply a way of helping an old friend.

One incident at the Dolder must be mentioned because of the significance attributed to it in the lawsuit that, as is well known, was brought by Stravinsky's children against his widow after his death. On October 9, 1968 Stravinsky telephoned from the hotel to Theodore, in Geneva, asking him to bring the manuscript of *The Rite of Spring* with him on his October 11 visit. The score had been in a Geneva vault since 1962, when Boosey &

Hawkes returned it to the composer for his eightieth birthday, even though it was his property in the first place.

Proofs that Stravinsky did not intend for Theodore to keep either the score or money from its sale are found in two letters from Stravinsky to his son. The first, December 7, 1962, gives him the "address of Erwin Rosenthal's son, whose first name is Albi [Albrecht]: 49A Belsize Park Gardens, London NW3. His father tells me that Albi is going to write to you, Theodore, and arrange a meeting with you, which might not be so easy, since you are in Leysin and the [*Rite of Spring*] manuscript (for which I want to obtain one hundred thousand dollars, to be deposited in your bank, and *then in mine*) is in Geneva." The second letter, dated June 1968, asks Theodore to have the *Rite* manuscript microfilmed, and to send the *film* to Boosey & Hawkes for inclusion in the archives, which is tantamount to saying that Stravinsky did not consider the *original* to belong with his other manuscripts.

October 23. Paris. Our rooms at the Ritz are not merely holding-actions against the "de-eroticization of the environment," in Herbert Marcuse's phrase, but veritable love nests, as strategically mirrored as brothels, though stylistically kin to Gavarni's foyer at the Opera. The beds—pink-silk spreads, goddess figureheads on the footboards—are double, and so, in an amorous squeeze, are the *chaises longues*. Moreover, the allotment of space for the boudoirs would be unthinkable in any city except Paris. Erotically conducive, as well, are the log-grate fireplaces, the coved doors, the carnival-mask (*cache-sexe*) lampshades, the key-and-keyhole light switches, the cushioned footrests for the *maquillage* and dressing tables, the chain in the bathtub to summon the *"femme de chambre,"* the bedside push button for *"service privé,"* and—not least—the window view of the great phallic monument in the Place Vendôme. Less erotic, even allowing for kinks, are the umbrella stand, the chandelier, the choke of the wall clock every five minutes, the tarnished gilt moldings, the striped upholstery, and the escritoire, but the only serious *an*aphrodisiac is the price.

According to the doorman, the hotel had only nineteen guests during last May's revolution-that-got-away, but the staff of four hundred was always on the job. From the second day, sugar had to be rationed, he says, but while he elaborated on this and other hardships, I wondered about the continuing provocation, to Cohn-Bendit and company, in the steady flow of Mercedes, Rolls-Royces, and Alfa Romeos stopping at the entrance.

1969

In New York at the beginning of July, we prepared to fly to Los Angeles, after Stravinsky's recovery from his latest hospital experiences. His physician, Dr. La Due, gave an account of the composer's recent medical history to Dr. Clarence Agress, 465 North Roxbury Drive, Beverly Hills: "Four days before he entered New York Hospital [on May 2], a thrombosis occurred in the left femoral artery. In the hospital, the arterial thrombosis was excised with a Fogarty catheter, and a left lumbar sympathectomy was performed— the latter after a re-extraction of a thrombus that had formed after the first operation . . . There is a necrosis in the right great toe, and he had severe post-operative Monilia infection and some mild pneumonia. But strength has increased and he can walk with help."

In Hollywood, midmonth, Vera Stravinsky wrote in her diary: "I do not know why everybody is glad to be home. It is not comfortable. We have no cook and must run up and down two flights of stairs. Of course, Igor is better, but someone who had not seen him in some years would be shocked . . . He hardly talks. Sometimes all of a sudden, he says: 'Where is Bob? I want music.' Now I will have three helpers, Bob, our secretary Marilyn, and Ed Allen, who is a librarian and who took a long leave of absence to be able to help me. After two operations Igor cannot get well very quickly. Sometimes it seems as if we pass the time expecting death, and when we realize that this is true we want to cry. I am hoping still that Igor will feel better."

On July 17, a lung scan was performed on Stravinsky in the Cedars of Lebanon Hospital. Two further entries from Vera Stravinsky's diary tell us that on July 19 "Igor" listened to music with me, and that on the 20th the three of us watched the moon landing on television.

On July 18 Laure Lourié warned the Stravinskys that "their" attorney, William Montapert, had been tapping her telephone and was capable of doing the same to theirs. On the 19th Laure arranged to telephone Vera Stravinsky while she was dining at Lawrence Morton's. On the 20th, when Montapert repeated the contents of this call to Mrs. Stravinsky, the composer and his wife dismissed him. They telephoned their New York attorney, L. Arnold Weissberger, who promptly flew to Los Angeles, met with Montapert in their home, and arranged the transfer of his power of attorney.[39]

Meanwhile, the main event in Stravinsky's personal history had already occurred. On August 16, by prearrangement, the Andre Marions and the Soulima Stravinskys met in a motel in Cambria, a resort 250 miles north of Los Angeles, long frequented by the Marions. There Stravinsky's children made the decision to enter into an agreement with Montapert, who had power of attorney to act for Stravinsky in his Swiss bank account, whereby Montapert would remove the composer's money and divide it 50 percent for himself and 50 percent for the progeny. On the night of the 16th, after

39. For the United States. At this date Weissberger did not know about the Swiss account.

driving to the Marion home in Los Angeles, Milene, Andre, Soulima, and Françoise signed the paper. (Theodore signed it later, in Geneva.) The next day, August 17, Milene, Soulima, and Françoise called on Stravinsky. Not wishing to see them, and to cut their visit short, he went to bed, pretending to be ill. None of the visitors inquired about Vera Stravinsky. The money was taken from the bank but returned when Montapert learned that he could be convicted of embezzlement even though the account was illegal, the monies, about four hundred thousand dollars, being undisclosed income.

On August 26, Christopher Isherwood came for his birthday dinner. A week later, as we prepared to move to New York, Mrs. Stravinsky arranged for their entire library to be placed in Beverly Hills Storage. Isherwood wrote to her at the Essex House, New York, on November 2:

> Dear Vera, Please forgive my delay in answering your sweet letter. I have written to no one for weeks because we have been toiling away at the screenplay of *I, Claudius* for Tony Richardson. I never thought it would end—but it's ready at last. We send it to England tomorrow! If we shall follow it soon, I don't know. It's possible—*if* Tony likes it and wants more work done on it. Also we have to make up our minds about our play *A Meeting by the River.* There's a possibility of getting it done in London in January.
>
> You *must* take care of yourself and not be "The Slave of the Slaves"—that was what they called one of the saints, Pedro Claver. If we can manage, we'll stop in New York either coming to or back from England. We miss you terribly and talk about you often. Many embraces and love to Igor, Bob, Ed, from your always loving Christopher.

On September 15 the Stravinskys left California forever, flew to New York, and installed themselves in the Plaza Hotel, moving to the Essex House a month later.

1970

Nicolas and Dominique Nabokov were guests for Mrs. Stravinsky's birthday dinner on January 7 in their suite at the Essex House. On the 16th, Hideki Takami, who had moved to New York ahead of us, was re-engaged as cook. Paul Horgan[40] gives an accurate picture of life in the Essex House ménage at this time:

---

40. *Encounters with Stravinsky, op. cit.*

Craft took me to Stravinsky, who was in his own room. It was a small, rather narrow room, but in its formal neatness it seemed larger than it was. The light was low everywhere but in one place—that was where Stravinsky was disposed, upright, in his small wheelchair, his back to the wall, and the lamp glowing over his shoulder upon the pages of a book which rested on a cushion, on a carefully folded throw, on his lap. He wore one of his cardigans. In his left hand he held a little dictionary. To his left was an ordered desk; to his right, a neat upright piano . . . He looked so frail that I was fearful of greeting him physically, but Craft said, "Go ahead—kiss him. He wants you to." I leaned down and touched his cheek with my lips. He responded with a small nod. I saw that the book he was reading was Henri Troyat's biography, *Pouchkine*. Merely to make sounds, I asked, "Is it a good book?" Stravinsky replied, so softly that Craft leaned down to him and repeated the words to me: "A biography of Pushkin is no ordinary affair," and bowed in the old way of confirmation of his own statement. The dictionary he held was in French. Even in his high literacy in that language, he enjoyed meditating on even familiar words with the aid of a lexicon—a lifelong habit . . .

Presently Craft, preparing Stravinsky for our absence for the remainder of the evening, said in a gentle subterfuge, "We are going downstairs for a little while to have a drink." Stravinsky caught a breath in his playful manner and said with longing in his almost vanished voice, so that Craft again had to repeat for him, "I will come with you."

The pathetic impossibility of this[41] resulted in Craft's instant decision not to leave at all. He was right: Stravinsky so plainly longed not to be abandoned. Craft said, with a fond air of daring to hope for an unexpected privilege, "If *you* will have a drink with *us*, we will stay here and have it with you." "*Merci*," Stravinsky indicated through a gesture.

Room service then responded to our altered plans. We ordered drinks and dinner. The waiter came, wheeled a rickety table in place, Stravinsky came in his rolling chair to the table, Craft next to him, Madame and myself facing them. A glass of watered-down Scotch was provided for Stravinsky. He made a social matter of pantomiming a toast.

What developed then was a miniature contest for life itself—for Craft, keeping up a running exhortation, like a coach putting "spirit" into his player, urged food upon Stravinsky, who responded like an earnest team member, so that the game took on a seriousness which stood for much more than the mere moment of its playing . . . In loving urgency, like one who is sure he can save what may soon be lost, Craft, throughout the dinner, devoted himself wholly to the nourishment of Stravinsky. A contest in a nursery style developed—

41. Horgan saw Stravinsky infrequently in the last years, and was not aware that the composer did go out when the weather permitted and also dined downstairs. Five days later, for example, on January 24, he hosted a birthday celebration for his nurse, Rita Christiansen, in the Essex House's street-level restaurant, and the next day dined with the Elliott Carters in his own suite.

though in deadly earnest—as Craft kept saying, *"Mangez,"* pointing to lima beans, and assuring the Maestro that there was much protein to be had in them; and the rare [diced] beef—*"Mangez-le,* it gives strength." Stravinsky took mouthful upon mouthful, in a determined effort to win, no matter what the odds. "He is eating better than for weeks," said Craft softly in an aside to Madame and me. And then, "Drink a little Scotch," he would say in his role of coach, and the striving tiny athlete did what he was cheered on to do. In French, Craft, watching every successful bite, said that with his strength recovered (it was coming fast now, all this excellent protein), in the spring, they would go to Paris, and stay at the Ritz, where, as Stravinsky must remember, the food was so good, the garden so charming, the wine so marvelous, remember the Richebourg '61 . . . He took a lima bean on his own fork, posed it to Stravinsky and said, *"Mangez. C'est la protéine"*—both of them hungry for the same great life, and so was I. . . .

After dinner Stravinsky was established on a sofa, his shoeless feet in neat plain black socks resting on a cushion on the floor, while Madame and I sat together at another side of the room. Craft, after bringing the scores, set the phonograph going. He came to sit beside Stravinsky to read scores with him, turning the pages, pointing out significant details in them, half conducting, indicating by finger on the page important entrances of instruments or various thematic matters.

At the end of January, Stephen Spender paid a visit, and on February 17, Elliott Carter and I attended an opera by Luciano Berio in Carnegie Hall, after which Carter visited Stravinsky in the Essex House.

My report to Eugene Berman, March 4, conveys something of the Essex House atmosphere:

The doctors say that nothing is essentially wrong with Stravinsky, yet one can see that he has lost ground. In December and the first part of January he seemed so much better that we decided to leave here on the first day of warm weather. Now I have no idea if we will be able to go at all. The house in California has been emptied and many of the contents are here in the hotel or in New York storage. But the house has not yet been sold. Mrs. Stravinsky hopes to dispose of everything except personal possessions, paintings, art objects, books. She is often tired and she reflects every fluctuation in Stravinsky's health, but when he is good she always seems able to recover her strength and spirits . . . The danger on the material side is that if Stravinsky is classified as "inactive"—as yet no tax official can say that he is not composing, or writing, even though works do not appear—his taxes will soar and he will be unable to stay even in this second-rate hotel. His home has always been accredited as his "factory," and he has been able to deduct household expenses. But if his status as working musician—composer-conductor—is contested, he would probably have to live in Europe . . . One advantage of life in New York is that he is never alone . . . We now see how very lonely he must have been during so many empty mornings in California.

The Elliott Carters visited him on the 8th, and on the 11th he autographed ten copies of the new edition of his *Poetics of Music* for Harvard Press. That same day a note came from Harold Schonberg answering Stravinsky's complaint about his review in the *Times* of the Juilliard *Rake*: "We have no argument on your comments on my review of *The Rake's Progress*. I have re-read it and it *was* a hasty and sloppy piece of work." This apology, surely very rare in the history of music criticism, struck Stravinsky as gallant.

On May 18, I wrote to Lawrence Morton: "We plan to fly to Geneva and from there drive to the Beau Rivage in Ouchy, until Mr. Stravinsky has recovered from the trip—assuming, of course, that his doctors discharge him. If he does go, it will be on the spur of the moment and not far into June. Summer in New York is impossible and so is any place near the city. Hideki leaves for Japan on June 3, and Rita, now in Mexico on vacation, will return for the Geneva trip. I cannot describe Mr. Stravinsky's condition. He will be 88 in less than a month! He bounced back amazingly after the hospital, but then went into a slump. He is now only about ten times more intelligent and aware than anybody either of us will ever know. He lusts for music and, listening to it, still grunts a second or two ahead of me at the right places."

We were driven from the Geneva airport to the Hôtel Royale, Evian.[42] The Stravinsky automobile followed from New York ten days or so later and was delivered at Brest. On its arrival at Evian, we drove first to the Chateau de Ripaille and Yvoire. The car was followed by the twelve Picassos and two Klees from the Stravinsky vault in the Chase Bank, rue Cambon, Paris, where Mrs. Stravinsky had deposited them on November 12, 1968. In Evian Stravinsky dined on the hotel terrace, weather permitting. Vera Stravinsky's diary notes that on August 1 we dined there "with Theodore, Denise, and Dr. Maurice Gilbert. Igor, unhappy, behaves nastily with all three of them."

In *Tracings*,[43] Paul Horgan records that in the summer of 1970

Miranda Masocco Levy was temporarily living in London, where her husband was producing films.[44] In California she had been a close companion and neighbor of the Stravinskys.[45] I now had a lively reunion with her; our shared inter-

42. The Stravinskys decided to spend the summer here on the recommendation of Sol Hurok.

43. Paul Horgan, *op. cit.*

44. Actually television programs starring Jack Benny, who also lived in the Pierre Hotel, and whom we often encountered in the elevators there.

45. See chapter 6.

est in everything concerning the Stravinskys gave us much to talk about . . . She had made a point of telephoning to Madame at Evian just before lunch so she could bring me the latest news.

"Marvelous," she said in the husky, humorous voice she kept for her best stories. "Vera sounded wonderful, she sent her love."

"How is the Maestro?"

"He is not very strong, but he seems comfortable. They take drives in the country, he enjoys seeing everything . . . But they are leaving tomorrow—no, day after tomorrow.[46] Back to New York. Vera was glad I called. She wanted me to do something for them. She said it was about the photographer. 'Please,' asked Madame, 'there is that photographer coming to photograph my husband. But we cannot. He is to come tomorrow. We are so busy. I am packing, packing. The airplane is to take us the next day. My husband is too tired. He should not be bothered. Why should there be photographers? Please tell him not to come.'

"But who is he?" asked Miranda.

"The name I do not think of at the moment. He has an appointment for a long time. He must not come."

"Do you want me to find him and cancel the appointment?"

"Yes, please."

"Then tell me how to look for him."

"He is married to a princess in England."

"Do you mean Lord Snowdon?"

"That is who! Please tell him we are so busy, I do not want my husband to be bothered."

"Is he at home, now, in London?"

"No, he is in Sardinia."

"Sardinia! But where in Sardinia?"

"He is with the Aga Khan," said Madame—surely a sufficient address for anyone.

"He is a very fine photographer," Miranda said, "an artist; and he is very sympathetic and moving in his pictures of old people. He would make some beautiful pictures of the Maestro."

"So, he should come?" asked Madame doubtfully.

"I would certainly let him come. After all, he needn't take all day."

"Very well. He may come. Do not do anything."

On August 24 I drove Mrs. Stravinsky to Geneva, where she deposited the Picassos and Klees in *Coffre-fort* No. 1879 NBS, 2, Place des Eaux-Vives. Back in Evian we dined with Snowden and a young companion of his.

On August 26 Paul François, husband of nurse Danielle, agreed to drive the Stravinsky car to Le Havre for shipment to New York. The hotel restau-

46. Actually August 26.

rant being closed, we lunched in the town, at La Bourgogne, with François-Michel, who had driven from Paris and who, with his friend André, drove us afterward to the Geneva airport.

The next day, one of Stravinsky's New York physicians, Dr. Elliott Howard, examined him and found no ill effects from the flight, and the day after that the Elliott Carters dined with us. On September 30, I informed Eugene Berman: "About two weeks after our return, a heat wave during which New York's already carcinogenic air became even more poisonous, aggravated Stravinsky's bronchial condition. He also suffered a bad reaction to a transfusion . . . The search for an apartment has so far been unsuccessful, the prices out of sight . . . It is obvious that he cannot spend another winter in New York. But where else? The Caribbean? A medically-civilized North African oasis? . . . Elliott and Helen Carter wrote from Bellaggio, but I suppose you'll be seeing them soon." I wrote to Berman again on October 15:

> Stravinsky needs change, not confinement to a small suite of rooms. He has not had a health crisis for seven months but he needs more stimulus than I can provide. Nabokov comes regularly, Natasha[47] is helpful, playing card games with him and reading to him in Russian; she cheers him up, but also tires him. Not that he is depressed at the moment; in fact he is livelier than he was two months ago. Still, he needs that change of surroundings, even saying that he would go back to California if only for the trip. He always smiles at the prospect of going south for the winter and immediately wants to know exactly when we plan to be under way. Francis Steegmuller asked for and received Mrs. Stravinsky's permission to write a biography, a "life" of Stravinsky apart from the music. But was there one? I mean, wasn't everything but the music simply a sideshow?

On November 3, I wrote to Nikita Magaloff[48] at his house in Ferney, next to Voltaire's: "The trip did not have any harmful effects on Stravinsky, who in fact has been remarkably well these last two months. I would be grateful if you would convey this to Theodore and Denise, to whom I promised to write but have not had a moment to do so. I should add that last summer's worries about Mr. Stravinsky's blood are over. His polycythemia has disappeared. Please keep the Stravinskys' needs in mind, and if you hear of an attractive house at a price somewhat lower than that of Walter Legge's,[49] kindly let us know."

47. Nabokov's first wife.
48. Joseph Szigeti's piano accompanist and son-in-law.
49. The Stravinskys had visited his villa outside Lausanne. He was the founder of the Philharmonia (London) and the husband of Elizabeth Schwarzkopf.

1971

On January 13, 1971, I wrote to Lawrence Morton, turning down some concerts he had offered:

> I was in Florida for twelve days at Christmas, the longest period I have been away from the Stravinskys since I conducted *Wozzeck* in Santa Fe four and a half years ago. No catastrophes occurred during this vacation, but if there had been a crisis, I could have returned quickly, as I did last April. No matter how immodest to say it, I see that I can have a good effect on Stravinsky's morale when I am here, at least through music, and I would therefore feel guilty in not doing whatever I can do for however long I will have an opportunity to do it. Not that he is in a bad way at the moment. Yet I found him in the dumps when I returned, and he has certainly picked up as a result of the music he has heard during the last few days. Dr. Lax says that according to the neurological evidence, no thrombosis, large or small, has occurred in nine months, and the heart, circulation, blood pressure, and lungs are all in good order. Still, we are only at the beginning of the winter.

On April 6, Stravinsky died. Paul Horgan's *Encounters with Stravinsky* recalls that on the ninth of June, two months later,

> Madame and Craft came to dine with me on the ninth of June 1971 in New York. Waiting for them, I was troubled to know what, or what not, to speak of concerning Stravinsky.
>
> But I need not have worried. They arrived, sat down with me, and almost at once began to tell of events which we had not previously talked of. I felt an almost exhausting strength in their love for Stravinsky as they spoke of him, even coming to some of the most intimate and difficult details of his death and afterward. They were still filled with the splendor and solemnity of the service in Venice . . . The world had come to pay its tribute—said Craft, though no official notice or message of any kind was sent by the United States.
>
> "The Mayor of Venice," he added with understated irony, "paid for the music at the funeral."
>
> The anonymous people of Venice hung over the bridges, filled the walks, crossed themselves as the cortège of gondolas went along the canals . . . [50]
>
> Madame said that, the day before the end, her husband kept trying to make the sign of the cross, over and over, but could only touch his brow . . . They described to me the astonishing strength of his handclasp as he reached for them. His fingers were curved into hooks to take his wife's and Craft's hands.

---

50. Only part of one canal, which debouched into the lagoon.

"He did not want to let go," said Madame.

Craft said to her now, "When he put your hand to his face he knew he was dying."

A death mask was taken. Craft said it was done without including the ears, as Beethoven's was—"That instrument of all great composers. Still, there is something noble about the mask, though the mouth is distorted."

"Have you seen it?" I asked Madame.

"No."

Craft said, "You must—you will find something true even so."

I left the following day for the West. We exchanged a few letters during the summer. They had again gone abroad. Craft wrote to me on July 27 from the Hôtel du Palais in Biarritz. He was kind enough to thank me for "helping to keep Madame's spirits up. I'm afraid," he wrote, "they fell rather far in Venice, which is why we are here. *Everything* reminded her, and she began to go out to the grave all alone, without telling me. It is quite a strenuous walk, as well as a long ride on the *vaporetto*." Craft continued, "An indication of the terrible loneliness she feels came on the road here [to Biarritz]. Suddenly, in a restaurant, south of Aix, she began to sob, but never said a word."[51]

51. Horgan, *Encounters, op. cit.*

Part III

Surviving the Legacy

Chapter 9

Confrontations

The 1970s

W hen Mrs. Stravinsky and I returned to New York from Stravinsky's grave in Venice at the beginning of May 1971, his attorney, L. Arnold Weissberger, had already listed the manuscript score of *The Rite of Spring* as an asset of the estate, disregarding her testimony that her husband had given it to her in Zurich in September 1968. Attorneys representing Stravinsky's descendants contested her claim, and though his will was probated in June, a decade and more of litigation began forthwith.

In June, on Stravinsky's birthday, I conducted the CBC Symphony, Toronto, in a memorial program. During my stay there my sister Phyllis lived in the Stravinsky apartment in New York helping Mrs. Stravinsky sort out personal effects. Following her wishes, the door to Stravinsky's studio was never left open during the first five months following his death, and even after that she never entered it.

In late August, Thomas Neurath of Thames & Hudson, London, commissioned a book from me, published five years later by Simon and Schuster as *Stravinsky in Pictures and Documents*. I was already working on another volume, *Stravinsky: Chronicle of a Friendship*, a compilation from my diaries, scheduled to appear in conjunction with the New York City Ballet's Stravinsky Festival in June 1972.

At the beginning of September, Robert B. Silvers, editor of *The New York Review of Books*, asked me to review Leonard Bernstein's "Mass," which was to be performed at the inauguration of the Kennedy Center in Washington. I accepted the assignment in order to escape, even briefly, the oppressive atmosphere of the Stravinsky apartment without Stravinsky.

In December, Phyllis, her husband, and I accompanied Mrs. Stravinsky to Florida in an attempt to distract her from thoughts of former birthday holidays. In the early part of the year, while Stravinsky was still alive, *Esquire* magazine had named him and Cole Porter as the most discriminating gourmets in their respective categories as composers. The prize was a dinner, restaurant and menu chosen by the winners. The feast that we consumed was served in the Down Under restaurant in Fort Lauderdale, food chosen by the widow.

I first met Rita Christiansen in Paris in the fall of 1968, when she was Stravinsky's nurse. The Stravinskys liked her and invited her to California with them when they returned home a few weeks later.

In early November 1968, the Paris Opéra presented a series of Stravinsky ballet evenings, one of which he decided to attend. We were given the center loge at the Palais Garnier, and Rita was asked to come and assist Stravinsky. His old friend Pierre Souvtchinsky came with us, and a sumptuous dinner was preordered to be served in the Stravinsky suite at the Ritz after the performance. What, I wondered, could Rita have thought of *The Rite of Spring*, never having seen a ballet or heard a symphony orchestra, let alone "modern music"? She said nothing and betrayed no emotion, but for the first time, I think, understood that her employer was a person of consequence. Stravinsky received an ovation, which infuriated him, the musical performance being poor and the choreography deplorable. The dinner had arrived in the hotel room long before we did, and the oysters, as indicated by the melted ice under their half-shells, had obviously been shucked well in advance. The Stravinskys did not eat them, but Rita and I were less prudent, and in consequence became violently ill. She missed two days of work.

New York's Pierre Hotel, when we arrived there in midmonth, was bustling with secret-service men and electricians installing special telephones for what had become Richard Nixon's preinauguration headquarters. Because of this nuisance, the Stravinskys cut their stay short and flew with Rita to Los Angeles. I followed but with a brief detour to see my parents in Florida. As it happened, fog had forced the Stravinskys' airplane to land a hundred miles to the east of Los Angeles, from where they were obliged to complete the trip in a limousine, an experience about which they were still complaining when I joined them a few days later.

Rita did not find the sprawling city congenial, despite the Stravinskys' efforts to make her comfortable. She had a large room in their house, with adjoining well-equipped bathroom and private outdoor entrance, but no place to go. Without being able to drive, and knowing no one, she became homesick for Paris. Jack Quinn, a young builder who was doing repair work in the Stravinsky home, escorted her to parties and to movies, and took her on ocean-side drives, imagining that he was in love with her, a flirtation that led nowhere, since he was attracted only to glabrous, good-looking boys.

I remember driving Rita one evening to the center of Beverly Hills, the nearest shopping district, but no substitute for the Galerie Lafayette. On a totally deserted Rodeo Drive we unthinkingly jaywalked across the street in the middle of a block, thereby setting off a police siren and dispatching in our direction a lights-flashing car of "blue fascists," to use the 1968 term. When they demanded to see my driver's license, I pointed out that we were walking—the Stravinsky car was parked some blocks away—and was roughly reminded that pedestrians are permitted to cross streets only at intersections. I responded that I was showing this internationally famous street to a friend from France, then conversed with Rita for a moment in French. They let us go.

Rita's life in Hollywood must also have been disappointing in that Stravinsky spent his evenings, and I with him, listening to music, Beethoven quartets above all. I disc-jockeyed, fetched the scores, and turned pages for him. These were the hours for which he waited all day, and he would accept no substitute for me. We invited Rita to listen with us, but she was not interested in music.

Rita and I recommenced the affair that had begun in Paris, until Mrs. Marilyn Stalvey, Stravinsky's secretary, invited her to dinner and revealed the sordidness of my past, the sowings with sopranos, mezzo-sopranos, *et al.* Rita reacted by asking the Stravinskys for a leave of absence, during which she flew to Puerta Vallarta, Mexico. Here she met, and became attracted to, a vacationing Air France pilot. She returned to her job in a more contented mood. In April we were back at the Pierre Hotel planning a trip to Holland, where a Stravinsky festival had been scheduled. Unfortunately Stravinsky was found to require an embolectomy, and the procedure took place in New York Hospital soon after his arrival in the city. Two months later he returned to Hollywood and Rita to France.

At the beginning of October, however, Rita resumed her position as the composer's nurse. By this time, the Stravinskys were permanent residents in New York, living in the Essex House on Fifty-ninth Street. They rented a room for her in the Wellington Hotel, around the corner and four blocks south on Seventh Avenue, but after a month or so, upgraded her accommodations to a front, park-side room in the Essex House on the same seventeenth floor as their own apartment. Mrs. Stravinsky purchased a fur coat for her, and found local nurses to relieve and assist her. In January 1970, by discovering a clot below Stravinsky's right knee, Rita prolonged his life. In New York she made friends, went to the theater, occasionally dined with me in restaurants, and generally enjoyed her life. She remained with us there until June 1970, when she accompanied Stravinsky to the Hôtel Royale in Evian, and again in New York from September 1970 until his death, April 6, 1971.

The best days in all of our relationships were during the summer in Evian. Under the supervision of Dr. Della Santa from Geneva, the polycythemia that had plagued Stravinsky for fifteen years disappeared. The Hôtel Royale's haute cuisine, although below the quality of the great restaurants in Saulieu, was nevertheless excellent, and the clientele was almost entirely French. Rita was more comfortable in the French world than in the American, and Mrs. Stravinsky was more at ease driving in France—on her still-valid 1920s license!—than in Los Angeles. We visited friends on the Swiss side of Le Lac Leman, and received others at the hotel, including Hugues Cuenod, who had created the part of Sellem in *The Rake's Progress* nineteen years before; Sol Babitz, Miranda, Arnold Weissberger and Milton Goldman; Souvtchinsky; Xenia Yurievna, Stravinsky's niece from Leningrad; and Natasha Nabokov, who was spending the summer with Vladimir and Vera Nabokov directly across the lake in Montreux. Our automobile excursions extended as far south as the Lac d'Annecy, and always included Rita, who, by now, really was becoming part of the family. In late August she visited her parents and two sisters in Copenhagen, then returned to New York with us.

The seven remaining months of Stravinsky's life distrained exhaustingly on Mrs. Stravinsky. She worked incessantly to prepare a home for him in the apartment she had purchased at the corner of Fifth Avenue and Seventy-third Street, a dilapidated fourteen-room establishment that had not been kept up by its previous owners, an elderly French countess and the movie director Elia Kazan, for whom we received telephone calls during an entire year after his departure. Every room had to be entirely refurbished. The lease in the Essex House also had to be rescinded—for an exorbitant sum—and our belongings shipped from a Hollywood warehouse. In January 1971, the 1218 North Wetherly Drive home was sold, at a loss, like the old one at 1260 N.W.D.

During Stravinsky's last illness, April 2–6, 1971, Rita's Scandinavian *sangfroid* melted, and the night before his death she came to me saying, "Robert, you must know that he cannot live any longer, and you must not want him to." She was still staying in the Essex House, and slept there that last night, on grounds that she would need a good rest for the morrow.

As I have recorded elsewhere, and as can be seen on an Italian television film, Rita stood with the *"Famiglia"* at the funeral in Venice, April 15. The next day she flew home to Copenhagen.

In the second week of May, Rita returned to New York to collect her possessions at the Essex House. Overwhelmed with Estate business, I invited her to stay in my small house in Pompano Beach, Florida, promising to join her there as soon as possible and to go together with her to Toronto in June for a Stravinsky memorial concert.

Our Florida interlude was a disaster. Completely alone for the first time, it became evident that we had no common interests, nothing to talk about, not Stravinsky's health, not music, literature, painting, which did not interest her. She also seemed to have undergone a personality change. Always very proper in the Stravinsky home, the new Rita now seemed to have shed what I could only see, thinking back, as a veneer. We began to quarrel and continued to do so in Toronto. She did not come to my rehearsals there or even to the concert. My niece, Diane, and her husband John Rumble, who were visiting a relative of his in Buffalo, drove us to Niagara Falls one night, the only occasion when we were together. Returning to New York, we reached the Stravinsky apartment in the middle of the night and were admitted by Phyllis. The next day Rita flew to Copenhagen.

A week later, Mrs. Stravinsky and I were in Venice. On our second day there, Rita called to say that she was planning to drive from Copenhagen to Rome with a doctor friend of hers and would like to visit us in Venice en route. She arrived with a female Danish friend.

Vera Stravinsky's return to Venice in June was a sorry mistake. Her memories of summers with Stravinsky there left her weeping and depressed. She began to visit the cemetery alone, not telling me she intended to do so. I wrote to Isaiah Berlin in Portofino, asking for help. He kindly offered to come but urged me to take her somewhere else. Since Lucia Davidova was in Monte Carlo, I called and arranged for us to go there for *le quatorze juillet*. But this was the wrong festivity and Monte Carlo the wrong place, since it was there that Mrs. Stravinsky had rehearsed the role of the Bride for the premiere of *Les Noces*. After a few days I drove her along the overcrowded Riviera to Arles and ultimately to Biarritz, which was equally rich in memories for her, as the city of the Basque restaurant that had been mismanaged by the brother-in-law of Stravinsky's first wife.

At the beginning of September, shortly after Mrs. Stravinsky and I had returned to New York, Rita showed up unexpectedly and announced that she was pregnant. She lived temporarily in the Stravinsky apartment until finding one of her own, also on East Seventy-third Street, three or four blocks from the Stravinskys'. She told Mrs. Stravinsky that she wanted the child and wanted it to have my name. Mrs. Stravinsky, whatever she thought, said nothing, but undoubtedly recognized that the matrimonial state would not endure. In January we entered it in a most unromantic two-minute civil ceremony in City Hall, New York.

1972

I spent the evening of the second of January discussing the June Stravinsky Festival repertory with George Balanchine. He was inspired with ideas and looking forward to the celebration, the greatest undertaking of his life. He knew which ballets he would do and which would go to Jerome Robbins, John Taras, and Lorca Massine. Remarkably, he was keener on choreographing concert pieces, concertos and symphonies, than de facto ballets such as *Petrushka, Renard, Noces, Jeu de cartes*. I tried but failed to squelch his strange insistence on having the early, clunky Symphony in E-flat performed on the first program.

A week later Paul Horgan brought the galley proofs of his *Encounters with Stravinsky,*[1] asking me to check his facts. I found a slew of errors, but his affectionate portrait greatly moved Mrs. Stravinsky and me. At this time, she was still unaware that her husband's sometime concert agent, Lillian Libman, had been preparing her own backstairs, self-important, and wildly off-target version. Mrs. Stravinsky innocently repeated her warm reaction to Horgan's *Encounters* to Libman and was dismayed and nonplussed by a vituperative outburst of jealousy.

On January 11, Wystan Auden, rumpled face now resembling that of a shar-pei, and Chester Kallman came for dinner. Conversation was like old times: Wagner—Chester very keen on Von Karajan's *Meistersinger* recording—life in Niederösterreich, and no-longer-risible anecdotes. W.H.A. was indignant about "Cal" Lowell's treatment of Elizabeth and Harriet[2] in his last poems, and he defended Ted Hughes's *Crow* against Chester's mockery of it. Promptly at nine o'clock W.H.A. announced that his bedtime hour had struck, but Chester admonished him, saying that *he* was not ready to leave, whereupon the reproved poet became petulant. Chester's anti-Isherwood animus was still alive, and not for the first time I suspected that he was the originator of the wisecrack about the novelist's "apparent candor."

At the beginning of February, I conducted a concert at the University of Tennessee in Knoxville, and met Donna Wright, an excellent flutist, good pianist, and attractive twenty-year-old "Daisy Mae." Primarily because of her I accepted an invitation to return to the school next year and perform Monteverdi's *Vespers.* I flew to New York, and, to attend the opening of Mrs. Stravinsky's exhibition in Washington, continued there by train, a snowstorm having canceled all flights.

On February 16, Paul Horgan escorted Mrs. Stravinsky and me to dinner at Alice Roosevelt Longworth's, a waspish lady with wicked repartee. Paul told us that since her double mastectomy three weeks ago her favorite quip has been: "I am the only topless octogenarian in Washington." To my right at table was the glamorous socialite Evangeline Bruce, who talked eighteenth-century French history, the romance between Axel von Fersen and Marie Antoinette. Her husband, David Bruce, was seated next to Mrs. Stravinsky, too far from me to explain to her that he was a Virginia grandee and a paladin of American diplomacy, former Ambassador to Paris, Bonn, Beijing, and the Court of St. James. Mrs. Longworth's beautiful granddaughter, Johanna Sturm, was there, and William Walton, the society painter and frequent escort of Jackie O.

On February 21, I shared a table with Lincoln and Fidelma Kirstein at the Coffee House on West 45th Street, for the Random House–*New York Review* Auden testimonial dinner, a combination birthday party and Last

---

1. Horgan, *op. cit.*
2. Robert Lowell's wife, Elizabeth Hardwick, and daughter.

Supper. When the mayhem and noise during cocktails subsided, and the guest of honor took his place at an elevated and Arthurianly round table, with Barbara Epstein on his right, the cenacle began. At one point glasses were tapped for silence, telegrams read in the pious hush that ensued, and a toast was proposed. A speaker from the publishing company opened with: "I don't know what genius is . . ." and was instantly interrupted by a loud, cranky "Well who does?" from Auden himself. The question was ignored. I saw Elizabeth Hardwick home afterward.

When Rita entered Doctors' Hospital the next day, a blizzard had already paralyzed the city. Her labor pains had just started, and the obstetrician told me that the delivery would probably not take place for several hours. I traipsed back to the Stravinsky apartment in the piling-up snow to dine with Paul Horgan, then hurried back to the hospital. While I was pacing the floor by a window overlooking the drifts in Gracie Square and John Finley Walk, our physician entered the room, shook my hand, and said, "You are the father of a healthy and beautiful boy." I could not have been happier, having wanted a boy as much as Rita wanted a girl. I was led to a glass-enclosed nursery in which an intern wearing a surgical mask and rubber gloves held up my infant son on the other side. Not sharing the immemorial fear about changelings, and stretching my ego along with my imagination, I thought he looked like me. We had agreed months before on the name Robert Alexander, or, if a girl, Anne.

Unfolding the *New York Times* on the morning of March 2, I saw a picture of myself and Stravinsky on the front page, just below one of Nixon arriving in China. The accompanying article was devoted to a scurrilous version of my life with Stravinsky.

On April 6, flowers and telegrams commemorating the anniversary of the composer's death filled the living room. On the same day, at a rehearsal of his Violin Concerto, which promised to be a new choreographic masterpiece, Balanchine asked me to set the tempos for Joseph Silverstein, my choice of soloist, who played it with dignity and élan.

Also on April 6, *The New York Review of Books* published a short piece by me titled "Fit to Print," in which I corrected some of the errors in the March 2 *Times* article, and in its Stravinsky obit. The former had claimed that the *Times*'s version of "a Stravinsky dinner at the White House in 1961 [amplified] Mr. Craft's." But the year was 1962, and the *Times* correspondent was not there. The obit further said that on the morning of Stravinsky's death, with him at his bedside "were his wife, Vera, his musical assistant and close friend, Robert Craft, Lillian Libman, his personal manager, and his nurse, Rita Christiansen." But Stravinsky never had a "personal manager," and Rita C. was miles away in a midtown hotel, having been replaced in the early evening of April 5 by Maigrehead Condon, R.N. The only people in the room with Stravinsky at the moment of death were Dr. Sam Berger, from Mt. Sinai Hospital, and Grace Buck, R.N. The remainder of my gentle rebuttal took on the *Times* for having published, without verification, the gushings of a self-described "intimate" of Stravinsky, who in truth knew him very little. I said that this person's "assertions of intimacy would have left him dumbfounded," and ended with the suggestion that she consider retitling her memoir, which the *Times* article was intended to publicize, "The Stravinsky Nobody Knew."

On May 2, Mrs. Stravinsky and I drove to Rhode Island University for my performances with Sarah Caldwell's Boston Opera of *Renard* and *Histoire du Soldat*, and arrived back in New York very late. Five days later, I flew with Rita to Boston for matinée and evening performances of the same pieces, and back to New York at 2 A.M.

On June 18, I conducted *Symphony in Three Movements* at the New York City Ballet's Stravinsky Gala opening. The only empty seat in the State Theater was Rita's, though I had sent a car for her. The Earl of Harewood[3] was at Nancy Lasalle's[4] reception afterward, with Andrew Porter.

On July 1, Rita took the baby to Denmark to visit her parents, while I flew to Florida with Phyllis and her husband to prepare the house I had purchased for my family in April, in Phyllis's name. Rita remained in Denmark until the end of the year.

In London, on October 10, Vera Stravinsky and I were the Earl of Drogheda's guests in the Royal Box at Covent Garden for the Royal Ballet's *Noces* and *Firebird*. Nijinska had changed her *Noces* choreography for the scene of the weeping mothers and the ending. The former, nearly static in the original, like the music, and enacted in front of the curtain, now employed the full stage and a Martha Graham-style dance, a peculiar solecism in relation to the otherwise angular movements. The new coda contradicted both the music and the libretto. Nijinska obviously saw the motionless original as too bleak by current standards, but her revision temporized to the extent that the entry of Bride and Groom into the nuptial chamber continued almost to the last chord. When the Groom sings alone, at which point all movement should cease, the dancers had just begun to form their concluding frieze. Like the music, the choreography should unwind as mechanically as a clock, not winding down, but stopping suddenly.

In *Firebird*, the *bolibotchki* and *kikimoras* were funny rather than fierce, the enchanted princesses and their golden apples insipid—only professional jugglers could save this episode—and Kastchei's beckoning yard-long Fu Manchu fingernail was a relic from bygone matinée kitsch. Yet the score should not be cut. The musical quality of the dramatic sections, as distin-

---

3. First cousin of Queen Elizabeth II, one-time Director of The Royal Opera House, Covent Garden, married to Marion Stein, the daughter of Schoenberg's pupil Erwin Stein.
4. Patroness of the New York City Ballet, daughter of the photographer Dorothy Norman, who had been married to Alfred Stieglitz.

guished from the dances, is higher than that of such numbers as "The Golden Apples," and the dramatic music points to *Petrushka* and *The Rite of Spring*. Every musical event was conceived so literally for stage action that to tamper with it is to misconstrue the piece. What could have been tolerated were a few orchestra rehearsals—a more dragged and ragged reading would be difficult to imagine—and at least one adjustment of costume: the Tsarevitch's should be returned to Santa Claus. But the Royal Ballet's "old-fashioned" and "Romantic" *Firebird* is the right one.

I was in Copenhagen on October 13 and 14. As instructed, I went directly from the airport to Rita's sister's apartment, where I found Rita bathing Alexander, who had grown like Pantagruel in the last three-and-a-half months. I took her to a restaurant that she suggested and discussed arrangements for her to return to New York, but since her U.S. visa had expired and she had not paid U.S. income taxes, this would require the services of an Immigration lawyer.

I met her at the Copenhagen airport the following afternoon. Shortly before boarding time, her sister and brother-in-law brought Alexander for a final hug. These last minutes with him were disturbing, the more so when at leave-taking the other man carried him away. From Heathrow I went straight to the Savoy Grill and, though looking scruffy and with my thoughts in disarray, dined with Stephen and Natasha Spender.

On October 23, we were Paul Horgan's guests at the Century Club, New York, together with the Goddard Liebersons, and the Snows, C. P. and Pamela Hansford Johnson. The "Two Cultures" debate with Leavis was cresting, and the avoidance of any mention of support for the Snovian side was noticeable.

On November 8, the Canadian Broadcasting Company began its Stravinsky oral-history project in his widow's apartment.

On November 28 and December 5, I lectured at the Metropolitan Museum of Art, then went to Florida. Vera Stravinsky spent the holidays in Connecticut with her old friends Tatiana Lieberman and husband, Alex, the sculptor. They dined with the Vladimir Horowitzes and the Arthur Millers. The photographer Inge Morath (Mrs. Miller) had recently done a series of portraits of Mrs. Stravinsky at home in New York.

Wishing to spend Christmas with her parents in Denmark, Rita postponed her travel date several times. When she finally returned to Pompano Beach, I had to be in New York for meetings with George Balanchine. At the New Year's party my parents gave for her at Pompano Beach, a revealing exchange took place between her and one of their friends: "Do you like Florida?" "I hate it." "Then why did you come?" "To get a divorce."

1973

On January 17, I flew from New York to Knoxville to conduct Monteverdi's *Vespers* at the University of Tennessee, and went from there to Pompano. Back in New York in February, I conducted a matinée concert (11th) at Columbia University, Ferris Booth Hall: the early versions of *Noces* and the premiere of "Two Sketches for a Sonata," played by Madeleine Malraux. Afterward, Balanchine, with Karen von Aroldingen, the Carters, the Francesco Carraros from Venice, Adriana and Jane Panni from Rome, dined with us at 920 Fifth Avenue. On the 20th, Leonard Bernstein's New York Philharmonic concert was notable for clean, restrained performances of a Haydn Mass, and of Stravinsky's Mass with the Newark Boys' Choir. Vera Stravinsky went to his green room afterward to thank him.

In March I was in Buffalo for two concerts with Michael Tilson Thomas's Philharmonic: Beethoven's First Symphony, the Brahms-Schoenberg, and Stravinsky's Violin Concerto, played by the concertmaster. A week later, I was in Ithaca for a lecture at Cornell and, in the absence of return flights, came back to New York by car, arriving just before dawn.

In April, after a lecture at the University of Chicago, I was invited by Milton Babbitt to a small party for Harold Rosenberg, the art critic, but, thinking that it would bore Donna Wright, who had come from Knoxville to see me, I stayed with her instead. The next morning's Chicago Symphony rehearsal exposed Georg Solti trying to learn *Erwartung* as he went along, and riding over most of the numerous tempo changes. Anja Silja was his soloist.

My absences from Florida to fulfill conducting and lecturing engagements were neither frequent nor long, and during them my parents helped to take care of Alexander, but by the end of January, Rita was preparing the baby's and her meals at odd hours in order to avoid the family dinner table. Though I knew that her wish to return to Denmark was not due to a preference for its snows to the sands of Florida, the discovery that she was consulting a divorce lawyer with the intention of forcing me to sell the Pompano house was upsetting. As Florida law sanctions, half of the proceeds would go to her. When the same lawyer informed her that I was not the actual owner of the property, she decided to leave for Copenhagen as soon as could be arranged.

One May morning my father telephoned to me in New York to say that Rita was gone. Later that same day a New York lawyer called to say that she would permit me to see Alexander in exchange for a certified check in five figures. At the designated time, I went to her hotel, the Wellington on Seventh Avenue, rang up from the lobby, and was instructed to wait in the street outside the entrance. When she finally appeared, pushing a perambulator, I gave an envelope to her containing the check. After verifying the figure, she turned away and wheeled the carriage around the corner, presumably in the direction of a bank. A little later, her lawyer again called to reassure me that she would fulfill her part of the agreement the next day, but the call that came in the morning was from the Goddard Liebersons in Oslo. Rita and the baby had been aboard the same New York-Copenhagen flight as theirs. I was stunned. Without a word to me, she had scarpered with the child to an unknown address in Denmark.

June 18. Paris. Driving to George Sand's chateau at Nohant, I was held up in Vierzon by a narrow street called—correctly, vis-à-vis my relationship with her literature—*Impasse George Sand.* A guidebook stated that *"Nohant n'a plus changé que la Vulgate,"* but the next edition will have to acknowledge an inn, a restaurant, a parking lot, a George Sand bookstall. Nor can the site be described as a retreat. During my visit, four pianists, as I took them to be from their keyboard postures, alighted in front of the chateau, posed for publicity photographs, swept on. Tourists will soon have to form queues before entering the shaded walks, gardens, pastures with period-piece, Rosa Bonheur cows. Of the main attractions, the chateau and the cemetery, the latter was more congenial, but, then, I find waxworks, tables set for dinners in 1840, "everything as it was," morbid. Nor did Sand's quill, Delacroix's umbrella, Chopin's white gloves help to revive the past. The chateau was haunted, not by the artists and writers who once resided here (Herbert Spencer strangely among them), but by the theater of leering puppets, the pride of Sand's children.

Not Sand but Delacroix had a sense of Chopin's genius, as is shown by the composer's remarks that the painter chose to immortalize in his diary: "[Chopin] would not admit sonority as a legitimate source of sensation," and was "indignant against those who attribute part of the charm of music to sonority." Admittedly, sonorities are subordinate to musical ideas, as are colors, volumes, dynamic shadings, yet Chopin exploited a larger spectrum of them than any other composer for the piano, using the pedal to create a Niagara of sixteenth notes in the final Etude, and, by means of tinkling effects in the treble, and a mechanical ostinato in the bass, making a Berceuse sound like a music box. Moreover, his music suggests the orchestra, from symphonic Beethoven to the *tempo primo* in the twenty-second Etude, and on to Iberian Debussy in the middle section of the Nocturne in F-Sharp, while at the same time defying orchestral transmutation. In respect to the orchestra, *Les Sylphides* is a misunderstanding.

"With Mozart, science is always on the level of inspiration," Chopin told Delacroix, who noted that "He adores Mozart" but "little resembles him." The same could be said of Chopin's reactions to, and negligible influence from, the biggest of the musical big bosses, Beethoven. Chopin alone succeeded in slipping through the German monopoly on musical genius. "What constitutes logic in music?" Delacroix asked one day. Chopin answered, "Bach fugues." Oddly, George du Maurier, the author of *Trilby*, also wrote perceptively about Chopin, having recognized that the Impromptu in A-Flat, from the first Bellini-like warble, is a coloratura aria.

Writing from Nohant, Delacroix sets the scene for a friend in Paris: "Chopin is at work in his room and every now and then a breath of his music blows through the window, which opens onto the garden, mingling with the song of the nightingales." Chopin himself wrote from Nohant that he had dreamed of death and pictured himself dead. Three years earlier he had written from Majorca, mocking the verdicts of three doctors: "The first said I was dead, the second that I was dying, and the third that I am going to die." For myself, I think of the Mazurkas, the Preludes, the Nocturnes as having always existed, life without them being difficult to imagine.

I returned to Paris via Vézelay, and dined with Mrs. Stravinsky and Souvtchinsky at L'Espadon, remembering former birthdays with Stravinsky.

On September 27 I accompanied Dominique Nabokov to the premiere of *Moïse et Aron* at the Paris Opéra, passionately conducted by Solti. At a postperformance party in the Café de la Paix, Rolf Liebermann introduced me to him, and to Antoine Goléa, who made the French translation of the opera, and had been Stravinsky's bête noire for the last thirty years.

In October Lincoln Kirstein wrote to me from London, where he was gathering material for a book on Nijinsky:

> Every day at eleven I go to talk with Mme Rambert, who, as Miriam Ramberg, a young Polish dancer of 22, was assigned by Jaques Dalcroze to Diaghilev for the purpose of helping Nijinsky [analyze] the counts . . . for *Le Sacre du printemps*. Now 87, she is rather frail but, if you ask the right questions, has a keen memory. I thought it would interest you to know what she said about the whole thing . . . Nijinsky was not a fool, although essentially non-verbal. He had no "personality," in contrast with Nureyev and other demonstrators of the self-as-negotiable-security. I think he was *polytropoi*.
>
> The Diaghilev company hated the rehearsals. They nicknamed Rambert "Rhythmichka." She and Vaslav Fomitch arbitrarily decided on what and how much would be tackled in a rehearsal session . . . There was a fat-bottomed German pianist they called "Kolossal," who played everything desperately slowly. When Stravinsky arrived he flew into a rage, yelling, pounding the piano, banging his fists on the piano cover to indicate the tempi he wanted. He was appalled at the way rehearsals were going. Stravinsky made Nijinsky very nervous. There was a dreadful scene at a rehearsal when, after Stravinsky had replaced Kolossal, Nijinsky said, "He can't do it and I can't do it." Mme

Rambert imagines there was some sort of conference with Diaghilev later that night, for the row was made up and rehearsals proceeded.

Nijinsky seemed defeated by the magnitude of the project. "What do you think we should do here?" he would ask, "Variations in big circles and small squares?"[5] Rambert was not involved in the invention of any arm or leg movements, but she did in some way give him courage because she could translate his wishes into terms that the corps de ballet could somehow accept.

When Diaghilev went off to Petersburg . . . Rambert and Vaslav Fomitch worked in Monte Carlo. She rather fell in love with him, but their sessions were interrupted every 20 minutes by Diaghilev's body servant Vasily Zhuikov, an awful man, rather like Dostoyevsky's Smerdiakov.

Mme Rambert daily tried to figure out the music for the next rehearsal session . . . They would go over it together . . . In the ballet she was one of the 4 small girls; there were 4 big girls, too. The elders moved twice as slowly as the youths and had to walk to a rhythm half that of the younger men.[6] The company hated all this. Were they trained as artists of the Imperial Ballet and graduates of the Academy for *this?* She wrote down the counts for the individual dancers, some of whom were much more musical than others, particularly the English girl known as Sokolova, and Grigoriev's wife, Tchernicheva.

The rehearsals in the Champs-Elysées Theater had gone badly; the theater was still being finished and workmen kept going through the rehearsal room; Nijinsky lost his temper and tried to throw a chair at a man coming through. Dress rehearsal was pandemonium chiefly because the dancers had not heard the orchestra before it. On stage at the premiere the dancers could not hear the orchestra at all. When the curtain went down Nijinsky, in the wings, was cursing: *"Dura Publica,"* stupid audience.

On October 5, minutes before Mrs. Stravinsky and I checked out of the Ritz for our flight to Zurich and meeting there with Albi Rosenthal, Chester Kallman telephoned from Vienna to say that Auden was dead. Chester had brought breakfast to him in a Vienna hotel room, where he had stayed after delivering a lecture, and was startled to find him lying on his left side. We were shocked, unbelieving, unable to accept the thought.

> *Stop all the clocks, cut off the telephone . . .*
> *[. . .]*
> *The stars are not wanted now: put out every one;*
> *Pack up the moon and dismantle the sun . . .*

5. The quadrature of the circle?
6. The polyrhythmic section leading to the "Kiss of the Earth."

The lines come to mind out of order. We decided to fly to Vienna from Zurich for the funeral, but the Zurich airport was fogged in. We landed in Basel and completed the trip in an unheated taxi, arriving at our Zurich hotel in the middle of the night with bad colds. All we could do was to send flowers. A great man had died, prematurely, someone we loved.

Soon after Auden's death came the death of my close friend of twenty-three years, Eugene Berman, in his apartment in the Doria Pamphili in Rome. When I first lived with the Stravinskys, he, of all the Stravinsky circle— Rieti, Nabokov—was genuinely sympathetic to me and my position. He cared very deeply for the Stravinskys but on occasions sided with me. One of the most cultivated persons I have ever known, he had learned Russian, German, French, and English from governesses in St. Petersburg but was self-taught in Italian, the language of his heart. He had resolved to live in Italy on his first visit there in 1920, as a refugee from the Russian Revolution. I owe much of my own Italophilia to excursions with him in Sicily, the Campania, and the Veneto.

1974

On January 19 I heard *Tristan* at the Met, sharing the director's loge with Phillip Johnson, the architect. Erich Leinsdorf conducted flabbily, the Isolde sang feebly. Five days later, Aaron Copland came to the apartment to record for the Canadian oral history.

Some weeks later I saw the Met's *Parsifal*. The production attempted to disguise opera's ranking solemnity as an opus of the Theater of the Absurd. The great bells that knell the king's death and the hour of the Crucifixion were replaced by a species of electric chimes in a key remote from the orchestra, and with a sonority rather like the steward's first-call to lunch on a Caribbean cruise. Moments after the approximately in-tune entrances of the chorus, the pitch drifted into microtonal regions that would have been impossible to find if required by an avant-garde score. Still, the musical faux pas were minor compared to the visual. Klingsor's spear, no more lethal-looking than a paper airplane, was effortlessly, nonchalantly plucked from the air by its intended target. The ithyphallic fantasy garden—pistils and stamens, like necks and corks of reheboams of champagne—was in radical disagreement with the Pre-Raphaelite tableaux of the other scenes, as well as with the final one in which, though the period is that of the Moorish conquest of Spain, the Grail Knights were dressed like Velasquez courtiers. Most egregious of all, the Flower Maidens' falsies, worn outside and just above nature's realities, suggested a Jean Genet drag scene with the self-castrated Klingsor as the transvestite, closet-pedophiliac madame. He even added a lip-smacking appoggiatura to the "K" in *"Er is schön, der Knabe."*

The only event of consequence in my personal life was my parents' decision to sell their house in Kingston and live in Florida. I had become attached to the upstate home in which, in recent years, I had spent many weekends in retreat from New York.

Also in 1974, and until the decline of Vera Stravinsky's health, Franklin and Helen Reeve, professors of Russian at Wesleyan University in Connecticut, became our close friends. Paul Horgan introduced us, thinking they might provide Mrs. Stravinsky with the Russian-language companionship she so sorely missed. Franklin, the father of Superman Christopher Reeve, was American-born, but Helen grew up in Yugoslavia and after the 1941 German invasion was interned in a labor camp in Germany for the duration of the war. In spite of sufferings and privations, she learned both German and Russian during these years. She and two of her American students in Russian, Mary Brown and Malcolm Macdonald, translated Stravinsky's entire Russian archive into English for me, not simply Stravinsky's side of his correspondence but the other sides as well, and not just letters but newspaper clippings, family documents, publishing and other professional contracts, and much more. I am grateful to them, and regret not seeing them in the last decades.

1975

On January 11 we dined with Victoria Ocampo at Louise Crane's, 820 Fifth Avenue. Victoria had a different menu from ours and a foot button to summon a personal waiter. During the meal Louise answered a call from her friend Elizabeth Bishop, who said she had to look up six words in my *Chronicle*.

On the 20th, Charles Wuorinen and Peter Lieberson came to dinner. I entrusted Stravinsky's last sketches to Wuorinen, who composed his *Reliquary* based on them. The next week I attended the Met's *La Forza del destino*, which I found an *"ennui mortelle"*—one of Stravinsky's favorite expressions—partly because my attention wanders from Piave's libretto.

In February, Gregor Piatigorsky came as an emissary from Hollywood, bringing a medal awarded to Stravinsky posthumously in the ridiculous category of "entertainer." As amusing and outgoing as always, he was gentle and considerate with Vera Stravinsky, an intimate friend of his first wife. Both were happy to be speaking Russian. His pronunciation of Stravinsky's patronymic eliminates all but the first vowel sound: "Igor Fy'd'r'v'ch."

Balanchine visited several times in March to discuss the repertory of his forthcoming Ravel Festival. On opening night we sat with Georges and

Nora Auric. Balanchine had told us that the score he commissioned from him turned out to be "department-store Webern," instead of the expected bygone neo-classicism.

Later in the spring I went with Donna Wright and Bob Silvers to Mick Jagger's Rolling Stones concert in Madison Square Garden but fled after twenty claustrophobic minutes fearing that our reverberating balcony would collapse from the ear-puncturing noise.

In July, Mrs. Stravinsky wanted to purchase Arthur Murray's house in Rye, New York, partly, I think, because the furnishings included Russian icons. She was greatly disappointed when Arthur Emil, the lawyer for the transaction, who advised her not to purchase it, did so himself. Her diary says that I was opposed to the idea of a summer country house, but this is not true. I did remark that the social life she so much enjoyed was only possible in New York, and so was the medical promptitude.

At the beginning of August we were in Salzburg. All approaches to the city, from Bahnhof, Flughafen, Autobahn, were displaying a poster of what, to judge by the white tie and tails, appeared to be a handsome headwaiter. These *affiches* were so close together that they almost blocked the route signs to Berchtesgaden. Suddenly the face seemed familiar, and the caption, *"Wir willkommen Sie bei den Salzburger Festspielen!,"* plus CBS trademark confirmed that it was Leonard Bernstein's.

We lingered outside the theater before *Così fan tutte*, watching the arrival of the Beautiful People on one side of the street and the gathering of the Fourth Estate to gape at them on the other, like masters and peasants in *Figaro*. The performance was dramatically, visually, and vocally (Gundula Janowitz) satisfying. Karl Böhm's slow tempi did not stifle the music's wit, and if his conception of the score was unusually mellow, this quality is implied in the opera's moral: *"La ragion guidar si fa."* The Bay of Naples was evoked by fishing nets, which is important because Neapolitan seductiveness, the aura of the South, is a primary influence on the conduct of the characters. The props establishing the eighteenth century were a swing and a flock of mechanical birds. Some of the sisters' clothing would have been more appropriate to a later date, but, mercifully, all trace of slapstick was absent from the Albanian disguises of the *amanti*.

In the early twentieth century the plot was condemned as unbelievable because the fidelity of the sisters does not survive a single day's siege by their "Albanian" suitors, whereas now, in the twenty-first century, a period as long as a day would challenge credibility. Unlike Don Giovanni and the Count in *Figaro*, the two young men disguised as Albanians do not at first wish to succeed in their seductions, and the wonder is that Mozart so successfully distinguishes between veritable and simulated desire. One of his means of doing so is to replace the round, full tones of the horns with the more acerbic and shallow trumpet sound, which is ordinarily a part of the remoter background. Trumpets here seem in perfect accordance with the insincerity of the sexual pursuit.

Così parodies operatic styles as it tweaks romantic sentiment. Thus *"Come scoglio"* "sends up" the clichés associated with the tempestuous prima donna, the bombastic recitative, the showy trill, the rapid scales, the exaggeratedly wide intervals, the meretricious high note, but at the same time the piece is perfectly "serious." So, too, Ferrando's *"Un'aura amorosa"* ridicules a new genre of high-flown feelings, and at the same time provides them to a tee. This aria demands attention to the words which actually say nothing, and again, the music, existing happily on two levels, is unquestionably "sincere."

Così shares one dramatic device with *The Magic Flute*: to achieve wisdom, the lovers in both operas undergo trials, worldly in one case, spiritual in the other. Here the *Così* libretto is more circumscribed than are those of *Figaro* and *Don Giovanni*, and more artificial. The anatomy of love is a subject of all Mozart operas, but in *Così* it is the only one.

Some directors, deaf to the tone-painting, the rippling muted violins in *"Soave sia il vento,"* load the puffing Vesuvius background with tendentious political interpretations. But the Revolution does not smolder in *Così*, and the Maid's impertinence has no more social significance than if her remarks had been part of the script of *Upstairs, Downstairs*. Even the crowd does not represent a class. What should be remarked is the absence of family, or duenna, to chaperone the nubile sisters, who surely should not be dressed in their boyfriends' uniforms, which begs the question of what these garments were doing in the homes of proper young ladies and belies their innocence and virtue.

In our hotel after the performance, I ran into my Santa Fe friend Regina Sarfaty, here to understudy the role of Despina. She came to our table without her husband, who was evidently embarrassed about his connection with the Stravinsky Swiss bank affair.[7]

On the next night we heard a dull *Figaro*, conducted by Von Karajan. At the end he bowed alone, stage-left, without so much as a glance of acknowledgment to the cast, huddled on stage-right. During intermissions we read the official program book, but failed to find a single image of Mozart among the two hundred glossy photos of jewelry, Jaguars, and banks. From Salzburg we flew to Geneva to photograph Stravinsky's residences in Morges, Montreux, Clarens, Chateau d'Oex, Les Diablerets. Why had he never mentioned the thirteenth-century Hohenstaufen fortress in Morges?

---

7. As a dual-citizen lawyer, Elwood Rickless was retained by Arnold Weissberger to close Stravinsky's Basel account and bring the assets to New York in the form of bearer bonds. Vera Stravinsky, who understood nothing about such matters, promptly converted the bonds to cash, a transaction that Bankers' Trust Company then reported to the I.R.S., which, of course, confiscated the money.

In December we met with Anthony Fell of Boosey & Hawkes at the Ritz Hotel in Paris, who told us that his company could not afford to continue work on the Stravinsky archives and would sell them back to Mrs. Stravinsky for ninety thousand dollars, the operating costs since 1968. She did not have that much money, nor the means of disposing of the archives elsewhere; hence they would have to be sold.

Mrs. Stravinsky's diary gives a more complete account of the year than mine, and it reminds me that throughout the period the family lawsuit was uppermost in our minds and foremost in demands on our time. Two or three afternoons a week were wasted in costly, protracted, fruitless meetings with lawyers. In March 1975 Mrs. Stravinsky gave two depositions. She was coached for them but never really understood what the suit was about in the first place, and why the provisions of her husband's will were superseded by settlement proposals.

1976

In February, Dwight Macdonald, Chairman of the Committee on Awards for Literature of the American Academy of Arts and Letters and the National Institute of Arts and Letters, informed me that I would receive three thousand dollars "in recognition of your creative work in literature. This award will be presented to you at our annual Ceremonial to be held on Wednesday, May 19."

On April 6 the fifth Panikhida service at the Russian Church began shortly before 6 P.M., when an old lady lighted candles around the room and next to a confessional where a priest was listening to a penitent. As an unseen choir began to chant antiphonally, we stood in the center of the room, holding candles. Balanchine remained on his knees throughout the long service. The following month Stravinsky was remembered by the installation of a plaque at the Ansonia Hotel, though he lived there for only a month in 1935.[8]

At the beginning of July, I entered Lenox Hill Hospital for a left inguinal herniorrhaphy, but also to escape the upcoming Bicentennial Independence Day hoopla. About seventy other patients were sworn in at the same hour, a process slowed by actuarial complexities resulting from the malpractice crisis. I had the feeling in Admissions that my identification bracelet manacled me to a "no-fault" system in which a fatal mistake, such as the transfusion of incompatible blood, becomes a "therapeutic accident." One of the new nonliability contracts that I was obliged to sign stated that "the charges incurred represent the fair and reasonable value of the services rendered." But how can this be known in advance?

8. Alexander Siloti, who had conducted Stravinsky's *Fireworks* in 1909 and convinced B. Schott in Mainz to publish the work, was a one-time resident, and in 1934 Schoenberg had lived in the hotel.

My eight by ten cell would have been expensive at a tenth of the price, and I was limited to paper towels: to have to blot the entire body with them after bathing was both tedious and skin-irritating. The thermostat did not modify the centrally controlled air-conditioning, set at fifty-five degrees, or the frigid drafts from a vent along the rim of the ceiling. The bed was extremely narrow, especially when the railings were raised, which no nurse managed to do without considerable trial and error, just as, at first try, they could not find the cranks for lifting and lowering the head and feet, each movement invariably beginning in the wrong direction. The secret of the "knee break" segment was never discovered, and that part of the bed remained uncomfortably elevated.

After exchanging my clothes for the immodest open-back, knee-length hospital gown, I climbed into bed and was perfused with intravenous fluids, while dictating an inventory of my personal effects. Are my teeth part of me or detachable? Thefts of dentures must be on the increase. Testing followed: blood pressure, pulse, temperature, a urine specimen. Pulse was still determined in the old-fashioned way, by human fingers on radial arteries. The nurse who took mine failed to conceal her alarm and asked if my beat was normally only forty-eight. No, I said, adding that the rate may be due to vagus inhibition. Still grasping at this straw, I mentioned the recent thermodynamics calculations by which the lifetime energy expenditure of the average human heart is thought to be the equivalent of that required to build the pyramid of Giza. I explained that sympathicotonics usually complete their pyramids, while vagotonics rarely reach the pinnacles of theirs, but the "vagos" live longer. Ignoring this information, she entered the pulse on the chart, and my metronome readings were recorded every hour thereafter.

Another consequence of soaring malpractice insurance rates was that patients had to be accompanied on each intramural excursion, lest they trip, fall, be kidnapped, or otherwise disappear. During the journey to Radiology, my escort, an elderly volunteer, watched me like a bailiff. On arrival I joined a queue of bathrobed women with worried expressions—the mammogram scare. In Cardiology, afterward, the line and the wait were longer, despite the three-nurse division of labor, one dabbing the jelly, another attaching the clamps and rubber bands, the third running the ticker tape. From here I tried to slip back to my room unescorted but was apprehended and made to join a convoy of wheelchairs.

The next preparatory step was the lathering and shaving of "Hesselbach's triangle" and the perineal and inguinal areas. The indignity of this was exacerbated by the tonsorialist's stale "pee-otomy" pun, and his ribald remarks warning of future itching from the stubble and the impossibility of scratching in public. But the razor was a lesser affront than the manner in which he manipulated the centerpiece, like a barber pushing a nose to the side while scraping an upper lip. However ridiculous the newborn look after the loss of pilosity, the episode served to loosen proprieties and, moments later, to lessen the embarrassment of being penetrated with a clyster by a teen-age girl, instead of by the male nurses of past experience. She ordered me to retain a substantial inundation for an excruciating ten minutes.

At 6 A.M. a remarkably cheerful anesthetist questioned me about allergies, reactions to sodium Pentothal, nitrous oxide, and ethyline chloride, as well as about details of previous operations, a childhood tonsillectomy, a fractured elbow seventeen years ago. An hour before the operation I would receive tranquilizing medication in my room, he said, but this was eventually postponed to make way for an emergency. After three painful attempts to find a vein in the left wrist, intravenous feeding was begun. Then in midafternoon I received two gluteal injections, which resulted in momentary euphoria, then grogginess, shimmering visions, oblivescence and dissolving time-sense, and the feeling of increasing isolation from Mrs. Stravinsky and Barbara Epstein, who had come to see me "off." I was not yet "under" when a masked figure in Shinto green apron, rubber cap, gloves, and galoshes, came for me with a gurney. I protested that the drugs had not "taken," but perhaps inaudibly, since I heard Mrs. Stravinsky tell Barbara, "He is fading."

The IV apparatus being part of the procession, the thought occurred to me that an onlooker might suppose the vehicle to be propelled by the bottled fuel. Though comatose, I was aware that the elevator to the floor above was bumpy and far from smoothly aligned at either dock. On the higher one I began to whistle, not out of bravado but because of a desire to know if my "inner" and "outer" ears were hearing the same thing (they were), and thereby to confirm my consciousness; but no one else seemed to notice my music. Crossing the threshold into the operating theater, wheeled to the center of the room, and transferred to a table—no signs of previous carnage—I lay in lonely splendor beneath a large green lamp, my day in the limelight. Green oxygen cylinders were rolled in, and human figures appeared, sacerdotalists, to judge by their uniforms and masks. As they closed in, one of them strapped my IV arm down, another stripped me, a third announced that "after this injection you will go to sleep." I did, and, mercifully, in a place without darkness or dreams.

"Time to wake up," female voices were saying nearly five hours later, and I was conscious of being on the same conveyance, this time guided by four nurses. Suddenly I found myself talking to Mrs. Stravinsky in voluble but, she told me later, incoherent French, and was aware of being hoisted to my bed ("upsy-dazy"), trembling from burning head to glacial feet. White "anti-embolism stockings" were pulled over my shanks. A note on the wrapper tickled my sick sense of sick humor—"Seamless stockings are contraindicated in cases of gangrene, heart failure, extreme deformity of leg"— but my giggling caused the fire in the left abdomen to burn so intensely that it had to be doused by morphine. Wakened in the night by the detonations of premature July 4 fireworks, I felt a wet-paint stickiness in my left hand. The IV needle had been dislodged, probably an hour before, since the *sang* on my fingers was already *froid*. Eventually an intern tore off the tapes, along with substantial patches of hair, and reinjected the feeder.

The pain was sharper the next morning, the anesthetics having worn off, and I slowly made my way to the bathroom held up by a nurse. The IV came loose again en route, as I realized seeing blood around my feet. Yet as soon as I was again decubitus, and even before the blood on the floor was mopped up, a lab technician extracted his daily vial from the other arm. Worse still, the rantipoling head nurse threatened me with a catheter unless I passed urine. When she brought a cold steel receptacle with a bull-size neck, I asked her to turn on a faucet, closed my eyes, and eventually brought forth a satisfactory flow, a rare instance, in my case, of mind triumphing over matter.

Dr. Lax, making his rounds, reported the discovery of a prehernial lipocele, larger than the rupture itself and the reason for the duration, double the surgeon's prediction, of the operation. The tumor was benign, but I remembered hearing that lipomas frequently return in the same place.

On the two hundredth July Fourth, my surgeon suddenly turned up to ask how I was—how would *I* know?—and departed in less than ten seconds. Concern was expressed by an intern over my low preoperation pulse, and another cardiogram was scheduled, though because of the holiday several hours passed before someone was found to take it. Finally, at 4 P.M., I was pushed along to Cardiology, where a truculent nurse allowed me to remain in my chair only because, so I suspect, the arm and leg straps reminded her, as they did me, of an execution.

By late afternoon my temperature had mounted, a reaction, at least in part, to the presidential platitudes pouring from the television. A further cause may have been the thought that a society which permits physicians to accept retainers from the rich to buy priority and preferential treatment should not be mouthing the equality formulas of the Philadelphia manifesto.

At midnight a new doctor wakened me to say that a cardiogram had been arranged for the next day. I protested that I had had one only hours ago, and asked why it had not been read, but he affected not to know about the matter, or why my bandage had not been changed in the more than fifty hours since surgery. On the hunch that the higher temperature indicated a pulmonary infection, he sent for a blow bottle, a plastic vessel, half filled with water, half with air, which forces the patient to breathe deeply in order to exhale through a hookah-like stem, displacing the water from the one area into the other. Since the transfer became progressively more strenuous, I feared that the exertion might result in a new hernia, yet every two hours throughout the night I was aroused from sleep to play Aeolus with this toy.

My surgeon's profile was even lower the day after the holiday: no visit at all. My chief pains were now gastric, and the nurse said the cure for this was to drink ginger ale and burp like a baby. Otherwise I felt almost back-to-normally bad and able to shuffle in the corridor with the other nonagenarians. Doing so in my blue hospital skirt, white support socks, green slippers, and thus in some measure resembling an emperor of China, I was probably regarded by them as undergoing psychiatric evaluation.

The next and penultimate day in the hospital, a new nurse arrived at dawn with an electrocardiograph. "Have you ever had an EKG in this hospital?" she asked, before adding to the lengthening record of them. A staff doctor described the "mattress-suturing" technique used on me, removed the bandage with one yank, and exclaimed: "A perfect job of mending." He asked me to look at the incision, but the sight of the red, yellow, and purple cross-quilting left me queasy. I could be discharged as soon as he returned with the surgeon, he said, but neither of them appeared. The next morning, when the same doctor peeked at my scar and promised to see me later, I decided that it was already too late, dressed, packed my bag, walked to the elevator, descended, and, undischarged, taxied home. So far as I know, my AWOL was never discovered.

In September, Rolf Liebermann's Paris Opéra opened a short guest season at the Metropolitan Opera with *Figaro*. Just before the Count's aria, *"Vedrò mentre io sospiro,"* Georg Solti, trying to evade the glare from a light on his conductor's stand, accidentally jabbed his right temple with his baton. The superficial wound bled profusely, temporarily blinding him, and the handkerchief that he grabbed with his left hand to stanch it did not help. He finished the number, signaled to stop the descent of the curtain, left the pit for first aid at the beginning of the recitative, and was back in place for the Sextet, which could not have been performed without him. After intermission, emerging for the final act, he received a meter-breaking ovation, but he deserved a Purple Heart as well.

When the curtain first rose on Figaro's realistically dingy digs, attention focused on the Count's newly pressed uniform, suspended from a hanger. During *"Se vuol ballare,"* Figaro thwacked this tunic with a cane, a gesture revealing deep hatred, as well as what might be expected from the staging thereafter by way of social commentary. Throughout the evening, Figaro and the Count—their detestation mutual—addressed each other through clenched teeth, in contrast to the routine nose-tweaking renditions of both roles. Act 3, dark and foreboding in decor and drab in costume, ended with the *contadini* flinging the Count's papers about and on the verge of seizing his palace in open rebellion.

This serious interpretation oddly reduced Figaro's prominence. Compared to his betrothed, he became inconspicuous, almost a background figure. Because he was not playing to the audience, or upstaging the rest of the cast, we were acutely aware that he does not have another solo *scena* after *Se vuol ballare* until *Tutto è disposto* in Act 4, during which his mood, albeit hidden beneath a frolicsome, ingratiating public manner, is the same as it was when he struck the effigy of oppression.

Giorgio Strehler's stage direction was ideologically consistent. While exposing signs of ferment in the lower orders, he also looked for corresponding moral corrosion in the Protected World. *Figaro* may be a comedy, he seemed to say, but the *liaisons* are truly *dangereuses.* In his production, the opera's inherent defects—the overly long part of the untowardly insistent gardener; the ubiquity of Cherubino in the first scenes versus the character's diminished importance in the last ones—were hardly noticeable. Strehler almost succeeded in showing that Cherubino's "love" is only his "libido," and that what he really wants is *"coucher avec n'importe qui."* No staging can account for the illogicality of this amorous adolescent's return so near the beginning of Act 2, after his regal farewell at the end of Act 1, but in spite of this I would not exchange a single bar of *"Non più andrai"* for all the logic of Aristotle.

The performance of the third and best overture, the one following *La Marseillaise* and *The Star-Spangled Banner,* was ragged because Solti gave two beats to the bar instead of one (the tempo is *Presto,* after all), but also because the players could not hear each other. The singers, too, continually anticipated the beat, which Sir Georg was obliged to accelerate from time to time to keep the performance from going agley. Balances, as well as rhythmic coordination, suffered from the acoustics. *"Di quel labbro menzonger?"* the Countess soliloquizes, and the response of the oboe and bassoon was louder than the lady herself, which can only mean that Solti was not hearing it that way.

Mrs. Stravinsky's fuller record of the year reminds me that in January two Californians, William Malloch and Fred Maroth, recorded some of her oral history of her husband. Several long sessions, during five or six days, were held in the Stravinsky dining room, but we never heard the tapes. Her diary entry for the 16th of the month reads: "Today I spoke, Bob said very well, for three hours."

By the beginning of February, Mrs. Stravinsky was unable to pay her lawyers—Arnold Weissberger, Martin Garbus, and Helene Kaplan—and the question of selling Stravinsky's music manuscripts arose. Mrs. Samuel Dushkin, widow of the violinist, the man closest to Stravinsky in the 1930s, had connections at the Pierpont Morgan Library, which had shown an interest in the *Nachlass* and which, because it already owned several important Stravinsky manuscripts, would be an ideal repository. Herbert Cahoon, the Joyce scholar and a Morgan curator, and Rigbie Turner, chief music librarian, examined the scores, sketches, and other materials, but failed to convince the library's governing board to acquire them. In the following year, the University of Texas and the University of California sent teams of musicologists for the same purpose and with the same results.

Another plan, proposed by Parmenia Miguel Ekstrom, was to establish a Stravinsky-Diaghilev museum in Venice. At that time the not-yet-restored Palazzo Grassi could have been purchased for less than a million dollars. Later the City of Venice offered a dilapidated palazzo in the Campo Santa Maria in Formosa, but funds were not forthcoming from either the American side, or UNESCO, whose president was a friend of Mrs. Ekstrom. Finally, in March, Albi Rosenthal, on behalf of Paul Sacher in Basel, purchased ten manuscript full scores, after a week's work with me during which we agreed on what were "fair market value" prices.

1977

On March 6 and 7, 1977, Mrs. Stravinsky, aged ninety-one, was deposed by an opposition lawyer, a Mr. Kunin, and defended by Martin Garbus. The subject was the conveyance of *The Rite of Spring* manuscript from Zurich to California. The following excerpt is typical:

Kunin: I take it you had clothes in your suitcase . . .
Mrs. Stravinsky: . . . usually no(t) closed . . . no lock.
Kunin: What kind of suitcase was it?
Mrs. Stravinsky: I have twenty suitcases. I don't remember what I had five
    years ago.
Kunin: Was it a suitcase?
Mrs. Stravinsky: A suitcase is a suitcase . . .
Kunin: You and your husband were talking about your birthday, I gather?
Mrs. Stravinsky: Name day.
Garbus: Her name day.
Kunin: Which you say is a birthday.
Garbus: No, it's better than a birthday, Mr. Kunin. You only have a birthday.
    Mrs. Stravinsky has a name day.
Kunin: "Bepa" is you?
Mrs. Stravinsky: Vera . . . in Russian . . .
Kunin: And the next (word) is?
Mrs. Stravinsky: "Hope," Nadiezhda . . .
Kunin: Who is that?
Mrs. Stravinsky: The saint; we have saints in the Russian Church.
Kunin: That is all it means?
Mrs. Stravinsky: You know . . . give me the blessings, Saint Vera, Saint
    Nadiezhda, and there is Charity.
Kunin: And that is all these things mean?

From Mrs. Stravinsky's and my own later experience, I began to understand the extent to which a deposition is a lawyers' game. The winner is the one who keeps his client from revealing anything and wastes the most time— arranging by telephone for a late beginning due to traffic, extending restroom visits and the lunch break, and setting up interruptions for urgent, but entirely bogus, phone calls. The defense lawyer instructs the deponent to delay in answering even the most obvious question and to answer noncommittally, if at all. "I am not sure that that is my handwriting; mine is easy to forge." Garbus is the absolute master of this sport, as of many other litigation techniques. He found an "objection" to every question by the opposition lawyer, a member of a Chicago firm, no match for him and hopelessly ill-informed as well.

At the beginning of May, I flew to Milwaukee, the Hotel Pfister, with our secretary, Pat Crane. The dean of the University's music department took us and Ernst and Gladys Krenek to dinner. Having lost contact after Stravinsky's death, the Kreneks were eager to have news of Vera Stravinsky. Ernst and I shared rehearsals for our half-and-half concert.

At the beginning of June we attended a memorial service for Goddard Lieberson at the Fifth Avenue Temple Emmanuel. Leonard Bernstein read a prayer in Hebrew. Afterward he was very gentle with Vera Stravinsky, and, in view of my critical mauling of his Mass, nice enough with me.

In Paris the next month, I read an interview in *Le Monde* with Karlheinz Stockhausen on the influence of astrology on the musical avant-garde. Condemned in Savonarola's *Tractato contra li Astrologi*, in general decline with Copernicus, losing every vestige of intellectual respectability with Newton, and derided in the nineteenth century as a medieval superstition, it is now redivivus, evidently, taught in universities, packaged and sold to the masses. Stockhausen claims to employ a notational system correlated to the zodiac. He compares his "new panthematicism resulting from all the parameters of sound" to the limited thematic treatment of Schoenberg, who "turned to serial music," and to Webern, who "reduced this to two or three intervals in a series of twelve pitches." Stockhausen believes that fantastic discoveries in perspective are ahead: "I dream of an apparatus that will finally give us the possibility of making sounds travel. Think of a sound crossing your nose, of a sound that stops in front of you, that circles your body, that passes back and forth in front of you at varying speeds . . . Music, when it becomes truly mobile, will give us new experiences."

No doubt. But who wants a sound to traverse his nose, or stop in front of him? And would this be music, or an experiment in physics? Perhaps some future technological genius will master the unlimited resources at his disposal and give birth to a new aural art. But Stockhausen's estimate concerning his own career—"it would take ten lifetimes to accomplish my objectives"—is not promising, and when he asserts that it would require "fifty musicologists, each one working for a year, to analyze the labyrinth of polyphonic relations in [my] *Sirius*," are we not justified in wondering whether the musical goal is worth the expenditure of time?

On our return to New York, Mrs. Stravinsky and I spent a week in London, partly to see *The Rake's Progress* at Glyndebourne, partly to visit her friend from the Russia and Paris years, Salomeya, Princess Andronica, a lively, but totally deaf ninety-plus. After flying to Miami, we drove to my house in Pompano Beach, where I learned that my father had had a stroke and was in Cypress Creek Hospital. As he seemed to be recovering, we returned to New York a few days later, but shortly after our arrival a call shocked me with the news of his death. Friends from my childhood came to his funeral in Kingston on August 15. At the Wiltwyck Cemetery, my mother, sisters, and nieces next to me faced the casket. A blue sky and warm sun made the burial more terrible. "How are the dead raised up? And with what body do they come? Thou fool, that which thou sowest is not quickened except it die . . . it is sown a natural body; it is raised a spiritual body." We were spared the ropes and boards, the lifting and lowering of the actual interment. Each of us took a rose from the blanket of flowers on the coffin, and I removed a red ribbon from a wreath with "Dad" on it, a word that cut like a knife: I had never used it in direct conversation with him since childhood. Driving to New York, I stopped at Cornwall-on-Hudson and my old, deeply hated school. I entered the grounds by the field where we were required to stand and cheer our football team and fight moronic mock battles while the real Battle of Britain was raging.

Back in New York, Balanchine spent an evening with me listening to Vivaldi concerti with the intent of choosing one or more of them for a ballet. He rarely agreed with the tempi of the recorded performances, maintaining, correctly I think, that one very fast three-meter finale should be played as a slow minuet. He chose the *"Santo Sepolcro"* Sinfonia for the centerpiece of his projected dance suite, but what excited him most was a concerto for piccolo, both the music and the instrument. It really "whistles," he said, and the sound is "so clean and unsentimental that Debussy's flute seems greasy in comparison." I told him about a newly discovered telegram from Stravinsky in Nice to Diaghilev in Monte Carlo, January 21, 1928, inviting him to "come with Balanchine tomorrow at four." When I asked if he had any recollections of Stravinsky playing *Apollo* at that time, he said, "Igor Fyodorovitch read the score at the piano, repeating the tempi to me over and over. Diaghilev later changed them. But Diaghilev never understood the music . . . And, though nobody will believe me, he did not know very much about dancing. His real interest in ballet was the male *joppa*. He could not bear the sight of Danilova[9] and would say to me, 'Her tits make me

9. Shura Danilova, d. 1997.

want to vomit.' Once when I was standing next to him at an *Apollo* rehearsal he said, 'How beautiful.' 'Yes,' I said, thinking he meant the music, but he corrected me: 'No, no. I mean Lifar's ass: it is like a rose.' "

Balanchine's superior staging of *Eugene Onegin* in Hamburg constantly came to mind a few weeks later, at the Met's revival of the opera. The Met performance was spiritless, and the only evidence of progress was that in 1957 it was sung in bad English, and in 1977, according to Vera Stravinsky, in reasonably good Russian. Why is the stage direction so ignorant of Russian life in the time of Pushkin's verse novel? Not that the presentation of period-piece operas is ever historically accurate in decor and decorum, but *Onegin* depends on a degree of verisimilitude in both, especially the latter. Admittedly, the time frames of the opera and the poem are often at loggerheads. In Pushkin, Lenski leaves Tatyana's name-day party almost immediately after the quarrel with Onegin, and Onegin himself leaves only a little later. The opera, on the contrary, expands the scene, keeping the antagonists on stage long enough to give the episode musical form. But the result is melodramatic and contradicts the code of conduct for men of Lenski's and Onegin's social positions. The Met's Onegin, oblivious of the qualities and impeccable manners of Pushkin's Byronic dandy, places Tatyana's letter by her side with all the graciousness of a bill collector. When she informs him of her decision to stay with her husband, he slumps to his knees in a maudlin gesture, while she assumes a stock firm-of-purpose pose, departing after the standard backward look from the doorway.

Tchaikovsky recognized that the poem does not give scope to full operatic treatment, yet believed that "the richness of the poetry, the simple human subject . . . will compensate for whatever it lacks in other ways." Wrong. Rich poetry is not a necessary or even a desirable ingredient for opera, and to cast a narrative poem in an operatic mold seems possible only by resorting, as Wagner did, to declamation. *Onegin* is additionally handicapped by its own institutional status as the best-known poem in the language. The fault of the libretto is not in its language, which incorporates a high proportion of Pushkin's lines, but in the nature of the operatic medium, which cannot project the psychology and sophistication of the poem.

In December we attended a dinner party at Thomas Messer's with Nina Kandinsky, last seen in Venice twenty years ago.

The year 1977 was a crisis one in the ongoing litigation launched six years ago by Stravinsky's children. In November, claiming title to all of his father's French royalties, Soulima Stravinsky brought an injunction in Paris to stop any distribution to Vera Stravinsky. In a counteraction Martin Garbus moved to have the French assets frozen, in which condition they remained until 1987, when a New York court ruled that Soulima's claim, based on his French citizenship and a French law of 1819, was illegal according to the terms of the 1979 settlement agreement.

1978

In January my book *Stravinsky in Pictures and Documents* was published, the result of six years of intermittent researching, selecting, translating, and writing. Unbelievably, but most agreeably, Simon and Schuster paid an advance of seventy-five thousand dollars, an unheard of amount for a volume of this kind. Martin Garbus, who brokered the sale, explained the "largesse" as a tax write-off for the publisher, which had reaped huge profits from books about Watergate and needed a few losses on books of presumed cultural merit. *SPD* was the first factual life of the composer, and the first to open doors that he would have preferred to have kept closed, wanting no biography beyond the catalog of his works.

SPD led to the idea of editing a selection of Stravinsky's correspondence, and much of my time after its publication was devoted to the three volumes of letters eventually issued. In them I tried to cast some light on the composer's less publicized personal associations, such as the one with Nicolas Nabokov. Stravinsky had known him very slightly in Paris in the late 1920s, but from the late 1940s in America the relationship became close and affectionate. True, Nabokov was an entrepreneur who presented prestigious arts festivals in Paris, Rome, Tokyo, and Berlin, in which Stravinsky's works and presence were focal. The friendship, albeit, was rooted not on this connection but in their shared cultures, languages, backgrounds, musical tastes, and sense of humor.

On the last day of February, Mrs. Stravinsky and I flew to London on the Concorde. Before boarding, we were given three sheets listing objects, among them aqualungs and thermometers, that could not be taken with us aboard the plane. During the steep takeoff our ears crackled and our nostrils filled with the stench of combusting fuel. The braking over Coney Island felt like the suspension before the plunge in an amusement park rollercoaster, and the engine noise thereafter remained at vacuum-cleaner level. The seats were too small, the ceiling too low—even moderately tall people had to crouch—and the pocket-mirror windows might have been designed for a maximum-security prison; basketball players would be well advised to travel subsonically. The Texan twang in the talk from the seats behind us about working for "oilionaire" sheiks contrasted radically to the British accents of the crew: "Pull the knob smartly downward," the attendant demonstrating a life jacket said, and he pointed to the buttons and dials in the "entertainment console" in the armrest, which provided a stolidly British earphone concert: Elgar, Walton, Britten. Within minutes, Long Island and snow-covered Connecticut were beneath us, as if on a vast curve-of-the-earth map. At 2 P.M. New York time an eerie twilight fell, like an eclipse.

The dinner-menu prose was vintage Brit Air: the Pauillac, "when in full cry," has a "curranty bouquet with dusty, cedary overtones. On the palate, the flavours are resinous and silky." The Echézeaux is "chewy," has "plenty of backbone," "performs well," and is "long in the mouth." The description of the Nuits St. George bordered on pornography: "well-structured, more masculine than other growths, with plenty of thrust and a phenomenally long, lush finish." The Chambertin's "nose of cassis and tobacco" did not attract, but the Petrus, the most expensive Bordeaux, was the least appealingly described: "tons of tannin, gobs of glycerin, and a plethora of Asian spices." Among champagnes, the Pol Roget is "pale lemon-gold with a hint of ginger," and its "full flavour seems to open up in the mouth." Where else?

"We will be landing fifteen minutes ahead of shedule," the cockpit informed us, and "in about three minutes from now will cease to be targets for satellites and enter the range of earth stations." Books and papers were stuffed into valises while the Mach meter registered the rapid deceleration. As a parting gift, passengers received boxes of candies, Sultana Squares, and Hazelnut.

In contrast to grungy, snowbound New York, still with yeti–sasquatch tracks in Central Park, Hyde Park was green, and the purple and yellow crocuses were in full bloom. We saw Peter Hall's *Cherry Orchard* and compared it favorably with the overstated production in the Vivian Beaumont Theater in New York. Strangely, the realistic staging—recorded clip-clopping of horses, a backdrop of telephone poles, and with Firs (Ralph Richardson) lying down at the end as if he really were dying—did not offer a glimpse of the orchard itself. Michael Frayn's translation was sprinkled with peculiar words—"litanies," for one, used in reference to the singing of peasants at work.

The Covent Garden *Idomeneo*, which I saw next, joined the first two acts without pause, a disastrously lopsided dramatic division. Another serious fault was that the staging centered distractingly on an enormous pair of self-animating staircases. But the terrifying monster that gobbled up some of the corps de ballet and belched smoke that filled the theater and emptied it more rapidly than usual at intermission was an unqualified success. After Elektra stabbed herself, holding the weapon like a sword-swallower, and as if she were the scabbard, the audience was obliged to watch as her corpse was shrouded and borne off. Even during the great third-act quartet, bodies, distributed all over the stage, were carried out one by one, an ambulance service that distracted from the music. Ilia sang *Se il padre perdei* seated on a stool, while Idomeneo listened on another one, as if the director wished to underline, for anyone who had not noticed, that the style of the staging had fallen somewhere between. Movement was never lacking, but billowing drapery and the raising and lowering of panels are no substitute for drama. *Idomeneo* anticipates Romantic opera, above all Verdi, in the choruses, the grandeur and complexity of the large scenes, the emotional extravagance, and, not least, the failure of credibility.

In New York on April 6, Nicolas Nabokov died in Mt. Sinai Hospital, shockingly, saddeningly, and, in spite of many heart attacks, unexpectedly.

It seems that when Dominique left him at about 1 A.M. he was in good spirits but did not have a night nurse. Then came the brutal telephone call. My Stravinsky world—Stravinsky died seven years ago on the same day—shrinks more with this loss than with any other in the interim. I think of Nabokov standing between Vera Stravinsky and her alienated stepchildren at the funeral in Venice, escorting her throughout the obsequies and formal obligations. I also think of how the Stravinskys enjoyed every visit from him as they did from no one else, and of how they looked forward to them. Poor Dominique, who took such loving care of him! Two days later, after the funeral at the Russian church, Elizabeth Hardwick, thinking about Lowell's death, cried on my shoulder. Later in the same month, we went to a memorial concert for Goddard Lieberson in Carnegie Hall, in which Bernstein conducted the *Symphony of Psalms* and Goddard's widow narrated *A Survivor from Warsaw*. (At intermission I was left alone with Jackie Onassis, who had invited Mrs. Stravinsky and myself to share her loge. Since her regular escorts—the painter Bill Walton, and the stage designer Oliver Smith—its only other occupants, went out to smoke, I was left alone to fend off Jackie's autograph seekers. She asked me to accompany her to the door of the W.C., but this did not stop her adulators from following her even there.)

A week later, Vanes Prazzi, our cook of the tall toque, having absconded, Mrs. Stravinsky hired Maria Kallami, from Morocco, to replace him, but soon fired her because she came with her small children and gave them the run of the house. Finally we found an excellent replacement, Mr. Ah-Ching, who agreed to sleep in.

In September, Tamara Geva filmed interviews with Balanchine in Mrs. Stravinsky's apartment for a television documentary about Diaghilev on the forthcoming fiftieth anniversary of his death. At the opening of the City Ballet season on November 14, Serge Lifar went backstage afterward with Mrs. Stravinsky, using her to gain access to Balanchine, who not only refused to be photographed with him but fled the theater.

In November we attended a gala sit-down dinner in the Metropolitan Museum of Art, inaugurating an exhibition of Ballets Russes costumes. The meal was followed by a masked ball, in which, nevertheless, everyone recognized everyone else. (Who could disguise William Buckley, Jr.?) The plainclothes police and large increase of museum guards created a sinister atmosphere. Lifar monopolized Mrs. Stravinsky all evening.

On December 4 Arnold Weissberger gave a birthday party for Mrs. Stravinsky. He photographed me with Jean Stein and Andrey Voznesensky, and with the writer Edna O'Brien, a redhead beauty.

1979

Dick Cavett dominated the beginning of our year. He presented two TV shows on Mrs. Stravinsky, after visits to her apartment with his wife. Having been a ballet dancer, Mrs. Cavett had at least heard of Stravinsky. The first show was aired at seven and again at eleven on January 12, but knowing nothing about the subject, Cavett had no follow-up questions, and, worse, interrupted his guest just when she was in stride. For the second show, the next night at 7 P.M. and at 12:30 A.M., Cavett, aware that the first evening could not have boosted his ratings, brought in Christopher Isherwood, with even duller results. Two weeks earlier, Mrs. Stravinsky had slipped and fallen on the ice only a few steps from the entrance to her building. She may have suffered a minor stroke but no apparent physical injuries, and she refused to be seen by her doctor.

In late March, Isherwood invited us to a preview of the play he had fashioned out of his novel *Meeting by the River*. Sam Jaffe added the luster of his name to the anonymous cast but no life. The piece was stillborn, and at the end of the first act we moved to the last row and from there to the street, hoping to avoid all eyes.

On May 1 Mrs. Stravinsky was in tears seeing Mikhail Baryshnikov in *Apollo* at the State Theater. Soon thereafter we went to Paris for an exhibition of her paintings, and to see the Diaghilev exhibition at the Bibliothèque Nationale. Most of the sources of the latter were French; hence the displays for *La Chatte* and *Le Dieu bleu* were more extensive than would have been the case in London or New York. The predominance of Cocteau was misleading, and would have appalled Diaghilev, but Cocteau's poster of Tamara Karsavina in *Le Spectre de la rose*, and his caricatures of dancers and balletomanes, composers and painters, Diaghilev and his entourage, and of backstage life with the Ballets Russes were highlights. Here, too, were his cartoon of Misia Sert in her loge, *chapeau à aigrette*, exclaiming to Diaghilev: *"Mais non, Serge, Fokine n'est pas épuisé";* and the drawing of himself with shirtsleeves too short, to make him look like a gangling youth outgrowing his clothes.

The most stunning pictures were Nikolay Roerich's delicately colored pencil, pen, and gouache costume design for the "third young girl" in part 2 of the *Rite*, and Picasso's 1917 green-ink portrait of Diaghilev with Léon Bakst and Léonide Massine. The major pictorial disappointments were Aleksander Benois's academic sets for *The Nightingale* and *Le Médecin malgré lui*, yet one of the former was reproduced in color in the catalog, in company with a Derain, a Bakst, an undistinguished Larionov and a, ditto, Goncharova. The *Mavra* exhibit revived Vera Stravinsky's memories of the private audition of the piece at the Hotel Continentale that Sudeykin forbade her to attend, provoking the argument that led to their separation. A description of Stravinsky, assisted at the piano that night by Nicolas Kopeikin, stirred memories in me as well, Kopeikin having helped me with *Mavra* when I presented it in New York twenty-seven years later. (All accounts of the event name Grzegorz Fitelberg as the conductor that night, but a drawing by Mikhail Larionov, discovered recently in an old vocal score at Boosey &

Hawkes, proves that the conductor was Ernest Ansermet; Larionov's portrait of Stravinsky at the piano is exceptionally good.)

Photographs were a feature of the show, but the best of them, the 1907 portrait of Rimsky-Korsakov and Saint-Saëns in a gathering of Russian and French musicians in the Salle Pleyel, did not appear in the catalog, which was largely limited to the familiar. On the credit side, the compilers identified the artists who *executed* the costumes and designs.

About 125 people came to Vera Stravinsky's exhibition in the Galérie André Pacitti, rue du Faubourg St.-Honoré, among them members of the Soviet Embassy and Boris Kochno, who, like Vera S., was obviously pleased to be kissing and making-up. Fifty-eight years ago she introduced him to Diaghilev. He asked her to send a copy of Michael Kuzmin's *Kusaja* manuscript. Lifar came, too, and Maya Plisetskaya telephoned, making the occasion a feast of Russian-speaking. But Americans bought the pictures.

Back in New York, we received a visit from the musical ex-prime minister Edward Heath on behalf of the London Sinfonietta's forthcoming Stravinsky festival. He was sporting as much blue (jacket, shirt, tie, cufflinks) as anyone in Gainsborough, and more, if one were to include his eyes. Conversation was confined to music. "None of the younger men can manage Haydn, Mozart, and Beethoven," he said, "and no audience can be nourished for long on Messiaen." He compared recordings of Bruckner's Seventh, deplored Lorin Maazel's Mahler ("without soul"), remarked that "after sixty years the so-called Second Viennese School has not gained any general acceptance." His accolades were reserved for the older performer-tycoons, Rubinstein, Heifetz, Horowitz.

In October, Jean Stein brought Joseph Brodsky for dinner. Looking at Vera Stravinsky's Russian Revolution salon album, he turned with disgust from the likenesses of the Stalinist "turncoats" Sergei Gorodetzky and Aleksey Tolstoi, but jumped to his feet, trembling with passion, when he saw the manuscript poem by Osip Mandelstam, which he recited from memory in a voice of such intensity that we hardly dared to look at him. It is still difficult to believe that he was only thirty-eight; my first guess would have been sixty-five. He recognized every poet and painter in the album and left its compiler and myself in a high state of emotion. A few days later Jean brought David Hockney for dinner. A lively and keen observer, he was much less shy and much more talkative than when we met him in London.

My main work of the year was in preparing Stravinsky's correspondence for publication and in writing introductions and appendices for it. In July, *The Musical Quarterly,* and in November, *The New York Review of Books,* published chapters from the first volume. Stravinsky preserved carbon copies and drafts of most of his business correspondence, but of the most interesting personal letters, dating from prerevolution Russia, the seventy good ones were published long ago in the U.S.S.R. In comparison, the correspondence of the French and American years reveals little about his artistic development and nothing about his creative processes, though much of this had already been established by the theorist Pieter Van den Toorn. Nor do the post-1921 letters, after the crisis in his love affair with Vera de Bosset Sudeykina, indulge in comments of a personal nature. All of his letters to his first wife were burned on his instructions after her death in 1939. The bulk of his outgoing mail consisted of missives to publishers, concert agents, impresarios, recording companies, performing musicians (most importantly Ansermet), and lawyers. Stravinsky was a persistent correspondent. His tone in business matters ranged from cantankerous to ferocious, and his diurnal correspondence was ungracious and petty. In general, the people Stravinsky cultivated were those who were useful to him.

His letters from the 1930s, moreover, are often politically incorrect. (On October 13, 1936, for example, he wrote from Paris accepting a concert engagement in Naples, and agreeing to conduct "L'Hymne Fasciste [the Giovenezza] avec joie.") Nor are they free of denigrating remarks about ethnicities and nationalities of the kind in general currency at the time, i.e., the Viennese are "flowery and false," the French "stingy and tergiversating," the Italians "clownish and unreliable," the Poles "bigoted." On occasion Vera Stravinsky, perhaps harboring some prejudice herself concerning her husband's Polish ancestry, would attribute this national trait to him. She used to tell a story about him reading George Antheil's Bad Boy of Music, flying into a rage at the book's references to him, vowing never to speak to the author again, then, a few days later, after hurrying past the Antheils in the same row in which they were seated at a concert and on reaching her seat, she glanced back and saw her husband in amicable conversation with Antheil and kissing his wife's hand.

In September, Mrs. Stravinsky attended a court hearing concerning a proposed settlement among the heirs of her husband's estate. When no acknowledgment of the ninety-one-year-old woman's presence was forthcoming from the opposition lawyers, nor any sign of courtesy to the widow of the man whose genius and labors had generated the money they were greedily devouring, she instructed her own lawyers to sign the agreement as soon as possible. The experience shattered her. She suffered a stroke shortly thereafter and from then until her death was rarely without nurses.

Chapter 10

Three Deaths and a New Life

The 1980s

I spent the 1979–1980 holidays with my mother and sister in Florida, returning to New York on January 2. After that I flew to Florida for three or four days every month, except during the summer, when my family came north. The remainder of my time was devoted to Mrs. Stravinsky. In the summer months, she and I, accompanied by Ed Allen, her librarian friend at Wesleyan University in Middletown, Connecticut, and by nurse Rita McCaffrey, spent weekends at Lake Mohonk in the Shawangunk Mountains near New Paltz. I had known this Quaker resort with its Victorian buildings since childhood, and in fact, the owner of the property in the 1860s was an ancestor of mine, from whom the two Quaker brothers who constructed the hotel in the 1870s purchased it. The attractions were a spectacular setting, with views of both the Rondout and the Wallkill Valleys, and, lying at the foot of granite cliffs and boulders, a clear, spring-fed lake. On its east side a path between, over, and under rocks led up a cliff to a tower that offered a view of the Hudson River. The ascent of the cliff, known as "the lemon squeezer," required stamina, good muscle tone, athletic skills that included jumping, and considerable nerve. I had climbed through many times, but when I brought my son Alexander there in 1984 and 1985, I could not keep up with him.

From the standpoint of modern comfort, however, Mohonk left too much to be desired. I still find it difficult to believe that Arturo Toscanini vacationed there, and, in the summer of 1945, Thomas Mann, who described it in his diary:

> With our daughter Monika we spent ten days in the country, at Lake Mohawk [sic],[1] Ulster County, in the foothills of the Catskills. The stately hotel called

1. Mann is thinking of James Fenimore Cooper. The actual lake is Mohonk, and the Indians who lived here were Lenapes, a tribe of the Algonquin Nation.

Mountain House, built in the Swiss style and run by Quakers, is situated in a parklike landscape of rugged hills, a kind of nature sanctuary in the Victorian taste. No outside automobile is permitted to enter its precincts, which are full of all sorts of outlooks and sprinkled quaintly with an assortment of turrets and little bridges—an old-fashioned *Kurort* without the "cure," unless we regard abstention from alcoholic beverages as a sort of cure. It was just the place for a rest, and at this time of year the air was a good deal cooler than sweltering, stuffy New York. Incidentally, the weather was exhausting and oppressive enough here, too; most of the time it thundered from morning to night.

Mrs. Stravinsky abominated the non-air-conditioned hotel, the Quaker prohibition in the dining room, and the rule against smoking anywhere. (She smoked throughout her life and even on her deathbed.) But she loved the lakeside, the walks on the woodland paths with their resting-place gazebos, and the magnificent flower gardens.

As for life in New York, I wrote the following paragraph at some undated point: "Channel J's 'Midnight Blue,' known hereabouts as 'the children's hour' (mommy and daddy being asleep by that time), pretends to promote sexual freedom, or, at least, decriminalized sex, while actually exploiting white and off-white slavery electronically packaged. At intervals a bedroom voice invites the viewer to 'Telephone for a discreet appointment on our exclusive out-call service,' while a Fugazy stretch-limo is shown delivering one of the service's overendowed layabouts. The slack between these commercials is taken up with old strip-tease films of flabby females of the 'forties; fashions in bodies change as rapidly as fashions in clothes. I learn from one of the purveyors that a girl trussed in chains is referred to in the market as 'gift-wrapped.' "

The summer issue of *Contemporary Keyboard* contained an interview with Glenn Gould very flattering to me:

> If insert 32, number 17, consists of exactly two notes, it should absolutely be possible to play those two notes in such as way as to conform to the line one has in mind. From the time that I first started recording, I was fascinated by the possibility that this could be done, but I had never seen it in action until 1961, when I recorded the Schoenberg Concerto with Robert Craft conducting. We were recording in Massey Hall here in Toronto, and Craft was connected by telephone with the producer backstage. He would get a phone call saying, "We need to do an insert starting at two bars after letter "L," and at no point did Craft ask to have a playback to find out what the tempo was. He had the most extraordinary ability to recall precisely what the musical context was within which that insert would have to fit. It is not just a metronomic consciousness, but a kind of complete structural comprehension that was there in his head. The ability to do that was something that I had never seen in any other artist. And I thought, "Damn it, I'm going to learn to do this."

In 1980 I published three essays in *The New York Review of Books* but devoted most of my time to the compilation of a photograph album called *Igor and Vera Stravinsky*. As noted earlier in the present book,[2] a partial biography of the composer in the 1920s and 1930s could be constructed from his captions on the hundreds of his and Vera Sudeykina's snapshots taken on their automobile travels. Both were keen photographers, and the three best portraits of him are by her: in Copenhagen in 1925, with monocle dangling on a tether around his neck; in Paris at about the same time; and seated on the staircase to the upper level of their Hollywood garden in the mid-1940s.

1981

Though Mrs. Stravinsky's high blood pressure became a major concern in 1981, she was able to appear in Tony Palmer's Stravinsky documentary, first in her own home and walking on Fifth Avenue, then in late August and early September in London, where, during my absence in the U.S.S.R. with Palmer, she looked at rushes of the film. On our return to New York, I was invited by Charles Schwartz, director of Composers' Showcase and Gershwin biographer, to conduct a Stravinsky concert in the Whitney Museum. He chose me partly because of my personal acquaintance with the three composers he had invited to participate as speakers in *Histoire du Soldat*: Virgil Thomson, whom I knew throughout my Stravinsky years; Roger Sessions, a Stravinsky friend from the late 1950s; and Aaron Copland, an acquaintance of Stravinsky from the 1920s in Paris, and of mine from Tanglewood in 1946. The program included premieres of the three-trumpet *Agon* fanfare, the flute and cimbalom version of *Sektanskaya*, and of the twelve-instrument version of the March for Alfredo Casella. After the concert three long-ago girlfriends greeted me backstage: Betty Rubinstein, from Barnard College, 1946; Sylvia Pfeiffer from Tanglewood later the same year; and Elaine, the Honolulu Symphony's harpist.

Soon after my return to Pompano, I witnessed two gruesome events. A two-seater stunt plane, flying at low altitude, plunged into the sea not very far offshore, in full view of scores of bathers. Helicopters and boats sped to the scene, but no trace of the plane was ever found. Hours later the body of the female copilot washed ashore just south of our beach. A day later the drowned bodies of thirty-three Haitian refugees were found on the sand at Hillsboro in front of, as if reproachfully, the most expensive homes in the area.

A week later I was in Boston, conducting the orchestra of the New England Conservatory in Jordan Hall in Stravinsky's *Symphonies of Winds*,

2. See chapter 6.

Vom Himmel hoch Variations, *Requiem Canticles,* and four excerpts from *The Flood.* This was the inaugural concert of the Stravinsky centenary that was observed worldwide.

1982

The year began with pourparlers about the New York City Ballet festival planned for June and modeled on the one of 1972. Unlike the earlier celebration, which had been efficiently organized months before, Balanchine had made only one decision: to choreograph *Perséphone* and *The Flood* himself. Initially he came to the Stravinsky apartment with Lincoln Kirstein, but our subsequent meetings took place in his office and at dinners with him and Barbara Horgan, his secretary (and executrix).

In February I conducted concerts, lectured, and participated in symposia at the University of Wisconsin, Madison, and at Carlton College, Minnesota. At the former I met my Columbia summer-school girlfriend of thirty-eight years earlier, Sydney Jacobs, and at the latter the poet John Lucas, with whom I have been in touch ever since. I was reluctant to leave Mrs. Stravinsky for more than a few days at a time, even though she was never alone during my absences. Besides the nurses and the new cook, Mr. Shu, she received the daily visits of such faithful friends as Lucia Davidova, and, during weekends, Ed Allen, from Connecticut.

In Pompano in early May, Phyllis, Kris, and I went to the beach hoping to observe the annual nesting of a herd of sea turtles. Since their eggs are prized as an aphrodisiac, the government protects them. But they did not show up, and we were left wondering whether this year's hatch might have been filled with cocaine. Every night between eight and eleven, lights in an upper floor of the neighboring condominium had been switching on and off in code-like patterns, signals to a darkened ship, we thought, because visible only on the ocean side. This stretch of coast being notorious for drug smuggling, we decided to ask the narcs to investigate, but our call to the police was so unwelcome that our fears increased, and were confirmed a few minutes later when the semaphoring stopped.

Balanchine's preparations proceeded very slowly. Having accepted his invitation to conduct both *Perséphone* and *The Flood,* I impatiently awaited the casting of singers and, in *The Flood,* speakers—eventually only one, John Houseman. Another worry was that long before the City Ballet proposal I had committed myself to direct the Ojai Festival in California on June 4, 5, and 6, in programs that included Haydn's *St. Anton* Divertimento, a Gabrieli Canzone, the Sinfonia from Bach's Cantata No. 174, the *Fidelio* Overture, and *Oedipus Rex.* By June 8, on my return from Los Angeles, I was in New York rehearsing the City Ballet Orchestra. Meanwhile, Leonard Bernstein had invited me to participate in a televised Stravinsky birthday concert in Washington, but the schedule for this proved to be in unresolvable conflict with my rehearsals for a New York Philharmonic concert (*Ebony Concerto, Abraham and Isaac* with John Shirley-Quirk, Mozart's Symphony No. 29, the *Symphony of Psalms*).

By June Balanchine's health—he was suffering from Creutzfeldt-Jakob disease, diagnosed only posthumously, then famously, as "mad-cow" disease—had deteriorated alarmingly. During the first dress rehearsal of *Perséphone*, he decided to repeat the orchestral introduction to Part Three, for the reason, I realized, that this was the only section he had finished choreographing—the remainder of the staging was eventually entrusted to John Taras—though ordinarily Balanchine would have been the first to perceive that this made no sense musically. The City Center Opera chorus was ill-prepared, and the tenor soloist, when he arrived from Germany with a bad cold just in time for the last rehearsal, did not know the music.

A Stravinsky symposium conceived by the musicologist Jann Passler and worked out with me in Boston and New York in November 1981 was moved from the University of Cincinnati in June to the University of California at San Diego in September, following the course of her own teaching career. By the beginning of September I understood that in spite of my year-long involvement with this event, I would not be able to participate in it. Ed Allen went, but Mrs. Stravinsky no longer recognized him when he returned three days before her death, on September 17.

At the New York funeral, Theodore alone of the Stravinsky family— two sons, a daughter, two grandchildren, and a great-granddaughter— acknowledged his stepmother's death with flowers. I packed and sent all of the family valuables, which included several crates of antique silverware, to him and his wife.

On my return to New York from her funeral in Venice, I noticed Herbert Read's and Bonamy Dobrée's *The London Book of English Verse* on the night table by her bed. It had been given to her by Brainerd Smith[3] in October 1949, and she had written three words in Russian on the flyleaf, as well as inserted a brightly colored paper bookmark. I turned to it and found Christina Rossetti's

> *Why were you born when the snow was falling?*
> *You should have come to the cuckoo's calling,*
> *Or when grapes are green in the cluster . . .*
> *[. . .]*
> *Why didn't you die when the lambs were cropping?*

She was born on Christmas Day, and on her second birthday discovered a baby lamb with a blue ribbon around its neck under the tree. She often spoke of this, and must have read the poem shortly before she died.

3. See chapter 5.

The weeks after that were almost as painful as those after Stravinsky's death. Every connection with my thirty-five-year Stravinsky past was now severed, including the one with my home of the last eleven years. I had loved the spacious Fifth Avenue apartment, its fourteen rooms three times the size of Gloria Swanson's on the ground floor, but could not bear to live alone in it. In any case, the bylaws of the co-op did not permit nonfamily heirs to reside there, a rule intended to prevent elderly and possibly non-compos owners from bequeathing their apartments to their servants. But I was unable to sell the residence and for four more years had to borrow in order to meet the astronomical monthly maintenance payments.

After only a few days in New York, the woman looking after my mother in Florida called to say that the eighty-five-year-old lady had become subject to fainting spells and could not be left alone. I went to her immediately, but soon had to return to New York in connection with the Stravinsky family litigation. In November, I conducted a concert in San Antonio and fled from there to Florida and a dismal holiday season.

1983

The event of the year was the reunion with my son. This was unanticipated, since all of my requests to see him during the ten-year separation had been refused. Before my every trip to Europe I had written to his mother seeking permission to visit him in Copenhagen or, alternatively, inviting her and a friend to come with him to another place of her choice. Her restrictions were always the same: a rendezvous could take place only in Copenhagen, out of doors, on a busy street rather than in a park, and at a location to be designated in a telephone call a few minutes before. She herself would not be present; Alexander would be accompanied by one of his uncles; and I would have to be alone. The spy-novel scenario indicated a fear, however unrealistic, that I entertained thoughts of kidnapping the child. Since neither of his family bodyguards nor he himself could speak a word of English, I wondered about the productiveness of sign-language exchanges on a crowded sidewalk.

At this time I did not know that when I finally gave up, my mother had continued to write to Alexander's mother. Then a telephone call from her to my mother revealed that he had seen me in Tony Palmer's televised Stravinsky documentary and wanted to meet me. His eleventh birthday was chosen as an appropriate time, and the conditions were that I provide round-trip tickets from Denmark for him, his mother, and one of her sisters serving as duenna, as well as transportation and accommodation for a side trip to Disney World. On February 16 I drove nervously to Miami airport to meet their flight. The tired threesome was there ahead of me and waiting with their bags on a curb. My son, a handsome eleven-year-old, extended his hand for a gentlemanly shake, but I swept him up and hugged him instead. Although he had been taught no English, and every word had to be translated, the visit was happy and successful. After it I took them to New York to stay in the Stravinsky apartment on their return journey.

At the end of March, I had to be in New York again to effect the transfer of Stravinsky's manuscripts and archives from his apartment to New York's Library of the Performing Arts. Soon after Vera Stravinsky's death an attorney for the Stravinsky heirs demanded the removal of the entire collection to the supposedly neutral ground and safekeeping of the Library. Though relieved of the responsibility for these uninsured treasures, I realized that the Library would microfilm them and thus reduce their value for a prospective buyer. The transfer was completed after days of sorting, counting, and signing-over, by me and Thor Wood, the chief music librarian. The difficulties of our work were compounded by discrepancies in physical descriptions and page counts between the two catalogs respectively prepared in 1969 by Andre Marion, Stravinsky's son-in-law, and in 1970 by Sigmund Rothshild, a government-accredited tax appraiser.

The archives—correspondence, photographs, clippings, family papers, etc.—could not be checked at all, for the reason that the microfilms of them, made without supervision in Hollywood in 1967–68, did not follow either a chronological or a subject order, and the task of identifying and describing the contents of the hundred or so boxes would have taken more than a year. As I feared, the Library immediately made its own microfilm, in violation of the contract agreement, and the collection was pirated in New York a full year before its exhibition in the Basel Kunstmuseum by the new owner, the Paul Sacher Stiftung.

At the end of April, I flew to London with my attorney, Martin Garbus, to meet with Albi Rosenthal, the musicologist and dealer in manuscripts who had been commissioned by Paul Sacher to acquire the Stravinsky *Nachlass*. I went on to Venice to look after the Stravinsky graves, and from there to Rome, where my friend Jane Panni drove me to Giacomo Manzù's home at Ardea to discuss the tombstone he had promised for Vera Stravinsky. I understood at once that he would not provide the *pietra*, and that I would have to employ a Venetian *marmorista* to copy Stravinsky's. Visitors to the grave note that her stone lacks Manzù's signature.

In New York, on June 20, the lawyers for the Stravinsky Trust offered his manuscripts and archives for sale, but only one bidder appeared, John Fleming, a New York dealer representing the Fred R. Koch Foundation as donor for the Pierpont Morgan Library. Rosenthal, representing Sacher, telephoned to Garbus that he would not compete against Koch because "his oil and pipeline fortune is unlimited." Fleming named his top price, $4.5 million, and his condition, that if not accepted by 5:30 P.M. that day, he would withdraw. Garbus called to say: "It is a little difficult to walk away from Fleming's four and a half when his previous offer was two." I replied that Albi knew the real value of the collection and would top the figure. The Koch Foundation's questions about the contents revealed that they were bidding for a prestigious, but to them wholly unknown, property. Fleming promised to keep his bid secret, at which point Garbus *did* walk away from it.

The next day Albi accused the Stravinsky Trust of dealing unfairly with Sacher, the terms of whose bona fide offer of $3.5 million, made in London on April 27 in my presence, were that the bid would stand for thirty days. The New York Public Library, custodian of the documents since March 26, contended that it had not been properly informed of the Sacher offer, and demanded a second thirty-day period, May 17 to June 17, for a fund-raising campaign. But this worked against the Library by attracting publicity and other bidders. At the end of the afternoon, Stravinsky's children instructed their lawyers to accept Koch's bid.

The following day Albi insisted that Garbus disclose Koch's offer, and that Sacher be allowed to match or improve it. Realizing that a leak would soon occur from Fleming or the Stravinsky children's lawyers, Garbus decided to send an acceptance agreement to Albi for the sale price of $5.25 million. "Sacher is away," Albi said, and Garbus responded: "But you know where he is, and a three-minute telephone call can conclude the purchase."

On the following day Albi told the children's lawyers that his top offer was $5 million. They quickly accepted, but Garbus refused, as I had asked him to do on grounds that in two years the collection would be worth at least $10 million, and by the end of the century five times that. Perhaps fearing a postponement, during which Koch would have the materials appraised, Albi at 2:11 P.M. signed the $5.25 million acceptance agreement. Stravinsky would have been amused to know that Valium and Librium (Sacher's fortune came from the F. Hoffman-LaRoche Pharmaceutical Company, found guilty of the thalidomide horrors and punished for them by a tap-on-the-wrist penalty of $600 million), had purchased his manuscripts, and that a drug manufacturer had reimbursed his heirs a millionfold for his lifelong expenditure on medications. Albi cabled to Sacher: *"Librium vincit omnia."*

In the summer I began to suffer from a recurring dream in which I was aware of being in a gondola, and of familiar other people being in one behind me. We stopped by a wall that I recognized as the canal front of S. Giorgio dei Greci, where Vera Stravinsky's funeral had taken place. In the courtyard, near the entrance, was a discarded self-portrait of her. (While preparing to change apartments I had trashed a badly damaged painting of hers—not a portrait, which she would never have attempted—and had been feeling guilty about it ever since.) Without transition, the passengers in the other gondola were inside a single room with the dimensions of the Greci gathered around her, whereas I was outside, unable to enter, watching through the upper window like the levitate Nicolas of Bari. Only one person, her friend Adriana Panni, was clearly recognizable. She embraced Mrs. Stravinsky, the features of whose face were indistinct. This reliving of the funeral continued to haunt me.

I stopped in London on my return to see Tony Fell of Boosey & Hawkes, and a performance of *Lulu* at Covent Garden. Götz Friedrich's production extended the menagerie metaphor of the Prologue through the opera. The stage arena and all of its entrances, including an elevator—the set had two levels—were cages, and the Animal Trainer of the Prologue reappeared to gloat upon each act of destruction resulting from involvement with Lulu. The part was accurately sung and perfectly enacted by my old California girlfriend, Karen Armstrong, now Frau Friedrich. In her first entrance, as a serpent, she rolled downstage on a gangplank wrapped in headless, armless, and legless black leather. Also on the plus side, the Act 2 film and its music were exactly coordinated, and in Act 3, Lulu as prostitute believably engaged her outdoors clients behind an open umbrella. On the minus, the director should have found ways of preventing the audience from laughing at the death of the Medizinalrat, and from giggling after each of Schigolch's asthmatic wheezes. But the opera itself disappointed me. Much of the thematic material seemed weak; the one-dimensional atonal harmony was exasperating; and the snarling muted brass and repeated *Hauptrhythmus* became monotonous. Nor did the completed Act 3 support the myth that Geschwitz is the one interesting character. The part is only slightly enlarged, and though her lesbian *Liebestod* remains the musical and dramatic high point, she does not have a single speech half as long as two or three by the insufferable Athlete.

In late October, after festivities marking my semi-centenarian birthday, I drove my mother and Phyllis to New Hampshire to see a friend. On the way, we visited Herman Melville's Arrowhead home near Pittsfield, which could be entered only through a souvenir shop, and only in groups. Although no more than four or five objects in the house belonged to Melville, a guide discoursed on the furniture and everything else at *Pierre*-like length (but mercifully without the archaic diction: "Oh, now methinks I a little see why of old men of Truth went barefoot"). No literary pilgrim, I bolted and resolved not to visit R. L. Stevenson's home in the Adirondacks, Kipling's in Vermont, or Thomas Hardy's in Maine.

My picture album, *A Stravinsky Scrapbook,* was published on November 28.

1984

Driving my mother and Phyllis to Florida in February, I noticed for the first time that beginning in the tall-barn tobacco country of South Carolina, most billboard faces are black. Having covered the distance from New York to North Carolina the day before, we stopped early in a Holiday Inn on the southwest curve of the Jacksonville beltway. After dinner I found my room stocked with unfamiliar clothes and baggage. The desk clerk told me that the previous occupant had checked out, but apparently kept the duplicate key and returned without reregistering. I was given another room but warned that the duplicate key was also missing, an unsettling thought, if only for the reason that a revolver was visible in the left hip pocket of the man at the next table in the restaurant.

The blight of roadside advertisements, and the quality of their jokes, worsened with the proximity to the Gold Coast. A restaurant sign said: "Chile today, hot tamale"; a sign for a hotel read, "Put Yourself in Our Place"; a bank ad with picture of a glitzy boat was captioned "Make Yachts of Money"; and another for a real estate development said, "What the World Is Coming To." Billboards on Federal Highway at the Pompano exit offered "Adult Motels," "Agape Lighthouses," and a "Centerfold Club" featuring two nudes, "Ms Illinois" and "Ms Kansas" (why "Ms" in these bastions of male chauvinism?). And what about "Wet T-shirts" (at "The Playpen")? No matter how torrid the atmosphere, mightn't someone catch cold? René Char's line came to mind: *"Tu as bien fait de partir Arthur Rimbaud."* On Federal Highway, Moonies sold flower bouquets at main intersections. An ad for Baird-Case Funeral Homes in Fort Lauderdale's *Sun Sentinel* was selling "Pre-paid Cremations." The customer need only mail in a coupon, placing an "X" next to his/her preference. Scatterings of ashes at sea are more expensive.

In mid-May we began our homeward trek, our automobile overloaded with possessions, including my collection of Indian miniatures. Since we had no room for bags, we stacked books, clothes, household items from floor to ceiling and in every cranny of the car and its trunk. Near Charleston in late afternoon, we strolled through the Magnolia Gardens, and stayed at the Francis Marion Hotel in the city. The next day we reached Florence, South Carolina, in heavy Saturday midtown traffic. The driver immediately in front of us stopped suddenly instead of making a left turn as signaled, and though I quickly applied our brakes, we skidded into his rear bumper. Fortunately no one in the front car, nor the car itself, was hurt, but our front was staved in, and my mother, asleep in the back seat, was thrown to the floor. Phyllis, next to me, though protected by her seat belt, was badly shaken, and I was pinned between the pushed-back steering wheel and my seat. Within moments the police and an ambulance were at the scene.

After the police and medics extricated me, I joined my mother in the ambulance, where she was electrically monitored. Phyllis rode with the driver. While the two of them were X-rayed in a nearby hospital, I described the accident to a polite state trooper, who drove me to an auto rental agency and to a compound containing our damaged car. He even helped me to transfer our possessions to a rented car—except that no vehicle was large enough for us and all of our cargo. This greatly complicated the continuation of our journey: rental cars could not be taken as far as New York, to fly home would involve transfers with long layovers, and only one Florida–New York train stopped in Florence, at four in the morning.

The courteous cop led me to a motel, where I rented rooms, then back to the hospital, where the patients were soon released. My eighty-six-year-old mother was contused to the color of a purple cow, but she walked unaided and with the same presence of mind shown from the first in having me check the daily medications in her purse.

We could do nothing about our smashed automobile on Sunday, but the next morning I had it towed to a garage. Here we saw a Mercedes undergoing what seemed to be a very minor repair. I proposed to purchase it, partly by a trade-in of our wrecked car. The terms were fair and the transaction was soon completed. The next day, after retransferring our belongings from the rented to the new car, we drove to a motel near the Virginia border. My mother's "blues" quickly disappeared, but she suffered spells of internal bleeding and nosebleeds thereafter, and on reaching home spent a week in the hospital.

In June, I traveled by way of Copenhagen to conduct three concerts in Karlsruhe. I saw Alexander's home for the first time, his school, and some of his friends. Karlsruhe is a charmless industrial city, its orchestra only a notch or so above competent. The French-speaking concertmistress, from Alsace, was helpful, and my friend the violinist Rolf Schulte played the Stravinsky Concerto with me in all three concerts. I enjoyed conducting a Beethoven Symphony, and I dined in the evenings at a delightful small inn in Ettlingen.

After the concerts I was driven to Basel by my German concert agent, Ruth Übel, to see the Kunstmuseum's huge—several-story—exhibition of Stravinsky manuscripts, documents, pictures, photographs, programs. Seeing this display, whose contents I had lived with for so long, was a shock, as was seeing my exclusion from the presentation of his last twenty-three years, to the extent that the recto of the Picasso drawing that he gave and affectionately inscribed to me had been turned to the wall so that the spectator saw only the verso, blank except for a three-line inked-in frame and a doodle. Hans Busch and his wife Caroline, stage directors I had known in Santa Fe, were there as well, but the crowd was so dense that I could not make my way through it to greet them.

The next day Alexander and his mother met me in London, and we spent an afternoon together at Sissinghurst, where Victoria Sackville-West is still a presence in the gardens and Tudor tower; one imagines her irrorating the buds and pruning the rose bushes. Of her celebrated one-color flowerbeds, only the white survives—in roses, peonies, dahlias, anemones, foxgloves, delphiniums, campanulas. (Together with fruit and potables, flowers seem to offer the closest comparisons for colors: buttercup-yellow, apple-green, vin-rosé Daphne.)

From London we continued to New York, where Alexander stayed on with me when his mother returned home. He came back to New York for the holidays and after New Year's departed for Copenhagen, while I flew to Milan for concerts in Padova, Mestre, Venice.

The burden of the monthly maintenance payments on the ghostly Stravinsky apartment, a constant anxiety, would continue for three more years. The desuetude of my home of fourteen years was apparent to prospective buyers, and I dreaded going there to show it to them.

1985

In May a French real-estate speculator made an offer for the Stravinsky apartment, backed with a 10 percent surety. The closing was to take place on the same day as my purchase of an apartment in Trump Tower, acquired on the assurance of a lawyer-friend heavily invested there that it could easily be resold at a substantial profit. (In fact I waited seventeen months before being able to sell it at a substantial loss.) At the appointed hour for the closing I went to the office of the buyer's attorney, only to find it locked. Monsieur had changed his mind, and a loophole in our agreement saved him from forfeiting his deposit.

Early in June, I spent several days with Alexander in Copenhagen. At the end of the month he came to New York by himself, and I drove him, my sister, and mother to Washington. After some sightseeing, we were joined by my grandnephew, Jonathan Rumble, four years younger than my son, at a railroad terminal in Lorton, Virginia, where we loaded our car on the overnight auto-train to Orlando. From there, emerging sleepless from our Wagon-Lit in the early morning, we drove to Cape Canaveral and its space museum, and on to Pompano.

In mid-July my son and I rode the jitney from Manhattan to the Hamptons, where we were houseguests of Jean Stein. We swam, bicycled, ping-ponged, and—unwisely, since we capsized—canoed, which left me without a change of clothes. When Alexander expressed a wish to visit a New York disco, Jean persuaded Victoria Leacock, a lovely young lady whose father had filmed Rolf Liebermann's Stravinsky documentary, to escort us to the Coliseum. Alexander being too obviously underage, we were not admitted, but we had better luck at the Area Club, where the clientele was almost entirely transvestite (boys will be girls), which I would not have known if not told. From the Area we were jostled along to a party on a boat moored in the Hudson River in the vicinity of Twenty-ninth Street. I wanted to depart immediately but had no means of transportation and was wary of walking in that neighborhood in the middle of the night. A friend of Victoria volunteered to drive us to a taxi stand but, being in an intoxicated state, collided on the way with another vehicle, driver in a similar condition, luckily without serious consequences. What was an exciting time for my adolescent son was a nightmare for me.

At the end of August, I accompanied Phyllis and my mother on a visit to a friend in a coastal town in Maine, stopping on the way for a few days in the Ritz-Carlton on Boston Common. In September I escorted Barbara Epstein to a New York City Opera performance of the *Rake*. The first duet, "In carefree May," had never sounded so despairing, partly because the singers were only sporadically in sync with the always-too-loud orchestra. Shadow's "The Progress of a Rake Begins" was followed by the lowering of the curtain in a totally dark house for seven minutes of backstage hammering and the crash of falling props. When the hero, in his London flat, asked "Is it for this I left the country?" the apartment-weary New York audience exploded with laughter. In Act 2, when he and the betrothed he has betrayed encounter each other in the street at night, neither showed the slightest surprise, despite their exclamations of startlement. The bread machine was a miserable pushcart instead of the splendid baroque contraption with wheels, funnels, pipes, pistons that it should have been, and nobody caught Auden's off-color joke: "Did your machine look anything like this?" But the zenith of zilch came when Shadow, prostrating himself in a coffin for his infernal exit, had to struggle with its resisting lid.

In October, Rita and Alexander came to Florida and then to New York, where I had wanted to enroll him in the United Nations School. Rita had agreed to stay with him in my apartment for three months, during which I would live in Florida. Jean Stein kindly arranged an interview with Brian Urquehart, the director of the school, but despite Rita's as well as my urgings, Alexander opted to return to Denmark. We drove to New Paltz to see my mother, who was struggling with walking pneumonia. Not being confident of her recovery, I discouraged Alexander from returning at Christmas.

On my birthday, October 20, Jean organized a party for me, Alexander, and his mother at an Italian restaurant in the East Fifties. At cake time a group of costumed Fellini-like revelers appeared and serenaded me, among them Ms. Leacock, easily recognizable under her disguise. Afterward we went to an exhibition of masks at Japan House.

In November I answered a request from *The New York Times Book Review* to contribute to a symposium on "What would you ask for from a Christmas muse?":

Poetry, the smallest mite, the tiniest touch of the wand to inspire the trying. I began with it, wrote nothing else, published a few attempts in the little mags of the 1950s, have not destroyed the folders full of failures. Trying to write it, one labors for oneself only, during the only time when impatience can be conquered. The joy of fitting a word, of combining two words, three . . . but that is already a hoard. Oh the waste of words in all other writing! *"Victorieusement fui le suicide beau."* Whatever Mallarmé meant, I like to imagine his pleasure when the startling adverb came to him. My heroes are poets. I have rejoiced in the unearned privilege of spending evenings with Eliot, days and weeks with Auden, two hours with Dylan Thomas, occasions with Cocteau, lunches with St.-John Perse, Henri Michaux, Borges, Robert Graves, dinners with Ingeborg Bachmann, Joseph Brodsky, Robert Lowell, lunch with Horace Gregory, Robert Penn Warren, a long afternoon with Marianne Moore, minutes with Eugenio Montale. I venerate them all.

Later in the month I went to an exhibition of Vera Stravinsky's paintings in the Imprimatur Gallery in St. Paul, Minnesota, a moving occasion for me, as I had not seen the pictures since her death and the 1970s exhibitions in London and Paris. They were perceptively juxtaposed by Christopher Frommer, the Gallery's co-proprietor with Mark Roberts. At a formal dinner after the opening, I was wedged between a woman who wanted to talk about George Steiner and Isaiah Berlin, and the Swiss conductor Charles Dutoit, there on a guest stint, who wanted to talk about music.

1986

During the first three months of the year I lived in Phyllis's home in New Paltz, helping to care for my mortally ill mother. Two or three nights a week I drove to New York after she was asleep and would not know that I had gone, to look after business affairs in my Manhattan apartment, returning between 3 and 4 A.M.

A little more than a year before, she had been given a choice between certain death in three to four months or having a kidney removed and possibly living longer, a high-risk, less-than-even-chance because of her eighty-eight years and damaged heart. She faced it with incredible pluck and the night before the surgery walked around the corridor of her floor in the Benedictine Hospital in Kingston with me and each of my sisters in turn, telling us about God's will and how we must be brave. At four o'clock the next afternoon, near breaking point after six hours in the waiting room, I was paged to the telephone—me, not one of my sisters, I feared, because bad news is broken to the man of the family. The surgeon said: "Your mother came through the operation; you can see her in about twenty minutes." Turning to my sisters and niece, all that I could choke out was: "Our great mother." A few months later I accompanied her to Florida by train, and in August drove her, as aforesaid, to Boston and Maine. But back in New Paltz her attacks of arrhythmia became more frequent, and in October pneumonia struck. After that the coughing from her bedroom was almost continual.

We realized that she could not live much longer, but my own and Phyllis's attitudes toward the impending death could hardly have been more dissimilar. Phyllis attempted to apply a death-acceptance psychology that counseled her to discuss the question openly with my mother. They read the obits of her coevals in the local newspaper together, and Phyllis went so far as to encourage her to write her own. I objected to this and pretended to her that she was gaining strength and would recover in the spring, now only a few weeks away. She did not believe me. "I am not getting any better," she would say, not despairingly but to help prepare me. "Bob so terribly wants me to get better," she told Phyllis, who opposed my acceptance of the tragic sense of life—Unamuno's "Man who dies and does not want to die"—with arguments about psychological and mental "preparation," as if death could be domesticated. My mother held on to life and fought for it every bit of the way. However, when discussing reincarnation with Phyllis, who believed in it, she became irate and said, "I am not coming back here. Once is enough."

In the third week of March, I conducted three rehearsals and a staged performance, in Tully Hall, New York, of *Histoire du Soldat*, with Tony Randall playing the Devil. Expecting each moment to be notified of the death, I had arranged for a substitute conductor, but the indomitable old lady stayed alive until after the concert, simply, as she told me, by resolving to do so. Alexander's school vacation coincided with the concert, and he came from Denmark to spend a week with me at Lake Mohonk. Our chief pastime there was table tennis, a game I usually won, though he was the better player, from which he may have learned something about psychological warfare.

During most of March my mother remained in her bedroom, but when I drove up from New York after my rehearsals, she made her way down the hall and called feebly from the top of the stairs: "Coming down," whence I helped her descend slowly from step to step and to the dinner table. When I kissed her forehead in the last days and she did not respond, I said, "Mother, you taught us that we should not receive without giving," after which I felt a gentle peck on my cheek, or the tips of her fingers touching my face.

Two weeks before she died, a hospital bed was installed downstairs, where she could listen to music—Orlando di Lasso's by her preference, over Monteverdi's dramatic *Vespers*. At about the same time we were blessed with the arrival of Andrée Ehrlich, a young charity worker from a nearby Hutterian work-sharing, wealth-sharing, Judeo-Christian community resettled from Germany via Paraguay, whose only condition was that we would not expose her to television or newspapers. Her family visited in the evenings and sang Bach around my mother's bed. Andrée, as bright in mood as her colorful cotton dress and bandanna, brought new light to our lives, and my mother responded to her, ate more when fed by her, and made greater efforts to sit up and to turn in bed.

We siblings grew up believing that our father was the "brains" of the family, partly because he could do math in his head, was quick-thinking, witty, caustic, and had always been first in his classes and valedictorian in his schools. He was wiry and fast-moving in body, quarterback on his Syracuse University team. A born debater, in his last years he often seemed to use his good command of English primarily to contradict me. But he placed a higher value on learning and the arts than anyone else in his society, seeking out and introducing me to the most interesting among the refugees from Germany who, in the 1930s, settled in the Woodstock and Catskill Mountain area. I remember a visit with him to an elderly musician near Saugerties who disparaged my discovery of Sibelius by comparing the opening of *Finlandia* with the opening of the *Coriolanus* Overture: "Beethoven keeps going."

My anti-clerical, church-avoiding, skeptical father ridiculed my mother's religion. He chided her for failing to appreciate his repartee, to see the joke, and it is true that she did not. Later we understood that the conflict between his wishful thinking and her plain-truth reality was deep, and that his scathing tongue and devastating comments offended her. But he was also a generous, kind-hearted man who gave secretly to people in need. My mother deflated his ego and punctured his pride. All pride was false, she said, while distinguishing it from amour propre. And while my mother may have been overemotional, my father was afraid of emotion, or emotionally immature. In old age, affection flowed from her, but he suppressed it in himself and turned away from it in others. There is more of him in me than of her, though she was the stronger character.

My mother used to say that while carrying me she played the piano from morning to night, and my earliest postnatal awareness of music is of her daily playing and singing. But though music was her gift, her vocation was to teach. I must believe what she wrote about herself in *The Kingston Daily Freeman*, that after her own children had grown up, teaching came first. How I admired her for going back to school to take refresher courses. How pleased she would be to know that the Ulster County Legislature adjourned in her memory on the day of her funeral, and that a ninety-year-old gentleman, last survivor of her class in Kingston Academy, came from Schenectady to place flowers on her grave.

My mother was the strict, implacable parent, my father the soft-touch, lenient one. She did not punish me the day when, trailing me to Public School No. 7, she caught me removing my galoshes and hiding them behind a tree (only sissies wore them); or the time after my recovery from measles when she found that I had been squirreling pills in the keyhole of my bedroom door. But when I returned from No. 7 one day with a coarse acquisition to my vocabulary, she literally washed my mouth out with soap, and when she found me with an older boy trading puffs on a cigarette that he had filched from his father, made me inhale one of my father's cigars until I was ill. I knew that "there would be the dickens to pay" when the mother of one of my younger sister's girlfriends complained that I had gone too far playing doctor and nurse, but I got off with being docked two weeks' allowance.

I never knew what either of my parents really thought about my relationship with the Stravinskys, apart from my mother's disappointment that, so she imagined, I gave up a career as a conductor to stay with them. I wonder if either my mother or father was ever wounded by gossip suggesting that I had exchanged my dowdy parents for glamorous ones, though both of them knew that from a very early age I had dedicated my life to music. The pain I live with now is that I came home for birthdays and holidays only rarely and spent most of them with the Stravinskys. In all my thirty-four Stravinsky years, my mother's letters, with their incidental sermons on right and wrong and no compromises, encouraged me, telling me that the Stravinskys needed me, that he was my destiny, and that what I did for him was important. She wanted me to give more time to conducting and to write different kinds of books: honey catches more flies than vinegar, she used to say of my review articles. What I should have written was a memoir for her—about our summer picnics at the Ashokan reservoir, our hikes to the top of Overlook Mountain, our drives in the Catskills, excursions to Kingston Point, the Dutchess County Fair and the Danbury Fair, riding the Rhinecliff Ferry past the lonely lighthouse in the Hudson beyond Rondout—about my love-filled childhood.

My mother was strong-willed, resolute, powerfully determined, independent, and highly structured: everything from spring and autumn housecleaning to Monday washday had its inalterable time. And place: we shelled nuts by the blue-tile dining room fireplace, worked on our stamp albums by the reddish-tile hall fireplace, played word games by the white-tile library fireplace. Most of our childhood games were educational, lessons in disguise. She was also compulsive, a compulsive worker, compulsive finisher of whatever she started, compulsive, perhaps, even in her charities: I remember the "sunshine baskets" that she used to fill up and take to hospitals, and the "club" she founded for the old and infirm called, speaking of euphemisms, "The Golden Age."

These fading older pictures are pushed away by sad later ones that intensify the regret for past happiness—or, as Eliot says, "What seems happiness when it is past." (Jane Austen, in *Sense and Sensibility*, places it in the future: "That sanguine expectation of happiness which is happiness itself.")

Reliving my mother's death, I am haunted by the ruminative, from-somewhere-beyond look in her eyes the afternoon before, as she emerged from deep slumber and intently studied my face. I left her reluctantly in order to drive Alexander to Kennedy Airport. On returning to New Paltz I found that her fever had vaulted and her pulse become wildly irregular. Still, she knew me, which may not have been the case in the afternoon.

Cranking up the hospital bed, I lifted her to the commode next to it, then removed her damp nightgown and replaced it with my pajama top. A few minutes after I had carried her emaciated body back to bed, the death rattle began—when she stopped breathing. I waited alone with her in the dark for several minutes before calling my sleeping sisters and niece Diane. Then I drove to Kingston, where the funeral would take place, and stayed in a motel. The next day I met with the minister who would conduct the service and chose texts with him, but I did not look in the direction of the coffin in the funeral "parlor."

The most terrible moment came not in Wiltwyck Cemetery ("Thou art the grave where buried love doth live"), but earlier, arriving for the funeral at St. John's Church and seeing the announcement of the service in a glass-covered case on the lawn: "Arpha Lawson Craft 1897–1986"—"Arpha," one of the Noah family; what led her parents to choose the name? The dates struck me like the "1882–1971" over the television screen on the day that Stravinsky died, the open end closed, the life completed and belonging to past time, "past perfect" time.

We were closest during my years in the choir in this church, where I learned so much music. When she visited La Scala in Milan in July 1963, shortly after I had conducted there, and saw a poster with my name, she told my father that she pictured me in her mind's eye as a choirboy. From the fifty cents a week I earned as a soprano soloist, I saved five dollars to buy her a Christmas present, a glass ship with sails of translucent shells floating on a blue-mirror sea. Fifty years later she told my sisters that this was her favorite of all gifts she had ever received. *"Je voudrais être enfant encore, avoir ma mère."* Laforgue's cry is achingly poignant.

At a Christmas Eve in St. John's only a few years ago, we stood together as she faintly sang hymns and recited prayers ("We have left undone those things which we ought to have done; and we have done those things which we ought not to have done") from books that she had opened for me but did not need to read herself. In this same place for her funeral, the female Hudson Valley Philharmonic String Quartet played Mozart's *Ave Verum* and the Adagio from Beethoven's last quartet. When a tenor, Henry Peyer, a friend of my mother, sang Tennyson's corny "Crossing the Bar," requested by her long ago and anticipated ever since with tears, I pulled the hairs on the back of my hand in an attempt not to cry.

After the service I gave a champagne-luncheon wake for my sisters' friends at New Paltz's Locust Tree Inn, where I had dined so many times with my mother. The last to arrive and disoriented, I looked at the empty chair that had been kept for me at the family's table, and said to Phyllis, "But where is mother?" I could not eat, but as soon as the observance was over, drove off on back roads by the Hurley Mountain to Woodstock, and to Pine Grove,

West Saugerties. No trace of my music camp survived, and the area was crowded with new houses. Dreading the thought of being alone in Florida, I went to the house of my sister Patricia, which overlooked the Hudson River at Port Ewen, and persuaded her and her husband to drive me to New York, then drive themselves to Florida.

Flying to Florida myself, I was surprised to find in the accumulated mail an intelligent and sympathetic review of my *Chronicle of a Friendship* by Paul Driver, music critic of the (London) *Sunday Times*. Dated January 23, 1986, and published in the *London Review of Books*, it is the most acute of the numerous speculations about my role in Stravinsky's life. The article quoted a sentence from the Cambridge philosopher Michael Tanner: "[Stravinsky's] prose is the greatest English prose of our time." Driver elaborated on this as follows:

> Craft's essayist prose is indistinguishable from what is ostensibly Stravinsky's in his answers to interview questions or in the various articles attributed to him . . . No one who has heard him talking on film or disc could credit him with the grasp of syntax and the virtuoso vocabulary required to produce a written result as coruscating, elaborate, searching, witty, and altogether remarkable . . . Only Nabokov, I take it, among émigré Russian *writers*, would have been thus capable, and I doubt whether even he could have essayed such mannered sentences as "My temperament and Mr. Cage's are hopelessly miscage-nated and his performances are often to me the frustration of time itself." Would Stravinsky have been inclined or able to use an expression like "alcoholic moistures?" . . .
>
> . . . The most satisfying interviews are those which are the most judiciously "worked up." . . . The influential dialogues of our culture, from Plato . . . have been the most conscientiously elaborated, while verbatim reporting essentially belongs to journalism. Robert Craft's industry, dedication and literary skill not only make more palatable the two books under review, but have elsewhere gone on to devise a persona in which Stravinsky could say, in English, the most marvellous and necessary things.
>
> I haven't doubted that the flow of the dialogues, their factual content and the angles of vision are very largely determined by the involvement of Stravinsky's mind . . . On the other hand the patina of the prose, the nuances of literary style, make all the difference in presenting Stravinsky, not as he *was*, but as a creation of Craft's. In the preface to his *Chronicle of a Friendship*, the latter insisted that he lacked "the novelist's talent that can make 'ordinary' people interesting." The "extraordinary ones," he went on, "take care of themselves with very little help from me." With a little help from him, Stravinsky, and indeed Auden (superbly evoked throughout the *Chronicle*), have been shaded off into fictional characters. We should be grateful for this.

In an effort to put the death out of mind, I adopted an early morning regimen of reading and writing, partly to meet two deadlines. Before leaving New York, I had found someone to look after my apartment and to do my word-processing.

I badly needed, wanted Alexander, and two weeks later flew to Copenhagen. This was the day, as it happened, of the Chernobyl disaster. Warnings had been posted at the airport that all Scandinavia was threatened with fallout, and so the very next day I returned to New York with him. On entering my apartment, we discovered an unknown young woman word-processing an unknown someone else's work. *The New York Review of Books* found a new computer operator for me, but, understanding little about the machine, he permanently erased more than a hundred pages of a book I had been working on. On the first of the next month I discovered that the same young woman had added more than five hundred dollars to my telephone bill in calls to her brother in Brussels.

After returning by way of Pompano to Mohonk, I took Alexander to London, where we stayed in the Connaught and undertook excursions to Oxford, Blenheim, Stratford, and Warwick Castle. After a week in Venice, and a few days in a quiet lakeside hotel outside Frankfurt, we flew to Copenhagen, where Rita told me she was contemplating remarriage and wanted Alexander to live with me for a time and go to school in the United States. On hearing this, he became recalcitrant and began to avoid me.

At the end of September both the Stravinsky apartment and the one in Trump Tower were sold, only a day apart. I shipped my most treasured possessions to Florida, stored the others, and moved to the Surrey Hotel on East Seventh-sixth Street. At the end of October, I drove with Phyllis to Amherst. A new book about the affair between Emily Dickinson's married brother, Austin, and their neighbor, Mabel, wife of the fully cognizant and unconcerned David Todd, piqued my curiosity to see the Dickinson home and Austin's, next door. But the visit overstrained credibility. How could Emily, who had never met Mabel and was seen by no one except her brother and his wife, act as watchdog during his very frequent noontime adulteries with Mrs. Todd on the Homestead dining-room couch? Why was there no danger of his wife stopping by on an errand?

Emily's preoccupation with death—"I noticed people disappearing / When but a little child"; "A wounded Deer / Leaps highest/I've heard the Hunter tell / 'Tis but the Ecstasy of *death*"; "'Twas just this time last year, I died"—haunted me more after the tour than before. On the way back to New Paltz, after leaving the poet's tombstone, my genealogy-minded sister explained our exceedingly remote connection to the great poet. It seems that we share a common Huguenot descent, from Hugo Frère, with Doris Frerichs, of the Juilliard piano faculty, my former teacher, whose grandmother was Emily Dickinson's first cousin. In 1715, Frère's son was one of 250 signatories to a declaration of allegiance to George the First, whom Louis XIV and the Pope were trying to unseat in favor of the Pretender James III, the self-proclaimed Prince of Wales under James II.

Phyllis told me that the Huguenot Society Archives, in the crypt under New Paltz's beautiful French church, contain a collection of Bibles, in Latin, French, Dutch, English, and one in a mixture of French and Dutch. As late as 1800 Dutch was apparently spoken in the vicinity of Kingston, and French in New Paltz. Indeed, the services in Saint Esprit, the Huguenot church on Sixty-first Street between Park and Lexington Avenues in New York, are still in French. I shall have to read up on Calvinism, since I know only Hazlitt's imaginary conversation between Calvin and Malancthon.

Also in October, Alexander, along with his mother, cousin, aunt, and uncle vacationed in my cramped and only partly furnished Florida condominium. After two confrontational evenings I retreated to New York, taking Alexander with me, confused though he was in his loyalties. By this time I had a new secretary, Julie Hartley, wife of a documentary filmmaker I had met in Minneapolis, who apartment-hunted for me, the Surrey being both rickety and expensive. She was accompanied on these expeditions by Alva Celauro, a charming lady working in real estate and recommended by my lawyer Robert Solomon. Thanks to her ministrations, on the last day of December I purchased an aerie on Central Park South. Meanwhile, I returned to my Florida apartment in Pompano to oversee the redecorating. Alexander came before Christmas and we drove to New York via Savannah and Washington.

1987

My newly acquired New York property not yet being habitable, I spent New Year's Eve in the Sherry Netherlands Hotel, joined by Alexander, Phyllis, and Jonathan Rumble. We drove to Battery Park, where Alexander had his first glimpse of the Statue of Liberty, then across the Brooklyn Bridge (same purpose), and, minutes before midnight, through Times Square. On January 1 my sister Patricia called from Kingston's Benedictine Hospital saying that a biopsy revealed inoperable cancer of the throat. A heavy snowfall prevented us from going to her. To relieve tensions we spent the evening in a mock snowball fight near the Wallman skating rink in Central Park. In the Benedictine the next day we heard an Indian surgeon brutally repeat the death sentence to us in front of the victim.

Feeling unable to face another deathwatch so soon after the one for my mother, I retreated to Florida to sort out the jetsam of my life and what remained to me of the Stravinskys' lives. Christopher Frommer came from Minneapolis to help, bringing his word-processor secretary, Lorelei, with him.

In February, I was in New York to audition singers for my March concert and to visit Patricia, now in Lenox Hill Hospital undergoing chemo-therapy. Back in Florida, I filed a lawsuit for plagiarism against John Kobler, who had written an inept biography of Stravinsky for Macmillan called *Firebird*, largely pilfered from my writings. The case was decided in my favor in August, but I was required to testify in New York months before.

While there I read the news of Lawrence Morton's death. Even though he had suffered several heart attacks and had been in poor health for the last three years, this came as a shock because he had sounded normal in recent telephone conversations. I thought of our expedition together on the Peloponnesus in 1966, and of how in Hollywood we would play har-monic progressions from Gesualdo to each other over the telephone in the morning from madrigals transcribed during the night. I remembered, too, that he carried a note in his wallet to the effect that, in the event of his sudden death, his assets should go to the NAACP. I admired him for that, and hope that his bequest was honored.

At the beginning of June I received a visit from John Bowlt, the Univer-sity of Texas Slavic languages professor I had commissioned to translate Vera Stravinsky's *Salon Album*. In July I went to Boulder to conduct concerts in Giora Bernstein's Colorado Music Festival, taking Phyllis, Alexander, and Jonathan with me. After a four-hour delay in a stifling plane on a crowded runway, due to an electrical storm in New York, and a long wait for a car in Denver, we reached the Boulderado Hotel to discover that the bag contain-ing *all* of my clothes had been lost, probably stolen on the sidewalk during check-in at La Guardia. I spent my first day in the mountains, before and after rehearsing the excellent orchestra, buying clothes, underwear, socks, shirts, a suit, ties. Claudio Spies shared some conducting chores with me, and we were joined in the symposia by Glenn Watkins, Jann Pasler, and Elmer Schönberger (from Amsterdam).

I had seen Alva in New York almost daily in the weeks before, and we had become very close. She had separated from her husband six months earlier and moved to an apartment. At the end of August, I wrote to her as follows:

I'm back in New York for meetings with people from the Colorado Festival about concerts here, and, next summer, there. The Hampshire House apart-ment looks bleak, horribly blue, and my room still does not have blackout shades, chairs, or the means of mixing hot and cold water. I can't understand Judith's lack of responsibility. Nothing has been right, and when I went through the place with her a month ago, pointing out what had to be done, she took no notes. Even the toilet seats that she bought did not fit and I had to pur-chase replacements from the Hampshire House. The shade she installed in the front window did not fit at the bottom. The loveseat that came while I was in Colorado is for midgets and one of the seats ejects you backwards. What kind of decorator puts a cabinet in a bathroom without checking to see if it could be blocking the only electrical outlet? This has been a frustrating summer.

Alexander has a week's vacation from September 11 and is begging me to come to Copenhagen. He manipulates me skillfully, and of course I want to see him, but the trip always flattens me for two weeks. I have a concert in California in mid-October and it coincides with another of his weeks off. I want him to come, but he will agree only if I go to him next weekend. I am too old to let him make my decisions for me.

I did not go to Denmark, and he did accompany me to Los Angeles, where I rehearsed for a concert in Ojai in memory of Lawrence Morton. After it we flew from Santa Barbara to San Francisco to spend a few days before returning to Florida.

On November 4 I read a lecture on *The Rite of Spring* at the Bruno Walter Auditorium in New York's Library of the Performing Arts. Afterwards the people who reconstructed the choreography, costumes, and decors for the Joffrey Ballet's revival of the work confronted me about the supposedly greater role of Nikolay Roerich in the creation of the piece than I had acknowledged. I invited them to discuss the question with me later in the afternoon at my apartment, and at that meeting agreed to give a copy of the four-hand score with Stravinsky's markings for Nijinsky to the Performing Arts Library. On November 5 I went with Louis Cyr[4] to the Joffrey Ballet performances of the *Rite, Parade,* and *Afternoon of a Faun* at the Fifty-fifth Street Mosque Theater. Afterward Alva and I indulged in caviar blini at the Russian Tea Room.

Alexander came back to Florida from Copenhagen before Christmas, and, on December 19, we drove to New York for the second time, stopping the first night at Savannah, the beautiful city with the outdoor staircases.

1988

On a return trip to Pompano in early January, I spent the first night in Richmond, going the next day to the Edgar Allan Poe Museum. It is uncertain if the creator of Monsieur Dupin, though a longtime resident in the vicinity, ever saw this 1730s stone house from the inside. Of the relics, only a walking stick, boot hooks, nail file, and the small bed in "The Raven Room" were Poe's. The brick-walled garden (Virginia creepers?) is a perfect Poe prop, like the ghosts, tombs, lost loves, remembered voices and eyes of the writer who exercised greater influence on continental European, but not English, literature than any other American. And not only on literature. Odilon Redon and Ravel were under Poe's spell at one time, as was Debussy, for whom the underground vaults and "vacant and eye-like win-

---

4. A Roman Catholic priest on an Indian reservation in Québec, and the editor of the *Firebird* facsimile score.

dows" of the *House of Usher* must have evoked an atmosphere similar to that of the castle in *Pelléas*. Baudelaire asks readers of his translation of "The Raven" to think of the most plaintive of Lamartine's strophes and the subtlest of Hugo's rhythms. (Poe's own rhythms "go on throbbing in your head," Eliot wrote.) For me, Baudelaire's "Raven," and Mallarmé's still more so (*"cet oiseau d'ébène"*), are comic poems: *"Le Corbeau dit: 'Jamais plus' . . . alors l'oiseau dit: 'Jamais plus.'"*

A feeling of dread enveloped me as I entered the Benedictine Hospital in Kingston on March 23, Phyllis having warned me that the ravages of Patricia's cancer had become much worse since I last saw her six days earlier. I found her sitting on the edge of a bed, legs and feet twitching, pressed to the bosom of a burly nurse trying to comfort her. Told that I had come to see her, she forced her drugged eyes open and clasped my hands, then stretched out on the bed, thrashing from side to side and moaning. After fifteen months of mental and physical torture, of chemotherapy, radiation, live-cell injection and laetrile treatment in Mexico, the fire in her throat had not burned out. The cancer's distention of her face had burst veins and capillaries and her skin looked smudged, like a charcoal drawing. The tumor had also extruded her tongue so that she could not form words clearly and sounded like someone with a speech impediment. Beloved little chain-smoking sister, what a horrible death, and tragic, thrown-away life! A week later Phyllis called me in Florida, saying that in spite of ever-increased doses of codeine, our sister was still screaming with pain. When would it end?

On May 12 I received a call from Phyllis to tell me that Patricia was dead. A few minutes before, she had asked Kris, who had been sitting with her, to hold her hand and not let go. Then she fell asleep. Kris said that during the last five days she had felt death was near, and, not having accepted it and continuing to grasp at straws, had resisted sleep in fear of not waking. Five days earlier, the pain had stopped, supposedly a sign of the imminence of death, the cancer having destroyed nerve endings.

Though the conclusion had been foregone since the death sentence, "inoperable cancer," a year and a half ago, the end came as a shock, the more so since two weeks ago, in an apparent remission, she seemed strong enough to go on for months, and was still talking about alternative methods of treatment. Always the actress, she put on a performance for Alexander when we visited her, made herself up, even tried to walk, but stumbled and fell back on her couch. Kris said that there was no struggle at the end, no gasping for breath, but only peace and a final heartbeat.

In the plane to New York the following day to meet Alexander's from Denmark, the second in two weeks, I could not banish the thought that Patricia was an enigma to me and had been since early childhood. Even then we disagreed about most things. She would mock the music I loved and annoy me by playing boogie-woogie on the piano. (Why, with such a talented ear, did she never learn to read music?) She seemed to enjoy exactly what I disliked: dancing, ice-skating, party-going. Whatever the origins of her "death wish"—born five years after me, she was probably an unplanned child and not long enough breast-fed—she did not know what to do with her love. I wonder if the change from the slender young woman (there are two photographs of her in the New York *Herald Tribune* of November 10, 1952 and one on a cover of *Cosmopolitan* magazine) to the obese older one indicated disturbances in the psyche. At thirty, after the bankruptcy of her and her first husband's once highly successful candle-manufacturing business, she gave up and allowed life to pass her by. Smoke was her element, and she made no resolve, no attempt to do without it until at last her throat caught fire. Obstinate and uncoercible, marrying a second time self-destructively—in the beautiful seventeenth-century Huguenot church in New Paltz—she was also the least aggressive of human beings.

In the flower-filled funeral home, I saw to my horror that the casket was open—on her husband's instructions—even though the face must have been unrecognizable to anyone but her family and would upset everyone else. When the cancer was first discovered she told me about nightmares of seeing herself in a coffin. The dreams had become the reality, and little Patricia, musical, a gifted painter, was not there anymore.

A moment before the funeral began, Alva turned up. How had she found out about it, and after taking the bus from New York to Kingston, made her way here? An Episcopal minister read prayers, though "Patricia," as he invoked her several painful times, had no religious affiliation. He discoursed briefly on the Pauline concept of change, describing her sickness as one transfiguration, her death as another. In the cemetery, standing before the open grave and the new hole in my life, I could only wonder why this way and not another. "When will indifference come?" John Berryman cries out in one of his *Dream Songs*.

I hired a car and driver who took Alexander and me to our respective air terminals in New York and returned Alva to her office. Two weeks later, back in Florida, I wrote to her: "How very kind of you to have made a contribution to the Cancer Society in memory of my sister. I thank you from as deep down as I go. (I'm sending the enclosed article only because I was correcting proofs of it in the car on the afternoon of the 16th. It is pretty shallow.) Phyllis and I collapsed last week. She'll go back north on the 9th. Alexander doesn't call, manages not to be there when I call, and is evidently not planning to come. I had entered him in a driving school. I'll be in New York in three weeks."

In July I returned to Boulder, again with Phyllis, Alexander, and Jonathan. Those summer experiences are best not repeated, and, after two weeks of conducting in the Music Festival—above all the Third Brandenburg Con-

certo, *Apollo*, Mozart's A-major Concerto, K. 488, with Garrick Ohlsson—
I found the altitude too tiring for me, though the Mozart, repeated at Estes
Park, was my musical peak of the year.

On our return to New York, Alexander met his mother at Kennedy
airport. After begging me to provide a ticket for her, he still could not bear
any confrontation between his homegrown Danish persona and the one
developed during his periods with me. When they arrived at my apartment,
he refused to speak English with his mother, and when she spoke it with
me, angrily broke in on her in Danish. Suddenly the clash became violent
and he demanded to return to Denmark immediately. I complied and arranged for this, most unwisely letting him have his own way, allowing his
headstrong rudeness to prevail, and wasting a lot of money. She accompanied him back to the airport, but, surprisingly, since he had almost total
control over her, resisted his pressuring to come with him. She stayed with
her niece on Long Island who was visiting her American fiancé.

Alexander was in a schizoid situation, obviously. I had been unable to
establish a relationship with him sufficiently intimate to counterbalance
the very close one he had with his mother. A week later Rita flew with me
to London, where he rejoined us for a brief trip to Venice. But he continued
to protest against seeing his parents together, refusing to walk with us *en
trois*. In Venice he went off with her alone, or stayed in her hotel room and
ignored me. I cut the holiday short and, by the time we separated at Heathrow,
had made up my mind to stop encouraging him to enter an American school.

At the end of August Alva and I flew to Florida, where Frommer, Roberts, and a secretary friend of theirs met us in my car three days later. Having promised to catalog my Stravinsky archives for the Library of Congress, I had employed them to help inventory the books and music in my
Florida residence. Since none of the three could read music or even identify
the foreign language books, the brunt of the work, which took three weeks,
devolved on me. Frommer packed these archival materials in my car and
drove it and me to the District of Columbia, where I displayed them in my
hotel room for scholars from the Library to study and appraise. During this
time I visited the Dumbarton Oaks Library to examine the manuscript full
score and the finely penciled *"brouillons"* of Stravinsky's Concerto in E-Flat—
which made me feel ancient. I still possess an invitation to a Mozart chamber music concert there, April 2, 1948, with "Mr. Auden" crossed out and
"Mr. Craft" written in, Auden suddenly having had to return to New York
before that date. "The chain of memory is resurrection," Charles Olson
wrote, yet I can recall everything about that evening except myself, being
wholly unable to imagine what I was then. I can still see the Stravinskys
vividly, hear their voices, and even remember some of the conversation en
route with them in a limousine, but of myself I recall only the inferiority
feelings that did not crush me only because I was with them. I can also

picture the chatelaine, Mildred Bliss; but, then, I saw her in later years in Athens, on her yacht during an excursion up the Bosphorus to the Symplegades, at lunches in her home in Washington with St.-John Perse, and, finally, in the Green Room at Constitution Hall after Stravinsky's and my concert there with the Philadelphia Orchestra in 1964. The Library of Congress did not purchase my Stravinskyana.

On my return to New York in September, I decided to live with Alva, who had returned to New York betweentimes to fulfill a film-acting engagement. In October I flew to Copenhagen, and from there, with Alexander, to Vienna, where I had planned to spend my birthday. We went first to the monastery at Melk, but the climb back up the stairs from the level of the Danube to the highway was too much for me. I was gasping for breath, perspiring profusely, feeling faint. The next day, my birthday, I again climbed too many stairs in two museums in Vienna. Having hot and cold flashes and fearing a heart attack, I telephoned to Alva in New York. Her MD brother returned the call and advised me to rest until I felt strong enough to return. Instead, and not wanting to be alone, I foolishly flew to Copenhagen with Alexander but failed to ask his mother, a nurse, for help. When I arrived in New York, October 22, exhausted from the flight, Alva, despite my protestations, escorted me to Lenox Hill Hospital and to Dr. Jeffrey Moses. I explained that I had long been aware of the eventual necessity of an operation to replace my congenitally defective aortic valve, and recounted the three recent experiences after which I felt abnormally tired: in addition to the "episode" in Vienna on my birthday, I had been ill with food-poisoning when I conducted an exceptionally demanding concert in Amsterdam in April, and I had suffered severe headaches and shortness of breath in Boulder last summer, conducting concerts at high altitudes.

After four hours of tests—radiological, chemical, electrical (EKG), supersonic (echogram)—Dr. Moses diagnosed stenosis of the aortic valve with the terrifying diktat: immediate surgery (open heart!). I decided to have an angiogram, a cardiac catheterization test, and was advised by my doctor friend George Meyer in Pompano that I should undergo this in Fort Lauderdale's North Ridge General Hospital, which I duly did on November 8. When I entered the lobby, it had been converted to an art gallery for a photographic exhibition: "The Many Faces of Percutaneous Transdermal Coronary Angioplasty." After processing, I was wheeled by a volunteer worker two decades older than myself to room 227, where I was glued and wired with electrodes, fettered with a transistor-size recorder, and plugged in for teletromic monitoring. Rubber tourniquets came next and puncturings for blood (more misses than hits), specimen gathering, pulse-taking, blood pressure pumping, and a female nurse's far-from-shy shaving of my groin. My roommate was a deaf elder tirelessly fond of TV soaps and suffering from, whatever else, resonant hiccoughing.

A 5:45 A.M. reveille on the morrow for measuring and weighing revealed that I was not taller, shorter, heavier, or lighter than the previous night. A five-hour delay in the angiogram scheduling was not conceded until 9 A.M., and four more hours elapsed before I was sedated and gurneyed to the operating laboratory, through a corridor decorated with bloodcurdling pictures of cardiovascular systems. Alva told me later that while being wheeled into an elevator I remarked that I wished I were going for a hair transplant. Inside, four insouciant young nurses in shower caps and surgical masks began to prepare me, placing a green towel with surgical instruments on my chest, as if it were a substitute tray. One of them inquired about my profession (that dreaded question, here as from the passenger in the next seat in an airplane: if I say "writer," he or she will ask the titles of my most famous novels, and if "musician," what instrument do I play; but fibs such as "engineer" weave tangled webs). I felt almost no effect, certainly no ataraxia, from the medications. But why was I so frightened? Werner Forsmann won a Nobel Prize for sliding a catheter inside his heart as long ago as 1929, with no medication, and while standing.

Dr. Ali Ghahramani, surgical hat and butcher's green apron, entered, offering facetious observations for the regalement of the four females, whose response suggested that the jokes were not altogether new. Going briskly to business, and clearly enjoying it, he talked about foods and vintages during some of the operation but in the more intense parts hummed softly, interrupting himself only to warn me of upcoming painful moments, and to encourage me with remarks such as "only one more needle" and "the worst is over."

The catheter that Ghahramani injected into my femoral artery was larger in circumference than I had anticipated and during the first part of the passage felt most unpleasant. Next, a machine resembling a hand-cranking laundry wringer winched the plastic tube into my heart, where a shadow seemed to fall as the intruder entered. The TVs were then switched on, the room darkened, and the explorations of the catheter, a slender black snake, screened. Ghahramani moved it to the aortic valve, showing me how it was blocked by calcium deposits, and prying one loose, whence it resembled a rock floating weightless in outer space. He passed the filament through the valve, which is like threading a needle at long range, a tricky and not immediately successful maneuver. Suffusing me with a dye, he warned me to expect sudden warmth and nausea, though what I actually felt was a burning sensation throughout the body that disappeared as quickly as it began. The position of the bed was changed several times to provide a variety of camera angles, fascinating but also frightening to watch—a look at my mortality? a premature autopsy? Several pictures were flashed of what might have been textbook illustrations of tuberose roots but were actually outlines of the coronary arteries, clean and uncoagulated in my case, Ghahramani said, adding that an aortic valve is less difficult to replace than a mitral.

The longest part of the procedure was the last, stopping the femoral bleeding. For about twelve minutes, until a clot had formed, the most muscular of the nurses pressed her thumbs on the area of the incision, wound thick bands of tape around the groin and leg, and placed a five-pound bag of sand on top to keep me flat and motionless for six hours.

Claiming he performed at least five of these operations a day, Ghahramani laughed (no doubt for the fifth time today) about the rusty knife he was saving for his next patient, a lawyer specializing in malpractice suits, then departed, referring to the job on me as "a piece of cake." "How do you feel?" he asked before he left, and, not wishing to destroy his bonhomie, I pretended I wouldn't have missed it for the world.

At the end of November, back in New York, I met with Dr. Ronald Drusin, Joseph Brodsky's cardiologist, a tall, balding man, soft-spoken but dour, and un-pin-downable except to the statistic that 5 percent do not survive the implant operation. I committed myself to it for January 5 and came away feeling relieved. I do not want a life of shipping water.

A week later Dr. James Malm, my surgeon, introduced himself to me, as no doubt to many others before me, with "I feel I know you from the inside out." He outlined the operating procedures, beginning with the sawing through the sternum in a vertical line, the insertion of the retractor, and the ratcheting back to expose the chest cavity. The bleeding edges of this incision are stanched with electric cauterizing, which leaves a smell of burning flesh that I will not notice. My pericardium, the sac that encases the heart, will be cut to expose the pulsating organ. The heart and lungs will be stopped and the blood shunted into a heart-lung machine filled with an electrolyte solution to prime the pump. When the blood starts to flow into the machine, oxygen is fed into it through sheets of porous plastic that function as surrogate lungs. The body temperature is lowered, which slows the metabolism of the tissues, thereby reducing their need for oxygen. "How is the heart stopped?" one naturally asks, and the answer is through flooding by ice-cold fluids rich in potassium, an ion that stops muscle contraction.

Malm showed me the St. Jude synthetic valve I was to receive, a black ring, made of pyrolitic carbon and double-velour Dacron—this in preference to a pig valve, which rarely lasts as long as a decade and often causes problems of immunology and rejection. Mine, he said, should stay with me all the way.

1989

Alexander and Henryk Falk, a Scandinavian Airlines employee who seems to be his surrogate father, came to New York on the last day of 1988, ostensibly to celebrate New Year's with Alva, me, and Phyllis. Alexander did not stay with me, but in a midtown hotel with Mr. Falk, which I thought odd, in that they and Rita live together in Copenhagen. I had met Mr. Falk only once, and that by an awkward accident in the Copenhagen airport.

The next day, as I prepared to enter Columbia Presbyterian Hospital, I noted in my diary: "In the hours before his return to Denmark, Alexander is unusually affectionate, alternately hugging, lunging at, and shadow-boxing with me, but he cannot bring himself to speak—or, when he does, can only ask me not to risk the operation." In August 1987, when Alexander was in Venice with me, overlapping a visit there by Mr. Falk guiding a party of SAS tourists, he refused to leave our hotel, fearing a chance encounter with him. Not seeing the harm in such a meeting, I deduced that he did not want to be caught in a contradiction about his attitude toward me as expressed at home. In any case, he was careful to ignore me at the 1989 New Year's shindig I gave for him, sitting as far from me as possible and speaking Danish only with Mr. Falk and a colleague of his at SAS, though Mr. Falk's English, like everyone else's, was fluent. Indications of the unhealthy life of double dissimulation that Alexander was in fact leading were to become increasingly frequent and open.

At Columbia Presbyterian's Harkness Pavilion my book-stuffed bags were taken to the tenth floor in a wheelchair while I walked alongside feeling foolish. My cell had a small bed, dirty and chipped walls, a dartboard on which to pin get-well cards, if not received posthumously. The same quarters at the end of the corridor were occupied by the partly living body of Sunny C. Von Bulow, tended here in macabre routine by physical therapists who exercised her atrophied leg and arm muscles, fed by nurses through a nose tube (her digestive system worked), coiffured by a mortician, and protected by a revolvered guard seated behind a screen in the corridor. Her eyes opened from time to time, apparently, but did not focus. I dreamed that I was reading my obituary.

Most of my first full day in the hospital was spent in coaching sessions with the cardiologist, the surgeon, and the anesthesiologist, but little was said about possible mental confusion on regaining consciousness. What I most feared was an alteration in my personality—not that I am deeply fond of the present version—and of mental dysfunction.

At about 7 A.M. on January 5 my entire body was painted with an iodine solution—I pictured myself as a Red Indian—and wheeled to the operating theater. The anaesthetizing process took two and a half hours, with six ingredients in the mix. One of them, a synthetic curare, added further Amerindian associations, being itself South American in origin and in effect erasing the patient's image of human sacrifice to the Mexican sun god, or any image of men poised with knives (Banquo: "It will rain tonight"; 1st Murderer: "Let it come down"). The operating table, like the stone on which the Mayan victims' hearts were cut out, similarly elevated the chest, suspending the head and shoulders over the top.

Consciousness came with a suffocating twist of the tracheal catheter, and with it the first shock, the awareness that my body was "dead," without proprioception, that it would not move, incline to one side or the other, or even budge, strongly as I willed it: I saw myself as an effigy on a catafalque. The second and greater shock was the simultaneous awareness that I could neither breathe nor speak, and that therefore the functions of the heart and lungs were on mechanical controls, the heart-lung machine. But without the participation of these organs—quite literally, *"Mon coeur mis à nu"*—was "I" still "I"? And was my mind not, in the strict sense of this disincarnation, posthumous?

At about 6 P.M. I was wheeled to Intensive Care. The surgery had been completed five hours before, but the IC unit had filled up with emergencies, and I had to be kept in the operating room waiting for a vacancy. Later I learned that Dr. Malm had emerged from it waving his arms like an orchestral maestro to indicate to my next of kin that I would conduct again. The anesthetic paralysis began to dissipate soon after, and, able to use my arms, I made a dumb show of writing and motioned for pen and pad. Incredibly, my scribbles, or grudges, proved legible: the one complaining about dryness of mouth immediately resulted in swabbing with water.

My heartbeat was so strong that it twitched my head on the pillow. Late in the evening I began to hallucinate: colored patterns kaleidoscopically rearranging red and gold speckles of what might be sand; scorched landscapes; malachites; square patches of light blue with a feathery texture. But this did not last, and instead of the amnesia the doctors had prepared me to expect, my mind swarmed with anamnesis, intense moments from my entire life. I listened to tapes of the *Rite* and *Così fan tutte*, but the asymmetries of the former, as much as the symmetries of the latter, were exasperatingly predictable.

The next morning I was breathing with my own lungs, and my heart was my own repaired one. I began to think of the operation as a journey, like Don Quixote's aerial one that never leaves the ground, into unknown realms of the mind that the anesthetics have both opened up and made frustratingly unrecallable. I was not "Lazarus . . . / Come back to tell you all." I remember a late-night tumult, loud voices, several TV channels screaming simultaneously, a nightmare in an inhuman place. In the cubicle next to mine, a team of medics, under freezing fluorescent light, struggled to revive someone in cardiac arrest.

By January 8 the surprisingly small scar looked like a filleted, still bloodflecked Dover sole, except that the imprint over the sternum was a zigzagging line, the Inca snake figure. Beneath and on each side was an incised "H," the surgical artist's colophon, it might be, but actually drains for medications and the solutions used during the operation. A vest-pocket bulge in my left abdomen was explained as a storage cell for the wiring system of a pacemaker, when and if required. In the afternoon, transferred to my own room, I answered telephone calls.

The following day, after checking the vital signs and breathing exercises, I ventured a brief, giddy, knee-buckling walk in the corridor, held up by Alva and a nurse. From behind several doors came an exotic muffled drumming, a communications system in ancient Mesoamerica, I mused, but actually the sound of physical therapists' fists pounding the ribs of postoperative cardiac patients to clear the lungs and prevent pulmonary complications. Later I was wheeled to radiology on a suspicion, so I learned afterward with alarm, that I might have a collapsed lung. I was becoming aware of a crunching sound in my chest, as loud to me as the "snapping" of a double-jointed knuckle. I wondered if my body was rejecting the new valve.

A second walk in the corridor brought back pictures of Stravinsky after his 1956 stroke, when the youthful spring in his legs disappeared. The discussions of blood chemistry, of prothrombin time, platelets, and hematocrit levels, were forcing the idea of a parallel between my new way of life and that of his later years.

During the night of January 12–13, the only one that Alva did not spend in the room with me, pain in the colon, constant and unchanging, not rhythmic or periodic, not increasing or diminishing, not with any variation in quality but only a steady intensity, made me cry out. I saw little burning threads of electricity when I closed my eyes. Nothing else existed. And pain cannot be "killed," but only the mind dulled. This new pain adjusted the perspectives of the old ones, and the severed muscles and ligaments in the area of the sternum that made coughing an agony had to be downgraded to severe soreness. Finally, after fourteen hours of appealing to the hospital system and letter-of-the-law doctors and nurses, I received a local anesthetic, but was more tired that night than three days ago. Pain exhausts, even on the cellular level.

Finally Dr. Todd, chief vascular surgeon, diagnosed the new affliction as a first-degree rectal prolapse, the most aggressive instance of it he had ever seen and for which I would have had to be hospitalized if I had not been already. Though unknown as a consequence of valvular implant surgery, it was obviously that in my case. But surely it was also simple bodily ecology: one area is violated and another breaks down in automatic reaction. According to Chinese medicine, which has a poiesis but no physiology, my collapsed Qi (Chi) is a result of the temporary "death" of the interconnected heart and lungs. In the words of Kaptchuk's *The Web That Has No Weaver*, "When there is collapsed Qi, such disorders as prolapse may occur." Palpating the excrescence revealed—cruel chrysalis—that it is shaped like a vulva (*aut vultus aut vulva*). I would have to change my body image, at least momentarily, to hermaphrodite.

On January 14 Dr. Todd warned that the prolapse would have to be shrunk before I could be paroled, and that I would also have to wait for the stabilization of the blood, or, rather, of the formula that will regulate a slower coagulation time: clots form more readily with a prosthetic device in the heart, and the blood must be kept thinner. I would have to try to avoid accidents and live like a hemophiliac Habsburg, in whose one-time domain this story began three months ago. Meanwhile, I lay propped on a mound of ice like a lobster in a restaurant.

Six weeks after the operation, the long scar line down the center of my chest had healed and looked like a zipper. I was permitted to return to Florida, but not by airplane. During the first day's drive to Washington, I felt light-headed and dizzy, and decided to rest there the next day, except for a visit to the Space Museum with Alexander.

We stopped at the old-fashioned Georgia resort of Sea Island. Bulrushes, live oaks draped with silver-gray moss, loblolly pines, and salt marshes— Sidney Lanier's "The Salt Marshes of Glyn": when I was in grammar school we had to memorize verses by Lanier, a minor poet and, in the 1870s, the first flutist in the orchestra at Peabody, Maryland. A Spanish Franciscan Mission was established here in the sixteenth century, followed in the eighteenth by Methodists, including the brothers Wesley themselves. The ruins of a slave hospital, made of tabby (spondylous) shells, lime, sand, salt water, are a reminder of subsequent history. Except for the repeal of the Eighteenth Amendment, the Cloisters Hotel, opened in 1928 with Calvin Coolidge planting an Oglethorpe Oak, can hardly be less rule-ridden now than it was then. Jim Crow is still only just beneath the surface, white suzerainty everywhere above. "The conquest of the earth," Marlow says in *Heart of Darkness*, "mostly means the taking away from those who have a different complexion or slightly flatter noses than ourselves." An echo of Deep South charm survives in the lilting chatter of the room maids ("Hush yo' mouth").

The hotel's dress code states that "men and boys twelve or over must wear a jacket and tie," and that "evening clothes are encouraged" at dinner. The "appropriate dress for ladies" is not spelled out beyond the clue that "extremes are to be avoided" (no topless). "Shirts must have collars" for tennis, and though "Bermuda shorts are permitted," the jogging kind are not. "Appropriate attire is required in the lobbies even for a brief errand, and shoes must be worn (no sandals, no sneakers)." Even the furniture is instructed to behave with proper modesty: "When in beach garb, all chairs must be covered with a towel." (Grammatical errors are apparently permitted.) On arrival, after monotonous hours through the mangrove-swamps along Route 95, we were obliged to upgrade our clothes before being admitted to the registration desk, which was difficult to accomplish in the back seat of a car.

I had received no briefing in the hospital about the mental and physical adjustments I could expect to face during my recuperation. While still in New York, I was unable to walk without assistance at first and had to have a pillow placed wherever I intended to sit. I could lift or carry nothing heavier than a thin book and was able to sleep only on my right side, any other position provoking a sharp pain in the sternum area. Worst of all were the recurrent dreams of being in a hospital bed and feeling caged by the side rails, or trapped in a maze-like cellar whose exit, when finally found, was blocked. I have since found similarities with the hallucinatory journeys described in the prose poems of Arthur Lundkvist (*Journeys in Dream and Imagination*), written after his recovery from a two-month coma in which he was thought to be brain-dead. Yet I was euphoric from the first moment outside the hospital. I had survived! Soon this feeling would turn into a live-while-you-can nihilism during which I spent money as inebriated sea-faring personnel are said to do on shore leave.

My recovery began in earnest with walks on the ocean-side pool deck of our Pompano condominium, once around the perimeter, then twice, locking arms with Alva at first but soon gaining strength and ambulating unaided. Three other resident open-heart-surgery patients were also shuffling the same path at the same twilight hour, and we began to joke about ourselves as a cardiac sodality. After increasing my pace, I began to swim, a right-side sidestroke.

In March we were obliged to vacate our apartment for three days during a termite fumigation. We moved to the Beach Club in Boca Raton (say Ratone, not Rat-on, or rattan, which describes the Club's furniture; the name means "rat's mouth," despite Chamber of Commerce claims for an older but no less apposite translation, "thieves' inlet"). The entrance, with drawbridge gates and fortified guard building, interrogations and telephonings to higher-ups, suggested an East European border crossing of an earlier period. Inside, a concierge brought identity cards, with a solemn warning to carry them at all times. As we reached our room, hoping for a brief respite from the atmosphere of lurking danger, the alarm on a small safe went off alarmingly, bringing the house police. Nor did anxiety about security entirely let up. While I was reading to Alva from a book about the Abaniki Indians, who lived here in the thirteenth century, a maid, who must have been listening at the door, burst in with the excuse, "I thought the television had been left on."

By the time we left for Europe in April my confidence had grown to the extent that I decided to conduct a concert in New York in December, though it would involve a great deal of organizing. I was nervous during our flights to New York and London, but the travel and the stair-climbing in Italy, without fear of passing out or of knees buckling, reassured me: I would soon be back to normal—or, as I should say, to better than normal, since I was already breathing more deeply and easily than before the operation.

In a taxi from London to Heathrow for our flight to Venice, I discovered that my passport was missing. After frantic but fruitless emptyings of bags, Alva decided to go on alone in order to meet Alexander's flight from Copenhagen—he had no money—and fly back to London with him. I returned to the Savoy, where a fine-comb search for the lost document, no doubt snaffled by a room waiter or maid aware of its value on the black market, yielded nothing. The experience had unnerved me, and I handled it less well than I would have done before turning that corner in my life in the hospital in January. Alva called from Venice to say that she had secured return seats via Paris.

The American Embassy in London was like a fortress with barricades inside the doors and guns-at-the-ready guards, but my new passport was issued expeditiously. Returning from a stroll through Temple Court, we watched the new Lord Mayor, in miniver-trimmed robe, on the way to his installation ceremony. Meanwhile the Savoy had been taken over by Frank Sinatra, his retinue, bodyguards, and a cavalcade of limousines.

We spent part of August in New York making arrangements for our end-of-year concert. One evening during the visit impressed us, a dinner at the San Domenico restaurant, a block from our Hampshire House. (I noticed that the *ticket* on our bottle of Sonoma Cutrer claimed that "All grapes . . . are hand-sorted and gently pressed," which made me wonder if any grape had ever been squeezed the least bit roughly.) A table for twenty-two suddenly filled up in the center of the main room, a Mafia gathering, we supposed, before hearing the language. In fact the host was Adnan Khashoggi, the multibillionaire munitions dealer, out of jail on $10 million bail. His bald pate and short stature brought D'Annunzio to mind, his mustache Hercule Poirot, and his thrusting chin and straight-arm manner of pointing as he ordered flunkies about, telling them where to sit and what to eat, Mussolini. His guests were swarthy Iranian bodyguards and a young blonde, with whom he conversed exclusively. No one else dared glance at either of them. A waiter told us that at an earlier dinner there Khashoggi brought ten veiled women, his Muslim harem.

In Pompano at the end of the month, we found our apartment infested with ants. The chemical sprays of the exterminators so aggravated my eyes and throat that I had to work outdoors, whereas the ants, in long caravans, did not seem to have minded at all. Myrmecologists tell us that socialism and caste systems work side by side in ant societies, but slavery and cannibalism are prevalent, too, and proletarian ants commit suicide to feed their younger sisters.

In September the news of Virgil Thomson's death revived many memories. I pictured him as he was in July 1948 at the Denver premiere of his *Mother of Us All*; at Carnegie Hall, February 1950, after the performance of his Cello Concerto with the Philadelphia Orchestra, which I heard in a loge with Stravinsky and Francis Poulenc; in the Foro Italico in Rome in the spring of 1954, conducting his *Wheat Field at Noon*, arms straight out sideways at the start, like airplane wings, as if to suggest the rectangular spread of Kansas. No less vivid was a lunch at the Stravinskys' in Hollywood in 1960, during which, monopolizing the conversation as he always did, he talked brilliantly about mescaline, comparing the experience of it to being transported to central China. At one of a number of parties with him in his Chelsea hideaway, I recalled meeting Gian Carlo Menotti, then on a Broadway roll with his double-bill *Medium* and *Telephone*. I remembered Auden, at a reception given by Robert Fizdale and Arthur Gold before the New York *Rake's Progress* premier, standing near Thomson and announcing loudly that "Virgil is not top-drawer, and, furthermore, he looks like Coleridge's death mask." The poet, in a snit of unknown provocation, was of course far-gone in his cups. I also remembered Virgil at Alexander Schneider's, with Nicolas Nabokov and Stravinsky, making a case for the survival of the Viennese Waltz in Schoenberg's Five Pieces for Orchestra, and remembered him in New York in March 1971 asking "How's Papa?," and when I said he was in Lenox Hill Hospital, Virgil remarking that this was the time of year in which, as a church organist in Missouri, he made the most money playing at funerals. He intended this kindly, to prepare me, and it proved to be prescient.

In London in October, Alva and I took Alexander to see *Hamlet* in the Olivier Theatre. The staging mixed periods in costumes and decors: Holbein headgear, eighteenth-century knee-breeches, and 1917 red flags carried by Fortinbras's army marching in the background. A statue of Hamlet's father, in full armor like the Commendatore, was a permanent and distracting prop. The intermission, after nearly three hours, robbed the too brief second part of intensity, but with the return of Laertes the play itself falls apart. Why, dying, does he suddenly know that the King is the murderer? And is his complicity in the plot to poison Hamlet less heinous than the King's? (Does Eliot's observation that Hamlet "occasioned the death of at least three innocent people, and two more insignificant ones," refer to Laertes as one of the three?) Laertes is dishonest, in any case, and in the dueling scene so is Hamlet, in his hollow claim of confederacy. Fortinbras's takeover and the silencing of Horatio, the witness, reminded me that in Ingmar Bergman's staging, Fortinbras actually shoots him. Horatio does not fulfill Hamlet's request to tell his "story," but merely gives an account of a stereotypical plot. (My pedantic side noticed that in Act 1 Horatio looks in our direction, saying, "yon high eastward hill," while Hamlet, later, saying "I am but mad north-north west," pointed to what would be due south.) The dybbuk doubling as "the old mole" was a nice touch.

The next night Götz Friedrich's *Die Walküre*, at Covent Garden, took place in a tunnel. The Valkyries were sheathed in black leather, some of them décolletés, some bare-shouldered, but Valkyries, in one get-up or another, are at least part of Wagner's cast. This cannot be said of Hunding's escort of flashlight-carrying Mafiosi in belted trench coats, dark glasses, and Humphrey Bogart hats. After plucking the sword from the ash-tree, Siegmund placed it between Sieglinde's inveigling legs, where she caressed the blade. An opera about incest, then, brother and sister, father and daughter, the tenderness in Wotan's farewell exceeding the merely paternal. But how unlike a god was this Wotan, henpecked and dominated by women, swooning and lurching about, to-ing and fro-ing in a white leather coat while toting a spear, deserting his earthlings, more racked with guilt than Freud's most despondent patient, ceaselessly bemoaning "the end." Surely a god should have some aplomb.

In November I was in Washington for an interview with Charlie Rose on "Nightwatch." The show aired at 2 A.M., and probably pushed insomniacs over the edge. The only viewer I knew of was the aunt of the conductor James Levine, who lived in the Wittington, our condominium in Pompano Beach. She actually said she enjoyed it.

In New York in December, I conducted the Tully Hall concert as planned: Varèse's *Ionisation*, Carter's Double Concerto (with Mark Wait and Tom Schultz playing piano and harpsichord respectively), Schoenberg's *Herzgewächse*, Stravinsky's *Pastorale*, Concertino, *Dumbarton Oaks*, *Pulcinella* Suite. Carter told me afterward that he was surprised to find the Varèse so nearly symmetrical. I was able to present the concert only with Alva's help and pampering, but it capped ten months of slowly climbing back to strength. I now felt that the shape of my life was being re-established. A few days later Alva and I saw *Wozzeck* at the Met, but the audience for the twentieth century's greatest opera was shockingly small, as well as bewildered, rustling programs and whispering to neighbors throughout, as if they had expected Lloyd Webber.

In 1989 I made a gift to the Library of Congress of my Stravinsky proof-scores, ozalids, and photocopies of scores, all corrected by him, along with acetate recordings of some of his live concerts in the 1940s and 1950s. I also published a few pieces in *The New York Review of Books*, and I read omnivorously, most touchingly a remark by Proust in the latest volume of the new collected edition of his letters, this one to Cocteau, December 31, 1918, on the death of his aviator friend Roland Garro: "You will have the comfort, you who loved him, of having made him live for ever, in a sky from which nothing ever falls . . ." And I wasted a good deal of time looking up words in the new *Oxford English Dictionary* that are not included in the old one. "Rinfrescative," which occurs in a letter by Gray of the *Elegy*, is still missing.

Chapter 11

My Return to Music

The 1990s

The main events of 1990 were the trips with Alva and Alexander to Nepal, in January, and, in May, to Tunisia.[1] On returning to New York from the former, Alva and I heard a fine *Rigoletto* at the Metropolitan Opera conducted by my old friend Marcello Panni. June Anderson, the Gilda, sang slightly behind his beat, waiting for the orchestra, Pavarotti, the Duke of Mantua, slightly ahead of it, knowing he would be followed. A few days later we dined with the Elliott Carters and Marcello. Before returning to Florida we saw the exhibition at the Met of Caravaggio's rediscovered *Lute Player.* The actual music portrayed in the painting, the *bassus* part of Arcadelt's first madrigal book, and the musical instruments, the honey-colored, beautifully ribbed lute, the violin, and the recorder, were also on display. But Georges de la Tour's *Fortune Teller,* in the same room, held us longer.

In 1990 my status as a Florida resident became official, though I had not been a New York resident, as the State's Revenue Department was claiming, since I went to California in 1949, having moved directly from there to Florida in 1968. Nor had I ever been a New York property owner. The Stravinsky apartment at 920 Fifth Avenue was willed to me, but the co-op rules denied nonblood heirs the right to live there or to own it in absentia. The two other apartments that I successively purchased while trying to sell it were intended as residences for my son and his mother during a period when he showed interest in going to school in New York.

At Tully Hall in April, I conducted two pieces and presented *The Rite of Spring* in the Dutch pianist Maarten Bon's eight-hand transcription. The music sounded more dissonant in the equal volumes produced by four pianos than it does in the orchestra, and the chord marking the kiss of

---

1. These are described in my book *Places* (Thames & Hudson, 2000).

the earth, primarily a color effect in the strings, became a startling, balanced, never-heard harmony in the pianos. But the triphammer blows of one of the players, a diminutive Japanese girl, snapped a string, which, though quickly replaced, broke the tension of the performance. The fast movements were more successful than the slow, which pianos cannot sustain.

In New York in June, I took Alexander to the "Rediscovering Pompeii" exhibition at the IBM Gallery of Science and Art, a lesson in computerized archaeology, especially papyrology. All texts with similarities to the one with the lacuna to be filled in, which is to say all others by the author, as well as those by the authors he mentions or quotes, are stored in base-file banks. The drudgery of inputting these data has been eliminated by an optical scanner, a machine that reads and transfers directly to the central memory. IBM's point, of course, is that our exposure to Roman realism and bienséance will leave us thinking how like ourselves the Pompeiians were, a functional society of urban planners and engineers, efficient, well-organized, abundantly supplied with tools and utensils. One caption claimed that an ancient hydraulic valve meets the requirements of the American Standards Association, and that the first-century B.C. kitchen, trays with movable handles, pastry molds (Pompeiians were fond of pizza), skillets, ladles, pots, pans, bowls, even samovars, was at least as well equipped as ours. The furniture was no less up-to-date, and the periform lamps might pass for Scandinavian Modern. As for the bone dice, the numerals are so placed that the sum of each pair of opposing sides is always equal to seven. Again, like our culture, the quality of the painting and sculpture is not high.

Later in the month Alva, Alexander, joined by his sidekick Jonathan, and I returned to Florida. The two teenagers rose to a level of comparative maturity during their nightly games of chess, then, glued to the tube, reverted to an abysmal adolescence, moaning along with a pop megastar, guffawing and squealing at every slapstick stupidity in *Christmas Vacation* (Chevy Chase), in which they characterized people as "nebbishes" and "nerds." But their competence with electronic machines humbled me. Whereas I do not know how to fix the fax or retrieve the lost pages from the computer software, they performed these operations merely by flipping the right dials and pressing the right buttons. Their perpetual need for action reminded me of the increasing imminence of my need for perpetual care.

In July we were in London, where Alexander wanted to see *Tosca*. Jonathan Miller's staging transposed the period from the Napoleonic Occupation of Rome to that of the Nazis in 1944. But not all the parallels were apt. The Cavaradossi, for one, brandishing a maulstick and palette, would be employed otherwise than as a portrait painter during that date in World War II. The stage was tilted laterally from the audience's perspective, perhaps to symbolize the angle of the change of period, but in the darkened theater the slant appeared to have been corrected on stage and transferred to the audience, which at intermission suffered a dizzy spell.

I devoted much of my time in 1990 to cataloging the remainder of my Stravinskyana—music manuscripts, letters, books, personal artifacts, including the Russian typewriter that Diaghilev had given to him, and his styluses for drawing different sizes of music staves. Since none of these items was insured, and since the Florida climate would corrode the gadgets and fade the paper, I offered the collection to the Paul Sacher Stiftung in Basel, already the world's largest Stravinsky library, and the best home for it. I then drew up a will bequeathing my assets to a Foundation for the support of projects in connection with Stravinsky's music, but not only his, on the moral, if not the chrematistical, grounds, that the money generated by his music should be used for its furtherance.

The letters from the Stiftung acknowledging the receipt of my twenty-four packing-cases contained a bill of lading describing them as my "Stravinsky Archives," the remaining tangible evidence of my life between 1948 and 1971, when I used to be Stravinsky's "Bob." (Who am I now?) But the de-acessioning was less painful than anticipated, and the burden of responsibility had been lifted. Perhaps I should have headed for the hills, if I could find them, lose the embonpoint assembled at the Côte Basque and La Caravelle and write up the outtakes.

In December I conducted Satie's *Parade*, Schoenberg's *Five Pieces*, and *The Rite of Spring* in Tully Hall.

1991

At the beginning of the year I recorded *The Rite* in a studio on West Forty-fourth Street, launching a Stravinsky series that by 2002 reached twenty-three CDs. A concert in Fisher Hall in April provided more recording opportunities. Through a connection with the actor Paul Newman's "Hole in the Wall Gang," a charity sponsoring a summer camp for terminally ill and underprivileged children, Alva convinced him to read the part of the Speaker in *Oedipus Rex*, the proceeds to go to this organization.

On a Sunday in late June, sunbathers draped themselves like drying laundry on the rounded, glacier-smoothed rocks just inside the south wall of Central Park at Seventh Avenue. The twenty-second annual Lesbian and Gay Pride Parade, from Columbus Circle to Fifth Avenue and down to Greenwich Village, on June 29, provoked near riots from young people with spiked hair and—the males—earrings, but the cheering, applauding, shouting, singing was at least a change in noise quality from the jackhammer drilling that serenaded us on weekdays. Most of the marchers were grouped into contingents of "Transsexuals for Change," "Females for Legalized Prostitution," and "Feminists: Protect Women's Rights." Some of the participants were tattooed, some of the females bare-breasted, while one male carried an ithyphallic dildo fitted with a condom. The term "pervs" is considered user-friendly.

After rusticating in Pompano for most of the rest of the summer, Alva, Alexander, and I spent a week in Basel, the city of banks, Burckhardt, Nietzsche, and Herzl. The Renaissance rooms in the Kunstmuseum were penetrated by the ghostly clatter of a playerless, electronically-controlled percussion ensemble. At a distance, Holbein's life-size Christ, body turned to the right, gashed in several places and everywhere blood-flecked, eyes partly open in the darkened face, could be mistaken for a sculpture, or an actual cadaver in a glass reliquary. The image was startlingly alive.

In the evening we climbed the hill to Münsterplatz and the Sacher Stiftung, which is in the rebuilt house of Charlotte Kestner, daughter of Goethe's Lotte. The open side of the Platz, facing a small park of lindens, was occupied by a traveling fair. We rode its Ferris wheel for the view of the Rhine from the top of the revolving circle. On returning to the hotel, half-way down what appeared to be a deserted street, we almost stumbled over an older man fellating a younger one in, of all places, the doorway of Erasmus's 1535 house.

The next day Paul Sacher personally escorted us in two bullet-proof Mercedes for lunch at his home in Pratteln, a half-hour drive of which the last few kilometers are on a narrow, eighteenth-century *pavé* road winding through a cherry orchard. The residence, inside prison-height electric-eye metal gates, is a reconstructed farmhouse-cum-fortress. (A few years ago the name of Sacher's young son was found in an abandoned car on the Italian side of the border at the head of a list of prospective candidates for kidnapping.) The Black Forest is in view in one direction and the Jura in another. The interior views are of Picassos, Braques, Chagalls, a large Ensor, and a collection of Chinese ivories.

At the table abundant helpings of large-bead Iranian caviar were followed by lamb and a smooth 1971 St. Emilion with which Felix, the sommelier, liberally replenished our glasses. When tongues loosened, Sacher reminisced about an earlier meeting with Stravinsky and me in a hotel in Zurich in 1961. He also described the initial rehearsal of Strauss's *Metamorphosen*, which he had commissioned. Asking to conduct it himself first, Strauss read it through without stopping. Sacher imitated the composer's famously small beat and showed us how it became larger, then shoulder-high and higher as a danger signal. "The composer said *'Ich danke'* to the players at the end but offered no comment." After the rehearsal Strauss told him that he had finished reading the complete Goethe the night before. Over coffee and kirsch, Sacher said to me directly, abruptly, and in view of his reputation for reticence, astonishingly: "I have always admired you and always been on your side. You were the most important person in Stravinsky's life. He was your destiny. You did what had to be done and did it brilliantly."

Back at the Stiftung, I signed the visitors' book just below Cage, Schnittke (in German), and the widows Leibowitz, Wolpe, and Dorati. Back in the hotel the concierge told us that our bill had been paid by Dr. Sacher. We drove to Milan.

One of my Christmas presents was Don Bachardy's *Last Drawings of Christopher Isherwood*. These close-ups of a man dying in agony, deteriorating mentally as well as physically from image to image, are Don's strongest work. One dreads to turn the pages. In a conversation recorded in the book between the artist and Stephen Spender, the latter compares Don's ordeal with mine: "Bob Craft had the same experience with Stravinsky, I think. Bob simply willed Stravinsky to stay alive. And I think that Bob felt he couldn't face life without Stravinsky."[2] Bachardy's last line in this dialogue refers to Spender's question as to whether Christopher went on thinking about Vedanta: "I think his attitude was: 'All right, I've worked at this thing all these years, I've given this my best effort—now let's see what's there.' " The last four drawings were actually done after the death, on January 4, 1986.

These reminders of my California years were no doubt responsible for a vivid New Year's dream of Aldous Huxley in the Stravinsky home, stepping gingerly, lifting his feet high in order not to stumble, spouting factoids; and of Gerald Heard, as he entered the pulpit of the Ivar Avenue temple, looking and sounding cold-blooded but quickly warming to his apocalyptic sermon.

Alexander came to New York for the holidays, and we saw the City Ballet's *Nutcracker*, sadly deteriorated since Balanchine's death, musically, scenically, and choreographically. On New Year's Eve, Elliott and Helen Carter came to watch the pyrotechnic display over Central Park from our thirty-first-floor window. What a long way from the Roman candles and sparklers of my childhood were the strobe stars and the limned pictures in fireworks of chrysanthemums and willow trees! But Joseph Wright of Derby's painting, and the girandola at Castel Sant'Angelo in Piranesi's and Desgardez's etching with colored washes, were far more spectacular than New York in 1992. Roman fireworks go back to at least 1410, but the display at Hadrian's tomb did not begin until 1540, when small rockets, holding three or four ounces of powder each, shot up and exploded just as they seemed about to fizzle out, releasing six or eight new rockets. In New York, police and TV

2. I wanted Stravinsky to stay alive because I loved him. He was a vital human being to the end. I knew that I could continue to live in different circumstances.

news helicopters hovered over the scene, and the sustained bombardment of the grand finale was followed by chokingly acrid smoke and a three-stage echo. Elliott talked about mixtures of serious and comic, as in Madame Verdurin, and *Lulu*, and about the foreseeable ebbing of the Mahler wave and the coming of the Bruckner.

1992

The event of the year came near the end of it, our late-November tour in China, the most memorable and mind-expanding of all our travel experiences.[3] I had prepared for it by an amount of reading, quadrupled afterward in Florida.

The musical highlight of the year came on the first day of spring with, appropriately, a performance of *Perséphone* in Tully Hall. The narrator was the pretty, petite Irène Jacob, star of the film *La Double vie de Véronique*, which we had seen months before and did not find altogether coherent. We dined with her after rehearsals but since her mother, brother, and other relatives live in Boston and New York, rarely saw her betweentimes. The performance was less successful than it should have been because her voice was amplified at the last minute, without testing, and distortions occurred. She also recited Debussy's *Chansons de Bilitis*, which I conducted along with Stravinsky's *Zvezdolikiy* and Beethoven's First Symphony. *Perséphone* and *Zvezdolikiy* were recorded at Purchase, New York, the day after the concert.

On the medical front, my prostate antigen screening indicated a sharp increase from a year ago, but I decided to do nothing about it, preferring to give up the ghost rather than become a capon. In mid-July I underwent minor surgery for the removal of a basal cell carcinoma on my left shoulder, the result of Florida sunburn. After the injection of the anesthetic I was aware of nothing until the beeps of the electronic needle that cauterizes the veins and produces the smell of burning. At one point I heard Alva mentioning Stravinsky's name and Dr. Hugo's response: "Didn't they just ship him back?" "No," I drowsily interjected, "that was Paderewski." I went on to explain that during World War I the two musicians had lived in the same building in Morges, Switzerland, but that Paderewski's remains were exhumed and interred in his native Poland, of which he had been its first president. I remembered my father talking about a childhood hearing of Paderewski in recital in New York after World War I.

Soon after our return to Pompano, an early morning news bulletin urged the immediate evacuation of all coastal areas in the path of Hurricane Andrew, which, with 140 to 150 mile winds, threatened to be the strongest in Florida history, a class-five disaster. By noon, the appeals to residents

3. *Places, op. cit.*

between Miami and the Keys to seek refuge inland were changed to police-mandated orders. But the only available space in nearby inland hotels was in their ballrooms, and in every case the supply of mattresses had been exhausted. Eventually we found a vacancy at the Marriott in Sawgrass, on the Jacksonville beaches, but were required to call Nebraska (!) to confirm our reservations. When our security guard latched our balcony shutters and told us that in twenty minutes the elevator would be shut off and the garage's electric doors closed, we packed medications, books, changes of clothes, and hurried to our car. The westbound traffic was dense. Turning north at Route 95, we joined a mass exodus, inching along behind boats attached to trailers and wedged between cars overloaded with people and their tied-on possessions. Movement was more rapid after West Palm Beach but bunchy and starting-and-stopping for another hundred miles. Meanwhile, the Miami radio alternated superfluous weather forecasts ("100 percent likelihood of rain"), ill-timed commercials ("Café l'Europa invites you to dine outside by candlelight"), useless information ("Visiting hours at Broward County Jail have been canceled"), dire warnings about loose objects becoming dangerous projectiles in high winds, and the hazard of electrocution from downed street and traffic lights. Statistics about deaths and property damage from the hurricanes of 1935, 1947, 1979 ("David," in which "1200 people died") were repeated, and, more pertinently, the locations of shelters and buses shuttling to them. At each turn-off for Orlando the number of retreating automobiles diminished, and at 9 P.M. we reached Sawgrass and our room, in a building a mile from the main one and in a jungle of live oaks. Centuries ago this was Timucuan Indian country.[4]

The televised scenes next day of devastated Homestead, Cutler Ridge, and the nearby migrant labor camps looked like those of a war zone: shattered homes and shops, people huddling in the corners of roofless buildings, uprooted trees, staved-in and blown-ashore boats. As always, the vic-

4. See *The Work of Jacques Le Moyne De Morgues, A Huguenot Artist in France, Florida and England* by Paul Hulton (British Museum Publications, 1977). This monograph of the painter and draughtsman is also a history of the French attempt to establish a foothold in Florida in 1564–65. Sailing from Le Havre on the day before Shakespeare was born, Le Moyne was a member of the Huguenot Laudonnière expedition, the second and more important of two. The route was by way of Tenerife (May 5), the West Indies, and Cape Canaveral. Le Moyne and his 150 shipmates landed on the south bank of the mouth of the St. Johns River on June 15. The Timucuans who met the ship were friendly and their chief, Solouriwa, proved to be more farsighted and sensible than the French. Spanish galleons patrolled the Florida coast and in little more than a year had destroyed the French fort and massacred the population of its colony. Le Moyne managed to escape and join a ship bound for England, where he lived at Blackfriars. He survived long enough to show his drawings of humans, birds, animals, and botanic life in the New World to Charles IX of France. Le Moyne's notes on North-East Florida Indian cultures comprise one of the great adventure books of sixteenth-century American history.

tims, the *sans-foyers*, the hungry and the property-less, 250,000 of them, were the worst-off already.

In preference to a local oyster bar, we drove twenty miles to Ponte Vedra and a waterfront lobster restaurant smelling sweetly of cedar wood. The accent of our waitress there was almost incomprehensible. Her word "Yawl" referred not to a type of boat but to ourselves collectively. Sawgrass is a tall, sharp-bladed species that grows on dunes.

The returning refugee traffic was light. We found our apartment intact, albeit with beetles scuttling hither and thither, accumulations of dirt beneath the vents, food spoiled, and, in the bedroom, an infestation of millions of mosquitoes on ceilings and walls. The vacuum cleaner failed to inhale all of them but brought down a torrent of stucco. The trees on the pool deck were bent to the ground, the thatched roof of the tiki hut had gone with the wind, and the beach and surf were littered with jetsam. Calling the executor of my estate to report that her services would not be needed quite yet, I learned that, being without electricity and air-conditioning, she left her front door ajar and the house was invaded by a snake. A friend called us from Coconut Grove to say that an acquaintance of hers returning home found his front door blown off and four non-apocalyptic horses in the living room, a Surrealist scene, the more so in that no horse had been seen in the region hitherto.

In New York on our way to China, we saw the Matisse exhibition at MOMA, pushed along at the pace of the swarm of viewers. Even in an emergency, retreat would have been impossible. The early pictures in the first five rooms were unremarkable, and the best in the Fauve section were by Derain. The 1930s and 1940s rooms did not show much development, and the wallpaper cutouts after that could have been skipped, except that skipping was out of the question. I do not care for Matisse's short-legged, thick-thighed, recessive-chinned women, in paint or bronze, and his pinks, oranges, celandines, and indigos are more pleasing in spacious canvases than in small, crowded ones. But "the red dancers" from the Hermitage was worth the aggravation and the stuffy air. The catalog stated that Diaghilev and Stravinsky visited the artist in Nice in June 1919 to commission the *Nightingale* sets and costumes, from which a sketch is shown, but the Matisse papers at the Getty Foundation establish that the visit took place in September 1919 in the painter's residence at Issy-les-Moulineaux, near Paris.

We also saw Philip Glass's *Voyage* at the Met, an opera intended to celebrate the five-hundredth anniversary of Columbus's mistake. The music never left the shallows of a harbor of repeated rhythms and simplistic melodies, while dramatic tension was confined to the audience's anxiety that the people floating about in outer space, especially "Stephen Hawkings" in his wheelchair, could crash to the floor.

1993

The event of the year was our marriage on November 7. Alva's divorce had become final the previous week, and we obtained our license at City Hall that same day. A brief ceremony, which took place in our apartment, was conducted by a non-denominational minister from the UN, a pleasant gent who read poetry. Phyllis and Alva's aunt Maria were the witnesses. We then dined at the Carlyle Hotel.

In Pompano in March, after three days during which six men filled four hundred packing cases with books and music, we moved thirteen miles north on the same road to 4111 S. Ocean Boulevard, Highland Beach. How suddenly, impulsively, this radical disruption came about! I first saw the new house only two weeks earlier and only once, disliking some of its features and fully aware that ocean-front structures must be caulked and painted like boats. But I wanted the spaciousness—the main room was large enough, and the ceiling tall enough, to stage chamber operas—the privacy, the sound of waves on the beach, and the light. I could not resume the cliff-dwelling condo life. The sale documents were signed only the day before. We began our new life with a cocktail-like shaking up in the Jacuzzi.

In May we were in New York for our concert performance of *The Rake's Progress* in Fisher Hall, and recording of it afterward at Purchase. While there I received a request for an autograph from a history teacher in Rakvere, Estonia, and a letter from an Edinburgh University music student who had read somewhere that Stravinsky preserved some of my crammed postcards to him and that he, Colin Dunn, had managed to fit 187 words into an area of four by three inches. A letter from our former California neighbor, Cynthia, said that she attended an open house at 1260 N. Wetherly Drive, found it unrecognizable as the former Stravinsky home, and fled when the realtor played a tape of *The Rite of Spring*.

In October, we opened the renovated Hunter College Playhouse, now the Sylvia and Danny Kaye Playhouse, with *Pierrot Lunaire* and *Histoire du Soldat*. This was the venue, in 1947, of my first professional concert

We were in New York again for the holidays, and watched the fireworks from our window, toasting the New Year with the Carters and Elizabeth Hardwick. At Christmas I received John Lucas's last book of poems, in which I found a

NOTE TO ROBERT CRAFT
PEN AND BATON TRUE
YOUR EVERY GLIMPSE AN INSIGHT
THANKS FOR BEING YOU

1994

At the beginning of the year I presented a second concert in the Kaye Playhouse: Stravinsky's viola *Elégie,* Carter's guitar piece, Schoenberg's Serenade, Mozart's Symphony No. 29, Stravinsky's *Monumentum* and *Abraham and Isaac.*

In March we learned that Alexei Haieff had died. I remembered him as I first knew him, interrupting his stories with fits of giggling and a chain-smoker's coughing. He came to my April 1987 concert with the Philarmonica Romana in the Teatro Olimpico, but looked frail, with trembling hands. Claudio Spies used to refer to him as "the Tsarevitch," in succession to Stravinsky, but Haieff failed to develop as a composer.

In London, in May, Simon Callow, the actor and writer, came to discuss *A Survivor from Warsaw,* which he would narrate on my recording with the London Symphony Orchestra. He had improved the text, changing "The next thing I *knew* was a soldier saying" to "The next thing I *heard* . . ."; and "the Sergeant ordered to do away with us" to "the Sergeant ordered *them* to . . ." Of his then new film, *Four Weddings and a Funeral,* he said, "Of course I play the gay who dies." At the recording session two of the London Symphony Orchestra players, the timpanist and a violinist, remembered me from our concert together in Rio de Janeiro in 1963!

In Paris the following month we visited Gustave Moreau's duplex atelier on rue Rochefoucauld. The upper and lower levels are connected by spiral stairs from which vantages alone the uppermost pictures are visible. Some four hundred canvases crowd the wall space to the very high ceilings, as in Diderot's descriptions of eighteenth-century exhibitions and in Panini's painting, *The Picture Gallery of Cardinal Silvio Valenti Gonzaga,* in which the pictures are fitted tightly together in seven and eight levels.

I prefer the largely, or partly, non-figurative paintings, such as the *Ebauche de couleurs,* the thickly pigmented oils with patches of gleaming white, red, pink, and gold, the reflected light of water, the luminous gyres and whirligigs, the veiled but transparent visions. I am not fond of the Nereids, Salomés, Ledas—was Moreau a gynophobe?—the pictures with Pre-Raphaelite influence (Hunt, Millais), or the scenes with angels, centaurs, monsters, and large human populations. Ensor comes to mind (both artists chose the Battle of Arbela as a subject), as well as Böcklin and the surrealists. But the tableau that kept calling me back was the *Angel of Death on Horseback.*

The three small rooms of Delacroix's atelier contain so few of his works that to justify the exorbitant admission fee the vitrines have been filled with photos, letters, bibelots associated with Baudelaire and George Sand, whom Baudelaire referred to as "a stupid cow." When I was last here in June 1973, the artist's drawings for that most famous of topless females, "Liberty," in *Liberty Guiding the People*, were on display. Now it is the small painting of Charles V at Yuste playing an organ, a reminder of both the artist's and the emperor's musical culture. Together with the bust of the painter showing the jutting jaw and the squint—Théophile Gautier described his eyes as tawny and feline, with thick, arched brows—this made the visit worthwhile. How I would like to live in this neighborhood, with the chestnut tree in the little square, and the market, the oysterers, the patiseries, the charcuteries, just beyond.

Back in Florida I received a letter from Elliott Carter, evidently intended as a blurb for my recording, though I had not asked for one:

> The Craft *Rake* is wonderful. It avoids the dragging gait of the Stravinsky which hurts the 3rd act especially. And what fine singing! I had forgotten that pervasive melancholy that surrounds the whole in some strange way, but adds a beauty . . . Perhaps Bedlam is the true artist's place in capitalist society.

A few days later, at the beginning of September, we were in Washington for the wedding of my grandniece, Wendy Rumble, Diane's daughter. Phyllis's younger daughter, Kristin, drove us across a landscape of rolling hills and white fences to Urbana, Maryland, where seats for one hundred or so had been placed on the sunny lawn of the Turning Point Inn. At the reception I was introduced to droves of unknown relatives and in-laws, while three young women played Bach, Pachelbel, and Vivaldi (a remarkable chaconne), on flute, oboe, cello.

In early October we were again in Paris. In a newspaper article on *"les reines de la Jet-Set,"* Oliver Stone was referred to as *"le célèbre très oscarisé metteur-en-scène."* The Musée Guimet being closed for repairs, we had to settle for the Cernuschi, which is rich in painted terra-cotta horses and Tang and Ming pieces, but poorly lighted, creaky, and unheated. After strolling in the Parc Monceau we dined at the Boule d'Or.

Our flight to New York the next day began nerve-wrackingly. In order to have more space in which to pack, Alva placed the first of our finally buckled-up bags into the hall, then sent for a porter, who, reasonably supposing this bulging, ponderous suitcase to be our only one, wheeled it into the street, where, unreasonably, he deposited it in the open trunk of a driverless white car. Meanwhile, no one having collected our remaining five bags and fearing to miss our flight, we schlepped them to the street ourselves. Thanks to snarled traffic, the white car had inched only a few yards ahead and our porter, recognizing his mistake, retrieved the missing first bag from the amazed driver. At Charles de Gaulle Airport, we were not allowed to check in before receiving our tax refund for the purchase of a Dictaphone in the Duty Free area two weeks before. At length a breathless Alva returned from the refund window, a kilometer and more from the check-in counter, only to report that the machine itself must be inspected. Since its components were distributed in three of our bags, which ones we no longer remembered, all had to be opened. By the time of her second return, with the machine and the francs, the flight had been closed, and we were escorted to the airplane door by a cadre of police shouldering guns.

On my birthday at Highland Beach we were awakened at dawn by avine cawing from our non-functional bedroom chimney, then greeted by a defecation from the fax. The next day we lowered our outside shutters against howling Hurricane Gordon, but because of electrical failure could not raise them again for two days. When lightning struck the house, our security alarms went off, and the police and fire department managed to stop the caterwauling only by pulling the alarm out of the wall and severing the wires. The ceiling fans swirled faster than ever and the doorbell beeped unintermittently, but most other electrical appliances, including lights, telephones, and stereo, were dead, and the elevator could not be unlocked.

The following week we read of the death of Soulima Stravinsky in the Emerald Oaks Nursing Home in Sarasota "after a long illness." But why, with all that royalty money, was he in a nursing home? I remembered him with affection from 1948–1949 and still have a manuscript that he copied for me of an interestingly intricate passage from Mozart's C-minor Mass.

1995

During the first two weeks of the year, I recorded *Le Baiser de la fée* with the London Symphony. (When we gave the Abbey Road address to our Italian-speaking driver, he talked about the *"Scarafaggi"* who made the name famous; when we turned into Brook Street he pointed out where Handel had lived.) I had reservations about parts of the *Baiser* when I began—the flaccid and seedy salon trio for cello, harp, clarinet, with its awkward clarinet fingering in the cadenza, the monotonous 6/8 figuration of the *"Entrée,"* the repetition, some twenty times, of the first tune in the *Village Fête,* fifteen too many. But then, and now, the "Apotheosis" seemed to me the most poignant music Stravinsky ever wrote. I also recorded *Orpheus,* thinking its pas de deux the lushest music of his late neoclassic phase.

While in London we watched Simon Callow's TV presentation of Pasolini's *Gospel According to Saint Matthew,* which made us nostalgic for Matera, the film's substitute Jerusalem, the Gravina its River Jordan. When Mary, played by Pasolini's mother, exits from one of the caves, the camera lingers on her face, as it does on the faces of the young men leading donkeys along the paths of the *sassi*. These strong, real faces, as distinguished from the prettified, cosmeticized ones in movies generally, are the film's greatest strength, together with the unobtrusive and tasteful use of Bach's *St. Matthew Passion*, and, as Christ prays in Gethsemane, his six-part ricercar. Callow contends that Pasolini sought abasing punishment, and that for him the Slaughter of the Innocents represents man's mother-worship and father-hatred.

While in London we met with Dr. Berke of Bärenreiter, a scholar and a gentleman, who had flown from Kassel, Germany, to discuss the possibility of a variorum Stravinsky *Gesamtausgabe*, which is what Stravinsky most wanted, and which was promised to him by Boosey & Hawkes in Paris in October 1968. His music is in disgraceful condition, teeming with errors, torn covers, cheap paper. But after a meeting with the publisher, we realized that this would not happen. I felt responsible for wasting Dr. Berke's time.

On our return to Florida a letter awaited us from Kris in Meherabad, India, with an enclosed rule sheet—bumpf—that had been posted on the door of the outhouse stalls. Item 10 reads, in her rendering of the Devanagri script: "Snake sticks: dead cobras may be thrown over the fence, but please replace the stick to areas near drinking water dispensers for the next cobra."

At the beginning of April, Alexander came from Denmark for a visit. At the end of the month Alva and I flew to Los Angeles for a music festival in Santa Barbara, in which I was to lecture and conduct. The views of the barren southwestern mountains brought back memories of the countless times I had flown this desert route, expecting to see the Stravinskys at the other end. The drive along the grisaille Pacific and the tacky beach bungalows added to the nostalgia. Evidence of landslides—long stretches of road open in only one lane—was apparent all the way. The Biltmore Hotel at Montecito, where we stayed, and where I had stayed with the Stravinskys more than once in the 1950s, faced ominous black oilrigs not far enough off shore. The hotel employed a dozen or more valets to park and retrieve its Rollses and stretch-limos, and as many waiters to drive the three-wheeled motorized rickshaws that deliver room-service orders to outlying cottages. Our unit was set in an exotic botanical garden with African tulip, Canton orchid, ficus trees, yellow and blue jacaranda, and oleander.

The next day we rented a car and drove to the UCSB campus, where we were obliged to park in lot twenty-three of twenty-three and to walk two miles from there to a rehearsal, competing with speeding bicycles, zooming skate-boards, and roller-blades; earthquakes are not the only peril in the Golden State. After two minutes rehearsing the Concertino, I realized that the cellist would not be able to play the part in a hundred hours of practice.

My lecture, on Stravinsky and Santa Barbara, explained that in the fall of 1943, working on the revision of the *Danse sacrale*, he contemplated moving here, and that in December 1943 part of the new version was actually written in Arthur Sachs's Hope Ranch mansion. I mentioned that from August 1941 until 1947 the Stravinskys spent many weekends there with the Sachs, and that Nadia Boulanger was another houseguest. On October 19, 1942 Nadia's ancilla, Marcelle de Manziarly, played as much as Stravinsky had finished of his four-hand Sonata with him. I also mentioned that U.S. Ambassador (to Argentina) and Mrs. Robert Woods Bliss lived here at the same time and had commissioned the *Dumbarton Oaks* Concerto. Bliss, a high-ranking official, helped obtain the entry permit from Europe for the second Mrs. Stravinsky and, in the same year, 1940, helped to make possible the Stravinskys' application for U.S. citizenship on the Mexican quota, the Russian having been closed. While in Santa Barbara the Stravinskys became friends with Mayette Meyneng, a French-born student and a member of the local De Gaullist circle, who had published a best-selling novel, *The Broken Arc*, which the Stravinskys read and admired. Stravinsky elicited her help with his French correspondence, and in editing his 1944 (French) Chicago lecture.

The following day we rehearsed the concert version of Parasha's *Mavra* aria at the University of Southern California in Los Angeles. The visit disturbed me: the uglification of the city, the heterogeneously horrible new buildings next to ramshackle old ones, above all the dislocation, the familiar names of unrecognizable streets. At Montecito the next morning we learned that after a giant truck had jack-knifed on the freeway nearby, traffic was scarcely moving by midafternoon. No matter that we would be late for our dress rehearsal, since the players were not there and did not arrive until concert time.

While packing medications on the morning of our departure, I accidentally read the label of the container from which I had been popping Coumadin pills for the past three weeks and discovered that they were seven-and-a-half strength, not five. This posological mistake, which could have caused a fatal hemorrhage, accounted for a feeling of weakness far exceeding my normal indolence and hebetude. We arranged to be driven to Los Angeles, where we boarded a flight to Miami, proceeding from there to Highland Beach by car. My prothrombin time was quickly corrected.

On the way to London we dined in New York with the Carters at the Century Club under the portrait of the young Henry James. In the waiting lounge at JFK Airport a man seated next to us, listening to classical CDs through earphones and following scores, proved to be Vladimir Ashkenazy, who had been importuning me via phone and fax during the last year for permission to arrange *The Rite* for eight pianos. In London, I recorded *The Rite* during a rare heat-wave. The lawn on the Thames side of the Savoy was strewn with pristine-white, never suntanned backs and legs. A story in the *Daily Telegraph* described a uxoricide in Newcastle-upon-Tyne that struck us as both compact and remarkably specific: "A husband bludgeoned his unfaithful wife to death, using a kitchen knife and a joiner's saw to cut her into seven pieces, which he stored in the freezer between vol-au-vent cases and packets of frozen peas. Michael Allen, 44, attacked his wife, Myrtle, 54, as she slept, inflicting at least 20 blows to the side of her head with a peened hammer. Paul Batty, the prosecuting QC, said the dismembering had been done in 'a very businesslike fashion.'"

In New York in mid-September, the filmmaker John Huszar interviewed me under melting lights in a studio on West Sixty-first Street for a "high definition television" program, then filmed me conducting the Juilliard student orchestra in the *Rite* for a TV "special." The stage was crowded with mobile cameras, and more than half of the allotted time was spent in repairing technical glitches and changing set-ups for camera angles.

On October 10 in Paris, half of our time in the labyrinthine Louvre was spent in queues: at the entrance to Pei's pyramid, at the basement ticket booths, and, on the return to ground level, in the climb to the Winged Victory, which used to mark the entrance to the galleries. Only a few pieces were better lighted and less ornately framed than when I was last here, and, though the windows were open, climate controls were still not in evidence. But among the few pictures properly lighted and displayed in vitrines were a marvelous Pisanello, and Cosmè Tura's stunning portrait of a man in a gray cloak. Unlike Ingres's small pencil study for *La Grande Odalisque*, the painting, because of the attenuated spine (extra-long rib cage), limits the voyeur's fantasies concerning the voluptuous malleability of the meniscuses, and what Kenneth Clark refers to as the "luxurious *débanchements*." As is, the curvaceous, never walked-upon thenars are the picture's main erotic attraction. And Baudelaire was right: Ingres's languorous ladies, like all of his sitters, are too present, too up-front: "they disturb our senses with their too visible and palpable extraneity," their too, too solid flesh. Ingres's most astute modern critic, André Lhote, wrote of the "amiable swellings of this flesh, the voluptuous undulations; it is she who will enter into him [Ingres], viscerally, and transform his scientific conception of the human body into a purely palpable one. From then on the exact number of vertebrae will matter little to him . . . This adorable curve of the back, so flowing, so supple, so long, he will lengthen still further . . ."

From the upper floor of the Louvre, the sight of the mother pyramid and her three little ones is grotesque.

During the final leg of our return flight to New York, I experienced what felt like a churning in the left side of my heart, accompanied by breathlessness, dizziness, perspiring. On arrival I spoke to a Dr. Levelli of the cardiac unit at Columbia-Presbyterian Hospital, who said that my symptoms suggested periocarditis. He directed me to a Dr. Romanioli in the hospital's downtown branch, only three blocks from our apartment, to have an electrocardiogram. The results indicated that I had "complete blockage of the heart" and must go immediately to the emergency entrance at nearby Lenox Hill. At the triage there, a few minutes later, two paramedics in police blue questioned me and filled out forms for me. They wished me "good luck," a reminder that heart surgery under emergency conditions is chancy. A Dr. Garcia, waiting inside, eased me into a wheelchair and quickly inserted an IV needle in the back of my right hand, explaining that in an emergency, when the blood pressure drops, finding a vein can take precious time. After pushing my conveyance to an elevator and from it on the fifth floor to the Cardiac Intensive Care Unit, he fitted me with an oxygen nose-mask and began tests that continued throughout the night. My pulse, blood pressure, and temperature were measured every few minutes, and I was echogrammed, X-rayed (twice), and cathoded for EKGs (four times), after which Garcia drew a diagram showing the dissociation of the atrial and ventricle rhythms, the breakdown in the impulse conduction system in the left bundle.

By midnight my pulse, 37 when I entered the hospital, had dropped to 20, and my blood pressure correspondingly. At about 4 A.M. Garcia injected atropine into a right-arm artery to stimulate the heart, warning me that I would feel flushed from it, nauseous, and dry in the mouth. The atropine evidently failed to act, and a half-hour later he and a team of assistants burst into the room. My pulse had fallen to 17—the new metronomy is so super-sensitive that even a blush will bring the monitor at the master console posthaste—and a temporary pacemaker had to be implanted at once. I was anesthetized, but the full effect had not yet taken when Garcia carved two incisions in the area of my right cervical. I also felt the insertion of the intermediate pacemaker and the threading of a wire into my jugular vein. Part of this filament, encased in a protective, accordion-like plastic wrapper, protruded from my neck between the two cuts like the side handle of a jug.

Within a short time, the pacemaker functioning and my pulse a stable 60 per beat, I was taken off the Coumadin that controlled my coagulation time, which was too slow and dangerous to permit more than "interventionary surgery," from which I deduced that I must have bled profusely from this so-called minimally invasive kind. I was then impaled on an IV containing heparin, an anticoagulant that metabolizes more quickly than Coumadin.

I had to wait three days for the switch in blood thinners to become effective, an intensely boring interval since any side-to-side move could disturb the position of the pacemaker wiring. Acedia sets in quickly in this near rigor mortis. It was hard to believe, as I lay there, that only a short while before I had been slogging up a mountain in Calabria, climbing steps in Noto and Piazza Armerina, walking long distances in Rome.[5] I tried to perspectivize the teetering on the brink during the night of October 25–26. If I had not gone to a doctor on the 25th, I would have retired early, exhausted and not yet recovered from jet lag, and, at about the time that Dr. Garcia came to the rescue, died.

The actual operation on October 30 took only forty minutes, including the suturing and the bandaging—in thin strips covered with thick padding. I was alert during most of it and conversed with the surgeon, the musically-minded, super-intelligent, and sympathetic Dr. Stelzer, who at one point asked me to indicate a 120 metronomic beat (I did), and at another to identify the pitch of a strange humming in the room (F-sharp). His two incisions, under the left cervical, were painless—I was under verséd and a narcotic—but I felt the insertion of the pacemaker and the movement of the wires to the atrium and ventricle. Only two days later, I was able to attend a midtown business meeting with one of Stravinsky's music publishers and several lawyers.

What I learned in the hospital is that the time between heartbeats varies in healthy hearts, but not in diseased ones on the verge of failure. Thus a perfectly steady heartbeat is more likely to be found in elderly, rigid bodies than in flexible young ones. The corollary of this is that fractal patterns of considerable complexity are linked to healthy heart functioning, and that when the complexity disappears, sudden death may follow.

In New York for New Year's, we invited the Carters, Elizabeth Hardwick, and Charles Rosen to see the Central Park fireworks from our window, but the intellectual form of them sent up by Charles distracted us from the visual competition. He was at the same time shy and self-assured, telling repertory stories about eminent musicians and writers, but laughing at them a little too long himself. Most of the evening was spent in one-upmanship exchanges of esoteric information between Elliott and him. Charles, who has the larger provision, expounded on his recent discoveries visiting the tombstones of artists and writers in Paris cemeteries.

1996

At the beginning of January we went to the Metropolitan Opera's performance of the *Makropulos Case*, on which, two days before, the curtain had to be rung down minutes after being raised owing to the heart-attack death onstage of a member of the cast. The production enthroned Jessye Norman on the Sphinx for most of the second act. The ending was borrowed from

5. *Places, op. cit.*

Götterdämmerung, and the story itself is as absurd as any in the annals of opera libretti, but no matter, the English being mostly indistinct. A blizzard began the next day, and narrow, mazelike trenches that had to be negotiated sideways were dug at street corners. We fled to Florida.

February 8 was spent listening to edits of our *Rite* and *Apollo* tapes. The *Rite* performance, as the Chicago critic Larry Kart would later write, "puts the shock back into the piece," and the excitement of it compared very favorably to the recent release of a bland, affectless, trudging read-through by Boulez.

I will not describe the kidney-stone surgery I had to undergo at North Ridge Hospital, Fort Lauderdale in February, but only the joy and relief as I emerged from Recovery on seeing Alva smiling outside the door. I got through the experience only with her aid and that of a morphine pump. I noted that on my Patient Discharge Instruction Sheet, "Activity as tolerated" had been O.K.'d but not "May resume sexual activity." On the way home, we visited our future house, but en route narrowly escaped being rammed by a truck of the "Bug Off Exterminator Company."

In mid-April we were in London, at the Hyde Park Hotel, to record Stravinsky's Variations and Concerto in D with the Royal Philharmonic in Henry Wood Hall. From there we went to Venice for a few days, continued to Rome by car over (or through) the Gran Sasso, then flew to Hamburg for a "Werkstatt Konzert" on May 9.

This took place in the too-reverberant Norddeutscher Rundfunk Studio 10 but was well received by a largely young audience. The "Werkstatt" format required me to conduct passages from the new edition of *Firebird* by way of illustration, and fortunately the shaky performances of these excerpts alerted me, as well as sober members of the orchestra, to the quasi-inebriation of many of the players, which should not have surprised me, since many of them had returned from the between-rehearsals lunch-breaks the worse for beer. Another requirement, about which I was not forewarned, was to deliver a pre-concert allocution, which I did in English with as many German words as I could remember. Someone asked a question about the relationship between Prinz Max Egon von Fürstenberg and Stravinsky. I said that they had known each other only briefly during 1957–1958, but that the death had shocked Stravinsky because the Prince appeared to be in robust health when they were last together in Donaueschingen a few months before. I said that Heinrich Strobel pressured Stravinsky to compose the *Grabmal,* with the hortatory argument that it would promote the cause of new music in Donaueschingen, but I asserted that the emotion of the piece is genuine.

I gave several interviews while in Hamburg and found the questions more sophisticated than would be the case in America. Asked how I would account for the drastic change of style between *Threni* and *Movements*, I said that a long sackcloth-and-ashes sacred-text piece and a short, lively, purely instrumental one could not be compared, and went on to limit the meaning of "style" to Stravinsky's own definition of it as a "fingerprint," the same in all of his music, not something that changed from piece to piece but that was extended by each new one. For examples I mentioned the melodic half-steps at the beginning of *Ebony* Concerto, *Orpheus*, the String Concerto, and also the incomplete triplets in the "Balalaika," in the first movement of the Symphony in Three, in the violins and violas in "The Building of the Ark," and in the Finale of the 1945 *Firebird*. I mentioned antipodal aspects—the extreme harmonic and polyphonic density of *Threni* versus the thin textures of *Movements*, the least inspissated of any Stravinsky opus to that date, and its new rhythmic language and instrumental variety, in contrast to the instrumental role in *Threni*, where the violins do not play at all during half of the piece, and, except for trombones at cadences, the Third Elegia is *a cappella*. *Movements*, I said, is the pivot to the later music.

A personal question followed as to whether I ever had tiffs with Stravinsky. I said that if he felt that tension had developed between us, he would send a repentant or apologetic note by hand, outside the postal system. I still have one of these in which, touchingly, he blames his age for speaking roughly to a young clarinetist in a recording session. The player, a young Israeli boy who worshipped him, began to cry. I had taken his side, saying he had not understood the composer's instruction. Stravinsky did not speak to me for three days, then sent our cook to me with a very touching note.

This provoked a related question: "You often conducted with Stravinsky by your side, and, conversely, he conducted with you at his side. What was that like? Did you ever feel as if you were in competition with each other?" "Never," I said. Sometimes I stood behind him on the same podium, where, being much taller, I could help by giving cues. Once, in a recording session, when I saw that he had forgotten to cut off the last chord of the *Symphony of Psalms*, I did it for him, to spare him, as well as the orchestra and chorus from having to do a long and tiring section over. I was criticized for this, but not by him. He needed help, I explained, because if you do not conduct regularly, as in his case, the sheer physical strain in a recording session can be exhausting.

Everyone wanted to know if my views of Stravinsky the man had changed since his death. I admitted that in the 1970s, when his 1920s–30s correspondence was translated for me, I realized that I could not have had a personal relationship with him as he was then. What upset me was the contrast between the arrogance and strident tone of his business letters at the time he was composing the dulcet music of *Apollo* and *Perséphone*. I said that it seemed to me that nothing of the character of the between-the-wars

Stravinsky comes into his correspondence with me, which suggests that he was transformed by his happy second marriage.

One interviewer said that hostility to Stravinsky's Russian roots had been perceived in me. I responded that no one in Russia could possibly be cognizant of my feelings about this or anything else. I noted that his daughter and daughters-in-law must have heard him say, as I did many times, that the underlying inspiration for *The Rite of Spring* was his wish to send the Russia of his background "to Hell." I reminded the interviewers that Soviet Russia had deprived him of family and friends, robbed him of his homes, his possessions, his copyrights, and made the use of his native tongue impracticable in his music. In turn, I wondered who could have expected him, at the time I entered his life, to be interested in Rimsky-Korsakov or Borodin, adding that Bach, Mozart, Beethoven, and the polyphonic music of the fourteenth to seventeenth centuries had become the focuses of his musical interests, and that after the *Rake*, when he began to study Schoenberg and Webern, he frequently regretted the narrowness and insufficiency of a musical background limited, as was that of the Russian Nationalists, to the nineteenth century. In Webern's case, the background extended as far back as Heinrich Isaac. Long before my time Stravinsky had come to regard *Firebird, Petrushka, The Rite of Spring,* and *Les Noces* as the end, indeed the eclipse, of "Russian musical traditions."

These music critics wanted to know what Stravinsky would have thought of today's music critics. I answered *"Plus ça change,"* adding that he was nevertheless intrigued by musicologists' discoveries of relationships in his music of which he was not consciously aware. I concurred that he was unkind about critics, referring to Antoine Goléa, for one, as "the hemorrhoid," and to Irving Kolodin of the New York *Sun* as "the bitch of the son." I said that a recent review of recordings of Stravinsky's violin and piano music in the *New York Times* made me imagine the composer decorating it with question and exclamation marks: "In 1924 Igor Stravinsky declared war on the violin," the notice began, and I could see Stravinsky red-penciling "not true" in the margin, and the words "Suite Italienne for Paul Kochanski, 1925," the arrangement that, together with the two from *Firebird* made for the same violinist in 1929, became the prototypes of Stravinsky's 1930s violin and piano repertory for Samuel Dushkin, except that the Kochanski arrangements are more difficult. The notice further asserted that the Duo concertant is "a sort of sonata in four movements," with "maniacal jigs and tarantellas." I said that Stravinsky would have written: "It is in five movements, in no sense 'a sort of sonata,' and has only one jig and one tarantella, neither in the least maniacal." I mentioned that Stravinsky had framed and attached to the wall of his studio a print-out of Eliot's remark: "Criticism is much too important to be left to the fellows who write for the papers."

The final question was: "Do you have any special goals in your own performances of Stravinsky's music?" I said that I hoped to convey something of what I know of his wishes concerning modes of attack, articulation, note lengths, and the different types of accentuation; that the Stravinsky phrase should not have the little tapering-off ritard at the end, still taught in music schools as "shaping a phrase"; and I admitted that Stravinsky's tempos in his recordings are not reliable as models, differing radically according to dates and circumstances of recording.

Leaving Hamburg, we tried to check in for an Air France flight to Paris, but were informed of a new rule restricting passengers to two bags each. Accordingly, we switched to Brit Air for Heathrow and checked four of our five bags through to New York.

On our return to Florida we began to pack for the move to our new home in Gulf Stream. The actual move, on July 2, the loading and unloading of furniture and boxes onto trucks, took twelve hours. Alexander had come to help, and was assisted by two muscular college girls. The unpacking of ten thousand books and uncounted music scores, and the shelving of them in some semblance of order continued for three weeks. We counted ourselves lucky when our Highland Beach house sold quickly, though at a loss, since ten newer houses had recently been completed within a mile of it.

Alexander visited me in Florida again in October. Returning from a restaurant with him one night, we found two of his Danish friends, a man and woman in their twenties, waiting outside our gate in a car rented at Orlando. Since this visit had to have been coordinated some time ago, I was surprised that he had said nothing about it. The ostensible reason for his trip was my birthday, but I quickly understood that his interest in the girl and his wish to lure her here was a deeper one. She turned out to be Denmark's bicycle-racing champion, which explained her closely-cropped blond hair. But why would he want her together with the boyfriend? I showed my collection of Danish literature in English to her and was interested to learn that she knew Peter Hoeg. After dinner she went to bed, leaving the three of us to sit by the pool until, realizing that the young people would want to speak Danish, I went to my room.

The Scandinavians were in the pool shortly after sun-up. When they emerged, I noticed that Alexander could not remove his eyes from the girl, which surprised me since she was flat-chested and her muscular thighs were surmounted by a boy's behind, or at any rate one very unlike the females of Dégas, Alma-Tadema, Bouguereau, and Klimt. On their second day I began to feel that the twosome would have liked to settle here permanently. They left soon after Alva returned from New York.

At the end of November we recorded *Firebird* with the London Phil-

harmonia, and went from there to Singapore, Bali, and Borobudur,[6] returning to the United States before the holidays. Dining with the Carters one
night, Elliott gave a new book of his music criticism to me.

The Times Literary Supplement had invited me to name two favorite books
of the year for a Christmas list, and I complied as follows:

> *The Western Greeks.*[7] The book's fifty-four richly diversified essays on the exten-
> sion of Greek culture to Southern Italy, that great pivot in the development of
> European civilization, comprehend the Minoan–Mycenian background, the
> evolution of Aegean scripts, political structure and history, and the Greek
> inquiry into philosophy and the physical world, the first expressions of scien-
> tific thought having emerged in the Italiot and Siceliot colonies. The studies
> of navigation and Early Bronze Age oared ships, of maritime communications,
> of the encounter with the Etruscan thalassocracy include the hypothesis that
> a taste for tunny, a deep-water fish, was the incentive of the earliest (ninth
> millennium) raft fishermen, bones of this scromboid having been found in the
> Mesolithic stratum of the Franchthi Cave (Argolid).
>
> The authorship of *Three Discourses,*[8] "Newly Identified Work of the Young
> Hobbes," is asserted here by "statistical wordprinting" and the matching of
> the subject matter, the pith, and the wit, to the paw prints of the Bear of
> Malmesbury. Visiting Rome in the second decade of his century, Hobbes re-
> marks that the empire of the popes "has more risen by encroachment than
> right." After seeing relics that included "Aaron's Rod" and the "Gridiron where-
> upon Saint Lawrence was broiled," he ridicules those who "believe in impossi-
> bilities for no other reason than because other men do so." He attended a
> conclave in which a Pontiff was elected, then abruptly deposed on the accusa-
> tion that this "head of church cannot speak a sentence without that scurrilous
> byword of the Lombards, *Cazzo* [prick]."

1997

In mid-January I became a traveling salesman for my recordings and books.
My first exposure in this enterprise was at Tower Records, Greenwich Village, where I autographed books and recording booklets. The buyers and
bystanders were a diverse group of NYU students, a culture maven or two,
a ballet teacher, a music engraver, a Rabbi, and a Talmudic scholar. They
were well informed and asked pertinent questions. One of them, Dr. Edward Polidi, a Holocaust survivor, flummoxed me with the statement that
Stravinsky had had an affair with his mother in Paris in 1934. The lady in
question was associated with Ida Rubinstein and was a member of the fam-

6. *Ibid.*
7. Bompiani: Milan, 1996.
8. The University of Chicago Press, 1995.

ily of Elias Canetti, but Polidi would not divulge her name. Suddenly I recognized my niece Kris in the group. Auden is right: "Private faces in public places are nicer than public faces in private places."

Toward the end of the month we flew to Heathrow. The human condition in London seemed even more dire than in New York, the beggars and bedded-down were like figures in Gustave Doré's drawings of a century ago. Having read that the Queen had asked her subjects to donate sixty thousand pounds toward a new royal yacht, we wondered why these panhandlers were not taxed to pay for it and the derelicts not obliged to pay sidewalk rent. I recorded *Petrushka* and *Pulcinella* with the Philharmonia in Abbey Road.

One midnight near the end of February we landed at Boston's Logan airport. After an hour's wait in zero weather for a taxi, the sedate, colonial Ritz-Carlton felt cozy, and a log fire was kindled in our sitting room while we swallowed briny Sheffield Maine oysters and took in the winter postcard scene of Boston Common with its icy trees, frozen pond, and picturesque bridge. A history of the hotel says that at one time Benny Goodman provided its dinner music. Our rooms were ghost-filled: I had stayed here with the Stravinskys in 1966, with my sister and mother in 1985, and at various times long ago with three different girlfriends.

The next afternoon I talked to students at the New England Conservatory. On entering the room, I recognized three old friends in the second row: the composers Arthur Berger, Leon Kirchner, and Harold Shapero. They told me later that my talk was necessary, since the audience, professors as well as students, were ignorant of the subject. When the symposium part of the session opened, Harold related an anecdote about one of his earliest meetings with Stravinsky, recollecting that when he asked the composer about the role of inspiration, he answered dryly: "You know better than that." The conversation was soon confined to the three composers and myself, each prodding the others' memories. In explaining that the canon, the basis of the *quattrocento* and *cinquecento* mass and motet, was the main device of Stravinsky's late music, I referred to his historical scope as being wider than Schoenberg's, who tended to regard Renaissance music as of antiquarian interest only. This prompted Leon to say that he happened to be present when the UCLA musicologist Walter Rubsamen showed a motet by Johannes Ockeghem to Schoenberg, who was fascinated by it. When I remarked that I found the vogue of octatonic analysis tiresome, Arthur, the acknowledged discoverer of Stravinsky's use of the device, chimed in with "So do I. I wish I had never mentioned it."

The four of us moved on to a restaurant down the block and continued to reminisce. Leon said that "One day during a class in Schoenberg's home, he suddenly walked to the window, pointed to a passing airplane, but gazed at it in silence. We wondered what could have attracted his attention, until he remarked that 'It neither accelerates nor decelerates, yet the sound changes.'" Leon said that he was present when René Leibowitz and his (and onetime my) inamorata, Ellen Adler, played their recording of Schoenberg's *Ode to Napoleon* in the composer's home. At the end, after a stunned silence, Gertrud Schoenberg blurted out: "I always knew that love is blind but now I know that it is also deaf." Leon imitated Schoenberg's Viennese accent and hand and head movements with an actor's skill.

Harold, still the Stravinsky freak I first knew in Tanglewood in 1946, said that when he sent an announcement of the birth of his daughter Hannah to Stravinsky, the composer arranged the letters of her name in palindromic form, enclosed them in a circle, and wrote on its circumference: "To little Hannah best birthday wishes, also to her gifted parents Harold and Esther Shapero from their friend Igor Stravinsky, Los Angeles. Sept./43."

Harold has a letter from Stravinsky praising his piano Variations: "This work is really remarkable: dimension, diatonics, Beethovenian spacing of voices, tastefulness of the rhythmical element (never overloaded), absolute clearness and convincingness of your musical speech."

Harold said that he was sitting with Aaron Copland at the Princeton premiere of *Requiem Canticles*. "Copland was speechless after it," he said, "then he opened his arms in the direction of the orchestra and exclaimed: 'Who at any age has composed music as completely new as that, but at eighty-five?'" Harold had always hated the marimba, he told us, but he thought that Stravinsky had "blotted out its vulgarity by blending it with bells and celesta."

Of the three elder statesmen, Arthur was the most cryptic and the softest spoken. All three complained about the splintering of styles in today's new music, about Cage's infantilism, and about the decline of the Boston Symphony after nineteen years of Ozawa.

The following day my extended hour at the Boston Conservatory of Music passed smoothly, but the only questions of substance came from the teachers. I mentioned that Stravinsky composed the third movement of his Symphony in C around the corner in the Hemenway Hotel, now, at street level, the "Hemenway Pharmacy." Incredibly, nobody was aware of this.

Before signing books at Borders in Chestnut Hill in the evening, I screened the *Grands Amants* film. The audience was Harvard-oriented and literary.

When a woman asked if I meant to use the expletive *Basta* with the same emphasis as Henry James, I was too surprised to ask where he used it. I signed a copy of my *Chronicle* for a Harvard student working on the Japanese translation of the book.[9] A distinguished-looking man astonished me by the request to record *The Rite of Spring* with the 1943 *Danse sacrale*. A middle-aged and apparently not addlepated lady said that the most thrilling musical experience of her life was playing oboe in the Orchestra of St. Luke's in my performance of Britten's *War Requiem.* Not wanting to embarrass her by saying that I had never conducted the piece, I inscribed her book and moved on, feeling a fraud, except that I *did* write the *book.*

On the morning of our last day in the city, the dean of Boston University's music department, Dr. Phyllis Hoffman, an attractive woman and perfect hostess, introduced me to an elderly but spry gentleman who addressed me in French. It was Roger Voisin, whose name I had deleted from my lecture, wrongly supposing that by this date he might no longer be among the quick. Instead, he proceeded to demonstrate how, in a three-sixteen bar between two two–four bars, Stravinsky would conduct all three sixteenths instead of beating the short bar in one. His imitation of Stravinsky's gestures was exact, and he himself was a charmer. I had first heard him play at Tanglewood in 1937 but had not seen him since I was in Boston with Stravinsky in 1949.

We returned to Florida, Baudelaire's *"Eldorado banal de touts les vieux garçons,"* to prepare for more hucksterism in upstate New York. Claudio Spies came as a houseguest. We talked about the Stravinskys as we had first known them, Claudio maintaining that Vera S.'s manners and deportment reflected her wealthy, aristocratic background, as I.S.'s did his middle-class one. But where did I.S. acquire those boorish table manners, pushing his plate aside when finished with it, blowing his nose in restaurant napkins, and swilkering his soup?

In mid-April, I addressed an audience at the Eastman School in Rochester, the best informed so far. One bright young man, who was blind, knew all of my records, and one of the teachers produced a 1962 program of the Hamburg State Opera, saying that he had met me when I conducted there, and showing me a program I had autographed. We dined with my grandniece, Wendy, whom I scarcely knew, and David, her husband, finding them smart, vivacious, and enjoyable company.[10] The next day we were taxied a half-hour late through wet snow to an outlying Borders. The sixty or more people waiting there were congenial and responsive, and at least half of them seemed to understand the French commentary of the *Amants* film. More books and records were sold here than at any other depot.

9. This was published in January 1999.
10. She is now a mother and pediatrician.

A grandnephew of Lyudmila Pitoëff, who danced the Princess in the first *Histoire du Soldat* in Lausanne in September 1918, introduced himself and said that the ballerina's granddaughter Svetlana Pitoëva lives in Pondicherry, India, a name out of Sherlock Holmes. A gentle, round-faced, white-haired lady, daughter of the conductor Albert Stoessel, told me that she played second flute in the Juilliard Orchestra in 1942 and remembered me conducting it. (I didn't.) A niece of my Juilliard teacher Elbert Lenrow presented herself, and the assistant manager of the store said that he was nine years old when Stravinsky died and recalls hearing the announcement on the morning radio. I told him that of the many telegrams received that day, the one I still think of was from the composer George Perle: "This is the first time in six hundred years that the world has been without a great composer," *i.e.*, since Guillaume de Machaut. We left this grim, cold, overcast city of ugly modern buildings and garishly painted turn-of-the-century clapboard houses—Simone de Beauvoir's diary for February 18, 1947 says: "I dearly hope I'm never fated to live in Rochester"—and drove through bleak farmlands and encroaching factories to Buffalo. Our Hyatt Hotel, "downtown," was surrounded by skyscrapers but no shops or stores. We were comfortably installed in a suite before becoming aware of the proximity of an elevator shaft in which arrivals and departures were as loud as subway trains. Repacking, we moved to a cramped single room on the far side of the hotel.

A Borders talk at Cheektowaga was followed by a two-hour seminar for the Buffalo University music faculty, one of them an intelligent and sophisticated young man named John Smith, another, of the same caliber, a female music-theorist, apostle of Pieter Van den Toorn, completing a thesis on the *Rake* and wishing to know why Ingmar Bergman's staging has been the most successful to date. A man-and-wife team was researching Stravinsky's relationship with Jacques and Raïssa Maritain at Meudon. All in all, I talked for three and a half hours. We dined at a restaurant in Mark Twain's sometime residence, decorated in the style of his period.

Very early the following morning, not the right time of day for selling my kind of merchandise, I was interviewed live on ABC National Television. The New York State Thruway, which cuts into the reservation territory of a Seneca Nation, had been shut down for one stretch, blocked off by a thousand Indians who had set fire to piles of old automobile tires. It seems that the price of gasoline was thirty cents lower on the Reservation, and that the Indians bootlegged it outside their territory, which resulted in a tax revenue deficit that threatened to raise the thruway tolls. The Seneca population in the region is about seven thousand, and dissension between the tribes is rife.

The oldest building in Buffalo—the territory was Dutch before the American Revolution—dates to the early 1830s. Two historical events are remembered: the attendance at a First Unitarian Church service, February

19, 1861, by President Millard Fillmore and President-Elect Abraham Lincoln; and, forty years later, the assassination of the pious fraud President William McKinley, whose favorite entertainment was watching nude theatricals in the White House's Lincoln Ballroom. After the shooting, his personal secretary was obliged to depart on the night train for Washington in order to shred the President's vast collection of pornography and compromising files.

The most gratifying of my Buffalo experiences was a radio interview by Mary Van Vorst, who had actually read my *Chronicle* and marked passages that she asked me to read. But our Buffalo mystery remained unsolved. Leaving our room for the television studio, we noticed a pair of large-size male shoes in our clothes closet and a bottle of vitamin pills. The hotel's security being tight, more so on our fifteenth floor than on lower levels, we deduced that one of the porters and the room maid, who saw us leave, must have trysted there while we were out. But how could a discalced porter go about his job, and why the vitamin pills?

In August we were in London recording the *Nightingale*. Our first session went slowly, since continuing microphone adjustments for the singers required that everything taped before each change had to be redone. The young Olga Trífonova, in the title role, bent the tempo too far in places and had learned the second cadenza in the Second Act incorrectly, leaving out three wiggles in the ornamentation. Ogling Olga was a constant distraction for the males in the cast, chorus, and orchestra.

Rudolf Bing's death a few weeks later took me back to evenings in his loge, beginning in December 1951, at the old Thirty-ninth Street Metropolitan Opera, after he had contracted to give the American premiere of *The Rake's Progress*. The Stravinskys had known his Russian wife, an ex-ballerina, in pre-war Paris, and they chatted with her in Russian during intermissions. On one occasion, when Eugene Ormandy conducted *Fledermaus* and the loge was full, Bing personally escorted me to a seat in the first row orchestra. I saw him several times in 1961, through his then girlfriend, Nancy King, later Mrs. William Zeckendorf Jr., a dancer in the Met ballet and friend there of my dancer friend Judith Chazin. But I remember him best at the eightieth-birthday reception for Stravinsky by the City of Hamburg, June 18, 1962, at which time we talked about *Lulu*. He hated the opera but was being pressured to present it in New York: "How can anyone be interested in any of those people?" he asked, and I agreed with him. Nonetheless I conducted the American premiere in Santa Fe a year later. When I saw him last, in the Carlyle Hotel restaurant in New York in 1986, he was suffering from Alzheimer's; his eyes were vacant, his face blank.

Unlike Bing's, Georg Solti's death was unexpected. He had been as active in his eighties as ever. In recent years he had called me every time he needed information about a Stravinsky piece that he intended to play. He wanted assurance that the *Petrushka* concert ending was really by Stravinsky. I said yes, but *Petrushka* is not *Petrushka* without the original last page. "That is exactly the problem," he said. "The Vienna Philharmonic trumpets cannot play it." They couldn't play it in January 1913, I told him, for which reason Stravinsky fled the city. On May 29, 1963, we heard the first two acts of Solti's *Marriage of Figaro* at Covent Garden. Stravinsky thought it "too high-powered, too dynamic, over-conducted: Mozart is simpler than that." (The next day at lunch he said the same thing to a London *Times* critic and musicologist friend of mine, in whose review this opinion turned up unattributed.) Solti had called Stravinsky in New York at the time of a performance there with the Chicago Symphony, in 1969 or 1970. I was moved to learn that the last recording he made was of Stravinsky's *Requiem Canticles.*

Returning to Gulf Stream we found our poolside patio fouled by raccoons. Alva engaged Grizzly's Wild Animal Service to set traps for them, but only after satisfying her ahimsa that the animal would not be hurt and, unless rabid, set free somewhere else.

In November we went to Hartford for a pair of concerts. On our arrival, I wrote a 250-word blurb about Jean Starobinski's *Largesse,* my book choice of the year, as requested by the *Times Literary Supplement:*

> For its quality of ideas, originality of subject, choice of texts and images, Jean Starobinski's *Largesse* belongs with Panofsky and Meyer Schapiro and demands to be read twice in succession. Starobinski examines the act of giving, in its multifarious and complex meanings, the "disinterested beneficence" versus the self-interest. The *sparsio* of the Roman Emperors, the showering of gold on the mob who then slaughter each other for it, exposes the giver's domination, contempt, destructiveness, and gratification in the spectacle of violence. "The first gift of every human existence is to itself, a given that art exalts . . . true sharing is the finality of art . . . the artist, detaching himself from what he has produced, surrenders his work to a receiver beyond himself." This sounds like Stephen Dedalus, but Starobinski's example is Michelangelo helping Sebastiano del Piombo "execute the figure of the dead Christ for an altarpiece by sending him a superb drawing of an ancient sleeping Cupid." This gift "attests to a generous superiority, and at the same time a desire to communicate the power of giving." Starobinski reminds us that "every thought ends in a throw [*sparsio*] of the dice," and that Diderot "imagined nature playing dice with the atoms of matter, creating the world and producing intelligent beings from a multitude of throws." The texts range from Epictetus to "Babette's Feast": "The only things which we may take with us from our life on earth are those which we have given away."

On November 6 I read my *Firebird* lecture at Hartt College (University of Connecticut) to about thirty composition students. My well-informed host introduced me to them, recommending my *Chronicle* but advising them to be equipped with a dictionary, "not Webster, but the twenty volumes of the OED, which could be a bit awkward if you read in bed." This very nice, droll man drove us back to the hotel, stopping on the way to show us the church where Charles Ives was married.

The rehearsals went smoothly, and we dined with Michael Lankaster, the orchestra's regular conductor, and his wife, Andrea, both of them British, bright, pleasant. A deluge made a washout of my appearance at a Borders, with only a dozen people turning up. An elderly German couple, called Johannes, told me that they were Balanchine's cooks and are in touch with Suzanne Farrell and Karen von Aroldingen, whose husband Balanchine used to refer to as "my husband-in-law." A physicist who bought several records and books said that he heard me conduct in New York in the 1950s.

The dress rehearsal at Bushnell Memorial, a converted cinema, brought unwelcome acoustical surprises: the balances were totally different from those in the rehearsal room, and the string volume was much weaker. We did not finish rehearsing the Haydn Cello Concerto, which Ralph Kirschbaum performed with a high degree of polish. At a makeshift dinner afterward, Mr. Kirschbaum lamented his failed efforts to obtain frequent-flyer mileage for his cello, even though he is obliged to pay full fare to have it strapped in a seat next to him.

Phyllis and Barbara Burge arrived for the second, and better, performance. We returned to New York in the morning and the next day received a young medical lady from Boston who brought a new machine, a wonder of the new medical technology, called a Coagu Chek System, a contrivance for prothrombin time self-testing. Smaller than a paperback book, it contains a laboratory for measuring the coagulation time of the blood, and in less than ten minutes. A two-inch computer screen converses with you when the machine is turned on, says "Good morning," asks whether you are ready to try the test, tells you to insert a strip and when to apply a drop of blood in a runnel on the strip leading to the interior. You then hold a small gadget next to one of your fingertips and press a button that releases the needle-prick into your flesh. You move your finger with the drop of blood over the strip and the computer screen begins to fill up from left to right with little angular figures that perform dance movements, one after the other until a chorus line of twenty of them has been completed, whereupon they vanish and the result, 2.5–3.5 in my case, is flashed on the screen. Hundreds of hours of driving to and waiting in laboratories are thus saved, and lab bills and contusions from the vein-missing punctures of nurses. This invention will become important in my future life.

At our first Florida breakfast the fire alarm rang and we did not know how to turn it off. In three minutes the police and a fire truck arrived to extinguish the bread that had curled and burned in our toaster while Alva was out of the room. Therewith I resolved to learn the switchboard of buttons and the workings of the electronically controlled front gate and garage doors, the house lights inside and out, the automatic shutters and window washers, the pool and Jacuzzi heaters, the insect zapper, the air-conditioning systems, the fax, the copier, the computer, and the extinguishing of the flames in the fake fireplace, as well as the slow-boat-to-China elevator, the side nozzles in the double shower, the transferring of telephone calls.

We saw *The Wings of the Dove* in Palm Beach and agreed that American Milly was not quite glamorous enough, whereas Kate, particularly in her final come-on scene, excited the Priapus in me. Milly's role, unlike what I recall of it in the novel, was too small, and she was too easily able to suppress her coughing spells in public and to save them for dramatic private moments. In a Venetian church under restoration, she somehow managed to climb a dozen ladders with the alacrity of a circus gymnast, and then, on the top scaffolding, to sport amorously and not breathlessly with Densher, all this only a few frames before she dies. When they have ditched Milly during the Venetian carnival, Kate makes love with Densher standing against a wall, but this sexually loose transposition of the novel deprives it of its tension. Moreover, bringing Densher back to Venice at the end is confusing. The next day we dined with George and Virginia Meyer, who described their boat trip around Tierra del Fuego and flight from Chile over northwest Antarctica. The most memorable moment, they said, was the view of a penguin rookery over the Antarctica coast and the discovery that the bird's excrement is a delicate pastel pink, the color of krill, the tiny crustaceans that are the bird's principal food.

1998

During our fourth night in the Dorchester Hotel in London, where we had come in mid-January for recording, I was awakened by an excruciating toothache in the next-to-last lower-right molar, the same that a Florida dentist warned me in October to "keep an eye on." (How would I do that?) Fortunately Alva had three codeine tablets, which abated the pain temporarily. She called the hotel doctor, who had been asleep but was pleasant and accommodating. He prescribed penicillin, and an analgesic, Nurofen, which he assured me would not disrupt my Coumadin balance. The concierge sent to a twenty-four-hour pharmacy for these, and the Nurofen brought relief. Just as I began to relax and doze, a shrill fire alarm went off in the ceiling of our bedroom. A moment later someone came to the door to announce that everyone was instructed to congregate by the Christmas-lighted tree in front of the hotel, from whence they (we) would be put up at Grosvenor House, a short walk up the street. We watched the evacuation of people in nightclothes and overcoats but did not join them, and an hour or so later were informed that the alarm had proved to be false. Thenceforth I napped for two hours before my early-morning recording session. Meanwhile, a letter arrived under our door from the general manager, apologizing for the ruckus and concluding, oddly, that " . . . it is highly unusual for the alarm to sound"—is it unreliable?—"and I do hope your sleep was not unduly disturbed"—unduly?

In the morning I conducted *Jeu de cartes* for three hours on nervous energy, but my sense of tempo was intact. The toothache returned on the way back to the hotel, where I read Thomas Bernhard's *The Voice Imitator,* 104 one-paragraph stories about murders, suicides, unnatural deaths, lunacies, and his other black-humor obsessions. Some were up to his best level, but some seemed pointless. The transparently autobiographical piece near the end should have been cut, while the equally transparent one about the death in Rome by fire of Ingeborg Bachmann required expansion and amplification. Bernhard's substitute device for the repeated, nervous-tic phrases in his novels is "in the nature of things," used like Vonnegut's "so it goes." A bonus: the reappearance of the comic character Irrsiegler from *Old Masters.*

In March we were in Poughkeepsie, where I signed books and records at Barnes and Noble, then dined in Highland with Alva, Phyllis, and Kristin, returning late-night to New York. A few days later I showed a film documentary at Borders, Park Avenue at Fifty-seventh Street, then signed books and records, the worst experience yet in my traveling-salesman adventures. As always at these affairs, the questions were answers providing people with opportunities to hear themselves talk. A madwoman challenged me with some belligerent blather about Stravinsky and vegetarianism. The sound system whistled and shrieked. Afterward, I finally met Olivia Pittet, my brilliant and attractive word-processor, for the first time and embraced her most warmly. The next afternoon, at Vassar, it was spring, and the audience was intelligent, informed, polite, the presentation well organized. The college paid me generously and sent me back to New York in a stretch limo.

From March 31 to April 13 we were at the Ritz in London for more recording, making daily use of the black brollies in our umbrella stand. The trees in Green Park were still bare, but the liveried room-waiters and white-tie-and-tails syces mooched about the lobby and tea salon (rose pouchong preferred), and downgraded our complaints about the weather ("a bit chilly"). In my experience of the city's posh inns, the service here was the least supercilious, erring, if at all, on the side of oversolicitude: we were rung up twice daily to ask if everything was satisfactory. But the waiters in the parkside restaurant had a technique of assiduously not looking. Dinner was accompanied by a medley of Noël Coward and moonlight music by Beethoven and Debussy. The menu recommended clafoutis of roasted vine tomatoes and black olive tapenade, pickled girolles and fig chutney, grilled ciabatta, and, as a savoury, Scottish woodcock.

We rehearsed the speakers for *The Flood* in our room: Robert Tear as Noah, Philippa Dame-Longworth as Mrs. Noah, a delightful lady and a

Plantagenet, who should sound bawdy in the farce, but instead grandly disdained her spouse's dinghy, suggesting by her tone in "Row forth, Noah" that her yacht was expected at any minute. We also listened to Anne-Sophie Mutter's recording of Stravinsky's Violin Concerto. She plays G-natural for G-flat at three after [71], E for F-sharp at one before [104], and omits the last triple-stop in the bar after [134]. Moreover, her glissandos on the double-stop (marked *"poco"*) in the first movement are exaggerated, and her gratuitous ritard before and at [7] (marked *"pocchissimo meno"*) is gross. The violinist Krzysztov Smietana says she has "simplified" the part in the final *Presto*.

On the return flight to New York, I finished Ted Hughes's *Tales from Ovid*, admiring it more than his *Birthday Letters* for Sylvia Plath. His poetry does not have as much personality as hers, but the Ovid reveals unsuspected verbal imagination, and the technical skill is enviable. Generally he is adroit at doctoring up clichés: "Heaven helps those who give it something to help." But how bloody were Ovid and his Greek sources! Hughes saves the goriest, Tereus, for last, perhaps to keep the reader from forgetting the book.

On reaching New York I was saddened by news of the death in Milan of Bill Congdon, at eighty-seven, feeling guilty that I had not found time to answer his letters or those of his other friends who had been gathering information about his paintings for a book. I remembered my first meeting with him in the airport canteen in the Azores in the middle of a March 1955 night, the happy times with him in Lisbon, Venice, Rome, Assisi, Palermo, and last seeing him at Stravinsky's and Vera Stravinsky's funerals in Venice. He should, but won't, be recognized as the last and best of the Betty Parsons stable of the School of New York.

The day before returning to Florida, a cold, misty one, we visited the Carters in their Twelfth Street apartment. Helen's new and not-yet-mastered hearing aid screeched from time to time. Both misunderstood key words, making the subject change constantly according to what they thought they had heard. When Elliott referred to comparatively recently deceased friends, he touchingly lowered his voice out of consideration for Helen's feelings, but she could not hear anyway. Elliott told amusing stories about Nadia Boulanger, Paul Bowles, Caroline Blackwood Lowell, Virgil Thomson, and the young Boulez vacationing in Acapulco, and he admitted that he cannot bear any music by Messiaen, though Paul Griffiths, the librettist of Elliott's opera, *What Next?*, is Messiaen's biographer.

An article in the *Times* (May 10) on Igor Markevitch by my good friend Richard Taruskin, redundantly headed "An Icarus Who Flew Too High," gave a fair account of his music but was wrong about some of the story. Described as "tall, gauntly handsome, icily cultivated," and "for more than five decades a spook of the first magnitude in the musical life of Europe," he was actually of medium height, puny, with a pinched, expressionless face, and was never more than a marginal figure whose sole claim to fame was that at age sixteen he became Diaghilev's catamite. In 1929 "Diaghilev romanced [him] with a whirlwind tour," the article goes on, then "returned to Venice exhausted, and died 12 days later." In truth Diaghilev, refusing insulin, had died of diabetes. Markevitch denied that he had had any sexual affair with him, but Stravinsky saw him enter Diaghilev's sleeping compartment on the same Paris-to-London night train in July 1929.

I remember meeting Markevitch on the terrace of the Baur Grünwald, Venice, in September 1951, when Stravinsky, Nabokov, and I had lunch with him. He had come for the premiere of *The Rake*. Seven years later we were fellow houseguests for several days in the Brussels palace of the Baroness Hansi Lambert-Rothschild. He had my recording of Schoenberg's Orchestra Variations, was fascinated by the piece, wanted to perform it, but was afraid to try. We talked about it and the rediscovery of Schoenberg at table and in a drawing room until late at night. I thought him shy, in spite of the ease with which he moved in the highest social circles. After marrying the Princess Caetani, he was referred to as "Prince Igor." A book of photographs of him taken in their Swiss home had recently been published, and Auden, happening to leaf through it in Stravinsky's hotel suite in New York and coming upon a picture of him in bed posing in a silk robe de chambre, recaptioned it with some *gros mots*. But Markevitch was kind to me after Brussels, going out of his way to write to a record company on my behalf. His recording of *The Rite of Spring* turned out to be generally correct, but strangely detached and devoid of excitement.

July 30. Venice. Our flight from Heathrow is late, but so is Alexander's from Copenhagen. We find him in the terminal, looking more svelte than when last seen, a year ago. He brings three Inuit carvings as a gift for me, all made in Greenland, one of a polar bear, and another of a man with a flat, nearly featureless face, dressed in a hooded garment that encloses the whole body like a space suit. Both are ancient and from the now uninhabited east coast of the island. The third, from the west coast, a shaman's "tupicak" carved from narwhal horn in 1902, is a work of high artistic accomplishment. The arms, large hands, and fingers extend to the ground between the legs and feet, and all four limbs are equal in length. The head, which looks skyward, shows three rows of teeth in a screaming open mouth, reminiscent of the horse in *Guernica*. After dinner we walk to the Rialto and return to the hotel on a crowded vaporetto, on which Alva is pleased to find Mel Brooks and Anne Bancroft, two close friends from her previous marriage.

August 5. While urinating this morning I feel intense pain of the same kind as in the days following my kidney operations in Florida. The concierge summons a doctor, Trevisan, who performs the color-band test in a urine sample and sends me to a urologist at the Ospedale. We go to the side entrance in a *motoscafo*, then lengthen the queue at the *"pronto soccorso"* (emergency) entrance. I absent myself from this every few minutes during the better part of an hour in order to visit the lavatory, the dirtiest imaginable, indeed unimaginable in a hospital. After being stabbed for a blood sample and filling out a lengthy form, we walk through an ancient cloister and climb to the third floor of a decrepit, and no less dirty, examination room, where a surly medic performs a sonogram and probes and manipulates my private parts. The results reveal nothing, which raises the hope that the stone has already departed. Back in the hotel Dr. Trevisan prescribes antibiotics (Cipro), a painkiller, and the consumption of three liters of water a day: I shall be spending much of the night in the *gabinetto*. Our vacated suite having been filled meanwhile, we are moved to a garret den designed for a single, very short room maid.

September 12. New York. I conduct Schoenberg's Chamber Symphony in Merkin Hall, an infectiously exuberant performance by New York's best players. The concert is sold out to an uptown audience of "elitists"—the derogatory downtown term—partly because *The Times*, in a moment of respite from the glut of Shostakovich, rose to the occasion with an unusually positive forecast: "Leading Music Astray? Yes, Down a Path of Wonder." In the roundtable discussion that followed the Symphony, Milton Babbitt is the readiest to talk. He begins by blocking an unanswerable question from the audience to James Levine about why Schoenberg did not finish *Moses und Aron:* "Because his application for a Guggenheim was turned down." At opposite extremes in girth, tonsorial matters, and complexions—ruddy vs. alabaster—Levine and Babbitt are of one mind about Schoenberg. Throughout the evening, "Jimmy" extends an affectionate and protective arm around the chair of his friend, pictorially as well as musically America's top egghead musician. Tradition and innovation in Schoenberg is the designated topic, but it should have been confined to the Symphony just heard, and perhaps to one or two other contrasting and less well-known works. When Babbitt sagaciously rules out any consideration of the sonata-form aspects of the opus, "Jimmy" turns to the more rewarding ones of instrumentation and performance, neatly refuting an objection from the floor about orchestral and emotional saturation.

October 12. London. Michael Berkeley, composer son of the composer Lennox B., interviewed me for a Third Programme broadcast in a series called "Private Passions." The interviewee provides a short list of his or her favorite recordings, and, while excerpts from them are played, talks with Berkeley about them. I chose Lasso (the *Missa Osculator*), Mozart (from the C-minor Mass), and Beethoven No. 5, First Movement, conducted by Furtwängler.

October 14. I begin my six-session, eighteen-hour marathon of recordings with the Philharmonia at Abbey Road. The orchestra has never played Schoenberg's Variations, but is determined to learn it, and we make solid progress. The music is anathema only to Hugh Bean, the orchestra's lovably cranky leader, now in his eighties, but as quick as the youngest fiddler. He complains to me that "Not a single phrase lies comfortably in the violin. Did Schoenberg hate the instrument?" Mr. Bean likes the concertos of Wieniawski, Viotti, Vieuxtemps, and only just tolerates Stravinsky's. He says that when Paul Sacher conducted the Stravinsky here with Anne-Sophie Mutter several years ago, "Sacher was a week behind her on every beat." When the first violins are late with a repeated off-beat twittering figure, he explains, "Mr. Craft, we do not chirp in time because we can't hear the clarinet at the beginning of the beat." At one point, when I vociferate against the chatter in the room, ending with "furthermore it is rude," he supports me entirely with "too much talk; furthermore it's *rude*." But the players are congenial. Many come to me to complain that Valery Gergiev, who was here last week, could not conduct *The Rite of Spring*.

October 15. The first clarinetist, Michael Whight, does not turn up this morning, and we cannot start to record. A substitute arrives nearly an hour late, time that will have to be made up by cutting the intermission and beginning a half-hour earlier tomorrow. When word spreads during the session that the missing musician is in Saudi Arabia, Mr. Bean's response is: "In that case he will definitely be late." Since visas are required for such excursions, we wonder whether the absentee might be a spy, drug dealer, white-slaver, or, more plausibly, hung-over and at home in bed.

I arrive at the Royal Philharmonic Society's lecture hall, 10 Stratford Place, fifteen minutes late, but Tony Fell's introductory speech smoothes over any ruffled feelings I may have caused. I recognize Lady Spender and Lady Berlin in the distinguished audience, and realize that certain references in my text will have to be skipped and connections improvised. The talk is warmly, even enthusiastically received. Aline Berlin is gracious and not disturbed by hearing my memento mori of her late spouse, telling me afterward that she wants his letters to me published. I inscribe books for Lord David Cecil's younger brother, and for Paul Driver, the *Sunday Times* music critic. And finally I meet Oliver Knussen, along with his former roommate Lucy Shelton and his young composer friend Julian Anderson. David Drew is also at the reception, as is his wife Judy, my old friend. A distinguished elderly gent questions me about Messiaen vis-à-vis Nadia Boulanger, and I give our new *Flood* record to Knussen, who won't like it.

October 20. When I enter the recording studio this morning, the Philharmonia plays "Happy Birthday" in Stravinsky's arrangement "conducted" by Greg Squires. A huge white cake with many, though fewer than seventy-five, candles is trundled in. I have been fearing something like this because Mansel Bebb, the orchestra manager, had asked me about the date, but everyone is very kind and pleasant, and the cake not too gooey. We record Bach's *Komm Gott* Chorale-Prelude in Schoenberg's arrangement and continue with the Brahms-Schoenberg.

On the return to New York, about twenty minutes from landing, smoke is detected, the upper cabin lights go out, and the green emergency lights along the floor go on. A cordon of police is waiting at the exit.

On the 26th, after a gracious introduction by Milton Babbitt, I talked to his Juilliard class on Schoenberg's instrumentation, the exploitation of the highest ranges of the strings, the expansion of the color palette (contrabass clarinet, flexaton, mandolin), the extraordinary doublings, and the preference for the clarinet family—all as demonstrated in the Songs, Opus 22. The next day Dr. Weld monitored my sonogram test (the Hewlett-Packard 5500 machine), a two-hour procedure. The results were good: the artificial aortic valve was found to be perfectly in place and likely to outlast me by thirty years. On the 29th, after several nervous days trying to decide the seating arrangements, we gave a catered dinner party for Elliott Carter. First, where to place Elliott himself, since he is on close terms with everyone? Finally we seat him with me and Carol Sherry. Edward Said and his wife go with Barbara Epstein (who, like most women, has a crush on him). Charles Rosen and Lizzy Hardwick go together, but does shy Richard Burgi belong at their table? He is as learned in Greek and Russian cultures as Rosen is in French, but I am the only one who knows him. Suzanne Farrell, as alluring as ever and not a prima donna, fitted smoothly with Claudio and Joan Accoccella, the new *New Yorker* dance critic.

On November 4, I was in Columbia-Presbyterian for a cystoscopy. A young female, not yet a nurse, led me to a small private room on the eleventh floor of the Milstein building, told me to remove all of my clothes, and seated me at the foot of the operating table. Her indifference while painting my penis with an orange-colored surface anesthetic did not totally deaden the erotic instinct, but her whispered "some men have erections" killed it. At this point Dr. Puckner, a man of few words and no small talk, appeared, injected an anesthetic into the groin, then, briskly and businesslike in manner, threaded an implement into my penis, an extremely disagreeable experience. After photographing the contents of the bladder, he told me that my prostate was enlarged but free of tumors. More urgently, three bladder stones must be pulverized as soon as possible, *i.e.*, after my concert in Miami next week. He prescribed a pill, Flomax, to shrink the prostate and ease micturation.

Driving from Gulf Stream to Florida International University in Miami on the 7th, we became hopelessly lost miles to the west of our destination and arrived two hours late for my rehearsal. The hour-long drive afterward to a small, dismal room in the Grand Bay Hotel in Coconut Grove convinced us to return to Gulf Stream in the morning, and drive back here the day after. The performance of *Noces* was gratifying.

Back in New York on December 6, Alva went to Carter's five o'clock concert uptown, and I to James Levine's at the same hour at Weill Recital Hall. The two lovely Brahms songs with viola obbligato opened the latter program, an apt choice in that the second of them uses the same Lope de Vega text set by Hugo Wolf in one of the songs set by Stravinsky for quintets of winds and strings that followed. These moved me, partly because I introduced Stravinsky to the music and was with him when he completed his instrumentations in a San Francisco hotel in May 1968.

On the 9th we taxied to Columbia-Presbyterian at 7 A.M. for my electro-hydraulic lithotripsy procedure. Hours later, after form-filling and answering an anesthetist's questions, I walked to an operating theater filled like a storage room with boxes and medical supplies. On my right was a Sony television screen, on my left, facing it, Dr. Peter Puckner, who greeted me saying he heard a broadcast of one of my recordings last night. The epidural injection was painful despite Novocain, but a minute later I was turned to stone from the hips down. Meanwhile I had been lifted from sitting to prone, with my legs hoisted to a higher elevation than my torso. The thought of smashing bladder stones through my tiny aperture had been preying on me since the cystoscopy three weeks earlier, but this time I felt nothing. The TV screen projected the interior of the bladder in bright colors: the scarlet tangle of blood vessels, the membrane of the small pouch, and, finally, the egg-shaped bright yellow stones themselves, rolling back and forth. They were presumed to be calcium and hence easier to break up than the uric-acid kind. The bladder wall was scruffy with dandruff-like fragments that seemed to be blowing in a wind. The charges of electrical force that Puckner aimed at fissures in the stones were like volleys of vibrations from a machine gun; but, seeing, hearing, and feeling nothing, I do not know how I was aware of this. The wreckage resembled cracked eggshells, and the broken, jagged, and sharp fragments did not augur well for the passage through my already very sore urethra.

At the end of the procedure Puckner's assistants wheeled me to a cubicle in the recovery room, where the temperature was more suited to a meatpacking plant. Electrically heated blankets were brought, and one of Puckner's nurses showed me a jar containing some of the resin-colored gravels quarried in my bladder. My left arm was wired to a blood-pressure monitor, the arm wrap-around inflating every ten minutes and automatically tabulating the rise or fall of the respiration, pulse, and nose-mask oxygen. The right arm was attached to an IV containing antibiotics and valium.

After four hours in this purgatory, able at last to raise my knees and twitch my toes, I was wheeled to a small double room with a bleak view of the Hudson, the Palisades, and the green lights of the Washington Bridge, which we see from our Fifty-ninth Street apartment. I spent most of the night urgently wanting to urinate through the catheter and was finally put to sleep by injections of Demerol. Puckner removed the catheter in the morning, a nurse bathed me, and at noon I returned to the Hampshire in a painfully bumpy taxi. A few days later, Puckner said the stones had not yet been analyzed so he could not tell us whether they were of the calcium kind or the uric-acid kind caused by "too good living," but he permitted me to fly to Florida.

The leader music column in this morning's *Times* (December 20) contained a number of inane remarks, any one of which should have brought about their author's immediate dismissal: "the *Grosse Fuge*, another late-Beethoven string-quartet piece, is as impenetrable to me today as it was on first hearing." (In 1968–70, Stravinsky listened to the *Fuge* every night for weeks at a time, "penetrating" new wonders in it on every hearing. I remember him asking for it again and again and declaring it the greatest music he knew.) Another howler was the statement "Just as we meet immediately dislikable people or animals . . . so I can hear the qualities in Schoenberg's music and feel only fleeting fondness." But do we "meet" animals? And is "fleeting fondness" the same as "immediately dislikable?" The writer continues with the nonargument, "Listeners can be conned for a time, but . . . they almost infallibly end up knowing what is good and what isn't," *i.e.*, the majority is right and truth will out.

On the day before Christmas we arrived at a snow-covered La Guardia Airport to find long queues for curbside check-ins, and still longer ones inside. I bribed a porter to bypass the line and check our six heavy bags through, but the mob inside beyond security became even more unruly when it was announced that our noontime flight had not yet left Florida. Four miserable hours later we were snugly aboard, but had to wait another three hours in the runway backup. Finally at home, we listened to Sweelinck's *Cantiones Sacrae*, which include polyphonic elaborations on "Alleluia," and Brahms's lovely Christmas Lullaby, which starts with the ancient version of the melody in the viola (*i.e.*, without words):

> *Josef, lieber, Josef mein, hilf mir wieg'n mein Kindlein fein,*
> *Gott der wird dein Lohnrer sein, im Himmelreich der Junfrau Sohn.*

The German version of the Lope de Vega text that follows, *"Es schlumert mein kind,"* is equally lovely.

1999

When Alexander arrived at the West Palm Beach Airport at the beginning of February, the carousels were cluttered with golfers' bags, while scalpers waved Super Bowl tickets at two thousand dollars each. Our pool was warm, and we swam, though my deltoids were rusty. At dinner Alexander adroitly avoided every question with a possible connection to what, if anything, he might be planning to do with his life.

On March 9 a call from Seattle at 3 A.M. announced the birth of Alva's grandson, Noah. Hosanna!

In London in mid-April, I discovered that my passport would expire in two days. We hastened to a photographer near the U.S. Embassy, and climbed three staircases to a small room wallpapered with passport photos of movie stars. The cameraman said that he is periodically obliged to rejuxtapose some of the portraits because of real-life realignments: viz., Mia Farrow from André Previn to Frank Sinatra to Woody Allen. Security at the Embassy was on the alert, St. Martin-in-the-Fields being surrounded with protesters carrying placards: STOP NATO BOMBING. My passport was held up because the computers were "down."

The air in the new ground-level wing of the National Gallery was stale, and coughers and sneezers crowded the rooms for the exhibition of Ingres portraits. With the exception of the drawing of the young Liszt, the pictures were not among the artist's finest. Blame the dullness of most of his subjects, in which people do not relate to backgrounds, and eyes are not windows to souls. The picture that held me longest was an unfinished painted sketch of a girl in profile, hair up in a bun in back. But Ingres's forte is female finery, jewelry, clothes, hairdos. I thought the best of the show was the late-period self-portrait.

May 26. New York. Paul Sacher is dead, not unexpectedly, since he was ninety-three, and ill, but I had known him, through Stravinsky, since 1948, and had a major role in his acquisition of the Stravinsky *"Nachlass."* We called Elliott Carter for advice on how to condole, since he is in touch with Sacher Foundation staff, and as the botched *New York Times* obit makes clear, the question is fraught with problems. "Mr. Sacher's wife is his only immediate survivor," the *Times* says. Actually she has been dead for several years. The survivors are three sons from her previous marriage to Fritz Hoffmann, now coheirs—with Paul Sacher's son Georg Sebastian Balthasar Schmidt (b. 1981), the natural issue of his young mistress, who predeceased his wife—of the Hoffmann-La Roche pharmaceutical empire. But the *Times* notice is wrong about nearly everything. Stravinsky's widow died in 1982, not 1983; the "protracted bidding war" for the Stravinsky archives lasted only a few days; the Morgan Library was not "involved" in it; and the "sale price" was $5.25 million not $5.2. The *Times* photo of Sacher with a young, not yet blonde Anne-Sophie Mutter was taken in Abbey Road, London, during their recording of the Stravinsky Violin Concerto. But how did the violinist's publicity agent get to the news-

paper ahead of the purveyors of photos of the deceased with Richard Strauss, Stravinsky, Bartók?

August 18. London. Dinner with Stanley Baron, who says that my lambdacisms, "l" for "r," in the China chapter of *Places,* are politically incorrect and must be deleted. In response I show him a Japanese CD of music by *Alnold* Schoenberg, but this carries no weight.

August 20. I awake with flu and fever. The hotel doctor comes promptly and bombards me with antibiotics, but today's session, which means that I shall have to do three days' work in two, and while feeling woozy.

August 21 and 23. I record Schoenberg's *Pelleas und Melisande* at Abbey Road.

August 27. New York. I have become a great-great uncle of Matthew, Wendy's son, born in Strong Memorial, the University of Rochester Hospital.

September 13. Gulf Stream. The lowered barometric pressure from Hurricane Floyd is also lowering our spirits and nerves. At 10 P.M. the police tell us that we must evacuate by morning. Alva finds rooms at the Longboat-Key Club in Sarasota.

September 14. After packing pills, pajamas, insurance and other documents, we drive through Alligator Alley, two-way and only two lanes when I was last here, in January 1948, now a divided, six-lane expressway. The Big Cypress Seminole Reservation, about halfway through, has expanded hideously. Since the storm warning had already been lifted in Miami last night, evacuee traffic is light, but at Fort Myers, a radar police car, lurking behind a hillock, stops us and awards Alva a speeding ticket (90 m.p.h. plus). She fights back, saying—truthfully—that every car on the road has passed her, but that our car is a target because it is Brit. Sarasota is half old-town, decrepit 1920s wooden shacks, and half Boca Raton glitz. Our hotel, a glorified golf club, is so crowded that we have no access to the restaurant but must go in a van to another one miles away.

September 16. Back home we find that the fearsome storm never arrived, that no rain fell, and that to all appearances no leaf has been blown away. After three days of doomsday television warnings, I am fuming: a nonevent and no work accomplished.

October 6. New York. Anja Silja comes at 4:00 P.M. for a *Pierrot Lunaire* rehearsal at Steinway Hall, with Christopher Oldfather at the piano. Sixtyish, taller than expected, blonde, and with blue eyes, she exudes joie-de-vivre. Intelligent, quick, and straightforward, she is happy with her life, as distinguished from self-satisfied. Conversation with her is easy and more American than Brit, which is natural since she lived for twenty-eight years in Shaker Heights, Cleveland, bringing up her three children by the conductor of the orchestra there, Christoph von Dohnányi. Within the first ten minutes she talks about the "love of her life," who turns out not to have been Wieland Wagner, as all the world would suppose, much less the father of her children, but André Cluytens, the French conductor with whom she lived in Paris for only two years before his death from cancer. Before she mentioned this, she had asked if I had the old LP of Cluytens conducting *Perséphone*, and, unthinkingly, I blurted out that the performance was so bad I had discarded the disc.

She must have been a beauty at seventeen when Wagner's grandson choreographed her as Salomé, a statement confirmed by photographs in her autobiography, some of them with Wieland, whose head and features could be mistaken for those of his grandfather. She talks freely and affectionately about him but refers to the present descendants of Wagner in Bayreuth and Milan as monsters and remarks on her good luck in not having borne children by Wieland, since she would now be living in Bayreuth. She claims not to have returned there since his death, which occurred when she was living with him in Berlin.

When we arrive at a rehearsal room in Steinway Hall, she is all business, working hard, repeating passages over and over. Though this is her first performance of the opus, she produces the first real *Sprechstimme* I have ever heard. Her voice is full and even in all registers, and the beauty of the German in her rendition is a new experience for me, as well as for the German-speaking Oldfather, a bright man and musician who knows the piece thoroughly. Her one fault is that she seems unable to count the beats before her entrances. At the Caravelle for dinner, she is enjoyable company, though the talk is largely about the world of music. She complains about Denmark, where she has been living until recently, with its "isolation," "small country nationalism," and the "strange remoteness of Danes."

October 8. Today's six-hour session starts in early morning, but Silja, who lets Alva and me know that she had a satisfying reunion with a former amour last night, is the brightest, most energetic, and self-demanding of all of us. She never sits but toward the end removes her shoes and stands in her bare feet. The musicians, who know the piece by heart, are eager to help with cues, suggestions about what to listen for, tone colors.

As guests of the Carters, we dine at La Caravelle with Rosamond Bernier and John Russell (her husband). Peggy is alert, keen, young-looking (at about eighty-five), and stunningly dressed. Elliott, at ninety-one, is a wonder, basking in the success of his opera in Berlin, and sharper than ever. He says that Daniel Barenboim conducted his opera much better than he did Schoenberg's *Von Heute auf Morgen*, its companion on the double-bill.

October 15. Gulf Stream. In this land of hurricanes, where comparatively mild storms provoke dire forecasts from television and radio, Hurricane Irene lands suddenly, totally unheralded in the media, bringing fierce wind and heavy rains. Losing electric power in mid-afternoon, we go to dinner at the Ocean Grand Hotel in South Palm Beach, where during the meal the manager tells us that the drawbridges to the mainland are out and that South Ocean Boulevard is blocked by fallen trees. We are obliged to rent a room and sleep in our clothes, only fifteen minutes from home.

November 6. Miami. After my concert with the excellent jazz clarinetist Eddie Daniels and the celebrated fluegelhornist Arturo Sandoval, we taxi to Joe's Stone Crab at the southern end of Collins Avenue in Miami Beach, but the return to our hotel entails a long wait on line for a taxi. Alva and I fly to Heathrow the next afternoon.

November 15. London. Michael White interviews me for two hours, except that he does most of the talking, whereas my other chats with the Brit press tend to become my monologues because I do not understand the accent and dislike having to ask for the questions to be repeated. We discuss the Earl of Harewood, the Queen's first cousin, and one of the few royals who has ever been intelligently involved in the arts. (Yes, Mendelssohn accompanied Victoria singing his and other songs, and George II took violin lessons from Handel, but both were long ago.) When I ask about the break-up of Harewood's first marriage, to Marion Stein, and her remarriage to Jeremy Thorpe, White tells us that at age twenty he was a solicitor on Thorpe's side during his trial, in spite of which he thinks "the not guilty verdict a gross miscarriage of justice. Thorpe was so very upper-class that he considered himself exempt from testifying in court. Nor did he, which must seem incredible to an American. He would have been convicted, of course, not only of putting out a contract on his lover, the male model blackmailing him, but also of using Labor Party money to do so. True, the funds were returned, but that would not acquit him of the theft. Thorpe is dying of Parkinson's disease."

Returning to Harewood, I remember him as pleasant in conversation and impressively informed about opera at a party after the gala opening of the New York City Ballet's 1972 Stravinsky Festival, in which I had conducted. White, who knows him well, says that he dreads his dinners with the Queen. "She does not read, is tone deaf, artistically blind, and interested only in horses, dogs, and soccer, knowing many of the names of the players and making admiring comments on their legs. Otherwise she says nothing at all, which burdens her guests with the decision as to whether or not they should talk."

November 28. New York. The Carters and Elizabeth Hardwick come for dinner, or rather, in Helen's case, for the view of the park from our windows. Lizzy, age eighty-five, is both jubilant and exhausted, having finished her book on Melville this afternoon. Elliott has brought the score and video of the Berlin performance of his opera. In the event, seeing and hearing this has to be postponed until we are in Florida tomorrow.

December 3. The *Times Literary Supplement* publishes my "book of the year" and "book of the millennium" contribution:

The Mummies of Ürümchi (Norton) by the archaeologist and authority on ancient textiles, Elizabeth Wayland Barber, has taught me more, while providing fascinating reading, than any other book this year. Ürümchi, in the Tarim Basin desert of Chinese Turkestan, first explored by Sir Aurel Stein at the beginning of this century, became world news in 1994 with the discovery of the mummified 3,000-year-old Chechen Man. He had blond hair, a thick beard, Caucasoid features—round eyes, a high-ridged nose—and was six foot six inches tall. The arid, sandy, salty land preserved his woolen clothes in the bright colors of the day on which they were woven. Sheep had been herded as a source of food for several millennia before they were cultivated for their wool, and, like the wheat grains found in a winnowing tray buried with the still older "Beauty of Loulan," did not exist in China in 2000 BC. Barber deduces that both commodities originated in the Fertile Crescent (the arc from Turkey to Mesopotamia), and she believes that the Ürümchi came from the grasslands of the Central Asian Steppes, attributing the migration to a change of climate. The move was possible only after the domestication of the horse and the invention of the spoked chariot-wheel. The Ürümchi language, Tokharian, belonged to the Indo-European group, with a special relationship to Celtic. Barber hypothesizes that at one period the Ürümchi were pushed westward and southward, settling in Northern India, where they became Buddhists. Eventually they returned along the Silk Road to the Tarim Basin, bringing their religion and possibly some influence of Alexandrian Greece. The book's illustrations are helpful, the text clearly written, proposing persuasive answers to questions that will occur to everyone, including the uses of DNA evidence.

As a scientific illiterate, I cannot nominate *On the Origin of Species* for the "book of the millennium," and my limited Italian keeps me from naming the obvious *trecento* candidate. Let it be Shakespeare's *Sonnets*.

December 19. Gulf Stream. During the night, eleven castaways, from India by way of the Bahamas, have been apprehended in a thicket only two hundred yards north of here. Nothing is said about their sufferings from exposure and hunger. We can only hope that, after such a voyage, they are not sent back.

December 23. Tonight the solstice moon brings it and the earth closer than they have been in 133 years. We walk along the beach at midnight. The temperature of the ocean is eighty-five degrees.

December 30. Ted Hughes's *Phèdre* reads smoothly, and the felicities offset such bumps in vocabulary as the too up-to-date "All Greece is buzzing with it." "Fists bunch" is redundant, and in "I mocked her captives in their ridiculous chains," one wonders how chains can be "ridiculous." "Thug," in Theseus' first speech, sticks out as Anglo-Indian, and "blackguard" as démodé Brit. Further, "This is the moment and we have to seize it" brings *Hamlet* too quickly to mind. More disturbing is Theseus' phrase "If the gods can be trusted," since it suggests a former certainty that they could be, and I like to believe in the progress of Euripides' desacralizing. The last act is completely ruled by the deities, alas. *Phèdre* says that her love is *"Vénus toute entière à son proie attachée."* Finally, the Aristotelian time/place restrictions make the off-stage action rush by in a few words of description.

December 31. At late-afternoon swimming time, a low-flying (50 feet), slow-moving, 1903-style parachute airplane, goggled and leather-helmeted pilot suspended in the open air, strapped in a swing-like, legs-dangling seat, patrols our beach and pool. The single, overhead wing is a parabolic yellow awning, and the motor throbs like an ancient auto. When Alva is adorning the pool, the aerial voyeur circles back for second and third runs, though she no longer bathes *au nature.*

Chapter 12

Not Going Gently

L ast night's celebration for the coming Millennium, at home in Gulf Stream, was quieter than any I can remember, partly because of Veronica and Andrew, the charming, well-behaved, sleepy young children of our guests, Terry and Julie Cudmore, who joined us with Drs. George and Virginia Meyer. When I was their age, eight or nine, I often wondered if I would live until the twenty-first century. I have. Hallelujah!

May 22. London. A visit from Michael Tanner, professor of philosophy and dean of Corpus Christi College, Oxford. We have sparred over Wagner and other matters since the 1960s, but today's meeting is amicable and stimulating.[1]

May 25–28. I record Schoenberg's Piano Concerto with Christopher Oldfather and the Philharmonia, as well as the Second Chamber Symphony, whose second movement I have only lately appreciated. It begins a bit like the hunt movement in Stravinsky's *Ode*—both pieces are in 6/8, and, partly, in G major—but whereas the Stravinsky merely temporizes and is thin in substance, the Schoenberg intensifies while discovering new areas of instrumental virtuosity. I remember recording the Symphony for broadcast in Baden-Baden in 1954 at slower tempos.

Paul Scofield has announced his intention to read Sonnet 71 at a memorial service for John Gielgud. This is slightly surprising, since he surely knows that number 72 comprises the second part of what is really an indivisible double sonnet, and is the stronger of the two arguments on the wisdom of the beloved forgetting the poet after his death. Number 72, as Helen Vendler perceptively remarks, has a chiastic structure, turning from the in-

1. His published interview in *Opera* for July manages to include my every indiscretion, but he repeats his evaluation, in a *TLS* of some years ago, of my *Chronicle*: "One of the great books of our century."

creasingly attenuating hopes expressed in number 71 to an aggressive defense of the poet's merits by the beloved. No doubt Scofield considers 71 the more mellifluous of the two, as well as, deceptively, the simpler-sounding. No doubt, too, he is thinking that Gielgud was well aware that the beloved is generally thought to have been a boy.

May 29. Tegel Airport, Berlin. Owing to gridlocks resulting from the simultaneous descent on the city of the W. J. Clinton entourage, and the consequent closing of the Brandenburg Gate area, the concierge sent by the Ritz-Carlton Schlosshotel to meet our flight is a half-hour late. Wearing striped trousers and tailcoat, like an attendant at a royal funeral or wedding (see R. Rehm's *Conflation of Wedding and Funeral Rituals in Greek Tragedy*), he attracts the ire of a husky policewoman, who tickets him for pausing to fetch us in a restricted zone.

The renovated Renaissance Schlosshotel on Brahmsstrasse—though Schumann (*"Im wunderschönen Monat Mai"*) is the composer I can't get out of my mind—is quiet and comfortable, except that we repeatedly bump our heads on the bulges in the wall formed by the windows in the steeply gabled roof. The living room reminds us of the one in the famous rear-view drawing of the young Goethe leaning on the windowsill and contemplating his *Seele*. The neighborhood is pleasantly woodsy, but then, more of Berlin is forest than any other city in the world.

May 30. At 6 P.M. we set off in a taxi for the American Academy. This is only a few miles away, on a slope overlooking the Wannsee, but since the driver has never heard of it, cannot find the street (Am Sandwerder) on his map, and the other taxis from whom he attempts to gather information at stoplights are equally at a loss, the expedition lasts more than an hour. Eventually reaching our destination, another ten minutes elapse before a young girl admits us and explains that the hosts and guests are at dinner, having despaired of us. (Why had no one called the hotel to inquire if we were en route?) Finally the president of the academy, Dr. Gary Smith, an ex-Harvard prof known for his translations of Walter Benjamin letters, appears, together with his assistant, Holly Austin, a Harvard musicologist, the most attractive member of the profession I have ever beheld. As the dining room empties, she escorts me upstairs to the seclusion of the "Arthur Miller Suite."

In the well-filled lecture hall, a young German musicologist introduces me by reading a version of my biography from a typescript with more pages than my talk, and lasting longer, since I read faster when nervous, and faster still when under the impression that most of the audience is German-speaking only and does not understand. At the end we move to the library, where I sign copies of the new Atlantis Verlag translations of two of my books. One of the buyers is the great Mozart scholar Ivan Nagel, whose study of the composer I reviewed very favorably a few years ago. He confirms that

Mozart's German, in his letters, is not impeccable, and that the spelling is inconsistent. At a late-night dinner in an Italian restaurant with Dr. Smith and Ms. Austin, I learn that the next lecturer will be Leon Botstein, and that the academy is actually part of an organization to promote relations between Germany and Israel. Smith's father was a former mayor of Berlin.

May 31. We much enjoy a late-afternoon visit from Heinz-Klaus Metzger and his companion, Rainer Rielin, co-authors of *Musik-Konzepte Sonderband Darmstadt-Dokumente,* a copy of which they inscribe to me. We break the language barrier, or avoid it, with a combination of my broken German and their broken English, in which they regale us with stories about the conductor Hermann Scherchen, who, it seems, on receiving the score of Henze's opera *König Hirsch,* excised all of the arias and told the composer, "*We* don't write arias anymore." When Messiaen's name comes up, Metzger declares that he likes the music "because I have bad taste." He tells us that at age twenty Theodor Adorno shocked Schoenberg by proposing that they collaborate on a book of philosophy. He asks me to describe Stravinsky's reaction to Adorno's *The Philosophy of New Music,* but I never knew how much, or little, of it he read. Later, flipping through the *Darmstadt* book, I am not surprised that its analytical charts are over my head, but I had not realized that Ernst Krenek was so deeply involved in the enterprise in the late 1940s–1950s.

June 1. An accommodating driver with as much English as we need takes us to Dresden and Leipzig. Not far into the country is the line of the former "Berlin Wall," large sections of which, as well as guard towers, remain. The houses and other buildings on the eastern side are much poorer, and the uneven, jolting, narrow prewar road reduces our speed by half. Thick patches of pine forest and fields with red poppies alternate in the sparsely populated countryside. The former East Germany feels grim and forlorn, little changed from what it must have been under the Soviets, and even the newest buildings, many in construction, emulate the drab Socialist style of decades ago. Nearing Dresden, the rolling hills of Saxony are studded with windmills, three metal blades shaped like airplane propellers topping steel poles. Many automobiles carry bicycles attached upright to their roofs. The newest bridge over the Elbe brings us to the center of the city.

Fifty-five years after the massacre of February 13–14, 1945, when an estimated 202,000 people, most of them women and children, perished in the criminally calculated three-phase Allied fire-bombing, the old city is still gutted, and because of bomb craters and rubble some streets are still impassable to automobiles. The first bombers, in the middle of the night, were British. The American second wave came after an interval, when survivors would be emerging from their hiding-places—the city had no bomb shelters, being beyond the range of *aller-retour* bombers, and some of its priceless paintings, including Raphael's *Sistine Madonna*, were stored in railroad tunnels. The third wave, again British, at daylight, was apparently intended to obliterate whomever and whatever remained. But most of the deaths seem to have been from suffocation, or carbon dioxide poisoning, the firestorms having depleted the oxygen in the atmosphere. In any case, the city could not be reentered for twelve days, as shown in photographs in David Irving's *The Destruction of Dresden* of relief forces wearing masks and collecting the remains of bodies into crematory pyres. Since Dresden, a city of 630,000, had no military or strategic importance and was known to be choking with refugees from the east, as well as all over Germany, historians now blame Winston Churchill for the attack, which is seen as the more barbaric in that the end of the war was obviously only weeks away. The Red Army reached Dresden three weeks after the catastrophe and immediately impounded the eight large buckets of gold wedding rings that had been collected from the dead all over the city and sent them as booty to Moscow. It seems that at first the Germans planned to execute an American POW for every German killed in this horror, but that Ribbentrop succeeded in convincing Hitler of the stupid and brutal folly of this.

The cobblestone pavements of the old city, not well aligned, are especially hard to negotiate in our case, since both of us are wearing slippery, thin-soled leather shoes. The one smooth promenade, the Brückische Terrasse, known as the "Balcony of Europe," is a broad elevated walk about forty-five yards above and bordering the southern embankment of the Elbe. Thronged with tourists, almost all of them German, it extends from the Albertinum, the New Masters Gallery (nineteenth- and twentieth-century German and French paintings) to the platz facing the opera house. During our several-hour visit to the city we do not hear a word of English or American, or, for that matter, French and Italian. Some of the German pedestrians are confrontational as to who steps aside; understandably, Dresdeners seem not to welcome the descendants of the people who wrought the disaster on them. Indeed, guidebooks warn visitors to the still-levelled Frauenkirche— until 1945, Germany's greatest Protestant church—to donate generously to the rebuilding fund if they visit the site. The Soviets decided to leave its ruins untouched as a memorial to the atrocity, but Dresdeners are determined to reconstruct it for the eight-hundredth anniversary of the city in 2006. At the Frauenkirche the horror of the fire-bombing, the crashing buildings, the mangled bodies, though unimaginable, is also impossible to banish from our thoughts. Every building in the old city is charred.

The high musical life of Dresden is fully active. The opera house, where Schumann heard the premiere of *Tannhäuser*, is currently presenting Mozart, Weber, Wagner, Verdi, Richard Strauss, and the top-class orchestra and four-hundred-voice boys' choir are concertizing. Still more remarkable is the abundance of music in the streets. Chamber-music ensembles—a trio of violin, recorder, and flauto traverso, a brass quintet, groups of strings—play baroque music in arcades, on bridges, at street corners, as they do in Bruges, and used to do in Vivaldi's Venice. A spirited musical culture thrives here.

Lacking time to visit the Museum of Musical Instruments and the Richard Wagner Museum, we follow Goethe's example on his first Dresden visit and spend our time in the Gemäldegalerie, the world's richest collection of paintings for a city of this size. Many of the contents were stored in a salt mine during the war. My old friend Lincoln Kirstein, then private first class, helped to retrieve them. Ticket-takers, attendants, and guards in the museum have learned very little, or no, English.

The Bernardo Bellotto rooms at the far end of the building display the "einst" of the "einst und jetzt," the "then" and "now," of the picture books sold everywhere. In these paintings the city of Bellotto ("Canaletto") is beautiful not only in its architecture but in its peace and tranquility. The eighteenth-century harbor is busy, but not teeming, with commercial vessels, barges with cargos, fishing boats, ferries. The sturdy but graceful stone bridge from the center of the old city to the Royal Castle on the north side has been restored, but the paddle-wheel tourist steamers must lower their smokestacks to pass under it. In fact the rebuilding of Dresden is based on Bellotto's paintings, as was the reconstruction of Warsaw. The gallery is spectacularly rich in pictures by the Venetian Rosalba Carriera (157 of them), the Tuscan Artemisia Gentileschi, and the Cremonese Sofonisba Anguissola, the best known female artist.

The collections are exhibited by nationality rather than chronologically. Thus a room of lordly British portraits of the Gainsborough period precedes vitrines of Flemish miniatures. Only a few of the greatest masterpieces—Antonella da Messina, Botticelli, Giovanni Bellini, Mantegna, Giorgione's *Sleeping Venus*, Titian's *Tribute Money*—are behind glass, albeit of the wrong kind, reflecting the viewer, or making the picture visible only from an impossibly awkward angle. The framing is often incongruous, as in the case of Raphael's *Sistine Madonna* and a Rembrandt in identical gilt rococo rectangles, and the lighting is everywhere insufficient. Nevertheless, the Lottos, the three by Velasquez, the Patinir, the Piero di Cosímo, the Durers, the Holbein, the Poussins, the Watteaus are all very fine. For myself, the most memorable picture in the museum is Francesco Mola's fantasy of the blind Homer playing a thirteen-string viola da gamba. As he sings, his poetry is taken down by a young man in a script that imitates classical Greek.

The Prince-Elector of Saxony, and, more so, his father, Augustus the Strong—partly so-called because of his amative prowess: the number of his bastards is estimated at over one thousand—were connoisseurs of art, as well as greedy collectors of it. Augustus III purchased the Este collection in

Modena for twelve tons of gold, and when trying to acquire the *Sistine Ma-donna* from Piacenza, over the protests of the people, he prevailed by apply-ing pressure through the Duke of Parma and the Pope.

On the way to Leipzig, via Meissen, of porcelain fame, I think about Victor Klemperer, cousin of the conductor Otto and author of *I Will Bear Witness: A Diary of the Nazi Years*, as well as of nine other volumes of diaries still in German. Victor was married to a Protestant, and in Dresden, Jews married to Gentiles were not sent to labor camps and worse. On the morn-ing before the raids, he received a notice ordering him to report to an as-sembly place in three days, saying that the mixed-marriage exemption rule had been revoked. It seems that about two hundred Jews to whom this rule applied survived in Dresden. After that night's first bombing, the Klemperers and others fled, tearing the yellow star from their coats, and making their way west to Munich, a three-month ordeal of scrounging and hiding, be-fore finally reaching the by-then American-occupied city. The Klemperers returned to Dresden and spent the remainder of their lives there.

Leipzig is a depressing, Soviet-era factory town, whose most promi-nent feature from the Dresden road is a ferris wheel. Johann Sebastian Bach's Thomaskirche is closed to us because of a Rakhmaninov concert now tak-ing place. The program, attached to the door, is in Russian. The oxidized statue of Bach standing in a patch of park near the right side door is over-shadowed by trees. It faces a street of souvenir shops selling Bach CDs, books, T-shirts. In the plaza behind the church's north side a rock band thuds and moans for a considerable crowd.

The Leipzig visit has touched my musical roots. Forty-one years ago I wrote album notes for my recording of Bach's *Trauer-Ode:*

> In 1697, the King-Elector Augustus II of Saxony assumed the Polish crown, adopting the Roman Catholic faith to do so and thereby betraying his Saxon subjects. His wife, Christiane Eberhardine, preferring her Lutheranism to her husband, renounced the throne and lived apart from him until her death, Sep-tember 6, 1727. She was deeply mourned in Saxony, where Hans von Kirchbach, a nobleman student at the University of Leipzig, organized a me-morial service in the Paulinerkirche, in which he would delivery a valedictory. Von Kirchbach commissioned a sometime librettist of Bach's, Johann Christoph Gottsched,[2] to write verses for a mourning ode, which Bach set to music. A difficulty arose because the choice of composer ignored the director of music at the University Church, a certain Herr Görner, who outranked Bach in the pecking-order and ordinarily would have supplied the music for a university function of this sort. When Görner protested, Kirchbach was required to pay twelve thalers compensation to him. (The penalty for musical discrimination

2. Bernard Berenson published an appreciation of him.

is always high.) Bach was then granted permission to compose the Ode, albeit with the reprimand that he was not thereafter "to assume the right to compose music for academic festivals." Permission was granted on October 12, but Bach must have had Gottsched's text a few days earlier, since the score was finished on the 15th, two days before the performance. A great catafalque bearing the Polish Queen's emblems stood in the center of the church, and the service began with the ringing of all the city's bells. Von Kirchbach—let us not forget a man who chose Bach—delivered his oration after the fugal second chorus, with its glorious accompaniment of flutes and gambas without *continuo.*

June 3. Berlin to Rome, over a cloudless Adriatic, Ancona, the Apennines, alighting smoothly at Fiumicino. I feel relieved from the first touchdown of the wheels, and from the Porta S. Sebastiano positively euphoric. "Every prospect pleases," as the poet wrote ("and only man is vile"). The mid-afternoon Hassler is deserted, and an assistant manager, whose siesta we have disturbed, escorts us to a refurbished room on the Via Sistina side with a view of the Spanish Steps. In the evening, we walk to the Pincio, past the obelisk of the Trinità dei Monte, that phallic center of a sex marketplace. Young females stroll in pairs, backs provocatively bare between skin-tight jeans and loose blouses that invite groping. At the Villa Medici, Claude Lorrain *dessins* of Roman landscapes are on exhibit, but we won't have time. Early to bed. Bliss to be in Rome.

June 4. A lazy morning, unwinding from two stressed-out weeks of recording, interviewing, dinners, packing and unpacking, and the arduous passages through airports. We walk down the Via Sistina to the Piazza Barberini. Here, in November 1951, Stravinsky pointed out for me the Albergo Italia, where he had completed *Petrushka* in the spring of 1911. The entrance to the recently reopened Galleria Doria Pamphili is from the Piazza del Collegio Romano side, beyond the entrance to what was once Eugene Berman's home. The Doria gallery was the residence, in succession, of the families Della Rovere, Borghese, Aldobrandini (primogeniture), and Camillo Pamphili (secondogeniture), Innocent X's nephew. Camillo's son, Cardinal Benedetto, is a familiar name to musicians as the friend and patron of Arcangelo Corelli and George Frideric Handel.

The vastness of the Galleria—the spacious corridors, huge salons, tall, over-decorated and overgilded neck-cricking ceilings—is not inviting. The Hall of Mirrors is lined on both sides by marble statues, sumptuous Renaissance curules, candelabra, sculptured grotesques, swags. Overhead are frescoes, putti, sculpted *giganti* holding up the roof—which, despite their bulging biceps, collapsed in 1951. A brisk walk through the Galleria, with only the briefest stops to admire the choicest paintings, would last an hour. We have come to see the three by Velasquez, of which the Innocent X is in an annex, with Bernini's bust of the same pope on a pedestal near the portrait.

The sculpture does not belong here, and the painting itself is roped off at too great a distance for full appreciation. Farther along in the same gallery are Titian's *Salome*, Raphael's *Double Portrait*, and Caravaggio's *Rest During the Flight Into Egypt* (the beautiful nude-boy angel), but it seems that the greatest Renaissance paintings, notably the Giovanni Bellinis, were sold in the *ottocento* after the Genovese branch of the Doria family, of Admiral Andrea of the sunken-ship notoriety, took possession of the place on the extinction of the Roman hereditary line. The entire wall space is covered with pictures, barely an inch between frames. The upper levels would be visible only through telescopes. Annibale Carracci, youngest of the family of the three Bolognese masters, is the featured artist, but the greatest paintings, beside the Velasquez, are by the elder Pieter Brueghel.

In his *Promenades dans Rome*, Stendhal says that Trajan's Column, farther along on the Via del Corso, was dedicated to the emperor in 99 A.D., by the Roman calendar 867, and that Trajan, in Syria at the time, died without seeing it. His bones, placed in a gold urn, were interred beneath it. Is the gold still there?

June 5. We spend the afternoon on the Aventine Hill, southernmost of the Seven, to see the fifth-century church of Santa Sabina. Long thought to have been a victim of Hadrian's persecution, she is now believed to have been martyred during Vespasian's reign. The basilica, rated the most beautifully proportioned in Early Christian Rome, is modeled on the basilicas of Ravenna, but is unlike them partly in that only one small area of mosaics remains. Light floods the room from thirty-four large windows—actually transparent sheets of selenite—above twenty-four fluted Corinthian columns of Parian marble appropriated from a nearby second-century temple. The spandrels of the arcades are decorated with marble inlay in opus sectile. The gold lettering in the mosaics above the doorway distinguishes the "Church of the Jews" (*"Ecclesia cum circumcisione"*) from the "Church of the Gentiles" (*"Ecclesia ex gentius"*), which goes back to the Pauline period, when the hill was a refuge for Jews in Rome. The treasure of the church is in the vestibule, a huge door of cypress, also early fifth-century, with eighteen carved panels of Scriptural scenes, one of which is claimed to be the oldest existing representation of the Crucifixion. This panel, top left, is too elevated to be seen at all distinctly. Although an obliging Dominican monk from the adjoining monastery trains a light on it, this brings it no closer. But I would be afraid to climb the ladder that is needed.

Santa Prisca, on the other side of the Aventine, a century older and excavated in 1958, protects a Mithraeum, with ancient frescoes and a statue of Mithras slaying the bull. The Aventine is secluded and, with comparatively little traffic, quiet. Its attractive parks and gardens are close to the center of the city and offer good views of St. Peter's, the Janiculum, and the Pantheon. Why do the books not mention that Hercules secreted his cattle in a cave here, where, according to Livy, their lowing betrayed their hiding place to Cacus, who stole them but was caught and killed by their rightful owner, who then erected the Ara Maxima altar to himself? Before we return to the Via Sistina, we visit Bramante's Tempietto.

June 6. On the seemingly endless and poorly serviced Alitalia flight to New York, I finish Roger Martin du Gard's *Lieutenant-Colonel de Maumort.* Of the younger generation, only Camus seems to have recognized how good du Gard is: "Those who have the honor of knowing him as a man realize his modesty is real, so real that it appears abnormal." Stravinsky knew him from 1930, and preserved photographs with him. I had previously read only his elegant little book on Gide and merely dipped into the *Thibaults.*

July 14. The *TLS* publishes my reply to John Warrack's review of Stephen Walsh's botched Stravinsky biography. Stanley Baron sends a fax:

> Dear Bob: WHAT a good letter published in today's TLS. It seemed to me nice and calm, to the point, and wonderfully witty to boot. Congratulations!

July 22–26. London. Cimmerian gloom, fog, rain. We drive to Putney for a rehearsal of Simon Joly's chorus of twelve superb BBC singers in the transpontine church where Cromwell is supposed to have decided in favor of the decapitation of Charles I.

July 27–28. I record *Die glückliche Hand* at Abbey Road. What a surprisingly different and new piece is this successor to *Erwartung!* The entire first scene is in ostinato, and scenes 1 and 4 form a symmetry unique in Schoenberg. The orchestration throughout and the rhythms of the middle scenes are entirely original and very good.

July 29. We approach Venice from Vittorio Veneto, a perspective described in Emilio Lussu's *Sardinian Brigade.* Over the city, Shelley's one-line description of Venice, "A peopled labyrinth of walls," suggests that he looked down on the city from the top of the bell tower. After our longish spell in London, I am of one mind with the *cinquecento* traveler Thomas Hoby, who journeyed through Calabria to "Cicilia," not only "to have a sight of the country, but also to absent myself for a while out of Englishmennes companie for the tung's sake." Alexander, waiting for us at the airport, has a beard, a butch haircut, and a bad cold. The prices of motorboats to the city now qualify as piracy, but at least the route follows most of the Grand Canal, and we are lucky enough to be in a traffic tie-up in front of the Fondamenta Tedeschi. Exhausted from yesterday's recording and the long wait standing at Heathrow for the delayed flight, we eat in the hotel. I promise to take Alexander to the Scuola Tedesca tomorrow, the oldest of the city's five synagogues, which still has its original *tevà*—pulpit—and *Aròn*—cabinet for the Tables of the Law—but have caught his cold and will have to rest.

August 1. San Michele. In view of the heat and the long walk, the number of people who pay their respects to Stravinsky's grave is impressive, as is the increase in floral tributes covering the wall and ground behind. Joseph Brodsky's tomb, not far from Ezra Pound's, is conventional in height and proportions, in contrast to the flat slabs of the Stravinskys'. The brevity of Brodsky's life—the dates on his stone—saddens us.

August 5. Nuria Schoenberg Nono shows us her Nono–Schoenberg archives on the Giudecca and dines with us at Cipriani Dolce nearby on the waterfront, which is as good as, and incomparably quieter than, the parent restaurant in San Marco. Last seen seventeen years ago, Nuria has been transformed from brunette to white. She seems to be little interested in her father's music and wholly devoted to the promotion of her husband's, even though they had been separated for years before his death. To her American past she relates not at all.

August 6. The direct flight on Delta from Venice to New York is excruciatingly long, over air-conditioned, and bereft of edible food, for which last we deposit our baggage at the Hampshire House on arrival and taxi to La Côte Basque.

August 13. Our return to Florida is prolonged by two hours in a holding pattern over the "Garden State" that necessitates a fueling stop at Orlando.

August 31. Boca Raton. *"Oh Wehe, das höchsten Schmerzentags!"* as Parsifal sings. Three injections of Novocain and one of lidocaine fail to produce the desired numbness, and only after an hour of further anesthetizing can the extraction of tooth #31 begin. Excavating the roots takes another hour, and so, after its departure, does the filling-in of the vacuum with "freeze-dried allogenic bone," tamped down granule by granule. The next stages will require the insertion of a ridge reconstruction and occlusal therapy, bone grafting on tooth #30 and "second-stage soft tissue augmentation." Dr. Leichter says that the procedure performed on Alva last week was also of her tooth #31, however improbable mathematically. At home, the antibiotics and injections of Lovenox are increased, but at the same time I am returned to my rat poison (Coumadin). A liquid dinner, but I promise myself an indulgence tomorrow with a merely soft one, caviar blini.

September 16. Alva's daughter, son-in-law, and eighteen-month-old grandson, Noah, arrive from Seattle for four days of swimming, digging in the sand, shopping, music, before continuing to New York and Fire Island. The little one is hungry at all hours and still turns to his mother's bosom for snacks.

October 1. I write two "Letters to the Editor" apropos my *Isherwood* review in the *Times Literary Supplement* of August 18. The first is as follows:

> Bernard Wasserstein wonders why "the bar in which Tony Bower picked up the young man who later murdered him in his Park Avenue apartment" could not have been on "Fifth Avenue in the West Forties." The answers are: 1) that

Fifth Avenue, a north-south thoroughfare, is not *in* the West Forties. It borders ten West Forties blocks but the building numbers on the West Forties streets begin west of, not on, Fifth Avenue. 2) Four of the ten Fifth Avenue blocks bordering the West Forties are occupied by the New York Public Library and Rockefeller Center, and, thanks to zoning requirements and high rents, the other six blocks did not have a bar.

The second reads:

Peter Parker cannot transcribe correctly. My review does not state that "K. Bucknell's glossaries are 'liberally strewn with *errors*.' " It states that they are "literally strewn with *catastrophes*." The word clearly refers not to Ms. Bucknell's work, but to the disasters that overtake so many of the people in her portrait gallery: three murders, three suicides, three drownings, an accidental gasecution.

Parker asserts that the Beesleys "prevailed" on John van Druten to undertake the stage adaptation of *I Am a Camera*. Ms. Bucknell, more circumspectly, says that they "connived" to have him do it. But in claiming that the producers could not have prevailed on Van Druten because his adaptation was "not yet written," Parker belittles the reader's intelligence. The producers could have chosen Van Druten simply because they did not like the existing version by Lamkin and Field. Isherwood did like it, but, as he complained to us, the producers prevailed, as they usually do.

Parker seems not to know that Isherwood's 1947 edition of his 1930 translation of Baudelaire is not "merely a reprint." It contains textual revisions by the author and a UCLA professor, as well as a September 1946 Preface that improves the whole.

I found *Kathleen and Frank* unreadable and hence am unaware that Isherwood wrote about his sexuality "in some detail" insignificantly earlier than in *Christopher and His Kind*.

October 23–26. I record the Schoenberg-Monn Concerto with Fred Sherry in the huge studio in Walthamstow Assembly Hall (the northwest Borough of Waltham Forest), a one-and-a-half to two-and-a-half hour drive from Central London, depending on the time of day. Our three sessions begin at, respectively, 9:30, 13:00, and 18:00, and each of the three drivers, none of them certain of the exact location, takes a radically different route. The neighborhood is extremely unattractive. Fred plays superlatively, and the orchestra, including its wide-eyed cello section, is soon applauding him. I think I prefer the sound of this dismal room to that of Abbey Road, but the absence of eye-contact with the control room is a major impediment. After dinner with the Sherrys, we return to the Ritz to find the street blocked, floodlit, and with scores of police patrolling the crowded walks: Princess

Margaret is birthday-partying in the dining room. Alva ducks under the cordon, is recognized by a doorman on the hotel steps, and the two of them pull me through.

October 27. Flying with Alexander from Gatwick, we arrive at Florence during rush hour. The Villa San Michele, on a ledge below Fiesole, has been improved and expanded since our last visit. This time we have a detached apartment beyond the hotel's back arbors, gravel walks, and up a steep flight of narrow stairs, on which Alva trips, spraining her left ankle. Our room is newly furnished with fake antique curules, prie-dieux, etc., and our neighbor is the U.N.'s Kofi Annan. In the dining room, only minutes before dinner, I tell Alexander that Alva's son, Ted, a gifted painter studying in Florence, will be joining us. This is unfair of me, I know, but if I had told him earlier he would not have come, simply out of shyness. But the meeting goes smoothly and we are soon relaxed by the fermented juice of Montepulciano's vineyards. Later, on our balcony, the two representatives of the young idea are actually smoking cigars together.

October 29. We visit the Marino Marini Museum, expecting to see the sculptor's two bronze heads of Stravinsky, the first of which I watched him model in 1950, but are disappointed to learn that one is in Milan, the other in Pistoia. A French film of *L'Après-midi d'un faune,* based on the Nijinsky photographs as pieced together by Nureyev and copied by another dancer, is screened continuously in the basement. The music is scarcely audible, but the climax of the masturbation draws a crowd.

October 30. After arranging to meet us two hours later in the Uffizi, Alva leaves early to see Ted's apartment. But the queue when we arrive is a mob, four and five abreast, that stretches around the building to the Arno. Neon signs announce a minimum 120-minute wait in the outside arcade and as much as that on the staircases inside. Not for me. I go with Alexander to the Piazza della Signoria to see Bandinelli's *Hercules and Cacus.* Hard to believe that he had hoped to surpass Michelangelo's *David* with this pile of stone. The original populace greeted the piece with scorn, and Benvenuto Cellini, in his *Autobiography,* wasted some of the most stinging invective in all art criticism on it: "If Hercules' beard and hair were shorn, the remaining noddle would not be sufficient to contain his brain; his muscles are not those of a man, but copies of a sack of melons; his shoulders are as ugly as the pommels of a donkey's packsaddle, and his head is awkwardly attached to his neck; one does not know on which leg he is standing; if the right calves were to be separated where they touch, both men would remain without calves at that point." At first glance, this diatribe seems perfectly targeted. At second, it seems maliciously exaggerated. And at third, it stands convicted of the old crime of criticizing the artist for not doing what he did not set out to do.

Graffiti on the walls here reads: "Clinton: Bomb Disneyland, not

Kosovo." Cameroons peddle imitation luxury goods and jewelry in front of the Uffizi, as they do on the streets of Venice. Their best-selling toy is a two-foot-tall plastic U.S. Marine in combat clothes crawling on his belly and firing a submachine gun. A turnoff to the left from our road back to Fiesole is called Via Tomasso Alva Edison, the derivation of Alva's name.

Learning from CNN that floods and hurricane-strength winds have closed all airports in Britain, we switch to an evening flight to Paris tomorrow, and from there, two days later, to New York.

October 30. After a four-hour wait at the Florence airport we scramble on board what, thanks to high winds, is the first flight to reach Paris in forty-eight hours. The George V Hotel is much less attractive than before its renovation, but the restaurant stays open for us at 11 P.M. and the Belons are large and succulent.

November 23. Gulf Stream. A sumptuous Thanksgiving feast at the Cudmores' with their children and a family of Finns, one of them a pretty nineteen-year-old girl who is a senior at Vanderbilt University. All talk is about the difference between pregnant and dimpled chads.

December 1. The *Times Literary Supplement* publishes my note on a "book-of-the-year" choice:

Pavimenti a Venezia: The Floors of Venice (Vianello Libri, Treviso). Text by Tudy Sammartini, translated by Giles Watson. Photographs by Gabriele Crozzolo. Impossible as it may seem, this is a newly informed history of the city from an unexplored perspective. Few readers can have had access to all of the palaces and even some of the churches, and only the authors will have seen these stone carpets in the lighting that, the photographer writes, was so difficult to procure. Inexplicably, Otto Demus's "exhaustive" *The Mosaics of San Marco* does not include the floor, which contains work by Uccello and Sansovino, and was much less damaged by flood tides and subsidence in their time than today. Signora Sammartini's theses are that a perfect iconographic correspondence obtains between the Basilica's vault mosaics and the geometric floor patterns, and that the city's floors are "the only remaining record of the riot of color" that was Venice in earlier centuries. For many, the value of the book will be in the discussions of restorations, particularly those in early ninth-century San Lorenzo, where, in 1987, fragments of colored floor marble cladding and cubes of tesserae were found a dozen feet below the surface. In twelfth-century Santi Maria e Donato, at Murano, the floor, apart from the peacocks of immortality, depicts a Star of David, a Solomon's seal, the sixty-four black and white squares of a chess board—symbol of wisdom in the Arab world when still a novelty in the West—two cockerels with fox strung from their shoulder pole (Charles VIII and Louis XII with the captive Ludoviso Sforza?), and, most curiously, a much magnified scene of two mating ants. These are the mosaics that Ruskin described as one of Italy's most precious monuments, "the beginning of that mighty spirit of Venetian color which was to be consummated in Titian." In the 1970s, when the floor was entirely "deconstructed," and each tessera individually cleaned, the church's five famous slabs of marble were discovered to be Roman gravestones turned back to front.

December 22. New York. We give a small, one-table dinner party for Helen and Elliott Carter, each of them recently turned ninety-two. Elliott talks with the vigor of a man half his age. Bob Silvers is amusing about Norman Mailer in Bayreuth last summer immediately identifying with Wotan. Suzanne Farrell, whose arms, hands, and legs are in constant graceful movement, discusses a possible collaboration in presenting stagings of Stravinsky's *Movements* and *Variations.* The Fred Sherrys, Claudio, and Lizzy Hardwick are early; Marty Garbus and his wife Sarina Tang come late. Alexander, who has just arrived, behaves well, for someone who was mugged in the middle of the night at Newark Airport, and robbed of his passport and cash.

December 24. Phyllis and Kristin come for Christmas Eve—and the night—on the way to the Rumbles' in Washington.

December 26. We spend the afternoon at the Metropolitan Museum's exhibition of Chinese calligraphy, "The Embodied Image." Sixteen centuries are represented and the collection, most of it from that of the J. B. Elliott in Princeton, is the largest outside China. Sarina, who has arranged for the chief curator, Maxwell K. Hearn, to guide us through privately, and her husband, join us. Oracle-Bone Writing (incised on tortoise plastrons and ox scapulae) is indistinguishable to me from Seal Script and Clerical Script, from Standard Script, and some Cursive from some Running Script, but Cursive seems the most dynamic of all. The point is that calligraphy transcends its linguistic meaning, that the physical presence of the words, or characters, not their content, is the object of appreciation. Wang Hsi-chih (303–61) is revered as the greatest of all calligraphers. Calligraphy conveys feelings of the most subtle kind, and Wang Shan-jen described it as "a mind print," or "reflection of the soul." One of the most interesting specimens, a sixth-century text, contains exactly one thousand characters, each used only once. Most of the texts on display are letters, official documents, poems. Two non-consecutive lines from a massive hanging scroll, *Poem on Lake T'ai yeh* in Peking, are translated as

> *The silver mountains rise from the world through mist*
> *The wild geese wheel round the air, never startled.*

But a poem by Yang Yin (1470–1524) I find deeply moving:

> *In the middle of the night, the moon is bright, and I listen*
> *   to dogs barking in the village;*
> *After the rain has passed orioles sing, and leaves blanket the town.*

The traveler has not yet returned, but another spring is passing;
With whom can I go arm and arm and sing a tune?

Mr. Hearn is gracious, acutely intelligent, and highly cultivated, a man one would like to listen to at length. I talk to him about Arthur Waley, Empson, I. A. Richards (*Mencius on the Mind*), Witter Brynner, and other Westerners who had studied and taught in China, but he is impressed only by my tiny acquaintanceship with Waley, whose reputation is continually rising, he says.

December 28. Night flight to London; several days earlier than expected because of tomorrow's blizzard forecast.

December 31. London, the Ritz. The rain has not stopped since our arrival. A dowdy party is underway on the ground floor. A few low, fizzling fireworks are visible from our park-side windows. But the manager sends us a bottle of top-year Dom Perignon.

2001

January 2. London. I record *Symphony of Psalms* at Abbey Road and in the next two days *Les Noces*, with the superb International Piano Quartet.

April 3. Rome. The Velasquez exhibition in the Palazzo Ruspoli contains a few masterpieces but many more pictures by minor contemporaries and followers. The same can be said of the Caravaggio at the Palazzo Giustiniani, a marvelous building I had not seen before. The surname of one of the insignificant painters on display here is "Craft."

April 4. Marcello and Jane Panni take us to a luncheon in a tennis club overlooking the Tiber. The other guests are Roman Vlad, my good friend of fifty years, Arnaldo Pomodoro (the sculptor), Alberto Arbesino (the writer), Francesco Pellizzi and his wife, an archaeologist working in the Mekong Delta.

Alexander comes from Copenhagen in time to dine with us on the Hassler Roof. As between the three "reconstructed" Nijinsky ballets at the Teatro Costanzi and the English Theater of Rome's presentation, "Freudian Slips and Other Underwear," we prefer to stroll in the Pincio.

April 7. To Viterbo, the city of marvelous fountains. The *uscita* through the sprawling suburbs of Rome takes longer than the rest of the forty-mile ride, but why is the capital of the Catholic world papered with the most lubricious affiches (Versace ads most teasingly) in all Europe? Spring is on time in the fields of Lazio, lilacs and bougainvillea, daisies and buttercups, sycamores putting out leaves, budding vineyards, groves of olive, chestnut, and hazelnut trees.

Viterbo—Viterbium—is a severe, windswept, isolated hilltop town, entirely surrounded by high brick walls. It was once the center of the "inner Etruria," where family ties were closer and inbreeding common. For this reason the Sicilian Vitaliano Brancati chose it as the setting for his novel of incestuous love, *A Traveler's Strange Adventure* (1934). Viterbo is famous today for its master printers in the *Casa Editrice Agnosotti.*

All streets in the medieval city are one-way, and most are closed to motor traffic, which means a lot of painful walking on cobblestones. The principal exhibits in the Etruscan archaeological museum, the first building inside the *porta principale,* are from the Acquarossa excavations of the Swedish Academy *(Scavi Svedesi)* in 1956–1978. I remember the Swedish King in the 1950s, when he occupied the floor above us at the Hassler Hotel, going out himself on early morning digs. The museum is poorly lighted, especially a top-floor oubliette containing the 2500-year-old skeleton of a young girl, the sight of which frightens us out into the sunlight wondering why her skull was fractured in so many places.

The Palazzo Papale, at the center of the city, is best-known for its openwork Gothic loggia, the *"merletti di pietra,"* lace made of stone, and it does look more like embroidery than sculpture. Between 1261 and the transfer of the Papal See to Avignon in 1309, Vitterbo was the scene of the election of five popes, and the deaths of four. Gregory X's elevation to the tiara in 1271 followed thirty-three months of deliberation by the College of Cardinals, which came to an end only when the military chief of the city locked the Cardinals in—*cum clave,* the origin of the word conclave—and had the roof removed, exposing the electors to the elements and forcing them to a conclusion. In 1271, as well, the child Prince Henry of Almain was murdered here, by his cousin Guido di Monforte, during Mass in the church of the Gesù. For this crime Dante includes Guido in the first—strictly for VIPs—circle in Hell, and condemns Adrian V, one of the five Viterbo popes, to the circle of the avaricious.

But Viterbo should be visited at night on September 3, to see the procession dedicated to Santa Rosa, who, at age ten, successfully rallied the population against a siege by the Emperor Federico Secondo, the *stupor mundi.* One hundred men wearing white turbans and suits raise a float to their shoulders carrying a Baroque machine ninety feet tall. They parade with it through the city, then lower it and charge up a hill to a sanctuary containing the mummified body of the beatified wunderkind.

Attached to the church of S. Maria Nuova on the north end of the façade is an elevated stone pulpit from which Thomas Aquinas preached, invited by his friend Gregory X, or so I suppose, this Pope having asked him to attend the Council of Lyon with him. (Soon after leaving Naples, however, Thomas died en route at his sister's house.) Dante placed Tommaso with his teacher Albertus Magnus and his friend St. Bonaventura among the *Spiriti sapienti* in the "Heaven of the Sun." We visit the Cathedral of San

Lorenzo, constructed on the site of a temple of Herakles. The city's best-known painting is the *Pietà* by Michelangelo's friend, Sebastiano del Piombo.

The Parco dei Mostri in the valley at Bomarzo, a few miles north, affords splendid views of the Orsini palace in the town high above. Returning to Rome on the autostrada, we stop at the hill towns of Attigliano (Attila) and, to see the Roman aqueduct, Orte.

June 25–29. London. Ted and Alexander, our respective sons, go to Wimbledon for the Agassi game. In the evening I record *Oedipus Rex* with a superior cast, chorus, and orchestra. Edward Fox, the soft-spoken narrator, has fine diction and he improves the translation of Cocteau's text with two emendations. I also record Stravinsky's *Lamentations of Jeremiah*, believing that this is the first time ever that all of the correct pitches have been sung.

June 30. Venice. Francis Ford Coppola, sitting on the awning side of the porch at the Gritti, watches our *motoscafo* dock. How I would like to talk to him about my recent visit to Cambodia. Venice is choking with tourists, to the extent that queues form to cross bridges, and it is impossible even to push our way into the Piazza. The prizewinner of this summer's Biennale exhibition is an empty room with walls painted green.

July 5. Our flight from Venice to Paris is so late that our bags miss the transfer to the connecting flight to Miami, and we have to sprint to catch the plane ourselves. Though it is only 9 P.M. in Florida when we land, the escalators have been turned off and we must walk four miles. The loudspeakers and the directing signs are in Spanish only, and the officials who take down our descriptions of missing bags and address and telephone information also speak no English.

July 25. New York. Fierce heat and a threatening storm. I read from *Places* to a surprisingly large audience at the Lincoln Center Barnes & Noble, and sign about fifty books. Solomon Volkov, here with his wife, gives me his Joseph Brodsky book and tells me that the poet mentioned having seen me conduct in Moscow in 1962.

September 11. Gulf Stream. Armageddon. As if to shock and depress us even more, while we watch the horrors on television, gardeners bring ladders and scythes and castrate our coconut palms.

September 21. The *Times* reports that a middle-aged English woman worked for six months alongside the pilot of the first kamikaze plane and remembers that on the day of the victorious bombing of the *Cole* in Yemen, he and his friends boisterously celebrated in one of their rented apartment rooms. Why did she not report this at the time?

September 22. Isaac Stern dies. I remember meeting him and his second wife, Vera, in October 1951 in Geneva, both he and Stravinsky having come to fill engagements with Ernest Ansermet's Orchestre de la Suisse

Romande. Stern played the Beethoven Concerto with Ansermet on a program with Stravinsky's *Orpheus* that the composer did not attend and obliging me to substitute for him in escorting Mme Ansermet. We sat with Denis de Rougemont, whose writings were in vogue at the time, and his young wife. We enjoyed two lively visits with the Sterns at the hotel. I recall another evening with him at the Luau on Rodeo Drive, a might-have-been-awkward occasion because we were dining with Dr. Edel, Stravinsky's physician, who had been having an affair with Nora Kaye when Stern married her in 1948. (The *Times* obit identifies her as "a dancer," whereas she was probably the best known American ballerina at the time [1947–48] and would go on to crown her career with the lead role in the Robbins–Stravinsky *The Cage.*) That night in the "Luau," the violinist and Edel shook hands but did not speak. My own participation was limited to some unsuccessful proselytizing for the Schoenberg Violin Concerto, which Stern did not regard as music, but as an unplayable cerebral exercise.

I began to know Stern well in June 1960 on his return to Los Angeles from a concert tour in Australia. He asked me to coach him in Stravinsky's Violin Concerto, which he would record with the composer in less than a week, and I spent most of the next three days with him in his suite at the Beverly Hills Hotel. In truth, he did not know the piece at all—for which reason the number of recording sessions had to be increased—but he graciously accepted my criticisms and comments on points of interpretation. I have wondered ever since how he could come to record the Concerto with its composer without having woodshedded it months before. He was nervous during the sessions, perhaps realizing that three players in the orchestra, Eudice Shapiro, Israel Baker, and Sol Babitz, had played it with Stravinsky. Let it be said that he came to love the piece, and that he convinced the young Itzkhak Perlman to learn it and perform it four times with me in Chicago and Honolulu.

Two days after the first bombing of Kabul, Alva and I flew from Miami to London. The entrance to the Miami airport was guarded by uniformed men carrying Uzis, but the building was virtually empty. After checking our bags, we spent five hours alone in the Brit Air lounge. If the plane had not been needed in the UK the next morning, our flight, with only a dozen passengers, would have been cancelled. When we arrived, Piccadilly was blocked to vehicular traffic by thousands of anti-bombing, anti-American demonstrators, and the Ritz was deserted and grim.

We recorded *Gurre-Lieder* in six sessions during the following week, an ordeal in that the venue was the Town Centre in Watford, a two-hour drive from our hotel. We had to rely on room service for after-midnight food, the recording sessions taking place in the evenings, the only time when singers, chorus, and orchestra were available. I enjoyed conducting this marvelous Romantic music more than anything in my life.

On October 21 I was interviewed by the editors of *Gramophone* and an American magazine, *Fanfare*. On October 22 we experienced a terrible scare, but retrospectively, when we learned that two bags had been checked through, then removed because the ticket holder failed to board the plane. We were not told what explosives they contained, but eight U.S. marshals met us on the ramp when we disembarked in Miami, and our baggage was put through an X-ray machine before we were allowed to leave the terminal. During the long ride to Gulf Stream, our driver talked about "biohazard suits" and bomb shelters coming on the market.

November 19. I finally get around to the *TLS*'s request for a contribution on the "book-of-the-year-choice":

Begin almost anywhere in Philip Larkin's *Further Requirements* (Faber), and the sordid underside of the "anti-Larkin crusade" (M. Amis) vanishes in the enjoyment of graceful prose, skewering wit, and keen insights. The collection lacks an essay as strong as the "Marvell" or the "What's Become of Wystan" (in *Required Writing*), but the compensatory interest in this successor volume is that some key pieces are Larkin's own rejects for that volume. They readjust his hierarchies in that Hardy has overtaken Yeats, Thomas is reinstated ("Plenty of people born after Thomas wrote quite nicely, but I don't think any of these was his equal"). Betjeman, early Auden, and Graves (despite an "uncertainty at the heart of his talent") hold their places, and Christina Rossetti is given an elevated one, as much for her "steely" stoicism as for a "body of work unequalled . . . for its objective expression of happiness denied."

Larkin's heroes have shifted: "Thomas Hardy [is] the most considerable English writer since Shakespeare before D. H. Lawrence." Never mind Donne, Herbert, Dryden, Pope, Keats, or even George Eliot. Larkin has always focused on his own century, and sought to find a place among the local and the low-key. What is striking here is that D. H. Lawrence is everything Larkin is not: "No writer of this century aimed himself more at the world, no writer took it on more completely, its countries and continents, people and philosophies, everything down to its smallest birds, beasts and flowers. It is this universality that is one of Lawrence's most compelling qualities, the sense he gives that . . . this is not only a world of men, but a vivid epiphany of life in all its alternatives, of which humanity is only one, and perhaps not the best one at that."

Three quibbles. Auden cannot be described as an "enthusiastic amateur pianist" (or any other kind). In an interview, the claim "still" not to "know what 'rood-lofts' are" can hardly be true of a librarian and close associate of John

Betjeman (see the glossary in his *English Parish Churches*). A review of Kingsley Amis's *Oxford Book of Light Verse* notes that Byron and Praed are "the opening bats" in the representation of the nineteenth century, and that "no one else comes near them." But can Praed, a minor poet from a different era, be coupled with Byron?

November 25. New York. It is still night as we leave for JFK, and the next night has fallen before we land in Paris, which is cold and wet. The Plaza Athénée seems almost empty, except that Alain Ducasse's restaurant is full; reservations must be booked two months in advance. From a *Guide Télévision* we learn that "details of films viewed" from pay-channel pornography are "not printed on the hotel bill." Unable to sleep, we watch Saudi TV, which shows the texts of sunrise prayers in yellow Arabic script as a tenor intones them. The beat is regular, the tempo steady, the pitch-range circumscribed, the contour of the chant diatonic and stepwise, and each verse begins with a 3-note upward incipit. Cantilation marks indicate quarter-tone tuning. Of the other five Arab channels, only the one from Dubai is functioning. It takes the viewer on a tour of private homes in an affluent neighborhood, in which framed photographs of Hitler are visible on most tables and walls.

November 30. The flight to Rome is smooth, but the Hassler Hotel has only the same impossibly small room that we occupied in April. When we explain to the manager that we need more space and that friends have offered us their apartment, he says that we may leave tomorrow without a penalty. Alva inspects a double-room, double-bathroom accommodation at the Majestic, a few blocks away, and places a deposit on it.

December 1. After packing and unpacking, we are resettled in a bright— red carpet, white couches and chairs—suite on the sunny side of the Majestic, not, of course, leaving any forwarding address at the Hassler. Dinner with Roman and Licia Vlad in their cozy—except for a flight of steps and a rickety elevator—fifth-floor apartment, which is just below the Quirinale. The Pannis arrive late, directly from Naples.

December 2. At 11 A.M. Vlad and I conduct a public dialogue in the Sala Casella, supposedly on Stravinsky's religious music. He translates for me. In the evening we go with the Vlads and Pannis to dinner at the Hotel de la Russie (Via del Babuino, near the Piazza del Popolo), which has a "Stravinsky Bar." Very good cuisine, better, it is said, than at the "Petrushka" restaurant.

December 3. Rehearse from 4 to 10 P.M. The bass-trombonist, Stan, an American from Chicago, translates for me. We dine with the Pannis, who persuade the proprietor of a restaurant near the Ludovisi Palace to stay open beyond closing time.

December 4. The second rehearsal, same time, same unsuccessful struggle for rhythmic steadiness, same failure to obtain a sense of ensemble. The chorus is amateur (unpaid), but has an admirably straight tone quality, attributable to its conductor, Padre Pablo, a priest who rehearses the Vatican choir.

December 5. The stage of the Teatro Olimpico, where the dress rehearsal takes place, is filled with Arnaldo Pomodoro's art, while the musicians are confined to a tiny platform above the pit. The scrims, huge abstract paintings in disguise, are attractive and appropriate, but the artist has constructed two levels of huge organ pipes and installed the singers inside them, three or four crowded together at each triangular flue, from which they are barely audible and in which they cannot hear the orchestra. Most of the rehearsal time is consumed in trying to remedy this situation, but neither Marcello P. nor Maestro R. C. is willing to tell Pomodoro, a dear man all too aware of his mistake, that the contraption will not work, and that the chorus should regroup at stage front.

December 6. The concert, at 9 P.M., is preceded by three hours of extra rehearsal, most of it used to try out the complicated and precarious exits and entrances of musicians and soloists, and to test the lighting. On arrival at my dressing room, I find a cellophane-wrapped white rose with a letter attached from "Dagmar Hader Lassander," an affectionate reminder that we last saw each other in Berlin thirty-eight years ago. She promises to be "watching from the front row." Just before curtain time a rip is discovered near the top of the first scrim. Ladders are set up and, in a mere thirty minutes and to the tune of several outbursts of protest applause, the damaged area is patched up. I am finally led out, in the semi-dark, over tangles of cables and down a creaky, nearly invisible wooden staircase, to a low podium. The first trumpet player manages to miscount in half a dozen places, leaving out the theme at one point, and his re-entries produce excruciating dissonances and confusion. I dare not stop, however, since in a restart he will simply make new mistakes. The violinist alternately rushes and drags, and the bassist fumbles his rhythms. The generous applause deservedly accorded to the contralto cannot be sustained because, like me, she must climb those stairs, and who, regaining stage level, would attempt to redescend? During intermission I foolishly give a live TV interview to RAI in my halting, inept French, the interviewer knowing no English. My only comfort is that the room is so full of noise and of comings and goings that the telecaster cannot have used it. The effort was fatiguing, all the same, and made the Mass more strenuous to conduct. The only passages that sounded as they should were the *a cappella* parts in the Sanctus and Agnus Dei.

After the concert I change my clothes in my dressing room while Alva barricades the unlockable door with her foot. Eventually some well-wishers enter, including an elderly lady who had waved to me from the first row during my bow. Backstage, she comes directly to me, encircles me in her arms, and says "You look just as you did conducting *Erwartung* in Washington forty years ago." This could only be Signora Mathilde Crespi, but confused by the communication from Dagmar, I do not recognize her. Another factor is that Signora Crespi was some years older than I am and had heart trouble, hence I assumed that she was deceased, especially since she did not attend my two other conducting appearances in Rome in the intervening years. When I respond with an irrelevant reference to Helga Pilarcycz, who sang the *Erwartung*, she turns and departs. I feel embarrassed by this encounter, and by ancient feelings of guilt.

At 11:45 we finally enter the club on the Tiber, where we had lunched in April, to join a post-concert dinner party. Among the forty people who applaud us are Francesco Carraro from Venice, the young, recently widowed wife of Giuseppe Sinopoli, the composer Aldo Clementi, who gives me a score of a new piece of his, and my old friend "Picci," to whom I would have liked to talk, but Alva and I are taken to a table with the president of the Filarmonica, who proves to be a likeable, bon-vivant *avogadro* speaking perfect English. Licia Vlad, on my left, talks wisely about the pleasures of old age, and learnedly about the recently excavated rooms in the Domus Aurea, which we had hoped to see tomorrow. Opposite me is a tall blond who looks like Meryl Streep, but turns out to be a pianist from Kiev. The party breaks up at 3:30 and we are in bed an hour later.

December 7. A wildcat Air France strike changes our plans, and we spend hours rearranging our return to Miami via London. No Domus Aurea, alas, which was one of the reasons for our trip, but Jane Panni makes a gift to us of a new Italian book on the subject.

December 8. I spend the morning with our Italian dictionary and the new book, which consists of reproductions of the Louvre album of the subterranean frescoes of the *"palazzo neroniono."* They were discovered at the end of the *quattrocento.* In 1504, the *Laocoön*—the one in the Vatican may be a Roman copy—which Trajan is supposed to have brought to Italy from Greece was found in an unfinished hall. In 1515 Raffaello conceived his Vatican loggia from torchlight study of the frescoes. Signorelli had been influenced by them, and Giovanni da Udine had made copies, as did the Portuguese painter Francisco d'Ollande, three of the latter being preserved in the Escorial. (The vogue of copying classic art seems to have started with Filippino Lippi and his work in the Carafa Chapel in Santa Maria sopra Minerva in 1489–1492.) The seventy pictures in the Louvre album were the work of three sixteenth-century artists, one of whom was Tsar Paul I's court painter. The copies are in watercolors, memorable for unknown shades of reds and blues and different tones of black. The subject matter features Aphrodites, Leda (the wife of the king of Sparta), birds, horses, and centaurs.

At 3 P.M. we fly to London for a single night in a tiny room at the Ritz.

December 9. The flight to Miami is intolerably long, but we arrive on time and are met by a car. Alas, our house is dark, and since the hurricane shutters are down we cannot open the door, the ultimate cruelty for battered, hungry, and exhausted travelers. The driver takes us to a nearby hotel and deposits us and our seven bags on the pavement. An hour later our college-age housekeeper, Marciella, turns up with a key through the garage, but in a car not capacious enough for both our baggage and ourselves, and we end this over-adventurous trip in a taxi.

December 31. A muted New Year's party at home. My wish: to find time to write another book and to make a few more recordings before time finds me.

2002

July 17, 2002. Arriving at our hotel in London for recording sessions with the Philharmonia, we find an invitation from St. James's Palace. His Royal Highness the Prince of Wales, Patron of the Philharmonia Orchestra, requests the pleasure of our company at a reception to be held at the Orchard Room, Highgrove, on Wednesday, July 24, 2002. Time: 4:15. Dress: Lounge Suit. A second letter tells us to expect a limousine and driver at 2 P.M. for the trip to the Gloucestershire estate and warns that we must show our invitations at the entrance and that our vehicle will be subject to a security search.

The limousine arrives promptly, but we are detained by an urgent problem concerning discrepancies between the scores and orchestral parts for our next recording, and are late in departing. Alas, we are no farther than Malmesbury at 4:15, and reach the Highgrove gate a half hour behind schedule. Here, surprisingly, a pair of constables waves us through without looking at our invitations or inspecting the car. Inside the grounds and around a bend in the road, our driver stops at the open front door of a palatial eighteenth-century residence. Two young toffs suddenly appear and usher us to a short threshold of stairs, where, to our astonishment, we recognize the Prince of Wales, standing at the top and seemingly waiting for us. Flustered, bewildered, we realized while mounting the steps that something is wrong. Where are the other people? And why is the interior not lighted, the Prince standing in semi-darkness? Clearly we do not belong here, and not knowing what to do about it, forget our freshly researched protocol. I actually introduce myself to him as a time-to-time conductor of the Philharmonia, and even extend my hand, which the Prince actually shakes. "But you *are* the King, the King of Bahrain, aren't you?," he asks. (As if conducting might be my part-time job.) Now looking at me and my complexion more closely, he recognizes the mistake and graciously invites us to join the tour-group already in his gardens, summoning an aide to accompany us. We retreat from the royal presence—not backwards, because of the stairs—whereupon the Prince courteously escorts me to the car and, in a stunning role-reversal, opens and closes the door for me.

Our recovery from this experience begins with the realization that the Prince was indeed awaiting the ruler of the Bahrain Sheikdom, a British protectorate until recently and the principal military base during the Persian Gulf War. The country and its neighbor Qatar are mentioned daily in British news speculating about the possibility of a new conflict with Iraq. Moreover, it is bruited that the Queen has been encouraging Prince Charles's participation in diplomatic affairs. The inadvertent incident with us has deprived his meeting of its secrecy.

The gardens are musical as well as fragrant; I recall no others so richly endowed with songbirds. The visitors have been parceled into smaller groups, each led by a young woman who provides the horticultural and dendrological facts as well as the history of the structures and statuary. An obstacle for us, but a superable one, is that the paths are sporadically paved with cobbles, pebbles, gravels, and bricks, the latter separated by varying depths of grass, and, though forewarned, we have neglected to wear the proper shoes. Although international and richly variegated, the gardens are also quirky and a little complicated in layout, as well as overstrewn with large terracotta pots, driftwood, and ingenious topiarizing. Hedges tilted in different angles and clipped into swirls and canapé-shaped squares of yew. Further, the pergolas, pavilions, arbors, the dovecote, the monuments (two of them for the Laureate Ted Hughes), the Léger-like collage of sculpted fragments ("tapestry of stone"), and the tree house for the young Princes William and Harry seem over-crowded. The copy of the "Versailles Diana" statue (with deer and quiver: Kenneth Clark believed that the original was by the same artist as the Apollo Belvedere) is avoided and mentioned without comment. All this is offset by vistas of fresh green meadows with grazing black Angus cows, sheep, and horses.

At six o'clock we go to the Orchard Room, a small concert hall next to the main residence. Here the VIP audience, which includes Bryn Terfel, sits in awkward silence for about fifteen minutes until HRH appears, acknowledges the warm applause, and takes his place at the center of the first row, flanked by empty chairs. The concert, conducted by Christopher Warren Green, the orchestra's leader, begins with a Vivaldi concerto for two trumpets, brilliantly played, and is followed by solo pieces for violin and cello. The Prince then chats about his own musical background, first as a trumpeter, then as a cellist, in his school orchestra, charmingly deprecating his abilities in contrast to those of the virtuosos just heard. Taking the baton, he conducts the grand finale himself, a medley of English tunes composed for Queen Victoria by the elder Johann Strauss, which cleverly turns "Rule Britannia" into a waltz and ends with the National Anthem. Whether HRH leads the orchestra or it leads him matters not. His beat-patterns, cues, and other gestures are elegant and merit the ovation in which the swell of national pride sweeps us along as well. The occasion has been a happy one.

As we leave, the manager of the Philharmonia, Mansell Bebb, tells me that the Prince asked if he knows "the conductor Robert Craft," which attests to a remarkable memory, in view of the long queue of curtsying and genuflecting patrons to whom HRH has just been introduced.

The twilight drive through Tetbury and the other oolitic villages and back across the Cotswolds is pleasant and the rarely cloudless sky is a blend of delicate English watercolors. The story has traveled to our hotel ahead of us and the concierges greet me as "Your Royal Highness of Bahrain."

Index

Acton, Baron John Emerich Edward Dalberg, 72

Adler, Stella, 189

Akhmatova, Anna, 126, 239

Ansermet, Ernest, 28, 68–69, 71, 79, 86, 87, 88, 90, 108 n. 127, 147, 176, 180–81, 185, 281, 332, 333, 431–32

Answers to 35 Questions (interview), 193

Aquinas, St. Thomas, 205

Aristotle, 3

Auden, W. H., 25–26, 54, 89, 92, 94, 98, 106, 108, 109, 126, 131, 134, 154, 165, 166, 173, 175, 198, 200, 206, 210, 213, 218, 219, 232, 238, 248, 257, 268, 275, 284, 306–7, 313–14, 359, 369, 393, 403; Barnard Lectures, 51–52; *Elegy for Young Lovers* (libretto), 226; *The Rake's Progress* (libretto), 59, 72, 95, 96, 100 n. 112, 151–53, 212, 243

Auerbach, Erich, 232

Avedon, Richard, 210

Ayer, Sir Alfred Jules, 222

Babbitt, Milton, 53, 123, 175, 179, 185, 198, 210, 248, 257, 310, 404, 406

Babin, Victor, 143–44, 188

Babitz, Sol, 83, 128–30, 140, 148, 153, 192, 202, 304, 432

Bach, Johann Sebastian, 30, 34, 68, 80, 129–30, 146, 157, 158, 164, 165, 175, 178, 182, 192, 198, 199, 237–38, 253, 254, 285; *Trauer-Ode*, 273, 320–21

Bachardy, Don, 131, 132, 187, 196, 201, 203, 243, 244, 245, 246; *Last Drawings of Christopher Isherwood*, 375

Balanchine, George, 23, 36, 73, 74, 75, 95, 110, 118, 126, 127, 135, 153, 156, 165, 167–68, 175–76, 178, 179, 191, 198, 215, 252, 255, 256, 258, 260, 268–69, 282, 283, 284, 286, 305, 307, 309, 310, 315–16, 318, 326–27, 330, 337–38

Ballet Society Productions, 19, 81, 94

Balthus (Count Balthasar Klossowski de Rola), 123

Baron, Stanley, 410, 423

Barrie, Michael, 134, 177–78, 202

Bartók, Béla, 49, 100, 162, 171, 207

Baudelaire, Charles, 380, 385, 395

Bean, Hugh, 405

Beauvoir, Simone de, 396

Beckett, Samuel, 256, 258

Beethoven, Ludwig van, 24, 26, 28, 30, 38, 90, 167, 172, 191, 202, 256, 298, 303, 310, 311, 332, 376; *Fidelio*, 165, 226, 238

Belline, Ira (Ira Beliankina), 76 n. 45, 246

Bellow, Saul, 281

Berg, Alban, 130, 283; *Altenberg Lieder*, 210, 285; Chamber Concerto, 106, 164, 244; *Lulu*, 130, 342, 376, 397; *Lyric Suite*, 208; Three Pieces for Orchestra, 190, 223, 224, 242; *Wozzeck*, 154, 286, 297

Berger, Arthure, 68, 90, 106, 109, 175, 393–94

Bergman, Ingmar, 252 n. 12, 270, 396

Bergman, Ingrid, 144

Berlin, Aline (Lady Berlin), 226, 242, 287, 405

Berlin, Sir Isaiah, 161, 209, 220–41, 242, 260, 287, 305

Berman, Eugene, 79–80, 100, 110, 118–21, 153, 178, 179, 186, 207, 216, 217, 247, 252, 260, 268, 293, 296, 313, 421

Bernhardt, Thomas, 401

Bernstein, Leonard, 53, 54–55, 62, 65, 66, 105, 189, 216, 219, 249, 256, 276, 286, 301, 310, 316, 325, 330, 337

Bliss, Mildred (Mrs. Robert Woods), 360, 384

Bohlen, Charles (U.S. ambassador), 269

Bohr, Niels, 213

Bolm, Adolph, 114–15, 147

Bolm, Beata, 61, 114–15, 202

Boosey & Hawkes, 63, 68, 84, 85, 87, 99, 100, 103, 154, 273, 288–89

Boothby, Lord "Bob," 223

Boston Symphony Orchestra, 53–54, 95

Boulanger, Nadia, 52, 118, 169, 179, 186, 208, 231, 271, 275, 384, 402, 405

Boulez, Pierre, 130, 179–80, 181, 182–83, 184, 190, 191, 193, 194, 200, 203, 207, 208, 215, 216, 273, 281, 388, 402; Eclat, 281; Le Marteau sans maître, 193, 195, 199, 203, 215, 216; Polyphonie, 154–55

Bowra, Sir Maurice, 221

Brahms, Johannes, 25, 172, 407

Britten, Benjamin, 25, 110, 328; Peter Grimes, 52, 54; War Requiem, 231

Brook, Peter, 182

Brown, Earle, 244

Brown, Marcia, 35, 36

Brown, Ruth (Mrs. Emmet), 35, 38

Brown, William Theophilus, 132, 270

Bruckner, Anton, 31, 376

Buketoff, Igor, 34

Burgi, Richard, 126, 406

Busch, Fritz, 36

Butor, Michel, 269

Bynner, Witter, 132, 144, 161, 215

Cage, John, 18, 100 n. 113, 286, 375, 394

Cagli, Corrado, 119

Caldwell, Sarah, 187, 307

Callas, Maria, 189

Callow, Simon, 380, 382–83

Capote, Truman, 25, 152; House of Flowers, 167–68

Carraro, Francesco and Dottoressa Chiara, 310, 436

Carril, Delia del, 245 n. 4

Carter, Elliott, 118, 123, 162; 169, 179, 182, 188, 190 n. 60, 253, 254, 256, 259 n. 19, 283, 285, 286, 293, 294, 296, 310, 370, 371, 375–76, 379, 380, 381, 384, 387, 392, 402, 406, 407, 409, 411, 412, 428; Double Concerto, 254

Carter, Helen, 118, 162, 169, 188, 253, 256, 294, 296, 310, 375, 379, 402, 412, 428

Casals, Pablo, 226, 230–31, 238

CBS documentary film, 281–82

Cecil, Lord David, 221

Celauro, Alva. See Craft, Alva

Chagall, Marc, 102, 247

Chamber Arts Society Concerts, 67, 68, 81

Chanel, Coco Gabrielle, 121

Char, René, 196

Charles (prince of Wales), 437–39

Chavez, Carlos, 258

Chazin, Judith, 252, 257–58, 397

Cherkassky, Shura, 170

Cherubini, Luigi, 31

Chirico, Giorgio de, 191

Chopin, Frédéric François, 102, 311–12

Christiansen, Rita. See Craft, Rita

Chrysippus, 59

Cingria, Charles-Albert, 83, 111 n. 137

Clark, Sir Kenneth, 385

Claudel, Paul, 217

Cocteau, Jean, 103, 190, 217–18, 256, 257, 271, 331

Congdon, Bill, 189, 259, 402

Connolly, Cyril, 210, 283

"Conversations with Stravinsky," 180, 194–95, 199, 231 n. 12, 243, 252

Copland, Aaron, 38, 53, 63, 141, 164, 175, 200, 286, 314, 336, 394

Couperin, François, 146, 157, 158, 182

Cowell, Henry, 18–19

Craft, Alva Celauro, 354, passim

Craft, Arpha Lawson, 3, 4–6, 8, 11, 12–13, 14–15, 17, 20, 25, 26–27, 29, 39, 45, 46, 47, 48, 51, 184, 195, 315, 334, 339, 342–44, 345, 346, 347–51

Craft, Patricia Jean, 4, 9, 26, 44, 351–52, 354–55, 357–58

Craft, Raymond E., 5, 8, 11, 12, 14–15, 23, 26, 34, 46, 51, 310, 315, 326, 349

Craft, Rita Christiansen, 294, 302–5, 306,

307–8, 309, 310–11, 339, 344–45, 346, 353, 354, 359, 360, 362

Craft, Robert Alexander, 307, 309, 310–11, 334, 339–40, 344–46, 348, 350, 353–54, 355, 356, 357–59, 360, 362–63, 366, 368, 369, 371, 372, 374–75, 383, 391, 403, 408–9, 423, 426, 429, 431

Crawford, Dorothy (author of Evenings On and Off the Roof), 130, 157–58, 160, 161, 174

Crawford, Kristin, 15, 176, 337, 357, 381, 383, 393, 401

Crawford, Phyllis Craft, 3, 7, 9, 11, 13, 23, 25, 30–31, 34, 35, 38, 46, 48, 50, 51, 103, 301–2, 305, 307–8, 334, 337, 342–44, 345–46, 347–48, 351, 353–54, 357–58, 381, 399, 401

Crespi, Signora Mathilde, 120–21, 247, 248, 252, 435–36

Cukor, George, 267

Cummings, Edward Estlin, 245–46

Dahl, Ingolf (Walter Ingolf Marcus), 79, 83, 98 n. 109, 130, 137, 148, 155–56, 161, 164, 249, 287

Dali, Salvador, 135, 136

Dallapiccolo, Luigi, 146, 169, 178, 181, 183, 184, 188, 199

Daniels, Eddie, 412

Davidova, Lucia, 74, 118, 126–27, 178, 181, 258, 269, 305, 337

Davidson, Robert, 132–33, 143

Davis, Sir Colin, 224

Day Lewis, Cecil, 173, 200 n. 78

Debussy, Claude, 73, 207, 211, 213, 254, 270; Chansons de Bilitis, 376

Delacroix, Eugène, 310–11, 380–81

DeMille, Agnes, 160

DeMille, Cecil B., 160

Diaghilev, Serge, 61 n. 4, 103, 114–15, 117, 126, 147, 203, 211, 243, 312–13, 326–27, 330, 331, 373, 378, 403

Dickinson, Emily, 353

Dietrich, Marlene, 128, 152–52

Dinesen, Isaak (Baroness Karen Blixen), 213

Domaine Musicale, La, 179–80, 209 n. 85

Drew, Mrs. David (Judith Sutherland), 188, 191

Driver, Paul, 352, 405

Duquette, Tony, 172, 173

Dushkin, Samuel, 54, 60, 67 n. 23, 76, 111 n. 137, 128, 146, 176, 256, 390

Edel, Dr. Maximillian, 79, 109, 127–28, 148, 165, 250, 256, 273, 432

Einstein, Alfred (author of The Italian Madrigal), 174

Eisler, Hanns, 139

Eliot, T. S., 131, 194–95, 199, 208, 210, 211–12, 213, 215–16, 218–19, 223, 253 n. 13, 255, 276

Enescu, George, 26

Epstein, Barbara, 307, 320, 346, 406

Erlanger, Catherine, Baroness d', 8, 78 n. 50, 117–18, 125, 127, 159, 161, 266, 270, 272, 274

Evenings on the Roof (concert series), 18, 83, 130, 137, 138, 139, 140, 154, 155–58, 161, 165

Falla, Manuel de, 106, 188

Farrell, Suzanne, 215, 282, 283, 399, 406, 428

Faulkner, William, 154

Fell, Anthony, 318, 342, 405

Feuchtwanger, Lion, 160

Fischer-Dieskau, Dietrich, 274

Fizdale, Robert, 76 n. 44, 175, 369

Fonteyn, Dame Margot, 232–34

Ford, Ford Maddox, 159

Forster, E. M., 222–23; Maurice, 184

Franck, César, 55

François-Michel, 207, 208, 216, 296

Fromm, Paul, 193–94, 210

Frommer, Christopher, 347, 354, 359

Fürstenberg, Prince Max Egon von, 204, 212, 388

Garbus, Martin, 246, 323–25, 328, 340–41, 428

Gates, Mrs. Yevgenia Petrovna, 113, 135, 142, 154

Gatwood, Elden, 55

Genet, Jean, 266, 275

Gesualdo, Don Carlo (prince of Venosa), 157–58, 165, 174–75, 177, 184, 185–86, 192, 194, 216, 217, 242

Ghiringhelli, Antonio (intendent of La Scala, Milan, 1951), 87

Giacometti, Alberto, 182, 190, 191, 284

Gielgud, John, 218, 415–16

Ginastera, Alberto, 244

Glass, Philip, 378

Glazunov, Alexander, 179, 241

Glinka, Michael, 79, 95

Gluck, Christoph Willibald von, 38
Godowsky, Dagmar, 115, 197–98
Gold, Arthur, 76 n. 44, 175, 369
Goldoni, Carlo, 189
Goncharova, Natalie, 219, 259
Goodman, Benny, 282, 393
Goossens, Eugene, 217
Gould, Glenn, 209, 244, 249–50, 258, 267–68, 335
Graham, Martha, 118
Grainger, Percy, 18–19
Grands Amants, Les (film), 203 n. 81, 394, 395
Graves, Robert, 226–28
Green, Henry (Henry Yorke), 209
Greissle, Felix, 210
Gross, Robert, 6, 13, 51–52
Guerzoni, Stephanie, 170
Guinness, Alec, 207

Hader, Dagmar (Signora Lassander), 269, 274–76, 435–36
Haieff, Alexei, 66 n. 20, 73, 113–14, 198
Handel, George Frideric, 217
Hardwick, Elizabeth (Mrs. Robert Lowell), 25–26, 306, 307, 330, 379, 387, 406, 412, 428
Harewood, George, Earl of, 308, 412
Harman, Carter, 19
Hawkes, Ralph, 68, 79, 81, 86, 87–89, 90, 98, 101, 105, 147–48
Haydn, Franz Josef, 154, 157, 191, 202, 213, 246, 271, 276, 332
Hayworth, Rita, 259–60
Heard, Gerald (H. F. Heard), 112, 131, 133–34, 135, 165, 168, 176, 177–78, 182, 184, 192, 196 n. 70, 202, 211, 243, 251, 267, 375
Heath, Sir Edward, 283, 332
Heifetz, Jascha, 54, 332
Henze, Hans Werner, 162, 169, 179, 274; Bohemian Fifths, 162–63; Elegy for Young Lovers, 226; König Hirsch, 417; Three Dithyrambs, 217
Herman, Woody, 113, 128
Hindemith, Paul, 32, 54, 60, 193, 211, 254
Hollander, John, 286
Horgan, Paul, 64, 118, 187, 211–12, 214–15, 217, 245–46, 248, 257, 270–71, 307, 309, 315; Encounters with Stravinsky, 193 n. 64, 270–71, 291–93, 297–98, 305–6; Tracings, 294–95

Horne, Marilyn, 158, 171, 175, 176, 178, 179, 202
Horowitz, Vladimir, 100, 309, 332
Hoyle, Fred, 282
Hubble, Edwin, 136
Hughes, Ted, 306, 402, 413–14
Hurok, Sol, 267, 268
Huston, John, 135
Huxley, Aldous, 87, 91, 112, 118, 121–22, 124, 131–32, 134, 135, 136, 143, 157–58, 159, 162, 165, 166, 168, 174–75, 177, 178, 187, 192, 200, 211, 215, 251, 254, 266, 267, 268, 268, 276, 375; Brave New World, 176, 198–99
Huxley, Julian, 188, 283
Huxley, Laura (Mrs. Aldous Huxley), 131–32, 177, 178, 192, 198, 200, 211, 268, 276
Huxley, Maria (Mrs. Aldous Huxley), 124, 136, 168

Ingres, Jean Auguste-Dominique, 385
Isherwood, Christopher, 25, 112, 131–32, 142–43, 165, 176, 183–84, 188, 201, 211, 223, 243, 254, 266, 291, 305, 330; Diaries, 172–73, 177–78, 184, 185, 186–87, 188, 196, 200, 202, 203, 214, 243, 244, 245–46, 291, 331, 375; I am a Camera, 152–53
Ives, Charles, 197

Jakobson, Roman, 235
James, Edward, 135–37, 159, 184, 186, 243–44
Jarnach, Phillip, 207
John XXIII (pope), 259
Johnson, Samuel, 71
Josquin des Prez, 192
Joyce, James, 61 n. 4
Juilliard School of Music, 30, 31, 32, 33–35, 36, 37–38, 49–52, 54–55, 60, 61, 385, 396, 406

Kallman, Chester, 95, 198, 210, 219, 243, 306, 313
Kassman, Elly, 55, 63, 70
Kassman, Vera, 53, 55, 73
Kennedy, President John F., 268, 272
King, Nancy (Mrs. William Zeckendorf, Jr.), 257–58, 397
Kirchner, Leon, 199, 393–94
Kirschbaum, Ralph, 399

Kirstein, Lincoln, 19, 73, 81, 94, 100, 118, 123, 153, 167, 180, 198, 254, 306, 312–13, 337, 419

Klemperer, Otto, 37, 75, 128, 138, 139, 148, 179, 217, 226, 420

Klemperer, Victor, 420

Knauer, Dr. Sigfrid, 127

Knussen, Oliver, 283, 405

Kochanska, Zosia (Mrs. Paul), 112

Kochansky, Paul, 112

Kollek, Theodore, 230, 234, 277

Koussevitzky, Serge, 35, 38, 53–54, 65, 66 n. 20, 70, 75, 76 n. 46, 87 n. 80, 96, 99, 103

Kraft, William, 196, 287

Krenek, Ernst, 138, 139–41, 168, 171–72, 183, 185–86, 191–92, 193–94, 201–3, 207, 242–43, 325, 417; Jonny spielt auf, 202; Sestina, 191, 194, 195–97, 198

Kubelik, Rafael, 149

Lalandi, Lina, 237–38, 273

Lambert, Baroness Hansi, 207, 221

Lambert, Baroness Lucie, 190, 207, 208, 221

Laretei, Käbi (Mrs. Ingmar Bergman), 270

Larionov, Michel, 219

Larkin, Philip, 433–34

Lasso, Orlandi di, 146, 192

Laszlo, Magda, 169–70, 178, 183

Laurentiis, Dino de, 273

Lawrence, D. H., 131, 143–44

Lawrence, Frieda, 132, 143

Leacock, Richard, 280–81, 283

Lebrun, Rico, 119

LeClercq, Tanaquil (Mrs. George Balanchine), 156

Lederman, Minna, 69 n. 27, 82–83

Lehmann, Rosamond, 200

Leibowitz, René, 54

Lenrow, Elbert, 55

Lenya, Lotte, 211

Lerche-Lerchenborg, Count, 249

Levant, Oscar, 36

Levi, Carlo, 191

Levine, James, 404, 407

Lhevinne, Josef and Rosina, 62

Lieberman, Rolf, 107 n. 124, 200, 207, 231, 232, 252, 269, 276, 280–81, 283, 312, 322; Acts et entractes, 189–90, 247–48

Lieberson, Brigitta (Mrs. Goddard Lieberson; also Mrs. George Balanchine). See Zorina, Vera

Lieberson, Goddard, 76, 127, 223, 242, 256, 282, 309, 311, 325, 330

Longworth, Alice Roosevelt, 306

Loos, Anita, 121–22

Lopokova, Lydia (Mrs. John Maynard Keynes), 283

Los Angeles Music Festival, 138

Lowell, Robert, 283, 306

Lucas, John, 337, 379

Machaut, Guillaume de, 157, 204–5, 396

Mahler, Fritz, 30

Mahler, Gustav, 30, 38, 137, 376

Mahler-Werfer, Alma, 78, 123–24, 211

Mann, Thomas, 78, 173, 233 n. 16, 250, 334–35; The Story of a Novel: The Genesis of Doctor Faustus, 250

Marion, Andre, 80, 99, 114, 125, 136, 152, 153–54, 163, 253, 290–91

Marion, Milene Stravinsky, 61, 80, 99, 114, 125, 139, 147, 152–53, 154, 163, 211, 254, 290–91

Markevitch, Igor, 209, 402–3

Marlowe, Sylvia (Mrs. Leonid Berman), 106, 175

Martin, Grace-Lynn, 182, 202, 253

Masocco, Miranda (Mrs. Ralph Levy), 90 n. 94, 132–33, 143, 187, 188, 294–95, 304

Massine, Léonide, 36, 252, 331

McCarthy, Mary, 74, 217

McClure, John, 244, 251, 256, 274

McLane, Reverend James, 79, 123–25

Menotti, Gian Carlo, 242, 272, 369

Menuhin, Yehudi, 232

Meyer, Dr. George, 360, 400, 415

Meyer, Dr. Virginia (Mrs. George), 415

Milhaud, Darius, 55, 139, 190, 240

Milhaud, Madeleine, 55, 64 n. 13, 98, 163, 190

Mitropoulos, Dimitri, 78, 86, 115, 139, 149, 156, 181, 210, 247

Monday Evening Concerts, 130, 140, 146, 161, 165, 173, 177, 182, 192, 198, 199, 211, 253–54, 284, 285

Montale, Eugenio, 151–52, 205–6

Montapert, William, 211, 253, 254, 290–91

Monteux, Pierre, 56, 165, 274

Monteverdi, Claudio, 130, 146, 157, 158, 174; Il Ballo dell'ingrate, 182; Orfeo, 110; Vespro della Beata Virgine (1610), 171, 178, 306, 310; "Zefiro torna," 179

Moore, Henry, 270, 283
Moore, Marianne, 123
Morandi, Giorgi, 217
Morante, Elsa (Mrs. Alberto Moravio), 191
Moravia, Alberto, 191
Moreau, Gustave, 380
Morton, Lawrence, 130, 137–38, 155–56,
    157–58, 165, 166, 173, 175, 176, 178,
    183, 187, 194, 200, 202, 217, 281, 285,
    290, 294, 297, 355, 356
Mozart, Wolfgang Amadeus, 34, 37, 38, 68,
    71, 72, 75, 82, 106, 144, 146, 157, 164,
    167, 168, 172, 178, 213, 246, 254, 311,
    332, 380; Così fan tutte, 36, 79, 316–17;
    Don Giovanni, 34, 175; Idomeneo, 329; The
    Magic Flute, 34, 38, 176, 317; The Marriage
    of Figaro, 317, 322–23
Murphy, Gerald and Sara, 219
Musical Quarterly, The, 187, 332

Nabokov, Dominique (Mrs. Nicolas
    Nabakov), 291, 312, 329
Nabokov, Natasha (Princess Natalie
    Shakhovskoy; Mrs. Nicolas Nabokov),
    118, 304
Nabokov, Nicolas, 61, 66 n. 21, 69 n. 27, 70,
    73, 74, 76 n. 45, 81, 82, 94, 97 n. 107
    and 108, 99, 100, 107 n. 124, 110 n. 136,
    132, 154, 169, 189, 196 n. 71, 219, 220,
    222, 223, 226, 227, 228, 229, 231, 232–
    33, 247, 252, 269, 274–76, 284, 287, 291,
    314, 328, 329–30, 369, 403
Nabokov, Vladimir, 81, 304; Lolita, 222
Nagel, Ivan, 416–17
Newman, Paul, 373
New York City Ballet, 232, 256–57
Nicolson, Sir Harold, 134, 209–10
Nietzsche, Friedrich, 102–3
Nijinsky, Vaslav, 114, 312–13, 426
Nono, Luigi, 176; Incontri, 176
Nono, Nuria Schoenberg, 156, 161–62, 163,
    424

Ocampo, Victoria, 98, 244, 245 n. 4, 315
Ojai Festival, 138, 164, 171–72, 178, 200,
    212–13, 337, 356
Oldfather, Christopher, 410, 411, 415
Olivier, Sir Laurence, 248
Oppenheim, David, 159, 187, 193, 219, 281,
    282
Oppenheimer, Robert, 216, 287

Ormandy, Eugene, 36, 82, 272, 397
Ortega y Gasset, José, 175
Osten-Sacken, Baron Fred, 115–16, 272
Ostrovsky, Marian, 246, 257
Oxford Bach Festival, 237–38, 273

Panni, Marcello, 371, 429, 434–35
Paoli, Domenico de', 87
Partisan Review, 180, 182
Pasternak, Boris, 222
Perlman, Itzhak, 287, 432
Petrarca, Francesco, 111 n. 137
Petrov, Vladimir Ivanovitch (Volodya), 260–
    66, 277–80
Piatigorsky, Gregor, 544, 139, 277, 315
Picasso, Pablo, 102, 167, 182, 219
Pirandello, Luigi, 178
Pitoëff, Lyudmila, 396
Porter, Cole, 118
Poulenc, Francis, 87, 162, 206
Pound, Ezra, 200, 224
Preble, Eleanor, 80 n. 58
Prokofiev, Serge, 18
Propes, Aron, 230, 233, 234
Protetch, Dr. David, 175, 248, 252
Proust, Marcel, 61 n. 4, 370
Puccini, Giacomo, 159, 372–73
Purcell, Henry, 71, 129, 165, 172, 213

Rakhmaninov, Serge, 34, 36–37, 60, 139,
    256, 420
Ramuz, C-F., 90
Ravel, Maurice, 52, 103, 164, 253
Reiner, Fritz, 27, 49, 51, 159
Renoir, Jean, 125, 267
Richardson, Ralph, 216
Rieti, Vittorio, 69 n. 27, 76, 84, 94, 314
Rimsky-Korsakov, Nikolay, 73, 332
Robbins, Jerome, 175, 282, 305
Rodzinsky, Artur, 25, 35
Roethke, Theodore, 211
Rogers, Shorty, 192
Rolland, Romain, 91
Rose, Charlie, 370
Rosen, Charles, 249, 387, 406
Rosenthal, Albi (Albrecht), 289, 313, 323,
    340–41
Rubinstein, Artur, 112, 139, 144, 190, 226,
    332
Rubinstein, Ida, 229, 392
Rubinstein, Nella (Mrs. Artur), 190

Ruggles, Charles, 249
Rumble, Diane Crawford, 15, 18, 51, 175, 285, 305, 381
Rumble, Dr. Wendy, 15, 395, 410
Rumble, Jonathan, 15, 345, 354, 355, 358, 372
Russell, Lord Bertrand, 37–38, 243; *Why I Am Not a Christian*, 31
Ryle, Gilbert, 234, 235–37

Sachs, Arthur, 66–67, 107–8, 110, 179, 384
Sandoval, Arturo, 412
Sarfaty, Regina (Mrs. Elwood Rickless), 214–15, 244, 285, 317
Satie, Erik, 103; *Parade*, 373; *Socrate*, 163
Scherchen, Hermann, 181, 183, 417
Schnecter, Dagmar, 190
Schoenberg, Arnold, 30, 31, 32, 53, 59, 60, 78, 86, 101, 123, 125, 128, 129, 130, 137, 140, 141, 146, 149–50, 156, 159, 169, 210, 250, 271–72, 274, 282, 284, 285, 393–94, 403, 404, 406, 415, 417; *Accompaniment to a Cinematographic Scene*, 156, 172, 202, 242, 282; Cello Concerto (Monn), 425; Chamber Symphony, 404; *Erwartung*, 232, 248, 267–68, 310; Five Pieces for Orchestra, "Premonitions," 130, 149, 190, 207, 210, 213, 270, 272, 373; *Genesis Prelude*, 256; *Die glückliche Hand*, 244, 250, 423; *Gurre-Lieder*, 149, 432–33; *Herzgewaechse*, 150, 370; *Kol Nidre*, 268; *Moses und Aron*, 161–62, 163, 207, 233, 312; *Pelleas und Melisande*, 37, 268, 410; Piano Concerto, 249–50, 415; *Pierrot Lunaire*, 42, 60, 130, 137, 148, 149, 184, 214, 379, 410; Second Chamber Symphony, 31; Septet-Suite, 149–50, 158, 271, 284, 380; Serenade, 149, 154, 182, 183, 284; Songs, Opus 22, 244; *A Survivor from Warsaw*, 256, 380; Three Little Pieces, 254; Variations for Orchestra, 38, 187, 209, 285, 403, 405; *Verklärte Nacht*, 149; Violin Concerto, 256, 432; *Von Heute auf Morgen*, 273
Schoenberg, Gertrud (Mrs. Arnold), 136, 156, 159, 161, 163, 176, 179, 182, 184, 251, 184, 394
Schoenberg, Nuria. *See* Nono, Nuria Schoenberg
Schoenberg, Ronald, 284

Schopenhauer, Arthur, 29
Schubert, Franz, 178, 213
Schumann, Robert, 416, 418
Schütz, Heinrich, 130, 157, 158, 162, 165, 178, 198
Scriabin, Alexander, 2677
Sessions, Roger, 216, 336
Shapero, Harold, 52–53, 54, 69 n. 27, 74, 91, 99, 187, 393–94
Sherry, Fred and Carol, 425, 428
Sibelius, Jean, 53, 271
Sibelius Prize, 270
Silja, Anja, 310, 410–11
Siloti, Alexander, 74 n. 39, 318 n. 10
Siloti, Kyriena, 74, 253
Silvers, Robert B., 301, 316, 428
Sitwell, Edith and Osbert, 96
Smith, Carlton Sprague, 180
Smith, Gregg, 253
Solti, Sir Georg, 172, 310, 312, 322–23, 397–98
Souvtchinsky, Pierre, 64, 76 n. 45, 181–82, 191, 207, 251, 282, 288, 302, 304, 312
Sparrow, John, 221
Spender, Natasha (Lady Spender), 213, 257, 309, 405
Spender, Sir Stephen, 154, 162, 209, 210, 211, 216, 221, 223, 235, 254, 255, 257, 266–67, 268, 270, 272, 282, 283, 293, 309, 375
Spies, Claudio, 52–53, 54, 63 n. 9, 64 n. 13, 187, 274, 355, 395, 406, 428
Spinoza, Baruch, 13
St. Léger, Alexis (St-John Perse), 253, 360
Staël, Nicolas de, 196
Stalvey, Mrs. Marilyn (Stravinsky's secretary, 1963–70), 290, 303
Stein, Jean (Mrs. Torsten Wiesel), 165, 178, 180, 182, 330, 332, 345–46
Stein, Leonard, 172, 254
Stern, Isaac, 226, 230, 243 n. 3, 277, 431–32
Stiftung, Paul Sacher, 105, 111, 254, 323, 340, 373, 374–75, 405, 409
Stockhausen, Karlheinz, 141, 181, 207, 325–26; *Caree*, 141; *Gruppen*, 141, 197, 207; *Zeitmasse*, 197 n. 74, 199
Stokowski, Leopold, 17, 27, 37, 67, 75, 76, 118, 148, 169, 210
Strauss, Richard, 31–32, 276, 374
Stravinsky, Denise Guerzoni (Mrs. Theodore), 170, 288, 294, 296

Stravinsky, Françoise (Mrs. Soulima), 60, 63–
    65, 76–77, 79, 81–82, 83, 87, 88, 90, 94,
    99, 104–5, 127, 148, 187, 254, 274, 287,
    290–91, 327
Stravinsky, Theodore, 61, 123, 147, 155,
    206, 254, 288–89, 291, 294, 296, 338; Le
    Message d'Igor Strawinsky, 153–54
Stravinsky, Vera de Bosset Sudeykina, 67 n.
    22, 74, 94, 96, 99, 103, 112, 113, 115,
    116, 118–19, 121, 124, 125, 126, 127,
    128, 133, 138, 142, 146–47, 152–53, 160,
    163, 169, 170, 172, 174, 176–77, 179,
    181, 187, 188, 196 n. 73, 197–98, 200,
    202, 203, 207, 208, 210, 211, 214–15,
    216 n. 96, 237, 239, 241, 243, 244, 245,
    246, 247, 249, 250, 254–55, 270, 271,
    272, 274, 284, 287, 290–91, 294–95,
    297–98, 301, 304–6, 307, 308–9, 312,
    313–14, 315, 316–18, 320, 323–25, 326,
    327, 328–33, 334–35, 336, 337, 338, 340,
    341–42, 347, 355, 395; correspondence,
    88, 91, 260–66, 277–80; diaries, 72, 73–
    75, 79–80, 127, 287–88, 290, 294
Strecker, Willy, 76 n. 45, 85 n. 73, 163, 198
Streifer, Ruth (Mrs. Martin Garbus), 246
Stuckenschmidt, Hans, 150, 179
Sudeykin, Sergey, 126, 127, 239, 331
Sweelinck, Jan Pieter, 408
Szigeti, Joseph, 139, 174

Takami, Hideki (the Stravinsky cook, 1962–
    71), 291, 294
Tallis, Thomas, 157, 182, 183, 198
Tang, Sarina (Mrs. Martin Garbus), 428
Tanglewood Music Center, 32, 52–54
Tchaikovsky, Peter Ilyich, 24, 25, 27, 75, 79,
    95, 143, 146, 164, 167; Eugene Onegin,
    327; The Nutcracker, 375; Sleeping Beauty,
    160; Swan Lake, 160
Thomas, Dylan, 176; "Do Not Go Gentle,"
    160, 162
Thomas, Michael Tilson, 130, 287, 310
Thomson, Virgil, 79, 100 n. 113, 162, 175,
    183, 246, 258, 336, 369, 402; Four Saints
    in Three Acts, 154; The Mother of Us All, 79;
    Wheatfield at Noon, 369
Toscanini, Arturo, 38, 108–9, 334
Trump, Donald, 25

Ustinov, Peter, 268

Vacchiano, William, 37
Varèse, Edgar, 4, 244, 252–52; Arcana, 251;
    Deserts, 251; Ecuatorial, 253; Ionisation, 198,
    370
Verdi, Giuseppe, 84; Ballo in Maschera, 233;
    Falstaff, 276; Rigoletto, 371
Verlaine, Paul, 102–3
Villa-Lobos, Heitor, 53
Villaseñor, Laura, 243, 246
Vivaldi, Antonio, 164, 198, 213, 326
Vlad, Mo. Roman and Dottoressa Licia, 162,
    169, 206, 429, 434, 436
Voltaire, François-Marie Arouet de, 10–11
Vronsky, Vitya, 143–44, 188

Wagner, Richard, 22, 24, 27, 28, 29, 30, 31,
    32, 34, 38, 55, 271; Lohengrin, 217;
    Meistersinger, 306; Parsifal, 314–15;
    Tannhäuser, 23, 36; Tristan, 314
Waley, Arthur, 188, 429
Walter, Bruno, 37, 38, 193
Walton, Sir William, 171, 328
Watkins, Dr. Glenn, 140, 183, 242, 248 n. 9,
    274, 355
Waugh, Evelyn, 86, 92
Weber, Karl Maria von, 27
Webern, Anton, 54, 137, 146, 150, 161,
    166–67, 169, 170, 172, 175, 176, 177,
    183, 185, 193, 276; Five Pieces for
    Strings, 202; Passacaglia, 208; Six Pieces
    for Orchestra, 190, 223, 242, 282;
    Variations for Orchestra, 217
Weissberger, L. Arnold, 180, 259, 290, 301,
    304, 317 n. 7, 323, 330
Wilson, Edmund, 219; The Dead Sea Scrolls,
    172; The Sixties, 219
Wind, Edgar, 221
Wolf, Hugo, 407
Wolpe, Stefan, 100 n. 113
Wright, Frank Lloyd, 134

Yates, Peter, 18, 129, 137, 154–55, 161, 165
Young, Stark, 74

Zeisl, Barbara (Mrs. Ronald Schoenberg),
    284
Zeisl, Eric, 85 n. 73, 98 n. 109, 129
Zorina, Vera (Mrs. Goddard Lieberson), 109,
    127, 211, 252, 254, 285, 309, 311, 330